T0320746

TYPE THEORY AND FORMAL PROOF

Type theory is a fast-evolving field at the crossroads of logic, computer science and mathematics. This gentle step-by-step introduction is ideal for graduate students and researchers who need to understand the ins and outs of the mathematical machinery, the role of logical rules therein, the essential contribution of definitions and the decisive nature of well-structured proofs.

The authors begin with untyped lambda calculus and proceed to several fundamental type systems, including the well-known and powerful Calculus of Constructions. The book also covers the essence of proof checking and proof development, and the use of dependent type theory to formalise mathematics.

The only prerequisite is a basic knowledge of undergraduate mathematics. Carefully chosen examples illustrate the theory throughout. Each chapter ends with a summary of the content, some historical context, suggestions for further reading and a selection of exercises to help readers familiarise themselves with the material.

ROB NEDERPELT was Lecturer in Logic for Computer Science until his retirement. Currently he is a guest researcher in the Faculty of Mathematics and Computer Science at Eindhoven University of Technology, the Netherlands.

HERMAN GEUVERS is Professor in Theoretical Informatics at the Radboud University Nijmegen, and Professor in Proving with Computer Assistance at Eindhoven University of Technology, both in the Netherlands.

TYPE THEORY AND FORMAL PROOF

An Introduction

ROB NEDERPELT

Eindhoven University of Technology,
The Netherlands

HERMAN GEUVERS

Radboud University Nijmegen,
and
Eindhoven University of Technology,
The Netherlands

CAMBRIDGE
UNIVERSITY PRESS

CAMBRIDGE
UNIVERSITY PRESS

University Printing House, Cambridge CB2 8BS, United Kingdom

Cambridge University Press is part of the University of Cambridge.

It furthers the University's mission by disseminating knowledge in the pursuit of
education, learning and research at the highest international levels of excellence.

www.cambridge.org
Information on this title: www.cambridge.org/9781107036505

© Rob Nederpelt and Herman Geuvers 2014

First published 2014

A catalogue record for this publication is available from the British Library

ISBN 978-1-107-03650-5 Hardback

To the memory of N.G. de Bruijn

Contents

Foreword

This book, *Type Theory and Formal Proof: An Introduction*, is a gentle, yet profound, introduction to systems of types and their inhabiting lambda-terms. The book appears shortly after *Lambda Calculus with Types* (Barendregt *et al.*, 2013). Although these books have a partial overlap, they have very different goals. The latter book studies the mathematical properties of some formalisms of types and lambda-terms. The book in your hands is focused on the use of types and lambda-terms for the complete formalisation of mathematics. For this reason it also treats higher order and dependent types. The act of defining new concepts, essential for mathematical reasoning, forms an integral part of the book. Formalising makes it possible that arbitrary mathematical concepts and proofs be represented on a computer and enables a machine verification of the well-formedness of definitions and of the correctness of proofs. The resulting technology elevates the subject of mathematics and its applications to its maximally complete and reliable form.

The endeavour to reach this level of precision was started by Aristotle, by his introduction of the axiomatic method and quest for logical rules. For classical logic Frege completed this quest (and Heyting for the intuitionistic logic of Brouwer). Frege did not get far with his intended formalisation of mathematics: he used an inconsistent foundation. In 1910 Whitehead and Russell introduced types to remedy this. These authors made proofs largely formal, except that substitutions still had to be understood and performed by the reader. In 1940 Church published a system with types, based on a variant of those of Whitehead and Russell, in which the mechanism of substitution was captured by lambda-terms and conversion. Around 1970 de Bruijn essentially extended the formalism of types by introducing *dependent types* with the explicit goal to formalise and verify mathematics. By 2004 this technique was perfected and George Gonthier established, using the mathematical assistant Coq, a full formalisation of the Four Colour Theorem.

The learning curve to formalise remains steep, however. One still needs to be an expert in a mathematical assistant in order to apply the technique. I hope and expect that this book will contribute to the familiarisation of formalising mathematical proofs and to improvements in the mathematical assistants, bringing this technique within the reach of the working mathematician and computer scientist.

Henk Barendregt

Preface

Aim and scope

The aim of the book is, firstly, to give an introduction to *type theory*, an evolving scientific field at the crossroads of logic, computer science and mathematics. Secondly, the book explains how type theory can be used for the verification of mathematical expressions and reasonings.

Type theory enables one to provide a 'coded' version – i.e. a full formalisation – of many mathematical topics. The formal system underlying type theory forces the user to work in a very precise manner. The real power of type theory is that well-formedness of the formalised expressions implies logical and mathematical correctness of the original content.

An attractive property of type theory is that it becomes possible and feasible to do the encoding in a 'natural' manner, such that one follows (and recognises) the way in which these subjects were presented originally. Another important feature of type theory is that proofs are treated as first-class citizens, in the sense that proofs do not remain meta-objects, but are coded as expressions (terms) of the same form as the rest of the formalisation.

The authors intend to address a broad audience, ranging from university students to professionals. The exposition is gentle and gradual, developing the material at a steady pace, with ample examples and comments, cross-references and motivations. Theoretical issues relevant for logic and computer science alternate with practical applications in the area of fundamental mathematical subjects.

History Important investigations in the machinery of *logic* were made by F.L.G. Frege, as early as the end of the nineteenth century (Frege, 1893). *Formal mathematics* started with B. Russell in the first decade of the twentieth century, by the publication of the famous *Principia Mathematica* (*The Principles of Mathematics*, see Russell, 1903). Other contributions were made by D. Hilbert (Hilbert, 1927) in the 1920s. An important step in the description of the essential mechanisms behind the mathematical way of thought was made by A. Church in the 1940s (Church, 1940). He invented the lambda calculus, an abstract mechanism for dealing with functions, and he introduced 'simple type theory' as the language for higher order logic.

At the end of the 1960s N.G. de Bruijn designed his 'mathematical language', Automath (de Bruijn, 1970), which he and his group tested thoroughly by translating a broad corpus of mathematical texts in it, and verifying it by means of a computer program. In the same period, the Polish Mizar group (Mizar, 1989) developed a language and a program to develop and store mathematical theories; they founded their efforts, however, not so much in a type-theoretic theory.

From approximately the 1980s there was an explosion of work in the area of type theory based on earlier work in the 1970s by J.-Y. Girard (Girard, 1986) and P. Martin-Löf (Martin-Löf, 1980). We mention the inspiring work of H.P. Barendregt, whose lambda-cube and the notion of Pure Type Systems based on that are by now a standard in the world of type theory (Barendregt, 1981, 1992).

The present book has been built on both Automath and the lambda-cube, which have been combined into a novel, concise system that enjoys the advantages of both respected predecessors.

Rationale Topics such as proven correctness and complete formalisation are essential in many areas of modern science. Type theory as an all-encompassing formalism has become more and more a standard benchmark for what formalisation of logico-mathematical content really means, and the more so because it also includes the essence of what a formal proof is. Thus, type theory is a valuable expedient to transform 'correctness' into a mechanisable issue, which is of great importance, in particular in mathematical proof development and correct computer programming.

There are many developments that build on the inherent force of type theory. We mention work on proving program correctness; on correct program construction; on automation of reasoning; on formalisation and archiving of mathematical subjects, including on-line consultable libraries of knowledge; on proof checking, (assistance for) proof development and construction. More about these subjects can be found in Chapter 16, in particular Sections 16.2 and 16.3.

For the benefit of any interested person who desires to get insight into the 'big points' of type theory, we note the following. Notwithstanding the momentum that formalisation of mathematics has gained, especially in computer science where it is used for the verification of software and systems by means of proof assistants, formalising is a considerable effort. For students and also for interested researchers, it is still a major investment to understand and use the systems. We expect this situation to improve in the future and this is where our book aims to fill a gap, by being a gentle introduction to the art of formalising mathematics on the basis of type theory, suitable for proof assistants and other systems. We believe that this book will be very useful for anyone starting to use such a system.

Approach This textbook describes a concise version of type theory that is immediately useable to represent mathematical theories and to verify them. The representation is close to the manner in which mathematicians write and think, and therefore easier to master and employ. It is a good means for students of mathematics and computer science to make a personal acquaintance with the ins and outs of the mathematical machinery, the role of logical rules therein, the essential contribution of definitions and the decisive nature of well-structured proofs.

For that purpose we build the material from scratch, gradually enlarging the influence of the types in the various systems described. The text starts with the untyped lambda calculus and then introduces several fundamental type systems, culminating in the well-known and powerful Calculus of Constructions. We continue by extending that system with a formal definition system and consecutively test the newly obtained system with several mathematical subjects, until we finally present a substantial piece of mathematics (Bézout's theorem and its proof) in the format described, in order to give a practical demonstration of how the formal system works, and how close the formal translation remains to the usual mathematical way of expressing such an item.

The main thread that runs through all the chapters is the development of a convincing and viable formal type system for mathematics. At the end of each chapter, the results are summarised in a section entitled Conclusions. In the final section of each chapter, called Further Reading, we look around, sketching a broader picture: we give a short historical justification of the topics described, an overview of the essential aspects of related research (past and present) not dealt with in the chapter, and suggest other literature as further reading to the interested reader.

Following each chapter there is a series of exercises, enabling the reader to get acquainted with the presented material. The exercises concentrate on the subjects treated in the chapter text as such (not in the Further Reading). Since we aim at a 'generic' approach to type theory as the basis of logical proofs and of mathematics in general, the exercises do not refer to, or make use of, specific proof assistants or software tools: we regard it as sensible to remain independent of the actual technical developments.

For answers to selected exercises, see `www.win.tue.nl/~wsinrpn/`.

Summary of contents

Chapter 1: Untyped lambda calculus

We start with an exposition of untyped lambda calculus, a fundamental topic originating from A. Church in the 1930s, which may be regarded as the calculus underlying the behaviour of functions, including variable binding and substitution – essential concepts in mathematics and computer science. The standard subjects in this area are discussed in detail, including β-reduction, normal forms, confluence, fixed points and the related theorems. We list the positive and negative aspects of this calculus.

Chapters 2 to 6

The drawbacks of the untyped calculus lead to a notion of *type*, which plays the main role in the rest of the book. In Chapters 2 to 6 we present the standard hierarchy of typed lambda calculi, as elaborated by H.P. Barendregt. In these chapters we introduce several systems, each with its own rationale, and contrast them with previous and coming ones as to their relative 'power'. Moreover, the reader becomes acquainted with derivation rules and their use, and with basic logical entities and their formal role in reasonings. The relevant properties of these systems are reviewed, with a selection of instructive proofs of these properties.

Chapter 2: Simply typed lambda calculus

In Chapter 2 we develop the simply typed lambda calculus in the explicit version, due to A. Church, which is called $\lambda{\to}$. We also mention the implicit version of H.B. Curry. We give a derivation system for $\lambda{\to}$ and examples of its use. The properties of the system are given, and contrasted with the properties of the untyped lambda calculus.

Chapter 3: Second order typed lambda calculus

We extend Church's $\lambda{\to}$ with terms depending on types, leading to the system $\lambda 2$, enjoying second order abstraction and application, and having Π-types. Again, examples show its usefulness.

Chapter 4: Types dependent on types

We extend $\lambda{\to}$ in another direction, adding types depending on types. Therefore we develop the notions 'type constructor' and 'kind'. Thus we obtain the system $\lambda\underline{\omega}$. We also adapt the derivation rules and include a conversion rule.

Chapter 5: Types dependent on terms

A third extension of $\lambda{\to}$ leads to λP, which enables us to formalise predicates. The far-reaching propositions-as-types concept, implying the Curry–Howard isomorphism, is one of the topics that pop up in a straightforward fashion. We discuss the correspondence with basic mathematical and logical notions.

Chapter 6: The Calculus of Constructions

Chapters 2 to 5 culminate in the powerful Calculus of Constructions (or λC), the theory on which the well-known proof assistant Coq has been built. In this chapter we explain the hierarchy and the structure present in the Barendregt cube, and we add the corresponding derivation system. The relevant properties are listed and contrasted with earlier results in the book.

Chapter 7: The encoding of logical notions in λC

We demonstrate how propositional logic and predicate logic fit naturally in the λC framework. For each of the usual logical connectives and quantifiers we give a type-theoretic encoding, for which we employ several times the second order possibilities of λC. Constructive logic is separated from classical logic, which needs a single axiom. A number of examples show how logical proofs can be embedded in type theory, thus deepening the reader's insight into logical reasonings and proofs.

Chapter 8: Definitions

In this chapter we look into the nature, the usage and the usefulness of definitions in logic and mathematics. We argue why one tends to give a specific object or notion a name of its own, often in a context of assumptions, and how these names are used afterwards. We explain the general format underlying the definition mechanism and discuss the various manners of instantiating these definitions. The differences and correspondences between variables, parameters and constants are reviewed, and we point at the possibility in type theory of giving names to proofs.

Chapter 9: Extension of λC with definitions

Here we extend the type theory λC with formal definitions, which is essential for making type theory practically useful. We formalise the common kind of definitions, which name a notion that is specified by a description. We discuss and analyse the extra derivation rules needed for the formal treatment of definitions: one for adding a definition, and one for instantiating a definition. We also introduce and elaborate a reduction mechanism for enabling the 'unfolding' of definitions, with a discussion of related notions. Finally, we obtain the system λD_0, a formal extension of λC treating definitions as first-class citizens.

Chapter 10: Rules and properties of λD

We introduce a second kind of definition, the primitive ones, which can be used for axioms and axiomatic notions. Their formal representation resembles the one for descriptive definitions, which is particularly apparent in the extra derivation rules necessary to encapsulate these primitive definitions. We thus obtain the system λD (i.e. λC + definitions + axioms) and we list the most important properties of the obtained formal system.

Chapter 11: Flag-style natural deduction in λD

In order to demonstrate how λD works in practice, we start with a more thorough investigation of formal logic in λD-style, as a sequel to Chapter 7. We illustrate how derivations in λD can be turned into a flag-style linear format, close to the familiar representation used in mathematics books, and therefore easy to understand. Natural deduction, the logical system that reflects the reasoning patterns employed by mathematicians, can be clearly presented in this format, as we demonstrate: the introduction and elimination rules for the standard connectives and quantifiers can be straightforwardly translated into λD. Examples show that natural deduction nicely agrees with the ideas and constructions present in type theory.

Chapter 12: Mathematics in λD: a first attempt

In this chapter we put λD to the test in the area of mathematics. A simple example, consisting of a theorem and a short proof, leads to investigations about equality, Leibniz's law, and orders, all directly transposable in the λD setting. Next, we discuss unique existence and the possibility to attach a name to uniquely existing objects and notions. In order to formalise this, we axiomatically introduce Frege's ι-descriptor.

Chapter 13: Sets and subsets

We discuss how to deal with sets and subsets in type theory. This is not straightforward, since sets and types are different concepts. For example, an element can be a member of several sets, whereas in the standard version of type theory that we develop in this book, each 'object' has a unique type (up to conversion). A crucial property of types is that it is decidable whether 'a has type T'. For sets this is not the case: '$a \in X$' is in general undecidable. This means we have to make a choice as to how to deal with sets in type theory. We make the choice to represent subsets as predicates over a type, which works out well, as we show with a number of examples. At the end of the chapter we compare our choice with other options.

Chapter 14: Numbers and arithmetic in λD

In order to investigate the usefulness of λD for formalising mathematics in a systematic manner, we focus on the integer numbers. Starting with Peano's axioms for the natural numbers, we give similar axioms for the integers, which turn out to be directly transposable into λD. The natural numbers then form a subset, with the desired properties. Thereby we obtain a viable approach to many parts of number theory. In order to demonstrate this, we develop basic arithmetic for the integers, concerning addition, subtraction, multiplication and the like. When formalising recursion, we make good use of the ι-descriptor introduced in a previous chapter. Inequalities, such as $\leq$, and divisibility follow relatively easy. We demonstrate the flexibility of the obtained formalisation by giving ample examples. In developing formal arithmetic, a long sequence of provable lemmas passes by, which shows the strength of the proposed encodings in type theory.

Chapter 15: An elaborated example
In order to demonstrate the reach and the power of the approach developed in this book, we formalise a non-trivial theorem and its proof in λD. Therefore we take a version of Bézout's Lemma: if two positive natural numbers are relatively prime, then there is a linear combination of the two which is equal to 1. We split the proof into a number of parts, which are formalised one by one. In the presentation we suppress a number of obvious details which are left to the reader, in order to keep a clear view of the overall picture. Our development of the proof of Bézout's Lemma shows that the chosen road is viable and feasible. Two auxiliary theorems (the Minimum Theorem and the Division Theorem) are considered in detail and also transposed in a λD setting.

Chapter 16: Further perspectives
This chapter summarises the useful points of a type-theoretic formalisation of mathematics as, for example, offered by λD. It also focuses on the general principles of type theory-based proof assistants and their power concerning proof checking and interactive proving. Finally, we outline our view on the future of the field, motivated by recent developments.

Appendix A: Logic in λD
Summary of the natural deduction rules described and used in the book.

Appendix B: Arithmetical axioms, definitions and lemmas
For the reader's convenience, we list the lemmas concerning arithmetic in $\mathbb{Z}$, as they are given in the text of Chapter 14.

Appendix C: Two complete example proofs in λD
We give complete versions of two λD proofs dealt with before, namely of the Closure Property of Addition in $\mathbb{N}$, and of the Division Theorem, in order to show what such formal proofs look like when all relevant details have been worked out.

Appendix D: Derivation rules for λD
This appendix summarises the derivation system as developed in the book, for easy reference.

Indexes
We add four sets: an Index of names (which contains the names of the persons mentioned in the main text of the book), an Index of definitions (listing the formal definitions presented in the figures of Chapters 8 to 15), an Index of symbols and an Index of subjects.

What's new?

The book has several new aspects in its presentation of type theory:

(1) A main novelty is that we present type theory in *flag-derivation style*. In modern presentations of type theory, one usually sees derivations presented in 'tree style', which enables a concise and precise way of defining the rules of type theory, and we will also employ it for that purpose. A tree style, however, is very impractical for giving real derivations. Derivation trees become too wide and big and enforce all kinds of basic typings to be derived several times (in different branches of the derivation tree). The flag style allows easy reuse of context elements. It also allows us, in combination with definitions (see below), to reuse derived results. Altogether it is very close to the usual 'book style', which builds up the mathematics in a linear order.

(2) Also new is the inclusion of *definitions*, which are often regarded as informal abbreviation mechanisms on the meta-level. Contrary to this, we give a formal treatment of definitions and show how they are used in practical derivations. Primitive notions, which are treated in a similar manner to definitions in our presentation of type theory, are used for adding elementary concepts and axioms to type theory.

Inductive notions can be defined by means of higher order logic and our definition mechanism allows us to give them a name. One can also define recursive functions over these inductive notions. Therefore we do not have inductive definitions as a basic concept, since this is not needed.

(3) We continually take care to give a *stepwise and gentle explanation* of the rules of type theory, illustrated with many examples of how these are used to formalise mathematics. In particular, given that it is not very common to devote a lot of attention to the notion of 'definition', our explicit description in Chapter 8 of the use and meaning of definitions stands out as a new look at what they are and intend to be. We contrast definitions with assumptions and differentiate between variables, parameters and constants. Thus we discuss a number of well-known mathematical concepts with a 'linguistic-philosophical flavour', which is not usual.

(4) The manner in which we represent definitions leads to a relatively small but powerful *extension* of λC. The system obtained in Chapter 10, called λD, has a simple, convincing format and is new: it has not yet been described as such in the literature. In Chapter 12 we introduce the descriptor ι in λD, which is straightforward, since λD permits primitive concepts such as axioms and axiomatic notions. Use of this ι, which enables uniquely identifiable objects, is not very common in dependent type theory. We note, however, that L.S. van Benthem Jutting already did this in his Automath translation of E. Landau's

book on Analysis (van Benthem Jutting, 1977), and that it is also present in the HOL system (see HOL system, 1988).

(5) At the end of Chapter 13 we give an overview discussion of how to deal with *subsets* in type theory. The new aspect is that we take a pragmatic viewpoint on subsets by making a conscious choice with a view to our aims.

Readership

Although the style of the book is expository, using a gradual pace of explanation with a continuous care for good understanding, including many examples, the subject has intrinsic difficulties because of the far-reaching and rather complex interweaving of type-related notions, which is inherent to type theory. Therefore, we consider this to be an *advanced textbook*. The intended readership may include certain undergraduate students, although the primary readership will range from graduate students to specialists:

– *Undergraduate students in mathematics and computer science* (second or third year) should be able to follow most of the text, from the beginning to the end. The main insight they get is to learn thoroughly what a proof 'is', how it should be read and how it can be obtained. Moreover, they see which 'fine structure' is present (albeit mostly hidden) behind a mathematical text; that extreme precision in mathematics is feasible; that logic can be framed as a highly systematic deduction apparatus; that proofs can be considered as mathematical objects, on a par with the usual mathematical entities; that definitions are an indispensable asset in the formal mathematical language.

– *Graduate students in mathematics and computer science* may profit more deeply from this book. They will enjoy the same benefits as sketched above, but they also learn from this book what the essence of types is, in particular of higher order and dependent types. This offers a useful lead into further investigations in type systems for programming languages. They get acquainted with important notions connected to function evaluation, by studying (typed and untyped) lambda calculus and their properties. They see, moreover, that (and how) mathematics can be formalised smoothly and hence that type theory is suitable for checking with computer assistance, for example by means of a proof assistant such as Coq.

– *Specialists and researchers in computer science and mathematics* not acquainted with type theory can get a good and thorough impression of what it's all about. They can easily browse through the text to pick up the essentials that interest them, in particular with respect to the important range of type systems combined in Barendregt's cube; the Calculus of Constructions and its properties; the essence and the value of (formal) definitions and how they can form part of a fully formal derivation system; the various approaches to formalising Set Theory; the approach to integers in the Peano style; and a worked-out example of a real formalised proof of a well-known, non-trivial theorem. As a by-product, the reader will understand the basic features of the system Automath (de Bruijn, 1970). A researcher may also be inspired by the possibility of formalising mathematics as demonstrated in this book, or by the overview of applications and perspectives at the end of the book.

Technical level

Since the book concerns a relatively new and self-contained subject, developed from scratch, no more prerequisites are required than a good knowledge of basic mathematical material such as (undergraduate) algebra and analysis. Some knowledge of logical systems and some experience with logico-mathematical reasoning and/or proofs may help, but it is not mandatory.

About the authors

Rob Nederpelt (born 1942) is a guest researcher in the faculty of Mathematics and Computer Science at the Eindhoven University of Technology (the Netherlands) and was, until his retirement, a lecturer in Logic for Computer Science at the same university. He studied mathematics at Leiden University and obtained his PhD at Eindhoven University in 1973, with N.G. de Bruijn as his thesis supervisor. The subject of his thesis was (weak and strong) normalisation in a typed lambda calculus narrowly related to the mathematical language Automath.

He has taught many courses at Eindhoven University, first in mathematics, later in logic, theoretical computer science, type theory and the language of mathematics.

His research interest is primarily logic, in particular type theory and typed lambda calculus. See www.win.tue.nl/~wsinrpn/publications.htm for his list of publications. It contains many papers and three books: *The Language of Mathematics* (Nederpelt, 1987), *A Modern Perspective on Type Theory* (Kamareddine et al., 2004), *Logical Reasoning* (Nederpelt & Kamareddine, 2011). He has also been one of the editors of *Selected Papers on Automath* (Nederpelt et al., 1994).

Herman Geuvers (born 1964) is professor in Theoretical Informatics at the Radboud University Nijmegen, and in Proving with Computer Assistance at the Eindhoven University of Technology, both in the Netherlands. He has studied mathematics in Nijmegen and wrote his PhD thesis in the Foundations of

Computer Science (Radboud University Nijmegen, the Netherlands; 1993) under the supervision of H.P. Barendregt on the Curry–Howard formulas-as-types interpretation that relates logic and type theory.

He has taught many courses, mainly on topics such as logic, theoretical computer science, type theory, proof assistants and semantics of programming languages. He has been a lecturer in type theory and proof assistants at various international PhD summer schools.

His research is in type theory, proof assistants and formalising mathematics. He has published over 60 papers (`www.cs.ru.nl/~herman/pubs.html`), has been a member of various programme committees and has organised various scientific events. Moreover, he co-edited the book *Selected Papers on Automath* (Nederpelt *et al.*, 1994). He was the leader of the 'FTA project' at the Radboud University Nijmegen, to formalise a constructive proof of the Fundamental Theorem of Algebra in Coq. This led to *CoRN*, the Constructive Coq Repository of formalised mathematics (`http://corn.cs.ru.nl`) at Nijmegen, which is a large library of formalised algebra and analysis by means of the proof assistant Coq.

Acknowledgements

This book is dedicated to N.G. de Bruijn (1918–2012). His pioneering work in the 1960s on the 'mathematical language' Automath and on formalising mathematics in type theory has greatly influenced the development of this book. His creative mind has been a great inspiration for us.

We thank H.P. Barendregt for sharing his deep insights in typed lambda calculus and for his thorough and convincing description of many important subjects in the field.

Since one of us is a student of N.G. de Bruijn, and the other one of H.P. Barendregt, the publication of this book is a way of thanking our teachers, and paying tribute to them.

We are particularly grateful to J.R. Hindley and C. Hemerik for their comments on the text. We thank F. Dechesne and H.L. de Champeaux for their useful remarks, A. Visser and R. Iemhoff for their valuable help and P. van Tilburg for his nice and convenient tool for making flag derivations in LaTeX.

We thank Eindhoven University of Technology for kindly offering us space, time and equipment to prepare the text. We are also grateful to Cambridge University Press, in particular to D. Tranah and G. Smith.

Rob Nederpelt, Herman Geuvers

Greek alphabet

For convenience, we list the letters of the Greek alphabet (small and capital) together with their names and English pronunciation.

α	A	alpha	/ˈælfə/	ν	N	nu	/njuː/
β	B	beta	/ˈbiːtə/	ξ	Ξ	xi	/gzaɪ/
γ	Γ	gamma	/ˈgæmə/	o	O	omicron	/əˈmaɪkrən/
δ	Δ	delta	/ˈdeltə/	π	Π	pi	/paɪ/
ε	E	epsilon	/ˈepsɪˌlɒn/	ρ	P	rho	/rəʊ/
ζ	Z	zeta	/ˈziːtə/	σ	Σ	sigma	/ˈsɪgmə/
η	H	eta	/ˈiːtə/	τ	T	tau	/tɔː/
ϑ	Θ	theta	/ˈθiːtə/	υ	Υ	upsilon	/ʌpˈsaɪlən/
ι	I	iota	/aɪˈəʊtə/	φ	Φ	phi	/faɪ/
κ	K	kappa	/ˈkæpə/	χ	X	chi	/kaɪ/
λ	Λ	lambda	/ˈlæmdə/	ψ	Ψ	psi	/psaɪ/
μ	M	mu	/mjuː/	ω	Ω	omega	/ˈəʊmɪgə/

1

Untyped lambda calculus

1.1 Input–output behaviour of functions

Many functions can be described by some kind of expression, e.g. $x^2 + 1$, that tells us how, given an *input value* for x, one can calculate an *output value*. In the present case this proceeds as follows: first determine the square of the input value and consequently add 1 to this. The so-called 'variable' x acts as an *arbitrary* (or abstract) input value. In a concrete case, for example when using input value 3, one must replace x with 3 in the expression. Function $x^2 + 1$ then delivers the output value $3^2 + 1$, which adds up to 10.

In order to emphasise the 'abstract' role of such a variable x in an expression for a function, it is customary to use the special symbol λ: one adds λx in front of the expression, followed by a dot as a separation marker. Hence, instead of $x^2 + 1$, one writes $\lambda x.\ x^2 + 1$, which means 'the function mapping x to $x^2 + 1$'. This notation expresses that x itself is not a concrete input value, but an abstraction. As soon as a concrete input value comes in sight, e.g. 3, we may give this as an argument to the function, thus making a start with the calculation. Usually, one expresses this first stage by writing the input value, embraced in a pair of parentheses, after the function: $(\lambda x.\ x^2 + 1)(3)$. (Compare with the case when one wishes to apply the function sin to argument π: this is conveniently expressed as $\sin(\pi)$.)

In what follows, we will concentrate on the general behaviour of functions. We will hardly ever take into account that we know how to 'calculate' in the real world, for example that we can evaluate $3^2 + 1$ to 10, and $\sin(\pi)$ to 0. Only later will we consider well-known elementary functions such as addition or multiplication of numbers, or call upon our knowledge about specific functions such as *square*: our initial intention is to analyse functions from an abstract point of view.

Our first attempts lead to a system called λ-*calculus*. This system encapsulates a formalisation of the basic aspects of functions, in particular their construction and their use. In the present chapter we do not yet consider *types*, being an abstraction of the well-known process of 'classifying' entities into greater units; for example, one may consider $\mathbb{N}$ as the type of all natural numbers. So this chapter deals with the *untyped λ-calculus*. In all the following chapters, however, we shall consider *typed* versions of λ-calculus, varying in nature, which will end up in a system suitable for doing mathematics in a formal manner.

1.2 The essence of functions

From the previous section we conclude that in dealing with functions there are two *construction principles* and one *evaluation rule*.

The construction principles for functions are the following:

Abstraction: From an expression M and a variable x we can construct a new expression: $\lambda x \,.\, M$. We call this *abstraction of x over M*.

Application: From expressions M and N we can construct expression $M\,N$. We call this *application of M to N*.

If necessary, some parentheses should be added during the construction process.

Examples 1.2.1   – Abstraction of x over $x^2 + 1$ gives $\lambda x \,.\, x^2 + 1$.
- Abstraction of y over $\lambda x \,.\, x - y$ gives $\lambda y \,.\, (\lambda x \,.\, x - y)$, i.e. the function mapping y to: $\lambda x \,.\, x - y$ (which is itself a function).
- Abstraction of y over 5 gives $\lambda y \,.\, 5$, i.e. the function mapping y to 5 (otherwise said: the 'constant function' with value 5).
- Application of $\lambda x \,.\, x^2 + 1$ to 3 gives $(\lambda x \,.\, x^2 + 1)(3)$.
- Application of $\lambda x \,.\, x$ to $\lambda y \,.\, y$ gives $(\lambda x \,.\, x)(\lambda y \,.\, y)$.
- Application of f to c gives fc. This can also be written, in a more familiar way, as $f(c)$, but this is not the style we use here.

Remarks 1.2.2   *(1) A 'free' usage of these construction principles allows expressions which do not have an obvious meaning, such as xx or $y(\lambda u \,.\, u)$. In this chapter, we treat these kinds of constructs just like the others, not worrying about their apparent lack of meaning.*

(2) The function 'square' now looks as follows: $\lambda x \,.\, x^2$. The stand-alone expression x^2 is still available, but it is no longer a function, but an abstract output value, viz. the square of (an unknown, but fixed) x. The difference is subtle and may become clearer as follows: let's assume that x ranges over $\mathbb{N}$,

the set of natural numbers. Then $\lambda x \,.\, x^2$ is a function, taking natural numbers
to natural numbers. But x^2 is not: it represents a natural number.

(3) The λ is particularly suited for the description of 'neat' functions, which
can be described by a mathematical expression. It takes some effort to use the
λ-notation to describe functions with a slightly more complicated description,
such as, for example:

— the function 'absolute value' with definition:
$$x \mapsto \begin{cases} x & \text{if } x \geq 0 \\ -x & \text{if } x < 0 \end{cases},$$
— or the function on domain $\{0,1,2,3\}$ with codomain $\{0,1,2,3\}$ that is described by: $0 \mapsto 2, 1 \mapsto 2, 2 \mapsto 1, 3 \mapsto 3$.

(In Exercise 1.14 we introduce an if-then-else function, which is helpful in such
cases.)

Next to the two construction principles described above, our intuitive function notion gives rise to a *rule* for the 'evaluation' of expressions. The formalisation of the *function evaluation process* is called 'β-reduction'. (An explanation
for this name, and a precise definition, will be given in Section 1.8.)

This β-reduction makes use of *substitution*, formally expressed by means of
square brackets '[' and ']': the expression $M[x := N]$ represents 'M in which N
has been substituted for x'. (Note, however, that substitution is more subtle
than one might expect. See Section 1.6 for a precise definition.)

β-*reduction:* An expression of the form $(\lambda x \,.\, M)N$ can be rewritten to
the expression $M[x := N]$, i.e. the expression M in which every x has
been replaced with N. We call this process β-*reduction of* $(\lambda x \,.\, M)N$ *to*
$M[x := N]$.

Examples 1.2.3 — $(\lambda x \,.\, x^2 + 1)(3)$ reduces to $(x^2 + 1)[x := 3]$, which is $3^2 + 1$.
— $(\lambda x \,.\, \sin(x) - \cos(x))(3 + 5)$ reduces to $\sin(3 + 5) - \cos(3 + 5)$.
— $(\lambda y \,.\, 5)(3)$ reduces to $5[y := 3]$, which is 5.
— $(\lambda x \,.\, x)(\lambda y \,.\, y)$ reduces to $x[x := \lambda y \,.\, y]$, which is $\lambda y \,.\, y$.

Reduction is also possible on suitable *parts* of expressions: when an expression of the form $(\lambda x \,.\, M)N$ is a subexpression of a bigger one, then this subexpression may be rewritten to $M[x := N]$, as described above, provided that
the rest of the expression is left unchanged. The *full* former expression (with
subexpression $(\lambda x \,.\, M)N$) is then said to reduce to the *full* latter expression
(with subexpression $M[x := N]$).

The rules describing how reduction extends from subexpressions to bigger
ones are called the *compatibility rules* for reduction (see Definition 1.8.1).

Example 1.2.4   By compatibility, $\lambda z \,.\, ((\lambda x \,.\, x)(\lambda y \,.\, y))$ reduces to $\lambda z \,.\, (\lambda y \,.\, y)$.

Remarks 1.2.5   *We emphasise that the word 'application' is deceptive: application of M to N is* not *the result of applying M to N, but only a first step in this procedure: all we can say is that 'application' is the construction of a new expression, MN, which, in a later stage, may* perhaps *lead to the actual execution of a function. For example, the application of function $\lambda x \,.\, \sqrt{x}$ to 7 gives expression $(\lambda x \,.\, \sqrt{x})(7)$, in which the function has not yet been executed. It is only after the reduction of the latter term that we obtain the result of 'application of the function to 7', namely the 'answer' $\sqrt{7}$.*

The λ-notation is for functions of *one* variable. A function of two or more variables does not fit in this notation. One could make the choice to extend the notation for this purpose. For example, consider the function f of two arguments, defined as $f(x, y) = x^2 + y$. We might express f as $\lambda(x, y) \,.\, (x^2 + y)$, with a *pair* as input. In this book, however, we will only consider functions of one argument. From the following remark it follows that this is not a real restriction.

Remark 1.2.6   *The behaviour of a function of two (or more) arguments can be simulated by converting it into a composite of functions of a single argument. For example, instead of the two-place function $\lambda(x, y) \,.\, (x^2 + y)$ one can write $\lambda x \,.\, (\lambda y \,.\, (x^2 + y))$. The latter function is called the* Curried *version of the former one, after the λ-calculus pioneer H.B. Curry; the idea of 'Currying' already can be found in the work of M. Schönfinkel (see Schönfinkel, 1924).*

There are subtle differences between the two versions when we provide them with two input values, for example:
– give $f = \lambda(x, y) \,.\, (x^2 + y)$ as argument the pair $(3, 5)$, then $f(3, 5)$ reduces to $3^2 + 5$;
– similarly, we can give $g = \lambda x \,.\, (\lambda y \,.\, (x^2 + y))$ these two arguments, but only *successively and in the 'correct' order, so first 3 and then 5; the result is $(g(3))(5)$, which reduces again to $3^2 + 5$ (use the reduction rule twice).*

By the way: with function g we have the liberty to give only one argument and then stop the process: $g(3)$ has a meaning in itself, it reduces to $\lambda y \,.\, (3^2 + y)$. This is not possible with function f, which always needs a pair of arguments.

1.3 Lambda-terms

The main concern of the discipline called *lambda calculus* is the behaviour of functions in the simplest, most abstract view. This means that we can even do without numbers, and consequently we neither consider, for the time being, the usual simple operations connected with numbers, such as addition and multiplication, nor more complex ones: exponentiation, the sine. Hence, many of the examples from the previous section are no longer useable.

What remains?

– To start with: *variables* $(x, y, \ldots)$.
– Moreover: the two construction principles mentioned in the previous section: *abstraction* and *application*.
– Finally: the 'calculation rule' called *β-reduction*.

In the rest of this chapter, we introduce the *untyped λ-calculus* as a formal system, giving precise definitions, including the important operations, and stating the main properties. We omit most of the proofs, for which we refer to the overview text of J.R. Hindley and J.P. Seldin (Hindley & Seldin, 2008) or the seminal work on untyped λ-calculus by H.P. Barendregt (Barendregt, 1981).

Remark 1.3.1 *Lambda calculus or λ-calculus was invented by A. Church in the 1930s (Church, 1933). (It is not completely clear why he used the Greek letter λ – which represents the letter l – for expressing abstraction; see Cardone & Hindley, 2009, Section 4.1, for more details.) Church's aim was to use his lambda calculus as a foundation for a formal theory of mathematics, in order to establish which functions are 'computable' by means of an algorithm (and which are not). See also Section 1.12.*

Expressions in the lambda calculus are called *λ-terms*. The following inductive definition establishes how the set Λ of all λ-terms is constructed. To start with, we assume the existence of an infinite set V of so-called *variables*: $V = \{x, y, z, \ldots\}$.

Definition 1.3.2   (The set Λ of all λ-terms)
(1) (Variable) If $u \in V$, then $u \in \Lambda$.
(2) (Application) If M and $N \in \Lambda$, then $(MN) \in \Lambda$.
(3) (Abstraction) If $u \in V$ and $M \in \Lambda$, then $(\lambda u \,.\, M) \in \Lambda$.

Saying that this is an *inductive definition* of Λ means that (1), (2) and (3) are the *only* ways to construct elements of Λ.

An alternative and shorter manner to define Λ is via *abstract syntax* (or a 'grammar'):

$$\Lambda = V | (\Lambda\Lambda) | (\lambda V \,.\, \Lambda)$$

One should read this as follows: following the symbol '=' one finds three possible ways of constructing elements of Λ. These three possibilities are separated by the vertical bar '|'.

For example, the second one is $(\Lambda\Lambda)$, which means the juxtaposition of an element of Λ and an element of Λ, enclosed in parentheses, gives again an element of Λ. (Note that the two elements taken successively from Λ may be the same element or different elements; both possibilities are covered by the notation $\Lambda\Lambda$.) What we get in this manner is clearly the same as expressed in Definition 1.3.2 (2).

Examples 1.3.3   Examples of λ-terms are:

- (with Variable as construction principle): x, y, z,
- (with Application as final construction step): $(x\,x)$, $(y\,x)$, $(x(x\,z))$,
- (with Abstraction as final step): $(\lambda x\,.\,(x\,z))$, $(\lambda y\,.\,(\lambda z\,.\,x))$, $(\lambda x\,.\,(\lambda x\,.\,(x\,x)))$,
- (and again, with Application as final step): $((\lambda x\,.\,(x\,z))\,y)$, $(y\,(\lambda x\,.\,(x\,z)))$, $((\lambda x\,.\,x)(\lambda x\,.\,x))$.

Notation 1.3.4   *(The representation of λ-terms; syntactical identity; $\equiv$)*
(1) We use the letters x, y, z and variants with subscripts and primes to denote variables in V.
(2) To denote elements of Λ, we use L, M, N, P, Q, R and variants thereof.
(3) Syntactical identity of two λ-terms will be denoted with the symbol $\equiv$.

So $(x\,z) \equiv (x\,z)$, but $(x\,z) \not\equiv (x\,y)$. Note that '$M \equiv N$' expresses that the actual λ-terms represented by M and N are identical.

With the following recursive definition we determine what the *subterms* of a given λ-term are; these form a *multiset*, since identical terms may occur more than once (see examples later).

Definition 1.3.5   (Multiset of subterms; Sub)
(1) (Basis) $\mathsf{Sub}(x) = \{x\}$, for each $x \in V$.
(2) (Application) $\mathsf{Sub}((MN)) = \mathsf{Sub}(M) \cup \mathsf{Sub}(N) \cup \{(MN)\}$.
(3) (Abstraction) $\mathsf{Sub}((\lambda x\,.\,M)) = \mathsf{Sub}(M) \cup \{(\lambda x\,.\,M)\}$.

We call L a subterm of M if $L \in \mathsf{Sub}(M)$.

From the above definition, the properties below follow.

Lemma 1.3.6   *(1) (Reflexivity) For all λ-terms M, we have $M \in \mathsf{Sub}(M)$.*
(2) (Transitivity) If $L \in \mathsf{Sub}(M)$ and $M \in \mathsf{Sub}(N)$, then $L \in \mathsf{Sub}(N)$.

Note that a certain λ-term can 'occur' several times as a subterm in a given term. For example, with $(x\,x)$ we have that $x \in \mathsf{Sub}((x\,x))$ for two reasons: the 'first' x in $(x\,x)$ is a subterm and also the 'second' x is a subterm. In such cases, one speaks about different *occurrences* of the subterm.

Examples 1.3.7 $-$ The only subterm of y is y itself.
$-$ The subterms of $(x\,z)$ are $(x\,z)$, x and z.

– Similarly, the λ-term $(\lambda x . (x\,x))$ has *four* subterms: (1) $(\lambda x . (x\,x))$ itself; (2) $(x\,x)$; (3) the *left* x in $(x\,x)$; and (4) the *right* x in $(x\,x)$. Note that the first occurrence of x in $(\lambda x . (x\,x))$, the one immediately following the λ, does not count as a *subterm*.

– $\mathrm{Sub}((\lambda x . (x\,x))(\lambda x . (x\,x)))$ consists of $((\lambda x . (x\,x))(\lambda x . (x\,x)))$, $(\lambda x . (x\,x))$ (twice), $(x\,x)$ (twice) and x (four times).

It is easy to find the subterms of a λ-term when this λ-term is given in *tree representation*. We do not describe specifically how such a tree representation can be constructed; an example should be enough. See Figure 1.1. The letter 'a' in this figure stands for 'application'.

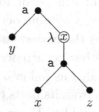

Figure 1.1 The tree of $(y\,(\lambda x . (x\,z)))$

A variable in a term M that immediately follows a λ symbol is drawn inside the corresponding node in the tree. The subterms of a λ-term M correspond to the *subtrees* in the tree representation of M. (We assume that the reader is familiar with the notion 'subtree'.) Check this in Figure 1.1. Note that the labels of the leaves in such a tree are always variables. And the other way round: a subterm consisting of a single variable corresponds to a labelled leaf. (Remember that a variable placed 'inside' a node is *not* a subterm; cf. Examples 1.3.7.)

There is also a notion of *proper* subterm, which excludes the Reflexivity in Lemma 1.3.6:

Definition 1.3.8 (Proper subterm)
L is a proper subterm of M if L is a subterm of M, but $L \not\equiv M$.

Example 1.3.9 The proper subterms of $(y(\lambda x . (x\,z)))$ are: y, $(\lambda x . (x\,z))$, $(x\,z)$, x and z.

Expressions constructed with Definition 1.3.2 have a lot of parentheses, which hampers readability. In order to be able to save on parentheses, the following conventions are followed:

Notation 1.3.10 – *Parentheses in an* outermost *position may be omitted, so MN stands for λ-term (MN) and $\lambda x . M$ for $(\lambda x . M)$.*

— *Application is left-associative, so MNL is an abbreviation for $((MN)L)$.*
— *Application takes precedence over abstraction, so we can write $\lambda x \,.\, MN$ instead of $\lambda x \,.\, (MN)$.*
— *Successive abstractions may be combined in a right-associative way under one λ, so we write $\lambda xy \,.\, M$ instead of $\lambda x \,.\, (\lambda y \,.\, M)$.*

These conventions are very useful, but also treacherous. As an example, note that $\lambda y \,.\, y\,(x\,y)$ should not be read as $(\lambda y \,.\, y)(x\,y)$, but as $\lambda y \,.\, (y(x\,y))$. Especially when substitution is involved (see Section 1.6), one must be careful.

1.4 Free and bound variables

Variable occurrences in a λ-term can be divided into three categories: *free* occurrences, *bound* occurrences and *binding* occurrences.

The last-mentioned category is the easiest to describe: these are the occurrences immediately after a λ. Other occurrences of variables in a λ-term are free or bound, which can be decided as follows.

In the construction of a λ-term from its parts (see Definition 1.3.2) we always start (see step (1)) with single variables. These are then *free*. In building more complicated terms via steps (2) and (3), it is only in the latter case that freeness may change: an occurrence of x which is free in M becomes *bound* in $\lambda x \,.\, M$. Otherwise said: abstraction of x over M *binds* all free occurrences of x in M; that is why the first x in $\lambda x \,.\, M$ is called a *binding* variable occurrence.

This discussion leads to the following recursive definition, in which $FV(L)$ denotes the set of free variables in λ-term L.

Definition 1.4.1   (*FV*, the set of free variables of a λ-term)
(1) (Variable) $FV(x) = \{x\}$,
(2) (Application) $FV(MN) = FV(M) \cup FV(N)$,
(3) (Abstraction) $FV(\lambda x \,.\, M) = FV(M) \setminus \{x\}$.

Examples 1.4.2

$$
\begin{aligned}
- FV(\lambda x \,.\, x\,y) \;&=\; FV(x\,y) \backslash \{x\} \\
&=\; (FV(x) \cup FV(y)) \backslash \{x\} \\
&=\; (\{x\} \cup \{y\}) \backslash \{x\} \\
&=\; \{x, y\} \backslash \{x\} \\
&=\; \{y\}.
\end{aligned}
$$

$$
- FV(x(\lambda x \,.\, xy)) \;=\; \{x, y\}.
$$

The last example demonstrates that Definition 1.4.1 collects the variables which are free *somewhere* in a λ-term. However, other occurrences of that variable in the same term may be bound. In the example term $x(\lambda x \,.\, x\,y)$, both x and y occur free, but only the first occurrence of x is free, the occurrence of x

just before y is bound. (The occurrence of x after the λ is a binding occurrence, being neither free nor bound.)

When inspecting the tree representation of a λ-term, it is easy to see whether a certain occurrence of a variable is free or bound: start with a variable occurrence, say x, at a leaf of the tree. Now follow the 'root path' upwards, that is: follow the branch from that leaf to the root (the uppermost node). If we pass an 'abstraction node' with the same x inside, then the original x is bound; otherwise it is free. Check these things for yourself with the tree representation of the term $x(\lambda x . \, x\, y)$.

Ending this section, we define an important subset of the set of all λ-terms by giving a name to terms without free variables:

Definition 1.4.3 (Closed λ-term; combinator; Λ^0)
The λ-term M is *closed* if $FV(M) = \emptyset$. A closed λ-term is also called a *combinator*. The set of all closed λ-terms is denoted by Λ^0.

Example: $\lambda xyz . \, xxy$ and $\lambda xy . \, xxy$ are closed λ-terms; $\lambda x . \, xxy$ is not.

1.5 Alpha conversion

Functions in the λ-notation (see Section 1.2) have the property that the *name* of the binding variable is not essential. The 'square function', for example, can be expressed by $\lambda x . \, x^2$ as well as by $\lambda u . \, u^2$. In both cases the expression means 'the function which calculates the square of an input value and gives the obtained number as its output value'. So the variable x (or u) serves as a temporary name for the input value, only meant to make it possible to *speak about* that value: the input called x gives output x^2, which describes the same procedure as 'input u gives output u^2'.

This is the reason why in the λ-calculus one is used to identify λ-terms which only differ in the *names* of the binding variables (together with the variables bound to them).

In order to describe this process formally, we define a relation called α-*conversion* or α-*equivalence*. It is based on the possibility of *renaming* binding (and bound) variables (cf. Hindley & Seldin, 2008, p. 278).

Definition 1.5.1 (Renaming; $M^{x \to y}$; $=_\alpha$)
Let $M^{x \to y}$ denote the result of replacing every free occurrence of x in M by y. The relation 'renaming', expressed with symbol $=_\alpha$, is defined as follows:
$\lambda x . \, M =_\alpha \lambda y . \, M^{x \to y}$, provided that $y \notin FV(M)$ and y is not a binding variable in M.

One says in this case: '$\lambda x . \, M$ has been renamed as $\lambda y . \, M^{x \to y}$'.

The intended effect is that the binding variable x in $\lambda x \,.\, M$, plus all the corresponding bound x's occurring in M, are renamed as y. Note that the mentioned bound x's are precisely the *free* x's in M.

Now, what about the two conditions in this definition?

(1) *First condition:* $y \notin FV(M)$. If there *were* a free y in M, then this y becomes *bound* to the binding variable y in $\lambda y \,.\, M^{x \to y}$, which is not what we want: renaming should not influence the free/bound status of variables.

Example: Take $\lambda x \,.\, M \equiv \lambda x \,.\, y$, so $y \in FV(M)$. Then $\lambda y \,.\, M^{x \to y} \equiv \lambda y \,.\, y$. Now the same variable occurrence y is first free, and then bound, which conflicts with our intentions regarding 'renaming'. Note that $\lambda x \,.\, y$ is essentially different from $\lambda y \,.\, y$: in the first expression, every input delivers the fixed output y, while in the second case each input returns itself as output.

(2) *Second condition:* y is not a binding variable in M. If this were permitted, then this binding y could unintentionally bind a 'new' y replacing an x.

Example: Take $\lambda x \,.\, M \equiv \lambda x \,.\, \lambda y \,.\, x$; then $\lambda y \,.\, M^{x \to y} \equiv \lambda y \,.\, \lambda y \,.\, y$. In the first expression, the final x is bound by the first λx; in the second expression, the final y, replacing the x, is bound by the *second* λy. So again, renaming would essentially change the situation. In terms of 'behaviour': originally, a first input followed by a second input returns the first input; but after illegitimate renaming, a first input followed by a second input returns the *second* input.

In short: in the renaming of $\lambda x \,.\, M$ to $\lambda y \,.\, M^{x \to y}$, it is prevented that the 'new' binding variable y binds 'old' free y's; and that any 'old' binding y binds a 'new' y.

Renaming in Definition 1.5.1 applies to the full λ-term only. In order to allow it more generally, we extend this definition to the following one:

Definition 1.5.2 (α-conversion or α-equivalence, $=_\alpha$)
(1) (Renaming) $\lambda x \,.\, M =_\alpha \lambda y \,.\, M^{x \to y}$ as in Definition 1.5.1, under the same conditions,
(2) (Compatibility) If $M =_\alpha N$, then $ML =_\alpha NL$, $LM =_\alpha LN$ and, for arbitrary z, $\lambda z \,.\, M =_\alpha \lambda z \,.\, N$,
(3a) (Reflexivity) $M =_\alpha M$,
(3b) (Symmetry) If $M =_\alpha N$ then $N =_\alpha M$,
(3c) (Transitivity) If both $L =_\alpha M$ and $M =_\alpha N$, then $L =_\alpha N$.

So renaming, expressed in (1), is the basis of α-equivalence.

The compatibility rules (2) have the effect that one may also rename binding and corresponding bound variables in an arbitrary *subterm* of a given λ-term.

Reflexivity (3a), symmetry (3b) and transitivity (3c) make α-conversion into an *equivalence relation*.

Examples 1.5.3

(1)　$(\lambda x \,.\, x \,(\lambda z \,.\, x\,y))\,z \;=_\alpha\; (\lambda x \,.\, x \,(\lambda z \,.\, x\,y))\,z,$

　　　$(\lambda x \,.\, x \,(\lambda z \,.\, x\,y))\,z \;=_\alpha\; (\lambda u \,.\, u \,(\lambda z \,.\, u\,y))\,z,$

　　　$(\lambda x \,.\, x \,(\lambda z \,.\, x\,y))\,z \;=_\alpha\; (\lambda z \,.\, z \,(\lambda x \,.\, z\,y))\,z,$

　　　$(\lambda x \,.\, x \,(\lambda z \,.\, x\,y))\,z \;\neq_\alpha\; (\lambda y \,.\, y \,(\lambda z \,.\, y\,y))\,z \quad (*_1),$

　　　$(\lambda x \,.\, x \,(\lambda z \,.\, x\,y))\,z \;\neq_\alpha\; (\lambda z \,.\, z \,(\lambda z \,.\, z\,y))\,z \quad (*_2),$

　　　$(\lambda x \,.\, x \,(\lambda z \,.\, x\,y))\,z \;\neq_\alpha\; (\lambda u \,.\, u \,(\lambda z \,.\, u\,y))\,v \quad (*_3)$

(2)　$\lambda x\,y \,.\, x\,z\,y \;=_\alpha\; \lambda v\,y \,.\, v\,z\,y,$

　　　$\lambda x\,y \,.\, x\,z\,y \;=_\alpha\; \lambda v\,u \,.\, v\,z\,u,$

　　　$\lambda x\,y \,.\, x\,z\,y \;\neq_\alpha\; \lambda y\,y \,.\, y\,z\,y \quad (*_4)$

　　　$\lambda x\,y \,.\, x\,z\,y \;\neq_\alpha\; \lambda z\,y \,.\, z\,z\,y \quad (*_5)$

Note that (1) uses the first case of the Compatibility rule: the renaming takes place in a subterm, viz. $\lambda x \,.\, x \,(\lambda z \,.\, x\,y)$.

In these examples, the most interesting cases are the ones where $=_\alpha$ does *not* hold (check the other cases yourself):

$(*_1)$: Renaming x as y in $\lambda x \,.\, x \,(\lambda z \,.\, x\,y)$ violates the first condition of Definition 1.5.1, since $y \in FV(x \,(\lambda z \,.\, x\,y))$.

$(*_2)$: Renaming x as z in $\lambda x \,.\, x \,(\lambda z \,.\, x\,y)$ violates the second condition, since z is a binding variable in $x \,(\lambda z \,.\, x\,y)$.

$(*_3)$: Renaming only applies to binding variables and (corresponding) bound ones, not to free variables. (Name change of a free variable does affect the 'intended meaning' of an expression.)

$(*_4)$: Renaming variable x as y is forbidden by the second condition of Definition 1.5.1, since y is a binding variable in $\lambda y \,.\, x\,z\,y$. Note that $\lambda y\,y \,.\, y\,z\,y =_\alpha \lambda x\,y \,.\, y\,z\,y$.

$(*_5)$: Conflicts with the first condition.

So, given a λ-term, there are many terms that are related to this term by the $=_\alpha$-relation.

Definition 1.5.4　(α-convertible; α-equivalent; α-variant)
If $M =_\alpha N$, then M and N are said to be α-*convertible* or α-*equivalent*. M is called an α-*variant* of N (and vice versa).

1.6 Substitution

In Section 1.2 we informally made use of substitution as a stepping stone to β-reduction. We denoted 'M in which N has been substituted for the free variable x' as $M[x := N]$. We are now in the position to give a precise formulation of this notion 'substitution'. It is defined as follows.

Definition 1.6.1   (Substitution)

(1a) $x[x := N] \equiv N$,

(1b) $y[x := N] \equiv y$ if $x \not\equiv y$,

(2) $(PQ)[x := N] \equiv (P[x := N])(Q[x := N])$,

(3) $(\lambda y \,.\, P)[x := N] \equiv \lambda z \,.\, (P^{y \to z}[x := N])$, if $\lambda z \,.\, P^{y \to z}$ is an α-variant of $\lambda y \,.\, P$ such that $z \notin FV(N)$.

Remarks 1.6.2   *In Definition 1.6.1 we make a liberal use of parentheses. For example, the two pairs of parentheses in $(P[x := N])(Q[x := N])$ are meant to make clear how the expression should be interpreted. They may well be erasable after elaboration. (See also Notation 1.3.10.)*

Before discussing these substitution rules in detail (see below), we note that terms of the form $P[x := N]$, as such, are not λ-terms, since the suffix $[x := N]$ does not occur in the definition of λ-terms (Definition 1.3.2). So $P[x := N]$ is meant to be *meta-notation* for a 'proper' λ-term, which can be found by applying the above definition until all suffixes $[x := N]$ have disappeared.

Now we take a closer look at the parts of Definition 1.6.1.

(1a) This is the heart of the matter: substituting N for x in the basic λ-term x naturally results in N.

(1b) But when y is different from x, then the substitution for x has, of course, no effect on y.

(2) Here the substitution is simply 'pushed inside' both sides of an application.

(3) This is how we push the substitution inside an abstraction. Thereby we have to be careful that free variables y of N do not become unintentionally bound by the binding variable y of $\lambda y \,.\, P$ when N is substituted for the free x's in P; this is the reason for taking a 'new' z (if necessary) such that $z \notin FV(N)$.

Remark 1.6.3   *(1) When $y \notin FV(N)$, then the definition permits us to let binding variable y stay as it is: $(\lambda y \,.\, P)[x := N] \equiv \lambda y \,.\, (P[x := N])$, since $P^{y \to y} \equiv P$.*

(2) This also holds when $x \notin FV(P)$, since then there is no x to substitute for.

(3) Renaming can be considered as a special case of substitution, since we can show that $M^{x \to u} =_\alpha M[x := u]$ if the conditions of renaming are satisfied.

Examples 1.6.4   (1) Consider $(\lambda y \,.\, y\, x)[x := x\, y]$.

When we disregard the condition in part (3) of Definition 1.6.1 and do not rename the y in $\lambda y \,.\, y\, x$, we obtain $\lambda y \,.\, ((y\, x)[x := x\, y])$, which is $\lambda y \,.\, y(x\, y)$. But this is clearly wrong, since the free y in $x\, y$ has become bound in $\lambda y \,.\, y(x\, y)$.

Hence, one first should rename all y's in $\lambda y \,.\, y\, x$, e.g. to z. Successive use of the substitution rules then gives:

$$
\begin{aligned}
(\lambda y \,.\, y\,x)[x := x\,y] \quad &\equiv \quad \lambda z \,.\, ((z\,x)[x := x\,y]), \\
&\equiv \quad \lambda z \,.\, ((z[x := x\,y])(x[x := x\,y])), \\
&\equiv \quad \lambda z \,.\, z(x\,y).
\end{aligned}
$$

$$
\begin{aligned}
(2) \quad (\lambda x \,.\, y\,x)[x := x\,y] \quad &\equiv \quad \lambda z \,.\, ((y\,z)[x := x\,y]), \\
&\equiv \quad \lambda z \,.\, ((y[x := x\,y])(z[x := x\,y])), \\
&\equiv \quad \lambda z \,.\, y\,z,
\end{aligned}
$$

Note: $\qquad =_\alpha \quad \lambda x \,.\, y\,x$ (cf. Remark 1.6.3 (2)).

$$
\begin{aligned}
(3) \quad (\lambda x\,y \,.\, z\,z\,x)[z := y] \quad &\equiv \quad \lambda u \,.\, ((\lambda y \,.\, z\,z\,u)[z := y]), \\
&\equiv \quad \lambda u \,.\, \lambda v \,.\, ((z\,z\,u)[z := y]), \\
&\vdots \\
&\equiv \quad \lambda u\,v \,.\, y\,y\,u,
\end{aligned}
$$

Note: $\qquad =_\alpha \quad \lambda x\,v \,.\, y\,y\,x$, but
$\qquad\qquad \neq_\alpha \quad \lambda x\,y \,.\, y\,y\,x.$

We conclude this section with the discussion of *sequential substitution*: doing a number of substitutions consecutively. For example, a twofold substitution may look like $M[x := N][y := L]$, which means: first substitute N for x in M, and next substitute L for y in the obtained result (so $(M[x := N])[y := L]$ would be a clearer notation).

An interesting point is the order of the substitutions: does $M[x := N][y := L]$ describe the same λ-term as $M[y := L][x := N]$? The answer is: in general, no. This can already be shown by means of a very simple counterexample: $x[x := y][y := x] \equiv x$, but $x[y := x][x := y] \equiv y$.

Therefore, we have to be careful in swapping substitutions. An educated guess is: $M[x := N][y := L] \equiv M[y := L][x := N[y := L]]$, in order to compensate on the right-hand side for the fact that, on the left-hand side, free y's in N become subject to the substitution $[y := L]$. Thus, on the right-hand side we have $N[y := L]$ instead of N, being substituted for x.

However, this still is not enough. One should also prevent free x's in L, which are left untouched on the left-hand side, becoming subject to the substitution $[x := N[y := L]]$ on the right-hand side. It suffices to require that $x \notin FV(L)$. So we obtain:

Lemma 1.6.5 *Let $x \not\equiv y$ and assume $x \notin FV(L)$. Then:*
$M[x := N][y := L] \equiv M[y := L][x := N[y := L]]\,.$

We do not give a proof for this lemma (such a proof is not hard, but rather boring), but make some suggestive drawings instead; see Figures 1.2 and 1.3.

In Figure 1.2 we give two pictorial representations of the λ-term M, which possibly contains the free variables x and y. On the left-hand side of the figure, we depict that N is substituted for x. This N may contain y. (It may also

$$M \equiv \boxed{\ldots\ldots x \ldots\ldots\ldots\ldots y \ldots\ldots} \qquad\qquad M \equiv \boxed{\ldots\ldots x \ldots\ldots\ldots\ldots y \ldots\ldots}$$

$$N \equiv \boxed{\ldots y \ldots} \qquad\qquad\qquad L \equiv \boxed{\textbf{no } x}$$

Figure 1.2 $M[x := N]$ (left) and $M[y := L]$ (right) in graphical form

contain x, but this is not relevant in the present case.) Similarly, on the right-hand side of the figure, we depict that L is substituted for y. In this picture we express, in accordance with one of the conditions in Lemma 1.6.5, that variable x does not occur free in L.

So Figure 1.2 represent the first steps on the left-hand side and the right-hand side of the lemma: $M[x := N]$ and $M[y := L]$, respectively.

Next, we depict how the second substitution steps, $[y := L]$ on the left-hand side and $[x := N[y := L]]$ on the right-hand side, contribute to the final result (see Figure 1.3). It will be intuitively clear that the results are the same. Note the importance of the fact that L in Figure 1.2 does not contain a free x.

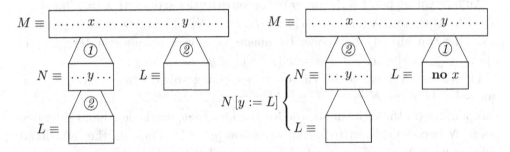

Figure 1.3 $M[x := N][y := L] \equiv M[y := L][x := N[y := L]]$

1.7 Lambda-terms modulo α-equivalence

In Section 1.5 we discussed α-conversion, meant to relate λ-terms that are in a sense 'equal': if $M =_\alpha N$, then the structures of M and N are the same but for the *names* of the binding variables and the corresponding bound ones. This implies that M and N have similar trees: a variable, λ or $\mathbf{a}$ in M's tree exactly matches with a corresponding one in N. Corresponding *free* variables have identical names; all combinations of binding and bound variables in M show exactly the same pattern as in N.

In a sense, such α-equivalent M and N represent the same λ-term. As to 'behaviour', there is no difference between them. Moreover, α-equivalence is conserved by elementary processes of term construction, as witnessed by the following lemma.

Lemma 1.7.1 *Let $M_1 =_\alpha N_1$ and $M_2 =_\alpha N_2$. Then also:*
(1) $M_1 N_1 =_\alpha M_2 N_2$,
(2) $\lambda x . M_1 =_\alpha \lambda x . M_2$,
(3) $M_1[x := N_1] =_\alpha M_2[x := N_2]$.

(In (1) and (2) we repeat (a variant of) the compatibility rules of Definition 1.5.2. Part (3) is stated without proof.)

As a consequence of the above, it does not really matter which one to choose in a class of α-equivalent λ-terms: the results of manipulating such terms are always α-equivalent again. Therefore we take the liberty to consider a full *class* of α-equivalent λ-terms as one *abstract* λ-term. We can also express this as follows: we *abstract from the names of the bound (and binding) variables*, by treating α-equivalent terms as 'equal'; that is to say, we consider λ-terms *modulo α-equivalence*.

Convention 1.7.2 *From now on, we identify α-convertible λ-terms.*

Notation 1.7.3 *With a slight abuse of Notation 1.3.4, we use $\equiv$ also for syntactical identity modulo α-equivalence.*

So the relation α-equivalence gets out of sight: for example, instead of $\lambda x . x =_\alpha \lambda y . y$ we simply write $\lambda x . x \equiv \lambda y . y$.

Since Convention 1.7.2 permits us to choose the names of binding and bound variables at will, it is convenient to agree on the following, which is called the *Barendregt convention* after H.P. Barendregt, a leading expert in λ-calculus (cf. Barendregt, 1981).

Convention 1.7.4 *(Barendregt convention)*
We choose the names for the binding variables in a λ-term in such a manner that they are all different, and such that each of them differs from all free variables occurring in the term.

Hence, we shall use a unique name after every λ occurring in a λ-term, and rename the bound variables accordingly. So, we do not write $(\lambda xy . xz)(\lambda xz . z)$, but e.g. $(\lambda xy . xz)(\lambda uv . v)$. By adopting the Barendregt convention, one is better able to read the λ-terms and to see how they are composed with respect to variable binding.

In order to exploit these matters to our benefit, we also stretch out the

Barendregt convention to 'intermediate' expressions with unexecuted substitutions; so we will not write $(\lambda x \, . \, x \, y \, z)[y := \lambda x \, . \, x]$, or $(\lambda x \, . \, x \, y \, z)[y := \lambda y \, . \, y]$, or $(\lambda x \, . \, x \, y \, z)[y := \lambda z \, . \, z]$, but, for example, $(\lambda x \, . \, x \, y \, z)[y := \lambda u \, . \, u]$, in line with the Barendregt convention.

1.8 Beta reduction

Now that we have formally introduced substitution, our reduction mechanism of Section 1.2 can be rephrased as a relation on λ-terms. It is generally called β-reduction, following H.B. Curry. (Why the letter β, the Greek b? The simple reason seems to be that α, the Greek a, was already occupied – see Definition 1.5.2 – and β was next; see Cardone & Hindley, 2009, for the history of λ-calculus.)

We start with a single β-reduction step:

Definition 1.8.1 (One-step β-reduction, $\to_\beta$)
(1) (Basis) $(\lambda x \, . \, M)N \to_\beta M[x := N]$,
(2) (Compatibility) If $M \to_\beta N$, then $ML \to_\beta NL$, $LM \to_\beta LN$ and $\lambda x \, . \, M \to_\beta \lambda x \, . \, N$.

Note that the suffix $[x := N]$ in (1), which (in Section 1.2) we inaccurately described as 'replacement', is now meant to be the (precisely defined) substitution of Section 1.6. The compatibility rules of (2) serve the same purpose as with α-conversion: they assure that $P \to_\beta Q$ also holds if a *subterm* of P of the form $(\lambda x \, . \, M)N$ has been changed into $M[x := N]$, resulting in Q.

In a picture, one-step β-reduction can be represented as in Figure 1.4.

$$\boxed{\ldots\ldots((\lambda x \, . \, M)N)\ldots\ldots} \quad \to_\beta \quad \boxed{\ldots\ldots(M[x := N])\ldots\ldots}$$

Figure 1.4 A pictorial representation of one-step β-reduction

The subterm of the form $(\lambda x \, . \, M)N$ on the left-hand side of this picture is called a *redex* (from '*red*ucible *ex*pression'). The subterm $M[x := N]$ on the right-hand side is called the *contractum* (of the redex).

We recall from Section 1.2 that the 'incentive' to defining the relation $\to_\beta$ is the presence of an application term (in the formal sense) where the first part is an abstraction: $\lambda x \, . \, M$. Since an abstraction can be thought of as representing a function, we can conceive of the part N as an *argument* for this function, which naturally leads to an 'outcome': $M[x := N]$.

The subterm M in $\lambda x \, . \, M$ is called the *body* of the abstraction. Note that the process of reduction can be described as: 'strip a redex down to the body

M of the abstraction and substitute argument N for all free x's occurring in this body'.

Relation '$\to_\beta$' is called *one-step* β-reduction because precisely *one* redex is replaced by its contractum (see again Figure 1.4).

We now give some examples.

Examples 1.8.2 (1) $(\lambda x \,.\, x(x\,y))N \to_\beta N(N\,y)$.

(2) In the term $(\lambda x \,.\, (\lambda y \,.\, y\,x)z)v$ we find *two* redexes:

    redex 1: the full term itself, and

    redex 2: the subterm $(\lambda y \,.\, y\,x)z$.

Hence, there are two possible one-step β-reductions:

    via redex 1:

$$\overbrace{(\lambda x \,.\, (\lambda y \,.\, y\,x)z)v} \to_\beta (\lambda y \,.\, y\,v)z$$

    or via redex 2:

$$(\lambda x \,.\, \overbrace{(\lambda y \,.\, y\,x)z})v \to_\beta (\lambda x \,.\, z\,x)v.$$

Note that the terms on the right-hand sides of the $\to_\beta$-symbols are not α-equivalent, hence not syntactically identical according to Convention 1.7.2.

The fact that one term reduces to two different terms demonstrates that the direct result of the reduction of a λ-term depends on the choice of the redex. Note, however, that, in the present example, both obtained terms can be reduced further to obtain a 'common reduct', viz. $z\,v$:

$$(\lambda y \,.\, y\,v)z \to_\beta z\,v, \text{ and } (\lambda x \,.\, z\,x)v \to_\beta z\,v.$$

(3) $(\lambda x \,.\, x\,x)(\lambda x \,.\, x\,x) \to_\beta (\lambda x \,.\, x\,x)(\lambda x \,.\, x\,x)$

This is a remarkable one. (To make this clearly visible, we temporarily ignore the Barendregt convention.)

First note that the full term is a redex: the abstraction $\lambda x \,.\, x\,x$ (the left half of the term) is applied to the argument $\lambda x \,.\, x\,x$ (being the right half of the term). It happens that both abstraction and argument are identical.

Check that the first subterm $x\,x$ is the body of the abstraction (in the left half), and that β-reduction amounts to substituting the argument for *both* free x's in this body (so the argument becomes 'duplicated'). This results in the same term we started with.

As shown in the second example above, we can often perform a second β-reduction step after the first one. Repeated one-step β-reduction leads to a more general relation, called β-reduction ('as such') and denoted $\twoheadrightarrow_\beta$.

Definition 1.8.3 (β-reduction (zero-or-more-step), $\twoheadrightarrow_\beta$)
$M \twoheadrightarrow_\beta N$ if there is an $n \geq 0$ and there are terms M_0 to M_n such that $M_0 \equiv M$, $M_n \equiv N$ and for all i such that $0 \leq i < n$:

$$M_i \to_\beta M_{i+1}.$$

Hence, if $M \twoheadrightarrow_\beta N$, there exists a *chain* of single-step β-reductions, starting with M and ending with N:

$$M \equiv M_0 \to_\beta M_1 \to_\beta M_2 \to_\beta \cdots \to_\beta M_{n-2} \to_\beta M_{n-1} \to_\beta M_n \equiv N.$$

For a demonstration of the relation $\twoheadrightarrow_\beta$, we refer to Example 1.8.2 (2), from which it follows that

$(\lambda x \,.\, (\lambda y \,.\, yx)z)v \twoheadrightarrow_\beta zv$.

(Example 1.8.2 even provides for *two* $\twoheadrightarrow_\beta$-chains from $(\lambda x \,.\, (\lambda y \,.\, yx)z)v$ to zv.)

The following holds for $\twoheadrightarrow_\beta$:

Lemma 1.8.4 *(1)* $\twoheadrightarrow_\beta$ *extends* $\to_\beta$, *i.e. if* $M \to_\beta N$, *then* $M \twoheadrightarrow_\beta N$.
(2) $\twoheadrightarrow_\beta$ *is reflexive and transitive, i.e.:*
  (refl): for all M: $M \twoheadrightarrow_\beta M$,
  (trans): for all L, M *and* N: *if* $L \twoheadrightarrow_\beta M$ *and* $M \twoheadrightarrow_\beta N$, *then* $L \twoheadrightarrow_\beta N$.

Proof *(1)* Take $n = 1$ in Definition 1.8.3.
(2) Reflexivity: take $n = 0$ in Definition 1.8.3. Transitivity: follows directly from the same definition. $\qquad\square$

An extension of this zero-or-more-step β-reduction is called β-conversion, denoted $=_\beta$.

Definition 1.8.5 *(β-conversion, β-equality; $=_\beta$)*
$M =_\beta N$ (to be read as: 'M and N are β-convertible' or 'β-equal') if there is an $n \geq 0$ and there are terms M_0 to M_n such that $M_0 \equiv M$, $M_n \equiv N$ and for all i such that $0 \leq i < n$:

either $M_i \to_\beta M_{i+1}$ *or* $M_{i+1} \to_\beta M_i$.

Note that each pair of M_i and M_{i+1} should now be related by the single-step relation $\to_\beta$, but not necessarily from left to right: it may also happen that some of these pairs are related the other way round (from right to left).

For instances of $=_\beta$, we refer again to Example 1.8.2 (2). Note that each pair in the following set of four terms is related by means of $=_\beta$:

$\{(\lambda x \,.\, (\lambda y \,.\, y \, x)z)v, \ (\lambda y \,.\, y \, v)z, \ (\lambda x \,.\, z \, x)v, \ z \, v\}$.

For example: $(\lambda y \,.\, y \, v)z =_\beta (\lambda x \,.\, z \, x)v$ since we have the following chain, where $\leftarrow_\beta$ is the inverse of $\to_\beta$:

$(\lambda y \,.\, y \, v)z \to_\beta z \, v \leftarrow_\beta (\lambda x \,.\, z \, x)v$.

Another chain giving the same result is:

$(\lambda y \,.\, y \, v)z \leftarrow_\beta (\lambda x \,.\, (\lambda y \,.\, y \, x)z)v \to_\beta (\lambda x \,.\, z \, x)v$.

The following holds for $=_\beta$:

Lemma 1.8.6 *(1)* $=_\beta$ *extends* $\twoheadrightarrow_\beta$ *in both directions, i.e. if* $M \twoheadrightarrow_\beta N$ *or* $N \twoheadrightarrow_\beta M$, *then* $M =_\beta N$.

(2) $=_\beta$ *is an equivalence relation, hence reflexive, symmetric and transitive, i.e.:*
(refl): for all M*:* $M =_\beta M$,
(symm): for all M *and* N*: if* $M =_\beta N$*, then* $N =_\beta M$,
(trans): for all L*,* M *and* N*: if* $L =_\beta M$ *and* $M =_\beta N$*, then* $L =_\beta N$.

Proof (1) and (2) follow directly from Definition 1.8.5. □

Check that it also holds that
− if $M \twoheadrightarrow_\beta L_1$ and $M \twoheadrightarrow_\beta L_2$, then $L_1 =_\beta L_2$,
− if $L_1 \twoheadrightarrow_\beta N$ and $L_2 \twoheadrightarrow_\beta N$, then $L_1 =_\beta L_2$.

1.9 Normal forms and confluence

As we have said before, β-*reduction* mimics, in a certain sense, a calculation. By applying a function to an argument, and using reduction, we get a kind of (temporary) outcome, which hopefully is closer to some *final outcome*. This process is comparable with ordinary numerical calculations, as for example in $(3 + 7) \times (8 - 2) \to 10 \times (8 - 2) \to 10 \times 6 \to 60$, with $\to$ a symbol for a 'calculation step'.

Moreover, we can see conversion as a calculation in which we can change the direction at will. Hence, one may replace $10 \times (8 - 2)$ by 10×6, but also the other way round. These apparently 'unnatural' calculation steps are not as uncommon as one would expect. For example, the following calculation is very suitable for finding the extreme value of a second order polynomial:

$$ax^2 + bx + c \leftarrow a(x^2 + \tfrac{b}{a}x) + c \leftarrow a(x^2 + 2\tfrac{b}{2a}x) + c \leftarrow a(x + \tfrac{b}{2a})^2 - \tfrac{b^2}{4a} + c,$$

which implies that $c - \tfrac{b^2}{4a}$ is the extreme value, obtained when $x = -\tfrac{b}{2a}$. In this calculation one continuously calculates 'in the wrong direction'.

In the present section, we take a closer look at these calculational aspects, concentrating on the notion of *outcome* of a term and its relation with reduction and conversion.

Definition 1.9.1 *(β-normal form; β-nf; β-normalising)*
(1) M *is in* β-*normal form* (or: is in β-nf) if M does not contain any redex.
(2) M *has a* β-*normal form* (has a β-nf), or is β-*normalising*, if there is an N in β-nf such that $M =_\beta N$. Such an N is a β-*normal form* of M.

One views β-normal forms of a λ-term M as the outcome of M. When M is in β-nf, then it *is* an outcome itself (it has no redex, so no further calculation is possible). The following lemma is obvious; a zero-or-more-step reduction starting from a β-normal form must be actually zero-step.

Lemma 1.9.2   *When M is in β-nf, then $M \twoheadrightarrow_\beta N$ implies $M \equiv N$.*

Examples 1.9.3   See Examples 1.8.2.

(1) $(\lambda x \,.\, (\lambda y \,.\, y\,x)z)v$ has a β-nf, viz. $z\,v$, since $(\lambda x \,.\, (\lambda y \,.\, y\,x)z)v \twoheadrightarrow_\beta z\,v$ and $z\,v$ is in β-nf.

(2) Define $\Omega := (\lambda x \,.\, x\,x)(\lambda x \,.\, x\,x)$. Then Ω is not in β-nf (the term itself is a redex) and does not reduce to a β-nf, since it β-reduces (only) to itself, and so one never gets rid of the redex.

(3) Define $\Delta := \lambda x \,.\, x\,x\,x$. Then $\Delta\Delta \to_\beta \Delta\Delta\Delta \to_\beta \Delta\Delta\Delta\Delta \to_\beta \cdots$. Hence it follows that also $\Delta\Delta$ does not reduce to a β-nf, since there are no other possibilities for one-step β-reduction than the ones given in the chain above. (Check this yourself.)

(4) Take Ω as above. Then $(\lambda u \,.\, v)\Omega$ contains two redexes: the full term and the subterm Ω. Reducing the first redex gives v, which is in β-nf, so $(\lambda u \,.\, v)\Omega$ has a β-nf. Note that one has to be careful with choosing one's redex: when continuously taking Ω as the redex, one never reaches a β-nf.

Remark 1.9.4   *From this example, part (2), it follows that the converse of Lemma 1.9.2 ('If $M \twoheadrightarrow_\beta N$ implies $M \equiv N$, then M is in β-nf') is not true: take $M \equiv N \equiv \Omega$ for a counterexample.*

From the last example, part (4), it follows that the choice of the 'reduction path' may be relevant. This notion is defined as follows.

Definition 1.9.5   (Reduction path)
A *finite reduction path* from M is a finite sequence of terms $N_0, N_1, N_2, \ldots, N_n$ such that $N_0 \equiv M$ and $N_i \to_\beta N_{i+1}$ for each i with $0 \le i < n$.
An *infinite reduction path* from M is an infinite sequence $N_0, N_1, N_2, \ldots$ with $N_0 \equiv M$ and $N_i \to_\beta N_{i+1}$ for all $i \in \mathbb{N}$.

One also writes such paths as $M\ (\equiv N_0) \to_\beta N_1 \to_\beta \cdots \to_\beta N_n$ (the finite case) or $M\ (\equiv N_0) \to_\beta N_1 \to_\beta \cdots$ (the infinite case). (Note that such paths are always constructed with consecutive *one-step* β-reductions.)

Now we can define two subcollections of terms which 'behave nicely': the terms for which there *exists* a reduction path leading to an outcome, and the terms for which *each* reduction path leads to an outcome:

Definition 1.9.6 (Weak normalisation, strong normalisation)
(1) M is *weakly normalising* if there is an N in β-normal form such that $M \twoheadrightarrow_\beta N$.
(2) M is *strongly normalising* if there are no infinite reduction paths starting from M.

It will be clear that when M is strongly normalising, then each reduction path can be *extended* to one ending in a β-nf (the process of choosing a redex, doing the matching β-reduction, and repeating this, cannot go on indefinitely). Hence, all strongly normalising terms are also weakly normalising.

Example 1.9.7 In Examples 1.9.3 we find a weakly normalising term in (4), viz. $(\lambda u \,.\, v)\Omega$, and a strongly normalising term in (1): $(\lambda x \,.\, (\lambda y \,.\, y\,x)z)v$. The terms Ω and Δ in (2) and (3) are not weakly normalising, so also not strongly normalising.

There is a very important theorem about β-reduction, which relates weak normalisation to having a β-normal form. It is usually accompanied by a picture such as in Figure 1.5. Its content is: if a term M reduces to both N_1 and N_2, then there exists a common reduct of these two.

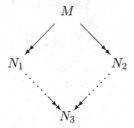

Figure 1.5 A pictorial representation of the Church–Rosser Theorem

The theorem is most commonly called the Church–Rosser Theorem (after the logicians A. Church and J.B. Rosser), abbreviated to CR. Another name is Confluence (the reduction paths 'flow together' again). Its formal statement is:

Theorem 1.9.8 *(Church–Rosser; CR; Confluence) Suppose that for a given λ-term M, we have $M \twoheadrightarrow_\beta N_1$ and $M \twoheadrightarrow_\beta N_2$. Then there is a λ-term N_3 such that $N_1 \twoheadrightarrow_\beta N_3$ and $N_2 \twoheadrightarrow_\beta N_3$.*

The proof of this theorem is much more complex than one would expect. Many proofs have been published in the past, some of considerable length. A complete proof can be found in H.P. Barendregt's standard work about the untyped lambda calculus (see Barendregt, 1981, p. 62) or in his 'Handbook paper' about typed lambda calculus, which has also been very influential (Barendregt, 1992, p. 136–141); in the latter book the proof takes a little more than four pages. We do not copy either of these proofs: the interested reader is referred to Barendregt's texts. (There also exists a short and elegant proof on an algebraic basis; see Takahashi, 1995.)

The importance of the Church–Rosser Theorem lies in the consequence that the outcome of a calculation (if it exists) is *independent* of the order in which the calculations are executed. (This follows from Lemma 1.9.10 (2) below.) This independence is what you intuitively expect from 'calculations': the consecutive choices of the redexes should not influence the final result.

For example, when calculating the outcome of $(3+5) \cdot (7-3)$, it should not matter whether one starts with redex $3+5$ or with redex $7-3$. And indeed, in both cases one obtains the same outcome:

$$(3+5) \cdot (7-3) \ \to \ 8 \cdot (7-3) \ \to \ 8 \cdot 4 \ \to \ 32,$$
$$(3+5) \cdot (7-3) \ \to \ (3+5) \cdot 4 \ \to \ 8 \cdot 4 \ \to \ 32.$$

For a diagram of this calculation, see Figure 1.6.

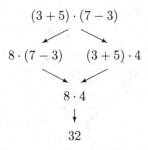

Figure 1.6 The various branches of a calculation

There is a corollary to the Church–Rosser Theorem, which says that any pair of convertible terms has a 'common reduct'; we shall also prove this:

Corollary 1.9.9 *Suppose that $M =_\beta N$. Then there is L such that $M \twoheadrightarrow_\beta L$ and $N \twoheadrightarrow_\beta L$.*

Proof Because $M =_\beta N$, we have by definition that, for some $n \in \mathbb{N}$:

$$M \equiv M_0 \ \overset{\to_\beta}{\underset{\leftarrow_\beta}{}} \ M_1 \ \ldots \ M_{n-1} \ \overset{\to_\beta}{\underset{\leftarrow_\beta}{}} \ M_n \equiv N \,.$$

(Here $M_i \ \overset{\to_\beta}{\underset{\leftarrow_\beta}{}} \ M_{i+1}$ denotes that either $M_i \to_\beta M_{i+1}$ or $M_{i+1} \to_\beta M_i$.)

We proceed by induction on n.

(1) $n = 0$: then $M \equiv N$. Take $L \equiv M(\equiv N)$, then $M \twoheadrightarrow_\beta L$ and $N \twoheadrightarrow_\beta L$ (in both cases in zero steps).

(2) $n = k > 0$: then M_{k-1} exists.

So we have that $M \equiv M_0 \ldots M_{k-1} \overset{\rightarrow_\beta}{\underset{\leftarrow_\beta}{}} M_k \equiv N$.

By induction, there is an L' such that $M_0 \twoheadrightarrow_\beta L'$ and $M_{k-1} \twoheadrightarrow_\beta L'$. This is shown graphically in Figure 1.7.

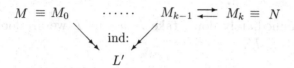

Figure 1.7 The induction case: $k > 0$

Now we distinguish between the two cases, $M_{k-1} \rightarrow_\beta M_k$ or $M_k \rightarrow_\beta M_{k-1}$.

(2a) In the first case, the situation is as in Figure 1.8.

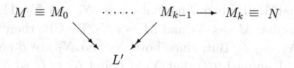

Figure 1.8 Subcase $M_{k-1} \rightarrow_\beta M_k$

Then we have that $M_{k-1} \twoheadrightarrow_\beta L'$ and $M_{k-1} \twoheadrightarrow_\beta M_k$. The latter reduction (in one step) is a special case of the more-step reduction $M_{k-1} \twoheadrightarrow_\beta M_k$. Hence, by CR, there is an L such that $L' \twoheadrightarrow_\beta L$ and $M_k \twoheadrightarrow_\beta L$. For a graphical representation, see Figure 1.9.

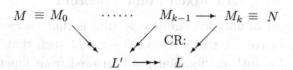

Figure 1.9 Subcase $M_{k-1} \rightarrow_\beta M_k$, extended by means of CR

Hence we found, as desired, the common reduct L, since $M \twoheadrightarrow_\beta L$ and $N \twoheadrightarrow_\beta L$.

(2b) In the second case, the situation is as in Figure 1.10.

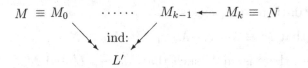

Figure 1.10 Subcase $M_k \to_\beta M_{k-1}$

Now we are immediately done: take L' as the L we are looking for, since $M \twoheadrightarrow_\beta L'$ and $N \twoheadrightarrow_\beta L'$. □

We conclude this section with two corollaries of the above.

Lemma 1.9.10   *(1) If M has N as β-normal form, then $M \twoheadrightarrow_\beta N$.*
  (2) A λ-term has at most one β-normal form.

Proof   (1) Assume $M =_\beta N$, with N in β-normal form. Then by the previous Corollary 1.9.9, there is an L such that $M \twoheadrightarrow_\beta L$ and $N \twoheadrightarrow_\beta L$. Since N is in β-nf, by Lemma 1.9.2: $N \equiv L$. Hence $M \twoheadrightarrow_\beta L \equiv N$, so $M \twoheadrightarrow_\beta N$.

(2) Assume that M has two β-normal forms, N_1 and N_2. Then by part (1) of the present lemma, $M \twoheadrightarrow_\beta N_1$ and $M \twoheadrightarrow_\beta N_2$. By CR, there is L such that $N_1 \twoheadrightarrow_\beta L$ and $N_2 \twoheadrightarrow_\beta L$. But, since both N_1 and N_2 are β-normal forms, it follows (again by Lemma 1.9.2) that $N_1 \equiv L$ and $N_2 \equiv L$, so $N_1 \equiv N_2$. □

Speaking informally, the consequences of this lemma are:
(1) If a λ-term has an outcome, then this outcome can be reached by 'forward calculation' (i.e. β-*reduction*).
(2) An outcome of a calculation, if it exists, is unique. (There cannot be two different outcomes for one λ-term.)

1.10 Fixed Point Theorem

A remarkable aspect of untyped lambda calculus is that *every* λ-term L has a 'fixed point', i.e. for each L there exists a λ-term M such that $LM =_\beta M$.

The term 'fixed point' (or 'fixpoint') is borrowed from functional analysis. There, a function f has fixed point a if $f(a) = a$, that is: function f applied to a returns a again, so a is 'fixed' by f. For example, the square function f on the natural numbers with $f(n) = n^2$ has two fixed points: 0 and 1. However, the so-called *successor function* s with $s(n) = n + 1$ has no fixed point at all and neither has g with $g(n) = 2^n$.

So untyped λ-calculus deviates from 'usual' calculus in this respect:

Theorem 1.10.1 *For all $L \in \Lambda$ there is $M \in \Lambda$ such that $LM =_\beta M$.*

Proof For given L, define $M := (\lambda x . L(xx))(\lambda x . L(xx))$.
  This M is a redex, so we have:

$$M \equiv (\lambda x . L(xx))(\lambda x . L(xx))$$
$$\rightarrow_\beta L((\lambda x . L(xx)) (\lambda x . L(xx)))$$
$$\equiv LM.$$

  Hence, $LM =_\beta M$. $\qquad\qquad\qquad\qquad\qquad\qquad\qquad\qquad\qquad\square$

Remark 1.10.2 *A λ-version of the successor function s mentioned above, e.g. $\lambda x . (x + 1)$, has a fixed point M according to Theorem 1.10.1. However, M does not represent a natural number. (About natural numbers in λ-form: see Exercise 1.10; see also Exercise 1.11.)*

From the method of the above proof, it follows that there even exists a so-called *fixed point combinator*, i.e. a closed term which 'constructs' a fixed point for an arbitrary input term. Such a fixed point combinator is

$$Y \equiv \lambda y . (\lambda x . y(xx))(\lambda x . y(xx)) .$$

Indeed, for each λ-term L, we have that YL is a fixed point of L, since $L(YL) =_\beta YL$, which can be shown as follows:

$$YL \rightarrow_\beta (\lambda x . L(xx))(\lambda x . L(xx))$$
$$\rightarrow_\beta L((\lambda x . L(xx))(\lambda x . L(xx)))$$
$$=_\beta L(YL).$$

Although this universal existence of a fixed point M for every λ-term L appears a bit exotic, it has a nice consequence, namely the solvability of recursive equations of the form

$$M =_\beta \boxed{\ \ldots\ldots M \ldots\ldots\ }$$

(Here we intend to express that one or more occurrences of M appear in the λ-term to the right of the $=_\beta$-symbol.)

So we claim: an M that makes such an equation true can always be found.

We show this as follows: let L be the expression on the right-hand side, but prefixed with $\lambda z .$, and with everywhere M replaced by the variable z. So we have that $L \equiv \lambda z . \boxed{\ \ldots\ldots z \ldots\ldots\ }$. Then $LM \rightarrow_\beta \boxed{\ \ldots\ldots M \ldots\ldots\ }$. Hence, it suffices to find an M such that $M =_\beta LM$. But such an M explicitly does exist, as shown in Theorem 1.10.1.

Examples 1.10.3 (1) Let's solve the question: does there exist a λ-term M such that $Mx =_\beta xMx$?
First rephrase the question to: is there an M such that $M =_\beta \lambda x . xMx$, because if so, then $Mx =_\beta xMx$.

Define $L := \lambda y \,.\, (\lambda x \,.\, xyx)$. Then $LM \twoheadrightarrow_\beta \lambda x \,.\, xMx$. So if we find M such that $M =_\beta LM$, we are done. Otherwise said: find a fixed point for L. But this is easy: use the fixed point combinator Y, which gives YL as the desired fixed point M of L.

(2) We can code the natural numbers 'nat' in untyped lambda calculus, including addition 'add' and multiplication 'mult' (cf. Exercise 1.10), a successor function 'suc' (Exercise 1.11), together with 'true', 'false' (Exercise 1.12), a zero-test 'iszero' (Exercise 1.13) and a conditional 'if–then–else' (Exercise 1.14). We can also code a predecessor function 'pred' in this setting, which is a bit harder to realise (see e.g. Hindley & Seldin, 2008).

The factorial 'fac' can now be defined by the recursive equation:

$\quad$ *fac* x $=_\beta$ $\;$ *if* (*iszero* x) *then* 1 *else* *mult* x (*fac*(*pred* x)).

Again, the desired 'fac' can be solved from this equation by means of a fixed point combinator.

1.11 Conclusions

We list some results about untyped lambda calculus:

(1) *on the positive side:*

- We have formally described the input–output behaviour of functions, including the essential construction principles (abstraction and application), and the evaluation rule (β-reduction).
- The λ-calculus is a clean and simple formalism for these purposes, which also deals neatly with variable binding.
- Substitution appears to be a fundamental mechanism for function evaluation. Its consequences are more subtle than expected. However, substitution can be treated rigorously in untyped lambda calculus.
- Conversion is an important extension of reduction, which can straightforwardly be introduced. It covers the notion 'being equivalent by means of calculations'.
- We have included the useful notion 'possible outcome of a calculation' by defining β-normal forms.
- Confluence, a property naturally desired for calculations, is guaranteed in lambda calculus.
- A nice consequence is the uniqueness of β-normal forms, if existing; so there cannot be more than one 'outcome' of a calculation.
- A number of recursive equations can be solved by means of fixed points.
- Finally, we mention the fact (which we discuss in the following section) that the untyped lambda calculus is *Turing-complete*.

(2) *on the negative side:*

- Self-applications (such as $x\,x$ or MM) are allowed in lambda calculus, although they are counter-intuitive.
- Existence of normal forms for λ-terms is not guaranteed, so we have the real possibility of undesired 'infinite calculations'.
- Each λ-term has a fixed point, which is not in accordance with what we know to be the usual behaviour of functions.

In the following chapters we will suppress the negative properties while maintaining the positive properties. The negative properties are removed by adding *types* to lambda calculus, which provide for natural restrictions on the terms allowed. In successive rounds, we will build up several 'classes' of types, each with their own special features and advantages.

1.12 Further reading

As we have already pointed out, the untyped lambda calculus was invented by A. Church to capture the notion of computability (Church, 1936b). He succeeded in giving a formal definition, on the basis of his lambda calculus: 'λ-definability'. In Exercises 1.10 to 1.14 we give an impression of how this Church-computability works, on the basis of the so-called Church numerals.

It turned out later that Church-computability is equivalent to a great number of other formulations of computability, defined in completely different settings. One such formalisation is Turing-computability, based on the notion of the Turing machine (Turing, 1936). (A Turing machine is an abstract kind of computer; cf. A.M. Turing's paper in Davis, 1965). Since 'computable' in the lambda calculus is equivalent to 'computable' using Turing machines, the lambda calculus is called *Turing-complete*.

Other formulations of effective computability are 'Herbrand–Gödel-computability' and 'general recursive function'. The first is based on specifying computable functions via a set of equations and the second inductively defines the collection of 'recursive functions' (see Mendelson, 2009). In Lewis & Papadimitriou (1981) you can find a nice exposition and proofs of the fact that the various approaches lead to the same results. This enhances the confidence that, indeed, a good formalisation of 'effective computability' has been found. This conviction is known under the name 'Church's thesis' or 'Church–Turing thesis'. This thesis states that any function that can be computed by using a mechanical device can be computed by a Turing machine (or equivalently by a λ-term).

Already before the lambda calculus, M. Schönfinkel (see Schönfinkel, 1924) had invented *combinatory logic*, which is even simpler and also Turing-complete.

Combinatory logic can be seen as the lambda calculus restricted to the terms K := $\lambda x\, y\,.\, x$ and S := $\lambda x\, y\, z\,.\, x\, z(y\, z)$ with the associated equality rules, $KPQ = P$ and $SPQR = PR(QR)$ (Curry, 1930; see also Exercise 1.9). Combinatory logic is a simpler system than lambda calculus, but the basic operations of variable binding and abstraction are not primitive, and therefore it is a slightly more difficult system to work with.

In lambda calculus, the issue of variable binding and substitution has raised a lot of attention, because these operations – though maybe intuitively clear – are quite subtle, involving renaming of bound variables. N.G. de Bruijn (see de Bruijn, 1972) invented a way of representing λ-terms without using named variables. This is now known as a representation using *de Bruijn indices*. The advantage is that all terms have a unique representation and one doesn't have to work 'modulo α-conversion'. A substitution now involves updating the indices, but that can rather easily be programmed. There has been quite a lot of work on how to do all this precisely and how to combine a de Bruijn nameless approach with a named calculus that one uses to communicate with the user.

Implementations of the untyped lambda calculus as a functional programming language have existed since 1958, when Lisp (McCarthy *et al.*, 1985) was invented by J. McCarthy. Lisp or variants of it are still used a lot, but the more recently developed functional languages are typed. One of the issues that comes up when actually implementing a (typed) lambda calculus as a programming language is the choice of an *evaluation strategy*, also known as *reduction strategy*. In a λ-term there will be many redexes that one can choose to contract. As we have seen, this choice doesn't matter for the 'end result' (the normal form that we obtain, if it exists), but it may matter for the amount of time it takes to compute the normal form. And if we always choose the 'wrong' redex, we may not find the normal form at all. For example, in the term $(\lambda u\,.\, v)\Omega$ we saw in Example 1.9.3 (4), there is an infinite reduction (contracting Ω) and a one-step reduction to normal form. In the lambda calculus one therefore studies reduction strategies: procedures that prescribe which redex to contract next. For example, it is known that the 'left-most reduction strategy' (always contract the left-most redex of the term) finds a normal form, if it exists.

In the early 1980s, H.P. Barendregt published a seminal book (Barendregt, 1981) on the untyped lambda calculus, more or less collecting all results that were known about its syntax and semantics at the time. This book serves as the standard reference on lambda calculus and has also been a starting point for a lot of new research into the field. It contains a proof of the Turing-completeness of the lambda calculus and also studies various reduction strategies and their properties.

A more introductory text about untyped (and typed) lambda calculus is the book *Lambda-Calculus and Combinators* (Hindley & Seldin, 2008), which also pays attention to the theory of combinatory logic. Another subject discussed in this book is how to construct *models* of the untyped lambda calculus and of combinatory logic; models are interpretations (mathematical structures) that reflect the 'behaviour' of the original calculi.

Exercises

1.1 Apply Notation 1.3.10 on the following λ-terms. So, remove parentheses and combine λ-abstractions:

   (a) $(\lambda x . (((x\,z)y)(x\,x)))$,
   (b) $((\lambda x . (\lambda y . (\lambda z . (z((x\,y)z))))))(\lambda u . u))$.

1.2 Find out for each of the following λ-terms whether it is α-equivalent, or not, to $\lambda x . x\,(\lambda x . x)$:

   (a) $\lambda y . y\,(\lambda x . x)$,
   (b) $\lambda y . y\,(\lambda x . y)$,
   (c) $\lambda y . y\,(\lambda y . x)$.

1.3 Use the definition of $=_\alpha$ to prove that $\lambda x . x(\lambda z . y) =_\alpha \lambda z . z(\lambda z . y)$, in spite of the fact that z occurs as a binding variable in $x(\lambda z . y)$.

1.4 Consider the following λ-term:

   $$U := (\lambda z . z\,x\,z)((\lambda y . x\,y)x) .$$

   (a) Give a list of all subterms of U.
   (b) Draw the tree representation of U.
   (c) Find the set of all free variables of U by a calculation, as in Examples 1.4.2.
   (d) Find out which of the following λ-terms are α-equivalent to U and give a motivation why; also check which of them satisfies the Barendregt convention:

   $(\lambda y . y\,x\,y)((\lambda z . x\,z)x)$,
   $(\lambda x . x\,y\,x)((\lambda z . y\,z)y)$,
   $(\lambda y . y\,x\,y)((\lambda y . x\,y)x)$,
   $(\lambda v . (v\,x)\,v)((\lambda u . u\,v)x)$.

1.5 Give the results of the following substitutions:

   (a) $(\lambda x . y(\lambda y . x\,y))[y := \lambda z . z\,x]$,
   (b) $((x\,y\,z)[x := y])[y := z]$,
   (c) $((\lambda x . x\,y\,z)[x := y])[y := z]$,
   (d) $(\lambda y . y\,y\,x)[x := y\,z]$.

1.6 Show that the following proposition is *not* always true:

$$M[x := N, y := L] \equiv M[x := N][y := L]$$

where the expression on the left-hand side means a *simultaneous* substitution; so, $M[x := N, y := L]$ is the result of replacing all free x's and y's in M at the same time ('together') by N and L, respectively. (The expression on the right-hand side is concerned with *sequential* substitution.)

1.7 Consider the λ-term U of Exercise 1.4, again.

(a) Mark all redexes in U.

(b) Find all reduction paths from U and the β-normal form of U (if it exists).

1.8 Show that the terms $(\lambda x .\, x\,x)y$ and $(\lambda xy .\, y\,x)x\,x$ are *not* β-convertible.

1.9 Consider the following λ-terms (cf. Section 1.12):

$\mathsf{K} := \lambda xy .\, x,$

$\mathsf{S} := \lambda xyz .\, x\,z(y\,z).$

(a) Check that $\mathsf{K}\,P\,Q \twoheadrightarrow_\beta P$ and $\mathsf{S}\,P\,Q\,R \twoheadrightarrow_\beta P\,R(Q\,R)$, for arbitrary λ-terms P, Q and R.

(b) Let $\mathsf{I} := \lambda x .\, x$. Prove that $\mathsf{S}\,\mathsf{K}\,\mathsf{K} \twoheadrightarrow_\beta \mathsf{I}$.

(c) Let $\mathsf{B} := \mathsf{S}(\mathsf{K}\,\mathsf{S})\mathsf{K}$. Prove that $\mathsf{B}\,U\,V\,W \twoheadrightarrow_\beta U(V\,W)$.

(d) Prove that $\mathsf{S}\,\mathsf{S}\,\mathsf{S}\,\mathsf{K}\,\mathsf{K} =_\beta \mathsf{S}\,\mathsf{K}\,\mathsf{K}\,\mathsf{K}$.

1.10 We define the λ-terms *zero, one, two* (the first three so-called *Church numerals*), and the λ-terms *add* and *mult* (which mimic addition and multiplication of Church numerals) by:

$zero := \lambda fx .\, x,$

$one := \lambda fx .\, f\,x,$

$two := \lambda fx .\, f(f\,x),$

$add := \lambda mnfx .\, m\,f(n\,f\,x),$

$mult := \lambda mnfx .\, m(n\,f)x.$

(a) Show that *add one one* $\twoheadrightarrow_\beta$ *two*.

(b) Prove that *add one one* $\neq_\beta$ *mult one zero*.

1.11 The *successor* is the function mapping natural number n to $n + 1$. It is represented in λ-calculus by $suc := \lambda m\,f\,x .\, f(m\,f\,x)$. Check the following for the Church numerals defined in the previous exercise:

(a) *suc zero* $=_\beta$ *one*,

(b) *suc one* $=_\beta$ *two*.

1.12 We define the λ-terms *true* and *false* (the *booleans*) and *not* (resembling the logical ¬-operator) by:

$true := \lambda xy .\, x$ (so it happens that $true \equiv \mathsf{K}$),

$false := \lambda xy .\, y$ (and $false \equiv zero$),

$not := \lambda z \,.\, z \, false \, true.$

Show that $not(not\,p) =_\beta p$ for all λ-terms p, in each of the following two cases: (a) $p \twoheadrightarrow_\beta true$ or (b) $p \twoheadrightarrow_\beta false$.

1.13 Consider the λ-terms *zero*, *true* and *false* from Exercises 1.10 and 1.12. Let $iszero := \lambda z \,.\, z(\lambda x \,.\, false)true.$

(a) Prove that *iszero zero* reduces to *true*.

(b) A natural number $n > 0$ may be represented by the following Church numeral: $\lambda fx \,.\, f(f(...(x)))$, with n copies of the variable f. (Cf. the definitions of *one* and *two* in Exercise 1.10.)

Prove that *iszero n* reduces to *false* for any Church numeral n except 0. (Consequently, *iszero* represents a test-for-zero.)

1.14 The term 'If x then u else v' is represented by $\lambda x \,.\, x\,u\,v$. Check this by calculating the β-normal forms of $(\lambda x \,.\, x\,u\,v)true$ and $(\lambda x \,.\, x\,u\,v)false$, respectively. (The booleans *true* and *false* are defined in Exercise 1.12.)

1.15 In Examples 1.9.3 we have seen that neither Ω nor Δ *reduces* to a β-nf. Prove that both λ-terms do not *have* a β-nf, as well.

1.16 Let M be a λ-term with the following properties:

(1) M has a β-normal form.

(2) There exists a reduction path $M \equiv M_0 \to_\beta M_1 \to_\beta M_2 \to_\beta \ldots$ of infinite length.

(a) Prove that *every* M_i has a β-normal form.

(b) Give an example of a λ-term with the mentioned two properties and show that it satisfies these properties.

1.17 Prove the following: if MN is strongly normalising, then both M and N are strongly normalising.

1.18 Let L, M and N be λ-terms such that $L =_\beta M$ and $L \twoheadrightarrow_\beta N$. Moreover, let N be in β-normal form. Prove that also $M \twoheadrightarrow_\beta N$.

1.19 We define $U := \lambda zx \,.\, x(zzx)$ and $Z := UU$. Prove that Z is a fixed point combinator, i.e. ZM is a fixed point for every λ-term M, so $M(ZM) =_\beta ZM$. Show that even holds: $ZM \twoheadrightarrow_\beta M(ZM)$.

(This Z is called the *Turing fixed point combinator* after the famous British mathematician A. Turing (1912–1954). The λ-term Y introduced in Section 1.10 is usually called the *Curry fixed point combinator*, after its inventor H.B. Curry (1900–1982); cf. Cardone & Hindley, 2009, Section 4.1. These two combinators are the most well-known among an infinite number of different fixed point combinators.)

1.20 (a) Construct a λ-term M such that $M =_\beta \lambda xy \,.\, x\,M\,y$.

(b) Construct a λ-term M such that $M\,x\,y\,z =_\beta x\,y\,z\,M$.

2

Simply typed lambda calculus

2.1 Adding types

In the previous chapter we saw that the abstract behaviour of functions can be expressed very well by means of λ-calculus. The system introduced in that chapter is highly concise and elegant. However, we also have seen that λ-calculus is sometimes 'too liberal' to conform to our intuitive demands concerning functions and how they should act as input–output devices. In the final section of Chapter 1 we listed a number of important drawbacks.

In order to get a firmer hold on the desired behaviour of functions, we will introduce *types* in the present chapter. This is a natural thing to do: functions are usually thought of as acting on objects belonging to a certain collection, e.g. the collection of the natural numbers or the collection of points on a line. Therefore, it is quite customary to talk about a function *on a domain*, for example the function 'square' on the natural numbers.

Hence, the addition of types gives certain restrictions on the input values permitted: a function defined on domain $\mathbb{N}$ may only take natural numbers as input values, even when it would be quite clear what the output value would be for some 'illegal' input value. For example, 'square' on $\mathbb{N}$ permits us to calculate three-squared, but excludes *by definition* the squaring of three-and-a-half. We could, however, define 'another' squaring function on a larger domain, e.g. $\mathbb{Q}$ or $\mathbb{R}$, in order to make it applicable to three-and-a-half. On the other hand, such an extension of the domain is often impossible: the function 'square root' on the naturals may not be extended to a function 'square root' on the integers, since the square root of a negative number is non-existent in the normal conception of what it means to be a root (even when complex numbers are permitted as an answer, *the* square root of -1 does not exist, since both i and $-i$ could serve as an answer).

Our hope is that the addition of types prevents the anomalies indicated in the previous chapter. And indeed, this turns out to be the case. The *simple types* that we introduce in the present chapter form a first important step, although they are in several senses *too restrictive*: we cannot represent a sufficient amount of functions by means of simple types, in particular when we want to express mathematics in a formal shape. In the subsequent chapters we will add more types to enlarge the expressivity of the system.

2.2 Simple types

A straightforward manner to add (abstract) types is to start with an infinite set of type *variables* and then add one production rule to build more complex types – so-called *function types*. This is done as follows, based on a famous paper of A. Church (Church, 1940).

We start with an infinite set of *type variables*: $\mathbb{V} = \{\alpha, \beta, \gamma, \ldots\}$.

Definition 2.2.1 (The set $\mathbb{T}$ of all simple types)
The set of simple types $\mathbb{T}$ is defined by:
(1) (Type variable) If $\alpha \in \mathbb{V}$, then $\alpha \in \mathbb{T}$,
(2) (Arrow type) If $\sigma, \tau \in \mathbb{T}$, then $(\sigma \to \tau) \in \mathbb{T}$.

In abstract syntax this is as follows: $\mathbb{T} = \mathbb{V} \mid \mathbb{T} \to \mathbb{T}$.

Examples of simple types are: γ, $(\beta \to \gamma)$, $((\gamma \to \alpha) \to (\alpha \to (\beta \to \gamma)))$.

Notation 2.2.2 *(1) The Greek letters α, β, ... and variants thereof are used for type variables belonging to $\mathbb{V}$. (Do not confuse this α and β with the symbols used for α-conversion and β-reduction.)*
(2) We use σ, τ, ... (occasionally A, B, ...) to denote arbitrary simple types.
(3) Outermost parentheses may be omitted.
(4) The parentheses in arrow types are right-*associative.*

Note the *right*-associativity of the arrow, in contrast with the *left*-associativity of application (cf. Notation 1.3.10). So $\alpha_1 \to \alpha_2 \to \alpha_3 \to \alpha_4$ is shorthand for the simple type $(\alpha_1 \to (\alpha_2 \to (\alpha_3 \to \alpha_4)))$, whereas $x_1\, x_2\, x_3\, x_4$ abbreviates $(((x_1 x_2)x_3)x_4)$.

Remarks 2.2.3 *Apart from the* type *variables α, β, ..., we also still have (ordinary) variables x, y, ... When we speak simply about* variables, *from now on we only mean the latter species.*

Now that we know what simple types are, we also want to know how to *use* them.

First of all, we discuss the *intended meaning* of the types. This is simple:
– *type variables* are abstract representations of *basic types* such as *nat* for natural numbers, *list* for lists, etcetera.

– *arrow types* represent *function types*, such as *nat* → *real* (the set of all functions from naturals to reals) or (*nat* → *integer*) → (*integer* → *nat*) (the set of all functions with *input* a function from naturals to integers and *output* a function from integers to naturals).

Remark 2.2.4 *We distinguish between the* sets ℕ *or* 𝕃 *and the types* nat *or* list, *because sets like* ℕ *belong to mathematics and types like* nat *to computer science. Otherwise said:* ℕ *is a collection of things in the 'real world' of mathematical entities, whereas* nat *is some* coding *of these entities in the 'virtual world' of computer programming. This distinction between sets and types will repeatedly play a role in the rest of this book.*

In order to express things like 'term M has type σ', we add so-called *statements* (or *typing statements*) to our formal language, of the form $M : \sigma$.

First of all, we assume that we have an infinitude of variables available for each type σ. If variable x has type σ, we denote this as $x : \sigma$. We thereby assume that each variable x has a *unique* type: if $x : \sigma$ and $x : \tau$, then $\sigma \equiv \tau$.

Now we investigate what the natural requirements are for the typing of *applications* and *abstractions*; these being the basic construction principles of λ-calculus.

(1) *(Application):* for the type of the application MN, we clearly have to know the types of M and N. The intention of MN is that ('function') M must be applied to ('input term') N. First, M should have a function type, say $\sigma \to \tau$. Second, N should be a 'proper' input for this function type, so the type of N must be the input type σ. Finally, the resulting type of MN should clearly be the output type τ.

Summarising: *if $M : \sigma \to \tau$ and $N : \sigma$, then $MN : \tau$.*

(2) *(Abstraction):* if $M : \tau$, what is the type of the abstraction $\lambda x . M$? The latter term is a function mapping x to M, so in order to know its type, it suffices to know the type of x (the type of M being known). Clearly, if x has type σ, then $\lambda x . M$ should have (function) type $\sigma \to \tau$.

Summarising: *if $x : \sigma$ and $M : \tau$, then $\lambda x . M : \sigma \to \tau$.*

The result of the above discussion is that it suffices to give the types of variables. The extension of the types to more complicated terms (if possible!) is then a question of calculation (see also Examples 2.2.6 below).

Remark 2.2.5 *Obviously, there are two side conditions which have to be satisfied in the typing of an* application $M N$: *the left-hand side M of the application must have a function type '$\ldots_1 \to \ldots_2$', and the right-hand side N of the application must* match *with the input type '$\ldots_1$'. Only when both conditions are met, can we derive the type of $M N$, being the output type '$\ldots_2$'.*

For the typing of an abstraction $\lambda x \,.\, M$, *we just need the types of x and M.*

Examples 2.2.6   (1) When x has type σ, then the identity function $\lambda x \,.\, x$ has type $\sigma \to \sigma$.

(2) By the side conditions mentioned above, the application $y\,x$ can only be typed if y has a function type (of the form $\sigma \to \tau$) and the type of x matches with the domain σ of this function type; the resulting type for $y\,x$ then is τ.

Compare this with the 'real world' of mathematics: one may only speak of $f(x)$ (i.e. f applied to x) if f is a function, say from input type A to output type B, and x is of the input type A; the result $f(x)$ then has type B.

(3) This suggests that $x\,x$ cannot have a type: if it had, then x should have type $\sigma \to \tau$ (for the first x) and also σ (for the second x). Since we presuppose that each variable has a unique type, $\sigma \to \tau \;\equiv\; \sigma$, which is obviously impossible.

Consequently, the following definition makes sense, since the conditions for the typing of applications really prevent the typing of a number of terms.

Definition 2.2.7   (Typable term) A term M is called *typable* if there is a type σ such that $M : \sigma$.

Remark 2.2.8   *The difference between the* right-*associativity of the arrow and the* left-*associativity of application (which we noticed after Notation 2.2.2) has a natural cause: assume that function f has type $\rho \to (\sigma \to \tau)$, and that $x : \rho$ and $y : \sigma$, then $f\,x : \sigma \to \tau$, so $(f\,x)\,y : \tau$. So, using both associativity conventions, we have that $f : \rho \to \sigma \to \tau$ (without parentheses) and $f\,x\,y : \tau$ (without parentheses). So, in a sense, both notation conventions correspond to each other.*

2.3 Church-typing and Curry-typing

Typing of a λ-term starts with typing its variables. There are two ways to give types to variables:

(1) Prescribe a (unique) type for each variable upon its introduction. This is called *typing à la Church* or *explicit typing*, since the types of variables are explicitly written down (as in Church's original paper: Church, 1940). The types of more complex terms now follow in an obvious manner, if one takes the restriction on typability of applications into account.

(2) Another way is not to give the types of variables, but to leave them open ('*implicit*') to some extent; this is called *typing à la Curry* or *implicit typing*. In this case, the typable terms are found by a search process, which may contain 'guesses' for the types of the variables. See the second example below.

Examples 2.3.1 *(1) (Typing à la Church)* Assume x has type $\alpha \to \alpha$ and y has type $(\alpha \to \alpha) \to \beta$, then yx has type β.

If, moreover, z has type β and u has type γ, then $\lambda zu \,.\, z$ has type $\beta \to \gamma \to \beta$. (We recall that $\beta \to \gamma \to \beta$ stands for $\beta \to (\gamma \to \beta)$; cf. Notation 2.2.2 (4).)

Hence, the application $(\lambda zu \,.\, z)(y\,x)$ is permitted, since the type β of $y\,x$ matches with the 'input type' β of $\lambda zu \,.\, z$. So $(\lambda zu \,.\, z)(y\,x)$ is typable, with type $\gamma \to \beta$.

(2) (Typing à la Curry) Look again at the λ-term $M \equiv (\lambda zu \,.\, z)(y\,x)$, but now assume that the types of the variables x, y, z and u have *not* been given beforehand. Can we make an educated guess about the 'possible' types of these variables, provided that we require that the full term must obtain a type?

First of all, we note that the term M is an *application* of $\lambda zu \,.\, z$ to $y\,x$. So $\lambda zu \,.\, z$ should have a function type, say $A \to B$, and then $y\,x$ must have type A. Consequently, M has type B.

The fact that $\lambda zu \,.\, z \,:\, A \to B$, implies that $z : A$ and $\lambda u \,.\, z \,:\, B$. In the latter typing statement, B is the type of a term starting with λ, hence B is a function type, so $B \equiv (C \to D)$ for some C and D, and it follows that $u : C$ and $z : D$.

In the second place, $y\,x$ itself is an application, so there must be E and F such that $y \,:\, E \to F$ and $x : E$. Then $y\,x : F$.

It follows that:

− $x : E$,

− $y : E \to F$,

− $z : A$ and $z : D$, so $A \equiv D$,

− $u : C$,

− $B \equiv (C \to D)$,

− $y\,x : A$ and $y\,x : F$, so $A \equiv F$.

Hence, we have that $A \equiv D \equiv F$, so, omitting the superfluous D and F (and B), we obtain:

$(*)$ $\quad x : E,\ y : E \to A,\ z : A,\ u : C$.

Since M has type B and $D \equiv A$, we can also say that $M \,:\, C \to A$. Thus we obtained a general scheme $(*)$ for the types of x, y, z and u, inducing a type for M.

We may fill the scheme $(*)$ with 'real' types, e.g.:

− $x : \beta$, $y : \beta \to \alpha$, $z : \alpha$, $u : \delta$, with $M : \delta \to \alpha$; or

− $x : \alpha \to \alpha$, $y : (\alpha \to \alpha) \to \beta$, $z : \beta$, $u : \gamma$, with $M : \gamma \to \beta$ (compare this with the typing-à-la-Church example above); or

− $x : \alpha$, $y : \alpha \to \alpha \to \beta$, $z : \alpha \to \beta$, $u : \alpha \to \alpha$, with $M : (\alpha \to \alpha) \to \alpha \to \beta$.

Apparently, each mentioned 'instance' of the general scheme shows that the λ-term $M \equiv (\lambda zu \,.\, z)(yx)$ is a *typable* term. Hence, as long as the restrictions imposed by the general scheme are respected, there is a rich choice of types for the four variables.

Typing à la Curry has interesting features, some of which have been hinted at above. We will discuss Curry-typing in some detail in Section 2.14. In the major part of this textbook, however, *we only consider typing à la Church* (explicit typing), because in 'real life' situations from mathematics and logic, types are usually fixed and given beforehand.

For a clear presentation, we denote the types of *bound* variables immediately after their introduction following a λ. The types of the *free* variables are given in a so-called *context* (sometimes called *basis*), in an order that may be chosen at will.

Example 2.3.2   Consider the term $(\lambda zu \,.\, z)(y\,x)$ again of Examples 2.3.1 (1), where z and u are bound and x and y are free. Assuming that z has type β and u has type γ, we write this term as follows: $(\lambda z : \beta \,.\, \lambda u : \gamma \,.\, z)(y\,x)$, with explicit typing of the bound variables z and u.

The context registering the types of the free variables x and y, as given in Examples 2.3.1 (1), becomes: $x : \alpha \to \alpha, \; y : (\alpha \to \alpha) \to \beta$.

Altogether, we write the content of this example in the following explicit format:

$$x : \alpha \to \alpha, \; y : (\alpha \to \alpha) \to \beta \;\vdash\; (\lambda z : \beta \,.\, \lambda u : \gamma \,.\, z)(y\,x) \;:\; \gamma \to \beta \,.$$

This *judgement* can be read as follows:

'In context $x : \alpha \to \alpha, \; y : (\alpha \to \alpha) \to \beta$, the term $(\lambda z : \beta \,.\, \lambda u : \gamma \,.\, z)(y\,x)$ has type $\gamma \to \beta$.'

The separation marker '$\vdash$' between context (left) and typable term (right) in the example judgement above, points at a technical connotation of 'derivability', which will be explained in the next section.

Remark 2.3.3   *We do not have β-reduction yet for 'typed terms' (for this, see Section 2.11), but an educated guess is that*

$$(\lambda z : \beta \,.\, \lambda u : \gamma \,.\, z)(y\,x) \;\to_\beta\; \lambda u : \gamma \,.\, y\,x \,.$$

Note that the latter term has the same type $\gamma \to \beta$ as the former one, since it can be shown that

$$x : \alpha \to \alpha, \; y : (\alpha \to \alpha) \to \beta \;\vdash\; \lambda u : \gamma \,.\, y\,x \;:\; \gamma \to \beta \,.$$

(Check this; see also Lemma 2.11.5.)

2.4 Derivation rules for Church's $\lambda\rightarrow$

Since we have decorated our terms with type information for the bound variables, we have to revise our definition of λ-terms, Λ. We call our new set of terms Λ_T, described by the following abstract syntax:

Definition 2.4.1 (Pre-typed λ-terms, Λ_T)
The set of pre-typed λ-terms is defined by:

$$\Lambda_T = V \,|\, (\Lambda_T \Lambda_T) \,|\, (\lambda V : \mathbb{T} . \Lambda_T) .$$

As already said in Section 2.2, we want to express things like 'λ-term M has type σ', relative to a context Γ, which we do by means of a *judgement*.

Definition 2.4.2 (Statement, declaration, context, judgement)
(1) A *statement* is of the form $M : \sigma$, where $M \in \Lambda_T$ and $\sigma \in \mathbb{T}$.
In such a statement, M is called the *subject* and σ the *type*.
(2) A *declaration* is a statement with a *variable* as subject.
(3) A *context* is a list of declarations with *different* subjects.
(4) A *judgement* has the form $\Gamma \vdash M : \sigma$, with Γ a context and $M : \sigma$ a statement.

So $x : \alpha \rightarrow \beta$ is a declaration, and $x_1 : \alpha$, $x_2 : \alpha \rightarrow \beta$, $x_3 : (\beta \rightarrow \alpha) \rightarrow \beta$ is an example of a context, where x_1, x_2 and x_3 must be different variables. A context may also consist of a single declaration, or even of none (a so-called *empty context*).

Notation 2.4.3 *We use similar notation conventions as in Notation 1.3.4 and Notation 1.3.10. So we write $\lambda x : \alpha . \lambda y : \beta . z$ for $(\lambda x : \alpha . (\lambda y : \beta . z))$. We import the notions 'free variable' and 'bound variable' in a straightforward manner from untyped λ-calculus.*
In a judgement $\Gamma \vdash M : \sigma$, we count the subject variables in the declarations of Γ as binding variables; they bind the corresponding free variables in M. We maintain the Barendregt convention 1.7.4 also for these 'new' binding variables. For example, in the judgement below Example 2.3.2, we take x, y, z and u as all different.

Since we are primarily interested in *typable* terms, it is profitable to have a kind of *method* to establish whether a term $t \in \Lambda_T$ is indeed typable and, if so, to compute a type for t. How this method works (in principle) has already been exemplified in the previous section. Now we give a set of formal rules which enable us to see whether a judgement $\Gamma \vdash M : \sigma$ is derivable, that is, whether M has type σ in context Γ.

The rules given below form a so-called *derivation system*: each rule explains

how certain judgements can be formally established. Each of the three derivation rules is in the so-called *premiss–conclusion format*, where a number of
premisses appear above a horizontal line, and the *conclusion* below.

In general, a derivation rule has the following format:

$$\frac{\texttt{premiss 1} \quad \texttt{premiss 2} \quad \ldots \quad \texttt{premiss } n}{\texttt{conclusion}}$$

The meaning of this *derivation scheme* is: *if* we 'know' that premiss 1 up
to premiss n hold, *then* the corresponding conclusion may be drawn.

The number of premisses may be zero, in which case one only writes the
conclusion (without the horizontal line).

Remark 2.4.4 *We use a different font for these notions* premiss *and* conclusion, *because we wish to distinguish the technical use of these words (as
pointing at expressions in a formal derivation) from their colloquial meanings
('presupposition' and 'final result').*

Below we give the three derivation rules for Church's $\lambda\!\rightarrow$, being the counterparts of our discussion in Section 2.2. Together, these rules form a *derivation
system* for Church's $\lambda\!\rightarrow$:

Definition 2.4.5 (Derivation rules for $\lambda\!\rightarrow$)

(var) $\Gamma \vdash x : \sigma$ if $x : \sigma \in \Gamma$

$(appl)$ $\dfrac{\Gamma \vdash M : \sigma \rightarrow \tau \quad \Gamma \vdash N : \sigma}{\Gamma \vdash MN : \tau}$

$(abst)$ $\dfrac{\Gamma,\, x : \sigma \vdash M : \tau}{\Gamma \vdash \lambda x : \sigma .\, M \,:\, \sigma \rightarrow \tau}$

The intention of these rules is *universal*, in the sense that they hold for
'arbitrary' Γ, σ, τ, x, M and N. In *using* these rules, we have to produce
instances of all of these, so we must provide actual specimens of Γ etcetera.

We discuss these derivation rules briefly:

The (var)-*rule.* This rule formally expresses that each declaration which occurs in the context is derivable with respect to that context. It thereby records
behind the $\vdash$-symbol what the type is of a *variable*, the simplest expression
in λ-calculus. This only applies to a variable that is already a subject in the
context; its type is copied from that context.

The rule has no premisses, but only contains a conclusion, so it can be
used as the *start* of a derivation.

The ($appl$)-*rule.* This rule concerns the typing of an *application*. It has two
premisses and one conclusion.

The rule establishes what we have seen before: if M has function type $\sigma \rightarrow \tau$ with respect to a certain context Γ, and N has type σ with respect to the same context Γ, then the application MN has type τ (with respect to the same Γ). Note that this means that the *conditions* on application, mentioned in Remark 2.2.5, have been satisfied.

The (abst)-rule. This rule enables us to type an *abstraction*. It has one premiss and one conclusion.

In the premiss, we have the context Γ, $x : \sigma$. This is a notation for the list Γ concatenated with $x : \sigma$, so for context Γ *extended with* one more declaration. The rule now establishes that, if M has type τ with respect to the extended context, then $\lambda x : \sigma . M$ has type $\sigma \rightarrow \tau$ with respect to Γ only.

The contents of this rule have already been explained in the previous sections. The only difficulty lies in the context, which becomes *smaller* from premiss to conclusion. What is the motivation for this? First note that in the term $\lambda x : \sigma . M$, variable x may occur free in M, since the term expresses a function 'mapping x to M'. So, if we look at a stand-alone M, as we do in the premiss, then we need type information concerning such an x. Therefore, we register its *type* (viz. σ) in the context.

On the other hand, this typing of x is no longer necessary in the conclusion: x has become a *bound* variable in $\lambda x : \sigma . M$, and gets its type within that term.

We give an example of a so-called *derivation*, built with the aid of Definition 2.4.5.

Example 2.4.6

(i) $y : \alpha \rightarrow \beta, z : \alpha \vdash y : \alpha \rightarrow \beta$ $\quad(ii)$ $y : \alpha \rightarrow \beta, z : \alpha \vdash z : \alpha$

(iii) $y : \alpha \rightarrow \beta, z : \alpha \vdash yz : \beta$

(iv) $y : \alpha \rightarrow \beta \vdash \lambda z : \alpha . yz : \alpha \rightarrow \beta$

(v) $\emptyset \vdash \lambda y : \alpha \rightarrow \beta . \lambda z : \alpha . yz : (\alpha \rightarrow \beta) \rightarrow \alpha \rightarrow \beta$

This derivation has been constructed as follows:

− First, a double use of the (var)-rule gives us (i) and (ii),
− then (iii) is obtained from (i) and (ii) by the $(appl)$-rule,
− and (iv) results from (iii) by the $(abst)$-rule;
− finally, we get (v) from (iv), again by the $(abst)$-rule.

The final result of the derivation in the above example can be found in the bottom line: (v). It says that in the empty context, $\lambda y : \alpha \rightarrow \beta . \lambda z : \alpha . yz$ has type $(\alpha \to \beta) \to \alpha \to \beta$. The derivation, exactly following the rules, thereby not only serves to *construct* judgement (v), but also to *justify* it.

Note that we may stop a certain derivation at an earlier point, or extend it to a later stage. For example, when restricting the example derivation to judgements (i) to (iv), we obtain a justifying construction of (iv).

Remark 2.4.7 *Derivation rules like the ones given in Definition 2.4.5 can be read in two directions: either from top to bottom or from bottom to top.*

From top to bottom: *when we are in a situation covered by the* **premisses***, then we may derive the* **conclusion** *as a result. This makes it possible to extend our knowledge step by step, as demonstrated in Example 2.4.6. This reading also emphasises that the derivation rules give an* inductive definition *of the set of derivable judgements.*

From bottom to top: *the rules can also be used as a* guide *to obtain some goal. For example, the* (appl)*-rule gives a guideline on how to find a type for an application MN, namely: try to find types for M and N, and see whether they match. The* (abst)*-rule tells us how to type an abstraction $\lambda x : \sigma . M$, namely by trying to type M, with respect to the same context extended with $x : \sigma$.*

There exists a strong parallel between Definition 2.4.1 of pre-typed λ-terms and Definition 2.4.5 of the derivation system: there are three kinds of terms (variables, applications and abstractions), and for each of these kinds of terms there is a corresponding derivation rule (one for deriving the type of a variable, one for the type of an application and one for the type of an abstraction).

It is worthwhile to compare the *(appl)*- and *(abst)*-rules in the derivation system of Definition 2.4.5 with well-known situations in mathematics and logic, as we do in the following two examples.

Example 2.4.8 *Mathematics:*

Read $A \to B$ as the set of all functions from A to B. Then we have:

$$(\textit{func-appl}): \quad \frac{\text{If } f \text{ is a member of } A \to B \text{ and } c \in A,}{\text{then } f(c) \in B}$$

and

$$(\textit{func-abst}): \quad \frac{\text{If for arbitrary } x \in A \text{ it holds that } f(x) \in B,}{\text{then } f \text{ is a member of } A \to B.}$$

Note the similarities between these rules and the *(appl)*- and *(abst)*-rules of Church's $\lambda\to$. The correspondence becomes even more striking if we recall that the function f in the **conclusion** of *(func-abst)* can also be written as $\lambda x \in A . f(x)$.

The context Γ of Definition 2.4.5 is empty here, but for the **premiss** of *(func-abst)*: the 'arbitrary' $x \in A$ mentioned there stands for $\Gamma \equiv x : A$.

Example 2.4.9   *Logic:*

Now read $A \to B$ as the *implication* $A \Rightarrow B$, which is 'A implies B'. So we 'identify' the function arrow $\to$ with the implication connective $\Rightarrow$, a basic symbol in logic.

In order to get a clear view on the logic behind the implication symbol, we refer to a formal system very appropriate for our purposes, namely that of *natural deduction*. In this system the 'natural' treatment of logical symbols, e.g. in mathematics, has been condensed. In the present book we often come back to natural deduction.

(For readers not acquainted with natural deduction as a logical system, we refer to van Dalen, 1994, or Pelletier, 1999.)

There are two standard rules for $\Rightarrow$ in natural deduction. The first rule is called the *elimination* rule for $\Rightarrow$, the second one the *introduction* rule for $\Rightarrow$:

$$(\Rightarrow\text{-}elim) \quad \frac{A \Rightarrow B \quad A}{B}$$

$$(\Rightarrow\text{-}intro) \quad \frac{\boxed{Assume : A} \\ \vdots \\ B}{A \Rightarrow B}$$

The ($\Rightarrow$-*elim*)-rule is also known under the name *Modus Ponens*. It is the rule to 'eliminate' an $\Rightarrow$. It expresses how to *use* an implication: if $A \Rightarrow B$ holds and A holds as well, then B is a legitimate conclusion.

The ($\Rightarrow$-*intro*)-rule gives a scheme suitable to 'introduce' an $\Rightarrow$, so to *obtain* an implication. This scheme formalises the following intuitive proof procedure: start with the assumption that A holds and then try to show that B holds. If we succeed (by filling the vertical dots with an appropriate argument), then we have shown that A implies B altogether – so we can conclude $A \Rightarrow B$.

Again, note the similarities with Definition 2.4.5 (in particular when identifying $\Rightarrow$ and $\to$). The context extension with $x : \sigma$ in the **premiss** of the (*abst*)-rule corresponds to the addition of a so-called 'flag' in the **premiss** of ($\Rightarrow$-*intro*). Such a flag marks an assumption, in this case of the proposition A. The 'flag pole' delimits the scope of the assumption.

Terms which are typable by the aid of a derivation system are called *legal*.

Definition 2.4.10   (Legal λ→-terms)
A pre-typed term M in λ→ is called *legal* if there exist context Γ and type ρ such that $\Gamma \vdash M : \rho$.

For example, entry (v) in the λ→-derivation given in Example 2.4.6, shows that the following term is legal: $\lambda y : \alpha \to \beta . \lambda z : \alpha . y\,z$, since there exist a context Γ and a type ρ such that

$$\Gamma \vdash \lambda y : \alpha \to \beta . \lambda z : \alpha . y\,z \; : \; \rho.$$

2.5 Different formats for a derivation in $\lambda\to$

A derivation that naturally follows the derivation rules has a *tree format*. See again the derivation given in Example 2.4.6. Its structure corresponds to the tree depicted in Figure 2.1.

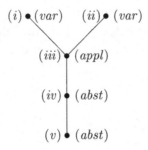

Figure 2.1 The tree structure of the derivation in Example 2.4.6

Such a tree format gives a good picture of the buildup of a derivation, but in more complicated cases a tree tends to spread out over the page, especially with longer judgements, and thereby this format loses its attraction. Another thing is that a more complex tree has many ramifications, and it may be difficult for a reader to get a good picture of how the separate construction steps have contributed to the final result.

This kind of inconvenience can be partly solved by imposing a *linear order* on the derivation steps, thus presenting the judgements one by one, as the lines in a book. Note that we already suggested an order in Example 2.4.6, since we numbered the judgements as (i) to (v).

The same derivation in *linear format* may look as the following list of judgements:

$$
\begin{array}{llll}
(i) & y : \alpha \to \beta, \, z : \alpha \;\vdash\; y \;:\; \alpha \to \beta & (var) \\
(ii) & y : \alpha \to \beta, \, z : \alpha \;\vdash\; z \;:\; \alpha & (var) \\
(iii) & y : \alpha \to \beta, \, z : \alpha \;\vdash\; y\,z \;:\; \beta & (appl) \text{ on } (i) \text{ and } (ii) \\
(iv) & y : \alpha \to \beta \;\vdash\; \lambda z : \alpha . \, y\,z \;:\; \alpha \to \beta & (abst) \text{ on } (iii) \\
(v) & \emptyset \;\vdash\; \lambda y : \alpha \to \beta . \, \lambda z : \alpha . \, y\,z \;:\; (\alpha \to \beta) \to \alpha \to \beta & (abst) \text{ on } (iv)
\end{array}
$$

The original tree structure being lost, we add an extra column with information about the construction process, giving the names of the rules and the numbers of the judgements involved. Note that the *order* in this list of judgements is not completely fixed. Taking it that a judgement $\mathcal{J}$ should follow all judgements used for its derivation, we see that (v) must follow (iv), which must follow (iii), which must follow both (i) and (ii). But the order of (i) and (ii) may be interchanged, without effect on the full derivation.

These *dependencies* between judgements in a derivation can be characterised as being a *strict partial order*. That is to say: it is *irreflexive* (no judgement $\mathcal{J}$ precedes itself), *asymmetric* (if one precedes another, then not the other way round) and *transitive* (if $\mathcal{J}_k$ precedes $\mathcal{J}_l$ and $\mathcal{J}_l$ precedes $\mathcal{J}_m$, then $\mathcal{J}_k$ precedes $\mathcal{J}_m$). This can easily be seen.

For a visualisation of such an order one often appeals to a kind of *diagram*, as has been drawn for example in Figure 2.1.

In the derivation above, either in tree format (Example 2.4.6) or in linear format, we observe many duplications of the declarations in the contexts, to the left of the $\vdash$-separators. Such duplications become annoying in more complex derivations. In order to prevent this, we present an alternative format for linear derivations, called the *flag notation*. In this notation, one displays each declaration in a '*flag*' (a rectangular box) and presumes that this declaration is part of the context for *all* statements behind the attached *flag pole*.

We illustrate this *flag format* of a derivation by rewriting the same example as above in flag notation:

(a) $\boxed{y : \alpha \to \beta}$

(b) $\boxed{z : \alpha}$

(1) $y : \alpha \to \beta$ (*var*) on (a)

(2) $z : \alpha$ (*var*) on (b)

(3) $y\,z : \beta$ (*appl*) on (1) and (2)

(4) $\lambda z : \alpha \,.\, y\,z \;:\; \alpha \to \beta$ (*abst*) on (3)

(5) $\lambda y : \alpha \to \beta \,.\, \lambda z : \alpha \,.\, y\,z \;:\; (\alpha \to \beta) \to \alpha \to \beta$ (*abst*) on (4)

The correspondence between the linear and the flag-style display of the derivation will be obvious:

    (i) $\leftrightarrow$ (a), (b) $\vdash$ (1)
   (ii) $\leftrightarrow$ (a), (b) $\vdash$ (2)
  (iii) $\leftrightarrow$ (a), (b) $\vdash$ (3)
  (iv) $\leftrightarrow$ (a) $\vdash$ (4)
   (v) $\leftrightarrow$ $\emptyset \vdash$ (5)

In what follows, we will allow a further shortening of a derivation by permit-

ting that the (*var*)-rule may be silently executed. With this convention, the
above flag derivation changes into the following shorter form:

(a) $\boxed{y : \alpha \to \beta}$

(b) $\boxed{z : \alpha}$

(1') $y\,z : \beta$ (*appl*) on (a) and (b)

(2') $\lambda z : \alpha \,.\, y\,z \; : \; \alpha \to \beta$ (*abst*) on (1')

(3') $\lambda y : \alpha \to \beta \,.\, \lambda z : \alpha \,.\, y \; : \; (\alpha \to \beta) \to \alpha \to \beta$ (*abst*) on (2')

As the above examples suggest, the linear format, and particularly the flag
format, are convenient manners of depicting derivations. This will become still
more apparent when we add definitions to typed lambda calculus, as we do from
Chapter 9 onwards. The flag format enables a writer to develop a derivation
step by step, and a reader to follow it in the specific order in which it has been
presented. Such a linear format corresponds to the natural way of knowledge
representation, as one finds, for example, in mathematics books: the accepted
style is to unfold the contents stepwise, line by line.

Since the flags make a linear derivation considerably more perspicuous, we
shall mostly use the flag format in the text to come for the representation of
derivations.

2.6 Kinds of problems to be solved in type theory

In general, there are three kinds of problems connected with judgements in
type theory:

(1) *Well-typedness* (also called *Typability*).

This problem will be posed in Section 2.7, which starts with a question of
the following form:

$$? \vdash \text{term} : ?,$$

namely: find out whether a term is legal. To be precise, the task is to find an
appropriate context and type if the term is indeed legal, and if not so, to show
where it goes wrong.

(1a) A variant of this is *Type Assignment*, where the context is given as well,
so that only the type has to be found:

$$\text{context} \vdash \text{term} : ?.$$

(2) *Type Checking.*

In Section 2.8 we give an example of how to check whether

$$\text{context} \overset{?}{\vdash} \text{ term } : \text{ type} ,$$

where 'context', 'term' and 'type' are given. The task is hence merely to check that a certain term has a certain type (relative to a certain context).

(3) *Term Finding* (also called *Term Construction* or *Inhabitation*).

There exists another important problem in this field, namely:

$$\text{context} \vdash ? : \text{ type} .$$

Thus, given a context and a type, find out whether a term exists with that type, corresponding to that specific context. A problem of this kind can be found in Section 2.9.

A particular case of Term Finding occurs when context $\equiv \emptyset$, so the problem boils down to:

$$\emptyset \vdash ? : \text{ type} .$$

An example of this problem can be found in the logic of natural deduction that we have mentioned in Example 2.4.9: the existence of a term of type σ in the empty context turns out to be equivalent to the provability of σ. We shall discuss this in Section 2.9.

We note that all of these problems are *decidable* in λ→, i.e. for each of these questions there is an *algorithm* that produces the answer, for given input in the form of 'context', 'term' and/or 'type'.

In more complicated systems, however, such as the ones we develop in the chapters to come, Term Finding is the real problem. It is *undecidable* in many cases. That is to say, there is no general *method* (or algorithm) to find out whether a term of the desired type exists, and if so, what this term is. We come back to this later.

2.7 Well-typedness in λ→

We have seen in Sections 2.4 and 2.5 that, given a derivation, it is a simple task to check its correctness.

If, however, the derivation has not been given, how should we try to find one? In this case, the derivation rules show the way, to some extent. We demonstrate this with the same example of Section 2.5, using the flag notation for displaying the context. At the same time, this is a good example of the Well-typedness problem.

So, let's start all over again. We want to show that the following λ-term M is legal: $M \equiv \lambda y : \alpha \to \beta . \lambda z : \alpha . y z$. Hence, our task is to find a context Γ and a type ρ such that $\Gamma \vdash M : \rho$.

First about the context Γ. It is a reasonable conjecture that $\Gamma \equiv \emptyset$ suffices, since a context is intended to give the types of the *free variables* in a λ-term, and there are no free variables in M. So all that's left is to find ρ. We can display this task as follows:

(n) $\lambda y : \alpha \to \beta . \lambda z : \alpha . y z \ : \ ?$

Now we browse through the three derivation rules of $\lambda \to$ in order to find a match. Obviously, only the (*abst*)-rule may be of help, since it is the only one to deliver an abstraction term in the **conclusion**. Looking at the **premiss** of (*abst*), we see that we can find a type for M *if* we can find a type for $\lambda z : \alpha . y z$, in a context *extended with* the declaration $y : \alpha \to \beta$. Hence, our new task is:

(a) $\boxed{y : \alpha \to \beta}$

      $\vdots$

(m) $\lambda z : \alpha . y z \ : \ ?$

(n) $\lambda y : \alpha \to \beta . \lambda z : \alpha . y z \ : \ \ldots$ (*abst*) on (m)

Our new goal is the type **?** in line (m). If that goal is solved, then this also solves the 'old' goal in line (n), by a simple use of the (*abst*)-rule.

So we have to find a type for $\lambda z : \alpha . y z$. Again, the main symbol is a λ, so we repeat the above procedure and we get:

(a) $\boxed{y : \alpha \to \beta}$

(b) $\boxed{z : \alpha}$

       $\vdots$

(l) $y z \ : \ ?$

(m) $\lambda z : \alpha . y z \ : \ \ldots$ (*abst*) on (l)

(n) $\lambda y : \alpha \to \beta . \lambda z : \alpha . y z \ : \ \ldots$ (*abst*) on (m)

The new term to be typed is $y z$. This is an application term, so only (*appl*) can help us further: it is the only rule with an application term in the **conclusion**.

Since (*appl*) has *two* **premisses**, we now obtain *two* new goals:

(a) $\boxed{y : \alpha \rightarrow \beta}$

(b) $\boxed{z : \alpha}$

         $\vdots$

(k_1) $y \;\; : \;\; ?_1$

         $\vdots$

(k_2) $z \;\; : \;\; ?_2$

(l) $y\, z \;\; : \;\; \ldots$ (*appl*) on (k_1) and (k_2)

(m) $\lambda z : \alpha \,.\, y\, z \;\; : \;\; \ldots$ (*abst*) on (l)

(n) $\lambda y : \alpha \rightarrow \beta \,.\, \lambda z : \alpha \,.\, y\, z \;\; : \;\; \ldots$ (*abst*) on (m)

Now we are at the heart of our expedition: the terms corresponding to the new goals are y and z, respectively. They are simple *variables*, and in that case the (*var*)-rule is the only candidate for a match. And indeed, both $?_1$ and $?_2$ can easily be solved by means of the (*var*)-rule, as we have demonstrated in the first flag derivation of Section 2.5.

The rest is routine: we find β for the type of term $y\, z$ in line (l), since the side conditions of (*appl*) are satisfied, and we easily deduce the other types.

Also here, an alternative is to skip lines k_1 and k_2, and to use (*appl*) directly on flags (a) and (b), as in the shortened flag derivation at the end of Section 2.5.

Remark 2.7.1   *The type α of z matches with the left-hand side of the type of y. If this were not the case, then our attempt at finding a type for $y\, z$ in line (l) would have failed. For example, if the type of z had been β instead of α, then there was no match.*

Hence, if we had started with the term $\lambda y : \alpha \rightarrow \beta \,.\, \lambda z : \beta \,.\, y\, z$, then at this point we would have come to the conclusion that a derivation of a type is impossible: the conclusion of the Well-typedness problem is that the term has no type.

Our final conclusion is that we have *succeeded* in finding a derivation which shows that $\lambda y : \alpha \rightarrow \beta \,.\, \lambda z : \alpha \,.\, y\, z$ is legal. Note that – but for the renumbering of the line-labels (k_1) up to (n) – we have obtained exactly the same derivation as the one in Section 2.5.

Remark 2.7.2   *In general, different derivations exist for showing that a particular term is legal. For example, we can take any Γ as a start of the above derivation, instead of $\Gamma \equiv \emptyset$. Moreover, lines (k_1) and (k_2) may be interchanged, as can easily be seen. There are many other reasons why derivations for the legality of a given term may vary, such as repetitions and detours, but also more essential differences may occur between derivations of the same term.*

2.8 Type Checking in $\lambda\rightarrow$

We continue with an example concerning the second kind of problem sketched in Section 2.6: Type Checking, i.e. checking the validity of a full judgement.

In order to illustrate this matter, we construct a derivation for the judgement we gave at the end of Section 2.3:

$$x : \alpha \rightarrow \alpha, \; y : (\alpha \rightarrow \alpha) \rightarrow \beta \vdash (\lambda z : \beta . \lambda u : \gamma . z)(y\,x) \; : \; \gamma \rightarrow \beta .$$

So our goal is now to fill the dots in:

(a) $\boxed{x : \alpha \rightarrow \alpha}$

(b) $\boxed{y : (\alpha \rightarrow \alpha) \rightarrow \beta}$

         $\vdots$

(n) $(\lambda z : \beta . \lambda u : \gamma . z)(y\,x) \; : \; \gamma \rightarrow \beta$

Since the term $(\lambda z : \beta . \lambda u : \gamma . z)(y\,x)$ is an application term, we use the (*appl*)-rule:

(a) $\boxed{x : \alpha \rightarrow \alpha}$

(b) $\boxed{y : (\alpha \rightarrow \alpha) \rightarrow \beta}$

         $\vdots$

(m_1) $\lambda z : \beta . \lambda u : \gamma . z \; : \; ?_1$

         $\vdots$

(m_2) $y\,x \; : \; ?_2$

(n) $(\lambda z : \beta . \lambda u : \gamma . z)(y\,x) \; : \; \gamma \rightarrow \beta$ (*appl*) on (m_1) and (m_2), (?)

Since use of the (*appl*)-rule is only allowed when the corresponding types match, we add a reminder (?) in the last line: at this moment we cannot yet check the match, since $?_1$ and $?_2$ are still unknown.

Now the final goal $?_2$ is easily solvable by using (*var*) twice, followed by (*appl*). Note that the types of y and x match as required. What remains is:

(a) $\boxed{x : \alpha \rightarrow \alpha}$

(b) $\boxed{y : (\alpha \rightarrow \alpha) \rightarrow \beta}$

         $\vdots$

(m_1) $\lambda z : \beta . \lambda u : \gamma . z \; : \; ?$

The goal in line (m_1) is easily solved by twice using the $(abst)$-rule, each for one of the λs in the term. This leads to the following complete derivation in the shortened version:

$$
\begin{array}{lll}
\text{(a)} & \boxed{x \,:\, \alpha \to \alpha} & \\
\text{(b)} & \quad\boxed{y \,:\, (\alpha \to \alpha) \to \beta} & \\
\text{(c)} & \quad\quad\boxed{z \,:\, \beta} & \\
\text{(d)} & \quad\quad\quad\boxed{u \,:\, \gamma} & \\
\text{(1)} & \quad\quad\quad\;\; z \,:\, \beta & (var) \text{ on (c)} \\
\text{(2)} & \quad\quad\;\; \lambda u : \gamma .\, z \,:\, \gamma \to \beta & (abst) \text{ on (1)} \\
(m_1) & \quad\quad\;\; \lambda z : \beta .\, \lambda u : \gamma .\, z \,:\, \beta \to \gamma \to \beta & (abst) \text{ on (2)} \\
(m_2) & \quad\quad\;\; y\,x \,:\, \beta & (appl) \text{ on (b) and (a)} \\
(n) & \quad\quad\;\; (\lambda z : \beta .\, \lambda u : \gamma .\, z)(y\,x) \,:\, \gamma \to \beta & (appl) \text{ on } (m_1) \text{ and } (m_2)\ \textbf{(?)}
\end{array}
$$

We have suppressed the non-essential uses of the (var)-rule (see line (m_2)), but we cannot suppress the mentioning of (var) in line (1), since we need that line for obtaining line (2).

So all that's left is our 'hanging' task to check the conditions on $(appl)$ in line (n), but these are clearly satisfied.

Hence we have succeeded in giving a proper derivation of the judgement of Section 2.3.

Remark 2.8.1 *In Remark 2.3.3 we noticed that*

$$(\lambda z : \beta .\, \lambda u : \gamma .\, z)(y\,x) \to_\beta \lambda u : \gamma .\, y\,x .$$

It is easy to establish that the latter term also has the type $\gamma \to \beta$, *in the same context for x and y as above.*

2.9 Term Finding in $\lambda_{\to}$

A final example in the present chapter concerns the third of the general problems in type theory mentioned in Section 2.6, namely Term Finding: find an appropriate term of a certain type, in a certain context.

A term which belongs to a certain type, is called an *inhabitant* of that type: one sees the type as a 'house' (or a city) which may (or may not) give accommodation to terms/residents.

Hence, the problem here is to find an inhabitant of a given type. We start with an empty context and explore the situation in which the type is an expression from logic: a *proposition*. Surprisingly, every inhabitant then codes a *proof* of this proposition, hence declaring it to be a 'true' one. We demonstrate this below.

As logical expression, we take $A \to B \to A$, where $\to$ should be read as 'implication'. This proposition is a *tautology*, which is to say that it holds as a general fact in logic. In this simple case our intuition immediately delivers a 'proof' of this, viz: assume that A holds and assume then that also B holds, then A of course still holds; hence we conclude: if A, then (if B then A).

Let's formalise this proof in $\lambda_\to$. So we take $A \to B \to A$ as a *type* and try to find an inhabitant in the empty context:

(n) ? : $A \to B \to A$

Our goal is to find a term of an $\to$-type, so the (*abst*)-rule of our derivation system (Definition 2.4.5) is obviously a first try. This gives (check it yourself):

(a) $\boxed{x \ : \ A}$

$\qquad \vdots$

(m) $\vert$? : $B \to A$
(n) ... : $A \to B \to A$ (*abst*) on (m)

The variable x in line (a) is a consequence of using the (*abst*)-rule.

Again, our goal concerns an $\to$-type, so we repeat the procedure. (Note that we take a *new* variable (y) here, as Definition 2.4.2 (3) requires.)

(a) $\boxed{x \ : \ A}$
(b) $\quad \boxed{y \ : \ B}$

$\qquad\qquad \vdots$

(l) $\quad$? : A
(m) $\vert$ ... : $B \to A$ (*abst*) on (l)
(n) ... : $A \to B \to A$ (*abst*) on (m)

Clearly, the goal ? can be solved by the x in line (a) and we obtain:

(a) $\boxed{x \ : \ A}$
(b) $\quad \boxed{y \ : \ B}$
(1) $\quad$ x : A (*var*) on (a)
(2) $\quad$ $\lambda y : B . x$: $B \to A$ (*abst*) on (1)
(3) $\lambda x : A . \lambda y : B . x$: $A \to B \to A$ (*abst*) on (2)

Thus we have finished the job.

Finally, we express this derivation in words, considering propositions as types and inhabitants of propositions as *proofs*, as mentioned above:

- (a)   Assume that x is a proof of proposition A.
- (b)   Also assume that y is a proof of proposition B.
- (1)   Then x is (still) a proof of A.
- (2)   So the function mapping y to x sends a proof of B to a proof of A, i.e. $\lambda y : B \,.\, x$ proves the *implication* $B \to A$.
- (3)   Consequently, $\lambda x : A \,.\, \lambda y : B \,.\, x$ proves $A \to B \to A$.

So we deal with an interpretation of proofs and logical expressions that works. It is generally called the *PAT-interpretation*, where 'PAT' means both 'propositions-as-types' and 'proofs-as-terms'. We will come back at length on this important idea in Section 5.4; see also Remark 5.1.1.

Remark 2.9.1   *When wishing to capture the derivation above, it suffices to store the final term* $\lambda x : A \,.\, \lambda y : B \,.\, x$ *only, because the full derivation can easily be reconstructed from this term. It is a complete 'coding' of the proof, and even more than that: the term implicitly includes the proposition it proves, since this is its type, being computable by the decidability of Well-typedness.*

Remark 2.9.2   *In Well-typedness and Type Checking, the development of the complete derivation roughly follows a pattern as illustrated in the left part of Figure 2.2: starting with a term (positioned on the lower left-hand side of the picture), one successively replaces it by simpler terms (upwards) until it can be typed (at the top of the picture); then the other types are calculated (downwards) until finally the type of the original term has been derived (on the place of the arrow head). See the examples in Sections 2.7 and 2.8 for derivations following this construction scheme.*

In Term Finding, on the other hand, the pattern is as in the right part of Figure 2.2. Here one starts with a type, replaces it by simpler types until one finds a term inhabiting such a type, and then terms are constructed corresponding to the types, until one obtains a term which inhabits the original type. See the example in the present section for a derivation construction that follows this scheme.

2.10 General properties of λ→

In this section we list a number of properties of Church's λ→ and explain their contents and importance. We do not give all the proofs of the lemmas; for the missing ones, we refer to Barendregt (1992).

First, we give a number of definitions about contexts, followed by examples.

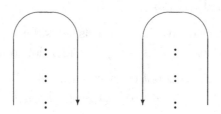

Figure 2.2 Construction schemes for typing problems

Definition 2.10.1   (Domain, dom, subcontext, $\subseteq$, permutation, projection, $\restriction$)
(1) If $\Gamma \equiv x_1 : \sigma_1, \ldots, x_n : \sigma_n$, then the *domain* of Γ or $\mathsf{dom}(\Gamma)$ is the list $(x_1, \ldots, x_n)$.
(2) Context Γ' is a *subcontext* of context Γ, or $\Gamma' \subseteq \Gamma$, if all declarations occurring in Γ' also occur in Γ, in the same order.
(3) Context Γ' is a *permutation* of context Γ, if all declarations in Γ' also occur in Γ, and vice versa.
(4) If Γ is a context and Φ a set of variables, then the *projection* of Γ on Φ, or $\Gamma \restriction \Phi$, is the subcontext Γ' of Γ with $\mathsf{dom}(\Gamma') = \mathsf{dom}(\Gamma) \cap \Phi$.

Examples 2.10.2   Let $\Gamma \equiv y : \sigma, \ x_1 : \rho_1, \ x_2 : \rho_2, \ z : \tau, \ x_3 : \rho_3$.
(1) $\mathsf{dom}(\emptyset) = (\ )$, the empty list; $\mathsf{dom}(\Gamma) = (y, x_1, x_2, z, x_3)$.
(2) $\emptyset \subseteq (x_1 : \rho_1, \ z : \tau) \subseteq \Gamma$.
(3) $x_2 : \rho_2, \ x_1 : \rho_1, \ z : \tau, \ x_3 : \rho_3, \ y : \sigma$ is a permutation of Γ.
(4) $\Gamma \restriction \{z, u, x_1\} = x_1 : \rho_1, \ z : \tau$.

An important property of $\lambda{\to}$ is the following, concerning the free variables occurring in a judgement:

Lemma 2.10.3   *(Free Variables Lemma)*
   If $\Gamma \vdash L : \sigma$, then $FV(L) \subseteq \mathsf{dom}(\Gamma)$.

As a consequence of the lemma, each *free* variable x that occurs in L has a *type*, which is recorded in a declaration $x : \sigma$ occurring in the context Γ. Therefore, in a judgement, there can be no confusion about the type of *any* variable whatsoever, since also *bound* variables get their type, namely upon introduction, behind the binding λ.

We now try to prove this lemma. The question is, of course, *how* to do this, so first we concentrate on the proof *method*. We have to show something for an arbitrary judgement $\Gamma \vdash L : \sigma$ (namely that all free variables of L occur in $\mathsf{dom}(\Gamma)$). What can we say about this judgement? Not very much, since it is 'arbitrary'. However, if it *is* a proper judgement, then by definition it must be derivable, so there must exist a *derivation* with this judgement as the final

conclusion. Derivations (as many notions in this field) are *inductively* defined, so our conjecture is that the proof of the lemma also needs induction.

The kind of induction that we use here is called *structural induction*. The principle is as follows. An inductive definition describes how to *construct* the expressions. So, to prove a general property $\mathcal{P}$ for an arbitrary expression $\mathcal{E}$ we can proceed by:

- assuming that $\mathcal{P}$ holds for all expressions $\mathcal{E}'$ used to construct $\mathcal{E}$ (this is called the *induction hypothesis*),
- and then proving that $\mathcal{P}$ also holds for $\mathcal{E}$ itself.

We apply this proof method to the lemma:

Proof of Lemma 2.10.3 The proof is by induction on the derivation of the judgement $\mathcal{J} \equiv \Gamma \vdash L : \sigma$, so we suppose that $\mathcal{J}$ is the final **conclusion** of a derivation and we assume that the content of the lemma already holds for the **premisses** that have been used to derive the **conclusion**.

By Definition 2.4.5, there are three possible cases: the final step to establish that $\mathcal{J}$ holds has been (1) the (*var*)-rule, or (2) the (*appl*)-rule, or (3) the (*abst*)-rule.

- *Case (1):* $\mathcal{J}$ is the **conclusion** of the (*var*)-rule.

  Then $\mathcal{J}$ has the form $\Gamma \vdash x : \sigma$ and this follows from $x : \sigma \in \Gamma$. Now the L mentioned in the lemma is x and we have to prove that $FV(x) \subseteq \mathrm{dom}(\Gamma)$. But this is an immediate consequence of $x : \sigma \in \Gamma$.

  (Note: the (*var*)-rule has no **premisses**, so there is no induction hypothesis about 'previously constructed' judgements.)

- *Case (2):* $\mathcal{J}$ is the **conclusion** of the (*appl*)-rule.

  Then $\mathcal{J}$ must have the form $\Gamma \vdash MN : \tau$ and we have to prove that $FV(MN) \in \mathrm{dom}(\Gamma)$.

  By induction, the lemma already holds for the **premisses** of the (*appl*)-rule, which are: $\Gamma \vdash M : \sigma \to \tau$ and $\Gamma \vdash N : \sigma$. Hence we may assume $FV(M) \subseteq \mathrm{dom}(\Gamma)$ and $FV(N) \subseteq \mathrm{dom}(\Gamma)$. Since by Definition 1.4.1, $FV(MN) = FV(M) \cup FV(N)$, it follows that $FV(MN) \subseteq \mathrm{dom}(\Gamma)$.

- *Case (3):* $\mathcal{J}$ is the **conclusion** of the (*abst*)-rule.

  Then $\mathcal{J}$ must have the form $\Gamma \vdash \lambda x : \sigma . M : \sigma \to \tau$ and we have to prove that $FV(\lambda x : \sigma . M) \subseteq \mathrm{dom}(\Gamma)$.

  By induction, the lemma already holds for the **premiss** $\Gamma, x : \sigma \vdash M : \tau$, so $FV(M) \subseteq \mathrm{dom}(\Gamma) \cup \{x\}$ (∗). Now $FV(\lambda x : \sigma . M) = FV(M) \backslash \{x\}$ (again by Definition 1.4.1), and by (∗) we have: $FV(M) \backslash \{x\} \subseteq \mathrm{dom}(\Gamma)$. $\square$

Remark 2.10.4 *A proof by induction apparently works* backwards*: in order to show a property of some expression, we appeal to previously constructed expressions. However, convince yourself that induction ultimately amounts to*

a forward *process: imagine yourself an arbitrary derivation, then the property*
$\mathcal{P}$ *can be thought of as being passed on from top to bottom, in parallel with*
the usage of the derivation rules. In every step, property $\mathcal{P}$ *is 'handed over'*
from premiss *(es) to* conclusion. *(If there is no* premiss *at all, then induction*
amounts to showing that the property holds 'immediately'; cf. the above proof,
case (1).)

We continue with three other properties of $\lambda{\rightarrow}$.

Lemma 2.10.5 *(Thinning, Condensing, Permutation)*
(1) (Thinning) Let Γ' *and* Γ'' *be contexts such that* $\Gamma' \subseteq \Gamma''$. *If* $\Gamma' \vdash M : \sigma$,
then also $\Gamma'' \vdash M : \sigma$.
(2) (Condensing) If $\Gamma \vdash M : \sigma$, *then also* $\Gamma \restriction FV(M) \vdash M : \sigma$.
(3) (Permutation) If $\Gamma \vdash M : \sigma$, *and* Γ' *is a permutation of* Γ, *then* Γ' *is*
also a context and moreover, $\Gamma' \vdash M : \sigma$.

We shall discuss these properties first, and then consider their proofs.

- The 'thinning' of a context is an extension of it obtained by adding extra
  declarations with 'new' subject variables. (So 'being thinner' is the converse of 'being a subcontext' – see Definition 2.10 (2).) Now the Thinning
  Lemma 2.10.5 (1) says: if M has type σ in some context Γ', then M also has
  type σ in a 'thinner' context Γ''.

  This is intuitively acceptable: Γ' already contains all the necessary type
  information for the free variables in M (otherwise $\Gamma' \vdash M : \sigma$ could not
  have been derived; see also Theorem 2.10.3). But all this type information
  is of course unaffected by thinning of the context, since then one merely
  adds some declarations of new, and hence 'non-essential', variables, but no
  declaration is removed or changed.
- On the other hand, the Condensing Lemma 2.10.5 (2) tells us that we may
  remove declarations $x : \rho$ from Γ for those x's which do not occur free in M,
  thus keeping only those declarations which are *relevant* for M.
- One could rephrase these two properties in a popular style as follows: 'One
  may either add or remove junk to/from a context, without affecting derivability', where 'junk' consists of declarations of variables which do not occur
  free in the term M. (Such variables play no role in the typing process.)
- Finally, the Permutation Lemma tells us that it is not important how the
  context is ordered. This is intuitively clear. Firstly, declarations are only
  used to store information about types of free variables; the *order* of these
  declarations is therefore irrelevant. Secondly, declarations in a context are
  mutually independent, so there is also no *technical* reason why they cannot
  be permuted.

Remark 2.10.6 *One can also define a context as a set – not a list: this is the usual approach in λ→. Such set-contexts are called* bases *(see e.g. Barendregt, 1992). We prefer (ordered) contexts over (unordered) bases, because richer systems – to be discussed in later sections – have dependent declarations, so there the order is important.*

We give an idea of the proofs of Lemma 2.10.5 (1) and (2) by considering some interesting cases. (For more complete proofs, see Barendregt, 1992, Proposition 3.2.7 or 3.1.7.) For Lemma 2.10.5 (3), we only give a hint.

Proof of Lemma 2.10.5

(1) We use induction on the derivation of the judgement $\mathcal{J} \equiv \Gamma' \vdash M : \sigma$, assuming that $\Gamma' \subseteq \Gamma''$, with Γ'' another context. Again, there are three cases to consider: $\mathcal{J}$ has been constructed with the (*var*)-, (*appl*)- or (*abst*)-rule. We only treat the last case:

– *Case (3):* $\mathcal{J}$ is the **conclusion** of the (*abst*)-rule.

   Then $\mathcal{J}$ must have the form $\Gamma' \vdash \lambda x : \rho . L : \rho \to \tau$. We have to prove that $\Gamma'' \vdash \lambda x : \rho . L : \rho \to \tau$. (We assume that $x \notin \text{dom}(\Gamma'')$; otherwise, rename x in $\lambda x : \rho . L$.)

   Now $\Gamma', x : \rho \vdash L : \tau$ must have been the **premiss** in the construction of $\mathcal{J}$, so by induction we have:

   (∗): Thinning already holds for $\Gamma', x : \rho \vdash L : \tau$.

   Since $x \notin \text{dom}(\Gamma'')$, it follows that $\Gamma'', x : \rho$ is a correct context and also $\Gamma', x : \rho \subseteq \Gamma'', x : \rho$. From the induction hypothesis (∗) it follows that $\Gamma'', x : \rho \vdash L : \tau$. From this, the (*abst*)-rule gives as **conclusion** that also $\Gamma'' \vdash \lambda x : \rho . L : \rho \to \tau$.

(2) Again, we use induction, this time on the construction of $\mathcal{J} \equiv \Gamma \vdash M : \sigma$. We only treat the (*appl*)-case:

– *Case (2):* $\mathcal{J}$ is the **conclusion** of the (*appl*)-rule.

   Then $\mathcal{J}$ has the form $\Gamma \vdash LN : \tau$. To prove: $\Gamma \upharpoonright FV(LN) \vdash LN : \tau$.

   By induction, the lemma already holds for the **premisses** $\Gamma \vdash L : \rho \to \tau$ and $\Gamma \vdash N : \rho$, so we know that $\Gamma \upharpoonright FV(L) \vdash L : \rho \to \tau$ (∗) and $\Gamma \upharpoonright FV(N) \vdash N : \rho$ (∗∗). Note that $\Gamma \upharpoonright FV(LN)$ is indeed a context. So by part (1) (the Thinning Lemma), since both $FV(L) \subseteq FV(LN)$ and $FV(N) \subseteq FV(LN)$, we obtain $\Gamma \upharpoonright FV(LN) \vdash L : \rho \to \tau$ from (∗) and $\Gamma \upharpoonright FV(LN) \vdash N : \rho$ from (∗∗). Using the (*appl*)-rule, we get from this $\Gamma \upharpoonright FV(LN) \vdash LN : \tau$.

(3) By induction on the derivation of $\Gamma \vdash M : \sigma$. (Try this yourself.) $\qquad\square$

In the following lemma, we establish that every derivation can be 'traced back' to the previous stage. That is to say, the legality of a variable, an application or an abstraction, can only follow from the (*var*)-rule, the (*appl*)-rule or the (*abst*)-rule, respectively. (One also says that derivations are *syntax-directed*: for each judgement there is *only one* rule possible for establishing that judgement as a `conclusion`, so the *syntax* of the term is a distinguishing factor in the construction of judgements.)

The lemma is called the Generation Lemma, since it says precisely how a certain judgement can be 'generated'.

Lemma 2.10.7   (*Generation Lemma*)

(1) *If* $\Gamma \vdash x : \sigma$, *then* $x : \sigma \in \Gamma$.

(2) *If* $\Gamma \vdash MN : \tau$, *then there is a type* σ *such that* $\Gamma \vdash M : \sigma \to \tau$ *and* $\Gamma \vdash N : \sigma$.

(3) *If* $\Gamma \vdash \lambda x : \sigma . M : \rho$, *then there is* τ *such that* $\Gamma, x : \sigma \vdash M : \tau$ *and* $\rho \equiv \sigma \to \tau$.

Proof   Inspection of the derivation rules for Church's $\lambda\to$ as given in Definition 2.4.5, shows that there are no other possibilities than the ones stated in this lemma. $\square$

Legal terms were defined as the typable ones (see Definition 2.4.10). So legal terms are the well-behaving constructs in $\lambda\to$-land. The following lemma expresses that all subterms of a well-behaving term are well-behaving as well. Here the notion 'subterm' is defined as in the untyped λ-calculus (Definition 1.3.5), reading $\lambda x : \sigma . M$ instead of $\lambda x . M$.

Lemma 2.10.8   (*Subterm Lemma*) *If M is legal, then every subterm of M is legal.*

(Given as Proposition 3.2.9 (see also 3.1.9) in Barendregt, 1992.)

Proof   Exercise 2.16. $\square$

So if there are Γ_1 and σ_1 such that $\Gamma_1 \vdash M : \sigma_1$, and if L is a subterm of M, then there are Γ_2 and σ_2 such that $\Gamma_2 \vdash L : \sigma_2$.

As an example, take the following judgement, derived in Section 2.8:

$$x : \alpha \to \alpha, \ y : (\alpha \to \alpha) \to \beta \ \vdash \ (\lambda z : \beta . \lambda u : \gamma . z)(y\,x) \ : \ \gamma \to \beta.$$

Hence, $M \equiv (\lambda z : \beta . \lambda u : \gamma . z)(y\,x)$ is legal.

(1) A subterm of M is $\lambda u : \gamma . z$. According to the Subterm Lemma, this term should be legal, as well. And indeed, as we showed in Section 2.8 (see line (2) in the last diagram of that section):

$$x : \alpha \to \alpha, \ y : (\alpha \to \alpha) \to \beta, \ z : \beta \ \vdash \ \lambda u : \gamma . z : \gamma \to \beta.$$

A simpler answer is, for arbitrary type δ:

$$z : \delta \ \vdash \ \lambda u : \gamma . z : \gamma \to \delta .$$

(2) Another subterm of M is $y\,x$. This term is legal, as shown in Section 2.8:

$$x : \alpha \to \alpha,\ y : (\alpha \to \alpha) \to \beta \vdash y\,x\ :\ \beta\,,$$

or, shorter yet:

$$x : \alpha,\ y : \alpha \to \beta \vdash y\,x\ :\ \beta\,.$$

To conclude this section, we mention the following important property of Church's $\lambda\to$ which expresses that, given a context, a term may have *at most one* type. Therefore, the type, if existing, is 'unique'. (This property does *not* hold for systems with typing à la Curry, as we noticed in Examples 2.3.1 (2). See also Barendregt, 1992, p. 159.)

Lemma 2.10.9 *(Uniqueness of Types) Assume* $\Gamma \vdash M : \sigma$ *and* $\Gamma \vdash M : \tau$. *Then* $\sigma \equiv \tau$.

Proof By induction on the construction of M (Exercise 2.17). $\qquad\qquad\square$

Finally, we repeat what we already noted in Section 2.6:

Theorem 2.10.10 *(Decidability of Well-typedness, Type Assignment, Type Checking and Term Finding) In* $\lambda\to$, *the following problems are decidable:*
(1) Well-typedness: $?\ \vdash\ \text{term}\ :\ ?$.
(1a) Type Assignment: $\text{context} \vdash \text{term}\ :\ ?$.
(2) Type Checking: $\text{context} \overset{?}{\vdash} \text{term}\ :\ \text{type}$.
(3) Term Finding: $\text{context} \vdash\ ?\ :\ \text{type}$.

Proofs can be found in Barendregt, 1992, Propositions 4.4.11 and 4.4.12.

2.11 Reduction and $\lambda\to$

In this section we examine the behaviour of $\lambda\to$ with regards to β-reduction. First we look at substitution, an operation at the heart of β-reduction.

In order to be able to treat substitution in $\lambda\to$, we have to adjust the related definition, viz. Definition 1.6.1; the only change concerns part (3), the abstraction case, because we have to add a type to the bound variable:

(3) $(\lambda y : \sigma\,.\,P)[x := N] \equiv \lambda z : \sigma\,.\,(P^{y\to z}[x := N])$, if $\lambda z : \sigma\,.\,P^{y\to z}$ is an α-variant of $\lambda y : \sigma\,.\,P$ such that $z \notin FV(N)$.

Now we have the following:

Lemma 2.11.1 *(Substitution Lemma) Assume* $\Gamma',\ x : \sigma,\ \Gamma'' \vdash M : \tau$ *and* $\Gamma' \vdash N : \sigma$. *Then* $\Gamma',\ \Gamma'' \vdash M[x := N] : \tau$.

This lemma says that if we substitute, in a legal term M, all occurrences of context variable x by a term N *of the same type as* x, then the result

$M[x := N]$ keeps the same type as M had. This is intuitively understandable: in order to calculate the type of M, it does not matter whether we deal with x's, or with N's *at the same place(s)* in the expression, given that the types of x and N are the same.

Note that the validity of the premiss $\Gamma' \vdash N : \sigma$, without the declaration $x : \sigma$ in the context, implies that x does not occur free in N (cf. the Free Variable Lemma 2.10.3). That's why the declaration $x : \sigma$ has been omitted in the final judgement since x consequently also does not occur free in $M[x := N]$.

Note also that $x : \sigma$ is a declaration occurring *somewhere* in the full context of the first judgement: the declaration $x : \sigma$ is preceded by context part Γ' and followed by context part Γ'' (either of these may be empty, of course). This is not essential: due to the Permutation Lemma 2.10.5 (3), we may shift $x : \sigma$ back and forth through the full context. However, if we omit the Γ'', the proof of the lemma would be more complicated, in particular the (*abst*)-case (see below).

We now discuss a proof of this Substitution Lemma. We spell out some important details, and ask the reader to complete the proof in the same vein.

Proof of Lemma 2.11.1   We use induction on the derivation of the judgement $\mathcal{J} \equiv \Gamma', \, x : \sigma, \, \Gamma'' \vdash M : \tau$. For the final step in the derivation of $\mathcal{J}$, there are three possibilities, depending on the 'shape' of M: whether it is a variable, an application or an abstraction.

We only look at the most complicated case, namely when M is an abstraction; say $M \equiv \lambda u : \rho . \, L$. Consequently, τ must be $\rho \to \zeta$ for some type ζ, so

$$\mathcal{J} \equiv \Gamma', \, x : \sigma, \, \Gamma'' \vdash \lambda u : \rho . \, L : \rho \to \zeta.$$

Then the derivation step by means of which this $\mathcal{J}$ has been obtained, must have been an instance of (*abst*), leading

– *from* $\mathcal{J}' \equiv \Gamma', \, x : \sigma, \, \Gamma'', \, u : \rho \vdash L : \zeta$
– *to* the $\mathcal{J}$ given just now.

The well-formedness of the context in $\mathcal{J}'$ implies that u cannot be a subject variable in Γ'. Hence, since $\Gamma' \vdash N : \sigma$ and by the Free Variables Lemma 2.10.3, we have that $u \notin FV(N)$.

Induction tells us that the lemma already holds for $\mathcal{J}'$. (This $\mathcal{J}'$ has an 'extended' Γ'', compared to $\mathcal{J}$, namely Γ'', $u : \rho$.) Putting the lemma into effect on $\mathcal{J}'$ and the supposition $\Gamma' \vdash N : \sigma$, we obtain:

$$\Gamma', \, \Gamma'', \, u : \rho \vdash L[x := N] : \zeta.$$

Now we may employ the (*abst*)-rule for this judgement, yielding:

$$\Gamma', \, \Gamma'' \vdash \lambda u : \rho . \, (L[x := N]) : \rho \to \zeta,$$

which (by what we noticed about substitution in the beginning of the present section and since $u \notin FV(N)$) is the same as

$\quad \Gamma', \Gamma'' \vdash (\lambda u : \rho . L)[x := N]) : \rho \rightarrow \zeta,$

hence

$\quad \Gamma', \Gamma'' \vdash M[x := N] : \tau.$ $\qquad\qquad\qquad\qquad\qquad$ $\square$

Another important lemma is concerned with β-*reduction*. We have defined β-reduction in an untyped setting (see Chapter 1), so we have to adjust it to the (pre-typed) terms of $\Lambda_{\mathbb{T}}$. This is straightforward: all we have to do is reconsider the Basis of one-step β-reduction (see Definition 1.8.1), since this contains a λ-abstraction over variable x, which now gets a type. All other things remain the same:

Definition 2.11.2 (One-step β-reduction, $\rightarrow_\beta$, for $\Lambda_{\mathbb{T}}$)
(1) (Basis) $(\lambda x : \sigma . M)N \rightarrow_\beta M[x := N]$.
(2) (Compatibility) As in Definition 1.8.1.

(Of course, in the third compatibility rule of Definition 1.8.1, we now have to read $\lambda x : \tau . M \rightarrow_\beta \lambda x : \tau . N$ instead of $\lambda x . M \rightarrow_\beta \lambda x . N$.)

We copy Definition 1.8.3 for *zero-or-more-step reduction*, $\twoheadrightarrow_\beta$, in $\Lambda_{\mathbb{T}}$ and Definition 1.8.5 for *conversion*, $=_\beta$.

Since types clearly play no role in the β-reduction process (see the (*Basis*)-rule above, where σ is neglected and, moreover, it is not required that x and N have the same type), the Church–Rosser Theorem (1.9.8) for untyped λ-calculus is also valid in the typed version $\lambda\rightarrow$:

Theorem 2.11.3 *(Church–Rosser Theorem; CR; Confluence) The Church–Rosser property also holds for* $\lambda\rightarrow$.

It is not hard to see that Corollary 1.9.9 also still holds in $\lambda\rightarrow$:

Corollary 2.11.4 *Suppose that* $M =_\beta N$. *Then there is* L *such that* $M \twoheadrightarrow_\beta L$ *and* $N \twoheadrightarrow_\beta L$.

An important lemma about β-reduction in $\lambda\rightarrow$ is the following:

Lemma 2.11.5 *(Subject Reduction) If* $\Gamma \vdash L : \rho$ *and if* $L \twoheadrightarrow_\beta L'$, *then* $\Gamma \vdash L' : \rho$.

We shall discuss this lemma first, and then prove it.

The lemma states that β-reduction does not affect typability. And even more: β-reduction of a term does not change the type of that term (and the same context will do).

This is of course a very welcome property: β-reduction is a formalisation of 'calculation', as we saw in Chapter 1. And we would not like calculations with a term to affect either the typability or the type of that term: $3+5$ is a natural number, and it remains so after evaluation to 8.

Take again the example of Section 2.8 and consider Remark 2.8.1. With Subject Reduction, we can now immediately conclude that:

$$x : \alpha \to \alpha, \; y : (\alpha \to \alpha) \to \beta \vdash \lambda u : \gamma . \, y \, x \; : \; \gamma \to \beta .$$

(This judgement can also be established on its own, of course, by means of a derivation, but an appeal to Subject Reduction is easier now.)

Proof of Lemma 2.11.5 We prove the case $L \to_\beta L'$, which is $L \twoheadrightarrow_\beta L'$ in *one step*; the lemma then follows by induction on the number of one-step β-reductions of $L \twoheadrightarrow_\beta L'$.

The case $L \to_\beta L'$ is proved by *induction on the generation of* $L \to_\beta L'$, that is to say: one distinguishes between the various possibilities for establishing that $L \to_\beta L'$, assuming that the lemma already holds for the assumptions leading to $L \to_\beta L'$ (cf. Definition 2.11.2):

(1) Basis: $L \equiv (\lambda x : \sigma . \, M)N$ and $L' \equiv M[x := N]$,

(2.1) Compatibility, case 1: $L \equiv MK$ and $L' \equiv M'K$,

(2.2) Compatibility, case 2: $L \equiv KM$ and $L' \equiv KM'$,

(2.3) Compatibility, case 3: $L \equiv \lambda x : \tau . \, M$ and $L' \equiv \lambda x : \tau . \, M'$.

The Basis case has no assumptions, so induction does not apply. In all three Compatibility cases the assumption is $M \to_\beta M'$.

We only treat the Basis case, because it is the most interesting case: we assume that $\Gamma \vdash (\lambda x : \sigma . \, M)N : \rho$ and prove that $\Gamma \vdash M[x := N] : \rho$.

By the Generation Lemma 2.10.7 (2), there must be a type τ such that $\Gamma \vdash \lambda x : \sigma . \, M : \tau \to \rho$ and $\Gamma \vdash N : \tau$. The first of these two judgements implies, by the Generation Lemma 2.10.7 (3), the existence of a φ such that $\Gamma, x : \sigma \vdash M : \varphi$ and $\tau \to \rho \equiv \sigma \to \varphi$. Hence, $\tau \equiv \sigma$ and $\rho \equiv \varphi$. We obtain $\Gamma, x : \sigma \vdash M : \rho$ and $\Gamma \vdash N : \sigma$. Then by the Substitution Lemma 2.11.1: $\Gamma \vdash M[x := N] : \rho$.

(Do the Compatibility cases yourself: Exercise 2.18.) $\qquad \square$

Finally, one can prove that there are no infinite reduction sequences in $\lambda_\to$, or 'every calculation is finite'. (See Definition 1.9.6 for the notion 'strong normalisation'.)

Theorem 2.11.6 *(Strong Normalisation Theorem or Termination Theorem)* *Every legal M is strongly normalising.*

The proof uses a kind of *measure* on legal terms which is always positive, and becomes smaller in each β-reduction step. These two facts clearly imply strong normalisation. We do not give the details of the proof here (see e.g. Geuvers & Nederpelt, 1994; see also Barendregt, 1992, Theorem 5.3.33).

Remark 2.11.7 *As already mentioned in Chapter 1, strong normalisation (or 'termination') always guarantees an outcome, whatever reduction path we choose. This of course is relevant for calculations, but also for programming: programs which do not end are undesirable. Algol 60 was one of the first well-structured, so-called 'high-level' programming languages in the history of computer science, but unfortunately, termination was not guaranteed. This is unavoidable: every programming language of sufficient power has non-terminating programs.*

On the other hand, one should not overestimate strong normalisability. Indeed, it guarantees termination within a finite amount of time, but this may nevertheless require waiting a long time. And since there is no upper bound on 'finiteness', one doesn't know beforehand how long this waiting will take.

2.12 Consequences

In the previous two sections we listed and proved a number of important properties of $\lambda{\to}$. These imply that all the negative aspects of *untyped* λ-calculus (see Section 1.11) disappear.

We show this one by one.

(1) *There is no self-application in* $\lambda{\to}$. (See also Example 2.2.6 (3).)

Proof Assume that MM is a legal term in $\lambda{\to}$. Then there are Γ and τ such that $\Gamma \vdash MM : \tau$. From the Generation Lemma 2.10.7 (2), it then follows that there is a type σ such that (for the first M:) $\Gamma \vdash M : \sigma \to \tau$ and (for the second M:) $\Gamma \vdash M : \sigma$. Hence, by the Uniqueness of Types Lemma 2.10.9, $\sigma \to \tau \equiv \sigma$. But this is clearly impossible: no function type can be equal to its own left-hand side. □

(2) *Existence of β-normal forms is guaranteed.*

This follows directly from the Strong Normalisation Theorem 2.11.6.

(3) *Not every legal λ-term has a fixed point.*

First note that the proof of Theorem 1.10.1 no longer works in $\lambda{\to}$: the term $M \equiv (\lambda x . L(xx))(\lambda x . L(xx))$ which is introduced in that proof makes heavy use of self-application (the term itself is of the form NN, and there are also two subterms xx).

But this is not enough to conclude that there are legal terms in Λ_{T} without a fixed point. So, let's give an example to show this.

Take two *different* types, σ and τ, and consider some legal function F of type $\sigma \to \tau$, in some context Γ, so $\Gamma \vdash F : \sigma \to \tau$. Now this F cannot have a fixed point within the system $\lambda_\to$, which we show now.

Assume that $FM =_\beta M$ where FM and M are legal. Then M must have type σ (by legality of FM, Uniqueness of Types and Generation Lemma (2)). Hence, by the (*appl*)-rule, FM has type τ. Now by Corollary 2.11.4, there must be N such that $FM \twoheadrightarrow_\beta N$ and $M \twoheadrightarrow_\beta N$, and by Subject Reduction (twice) we obtain both $\Gamma \vdash N : \tau$ and $\Gamma \vdash N : \sigma$. This contradicts Uniqueness of Types.

2.13 Conclusions

In this chapter we have added simple types to lambda calculus. These types do not have much structure: starting from type variables, the only way to construct other types is by repeatedly writing the binary $\to$-symbol between types. By their simplicity, they do not contain much 'information' about the terms. We preferred explicit typing (à la Church) over implicit typing (à la Curry).

The derivation system for Church's $\lambda_\to$ reflects the structure of λ-terms in that it has one rule for variables, one for applications and one for abstractions. Thus it is very concise and to the point. It also conforms neatly to intuition. We gave examples of derivations, which demonstrated the smooth behaviour of the system-in-action.

The system $\lambda_\to$ satisfies many nice and desirable properties, in particular concerning β-reduction. These properties also cause the drawbacks encountered in *untyped* lambda calculus to be eliminated. In other words, there is no more self-application, there are no infinite reduction sequences and we no longer have fixed points for *every* function. And there is more: the *positive points* of untyped lambda calculus extend to the simply typed version of lambda calculus. There is only one important drawback, which we mention here without a proof: the system $\lambda_\to$ is much too weak to encapsulate all computable functions and is hence not useable for the formalisation of mathematics.

Therefore, we have to extend $\lambda_\to$ to more powerful systems of typed lambda calculus, which we shall do in the following chapters: we gradually introduce more complex types, which are suitable for more 'realistic' situations, in particular for general use in logic and mathematics, as we shall show with various examples.

Important to note is that these extensions will be without harm: the undesired aspects of *untyped* lambda calculus will stay away.

2.14 Further reading

Historically, the British mathematician and philosopher B. Russell was the first
to formulate a type theory. He developed this type theory (called the *Ramified
Theory of Types*, or *RTT*; see also Section 13.8) for his thorough investigations
into the foundations of mathematics. Russell did not yet employ the λ-notation.
A few decades later, A. Church presented the simply typed lambda calculus
– the subject of the present chapter – which is a simplification of RTT, as it
removes the ramification. Church's goal was to define higher order logic; simple
type theory defines the language of higher order logic. Church's paper (Church,
1940) is still very accessible.

In this chapter we have mainly discussed the explicit typing variant of simple
type theory, or typing à la Church. With explicit typing, the decidability of
typing is almost immediate: the free variables have a type in the context and
the bound variables have a type in the lambda abstraction (we write $\lambda x : \sigma . M$
instead of just $\lambda x . M$). From that information one straightforwardly computes
the (unique) type of the whole term, if it exists.

For functional programming languages, the system à la Curry, with implicit
types, is relevant. That is because, when programming, one wants to avoid
writing the types, and instead let the compiler compute a type (if the term is
typable; and return 'fail' if the term is not typable). For the Curry system, the
type of a term is not unique. J.R. Hindley (see Hindley, 1969, 1997), H.B. Curry
(Curry, 1969) and R. Milner (Milner, 1978) have independently developed the
principal type algorithm, that, given a closed untyped term M, computes a
type σ of M (if M is typable) and 'fail' if M is not typable in simple type
theory à la Curry. Moreover, the computed type σ is 'minimal' in the sense
that all possible types for M are substitution instances of σ. (Such a type is
called a *principal* type.) A more modern exposition of this algorithm is given
by M. Wand (Wand, 1987), where a type checking problem is reduced to a
unification problem over type expressions, and then the *most general unifier*
of J.A. Robinson's unification algorithm (Robinson, 1965) yields the principal
type.

Readers particularly interested in the value of types for computer science are
referred to the books of B.C. Pierce (Pierce, 2002, 2004). A good introductory
text on simple type theory for logic is Hindley (1997); another one, focusing
on computation, is Simmons (2000).

Untyped lambda calculus is Turing-complete, but the expressivity of simple
type theory is limited. It can be shown that one can encode natural numbers
as the closed terms of type $(\alpha \to \alpha) \to \alpha \to \alpha$. The encoding represents
the number n as the expression $\lambda f : \alpha \to \alpha . \lambda x : \alpha . f(\dots(f\,x)\dots)$ with n
times an f. These are called the (typed) Church numerals (Church, 1940).

(See Exercise 2.2; compare this with Exercise 1.10.) On these numerals, one can then define addition and multiplication, but that's about it: the class of functions definable on the Church numerals in simple type theory is the class of generalised polynomials (Schwichtenberg, 1976).

The limited expressivity of simple type theory can be overcome by extending the system with a fixed point combinator. This has been done in the system PCF (Plotkin, 1977), where for every type σ, a constant $Y_\sigma : (\sigma \to \sigma) \to \sigma$ is added, satisfying the reduction rule $Y_\sigma f \to f(Y_\sigma f)$. This renders the system Turing-complete and therefore it has been studied as the theoretical basis of functional programming languages. It is also a good basis to study various evaluation strategies that are known from functional programming, for example 'call-by-value' (to reduce $(\lambda x : \sigma . M)N$, first reduce N to a value) and 'call-by-name' (to reduce $(\lambda x : \sigma . M)N$, first contract the redex itself to $M[x := N]$).

A non-trivial property of simple type theory is normalisation. For simple type theory, Weak Normalisation (cf. Definition 1.9.6) was first proved by A.M. Turing in the 1940s, but only written up by his student R.O. Gandy much later (see Gandy, 1980). Strong Normalisation was first proved by L.E. Sanchis in 1965 and published in Sanchis (1967). Probably the most well-known proof of Strong Normalisation is due to W.W. Tait, using an ingenious semantic interpretation. In Tait (1967) he only proves Weak Normalisation, but the proof can immediately be extended to Strong Normalisation. See Section 8.2 of Cardone & Hindley (2009) for a more detailed historic overview.

Exercises

2.1 Investigate for each of the following λ-terms whether they can be typed with a simple type. If so, give a type for the term and the corresponding types for x and y. If not, explain why.

    (a) $x \, x \, y$,

    (b) $x \, y \, y$,

    (c) $x \, y \, x$,

    (d) $x(x \, y)$,

    (e) $x(y \, x)$.

2.2 Find types for *zero*, *one* and *two* (see Exercise 1.10).

2.3 Find types for K and S (see Exercise 1.9).

2.4 Add types to the bound variables in the following λ-terms such that they become pre-typed λ-terms which are legal, and give their types:

    (a) $\lambda xyz \, . \, x(y \, z)$,

    (b) $\lambda xyz \, . \, y(x \, z)x$.

2.5 For each of the following terms, try to find a pre-typed variant which is typable. If this is not possible, show why.

    (a) $\lambda xy \,.\, x(\lambda z \,.\, y)y$,

    (b) $\lambda xy \,.\, x(\lambda z \,.\, x)y$.

2.6 (a) Prove that the following pre-typed λ-term is legal, using the tree format:
$$\lambda x : ((\alpha \to \beta) \to \alpha) \,.\, x \,(\lambda z : \alpha \,.\, y).$$

    (b) Transform the derivation into flag format.

2.7 (a) Prove the following by giving a kind of derivation, with the rules (*func-appl*) and (*func-abst*) described in Example 2.4.8:

        If $f : A \to B$ and $g : B \to C$, then $g \circ f : A \to C$.

    (Note: $g \circ f$ is the *composition* of f and g, being the function mapping x to $g(f\,x)$.)

    (b) Give a derivation in natural deduction of the following expression, using the rules $\Rightarrow$-*elim* and $\Rightarrow$-*intro* described in Example 2.4.9:
$$(A \Rightarrow B) \Rightarrow ((B \Rightarrow C) \Rightarrow (A \Rightarrow C)).$$

    (c) Prove that the following pre-typed λ-term is legal, using the flag format:
$$\lambda z : \alpha \,.\, y(x\,z).$$

    (d) Indicate the similarities between the derivations in (a), (b) and (c).

2.8 (a) Add types to the bound variables in the λ-term $\lambda xy \,.\, y(\lambda z \,.\, y\,x)$ such that the type of this term becomes
$$(\gamma \to \beta) \to ((\gamma \to \beta) \to \beta) \to \beta.$$

    (b) Give a derivation in tree format, proving this.

    (c) Sketch a diagram of the tree structure, as in Section 2.5.

    (d) Transform the derivation into flag format.

2.9 Give derivations by means of which the following judgements become type-checked. You may use the flag notation. In part (b), you may use flag notation in its 'shortened' form, i.e. suppress steps involving the (*var*)-rule.

    (a) $x : \delta \to \delta \to \alpha, \; y : \gamma \to \alpha, \; z : \alpha \to \beta \;\vdash$
$$\lambda u : \delta \,.\, \lambda v : \gamma \,.\, z(y\,v) : \delta \to \gamma \to \beta,$$

    (b) $x : \delta \to \delta \to \alpha, \; y : \gamma \to \alpha, \; z : \alpha \to \beta \;\vdash$
$$\lambda u : \delta \,.\, \lambda v : \gamma \,.\, z(x\,u\,u) : \delta \to \gamma \to \beta.$$

2.10 Prove that the following pre-typed λ-terms are legal, by giving derivations in (shortened) flag notation.

    (a) $x\,z\,(y\,z)$,

    (b) $\lambda x : (\alpha \to \beta) \to \beta \,.\, x(y\,z)$,

    (c) $\lambda y : \alpha \,.\, \lambda z : \beta \to \gamma \,.\, z(x\,y\,y)$,

    (d) $\lambda x : \alpha \to \beta \,.\, y(x\,z)z$.

2.11 Find inhabitants of the following types in the empty context, by giving appropriate derivations.

(a) $(\alpha \to \alpha \to \gamma) \to \alpha \to \beta \to \gamma$,

(b) $((\alpha \to \gamma) \to \alpha) \to (\alpha \to \gamma) \to \beta \to \gamma$.

2.12 (a) Construct a term of type $((\alpha \to \beta) \to \alpha) \to (\alpha \to \alpha \to \beta) \to \alpha$.

(b) Construct a term of type $((\alpha \to \beta) \to \alpha) \to (\alpha \to \alpha \to \beta) \to \beta$. (Hint: use (a).)

2.13 Find a term of type τ in context Γ, with:

(a) $\tau \equiv (\alpha \to \beta) \to \alpha \to \gamma$, $\Gamma \equiv x : \alpha \to \beta \to \gamma$,

(b) $\tau \equiv \alpha \to (\alpha \to \beta) \to \gamma$, $\Gamma \equiv x : \alpha \to \beta \to \alpha \to \gamma$,

(c) $\tau \equiv (\alpha \to \gamma) \to (\beta \to \alpha) \to \gamma$, $\Gamma \equiv x : (\beta \to \gamma) \to \gamma$.

Give appropriate derivations.

2.14 Find an inhabitant of the type $\alpha \to \beta \to \gamma$ in the following context:
$$\Gamma \equiv x : (\gamma \to \beta) \to \alpha \to \gamma.$$
Give an appropriate derivation.

(Hint: if τ is inhabited, then also $\sigma \to \tau$ is inhabited.)

2.15 Give the (*var*)- and (*appl*)-cases of the proof of Lemma 2.10.5 (1) (the 'Thinning Lemma').

2.16 Prove Lemma 2.10.8 (the 'Subterm Lemma').

2.17 Prove Lemma 2.10.9 (the 'Uniqueness of Types Lemma').

(Hint: use Lemma 2.10.7 (the 'Generation Lemma').)

2.18 Prove the Compatibility cases in the proof of Lemma 2.11.5.

3

Second order typed lambda calculus

3.1 Type-abstraction and type-application

In Church's $\lambda\to$, we only encounter abstraction and application on the term level:

— Look at the *abstraction* process. We start with term M, in which x may occur as a free variable. Assuming that x has type σ, we then may *abstract* M from x by means of a λ, in order to obtain $\lambda x : \sigma \,.\, M$. As a side effect, every free occurrence of x in M becomes *bound* in $\lambda x : \sigma \,.\, M$.

    The variable x is itself a term. Consequently, by *abstracting the term M from the term x*, we obtain a new term: $\lambda x : \sigma \,.\, M$. One describes this situation by saying:

    the term $\lambda x : \sigma \,.\, M$ depends on the term x .

    Hence, in $\lambda\to$ we can construct **terms depending on terms**.

— The counterpart of abstraction is *application*. And when we can 'abstract a term from a term', then it is natural that we also can 'apply a term to a term'. And indeed, we can: for the construction of MN we *apply the term M to the term N*. Also now, the result is a term, namely MN.

Here one speaks of *first order* abstraction, or first order dependency, since the abstraction is over *terms*. Its companion, application, is first order as well.

In the present chapter, we also introduce **terms depending on types**. In this case one speaks of *second order* operations (or second order dependency).

The system that we obtain is called the *second order typed lambda calculus*, or $\lambda 2$ for short. Its precise definition and derivation rules follow later in this chapter.

We start with motivating examples.

Examples 3.1.1 (1) First, we consider the *identity function*, i.e. the function which, after taking an input, returns it unchanged:

– On the natural numbers, *nat*, this identity function is $\lambda x : nat \, . \, x$.
– On the booleans, *bool*, this is $\lambda x : bool \, . \, x$.
– On *nat* $\to$ *bool* (the set of functions from *nat* to *bool*), we have the identity function $\lambda x : (nat \to bool) \, . \, x$.

So there are many identity functions, one per type. But what about 'the' identity function? It apparently does not exist in $\lambda{\to}$. The best we can do is to consider an *'arbitrary'* type α and construct the function $f \equiv \lambda x : \alpha \, . \, x$.

But now, given an M of type *nat*, we cannot write fM, because this term is not legal: the types do not match. (Since $\alpha \not\equiv nat$, the (*appl*)-rule of Definition 2.4.5 fails.) Similar considerations hold for a B of type *bool*: also fB is not legal.

Concluding, we want to have the possibility of 'tuning' this general function $\lambda x : \alpha \, . \, x$ in such a manner that it can deal with all kinds of types. The trick for this is to add *another abstraction* at the front:

$\lambda\alpha : * . \, \lambda x : \alpha \, . \, x$.

The novelty in this new kind of abstraction is the *type* variable α occurring behind the first λ. The symbol $*$ denotes *the type of all types*, so in particular $\alpha : *$.

Note that $\lambda\alpha : * . \, \lambda x : \alpha \, . \, x$ acts by itself as a term again, but this time it is *a term depending on a type*. The type it depends on is α.

The obtained (second order) term is called the *polymorphic* identity function. Note that it is not an identity function itself, but only a potential one (an 'identity-function-to-be'). We have to do (second order) *application* and β-reduction to obtain a 'genuine' identity function. For example:

– $(\lambda\alpha : * . \, \lambda x : \alpha \, . \, x)nat \to_\beta \lambda x : nat \, . \, x$, which is the identity on *nat*,
– $(\lambda\alpha : * . \, \lambda x : \alpha \, . \, x)(nat \to bool) \to_\beta \lambda x : (nat \to bool) \, . \, x$, which is the identity on *nat* $\to$ *bool*.

So when extending $\lambda{\to}$ in this manner, we have to add second order abstraction and application. Moreover, we need β-reduction for second order terms.

(2) Our second example is about *iteration*, i.e. the repeated application of the same function.

Take a type σ and a function F of type $\sigma \to \sigma$. We define $D_{\sigma,F}$ as the function mapping x in σ to $F(F(x))$. So $D_{\sigma,F}$ is the *second iteration* of F, also denoted as $F \circ F$ (the composition of F with itself).

This $D_{\sigma,F}$ can easily be expressed in $\lambda{\to}$ already, viz. as $\lambda x : \sigma \, . \, F(F x)$. Now we want to consider such a D for *arbitrary* σ and *arbitrary* $F : \sigma \to \sigma$, so instead of the fixed type σ we take type *variable* α, and instead of the fixed function F we take term *variable* f, where $f : \alpha \to \alpha$. By means of abstraction from f and α we obtain:

$$D \equiv \lambda \alpha : *. \, \lambda f : \alpha \to \alpha . \, \lambda x : \alpha . \, f(fx) .$$

D is called a *polymorphic function*, since it generalises over types: the first abstraction is second order. We can apply D, for example, to the type *nat*, using second order application. Reduction gives:

$$D \, nat \, \to_\beta \, \lambda f : nat \to nat . \, \lambda x : nat . \, f(fx) ,$$

so $D \, nat$ is the function that maps f to its second iteration $f \circ f$.

Assume that s is the *successor function* on the naturals, that is the function mapping n to $n + 1$, having type $nat \to nat$. Then:

$$D \, nat \, s \, \twoheadrightarrow_\beta \, \lambda x : nat . \, s(s \, x) .$$

This is the function mapping n to $n + 2$.

(3) Iteration as in the previous example is a special case of general *function composition*, i.e. the application of one function after another.

We immediately give the function composition operator, $\circ$, in $\lambda 2$:

$$\circ \equiv \lambda \alpha : *. \, \lambda \beta : *. \, \lambda \gamma : *. \, \lambda f : \alpha \to \beta . \, \lambda g : \beta \to \gamma . \, \lambda x : \alpha . \, g(fx) .$$

So for given types A, B and C, and functions $F : A \to B$ and $G : B \to C$, we have that $\circ \, A \, B \, C \, F \, G$ 'is' (i.e. is β-convertible to) the composition $G \circ F$, being the function $\lambda x : A . \, G(F(x))$.

3.2 Π-types

In the previous section we introduced *second order λ-abstraction* or *type-abstraction*; see for example the first λ of the polymorphic identity:

$$\lambda \alpha : *. \, \lambda x : \alpha . \, x .$$

Since we work in *typed* lambda calculus, it is natural to ask what the type is of this second order term. Now we know already from $\lambda{\to}$ that $\lambda x : \alpha . \, x \, : \, \alpha \to \alpha$, so an educated guess is:

$$\lambda \alpha : *. \, \lambda x : \alpha . \, x \quad : \quad * \to (\alpha \to \alpha) .$$

But now we have a problem. We saw earlier (Section 1.5) that we identify terms which only differ in the names of their binding (and corresponding bound) variables. In our second order expression above, the type α has become a *binding* variable, since it appears behind a λ (it is no longer a free variable, as in Chapter 2).

It is natural to identify $\lambda \alpha : *.\, \lambda x : \alpha .\, x$ with e.g. $\lambda \beta : *.\, \lambda x : \beta .\, x$. However, then we have:

$$\lambda \alpha : *.\, \lambda x : \alpha .\, x \quad : \quad * \to (\alpha \to \alpha)$$

$$|||\qquad\qquad\qquad \text{||||}$$

$$\lambda \beta : *.\, \lambda x : \beta .\, x \quad : \quad * \to (\beta \to \beta)\,,$$

implying that two *'identical'* terms (left) have *different* types (right). This is clearly not what we intended.

It is easy to pinpoint the trouble: in both left-hand sides, we treat α and β as bound variables, but in the right-hand sides, α and β act as *free* variables, which is not what we want. Therefore we introduce a new binder, the *type-binder* or Π-*binder*, denoted by the Greek capital Π (pronounced 'pi'). We write $\Pi \alpha : *.\, \alpha \to \alpha$ for the type of functions sending an *arbitrary* type α to a term of type $\alpha \to \alpha$.

By an obvious extension of the notion of α-conversion (see Section 1.5), we obtain $\Pi \alpha : *.\, \alpha \to \alpha \equiv_\alpha \Pi \beta : *.\, \beta \to \beta$, so now we have:

$$\lambda \alpha : *.\, \lambda x : \alpha .\, x \quad : \quad \Pi \alpha : *.\, \alpha \to \alpha$$

$$|||\qquad\qquad\qquad |||$$

$$\lambda \beta : *.\, \lambda x : \beta .\, x \quad : \quad \Pi \beta : *.\, \beta \to \beta\,,$$

and our problem has been solved.

Looking at the second order terms in (2) and (3) from Examples 3.1.1, it is not hard to guess what their Π-types will be (see also Section 3.5):

$$\lambda \alpha : *.\, \lambda f : \alpha \to \alpha .\, \lambda x : \alpha .\, f(fx) \quad : \quad \Pi \alpha : *.\, (\alpha \to \alpha) \to \alpha \to \alpha\,,$$

$$\lambda \alpha : *.\, \lambda \beta : *.\, \lambda \gamma : *.\, \lambda f : \alpha \to \beta .\, \lambda g : \beta \to \gamma .\, \lambda x : \alpha .\, g(fx) \quad :$$
$$\Pi \alpha : *.\, \Pi \beta : *.\, \Pi \gamma : *.\, (\alpha \to \beta) \to (\beta \to \gamma) \to \alpha \to \gamma\,.$$

Remark 3.2.1   *In mathematics, the letter Π (the Greek P) is usually reserved for a product, just as Σ (the Greek S) is reserved for sums. Π-types are also called product types; cf. Remark 5.2.2.*

3.3 Second order abstraction and application rules

Since we allow second order abstraction, second order application and Π-types, our derivation system for $\lambda{\to}$ has to be extended.

To begin with, we need an extra abstraction rule, in order to make the connection between second order terms and Π-types. This rule is:

Definition 3.3.1   (Second order abstraction rule)

$$(abst_2) \quad \frac{\Gamma,\, \alpha : * \;\vdash\; M : A}{\Gamma \;\vdash\; \lambda \alpha : *.\, M \;:\; \Pi \alpha : *.\, A}$$

So when M has type A in a context where α has type $*$, then $\lambda\alpha : *.\ M$ has type $\Pi\alpha : *.\ A$. This rule corresponds to our expectations after the examples in the previous section. There is one novelty: we allow second order declarations in the context, such as $\alpha : *$.

How about *applications* in the presence of Π-types? Let's observe an example, again. We know that $\lambda\alpha : *.\ \lambda x : \alpha.\ x\ :\ \Pi\alpha : *.\ \alpha \to \alpha$.

Now we apply the left-hand side to, say, nat. This is a type, so it does 'fit' in the second order term. We obtain the term:

$(\lambda\alpha : *.\ \lambda x : \alpha.\ x)nat$,

which β-reduces to $\lambda x : nat.\ x$. (It is easy to see how reduction must be extended to second order terms.) The latter term has type $nat \to nat$, so a good guess is:

$(\lambda\alpha : *.\ \lambda x : \alpha.\ x)nat\ :\ nat \to nat$.

This is indeed also a natural thing to do: we start with a function belonging to the specific Π-type $\Pi\alpha : *.\ \alpha \to \alpha$, which is *the type of all functions sending an arbitrary type α to a term of type $\alpha \to \alpha$*. So, when applying such a function to nat, we obtain *a term of type $nat \to nat$*, and that's exactly what we have above.

Recapitulating the above in a more general setting:

If $M\ :\ \Pi\alpha : *.\ \alpha \to \alpha$, then:

$MB\ :\ B \to B$,

and even more generally:

If $M\ :\ \Pi\alpha : *.\ A$, then:

$MB\ :\ A[\alpha := B]$.

Of course, we have to be certain that B matches with the domain of M in the last two cases, so B should be a type, i.e. $B : *$. This leads us to the following second order application rule:

Definition 3.3.2 (Second order application rule)

$$(appl_2)\ \frac{\Gamma \vdash M\ :\ \Pi\alpha : *.\ A \qquad \Gamma \vdash B\ :\ *}{\Gamma \vdash MB\ :\ A[\alpha := B]}$$

3.4 The system λ2

In this section we describe the complete system λ2.

Firstly, we have to extend our definition of types (cf. Definition 2.2.1). This is the abstract syntax for λ2-types:

$\mathbb{T}2\ =\ \mathbb{V}\ |\ (\mathbb{T}2 \to \mathbb{T}2)\ |\ (\Pi\mathbb{V} : *.\ \mathbb{T}2)$, with $\mathbb{V}$ the set of type variables. For these we take $\alpha, \beta, \gamma, \ldots$.

Secondly, we extend our set of pre-typed λ-terms ($\Lambda_{\mathbb{T}}$, cf. Definition 2.4.1) to terms where also second order abstraction and application are allowed:

Definition 3.4.1 (Second order pre-typed λ-terms, $\lambda 2$-terms, $\Lambda_{\mathbb{T}2}$)
The set of second order pre-typed λ-terms, or $\lambda 2$-terms, is defined by:

$$\Lambda_{\mathbb{T}2} = V | (\Lambda_{\mathbb{T}2}\Lambda_{\mathbb{T}2}) | (\Lambda_{\mathbb{T}2}\mathbb{T}2) | (\lambda V : \mathbb{T}2 . \Lambda_{\mathbb{T}2}) | (\lambda \mathbb{V} : * . \Lambda_{\mathbb{T}2}).$$

Note that we now have *two* classes of variables at our disposal: object variables V (such as x, y, $\ldots$) and type variables $\mathbb{V}$ (such as α, β, $\ldots$). As a consequence, we have *first order* abstraction ($\lambda V : \mathbb{T}2 . \Lambda_{\mathbb{T}2}$) from object variables, and *second order* abstraction ($\lambda \mathbb{V} : * . \Lambda_{\mathbb{T}2}$) from type variables.

Correspondingly, we have first order application ($\Lambda_{\mathbb{T}2}\Lambda_{\mathbb{T}2}$) and second order application ($\Lambda_{\mathbb{T}2}\mathbb{T}2$).

In $\lambda 2$, we save on parentheses and λs in a similar manner as we have done for untyped lambda calculus and for simply typed lambda calculus (see Notations 1.3.10 and 2.2.2). This convention extends to arrows ($\rightarrow$) and Πs:

Notation 3.4.2 – *Outermost parentheses may be omitted.*
– *Application is left-associative.*
– *Application and $\rightarrow$ take precedence over both λ- and Π-abstraction.*
– *Successive λ- or Π-abstractions* concerning the same types *may be combined in a right-associative way.*
– *Arrow types are denoted in a right-associative way.*

For example: we write $\Pi\alpha, \beta : * . \alpha \rightarrow \beta \rightarrow \alpha$ as an abbreviating notation for $(\Pi\alpha : * . (\Pi\beta : * . (\alpha \rightarrow (\beta \rightarrow \alpha))))$.

Next, we extend our notion of 'declaration' (see Definition 2.4.2) by allowing second order declarations:

Definition 3.4.3 (Statement, declaration)
(1) A *statement* is either of the form $M : \sigma$, where $M \in \Lambda_{\mathbb{T}2}$ and $\sigma \in \mathbb{T}2$, or of the form $\sigma : *$, where $\sigma \in \mathbb{T}2$.
(2) A *declaration* is a statement with a *term variable* or a *type variable* as subject.

In $\lambda \rightarrow$, a *context* was just a list of term declarations. In $\lambda 2$, however, we are a bit more strict. Since the type *constants* of $\lambda \rightarrow$ have become type *variables* in $\lambda 2$, we treat these type variables on a par with *term* variables, in the sense that *all variables must be declared before they can be used*. This guarantees that we 'know' the types of *all* variables before we use them.

That is to say, a declaration such as $x : \alpha \rightarrow \alpha$ must be *preceded* by the declaration of type variable α (having type $*$). Furthermore, the declaration $x : \alpha \to \beta$ presupposes the declarations of both α and β.

This is the motivation for the following recursive definition of λ2-context, which we combine with a new definition of the *domain* of a context. In this definition, part (3), we speak about *free* type variables. We leave it as an exercise to the reader to say what freeness for type variables comprises (Exercise 3.21).

Definition 3.4.4 (λ2-context; domain; dom)
(1) $\emptyset$ is a λ2-context;
$\mathrm{dom}(\emptyset) = (\ )$, the empty list.
(2) If Γ is a λ2-context, $\alpha \in \mathbb{V}$ and $\alpha \notin \mathrm{dom}(\Gamma)$, then $\Gamma, \alpha : *$ is a λ2-context;
$\mathrm{dom}(\Gamma, \alpha : *) = (\mathrm{dom}(\Gamma), \alpha)$, i.e. $\mathrm{dom}(\Gamma)$ concatenated with α.
(3) If Γ is a λ2-context, if $\rho \in \mathbb{T}2$ such that $\alpha \in \mathrm{dom}(\Gamma)$ for all free type variables α occurring in ρ and if $x \notin \mathrm{dom}(\Gamma)$, then $\Gamma, x : \rho$ is a λ2-context;
$\mathrm{dom}(\Gamma, x : \rho) = (\mathrm{dom}(\Gamma), x)$.

Note that this definition entails that all term variables and type variables in a λ2-context are mutually distinct.

Example 3.4.5
- $\emptyset$ is a λ2-context by (1).
- So $\alpha : *$ is a λ2-context by (2).
- Hence, $\alpha : *,\ x : \alpha \to \alpha$ is a λ2-context by (3). (Note that type variable α in type $\alpha \to \alpha$ has already been declared in the context.)
- Also, $\alpha : *,\ x : \alpha \to \alpha,\ \beta : *$ is a λ2-context by (2).
- Hence, $\Gamma \equiv \alpha : *,\ x : \alpha \to \alpha,\ \beta : *,\ y : (\alpha \to \alpha) \to \beta$ is a λ2-context by (3), with $\mathrm{dom}(\Gamma) = (\alpha, x, \beta, y)$.

Conforming with our new notion of context, we adapt the *(var)*-rule of λ→ (cf. Definition 2.4.5) in order to start the derivation of the type of a variable relative to a 'proper' λ2-context:

Definition 3.4.6 (Var-rule for λ2)
$\quad$ *(var)* $\quad \Gamma \vdash x : \sigma$ if Γ is a λ2-context and $x : \sigma \in \Gamma$.

Note that this *(var)*-rule for λ2 is, again, a rule without a **premiss**.

Now we have most of the rules for derivations in λ2: we reuse *(appl)* and *(abst)* from λ→ (see Definition 2.4.5), we take the new *(var)*-rule as above and we add the rules $(appl_2)$ and $(abst_2)$ from the previous section.

There is one complication, however: when employing these five rules, we will never be able to use the $(appl_2)$-rule. The reason is that the second **premiss** of this rule is $\Gamma \vdash B : *$, and there is *no* rule to establish that something has type $*$ (verify this: no **conclusion** is of the form $\ldots \vdash \ldots : *$).

It is not hard to repair this. Our intuition is that $B : *$ holds as soon as B is a type and all type variables in B are 'known'. So we add:

Definition 3.4.7   (Formation rule)

$(form)$ $\Gamma \vdash B : *$ if Γ is a $\lambda 2$-context, $B \in \mathbb{T}2$ and all free type variables in B are declared in Γ.

This rule is called the *formation*-rule, since it tells us what the type is (namely, $*$) of a B which is itself a properly *formed* $\lambda 2$-type.

Note that the $(form)$-rule has three side conditions, but no **premisses**. So, just like the (var)-rule, it can only occur in the leaves of a derivation tree.

For convenience, we display all derivation rules of $\lambda 2$ in Figure 3.1:

(var) $\Gamma \vdash x : \sigma$ if Γ is a $\lambda 2$-context and $x : \sigma \in \Gamma$

$(appl)$ $\dfrac{\Gamma \vdash M : \sigma \to \tau \quad \Gamma \vdash N : \sigma}{\Gamma \vdash MN : \tau}$

$(abst)$ $\dfrac{\Gamma, x : \sigma \vdash M : \tau}{\Gamma \vdash \lambda x : \sigma . M \; : \; \sigma \to \tau}$

$(form)$ $\Gamma \vdash B : *$ if Γ is a $\lambda 2$-context, $B \in \mathbb{T}2$ and all free type variables in B are declared in Γ

$(appl_2)$ $\dfrac{\Gamma \vdash M : (\Pi\alpha : * . A) \quad \Gamma \vdash B : *}{\Gamma \vdash MB : A[\alpha := B]}$

$(abst_2)$ $\dfrac{\Gamma, \alpha : * \vdash M : A}{\Gamma \vdash \lambda\alpha : * . M \; : \; \Pi\alpha : * . A}$

Figure 3.1 Derivation rules for $\lambda 2$

We translate the notion 'legality' from Definition 2.4.10 to $\lambda 2$:

Definition 3.4.8   (Legal $\lambda 2$-terms) A term M in $\Lambda_{\mathbb{T}2}$ is called *legal* if there exists a $\lambda 2$-context Γ and a type ρ in $\mathbb{T}2$ such that $\Gamma \vdash M : \rho$.

3.5 Example of a derivation in $\lambda 2$

In Section 3.2 we 'guessed' the type of $M \equiv \lambda\alpha : * . \lambda f : \alpha \to \alpha . \lambda x : \alpha . f(fx)$.

Now we show how this type can be *derived* by the aid of the rules. So, our task is to find a context Γ and a type ρ such that $\Gamma \vdash M : \rho$. Since M has no free term or type variables, we take $\Gamma \equiv \emptyset$. Thus, we start with the goal:

(n) $\lambda\alpha : *. \lambda f : \alpha \to \alpha. \lambda x : \alpha. f(fx)$: ?

Since the term-to-be-typed starts with a *'second order* λ', we use the rule $(abst_2)$, in reverse order:

(a) $\boxed{\alpha : *}$
    $\vdots$

(m) $\lambda f : \alpha \to \alpha. \lambda x : \alpha. f(fx)$: ?

(n) $\lambda\alpha : *. \lambda f : \alpha \to \alpha. \lambda x : \alpha. f(fx)$: ... $(abst_2)$ on (m)

The new goal starts with $\lambda f : \alpha \to \alpha. \ldots$, which is an 'ordinary' first order abstraction, so $(abst)$ is the suitable rule to use – again, in reverse order. Obviously, we may use this rule twice:

(a) $\boxed{\alpha : *}$
(b) $\boxed{f : \alpha \to \alpha}$
(c) $\boxed{x : \alpha}$
    $\vdots$

(k) $f(fx)$: ?

(l) $\lambda x : \alpha. f(fx)$: ... $(abst)$ on (k)

(m) $\lambda f : \alpha \to \alpha. \lambda x : \alpha. f(fx)$: ... $(abst)$ on (l)

(n) $\lambda\alpha : *. \lambda f : \alpha \to \alpha. \lambda x : \alpha. f(fx)$: ... $(abst_2)$ on (m)

The remainder is just a typing problem in $\lambda{\to}$, which we know how to solve (we give a *shortened* derivation, as in the previous chapter):

(a) $\boxed{\alpha : *}$
(b) $\boxed{f : \alpha \to \alpha}$
(c) $\boxed{x : \alpha}$
(1) fx : α $(appl)$ on (b) and (c)
(2) $f(fx)$: α $(appl)$ on (b) and (1)
(3) $\lambda x : \alpha. f(fx)$: $type_1$ $(abst)$ on (2)
(4) $\lambda f : \alpha \to \alpha. \lambda x : \alpha. f(fx)$: $type_2$ $(abst)$ on (3)
(5) $\lambda\alpha : *. \lambda f : \alpha \to \alpha. \lambda x : \alpha. f(fx)$: $type_3$ $(abst_2)$ on (4)

Now all that's left is to fill in $type_1$, $type_2$ and $type_3$, which immediately follows from the $(abst)$- and $(abst_2)$-rules:

$type_1 \equiv \alpha \to \alpha$,
$type_2 \equiv (\alpha \to \alpha) \to \alpha \to \alpha$, and
$type_3 \equiv \Pi\alpha : *. (\alpha \to \alpha) \to \alpha \to \alpha$.

So our conclusion, the completion of line (5), is:

(5) $\emptyset \vdash \lambda \alpha : *. \, \lambda f : \alpha \rightarrow \alpha . \, \lambda x : \alpha . \, f(fx) \; : \; \Pi \alpha : *. \, (\alpha \rightarrow \alpha) \rightarrow \alpha \rightarrow \alpha$.

From this we can conclude by the Thinning Lemma (see Lemma 3.6.4), that for every $\lambda 2$-context Γ:

(6) $\Gamma \vdash \lambda \alpha : *. \, \lambda f : \alpha \rightarrow \alpha . \, \lambda x : \alpha . \, f(fx) \; : \; \Pi \alpha : *. \, (\alpha \rightarrow \alpha) \rightarrow \alpha \rightarrow \alpha$.

Suppose we have a type *nat* that we can form in Γ, that is we have:

(7) $\Gamma \vdash nat : *$.

From (6) and (7) follows by $(appl_2)$:

(8) $\Gamma \vdash (\lambda \alpha : *. \, \lambda f : \alpha \rightarrow \alpha . \, \lambda x : \alpha . \, f(fx)) \; nat \; :$
      $(nat \rightarrow nat) \rightarrow nat \rightarrow nat$.

Suppose we also have:

(9) $\Gamma \vdash suc \; : \; nat \rightarrow nat$,

then with $(appl)$ on (8) and (9) we get:

(10) $\Gamma \vdash (\lambda \alpha : *. \, \lambda f : \alpha \rightarrow \alpha . \, \lambda x : \alpha . \, f(fx)) \; nat \; suc \; : \; nat \rightarrow nat$,

and so, if we also have $\Gamma \vdash two : nat$, we obtain:

(11) $\Gamma \vdash (\lambda \alpha : *. \, \lambda f : \alpha \rightarrow \alpha . \, \lambda x : \alpha . \, f(fx)) \; nat \; suc \; two \; : \; nat$.

3.6 Properties of $\lambda 2$

We have to adapt our Definition 1.5.2 of α-conversion, in order to accommodate Π-types:

Definition 3.6.1   (α-conversion or α-equivalence, extended)
(1a) (Renaming of term variable)
$\lambda x : \sigma . \, M =_\alpha \lambda y : \sigma . \, M^{x \rightarrow y}$ if $y \notin FV(M)$ and y does not occur as a binding variable in M.
(1b) (Renaming of type variable)
$\lambda \alpha : *. \, M =_\alpha \lambda \beta : *. \, M[\alpha := \beta]$ if β does not occur in M,
$\Pi \alpha : *. \, M =_\alpha \Pi \beta : *. \, M[\alpha := \beta]$ if β does not occur in M.
(2), (3a), (3b), (3c) (Compatibility, Reflexivity, Symmetry, Transitivity)
As in Definition 1.5.2.

We also extend β-reduction to $\lambda 2$ in the obvious way (cf. Definitions 1.8.1 and 2.11.2):

Definition 3.6.2 (One-step β-reduction, $\to_\beta$ for Λ_2-terms)
(1a) (Basis, first order) $(\lambda x : \sigma .\, M)N \to_\beta M[x := N]$
(1b) (Basis, second order) $(\lambda \alpha : * .\, M)T \to_\beta M[\alpha := T]$
(2) (Compatibility) As in Definition 1.8.1.

Example 3.6.3 We can start a β-reduction on the term in judgement (11) of the previous section:

$(\lambda \alpha : * .\, \lambda f : \alpha \to \alpha .\, \lambda x : \alpha .\, f(fx))\ nat\ suc\ two\ \to_\beta$
$(\lambda f : nat \to nat .\, \lambda x : nat .\, f(fx))\ suc\ two\ \to_\beta$
$(\lambda x : nat .\, suc(suc\ x))\ two\ \to_\beta$
$suc(suc\ two).$

Each of the four terms in this β-reduction chain has the same type, viz. *nat*. This can be established in two ways:
(1) By giving type derivations for each of them, as we did in Section 3.5 for the first one (this is the laborious way);
(2) But also: by using Subject Reduction (see Lemma 3.6.4 below) – this is apparently the easy way here, because we have already derived judgement (11).

In Chapter 2 we established a number of properties for $\lambda\to$. Most of these may be transferred to $\lambda 2$.

Lemma 3.6.4 *The following lemmas and theorems also hold for $\lambda 2$:*

– *Free Variables Lemma (cf. Lemma 2.10.3),*
– *Thinning Lemma (cf. Lemma 2.10.5 (1)),*
– *Condensing Lemma (cf. Lemma 2.10.5 (3)),*
– *Generation Lemma (cf. Lemma 2.10.7),*
– *Subterm Lemma (cf. Lemma 2.10.8),*
– *Uniqueness of Types (cf. Lemma 2.10.9),*
– *Substitution Lemma (cf. Lemma 2.11.1),*
– *Church–Rosser Theorem (cf. Theorem 2.11.3),*
– *Subject Reduction (cf. Lemma 2.11.5),*
– *Strong Normalisation Theorem (cf. Theorem 2.11.6).*

We omit proofs of these properties.

Note that the only lemma from Chapter 2 that we have to adapt is the Permutation Lemma (cf. Lemma 2.10.5): it is no longer allowed to arbitrarily permute the declarations in a context Γ occurring in a judgement $\Gamma \vdash M : T$, since a declaration occurring later in that context may *depend* on an earlier one, as we have explained in Section 3.4. If we require, however, that the permuted context is a $\lambda 2$-context, again, then it holds.

3.7 Conclusions

In this chapter we have extended Church's $\lambda\to$ with terms depending on *types*. The motivation is that a natural desire exists to 'abstract away' from a certain type in order to get a more general notion, such as the (polymorphic) identity function or generic function composition.

The extension has led to terms incorporating *second order* abstraction and application. As a consequence of the extension, Π-types have been introduced, being types of functions which send a type to a term.

The system obtained is $\lambda 2$, having first order *and* second order abstraction and application rules. Most of the nice properties of $\lambda\to$ still hold for the new system $\lambda 2$.

3.8 Further reading

The second order typed lambda calculus was first defined by J.-Y. Girard in his PhD thesis (Girard, 1972), where it was called 'system F'. Girard defined system F for proof-theoretic reasons: to capture the functions that one can prove to be total in second order arithmetic. We have not taken that angle here, but there is a vast literature on second order lambda calculus that builds on it (see Girard, 1986, and Girard *et al.*, 1989, for a comprehensible overview).

A powerful aspect of second order types is that one can define various data types, such as natural numbers, lists and trees, as closed second order types. One can also define functions over these data types such as addition and multiplication. For example, the data type of the natural numbers is $\Pi\alpha : *. (\alpha \to \alpha) \to \alpha \to \alpha$ and the natural numbers are represented as the *polymorphic Church numerals*: natural number n is represented as $\lambda\alpha : *. \lambda f : \alpha \to \alpha. \lambda x : \alpha. f(\dots(f\,x)\dots)$ with n times an f (cf. what we said about this in Section 2.14). C. Böhm and A. Berarducci have given a general method of representing algebraic data types in $\lambda 2$ (Böhm & Berarducci, 1985). They also show how a large class of functions can be defined on those data types in $\lambda 2$.

Polymorphic types are also called 'impredicative' types. One speaks of *impredicativity* if an element of a set X is identified by referring to the set X itself. A famous example of impredicativity occurs in the so-called Naive Set Theory, where we have the notion *powerset* of a set X. (The powerset $\mathcal{P}(X)$ of a set X is the set of all subsets of X.) Now it is tempting to introduce *the set of all sets*, say Set. Then we must also allow the powerset of Set, and we have $\mathcal{P}(\text{Set}) \in \text{Set}$. In this case we identify the element $\mathcal{P}(\text{Set})$ by referring to the set Set to which it belongs. Impredicativity was seen as a source of inconsistency by B. Russell and A.N. Whitehead in the book *Principia Mathematica*

(Whitehead & Russell, 1910; cf. Section 2.14) and therefore banned from their type theory (see also Section 13.8).

In the definition of a polymorphic type like $\sigma := \Pi\alpha : *. \alpha \to \alpha$, itself being of type $*$, we also refer to (i.e. quantify over) the *whole collection of types* (the type $*$ of the αs). Therefore, σ is called an impredicative type. Fortunately, it has been shown by J.-Y. Girard that polymorphic types are consistent, so the seemingly 'vicious circle' in the definition of polymorphic types is harmless. To be precise, we mean here that the type theory is *(logically) consistent* if we view the types as propositional formulas under the so-called propositions-as-types isomorphism (*'PAT'*; see the end of Section 2.9 or Section 5.4) and we can prove that there are 'empty types', i.e. types σ for which there is no closed term $M : \sigma$.

Independent of Girard, J.C. Reynolds (see Reynolds, 1974) invented a similar typed lambda calculus that he called the *polymorphic lambda calculus*. He constructed this system in order to capture the notion of *parametricity*. Parametricity is the aspect that we have been focusing on in this chapter: a function f of type $\Pi\alpha : *. \alpha \to \alpha$ treats the input type as a parameter. Such an f, applied to an arbitrary type τ, maps an object of τ to an object of that same type τ *without the possibility to look deeper into the structure of* τ. Therefore, an 'overloaded' function F that maps a natural number n to $n+1$, *and* a real number x to $|x|$, *and* a list l to the empty list, is not parametric, because F has to distinguish cases according to the *type* of its argument. In order to compute the value of $F\,t$, one has to inspect the type of t, and depending on that, apply a certain algorithm. Actually, it can be shown that the only function $f : \alpha \to \alpha$ that is parametric is the identity. This fits precisely with the fact that the polymorphic identity $\lambda\alpha : *. \lambda x : \alpha . x$ is the only closed term of type $\Pi\alpha : *. \alpha \to \alpha$.

The polymorphic lambda calculus of Reynolds has inspired researchers in functional programming languages to extend their languages with more powerful typing disciplines. However, in a programming language, one wants to write as few types as possible and let the compiler do *type inference*: i.e. do the check whether the term we have is typable, and if so, to compute a 'most general type' for us. This amounts to the implicit (à la Curry) typing that we have alluded to in Chapter 2.

For second order typed lambda calculus, some of the basic questions are much more difficult than for simple type theory.

For example, self-application is possible in $\lambda2$: we can add type information to the term $\lambda x . x\,x$ that makes it typable. This can be observed by looking at the term $\lambda x : (\Pi\alpha : *. \alpha \to \alpha) . x\,(\sigma \to \sigma)\,(x\,\sigma)$, which is a proper way of adding type information to $\lambda x . x\,x$. For $(\lambda x . x\,x)(\lambda x . x\,x)$, however, this is not possible, but that is far from obvious. A type inference algorithm should be able to see that $\lambda x . \, x\,x$ is typable while the other term is not. It was an open question for a long time whether type inference in polymorphic lambda calculus is decidable, until this question was answered in the negative by J.B. Wells (see Wells, 1994).

In modern functional languages, various 'weak' versions of polymorphism are used that allow parametricity while preserving the decidability of type inference. These type inference algorithms build on the work of R. Milner (Milner, 1978), who was the first to develop typing algorithms for polymorphic languages (see also Damas & Milner, 1982).

As for the meta-theory of polymorphic λ-calculus, Girard extended the original strong normalisation proof of the simple type theory by W.W. Tait (Tait, 1967) in an ingenious way to $\lambda 2$ (Girard, 1971; Girard *et al.*, 1989). Another interesting aspect to mention of the polymorphic λ-calculus is that it has no 'set-theoretic' models, as was proved by J.C. Reynolds (1984). This means that in a semantics of $\lambda 2$, the type $\sigma \to \tau$ cannot be interpreted as the full set of functions from the interpretation of σ to the interpretation of τ.

Exercises

3.1 How many $\lambda 2$-contexts are there consisting of the four declarations $\alpha : *$, $\beta : *$, $f : \alpha \to \beta$, $x : \alpha$?

3.2 Give a full (i.e. not-shortened) derivation in $\lambda 2$ to show that the following term is legal; use the flag format. (Cf. Example 3.1.1 (3).)
$$M \equiv \lambda \alpha, \beta, \gamma : * . \, \lambda f : \alpha \to \beta . \, \lambda g : \beta \to \gamma . \, \lambda x : \alpha . \, g(f\,x).$$

3.3 Take M as in Exercise 3.2. Assume $nat : *$, $bool : *$, $suc : nat \to nat$ and $even : nat \to bool$.

   (a) Prove that M nat nat $bool$ suc $even$ is legal.
   (b) Prove that $\lambda x : nat . \, even(suc\,x)$ is legal, in two ways:
       (1) using Exercise 3.3 (a) and Subject Reduction; (2) directly.

3.4 Give a shortened derivation in $\lambda 2$ to show that the following term is legal in the context $\Gamma \equiv nat : *, bool : *$:
$$(\lambda \alpha, \beta : * . \, \lambda f : \alpha \to \alpha . \, \lambda g : \alpha \to \beta . \, \lambda x : \alpha . \, g(f(f\,x))) \, nat \, bool.$$

3.5 Let $\perp \equiv \Pi \alpha : * . \, \alpha$ and $\Gamma \equiv \beta : *, \, x : \perp$.

   (a) Prove that $\perp$ is legal.
   (b) Find an inhabitant of β in context Γ.
   (c) Give three not β-convertible inhabitants of $\beta \to \beta$ in context Γ, each in β-normal form.
   (d) Prove that the following terms inhabit the same type in context Γ:
       $\lambda f : \beta \to \beta \to \beta . \, f(x\,\beta)(x\,\beta), \quad x((\beta \to \beta \to \beta) \to \beta).$

3.6 Find terms in Λ_{T2} that are inhabitants of the following $\lambda 2$-types, each in the given context Γ:

   (a) $\Pi\alpha, \beta : *.\ (nat \to \alpha) \to (\alpha \to nat \to \beta) \to nat \to \beta$,
      where $\Gamma \equiv nat : *$.

   (b) $\Pi\delta : *.\ ((\alpha \to \gamma) \to \delta) \to (\alpha \to \beta) \to (\beta \to \gamma) \to \delta$,
      where $\Gamma \equiv \alpha : *,\ \beta : *,\ \gamma : *$.

   (c) $\Pi\alpha, \beta, \gamma : *.\ (\alpha \to (\beta \to \alpha) \to \gamma) \to \alpha \to \gamma$, in the empty context.

3.7 Take $\bot$ as in Exercise 3.5.

   Let context Γ be $\alpha : *,\ \beta : *,\ x : \alpha \to \bot,\ f : (\alpha \to \alpha) \to \alpha$.

   Give a derivation to successively calculate an inhabitant of α and an inhabitant of β, both in context Γ.

3.8 Recall that $\mathsf{K} \equiv \lambda xy.\ x$ in untyped lambda calculus.

   Consider the following types:

   $T_1 \equiv \Pi\alpha, \beta : *.\ \alpha \to \beta \to \alpha$ and $T_2 \equiv \Pi\alpha : *.\ \alpha \to (\Pi\beta : *.\ \beta \to \alpha)$.

   Find inhabitants t_1 and t_2 of T_1 and T_2, which may be considered as different closed $\lambda 2$-versions of K.

3.9 Find a closed $\lambda 2$-version of $\mathsf{S} \equiv \lambda xyz.\ x\,z(y\,z)$, and establish its type.

3.10 Let $M \equiv \lambda x : (\Pi\alpha : *.\ \alpha \to \alpha)\ .\ x(\sigma \to \sigma)(x\,\sigma)$. (Cf. Section 3.8.)

   (a) Prove that M is legal in $\lambda 2$.

   (b) Find a term N such that $M\,N$ is legal in $\lambda 2$ and may be considered to be a proper way of adding type information to $(\lambda x.\ x\,x)(\lambda y.\ y)$.

3.11 Take $\bot$ as in Exercise 3.5. Prove that the following term is legal in the empty context:

   $\lambda x : \bot.\ x(\bot \to \bot \to \bot)(x(\bot \to \bot)x)(x(\bot \to \bot \to \bot)x\,x)$.

   What is its type?

3.12 As mentioned in Section 3.8, we have in $\lambda 2$ the polymorphic Church numerals. They resemble the untyped Church numerals, as described in Exercises 1.10 and 1.13 (b). For example:

   $Nat \equiv \Pi\alpha : *.\ (\alpha \to \alpha) \to \alpha \to \alpha$,

   $Zero \equiv \lambda\alpha : *.\ \lambda f : \alpha \to \alpha.\ \lambda x : \alpha.\ x$, having type Nat,

   $One \equiv \lambda\alpha : *.\ \lambda f : \alpha \to \alpha.\ \lambda x : \alpha.\ f\,x$, with type Nat, as well,

   $Two \equiv \lambda\alpha : *.\ \lambda f : \alpha \to \alpha.\ \lambda x : \alpha.\ f(f\,x)$.

   We define Suc as follows as a $\lambda 2$-term:

   $Suc \equiv \lambda n : Nat.\ \lambda\beta : *.\ \lambda f : \beta \to \beta.\ \lambda x : \beta.\ f(n\,\beta\,f\,x)$.

   Check that Suc acts as a successor function for the polymorphic Church numerals, by proving that $Suc\ Zero =_\beta One$ and $Suc\ One =_\beta Two$.

3.13 See the previous exercise.

   (a) We define Add in $\lambda 2$ as follows:

      $Add \equiv \lambda m, n : Nat.\ \lambda\alpha : *.\ \lambda f : \alpha \to \alpha.\ \lambda x : Nat.\ m\,\alpha\,f(n\,\alpha\,f\,x)$.

      Show that Add simulates addition, by evaluating $Add\ One\ One$.

(b) Find a λ2-term *Mult* that simulates multiplication on *Nat*. (Hint: see Exercise 1.10.)

3.14 We may also introduce the polymorphic booleans in λ2:

$Bool \equiv \Pi\alpha : *. \alpha \to \alpha \to \alpha,$

$True \equiv \lambda\alpha : *. \lambda x, y : \alpha . x,$

$False \equiv \lambda\alpha : *. \lambda x, y : \alpha . y.$

Construct a λ2-term $Neg : Bool \to Bool$ such that $Neg\ True =_\beta False$ and $Neg\ False =_\beta True$. Prove the correctness of your answer.

3.15 See Exercise 3.14. Define M by

$M \equiv \lambda u, v : Bool . \lambda\beta : *. \lambda x, y : \beta . u\,\beta(v\,\beta\,x\,y)(v\,\beta\,y\,y).$

(a) Reduce the following terms to β-normal form:

$M\ True\ True,\ M\ True\ False,\ M\ False\ True,\ M\ False\ False.$

(b) Which logical operator is represented by M?

3.16 See the previous exercises. Find λ2-terms that represent the logical operators 'inclusive or', 'exclusive or' and 'implication'.

3.17 See the previous exercises. Find a λ2-term *Iszero* that represents the test-for-zero. That is, define a λ2-term such that $Iszero\ Zero =_\beta True$ and $Iszero\ n =_\beta False$ for all polymorphic Church numerals n except *Zero*. (Hint: see Exercise 1.14.)

3.18 See Exercise 3.14. We define the type *Tree*, representing the set of binary trees with boolean-labelled nodes and leaves, by

$Tree \equiv \Pi\alpha : *. (Bool \to \alpha) \to (Bool \to \alpha \to \alpha \to \alpha) \to \alpha.$

Then $\lambda\alpha : *. \lambda u : Bool \to \alpha . \lambda v : Bool \to \alpha \to \alpha \to \alpha . M$ has type *Tree*, for every λ2-term M of type α.

(a) Sketch the three trees that are represented if we take for M, respectively:

$u\ False,$

$v\ True(u\ False)(u\ True),$

$v\ True(u\ True)(v\ False(u\ True)(u\ False)).$

(b) Give a λ2-term which, on input a polymorphic boolean p and two trees s and t, delivers the combined tree with p on top, left subtree s and right subtree t.

3.19 Prove: if $\Gamma \vdash L : \sigma$, then Γ is a λ2-context.

3.20 Prove the Free Variables Lemma for λ2 (cf. Lemma 3.6.4): if $\Gamma \vdash L : \sigma$, then $FV(L) \subseteq \mathsf{dom}(\Gamma)$.

3.21 Give a recursive definition for $FTV(A)$, the set of free type variables in A, for an expression A in 𝕋2 or in $\Lambda_{\mathbb{T}2}$.

4

Types dependent on types

4.1 Type constructors

In the previous chapter we introduced the possibility of constructing *generalised terms*, by abstracting a term from a type variable. For example, the term $\lambda x : \sigma . \, x$ (which is the identity on the fixed type σ) can be generalised to the term $\lambda \alpha : * . \, \lambda x : \alpha . \, x$ (the 'polymorphic' identity, i.e. the identity on variable type α, abstracted from this α).

In a similar manner, there is a natural wish to construct generalised *types*. For example, types like $\beta \to \beta$, $\gamma \to \gamma$, $(\gamma \to \beta) \to (\gamma \to \beta)$, ..., all have the general structure $\Diamond \to \Diamond$, with the same type both left and right of the arrow. Abstracting over $\Diamond$ makes it possible to describe the whole family of types with this structure.

In order to handle this, we introduce a generalised expression that embodies the essence of this structure: $\lambda \alpha : * . \, \alpha \to \alpha$. This is itself not a type, but a function with a type as a *value*. It is therefore called a *type constructor*. Only when we 'feed' it with e.g. β, γ or $(\gamma \to \beta)$, we obtain types:

$$(\lambda \alpha : * . \, \alpha \to \alpha) \, \beta \qquad \to_\beta \quad \beta \to \beta \, ,$$
$$(\lambda \alpha : * . \, \alpha \to \alpha) \, \gamma \qquad \to_\beta \quad \gamma \to \gamma \, ,$$
$$(\lambda \alpha : * . \, \alpha \to \alpha) \, (\gamma \to \beta) \quad \to_\beta \quad (\gamma \to \beta) \to (\gamma \to \beta) \, .$$

We obtain the type constructor $\lambda \alpha : * . \, \alpha \to \alpha$ by abstracting the type $\alpha \to \alpha$ from the type α. In a similar manner, we can make more complex type constructors, such as $\lambda \alpha : * . \, \lambda \beta : * . \, \alpha \to \beta$.

An obvious question is: what are the *types* of these type constructors? We already know that $\alpha \to \alpha$ is a type. Hence, one may consider $\lambda \alpha : * . \, \alpha \to \alpha$ as a function mapping the type α to the type $\alpha \to \alpha$. Since $\alpha : *$ and $\alpha \to \alpha : *$, we obtain:

$$\lambda \alpha : * . \, \alpha \to \alpha \; : \; * \to * \, .$$

Therefore, we need, next to $*$, a *new* 'super-type', viz. $* \to *$.

Similarly, we may conclude:

$$\lambda\alpha : * . \, \lambda\beta : * . \, \alpha \to \beta \, : \, * \to (* \to *) \, .$$

When adding things like $* \to *$ and $* \to (* \to *)$ as new super-types, it is natural to also allow variables belonging to these super-types.

Examples 4.1.1

(1) Suppose we have a variable $\alpha : * \to *$, then for $\gamma : *$, we have:

$$\alpha\gamma : *.$$

It is then also natural to *abstract* from this variable α, obtaining:

$$\lambda\alpha : * \to * . \, \alpha\gamma \, : \, (* \to *) \to *.$$

And we can apply this type constructor to the identity on types $\lambda\beta : * . \, \beta$, since $\lambda\beta : * . \, \beta$ has type $* \to *$:

$$(\lambda\alpha : * \to * . \, \alpha\gamma)(\lambda\beta : * . \, \beta) \, : \, *.$$

(2) We also may abstract from an α of type $* \to *$ and infer:

$$\lambda\alpha : * \to * . \, \alpha \, : \, (* \to *) \to (* \to *) \, .$$

The extensions described above can be summarised as the addition of **types depending on types**, which will lead to the system $\lambda\underline{\omega}$ to be described in the present chapter.

Remark 4.1.2 *When using this kind of general explanatory expression, such as 'terms depending on types' or 'types depending on types', we now have to extend the meaning of the word 'type', since we deal with both* ordinary *types* and *type constructors. Similar things hold for expressions such as 'abstracting a term from a type'.*

Above we have met the following examples of types (better: type constructors) depending on a type, which here is, in all cases, α:

- $\lambda\alpha : * . \, \alpha \to \alpha$,
- $\lambda\alpha : * . \, \lambda\beta : * . \, \alpha \to \beta$,
- $\lambda\alpha : * \to * . \, \alpha$,
- $\lambda\alpha : * \to * . \, \alpha\gamma$.

The 'super-types' which we have met above, consisting of $*$ alone and of $*$-symbols with arrows in between, are called *kinds*. Abstract syntax for the set $\mathbb{K}$ of all kinds is:

$$\mathbb{K} = * \, | \, (\mathbb{K} \to \mathbb{K}) \, .$$

Notation 4.1.3 *We use similar conventions for the omission of parentheses, as for simple types. So outermost parentheses may be omitted, and the kinds are denoted* right-associatively. *(Cf. Notation 2.2.2.)*

Examples of kinds are:

$$*, * \to *, * \to * \to *, (* \to *) \to *, (* \to *) \to * \to *, * \to (* \to *) \to *.$$

We introduce a new symbol for the *type of all kinds*, namely $\square$, which is so to speak the one and only 'super-super-type'. We have now e.g. that $* : \square$, but also $* \to * : \square$, etcetera. If κ is a kind, then often *each M* 'of type' κ (this is colloquial for $M : \kappa$) is called a type constructor, or simply *constructor*. Then all 'old' types – like α or $\alpha \to \alpha$ – are also called constructors, although there is 'nothing to construct' in these cases. So $\lambda\alpha : *. \; \alpha \to \alpha$ is a constructor of kind $* \to *$ and the 'old' type $\alpha \to \alpha$ itself is a constructor of kind $*$.

We use the term *proper constructor* for constructors which are *not* types. So the set of constructors splits apart into ('old') *types* and *proper constructors*.

Finally, the word *sort* is used for either $*$ or $\square$, so:

Definition 4.1.4 (Constructor, proper constructor, sort)
(1) If $\kappa : \square$ and $M : \kappa$, then M is a *constructor*. If $\kappa \not\equiv *$, then M is a *proper constructor*.
(2) The set of *sorts* is $\{*, \square\}$.

Notation 4.1.5 *From now on, we reserve symbol s as meta-variable for a sort (so s represents either $*$ or $\square$).*

With the addition of $\square$, we now have *four* levels in our syntax:

Definition 4.1.6 (Levels)
Level 1: here we find the terms;
level 2: where the constructors are (so the types plus the proper constructors);
level 3: that of the kinds;
level 4: consists solely of $\square$.

By gluing things together, we informally write *judgement chains* such as $t : \sigma : * \to *$, or even $t : \sigma : * \to * : \square$, expressing $t : \sigma$ and $\sigma : * \to *$ and $* \to * : \square$. In the last example we have levels 1 to 4 combined into one judgement chain.

When σ is a *proper* constructor, then it cannot be inhabited, so we have to omit the t from the chain. We then obtain the shorter judgement chain $\sigma : \kappa : \square$, with, for example, $\kappa \equiv * \to *$. But again, we observe several levels in this chain, viz. levels 2 to 4.

Remark 4.1.7 *It is worthwhile noticing that also statements $A : B$ are influenced by the richer choice in levels. Since the level of B must be one higher than that of A, we have:*
 If A has level 1, then A must be a term and B a type.
 In $\lambda 2$, A may also have level 2. Then A is a type and $B \equiv *$. In $\lambda\underline{\omega}$, A may

also be a type constructor and consequently B can be a more complicated kind, such as $* \to *$.

In $\lambda\underline{\omega}$*, it is possible that A has level 3; then A is a kind and* $B \equiv \square$.

Consequently, the roles of subject and type in a statement also range over several levels. These roles (and therefore their constructions) become increasingly interwoven, which will be an essential feature of the type systems to be discussed in the present chapter and thereafter.

4.2 Sort-rule and var-rule in $\lambda\underline{\omega}$

The system we consider in the present chapter is called $\lambda\underline{\omega}$. It is another extension of $\lambda{\to}$:

- $\lambda2 = \lambda{\to}$ plus *terms*-depending-on-types,
- $\lambda\underline{\omega} = \lambda{\to}$ plus *types*-depending-on-types.

We now continue with describing the specific derivation rules of $\lambda\underline{\omega}$. First, we formalise the fact that the super-type $*$ is of type $\square$. (That also all other kinds are of type $\square$, follows in Section 4.4.) This rule is called the *sort*-rule:

Definition 4.2.1 (Sort-rule)

(*sort*) $\emptyset \vdash * : \square$

Our next desire is a rule to establish that all declarations occurring in a context are derivable in that context. In $\lambda{\to}$ and $\lambda2$, we used the (*var*)-rule for this purpose (see Definition 2.4.5 and Figure 3.1, respectively). In $\lambda\underline{\omega}$, we use a slightly different approach: we neatly combine derivability of context declarations with the *construction of the context proper*.

The reason for this is that types are more complex in $\lambda\underline{\omega}$, so we have to make sure that the types are well-formed. In $\lambda{\to}$, where the set of permissible types was given beforehand, there was no problem at all. In $\lambda2$, things were a bit more complicated, so we had to establish what a (proper) $\lambda2$-context was (see Definition 3.4.4), which led in particular to requirements on the *types* used in such contexts. Hence, the permissibility of types occurring in a judgement could no longer be decided by referring to an *outside* set, but should depend on an inspection of the judgement itself, including its context.

In the present system, the requirements imposed on the types are still more severe: the permissibility of a type occurring in a judgement now only follows if we can formally *derive* it.

Our new approach is the following: we only extend a context with a declaration $x : A$ if the type A itself is already 'permissible'. And 'permissible types' of a statement occur in either level 2 or 3, and therefore are a type or a kind.

These things can be expressed in a rule, as follows:

Definition 4.2.2 (Var-rule)

$$(var) \; \frac{\Gamma \vdash A : s}{\Gamma, \; x : A \vdash x : A} \quad \text{if } x \notin \Gamma.$$

Recall that s ranges over *sorts* (cf. Notation 4.1.5). So, the **premiss** of this (var)-rule, $\Gamma \vdash A : s$, requires that A itself is a type (if $s \equiv *$) or a kind (if $s \equiv \square$). Notice that the letter 'x' may hence stand for either a *term variable* or a *type variable*. The (var)-rule allows us to extend context Γ with a declaration $x : A$, *and* to derive the same declaration as a statement in the extended context.

The restriction $x \notin \Gamma$ guarantees that variable x is 'fresh', i.e. x does not occur in Γ. From this follows that *all* variables declared in a context are *different*, which is a natural requirement, again: a context serves for typing possibly free variables in a statement and it is obviously unnecessary to declare a variable more than once in a context (and even confusing if the corresponding types happen to be different).

We emphasise the fact that this (var)-rule plays a *double role*, due to the two possibilities for s. Since s may be either $*$ (of level 3) or $\square$ (of level 4), the rule-as-a-whole covers *two* levels. We show this in the following example, by giving several realisations of the statements $A : s$ and $x : A$ occurring in Definition 4.2.2:

Example 4.2.3

	$s \equiv \square$			$s \equiv *$	
$A : s$	$* : \square$	$* \to * : \square$	$\alpha : *$	$\alpha \to \beta : *$	
$x : A$	$\alpha : *$	$\beta : * \to *$	$x : \alpha$	$y : \alpha \to \beta$	

Now we can start a derivation with the $(sort)$- and (var)-rules as given above. We give an example in tree format, which clearly demonstrates how these rules work.

$$\frac{\quad (1) \;\; \emptyset \vdash * : \square \quad}{\dfrac{(2) \;\; \alpha : * \vdash \alpha : *}{(3) \;\; \alpha : *, \; x : \alpha \vdash x : \alpha}\;(var)} \; (var)$$

The $(sort)$-rule gives line (1). The (var)-rule has been used in its two roles, with $s \equiv \square$ in line (2), and with $s \equiv *$ in line (3).

Of course, a similar derivation can be made for a type β.

In Section 2.5 we have mentioned that we prefer a flag format over a tree format in this book. Therefore we repeat the above derivation in flag format:

(1) $* : \square$ (*sort*)

$$\boxed{\alpha : *}$$

(2) $\alpha : *$ (*var*) on (1)

$$\boxed{x : \alpha}$$

(3) $x : \alpha$ (*var*) on (2)

It becomes also clear from this example that the (*var*)-rule introduced in the present chapter is less general than the one in e.g. the system $\lambda{\to}$ (see Definition 2.4.5), since the present (*var*)-rule only allows the derivation of the newly added, *final* declaration $x : A$ of the context. See lines (2) and (3) in the derivation. In $\lambda{\to}$, however, *any* declaration $x : \sigma$ occurring in Γ, is derivable with respect to this Γ.

It is a natural desire that we can do as much in our present system $\lambda\underline{\omega}$ as in $\lambda{\to}$. So, for example, we want to be able to derive not only $\alpha : *,\ x : \alpha \vdash x : \alpha$, but also:

($?_1$) $\alpha : *,\ x : \alpha \vdash \alpha : *$,

which is impossible with the present rules. Another judgement that we cannot make yet, is:

($?_2$) $\alpha : *,\ \beta : * \vdash \alpha : *$.

When we come to think about it, even the derivation of

($?_3$) $\alpha : *,\ \beta : * \vdash \beta : *$

is not possible, although $\beta : *$ is the final declaration of the context $\alpha : *,\ \beta : *$. The reason is that we cannot yet obtain the **premiss**:

($?_4$) $\alpha : * \vdash * : \square$,

which is necessary for deriving ($?_3$) with the (*var*)-rule.

All this will be repaired in the following section by the addition of the so-called 'weakening rule'.

4.3 The weakening rule in $\lambda\underline{\omega}$

The solution to the previously explained problem is the addition of a new rule. This rule, called *Weakening*, allows us to 'weaken' the context of a judgement by adding new declarations, provided that the 'types' of the new declarations are 'well-formed'. We first state the rule and discuss it afterwards:

Definition 4.3.1   (Weakening rule)

$$(weak)\ \frac{\Gamma \vdash A : B \quad \Gamma \vdash C : s}{\Gamma,\ x : C \vdash A : B}\quad \text{if } x \notin \Gamma.$$

The main effect of this rule can be described as follows. Assuming that we have derived the judgement $\Gamma \vdash A : B$ (first **premiss**), then we may 'weaken' the context Γ by adding an arbitrary declaration at the end. So, the resulting **conclusion** is $\Gamma,\ x : C \mid A : B$, i.e. $A : B$ is also derivable in the extended context.

There is one proviso: the type C of the added declaration should be well-formed itself. This is expressed in the requirement given in the second **premiss**: it should hold that $\Gamma \vdash C : s$, i.e. C itself is derivable in the same context Γ as something at level 2 when $s \equiv *$, or level 3 when $s \equiv \Box$.

The fact that the context extension in the (*weak*)-rule is only allowed *at the end* is easy to express and turns out to be sufficient. It is provable that *any* extension of the context with a well-formed declaration is permissible, which is a result of the Thinning Lemma which also holds for $\lambda\underline{\omega}$ (cf. Lemmas 2.10.5 (1) and 3.6.4).

Remark 4.3.2 *In type theory, one prefers the word 'thinning' for the general process of inserting a new declaration in a given list of declarations, at an arbitrary place. 'Weakening', however, is preferably used for extending such a list at the end* only. *In both situations one adds* more *assumptions, and this has indeed a 'weakening' (or 'thinning') effect on what we express.*

Now we are able to derive the missing judgements $(?_1)$ to $(?_4)$, mentioned at the end of the previous section. We first give the tree versions of the derivations, in order to maintain a close correspondence to the format of the rules.

$(?_1)$ This is the resulting judgement (4) in the following derivation, in which the (*weak*)-rule plays an important role.

$$\frac{(1)\ \ \emptyset \vdash *:\Box}{(2)\ \ \alpha : * \vdash \alpha : *}\ (var) \qquad\qquad \frac{\dfrac{(1)\ \ \emptyset \vdash *:\Box}{(2)\ \ \alpha : * \vdash \alpha : *}\ (var)}{(4)\ \ \alpha : *,\ x : \alpha \vdash \alpha : *}\ (weak)$$

It is interesting to see how two copies of line (2) have been used here as the first *and* the second **premiss** of the (*weak*)-rule, in order to obtain line (4) as a **conclusion**. We take $s \equiv *$. Please check carefully what is happening here.

$(?_2)$ and $(?_4)$ In the following derivation, the final conclusion (line (6)) solves question $(?_2)$. As a subresult, we also obtain an answer to question $(?_4)$: see line (5), for which, again, two copies of the same judgement have been used as left and right **premisses**.

$$\frac{(1) \; \emptyset \vdash * : \square}{(2) \; \alpha : * \vdash \alpha : *} \; (var)$$

$$\frac{(1) \; \emptyset \vdash * : \square \qquad (1) \; \emptyset \vdash * : \square}{(5) \; \alpha : * \vdash * : \square} \; (weak)$$

$$\frac{(6) \; \alpha : *, \; \beta : * \vdash \alpha : *}{} \; (weak)$$

Both cases of (*weak*) here are based on $s \equiv \square$.

($?_3$) The remaining question is solved in line (7) below.

$$\frac{(1) \; \emptyset \vdash * : \square \qquad (1) \; \emptyset \vdash * : \square}{(5) \; \alpha : * \vdash * : \square} \; (weak)$$

$$\frac{}{(7) \; \alpha : *, \; \beta : * \vdash \beta : *} \; (var)$$

Finally, we condense all tree derivations as given in this and the previous section into one flag derivation:

$$\begin{array}{lll}
(1) & * : \square & (sort) \\
 & \boxed{\alpha : *} & \\
(2) & \alpha : * & (var) \text{ on } (1) \\
 & \boxed{x : \alpha} & \\
(3) & x : \alpha & (var) \text{ on } (2) \\
(4) & \alpha : * & (weak) \text{ on } (2) \text{ and } (2) \\
(5) & * : \square & (weak) \text{ on } (1) \text{ and } (1) \\
 & \boxed{\beta : *} & \\
(6) & \alpha : * & (weak) \text{ on } (2) \text{ and } (5) \\
(7) & \beta : * & (var) \text{ on } (5)
\end{array}$$

Remark 4.3.3 *Albeit that tree derivations reflect the derivation rules faithfully, they are not always easy to read, as we mentioned already in Section 2.5. Firstly, tree derivations soon become inconveniently large and complex. Secondly, tree derivations tend to contain many repetitions of judgements, and also of subtrees. See the trees above, for example, where line (1) has been written seven times. The tree consisting of lines (1) and (2) has been repeated three times.*

A linear representation such as the flag format is more distant from the derivation rules as presented. It gives, however, a step-by-step impression of the development of a derivation. Moreover, flag derivations are considerably more compact, as the above example demonstrates. In particular, the repetitions that are inherent to a tree derivation are no longer necessary, since each line in a flag derivation can be used arbitrarily often. See, for example, the flag derivation above, where line (2) has been given only once, but has been appealed to four times.

4.4 The formation rule in λω̲

In λ2 we had a formation rule called (*form*) for the construction of typing statements in a context. The rule was based on a set 𝕋2 of λ2-types (see the beginning of Section 3.4). As already noted in Section 4.2, types in λω̲ are more complex. Therefore, we introduce a 'real' derivation rule, with **premisses** and **conclusion**, for the construction of types.

Moreover, we have also *kinds* in λω̲. But, thanks to the possibility of 'double roles' in λω̲, things become easier than expected. The new (*form*)-rule, enabling to *form* types *and* kinds, looks as follows:

Definition 4.4.1 (Formation rule)

$$(form) \quad \frac{\Gamma \vdash A : s \quad \Gamma \vdash B : s}{\Gamma \vdash A \to B : s}$$

This covers all the types and kinds that we want. (Note that there are no *terms depending on types* in λω̲, which has as a consequence that there are no Π-types in λω̲.)

We give two examples of this rule, the first one with $s \equiv *$. The omitted subtrees above lines (6) and (7) can be found in the previous section.

$$\frac{(6) \ \ \alpha : *, \ \beta : * \vdash \alpha : * \qquad (7) \ \ \alpha : *, \ \beta : * \vdash \beta : *}{(8) \ \ \alpha : *, \ \beta : * \vdash \alpha \to \beta : *} \ (form)$$

Our second example has $s \equiv \square$:

$$\frac{(5) \ \ \alpha : * \vdash * : \square \qquad (5) \ \ \alpha : * \vdash * : \square}{(9) \ \ \alpha : * \vdash * \to * : \square} \ (form)$$

We can also give these results in flag format, by extending the flag derivation of the previous section with two more lines:

$$\vdots$$

(8) $\alpha \to \beta : *$ (*form*) on (6) and (7)

(9) $* \to * : \square$ (*form*) on (5) and (5)

4.5 Application and abstraction rules in $\lambda \underline{\omega}$

What remains are the (*appl*)- and (*abst*)-rules. We give them below.

The rules slightly differ from the rules in Chapter 3 (see Figure 3.1). Firstly, the names of the meta-variables for the types are different (A instead of σ, etcetera), because types in $\lambda\underline{\omega}$ are more general. And secondly, in the (*abst*)-rule we must be sure that $A \to B$ is a well-formed type. (Recall that we have no Π-types in $\lambda\underline{\omega}$.) This is expressed as a second **premiss** of that rule in a manner similar to what we did earlier in the present chapter.

$$(appl) \quad \frac{\Gamma \vdash M : A \to B \qquad \Gamma \vdash N : A}{\Gamma \vdash MN : B}$$

$$(abst) \quad \frac{\Gamma, x : A \vdash M : B \qquad \Gamma \vdash A \to B : s}{\Gamma \vdash \lambda x : A.\, M \; : \; A \to B}$$

Note that both have a double role again, since $s \in \{*, \square\}$. Hence, the type $A \to B$, occurring in both (*appl*) and in (*abst*), may be a second level type such as $(\alpha \to \beta) \to \gamma$, when $s \equiv *$. But $A \to B$ can also be a third level type, or kind, such as $(* \to *) \to *$, when $s \equiv \square$.

We still have not explained exactly how to extend β-reduction and β-conversion to $\lambda\underline{\omega}$. This is a natural thing to do. We postpone the real definition until later, and refer to the beginning of Section 4.1 for examples to show how it works.

One of these examples was:

$$(\lambda \alpha : *.\, \alpha \to \alpha)\, \beta \quad \to_\beta \quad \beta \to \beta\,.$$

As a little exercise, let's calculate the types of the two expressions. We start with the left-hand side $(\lambda \alpha : *.\, \alpha \to \alpha)\, \beta$, and derive its type in flag format, again as a continuation of the previous flag derivation, but with an empty context to start with.

Both (*abst*) and (*appl*) are used in the derivation: see lines (14) and (16). In order to demonstrate graphically how these rules have been implemented, we also give the corresponding part of the tree-formatted derivation.

$\vdots$

$$\boxed{\beta : *}$$

(10) $\quad * : \square$ $\qquad\qquad$ (*weak*) on (1) and (1)

$$\boxed{\alpha : *}$$

(11) $\quad\quad \alpha : *$ $\qquad\qquad$ (*var*) on (10)

(12) $\quad\quad \alpha \to \alpha \; : \; *$ $\qquad$ (*form*) on (11) and (11)

(13) $\quad * \to * : \square$ $\qquad\qquad$ (*form*) on (10) and (10)

(14) $\quad \lambda\alpha : * . \; \alpha \to \alpha \; : \; * \to *$ $\quad$ (*abst*) on (12) and (13)

(15) $\quad \beta : *$ $\qquad\qquad$ (*var*) on (1)

(16) $\quad (\lambda\alpha : * . \; \alpha \to \alpha) \, \beta \; : \; *$ $\quad$ (*appl*) on (14) and (15)

$$\frac{\text{(12)} \; \beta : *, \; \alpha : * \vdash \alpha \to \alpha \; : \; * \qquad \text{(13)} \; \beta : * \vdash * \to * \; : \; \square}{\text{(14)} \; \beta : * \vdash \lambda\alpha : * . \; \alpha \to \alpha \; : \; * \to *} \; (abst)$$

$$\frac{\text{(14)} \; \beta : * \vdash \lambda\alpha : * . \; \alpha \to \alpha \; : \; * \to * \qquad \text{(15)} \; \beta : * \vdash \beta : *}{\text{(16)} \; \beta : * \vdash (\lambda\alpha : * . \; \alpha \to \alpha) \, \beta \; : \; *} \; (appl)$$

The derivation corresponding to the right-hand side, $\beta \to \beta$, is simple; we only need line (15) for this:

$\vdots$

(17) $\quad \beta \to \beta \; : \; *$ $\qquad\qquad$ (*form*) on (15) and (15)

Judgements (16) and (17) demonstrate that left-hand side and right-hand side of the example β-reduction have the same types, corresponding to the same contexts. This is as expected: cf. the Subject Reduction Lemma 2.11.5.

4.6 Shortened derivations

Derivations like the ones given in the previous sections, leading to a judgement in $\lambda\underline{\omega}$, have both interesting and uninteresting components. For example, the judgement

(8) $\quad \alpha : *, \; \beta : * \; \vdash \; \alpha \to \beta : *$

has been constructed from judgements (6) and (7) by means of the (*form*)-rule. These judgements, in turn, depend on (1), (2) and (5), as can be established by inspecting either the trees or the flag derivations.

We list these judgements below:

(1) $\emptyset \vdash * : \square$ (*sort*),
(2) $\alpha : * \vdash \alpha : *$ (*var*),
(5) $\alpha : * \vdash * : \square$ (*weak*),
(6) $\alpha : *, \beta : * \vdash \alpha : *$ (*weak*),
(7) $\alpha : *, \beta : * \vdash \beta : *$ (*var*).

No less than five judgements are needed to establish (8). However, all the judgements mentioned, including (8), look very obvious.

These kinds of not-so-interesting steps occur in particular in three cases:
(i) when using the rules (*sort*), (*var*) and (*weak*),
(ii) when using (*form*), and
(iii) when establishing the validity of the second **premiss** of the (*abst*)-rule.

Note that case *(i)* applies to all five judgements used in the derivation of (8). All these are 'obviously' *well-formed judgements*. Case *(ii)* applies to (8). Cases *(ii)* and *(iii)* are precisely the cases when we want to make sure that something is a *well-formed type*.

We like to focus our attention on the really interesting steps, as in Chapters 2 and 3 (see, for example, the *shortened* derivation in Section 2.5). Therefore we will allow *skipping all judgements which are obvious as such, or only intended to establish that something is a well-formed type*.

Remark 4.6.1 *This is of course a debatable decision, since we are no longer as precise as we actually should be. But humans tend to make errors when they lose their concentration, and this easily happens when one does uninteresting steps. Moreover, our system being completely formal enables us to leave the final check to a computer program, which has no problems in filling in the omitted judgements. Therefore, we feel it is permissible to skip 'uninteresting' steps in the rest of this book.*

A consequence is that the (*form*)-rule will be rarely appealed to from now on, and the use of (*sort*), (*var*) and (*weak*) will be minimal.

To demonstrate what we win when employing this convention, we give the shortened version of the flag derivation of (16), as given in the previous section:

(a) $\boxed{\beta : *}$

(b) $\boxed{\alpha : *}$

(12) $\alpha \to \alpha : *$ (*form*) on (b) and (b)

(14) $\lambda \alpha : * . \, \alpha \to \alpha : * \to *$ (*abst*) on (12)

(16) $(\lambda \alpha : * . \, \alpha \to \alpha)\beta : *$ (*appl*) on (14) and (a)

Comparing these two derivations, the following may be noticed:

- The second derivation is compact and directly understandable, in particular when read in the goal-directed (bottom-to-top) direction.
- We may immediately refer to what is in the *flags*: compare the two versions of (12), and of (16).
- The rule (*form*) has been skipped in the shortened version, but judgement (12) must remain since it is necessary for (14).
- We allow (*abst*) to be used with a reference to the first **premiss** only, neglecting the second one: see the new (14).

4.7 The conversion rule

In this section we come back to β-reduction and β-conversion in $\lambda\underline{\omega}$, and their consequences for typing. We recall the following $\lambda\underline{\omega}$ example of β-reduction, discussed in Sections 4.1 and 4.5:

$$(\lambda\alpha : * . \, \alpha \to \alpha)\,\beta \quad \to_\beta \quad \beta \to \beta \, .$$

We derived type $*$ for the left-hand side in the previous section, in context $\beta : *$ (see line (16)). By the (*var*)-rule then follows:

$$\beta : *, \; x \; : \; (\lambda\alpha : * . \, \alpha \to \alpha)\,\beta \;\; \vdash \;\; x \; : \; (\lambda\alpha : * . \, \alpha \to \alpha)\,\beta.$$

What we naturally want is that also:

$$\beta : *, \; x \; : \; (\lambda\alpha : * . \, \alpha \to \alpha)\,\beta \;\; \vdash \;\; x \; : \; \beta \to \beta,$$

since β-convertible types are intentionally 'the same' types.

However (and this may come as a surprise), the latter judgement cannot be derived, because our derivation system is too weak to draw that conclusion. The transition from the type $(\lambda\alpha : * . \, \alpha \to \alpha)\beta$ to the type $\beta \to \beta$ is a case of the more general β-conversion. Obviously, the following is what we want:

> If M has type B and $B =_\beta B'$, then M also has type B'
> (provided that both B and B' are well-formed types or kinds).

Since we cannot yet derive this in our system $\lambda\underline{\omega}$, we need an extra derivation rule. This rule, called the *conversion rule*, is expressed as follows:

Definition 4.7.1 (Conversion rule)

$$(conv) \; \frac{\Gamma \vdash A : B \quad \Gamma \vdash B' : s}{\Gamma \vdash A : B'} \quad \text{if } B =_\beta B'.$$

Note that, in the above rule, B is already well-formed since it appears as a type in the judgement $\Gamma \vdash A : B$. In order to guarantee that B' is well-formed as well, we add the second **premiss**: $\Gamma \vdash B' : s$. (So when $s \equiv *$, we have that B' is a well-formed *type*, and when $s \equiv \Box$, we have that B' is a well-formed *kind*.)

Remark 4.7.2   *One could wonder whether the second* **premiss** *in the conversion rule is really necessary: the first* **premiss** *implies that B is well-formed; isn't B′ then automatically well-formed, as well, since B =$_\beta$ B′?*

The answer is: no. It holds, for example, that $\beta \to \gamma$ =$_\beta$ $(\lambda \alpha : *.\ \beta \to \gamma)\, M$, for any term M. Now the left-hand side $\beta \to \gamma$ is a well-formed type, but the right-hand side $(\lambda \alpha : *.\ \beta \to \gamma)\, M$ may easily be 'wrong', e.g. when M has not the type $*$.

As an example, we picture the key part of the tree derivation corresponding to the judgements above. Let $\Gamma \equiv \beta : *,\ x\ :\ (\lambda \alpha : *.\ \alpha \to \alpha)\beta$.

$$\frac{(18)\ \ \Gamma \vdash\ x\ :\ (\lambda\alpha : *.\ \alpha \to \alpha)\beta \qquad (19)\ \ \Gamma \vdash\ \beta \to \beta\ :\ *}{(20)\ \ \Gamma \vdash\ x\ :\ \beta \to \beta}\ (conv)$$

Notwithstanding what has been said in Remark 4.7.2, we allow that the second **premiss** in the conversion rule is suppressed in a *shortened derivation*, as soon as it is immediately clear that the B' under consideration is a well-formed type. This is in line with our convention in the previous section.

As an example, we express the part of the tree given above as a flag-formatted, shortened derivation; hence, we omit the second **premiss** of $(conv)$, viz. line (19).

	$\vdots$	
	$\boxed{x\ :\ (\lambda\alpha : *.\ \alpha \to \alpha)\,\beta}$	
(18)	$x\ :\ (\lambda\alpha : *.\ \alpha \to \alpha)\,\beta$	(var) on (16)
(20)	$x\ :\ \beta \to \beta$	$(conv)$ on (18)

In order to make perfectly clear what the difference is between subject reduction and the conversion rule, we give the following scheme:

$$
\begin{array}{c|c|c}
\Gamma \ \vdash\ A\ :\ B & \Gamma \ \vdash\ A\ :\ B & \Gamma \ \vdash\ A\ :\ B \\
\quad\downarrow_\beta & \quad\downarrow_\beta & \quad =_\beta \\
A' & B' & B' \\
\hline
\Gamma \ \vdash\ A'\ :\ B & \Gamma \ \vdash\ A\ :\ B' & \Gamma \ \vdash\ A\ :\ B' \\
 & \text{if } \Gamma \vdash B' : s & \text{if } \Gamma \vdash B' : s \\
\\
\text{Subject Reduction} & \text{Type Reduction} & \text{Conversion} \\
\text{(a theorem)} & \text{(subcase of } (conv)) & \text{(the rule } (conv))
\end{array}
$$

Subject Reduction states that if we reduce the *subject* of a judgement, keeping the type as it is, we obtain a judgement that is derivable again. It can be proved in $\lambda\underline{\omega}$ without the Conversion rule.

Type Reduction states that if we reduce the *type* of a judgement, we obtain a derivable judgement again. But this is *not* provable in $\lambda\underline{\omega}$ without the Conversion rule. Note that Type Reduction is a special case of the Conversion rule.

For convenience, we end this section with a list of all $\lambda\underline{\omega}$-rules (see Figure 4.1).

$$(sort) \quad \emptyset \vdash * : \square$$

$$(var) \quad \frac{\Gamma \vdash A : s}{\Gamma,\, x : A \vdash x : A} \quad \text{if } x \notin \Gamma$$

$$(weak) \quad \frac{\Gamma \vdash A : B \quad \Gamma \vdash C : s}{\Gamma,\, x : C \vdash A : B} \quad \text{if } x \notin \Gamma$$

$$(form) \quad \frac{\Gamma \vdash A : s \quad \Gamma \vdash B : s}{\Gamma \vdash A \to B : s}$$

$$(appl) \quad \frac{\Gamma \vdash M : A \to B \quad \Gamma \vdash N : A}{\Gamma \vdash MN : B}$$

$$(abst) \quad \frac{\Gamma,\, x : A \vdash M : B \quad \Gamma \vdash A \to B : s}{\Gamma \vdash \lambda x : A.\, M \; : \; A \to B}$$

$$(conv) \quad \frac{\Gamma \vdash A : B \quad \Gamma \vdash B' : s}{\Gamma \vdash A : B'} \quad \text{if } B =_\beta B'$$

Figure 4.1 Derivation rules for $\lambda\underline{\omega}$

4.8 Properties of $\lambda\underline{\omega}$

The system $\lambda\underline{\omega}$ satisfies the majority of the nice properties of previous systems (see Sections 2.10, 2.11 and 3.6).

However, the conversion rule requires a slight modification of the Uniqueness of Types Lemma: types need no longer be literally unique, but they are unique *up to conversion*:

Lemma 4.8.1   *(Uniqueness of Types up to Conversion)*
If $\Gamma \vdash A : B_1$ *and* $\Gamma \vdash A : B_2$, *then* $B_1 =_\beta B_2$.

We do not give a proof of this lemma.

4.9 Conclusions

We have studied generalised types, which themselves also depend on types. Some of the constructs obtained are (proper) type *constructors*, i.e. functions that are not types, but that deliver types when applied to the right arguments. In extending our set of types, we also needed to extend our singleton set of super-types: $*$ alone is not enough, we obtain *kinds* built from $*$ and $\to$. We also extended the already obtained three levels by a fourth: that of the super-super-type $\square$. The system resulting from these extensions is $\lambda\underline{\omega}$.

As to the derivation rules for $\lambda\underline{\omega}$, we have a (*sort*)-rule stating that $*$ is of type $\square$. Moreover, we need a new (*var*)-rule for variables, and a weakening rule (*weak*) for contexts of judgements. In order to construct types *inside* the derivation system, we have introduced the formation rule (*form*).

The application rule (*appl*) and abstraction rule (*abst*) in $\lambda\underline{\omega}$ are more or less as expected. They are single, straightforward rules, which need not be doubled as in $\lambda 2$. One reason for this is that there are no Π-types in $\lambda\underline{\omega}$. Another reason is the important *double role* of most of the rules in $\lambda\underline{\omega}$, in particular of (*appl*) and (*abst*).

When making actual derivations in $\lambda\underline{\omega}$, it turns out that many steps are not very interesting. To cope with this, we have allowed *shortened* derivations, in which some of the necessary checks are deliberately left out. Although this is a debatable decision, it makes the derivations shorter and more manageable for humans.

Finally, we have added the conversion rule (*conv*), which allows us to replace a type by a ('well-formed') convertible type.

The system $\lambda\underline{\omega}$ satisfies many of the nice properties of previous systems ($\lambda\to$, $\lambda 2$). But, in order to deal with convertible types originating from the conversion rule, the Uniqueness of Types Lemma has to be adapted.

4.10 Further reading

J.-Y. Girard was the first one to study the phenomenon of 'types depending on types' in his PhD thesis (Girard, 1972), as an extension of his system F (see Section 3.8) to system Fω. His goal was to study the class of functions that one can prove to be total in higher order arithmetic. It turns out that this class coincides exactly with the functions that can be defined in Fω.

The 'types depending on types' feature is usually not studied in isolation, but combined with polymorphism as introduced in Chapter 3 (see Examples 3.1.1 (2)). The system $\lambda\underline{\omega}$ is basically only defined as a transition to Fω or the Calculus of Constructions (see Chapter 6).

In modern functional languages, e.g. in Haskell (Peyton Jones *et al.*, 1998), we see 'types depending on types' in the form of *type constructors*: if List_σ is the type of lists over the carrier type σ (so $l : \mathsf{List}_\sigma$ is a list consisting of terms of type σ), then one would like to abstract from the carrier. Then we view $\mathsf{List} : * \to *$ as a 'type constructor', taking a type σ to the type of lists over σ. The 'length' function then can be given the polymorphic type $\Pi\alpha : *.\ \mathsf{List}\,\alpha \to nat$, which is 'borrowed' from $\lambda 2$.

Exercises

4.1 Give a diagram of the tree corresponding to the complete tree derivation of line (16) of Section 4.5.

4.2 Give complete $\lambda\underline{\omega}$-derivations, first in tree format and then in flag format (not shortened), of the following judgements:

   (a) $\emptyset \vdash (* \to *) \to * : \square$,

   (b) $\alpha : *,\ \beta : * \vdash (\alpha \to \beta) \to \alpha : *$.

4.3 (a) Give a complete (i.e. not shortened) $\lambda\underline{\omega}$-derivation in flag format of
     $\alpha, \beta : *,\ x : \alpha,\ y : \alpha \to \beta \vdash y\,x : \beta$.

   (b) Give a shortened $\lambda\underline{\omega}$-derivation in flag format of
     $\alpha, \beta : *,\ x : \alpha,\ y : \alpha \to \beta,\ z : \beta \to \alpha \vdash z(y\,x) : \alpha$.

4.4 Give shortened $\lambda\underline{\omega}$-derivations in flag format of the following judgements:

   (a) $\alpha : *,\ \beta : * \to * \vdash \beta(\beta\,\alpha) : *$,

   (b) $\alpha : *,\ \beta : * \to *,\ x : \beta(\beta\,\alpha) \vdash \lambda y : \alpha.\,x\ :\ \alpha \to \beta(\beta\,\alpha)$,

   (c) $\emptyset \vdash \lambda\alpha : *.\,\lambda\beta : * \to *.\,\beta(\beta\,\alpha)\ :\ * \to (* \to *) \to *$,

   (d) $\emptyset \vdash (\lambda\alpha : *.\,\lambda\beta : * \to *.\,\beta(\beta\,\alpha))\,nat\,(\lambda\gamma : *.\,\gamma)\ :\ *$, assuming that nat is a constant of type $*$.

4.5 Give a shortened $\lambda\underline{\omega}$-derivation in flag format of the following judgement:
     $\alpha : *,\ x : \alpha \vdash \lambda y : \alpha.\,x\ :\ (\lambda\beta : *.\,\beta \to \beta)\alpha$.

4.6 (a) Prove that there are no Γ and N in $\lambda\underline{\omega}$ such that $\Gamma \vdash \square : N$ is derivable.

   (b) Prove that there are no Γ, M and N in $\lambda\underline{\omega}$ such that $\Gamma \vdash M \to \square : N$ is derivable.

4.7 (a) Give $\lambda\underline{\omega}$-definitions of the notions legal term, statement, $\lambda\underline{\omega}$-context and domain.

   (b) Formulate the following theorems for $\lambda\underline{\omega}$: Free Variables Lemma, Thinning Lemma, Substitution Lemma.

5

Types dependent on terms

5.1 The missing extension

In the previous three chapters, we have met the following dependencies:

- Chapter 2: *terms depending on terms*, in the *basic system* $\lambda{\to}$.
- Chapter 3: terms depending on terms + *terms depending on types*, in the system $\lambda2$, extending $\lambda{\to}$.
- Chapter 4: terms depending on terms + *types depending on types*, in the system $\lambda\underline{\omega}$, also extending $\lambda{\to}$.

Clearly, there is one extension missing, and that's the one we deal with now:

- Chapter 5: terms depending on terms + **types depending on terms**. This gives us the system λP, another extension of $\lambda{\to}$.

A type depending on a term has the general format:

$$\lambda x : A . M ,$$

where M is a type, and x a term-variable (then A must be a type). The abstraction $\lambda x : A . M$ then *depends on* the term x.

In correspondence with Remark 4.1.2, we note that 'a *type* depending on a term', such as $\lambda x : A . M$, is actually a *type-valued function* or type *constructor*.

We start with motivating examples, showing some of the useful features of the novel extension, particularly when using type theory for logic and mathematics.

In order to get an idea of the usefulness of types-depending-on-terms, we specialise the type M in the general expression $\lambda x : A . M$ to either sets or propositions:

(1) Let S_n be a *set* for each $n : nat$. Informally speaking, each of those sets can be considered as a *type*. Then $\lambda n : nat . S_n$ is also a type (to be precise: a type *constructor*), depending on the term n. One can also say: $\lambda n : nat . S_n$ is the function mapping term n to the set S_n, a so-called *set-valued function*.

Other terminology that is used for $\lambda n : nat. \, S_n$ is that it is a *family of types* (one type for every $n : nat$) or an *indexed type* (indexed by $n : nat$).

For example, let $S_n = \{0, n, 2n, 3n, \ldots\}$, the set of all non-negative multiples of n. Then $\lambda n : nat. \, S_n$ maps:

– natural number 0 to the set $\{0\}$,
– natural number 1 to the set *nat* (the set of all natural numbers),
– natural number 2 to the set $\{0, 2, 4, 6, \ldots\}$ (the set of the even naturals), etcetera.

What is the *type* of $\lambda n : nat. \, S_n$? Since $n : nat$ and $S_n : *$, this type clearly should be $nat \to *$.

A more common example is the following, presupposing that we have the notion 'finite sequence of naturals' at our disposal: assume that $\langle v_1, \ldots, v_n \rangle$ represents a sequence of n natural numbers.

Now let $V_n = \{\langle v_1, \ldots, v_n \rangle \mid v_i \in \mathbb{N}\}$, the set of all natural number sequences ('*vectors*') of length n. Then $\lambda n : nat. \, V_n$ maps n to the set of all vectors of length n.

The type of $\lambda n : nat. \, V_n$ is again $nat \to *$.

(2) Now take P_n to be a *proposition* for each $n : nat$. Let's consider propositions as *types*, again. Then $\lambda n : nat. \, P_n$ is also a type (to be precise: a type *constructor*), depending on the term n. One can also say: $\lambda n : nat. \, P_n$ is the function mapping term n to the proposition P_n, so it is a *proposition-valued function*.

Such a function represents what in logic is called a *predicate*. For example, take P_n to be the proposition 'n is a prime number'. Then $\lambda n : nat. \, P_n$ is the logical predicate 'to be a prime number' (for naturals).

The logical predicate $\lambda n : nat. \, P_n$, applied to a given n, may hold (be true for that n) or not (be false for that n).

With P_n as above, the predicate $\lambda n : nat. \, P_n$ maps for example:

– natural number 3 to the proposition '3 is a prime number' (which is true),
– natural number 4 to the proposition '4 is a prime number' (which is false).

Again, the type of $\lambda n : nat. \, P_n$ is $nat \to *$.

In mathematics there are many set-valued functions, and both in logic and mathematics the notion 'predicate' is of paramount importance. So the extension of $\lambda \to$ with types-depending-on-terms has useful applications.

Remark 5.1.1 *In part (2) above, we consider propositions as* types. *This is the so-called PAT-interpretation, which we have already mentioned in Section 2.9. It is the first step to a very fruitful treatment of proofs in formal logic* *and mathematics. See the forthcoming Section 5.4 for examples that provide a convincing introduction to this powerful and fundamental pillar of type theory.*

As we have mentioned before, the system obtained from $\lambda\!\to$ by extending it with types-dependent-on-terms, is called λP. It will not come as a surprise now, that the letter 'P' in λP comes from *predicate*.

By applying the above-mentioned type constructors to a term we obtain:

− $(\lambda n : nat . S_n)\, 3$,
− $(\lambda n : nat . P_n)\, 3$.

Both expressions represent types, depending on a term (viz. 3). In the first case, β-reduction gives S_3 (which is the set of all non-negative multiples of 3); in the second case we obtain P_3 (the proposition '3 is a prime number').

5.2 Derivation rules of λP

The derivation rules of λP have a great resemblance to the rules of $\lambda\underline{\omega}$ (see Figure 4.1 on page 99). The rules (*sort*), (*var*) and (*weak*) in λP are even identical to the ones in $\lambda\underline{\omega}$. The same holds for (*conv*), the Conversion rule.

In Figure 5.1 we give a list of all λP-rules.

$(sort)\quad \emptyset \vdash * : \square$

$(var)\quad \dfrac{\Gamma \vdash A : s}{\Gamma,\, x : A \vdash x : A}\quad \text{if } x \notin \Gamma$

$(weak)\quad \dfrac{\Gamma \vdash A : B \quad \Gamma \vdash C : s}{\Gamma,\, x : C \vdash A : B}\quad \text{if } x \notin \Gamma$

$(form)\quad \dfrac{\Gamma \vdash A : * \quad \Gamma,\, x : A \vdash B : s}{\Gamma \vdash \Pi x : A .\, B \ : \ s}$

$(appl)\quad \dfrac{\Gamma \vdash M \ : \ \Pi x : A .\, B \quad \Gamma \vdash N : A}{\Gamma \vdash MN \ : \ B[x := N]}$

$(abst)\quad \dfrac{\Gamma,\, x : A \vdash M : B \quad \Gamma \vdash \Pi x : A .\, B \ : \ s}{\Gamma \vdash \lambda x : A .\, M \ : \ \Pi x : A .\, B}$

$(conv)\quad \dfrac{\Gamma \vdash A : B \quad \Gamma \vdash B' : s}{\Gamma \vdash A : B'}\quad \text{if } B =_\beta B'$

Figure 5.1 Derivation rules for λP

The main differences with respect to $\lambda\underline{\omega}$ are:

(*i*) *An upgrading of the $\rightarrow$-types.* The main novelty is the reappearance of Π-types. In the rules (*form*), (*appl*) and (*abst*) of λP, we do not find $\rightarrow$-types $A \rightarrow B$, but Π-types $\Pi x : A . B$ instead. Of course, this is more than a simple change in notation: it is a real generalisation, since variable x may occur as a free variable in B. As a consequence, we no longer have the simple situation of a function type, consisting of all functions from input type A to a *fixed* output type B. Instead, we have a *dependent product* in which the output type *depends on* the value x chosen in the input type A.

(*ii*) *A downgrading of the input types.* In λP, we have types dependent on terms, but *no* types dependent on types, such as $\Pi\alpha : * . \alpha \rightarrow \alpha$ in $\lambda\underline{\omega}$. Hence, a type $\Pi x : A . B$ in λP has the property that x is a *term*, so A can only have type $*$, not $\square$. See the (*form*)-rules of λP and $\lambda\underline{\omega}$.

Apart from the mentioned differences between $\lambda\underline{\omega}$ and λP, we note the following consequences of the fact that B in $\Pi x : A . B$ may depend on x:

As to (form): We have to *extend* the context of the second **premiss**, by changing Γ into $\Gamma, x : A$.

As to (appl): We have to choose the 'proper' output type $B[x := N]$, corresponding to the input value N taken for x.

Note again the double role of many of the rules, so that they are useable at different levels.

For example, for the (*form*)-rule we have the following possibilities:

(1) $s = *$. Then $A : *$, $B : *$ and $\Pi x : A . B : *$,
(2) $s = \square$. Then $A : *$, $B : \square$ and $\Pi x : A . B : \square$.

Consider the following concrete examples of the above Π-types:

(1) $\Pi n : nat . nat : *$,
(2) $\Pi n : nat . * : \square$.

We have already met inhabitants of these Π-types:

(1) $\lambda n : nat . f(fn) : \Pi n : nat . nat$ (cf. Examples 3.1.1 (2)),
(2a) $\lambda n : nat . S_n : \Pi n : nat . *$ (Section 5.1 (1)),
(2b) $\lambda n : nat . P_n : \Pi n : nat . *$ (Section 5.1 (2)).

Notation 5.2.1 *In λP, we write $A \rightarrow B$ for Π-type $\Pi x : A . B$ if we are sure that x does not occur free in B. However, 'officially' we have only Π-types in λP, and no $\rightarrow$-types.*

System λP has the same nice properties as $\lambda 2$ and $\lambda\underline{\omega}$, albeit in a slightly different format because our terms and types are a bit different. We do not give a list of these properties now, but postpone this to the following chapter, where all relevant properties are given and described in a general format.

Remark 5.2.2 *The Formation rule, (form), is also called the Product rule, since it enables the construction and typing of a Π-type (see Section 3.2).*

Martin-Löf (1980) calls a Π-type the Cartesian product of a family of types. If one considers A to be a finite type, say with two elements a_1 and a_2, then $\Pi x : A \,.\, B$ is indeed the same as $B[x := a_1] \times B[x := a_2]$, the Cartesian product. So, Π-types can both be seen as a generalisation of the Cartesian product and as a generalisation of the function space (if $x \notin FV(B)$, then $\Pi x : A \,.\, B$ is just $A \to B$).

5.3 An example derivation in λP

We give an example of a derivation in λP, starting from scratch. We use the flag format and leave it as an exercise to the reader to verify that the λP-rules are properly used.

We first derive the following simple judgements in λP:

(1) $* : \square$ (*sort*)

        $\boxed{A : *}$

(2) $A : *$ (*var*) on (1)

(3) $* : \square$ (*weak*) on (1) and (1)

          $\boxed{x : A}$

(4) $* : \square$ (*weak*) on (3) and (2)

(5) $A \to * : \square$ (*form*) on (2) and (4)

All of these are also derivable in λ$\underline{\omega}$, as shown in the previous chapter, *except* the last one. In line (5) we derive the super-type $A \to *$, i.e. $\Pi x : A \,.\, *$. Here we have types of *different level* left and right of the $\to$. This was not possible in λ$\underline{\omega}$. Note that $A \to *$ is a *kind depending on a term*, and a $P : A \to *$ is a *type depending on a term*, although this is not immediately visible: the term they depend on is the x in the unabbreviated form of $A \to *$, viz. $\Pi x : A \,.\, *$.

The new type $A \to *$ may have inhabitants. For example, we may *assume* that P is an inhabitant and continue the derivation with this assumption:

       $\vdots$

        $\boxed{P : A \to *}$

(6) $P : A \to *$ (*var*) on (5)

(7) $A : *$ (*weak*) on (2) and (5)

(8) $* : \square$ (*weak*) on (3) and (5)

Adding a variable x of type A, again, gives more possibilities; for example, we can *apply* P to x to obtain the type $P\,x$:

$$\vdots$$

$\boxed{x : A}$

(9) $x : A$ (*var*) on (7)
(10) $P : A \to *$ (*weak*) on (6) and (7)
(11) $P\,x : *$ (*appl*) on (10) and (9)

Line (11) enables us to construct a 'real' dependent type, $\Pi x : A \,.\, P\,x$, with variable x occurring in 'body' $P\,x$:

$$\vdots$$

(12) $\Pi x : A \,.\, P\,x \;:\; *$ (*form*) on (7) and (11)

After raising a new flag $x : A$ (with a 'new' variable, called x again by abuse of notation), we can derive other consequences of line (11): first, we show that also the type $P\,x \to P\,x$ is derivable, and next we construct another Π-type, viz. $\Pi x : A \,.\, P\,x \to P\,x$. It is mere technique to show the validity of these judgements and we leave it to the reader to see what's happening:

$$\vdots$$

$\boxed{x : A}$

$\boxed{y : P\,x}$

(13) $P\,x : *$ (*weak*) on (11) and (11)
(14) $P\,x \to P\,x : *$ (*form*) on (11) and (13)
(15) $\Pi x : A \,.\, P\,x \to P\,x \;:\; *$ (*form*) on (7) and (14)

Finally, we show that this $\Pi x : A \,.\, P\,x \to P\,x$ is *inhabited*, i.e. there is a term of this type. This requires new flags $x : A$ and $y : P\,x$, and the use of the (*abst*)-rule, twice:

$$\vdots$$

$\boxed{x : A}$

$\boxed{y : P\,x}$

(16) $y : P\,x$ (*var*) on (11)
(17) $\lambda y : P\,x \,.\, y \;:\; P\,x \to P\,x$ (*abst*) on (16) and (14)
(18) $\lambda x : A \,.\, \lambda y : P\,x \,.\, y \;:\; \Pi x : A \,.\, P\,x \to P\,x$ (*abst*) on (17) and (15)

Remark 5.3.1   *Also in λP, many rules have a double role, since the s may be either $*$ or $\square$. Check yourself that $s \equiv \square$ has been used in lines (2), (3), and (5) to (8) of the above derivation, whereas $s \equiv *$ holds for the justifications of lines (4), (9), (10), and (12) to (18).*

So altogether, we have obtained a derivation which can be seen as a solution to several questions (cf. Section 2.6), all condensed in line (18):

(Q1)   *Well-typedness:* find out whether $\lambda x : A . \lambda y : P x . y$ is well-typed.

(Q2)   *Type Checking:* check that
$$A : *, \; P \; : \; A \to * \vdash \; \lambda x : A . \lambda y : P x . y \; : \; \Pi x : A . P x \to P x.$$

(Q3)   *Term Finding:* find a term of type $\Pi x : A . P x \to P x$ in the context $A : *, \; P \; : \; A \to *$.

We solved these questions 'linearly', starting from $\emptyset \vdash * : \square$ and building our derivation step by step. Almost accidentally this culminated in judgement (18). If one of the three questions above had been our starting point, then a linear ('forward') build-up of the derivation is not the best approach: see Remark 2.9.2.

As we did with $\lambda \underline{\omega}$-derivations (see Section 4.6), we may restrict ourselves to *shortened* derivations in λP by omitting the majority of lines based on (*sort*), (*var*), (*weak*) and (*form*), and by suppressing references to the second **premiss** of the (*abst*)-rule.

When we apply this convention to the derivation above, we obtain the following, considerably shorter derivation:

(a)	$\boxed{A : *}$	
(b)	$\boxed{P \; : \; A \to *}$	
(c)	$\boxed{x : A}$	
(11)	$P x : *$	(*appl*) on (b) and (c)
(e)	$\boxed{y : P x}$	
(16)	$y : P x$	(*var*) on (11)
(17)	$\lambda y : P x . y \; : \; P x \to P x$	(*abst*) on (16)
(18)	$\lambda x : A . \lambda y : P x . y \; :$	
	$\Pi x : A . P x \to P x$	(*abst*) on (17)

5.4 Minimal predicate logic in λP

In λP it is possible to code a very simple form of logic, called *minimal predicate logic*, which only has *implication* and *universal quantification* as logical operations. The basic entities of this predicate logic are *propositions*, *sets* and *predicates over sets*.

We already mentioned in Section 2.9 that the propositions-as-types interpretation of logic (cf. Remark 5.1.1) also implies another nice and useful interpretation: proofs-as-terms. Both notions are abbreviated by PAT and one speaks about the PAT-interpretation of logic, covering both aspects.

We summarise the meaning of PAT as follows:

− If a term b inhabits type B (i.e. $b : B$), where B is interpreted as a proposition, then we interpret b as a *proof* of B. Such a term b in type theory is called a *proof object*.
− On the other hand, when *no* inhabitant of the proposition B exists (there is no b with $b : B$), then there exists no proof of B, so B must be *false*.

Of course, the existence of an inhabitant of type B should be checked in a type system such as λP, so one has to deliver a context Γ and a term b such that $\Gamma \vdash b : B$.

So the PAT-interpretation implies:

> Proposition B is inhabited *iff* B is true;
> proposition B is not inhabited *iff* B is false.

We now investigate the coding of the basic entities of minimal predicate logic and apply the full PAT-interpretation in the appropriate cases.

I. Sets

We code a set S as a type, so $S : *$. *Elements* of sets are terms. So if a is an element of set S, then $a : S$. (Of course, if S is the empty set, then there should be no derivable term a with $a : S$.)

Examples: $nat : *$, $nat \rightarrow nat : *$; $3 : nat$, $\lambda n : nat \, . \, n \, : \, nat \rightarrow nat$.

II. Propositions

We also code propositions as types. So if A is a proposition, then $A : *$. According to the PAT-interpretation, a term p inhabiting such A codes a *proof* of A. So if A is a true proposition, p being a proof of A, then $p : A$. (If there is no proof of A, i.e. if A is false, then there is no such p inhabiting A.)

III. Predicates

As we saw in Section 5.1, a predicate P is a function from a *set S* to *the set of all propositions*. So $P : S \rightarrow *$.

We investigate this situation a bit further. If P is an arbitrary predicate on S, i.e. $P : S \rightarrow *$, then for each $a : S$ we have that $P\,a : *$. All these $P\,a$

are propositions, which are types (level 2), so each $P\,a$ may be inhabited. To be precise:

(1) If $P\,a$ is inhabited, so $t : P\,a$ for some t, then the predicate *holds* for a.
(2) If $P\,b$ is *not* inhabited, then the predicate does *not hold* for b.

Let's now have a closer look at the *logical operations* of minimal predicate logic, viz. implication and universal quantification:

IV. Implication

In Section 2.4 (Example 2.4.9) we identified the logical implication $A \Rightarrow B$ with the type $A \to B$. Using the PAT-interpretation, we can easily justify this coding of $\Rightarrow$ as $\to$, by considering the following string of equivalences:

$A \Rightarrow B$ is true;
if A is true, then also B is true;
if A is inhabited, then also B is inhabited;
there is a *function* mapping inhabitants of A to inhabitants of B;
there is an f with $f : A \to B$;
$A \to B$ is inhabited.

So the truth of $A \Rightarrow B$ is equivalent to the inhabitation of $A \to B$. And since in PAT, 'truth' is the interpretation of being inhabited, the following is intuitively permitted:

We code the implication $A \Rightarrow B$ *in type theory as the function type* $A \to B$.

Remark 5.4.1 *The propositions A and B are 'independent', hence we may write $A \to B$ in case of an implication, instead of $\Pi x : A \,.\, B$, because x cannot occur free in B.*

A remarkable thing is now that we get the elimination rule and introduction rule of the implication for free. We discussed this already for $\lambda{\to}$ in Example 2.4.9: there are narrow correspondences between the $\Rightarrow$-elimination rule from natural deduction and the (*appl*)-rule, and between the $\Rightarrow$-introduction rule and the (*abst*)-rule.

This is still the case for implications in λP. Writing $A \to B$ for $\Pi x : A \,.\, B$, we obtain the following version of the (*appl*)-rule (familiar from $\lambda\underline{\omega}$):

$$(appl) \ \frac{\Gamma \vdash M \ : \ A \to B \quad \Gamma \vdash N : A}{\Gamma \vdash MN \ : \ B}$$

Similarly, we obtain the following version of the (*abst*)-rule:

$$(abst) \ \frac{\Gamma, \ x : A \vdash M : B \quad \Gamma \vdash A \to B \ : \ s}{\Gamma \vdash \lambda x : A \,.\, M \ : \ A \to B}$$

We invite the reader to compare these rules with the ($\Rightarrow$-*elim*)-rule and the ($\Rightarrow$-*intro*)-rule given in Example 2.4.9.

V. *Universal quantification*

Now consider the universal quantification $\forall_{x \in S}(P(x))$ of some predicate P depending on x, over a set S. What is $\forall_{x \in S}(P(x))$ under the PAT-interpretation?

Again, we can make a string of equivalences:

$\forall_{x \in S}(P(x))$ is true;
for each x in the set S, the proposition $P(x)$ is true;
for each x in S, the type $P\,x$ is inhabited;
there is a *function* mapping each x in S to an inhabitant of $P\,x$
(such a function has type $\Pi x : S\,.\,P\,x$);
there is an f with $f\ :\ \Pi x : S\,.\,P\,x$;
$\Pi x : S\,.\,P\,x$ is inhabited.

So, similarly to the case of implication, we have found a way to code universal quantification in type theory: *we code the universal quantification $\forall_{x \in S}(P(x))$ as the Π-type $\Pi x : S\,.\,P\,x$.*

Remarks 5.4.2 *(1) The 'logico-mathematical' proposition $P(x)$, i.e. predicate P for value x, has been coded as the type-theoretic term $P\,x$.*

(2) $\Pi x : S\,.\,P\,x$ is a type (constructor) depending on a term, x, which actually occurs in the body $P\,x$.

Just as in the case of implication, the elimination and introduction rules for $\forall$ turn out to be a special case of the (*appl*)- and (*abst*)-rules of λP.

Va. *($\forall$-elim) versus (appl)*

First we recapitulate the ($\forall$-*elim*)-rule:

$$(\forall\text{-}elim) \ \frac{\forall_{x \in S}(P(x)) \qquad N \in S}{P(N)}$$

The content of this rule is: 'If we know that for all x in set S, proposition P holds for x, then we may conclude that P holds for N, for given N in S.'

Next, we repeat (*appl*):

$$(appl) \ \frac{\Gamma \vdash M\ :\ \Pi x : A\,.\,B \qquad \Gamma \vdash N : A}{\Gamma \vdash MN\ :\ B[x := N]}$$

The correspondences are clear, when we consider the following:
(1) The $\forall$ in ($\forall$-*elim*) is coded as Π in (*appl*).
(2) The S corresponds to A.

(3) The $P(x)$ in ($\forall$-*elim*) is B in (*appl*), hence $P(N)$ becomes $B[x := N]$.

(4) In (*appl*), every judgement has a context. In ($\forall$-*elim*) the context is traditionally left implicit.

(5) In (*appl*) there are proof objects added for the proposition $\Pi x : A . B$ (viz. M) and for the proposition $B[x := N]$ (viz. MN). This is *possible* by the PAT-interpretation, and *necessary* because we need 'full' judgements in λP.

The corresponding reading of (*appl*) in the $\Pi{=}\forall$-case is: 'If we know that (in a certain context) M is a proof of $\forall x : A . B$, and if (in the same context) N is of type A, then MN is (in that context) a proof of $B[x := N]$.'

This matches the earlier given reading of ($\forall$-*elim*).

Vb. (∀-*intro*) *versus* (*abst*)

The correspondence between ($\forall$-*intro*) and (*abst*) is similar, as we show below. First, we give the ($\forall$-*intro*)-rule in flag style:

$$
(\forall\text{-}intro) \quad \frac{\begin{array}{|l}\hline \text{Let } x \in S \\ \hline \vdots \\ P(x) \end{array}}{\forall_{x \in S}(P(x))}
$$

The rule says the following: 'If we can show, for arbitrary $x \in S$, that predicate P holds for x, then we may conclude that P holds for *all* $x \in S$.' The 'arbitrariness' of x is expressed by putting x in a flag.

The type-theoretic counterpart of this rule is (*abst*), which we repeat below:

$$
(abst) \quad \frac{\Gamma, x : A \vdash M : B \qquad \Gamma \vdash \Pi x : A . B : s}{\Gamma \vdash \lambda x : A . M : \Pi x : A . B}
$$

The correspondences (and differences) are obvious:

(1) The second **premiss** in (*abst*) does not occur in ($\forall$-*intro*), so we should dismiss it in our comparison. This second **premiss** only serves to ensure that $\Pi x : A . B$ is well-formed, whereas in ($\forall$-*intro*) it was taken for granted that $\forall_{x \in A}(P(x))$ is an 'acceptable' expression.

(2) Again, $\forall$ is coded as Π.

(3) In ($\forall$-*intro*), the context Γ is implicit. Only the context *extension* with $x : S$ (in the flag) is given explicitly.

(4) Again, the S has been changed into A, and the $P(x)$ has become a B.

(5) Finally, proof objects have been added in (*abst*) with respect to ($\forall$-*intro*), namely: M as a proof of B, and $\lambda x : A . M$ as a proof of $\Pi x : A . B$.

Remark 5.4.3 *In retrospect, we now have some interesting interpretations for judgements in Section 5.3. Let* $\Gamma \equiv A : *,\ P\ :\ A \to *.$

(12) $\Gamma \vdash \Pi x : A \,.\, P\, x\ :\ *$ *, can be read as:*
'*If* A *is a set and* P *a predicate over* A, *then* $\forall_{x \in A}(P(x))$ *is a proposition.*'

(15) $\Gamma \vdash \Pi x : A \,.\, P\, x \to P\, x\ :\ *$ *, expresses:*
'*In the same setting,* $\forall_{x \in A}(P(x) \Rightarrow P(x))$ *is a proposition.*'

(18) $\Gamma \vdash \lambda x : A \,.\, \lambda y : P\, x \,.\, y\ :\ \Pi x : A \,.\, P\, x \to P\, x$ *, says:*
'*And moreover, there is an inhabitant* $\lambda x : A \,.\, \lambda y : P\, x \,.\, y$ *of the proposition* $\forall_{x \in A}(P(x) \Rightarrow P(x)).$' *Hence, by the PAT-interpretation,* $\forall_{x \in A}(P(x) \Rightarrow P(x))$ *is a logical* tautology, *and* $\lambda x : A \,.\, \lambda y : P\, x \,.\, y$ *a coded version of its proof.*

Note that $\forall_{x \in A}(P(x))$ *is not a tautology, and indeed, no inhabitant can be found for* $\Pi x : A \,.\, P\, x.$

So we now have a coding of minimal predicate logic by means of the derivation rules of λP.

In Figure 5.2 we summarise what we have found. Note that we have neither negation in minimal predicate logic (or λP), nor do we have conjunction, disjunction or the existential quantifier. These things are not available in λP: we need more, as we explain in the following chapter, where we *combine* several systems. (In Chapter 7 we come back to the coding of logic in type theory. General remarks about natural deduction can be found in Section 11.4.)

Minimal predicate logic	The type theory of λP
S is a set A is a proposition	$S : *$ $A : *$
$a \in S$ p proves A	$a : S$ $p : A$
P is a predicate on S	$P : S \to *$
$A \Rightarrow B$ $\forall_{x \in S}(P(x))$	$A \to B\ (= \Pi x : A \,.\, B)$ $\Pi x : S \,.\, P\, x$
$(\Rightarrow\text{-}elim)$ $(\Rightarrow\text{-}intro)$	$(appl)$ $(abst)$
$(\forall\text{-}elim)$ $(\forall\text{-}intro)$	$(appl)$ $(abst)$

Figure 5.2 Coding minimal predicate logic in λP

5.5 Example of a logical derivation in λP

In Section 5.3, when practising with the derivation rules of λP, we finally obtained a judgement allowing a logical interpretation: line (18) can be seen as a proof of the proposition $\forall_{x \in A}(P(x) \Rightarrow P(x))$, as we mentioned in Remark 5.4.3.

In the present section, we demonstrate how such a result can be obtained in a systematic manner, starting from the proposition-to-prove. We give an example in minimal predicate logic, coded in λP.

Let S be a set and Q a binary predicate over S. Then the following proposition is provable in minimal predicate logic:

$$\forall_{x \in S} \forall_{y \in S}(Q(x, y)) \ \Rightarrow \ \forall_{u \in S}(Q(u, u)) \, .$$

We first give its natural deduction proof, which is straightforward:

(a)	Assume : $\forall_{x \in S} \forall_{y \in S}(Q(x, y))$	
(b)	Let $u \in S$	
(1)	$\forall_{y \in S}(Q(u, y))$	($\forall$-*elim*) on (a) and (b)
(2)	$Q(u, u)$	($\forall$-*elim*) on (1) and (b)
(3)	$\forall_{u \in S}(Q(u, u))$	($\forall$-*intro*) on (2)
(4)	$\forall_{x \in S} \forall_{y \in S}(Q(x, y)) \ \Rightarrow \ \forall_{u \in S}(Q(u, u))$	($\Rightarrow$-*intro*) on (3)

Remark 5.5.1   *Line number* (1) *is a result of the (*$\forall$*-elim)-rule:*
- *Flag (a) matches the first* **premiss** $\forall_{x \in S}(P(x))$ *in the (*$\forall$*-elim)-rule, if we take* P *such that* $P(x) \equiv \forall_{y \in S} Q(x, y)$.
- *For the second* **premiss** $N \in S$, *we take flag (b), i.e.* $u \in S$.
- *Then the* **conclusion** $P(N)$ *of the (*$\forall$*-elim)-rule becomes* $P(u)$, *which is in the present case:* $\forall_{y \in S}(Q(u, y))$. *(Note the* u *in the place of the* x.)

Now we code the expression and its proof in λP.

First, we have to decide how to code the *binary* predicate Q over $S \times S$. At first sight, this is an inhabitant of the type $(S \times S) \to *$, so we have to find a coding for the Cartesian product $S \times S$.

However, we may also get round this by using Currying (see Remark 1.2.6): we consider Q to be a *composite unary* predicate of type $S \to S \to *$, which is $S \to (S \to *)$. Hence, instead of 'feeding' Q immediately with a *pair* (a, b), denoted $Q(a, b)$, we give it a first and b afterwards. This leads to $Q\, a\, b$, which is $(Q\, a)b$, hence Q applied to a where the *result* has been applied to b. Our coding of the original proposition from minimal predicate logic now becomes:

$$\Pi x : S \, . \, \Pi y : S \, . \, Q\, x\, y \ \to \ \Pi u : S \, . \, Q\, u\, u \, .$$

We have to find an inhabitant of this, so our task is:

(n)   ? : $\Pi x : S . \Pi y : S . Q\, x\, y \ \rightarrow\ \Pi u : S . Q\, u\, u .$

In the above expression, both S and Q are untyped (or free) variables. Since this is undesirable in a derivation system, we add a context of two flags:

(a) $S : *$

(b) $Q : S \rightarrow S \rightarrow *$

   $\vdots$

(n)   ? : $\Pi x : S . \Pi y : S . Q\, x\, y \ \rightarrow\ \Pi u : S . Q\, u\, u$

The type in (n) is an $\rightarrow$-type, which reflects that the original logical proposition is an implication. So it is natural to try the λP-variant of the ($\Rightarrow$-*intro*)-rule. In part IV of Section 5.4 we formulated a simplified (*abst*)-rule for this purpose. We can use this simplified (*abst*)-rule bottom-up; thereby we forget about the second **premiss** (we make *shortened* derivations, as described in Section 4.5):

(a) $S : *$

(b) $Q : S \rightarrow S \rightarrow *$

(c) $z : (\Pi x : S . \Pi y : S . Q\, x\, y)$

   $\vdots$

(m)   ? : $\Pi u : S . Q\, u\, u$

(n)   ... : $\Pi x : S . \Pi y : S . Q\, x\, y \ \rightarrow\ \Pi u : S . Q\, u\, u$ (*abst*)

Line (m) asks for (*abst*), again. Note that this time we cannot appeal to the $\rightarrow$-version of the (*abst*)-rule, described in Section 5.4, IV, since we have a 'real' Π-type. This is also visible in the natural deduction proof, where we use ($\forall$-*intro*), and not ($\Rightarrow$-*intro*), in the corresponding step. We obtain:

(a) $S : *$

(b) $Q : S \rightarrow S \rightarrow *$

(c) $z : (\Pi x : S . \Pi y : S . Q\, x\, y)$

(d) $u : S$

   $\vdots$

(l)   ? : $Q\, u\, u$

(m)   ... : $\Pi u : S . Q\, u\, u$ (*abst*)

(n)   ... : $\Pi x : S . \Pi y : S . Q\, x\, y \ \rightarrow\ \Pi u : S . Q\, u\, u$ (*abst*)

The rest is not hard. Combining lines (c) and (d) with the ($appl$)-rule, twice, gives exactly the desired result, since:

$z\,u\ :\ \Pi y : S\,.\,Q\,u\,y$ (note the u instead of the x), hence

$z\,u\,u\ :\ Q\,u\,u$.

So finally, we can fill in everything that is left open; as usual, we include the arguments:

(a) $\boxed{S : *}$

(b) $\boxed{Q\ :\ S \to S \to *}$

(c) $\boxed{z\ :\ (\Pi x : S\,.\,\Pi y : S\,.\,Q\,x\,y)}$

(d) $\boxed{u : S}$

(1) $z\,u\ :\ \Pi y : S\,.\,Q\,u\,y$ ($appl$) on (c), (d)

(2) $z\,u\,u\ :\ Q\,u\,u$ ($appl$) on (1), (d)

(3) $\lambda u : S\,.\,z\,u\,u\ :\ \Pi u : S\,.\,Q\,u\,u$ ($abst$) on (2)

(4) $\lambda z : (\Pi x : S\,.\,\Pi y : S\,.\,Q\,x\,y)\,.\,\lambda u : S\,.\,z\,u\,u\ :$
         $\Pi x : S\,.\,\Pi y : S\,.\,Q\,x\,y\ \to\ \Pi u : S\,.\,Q\,u\,u$ ($abst$) on (3)

Compare this derivation with the logical one in the beginning of this section. The derivation is a bit longer than the natural deduction proof, but it captures the same content. Note that the derivation includes all the proof objects and hence tells us exactly how the proof has been constructed. So the derivation contains *more* information.

The final conclusion in this derivation is the judgement (a), (b) $\vdash$ (4), i.e.:

$S : *,\ Q\ :\ S \to S \to *\ \vdash\ \lambda z : (\Pi x : S\,.\,\Pi y : S\,.\,Q\,x\,y)\,.\,\lambda u : S\,.\,z\,u\,u\ :$
                          $\Pi x : S\,.\,\Pi y : S\,.\,Q\,x\,y\ \to\ \Pi u : S\,.\,Q\,u\,u$.

So we have indeed found an *inhabitant* of the original goal type, namely

$\lambda z : (\Pi x : S\,.\,\Pi y : S\,.\,Q\,x\,y)\,.\,\lambda u : S\,.\,z\,u\,u$.

This is the *proof object* proving the proposition. The proof object codes the *full proof* of the theorem it proves. That is to say: from the proof object alone one can already reconstruct the full derivation. So the above derivation contains, in a sense, *too much* information. Of course, for a human reader the above version is preferable, since it concisely shows how the proof has been constructed.

Remark 5.5.2 *By calculating the* type *of a proof object, one obtains a coding of the proposition it proves. There is a slight complication due to the ($conv$)-rule. Assume that M is a proof object, and that a direct calculation of its type gives expression N. Then it may be the case that the direct representation of the* *proposition-to-prove is a different expression N'. However, if $N =_\beta N'$ there is no problem, since proof object M then also proves N' by the (conv)-rule.*

The context Γ of judgement (4), consisting of the declarations (a) and (b), gives type information about S and Q. Note that in the above shortened derivation, we do not call upon this information. However, when giving the *full* derivation, we *do* need (a) and (b), as follows from Exercise 5.3.

5.6 Conclusions

In the present section we have extended the basic system $\lambda\!\to$ with *types depending on terms*. The system obtained, λP, differs from $\lambda\underline{\omega}$ in several aspects. For example, the *(form)*-rule is less general; on the other hand: Π-types are back as first-class citizens.

System λP is particularly suited for coding set-valued functions and proposition-valued functions. The latter functions are generally known as 'predicates'.

In λP we have the opportunity to investigate and use an extremely important interpretation, being a foundational idea behind type theory as a whole: the so-called *propositions-as-types* notion, or PAT. In this conception, propositions are coded as types, and inhabitants of these types represent the *proofs* of these propositions (*'proofs-as-terms'*, which is a second reading of 'PAT'). By means of this PAT-interpretation, *propositions* are treated on a par (at least, to a large extent) with *sets*, since propositions *and* sets are coded as types. Similarly, there is a correspondence between *proofs* of propositions and *elements* of sets: both are coded as terms of the types concerned.

This 'double' PAT-approach has already widely demonstrated its power and fruitfulness. It enables type theory to be employed as a foundation of logic and mathematics. In the present chapter we have given a hunch about how this can be started.

Interesting features of λP are its possibilities of encoding
(1) *basic mathematical notions*, in particular: sets, propositions and predicates;
(2) *basic logical notions:* implication and universal quantification.

These are the ingredients of *minimal predicate logic*.

There is a striking correspondence between the traditional way of reasoning in minimal predicate logic and the corresponding derivational approach in λP. System λP can be seen as a more complete variant of minimal predicate logic, including proof objects that encode the reasoning. The type-theoretic translation of logical formulas is rather straightforward: $\Rightarrow$ becomes $\to$, and $\forall$ is represented by Π. The derivation rules of natural deduction in minimal predicate logic on the one hand, and the derivation rules of λP on the other, are comparable to a high degree.

5.7 Further reading

Ideas about dependent types were already present in the work of H.B. Curry on 'illative logic' (see e.g. Curry & Feys, 1958, Appendix A). The idea was to add a constant to untyped λ-calculus (or combinatory logic) to single out the terms representing well-formed propositions, and a constant to denote derivability. A formal system based on these ideas was developed by J.P. Seldin in 1975, but only published in Seldin (1979). See also the historic overview in Cardone & Hindley (2009).

The first system to actually use type theory to formalise mathematics was the Automath system, developed by N.G. de Bruijn and his research team in the early 1970s (de Bruijn, 1980; Nederpelt *et al.*, 1994). See also the Automath Archive (2004), a database containing copies of many original papers about Automath. There are various Automath type theories and several of them have been implemented as proof checkers. For two of the Automath languages, AUT-68 and AUT-QE, F. Wiedijk has made new computer implementations, written in C (see Wiedijk, 1999).

An interesting aspect of Automath is that it also used type theory and the propositions-as-types interpretation in a different way than as described in this chapter. The first Automath systems used what can be called the 'Logical Framework' interpretation of propositions-as-types (see below), which was invented by de Bruijn in the late 1960s.

The propositions-as-types interpretation of minimal predicate logic into λP we have described in the present chapter can be called the 'Curry–Howard' interpretation (or isomorphism), which was first formally described in a paper by W. Howard of 1968, which only appeared in print 12 years later (Howard, 1980). Later Automath systems, such as AUT-QE (1970; cf. Nederpelt *et al.*, 1994), also used the Curry–Howard interpretation, or combined the two. Therefore, the 'propositions-as-types' interpretation is now often referred to as the 'Curry–Howard–de Bruijn' embedding.

The idea of the 'Logical Framework' interpretation is that we use λP as a 'meta-calculus' for doing logic: one can define a logic L in λP by choosing an appropriate context Γ_L. In Γ_L, the language and the logical rules are declared. Then one can employ the logic L by working in the context Γ_L within the type theory λP. The strength of this approach lies in the fact that λP deals with the 'meta-operations' of binding and substitution that are present in any formal system of logic. Important aspects that are usually left implicit in a paper description of the logic, like avoiding the capture of free variables when performing a substitution, are taken care of by the system λP.

The logical framework approach has been revived in the Edinburgh LF system (Harper *et al.*, 1987). There also the presentation with contexts was used. (Automath uses a system with so-called 'books' and 'lines'; see also Chapters 9 and 11, where we follow similar ideas.) The system Twelf (see Twelf Project, 1999) is a direct successor of Edinburgh LF; it is widely used in the United States of America for formalisation and verification in computer science.

In the period when de Bruijn introduced Automath, P. Martin-Löf introduced his Intuitionistic Type Theory (Martin-Löf, 1980; Nordström *et al.*, 1990), which can be seen as an extension of λP with specific features to be a foundation of intuitionistic mathematics. Martin-Löf's primary aim was not to lay the basis for a system for formalising mathematics, but to develop a foundational system to capture the Brouwer–Heyting–Kolmogorov interpretation (Troelstra & van Dalen, 1988) of proofs. There are various versions of intuitionistic type theory, some being *intensional* like λP and some being *extensional*. In extensional type theory, two types have the same inhabitants if they are provably equal (not only if they are β-convertible). This conforms with a set-theoretic view of mathematics, but it renders the type checking undecidable, so therefore it has been abandoned by Martin-Löf.

Martin-Löf's systems have been very influential in type theory. He extended type theory with Σ-types to represent dependent products, and with inductive types to make proofs by induction (and also functions defined by well-founded recursion) a primitive in the system. A Σ-*type* $\Sigma x : A . B$ represents the type of the pairs $\langle a, b \rangle$, such that $a : A$ and $b : B[x := a]$; so the type B may depend on the x of type A. These Σ-types (or a variant thereof) are very useful for representing abstract mathematical structures, like 'symmetric relations', consisting of tuples $\langle A, R \rangle$ where A is a type and R is a binary relation on A that is symmetric. See also Sections 6.5 and 13.8 for more information on Σ-types. *Inductive* types as primitives allow proofs by induction, but are also very useful for representing data types and functional programs over them. This enables one to specify functional programs and prove them correct.

These ideas have been followed by other systems, for example in the type theory of the proof assistant Coq (see Coquand & Huet, 1988; Coq Development Team, 2012), called the Calculus of Inductive Constructions (Bertot & Castéran, 2004). Martin-Löf's type theory itself has been implemented as a proof assistant in the systems Nuprl (Constable *et al.*, 1986), ALF (Magnusson & Nordström, 1994) and Agda (Bove *et al.*, 2009).

A recent text with special emphasis on the Curry–Howard isomorphism is M.H. Sørensen and P. Urzyczyn's *Lectures on the Curry–Howard Isomorphism* (2006), which also treats other topics related to this book, such as simply typed λ-calculus (cf. our Chapter 2), dependent types, the λ-cube (Chapter 6), sequent calculus (Section 11.13) and arithmetic (Chapter 14). Another text that explains 'Curry–Howard' is Simmons (2000), but its types are only simple and its emphasis is more on computation than derivation.

Exercises

5.1 Give a diagram of the tree corresponding to the complete tree derivation of line (18) of Section 5.3.

5.2 Give a complete (i.e. unshortened) λP-derivation of
$$S : * \vdash S \to S \to * : \square,$$
(a) in tree format,
(b) in flag format.

5.3 Extend the flag derivation of Exercise 5.2 (b) to a complete derivation of
$$S : *, \ Q : S \to S \to * \vdash \Pi x : S . \Pi y : S . Q x y : *.$$

5.4 Prove that $*$ is the only legal *kind* in λP.

5.5 Prove that $A \Rightarrow ((A \Rightarrow B) \Rightarrow B)$ is a tautology by giving a shortened λP-derivation.

5.6 Prove that $(A \Rightarrow (A \Rightarrow B)) \Rightarrow (A \Rightarrow B)$ is a tautology, (first) in natural deduction and (second) by means of a shortened λP-derivation.

5.7 Prove that the following propositions are tautologies by giving shortened λP-derivations:
(a) $(A \Rightarrow B) \Rightarrow ((B \Rightarrow C) \Rightarrow (A \Rightarrow C))$,
(b) $((A \Rightarrow B) \Rightarrow A) \Rightarrow ((A \Rightarrow B) \Rightarrow B)$,
(c) $(A \Rightarrow (B \Rightarrow C)) \Rightarrow ((A \Rightarrow B) \Rightarrow (A \Rightarrow C))$.

5.8 (a) Let $\Gamma \equiv S : *, \ P : S \to *, \ Q : S \to *$. Find an inhabitant of $\Pi x : S . P x \to Q x \to P x$ with respect to Γ, and give a corresponding (shortened) derivation.
(b) Give a natural deduction proof of the corresponding logical expression.

5.9 Give proofs that the following propositions are tautologies, (first) in natural deduction and (second) by means of a shortened λP-derivation.
(a) $\forall_{x \in S} (Q(x)) \Rightarrow \forall_{y \in S}(P(y) \Rightarrow Q(y))$,
(b) $\forall_{x \in S}(P(x) \Rightarrow Q(x)) \Rightarrow (\forall_{y \in S} (P(y)) \Rightarrow \forall_{z \in S} (Q(z)))$.

5.10 Consider the following context:
$$\Gamma \equiv S : *, \ P : S \to *, \ f : S \to S, \ g : S \to S,$$
$$u : \Pi x : S . (P(f x) \to P(g x)), \ v : \Pi x, y : S . ((P x \to P y) \to P(f x))$$
(cf. Notation 3.4.2).
Let $M \equiv \lambda x : S . v(f x)(g x)(u x)$.

(a) Make a guess at which type N may satisfy $\Gamma \vdash M : N$.

(b) Demonstrate that the proof object M does indeed code a proof of the proposition N you have guessed, by elaborating the λP-derivation corresponding to M.

5.11 Let S be a set, with Q and R relations on $S \times S$, and let f and g be functions from S to S. Assume that $\forall_{x,y \in S}(Q(x, f(y)) \Rightarrow Q(g(x), y))$, $\forall_{x,y \in S}(Q(x, f(y)) \Rightarrow R(x, y))$, and $\forall_{x \in S}(Q(x, f(f(x))))$.

Prove that $\forall_{x \in S}(R(g(g(x)), g(x)))$ by giving a context Γ and finding a term M such that:

$$\Gamma \vdash M : \Pi x : S . R (g(g\,x)) (g\,x).$$

Give the corresponding (shortened) λP-derivation.

5.12 In λP, consider the context

$$\Gamma \equiv S : *, \; R : S \to S \to *, \; u : \Pi x, y : S . R\,x\,y \to R\,y\,x,$$
$$v : \Pi x, y, z : S . R\,x\,y \to R\,x\,z \to R\,y\,z.$$

(a) Show that R is 'reflexive on its domain', by constructing an inhabitant of the type $\Pi x, y : S . R\,x\,y \to R\,x\,x$ in context Γ; give a corresponding (shortened) derivation.

(b) Show that R is transitive by constructing an inhabitant of the type $\Pi x, y, z : S . R\,x\,y \to R\,y\,z \to R\,x\,z$ in context Γ; give a corresponding (shortened) derivation.

6

The Calculus of Constructions

6.1 The system λC

In this section we combine the systems of Chapters 2 to 5, so we obtain a system with all four possible choices of 'terms/types depending on terms/types' (see the beginning of Section 5.1).

The system thus obtained is known as λC, but also as *Calculus of Constructions* or λ-Coquand, after one of its founders, Th. Coquand (see Coquand, 1985, and Coquand & Huet, 1988). So the letter 'C' in the name λC has many references, and there's still one more to come: the 'c' in the word λ-cube (see below).

Technically, there is only one difference between λP and λC, but this is enough to extend λP to λC $= \lambda 2 + \lambda\underline{\omega} + \lambda$P. The difference concerns the rule (*form*), the formation rule. In λP this rule looks as follows:

$$(form_{\lambda P}) \quad \frac{\Gamma \vdash A : * \quad \Gamma, x : A \vdash B : s}{\Gamma \vdash \Pi x : A . B \ : \ s}$$

As we noted in Section 5.2, the crucial point for λP in this rule is that A must have type $*$, in order to guarantee that the inhabitants of $\Pi x : A . B$ are terms or types dependent on *terms* only (since x is a term, of level 1). But when we lift this restriction, we get the generalisation we want: terms or types depending on terms *or types*.

Hence, it appears to be sufficient to replace $A : *$ in the rule by $A : s$, with s in $\{*, \square\}$. However, we already have an s in the rule, since also $B : s$, and we want to be able to choose the two s's independently of each other.

Compare this with the (*form*)-rule of $\lambda\underline{\omega}$, where there is only one s involved, so that we only have terms-dependent-on-terms and types-dependent-on-types, but not the 'cross-overs':

$$(form_{\lambda\underline{\omega}}) \quad \frac{\Gamma \vdash A : s \quad \Gamma \vdash B : s}{\Gamma \vdash A \to B : s}$$

A neat way out is to use two s's: an s_1 and an s_2. And this is exactly what we do in the (*form*)-rule of system λC:

$$(\textit{form}_{\lambda C}) \ \frac{\Gamma \vdash A : s_1 \quad \Gamma, \, x : A \vdash B : s_2}{\Gamma \vdash \Pi x : A . \, B \ : \ s_2}$$

So in the first **premiss** we have s_1 and in the second **premiss** we have s_2, which may be chosen independently of each other from $\{*, \square\}$ (*four* possible choices). In the **conclusion** of the rule, s_2 appears, again. So the type of $\Pi x : A . \, B$ is inherited from its body, viz. B. This is acceptable because:

(1) *intuitively:* if B is a type, then the generalised ('dependent') type $\Pi x : A . \, B$ should be a type as well; and if B is a kind, then $\Pi x : A . \, B$ should be one, too. This may not be a very convincing argument, since there are more general systems of type theory where the type of $\Pi x : A . \, B$ may be different from s_1 and s_2. (Such systems, developed by S. Berardi and J. Terlouw, are called '*pure type systems*' or *PTS*s. In a PTS, the type of $\Pi x : A . \, B$ becomes s_3; this leads to *eight* possible choices for (s_1, s_2, s_3).)

(2) *technically:* in the (*form*)-rule of λC we just copy the features of the rules (*form*$_{\lambda P}$) and (*form*$_{\lambda \underline{\omega}}$), in which the types of B and $\Pi x : A . \, B$ (or $A \to B$) are the same.

So what can we obtain with this rule (*form*$_{\lambda C}$)? Assume we have a function $\lambda x : A . \, b$ of type $\Pi x : A . \, B$, that is constructed with the (*abst*)-rule (which is identical to the one in λP, so b must be of type B). Then A is of type s_1 and B is of type s_2 by the (*form*)-rule. This leads to the following possibilities:

$x : A : s_1$	$b : B : s_2$	(s_1, s_2)	$\lambda x : A . \, b$	from
$*$	$*$	$(*, *)$	term-depending-on-term	$\lambda {\to}$
$\square$	$*$	$(\square, *)$	term-depending-on-type	$\lambda 2$
$\square$	$\square$	$(\square, \square)$	type-depending-on-type	$\lambda \underline{\omega}$
$*$	$\square$	$(*, \square)$	type-depending-on-term	λP

Clearly, all four possibilities from Chapters 2 to 5 can be realised. For example, when $(s_1, s_2) = (\square, *)$, then we have terms dependent on types as in $\lambda 2$; from the table it follows that x then has level 2, that A has level 3 and that b has level 1.

In order to be able to quickly recognise the nature of the dependencies in λ- and Π-abstractions, we give the following diagrams:

$$
\boxed{\begin{array}{c} \lambda x : A . \ b \\ \cdot \cdot \ \ \cdot \cdot \\ s_1 \ \ B \\ \cdot \cdot \\ s_2 \end{array}}
$$

$$
\boxed{\begin{array}{c} \Pi x : A . \ B \\ \cdot \cdot \ \ \cdot \cdot \\ s_1 \ \ s_2 \end{array}}
$$

For example, in order to know in which subsystem of λC a certain λ-expression $\lambda x : A . \ b$ can be formed, we calculate the type of A (say s_1) and the *type of the type* of b (say s_2). Then the pair (s_1, s_2) tells us which combination we need to have.

For a Π-expression $\Pi x : A . \ B$ we calculate the types of A and B.

6.2 The λ-cube

We have encountered three extensions of the simplest system, λ→:
- with terms depending on types: λ2,
- with types depending on types: λ$\underline{\omega}$,
- with types depending on terms: λP.

These three possibilities are mutually independent. They may be visualised as three perpendicular *directions* of extending λ→, giving a three-dimensional system of coordinate axes (see Figure 6.1).

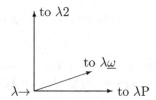

Figure 6.1 Directions of extending λ→

All three extensions *together* give λC, as we have seen in the previous section. There are, of course, other possibilities of extension, by combining λ → with *two* of the three possibilities. The obtained systems are called λω, λP2 and λP$\underline{\omega}$, respectively. The decisive choice is what combinations of s_1 and s_2 are allowed in the (*form*)-rule. These combinations are listed in Figure 6.2.

All eight systems can be positioned in a cube, the so-called λ-*cube* or *Barendregt cube* (see Figure 6.3).

Remark 6.2.1 *The unifying framework for the eight systems was discovered and described by H.P. Barendregt (see Barendregt, 1992). He investigated the common properties and differences of existing type-theoretic systems and*

system:	combinations (s_1, s_2) allowed:			
$\lambda{\to}$	$(*,*)$			
$\lambda 2$	$(*,*)$	$(\square,*)$		
$\lambda\underline{\omega}$	$(*,*)$		$(\square,\square)$	
λP	$(*,*)$			$(*,\square)$
$\lambda\omega$	$(*,*)$	$(\square,*)$	$(\square,\square)$	
$\lambda P2$	$(*,*)$	$(\square,*)$		$(*,\square)$
$\lambda P\underline{\omega}$	$(*,*)$		$(\square,\square)$	$(*,\square)$
$\lambda P\omega = \lambda C$	$(*,*)$	$(\square,*)$	$(\square,\square)$	$(*,\square)$

Figure 6.2 The eight systems of the λ-cube

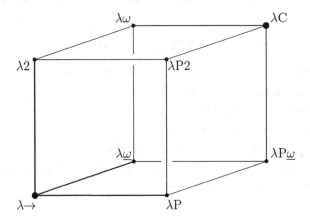

Figure 6.3 The λ-cube or Barendregt cube

investigated their relation. Thus he could identify some of these systems as (essentially) $\lambda 2$, $\lambda\underline{\omega}$, λP, *and others as* $\lambda P2$, $\lambda\omega$ *or* λC.

The most striking result of Barendregt's investigations is that the eight different systems can be described with only one set of derivation rules (see Figure 6.4). This set of rules is relatively simple: apart from three *initialisation rules* (viz. (*sort*), (*var*) and (*weak*)), all that we need are a formation rule (*form*) for Π-types, a conversion rule (*conv*) and the two fundamental rules for every lambda calculus system, concerning application and abstraction.

Remark 6.2.2 *N.G. de Bruijn's* Automath, *the first operative formal system for formalising and checking mathematics, enjoys all relevant features of* λP, *but is richer, as has been demonstrated by Kamareddine et al. (2004); also some aspects of* $\lambda 2$ *and* $\lambda\underline{\omega}$ *are incorporated in it. In fact, one could position Automath in the centre of the lateral face on the right-hand side of the depicted* λ-cube. *Moreover, definitions are a core notion in Automath (their indispens-*

ability will be argued in Chapter 8 and further). In other words, Automath ∼ λP + $\frac{1}{2}$λ2 + $\frac{1}{2}$λ$\underline{\omega}$ + definitions.

In Figure 6.4 we give the complete list of rules for the eight systems of the λ-cube. In which system we are depends on the combinations of (s_1, s_2) we allow in the *(form)*-rule, according to the table in Figure 6.2.

$$(sort) \quad \emptyset \vdash *:\square$$

$$(var) \quad \frac{\Gamma \vdash A:s}{\Gamma,\ x:A \vdash x:A} \quad \text{if } x \notin \Gamma$$

$$(weak) \quad \frac{\Gamma \vdash A:B \quad \Gamma \vdash C:s}{\Gamma,\ x:C \vdash A:B} \quad \text{if } x \notin \Gamma$$

$$(form) \quad \frac{\Gamma \vdash A:s_1 \quad \Gamma,\ x:A \vdash B:s_2}{\Gamma \vdash \Pi x:A.\,B\ :\ s_2}$$

$$(appl) \quad \frac{\Gamma \vdash M\ :\ \Pi x:A.\,B \quad \Gamma \vdash N:A}{\Gamma \vdash MN\ :\ B[x:=N]}$$

$$(abst) \quad \frac{\Gamma,\ x:A \vdash M:B \quad \Gamma \vdash \Pi x:A.\,B\ :\ s}{\Gamma \vdash \lambda x:A.\,M\ :\ \Pi x:A.\,B}$$

$$(conv) \quad \frac{\Gamma \vdash A:B \quad \Gamma \vdash B':s}{\Gamma \vdash A:B'} \quad \text{if } B =_\beta B'$$

Figure 6.4 Derivation rules for the systems of the λ-cube

Remark 6.2.3 *It will immediately be clear how the systems λ$\underline{\omega}$ and λP, as respectively described in Chapters 4 and 5, fit in the general framework of Figure 6.4:*

- *For λ$\underline{\omega}$, just see $A \to B$ as an abbreviation of $\Pi x:A.\,B$, and the rules given in Figures 4.1 and 6.4 coincide. (Since $(s_1, s_2) \in \{(*, *), (\square, \square)\}$ in λ$\underline{\omega}$, we may take $s_1 = s_2 = s$.)*
- *For λP, restrict s_1 of Figure 6.4 to $s_1 = *$, and we obtain the rules in Figure 5.1.*

For λ→ and λ2 we have to do a little more work to see that their original definitions in Chapters 2 and 3 fit in Figure 6.4. In the original versions of λ→ and λ2, the types are given beforehand as a fixed set, while in the λ-cube definition, they need to be constructed during a derivation by means of (sort), (weak) and (form). Moreover, the (conv)-rule is superfluous in these systems, since there $B =_\beta B'$ implies that $B \equiv B'$. It is not too hard to show, however,

*that the original $\lambda\!\to$ and $\lambda 2$ are precisely covered by the rules in the λ-cube, of
course when restricting the admissible (s_1, s_2)-combinations to the sets $\{(*, *)\}$
and $\{(*, *), (\Box, *)\}$, respectively.*

6.3 Properties of λC

Most of the properties of the previously described systems also hold for the
'combined' system λC. Of course, the phrasing of the lemmas should sometimes
be a little bit different, because we are in a more general environment (no fixed
types, more than two or three levels, etcetera).

Below we give the lemmas for λC in their general shape. For comments on
their content, in particular regarding their intuition and relevance, we refer to
Sections 2.10 and 2.11, and to Section 4.8 for the necessary extension of the
Uniqueness of Types Lemma.

Some notions have to be redefined in the more general environment of λC.
For example, the description of the domain (dom) of a $\lambda\!\to$-context, given in
Definition 2.10, should be slightly adapted for the case of a λC-context. Many
of these changes in definition are straightforward and therefore we do not spell
them out.

We do not give proofs of the lemmas below, since they are rather laborious for
the λC case. In particular, the proof of Strong Normalisation (Theorem 6.3.14)
is very complicated. The proof in Geuvers (1995) is four pages long and that
in Barendregt (1992) is even longer, almost 19 pages.

First we summarise what the *expressions* are in λC:

Definition 6.3.1   (Expressions of λC, $\mathcal{E}$)
The set $\mathcal{E}$ of λC-expressions is defined by:

$$\mathcal{E} = V\,|\,\Box\,|*\,|(\mathcal{E}\mathcal{E})|(\lambda V : \mathcal{E} \,.\, \mathcal{E})|(\Pi V : \mathcal{E} \,.\, \mathcal{E})\,.$$

Notation 6.3.2   *In λC, we employ the same notation conventions as before,
in particular about variables (see Notation 1.3.4), parentheses, successive abstractions (Notations 1.3.10, 3.4.2), sorts (Notation 4.1.5) and the abbreviation
$A \to B$ for $\Pi x : A \,.\, B$, in case $x \notin FV(B)$ (Notation 5.2.1).*

Now we give a list of important lemmas and theorems, provided with a short
comment.

Lemma 6.3.3   *(Free Variables Lemma)*
   If $\Gamma \vdash A : B$, then $FV(A)$, $FV(B) \subseteq \mathtt{dom}(\Gamma)$.

Comment: Cf. Lemma 2.10.3. See also Barendregt (1992), Lemma 5.2.8, 2.

We say that a context is *well-formed* if it forms part of a derivable judgement:

Definition 6.3.4 (Well-formed context)
A context Γ is *well-formed* if there are A and B such that $\Gamma \vdash A : B$.

Lemma 6.3.5 *(Thinning Lemma, Permutation Lemma, Condensing Lemma)*
(1) (Thinning) Let Γ' and Γ'' be contexts such that $\Gamma' \subseteq \Gamma''$. If $\Gamma' \vdash A : B$ and Γ'' is well-formed, then also $\Gamma'' \vdash A : B$.
(2) (Permutation) Let Γ' and Γ'' be contexts such that Γ'' is a permutation of Γ'. If $\Gamma' \vdash A : B$ and Γ'' is well-formed, then also $\Gamma'' \vdash A : B$.
(3) (Condensing) If $\Gamma', x : A, \Gamma'' \vdash B : C$ and x does not occur in Γ'', B or C, then also $\Gamma, \Gamma'' \vdash B : C$.

Comment: Cf. Lemma 2.10.5; we do not give the general notion of context-inclusion $(\Gamma' \subseteq \Gamma'')$ – it is similar to the one in Definition 2.10 (2).

As to the Condensing Lemma: we recall that $\Gamma', x : A, \Gamma''$ is a context in which the declaration $x : A$ occurs *somewhere*. Note that the present Condensing Lemma is slightly different from the one in Lemma 2.10.5: here we state that it is allowed to take out an *arbitrary* 'superfluous' declaration $x : A$ from the context, while in the $\lambda{\to}$-version we projected out *all* the superfluous context declarations 'in one sweep'.

For proofs of the three parts of Lemma 6.3.5, see Barendregt, 1992 (Lemmas 5.2.12 and 5.2.17).

Lemma 6.3.6 *(Generation Lemma)*
(1) If $\Gamma \vdash x : C$, then there exist a sort s and an expression B such that $B =_\beta C$, $\Gamma \vdash B : s$ and $x : B \in \Gamma$.
(2) If $\Gamma \vdash MN : C$, then M has a Π-type, i.e. there exist expressions A and B such that $\Gamma \vdash M : \Pi x : A . B$; moreover, N fits in this Π-type: $\Gamma \vdash N : A$, and finally, $C =_\beta B[x := N]$.
(3) If $\Gamma \vdash \lambda x : A . b : C$, then there are a sort s and an expression B such that $C =_\beta \Pi x : A . B$, where $\Gamma \vdash \Pi x : A . B : s$ and moreover: $\Gamma, x : A \vdash b : B$.
(4) If $\Gamma \vdash \Pi x : A . B : C$, then there are s_1 and s_2 such that $C \equiv s_2$, and moreover: $\Gamma \vdash A : s_1$ and $\Gamma, x : A \vdash B : s_2$.

Comment: Cf. Lemma 2.10.7. See Barendregt, 1992 (Lemma 5.2.13) for a proof.

Note that we distinguish *four* cases here: except (1) for variable x, (2) for application MN and (3) for λ-abstraction $\lambda x : A . b$, as in Lemma 2.10.7, we need the extra case (4) for Π-abstraction $\Pi x : A . B$ here. All four cases are more complicated because of the $(conv)$-rule, which allows a type to be replaced by a β-convertible one. If we forget about this complication, then the four cases reflect rather directly the corresponding rules: (var), $(appl)$, $(abst)$ and $(form)$.

One employs a more general notion of legality (cf. Definition 2.4.10) in λC. This is defined as follows:

Definition 6.3.7   An expression M in λC is *legal* if there exist Γ and N such that $\Gamma \vdash M : N$ or $\Gamma \vdash N : M$ (so when M is either *typable* or *inhabited*).

Then we have:

Lemma 6.3.8   *(Subexpression Lemma)*
  If M is legal, then every subexpression of M is legal.

Comment: Cf. Lemma 2.10.8 and Barendregt, 1992 (Corollary 5.2.14, 4).

Lemma 6.3.9   *(Uniqueness of Types up to Conversion)*
  If $\Gamma \vdash A : B_1$ and $\Gamma \vdash A : B_2$, then $B_1 =_\beta B_2$.

Comment: Cf. Lemmas 2.10.9 and 4.8.1. A proof can be found in Barendregt, 1992 (Lemma 5.2.21).

Lemma 6.3.10   *(Substitution Lemma)*
  Let Γ', $x : A$, $\Gamma'' \vdash B : C$ and $\Gamma' \vdash D : A$.
  Then Γ', $\Gamma''[x := D] \vdash B[x := D] : C[x := D]$.

Comment: Cf. Lemma 2.11.1 and the explanation following that lemma. Here we substitute D for x in the judgement Γ', $x : A$, $\Gamma'' \vdash B : C$, where D and x have the same type, viz. A. The lemma says that the resulting judgement is still derivable (we may even leave out the declaration $x : A$, for obvious reasons). The substitutions should take place *everywhere*, so not only in B and C, but also in the part of the context in which x's may occur (viz. Γ''). The latter substitution, $\Gamma''[x := D]$, has not yet been defined. However, it will be obvious how this should be done.
  For a proof of Lemma 6.3.10, see Barendregt, 1992 (Lemma 5.2.11).

Theorem 6.3.11   *(Church–Rosser Theorem; CR; Confluence)*
  The Church–Rosser property holds for λC, i.e. if M in $\mathcal{E}$, $M \twoheadrightarrow_\beta N_1$ and $M \twoheadrightarrow_\beta N_2$, then there is N_3 such that $N_1 \twoheadrightarrow_\beta N_3$ and $N_2 \twoheadrightarrow_\beta N_3$.

Comment: Cf. Theorems 1.9.8 and 2.11.3. The notions of β-reduction and β-conversion have to be adapted to the expressions of λC. This is straightforward (see also Definitions 1.8.1, 1.8.3, 1.8.5, 2.11.2 and 3.6.2).

Corollary 6.3.12   *Suppose that M, N in $\mathcal{E}$ and $M =_\beta N$. Then there is L such that $M \twoheadrightarrow_\beta L$ and $N \twoheadrightarrow_\beta L$.*

Comment: Cf. Corollaries 1.9.9 and 2.11.4.

Lemma 6.3.13   *(Subject Reduction)*
  If $\Gamma \vdash A : B$ and $A \twoheadrightarrow_\beta A'$, then $\Gamma \vdash A' : B$.

Comment: Cf. Lemma 2.11.5. For a proof, see Barendregt, 1992 (Theorem 5.2.15).

Theorem 6.3.14   *(Strong Normalisation Theorem or Termination Theorem)*
Every legal M is strongly normalising.

Comment: Cf. Theorem 2.11.6. The proof is complicated. See e.g. Barendregt, 1992 (Theorem 5.3.33), or Geuvers, 1995.

Finally, we concentrate on the three main questions in type theory, namely: Well-typedness, Type Checking and Term Finding (cf. Section 2.6). The first two of these are decidable; for a proof, see van Benthem Jutting (1993).

Theorem 6.3.15   *(Decidability of Well-typedness and Type Checking)*
    In λC *and its subsystems, the questions of Well-typedness and Type Checking are decidable.*

So it is possible to conceive of *a computer program* which solves these problems automatically: on input of either a sole 'term' or a combination 'term + type' (with or without context), the program finds out whether a corresponding derivation exists and, if so, *gives* this derivation.

The question of Term *Finding*, however, is decidable in $\lambda\!\to$ and $\lambda\underline{\omega}$, but *undecidable* in all other systems. This is understandable if we recall that there is no general method to *prove or disprove* an arbitrary theorem in mathematics. This famous result, called the Church–Turing Undecidability Theorem, comes from A. Church and, independently, A.M. Turing (see Church, 1935, 1936a,b; Turing, 1936). As we saw, the assignment to prove or disprove a proposition M can be translated into finding a *term* of type M in type theory, or to show that no such inhabitant exists. Hence, decidability of Term Finding would imply that there was an algorithm which could prove or disprove every mathematical proposition.

As a consequence, logic and mathematics cannot be fully handed over to a machine that solves all problems that you pose. That may be a pity for science in general, but not for the scientists, who are still necessary not only to *invent* the problems, but also to *solve* them. Hence, in a type-theoretic setting: humans formulate the types and human intervention is also required to find the inhabitants.

Nevertheless, computers can be of substantial aid in solving these problems. They can administer the problem and the derivation as it develops, be of help in listing the open goals that have not (yet) been solved and check whether the development of the derivation occurs exactly according to the rules.

Such computer programs, called '*proof assistants*', become more and more useful in helping a human solving logical or mathematical problems. They are also employed for proving *correctness of computer programs* in general, i.e. giving a formal proof that a given computer program satisfies its specifications. Last but not least, proof assistants may be of help in the *development* of provably correct computer programs.

6.4 Conclusions

Different combinations of the systems encountered in the previous chapters are possible. All systems ($\lambda{\rightarrow}$, $\lambda 2$, $\lambda\underline{\omega}$ and λP), and therefore all combinations thereof, include the simply typed lambda calculus ($\lambda{\rightarrow}$), this being the foundation on which the enlargements are built.

Different dependencies of terms and/or types on terms and/or types are realised in these combinations; these combinations can be positioned in a cube: the λ-cube or Barendregt cube.

All these systems – eight of them, altogether – can be described concisely and very elegantly by means of *one* single set of derivation rules (see Figure 6.4), in which the tuning of one parameter (the choice of the permitted combinations (s_1, s_2) in the *(form)*-rule) determines which system we have at hand. Among these rules there are many that are already familiar from the four basic systems. They are presented here in a uniform format, in which they get their definite description.

One recognises, for instance, the application and abstraction rules, fundamental to every system of lambda calculus. The *sort*-rule is the start of every derivation. Moreover, we have a variable rule and a weakening rule to manipulate contexts and a formation rule to construct dependent types. Finally, there is a conversion rule, which allows us to replace a type in a derivation by a legal β-convertible one.

The most extensive combination, combining *all* the mentioned systems, is λC, the Calculus of Constructions. Every combination of s_1 and s_2 is allowed in this 'jewel of type theory'. Moreover, it satisfies all the nice properties already formulated for the underlying systems, albeit sometimes in a slightly more general phrasing. Among these are the Uniqueness of Types Lemma (up to conversion), the Church–Rosser Theorem, the Subject Reduction Lemma, the Termination Theorem and the Decidability of Well-typedness and Type Checking.

These remarkable results establish the power of these systems and their suitability to be used as a foundation for proof assistants. Their proofs ensure the reliability and useability of λC and its subsystems.

6.5 Further reading

The Calculus of Constructions (Coquand & Huet, 1988), also called *CC*, was implemented as a proof checker in the 1980s. It combines all features of λP and $\lambda\omega$ (where $\lambda\omega = \lambda 2 + \lambda\underline{\omega}$, see Section 6.2). It has been introduced to do exactly that: it was conceived as a type theory that unites ideas of A. Church, N.G. de Bruijn, P. Martin-Löf and J.-Y. Girard. Thus it includes higher order predicate logic and polymorphic data types. The λ-cube was constructed to make this explicit, defining the Calculus of Constructions as the union of λP and $\lambda\omega$ (cf. Figure 6.2). Thus it became explicit how the typing rules correspond to the term/type dependencies (see Barendregt, 1992, or Sørensen & Urzyczyn, 2006, for further reading).

CC was used a lot for proving functional programs correct. The data types used were the definable polymorphic data types, because there were no primitive inductive types. These were added later, because the polymorphic data types are a bit less expressive and don't yield an induction proof principle (which has to be added axiomatically). The extension with inductive types (mentioned already in Section 5.7) was called the 'Calculus of Inductive Constructions' or *CIC* (see Bertot & Castéran, 2004, for further reading).

Another variant of the Calculus of Constructions is where 'universes' are added. This means we add 'super-kinds' $\square_i$ (for $i \in \mathbb{N}$; we identify $\square_0$ with our old sort $\square$), where $\square_i : \square_{i+1}$ and as (*form*)-rule we have:

$$\frac{\Gamma \vdash A : \square_i \quad \Gamma, x : A \vdash B : \square_j}{\Gamma \vdash \Pi x : A . B : \square_{\max(i,j)}}$$

The reason for not taking $\square_j$ in the `conclusion` is that if $j < i$, we can get an inconsistency: one can construct a term of type $\bot$. This system was first defined and analysed by Z. Luo (see Luo, 1994) and called the 'Extended Calculus of Constructions', *ECC*. In ECC, the universes are also subsets of each other: $\square_i \subseteq \square_{i+1}$. This is usually phrased as 'cumulativity' of the universe hierarchy and it amounts to the following typing rules:

$$\frac{\Gamma \vdash A : *}{\Gamma \vdash A : \square_0} \qquad \frac{\Gamma \vdash A : \square_i}{\Gamma \vdash A : \square_{i+1}}$$

Furthermore, ECC also has Σ-types (see Section 5.7, again), with the formation rules:

$$\frac{\Gamma \vdash A : * \quad \Gamma, x : A \vdash B : *}{\Gamma \vdash \Sigma x : A . B : *} \qquad \frac{\Gamma \vdash A : \square_i \quad \Gamma, x : A \vdash B : \square_j}{\Gamma \vdash \Sigma x : A . B : \square_{\max(i,j)}}$$

The reason for not allowing 'impredicative Σ-types', like $\Sigma\alpha : * . \alpha \to \alpha : *$, is that we lose consistency.

In Section 5.7 we already mentioned a number of proof assistants, such as

Coq. Many of these are based on the Calculus of Constructions, so not only on λP. For a general paper on proof assistants, see Barendregt & Geuvers (2001).

Exercises

6.1 (a) Give a complete derivation in tree format showing that $\bot \equiv \Pi\alpha : *.\, \alpha$ is legal in λC (cf. Exercise 3.5).
   (b) The same for $\bot \to \bot$.
   (c) To which systems of the λ-cube does $\bot$ belong? And $\bot \to \bot$?

6.2 Let $\Gamma \equiv S : *,\ P : S \to *,\ A : *$.
   Prove by means of a flag derivation that the following expression is inhabited in λC with respect to Γ:
   $$(\Pi x : S.\, (A \to P\,x)) \to A \to \Pi y : S.\, P\,y.$$
   (You may shorten the derivation, as explained in Section 4.5.)

6.3 Let $\mathcal{J}$ be the judgement:
   $$S : *,\ P : S \to * \vdash \lambda x : S.\, (P\,x \to \bot) : S \to *.$$
   (a) Give a shortened λC-derivation of $\mathcal{J}$.
   (b) Determine the (s_1, s_2)-combinations corresponding to all Πs (or arrows) occurring in $\mathcal{J}$. (For $\bot$, see Exercise 6.1.)
   (c) Which is the 'smallest' system in the λ-cube to which $\mathcal{J}$ belongs?

6.4 Let $\Gamma \equiv S : *,\ Q : S \to S \to *$ and let M be the following expression:
   $$M \equiv (\Pi x, y : S.\, (Q\,x\,y \to Q\,y\,x \to \bot)) \to \Pi z : S.\, (Q\,z\,z \to \bot).$$
   (a) Give a shortened derivation of $\Gamma \vdash M : *$ and determine the smallest subsystem to which this judgement belongs.
   (b) Prove in λC that M is inhabited in context Γ. You may use a shortened derivation.
   (c) We may consider Q to be a relation on set S. Moreover, it is reasonable to see $A \to \bot$ as the negation $\neg A$ of proposition A. (We shall explain this in Section 7.1.) How can M then be interpreted, if we also take Figure 5.2 into account? And what is a plausible interpretation of the inhabiting term you found in (b)?

6.5 Let $\mathcal{J}$ be the following judgement:
   $$S : * \vdash \lambda Q : S \to S \to *.\, \lambda x : S.\, Q\,x\,x : (S \to S \to *) \to S \to *.$$
   (a) Give a shortened derivation of $\mathcal{J}$ and determine the smallest subsystem to which $\mathcal{J}$ belongs.
   (b) We may consider the variable Q in $\mathcal{J}$ as expressing a relation on set S. How could you describe the subexpression $\lambda x : S.\, Q\,x\,x$ in this setting? And what is then the interpretation of the judgement $\mathcal{J}$?

6.6 Let $M \equiv \lambda S : *.\ \lambda P : S \to *.\ \lambda x : S.\ (P\,x \to \bot).$

(a) Which is the smallest system in the λ-cube in which M may occur?

(b) Prove that M is legal and determine its type.

(c) How could you interpret the constructor M, if $A \to \bot$ encodes $\neg A$?

6.7 Given $\Gamma \equiv S : *,\ Q : S \to S \to *$, we define in λC the expressions:

$\quad M_1 \equiv \lambda x, y : S.\ \Pi R : S \to S \to *.\ ((\Pi z : S.\ R\,z\,z) \to R\,x\,y),$

$\quad M_2 \equiv \lambda x, y : S.\ \Pi R : S \to S \to *.$

$\qquad ((\Pi u, v : S.\ (Q\,u\,v \to R\,u\,v)) \to R\,x\,y).$

(a) Give an inhabitant of $\Pi a : S.\ M_1\,a\,a$ and a shortened derivation proving your answer.

(b) Give an inhabitant of $\Pi a, b : S.\ (Q\,a\,b \to M_2\,a\,b)$ and a shortened derivation proving your answer.

6.8 (a) Let $\Gamma \equiv S : *,\ P : S \to *$. Find an inhabitant of the following type N in context Γ, and prove your answer by means of a shortened derivation:

$\quad N \equiv [\Pi \alpha : *.\ ((\Pi x : S.\ (P\,x \to \alpha)) \to \alpha)] \to$

$\qquad [\Pi x : S.\ (P\,x \to \bot)] \to \bot.$

(b) Which is the smallest system in the λ-cube in which your derivation may be executed?

(c) The expression $\Pi \alpha : *.\ ((\Pi x : S.\ (P\,x \to \alpha)) \to \alpha$ may be considered as an encoding of $\exists_{x \in S}(P(x))$. (We shall show this in Section 7.5.) In Section 7.1 we make plausible that $A \to \bot$ may be considered as an encoding of the negation $\neg A$. With these things in mind, how can we interpret the content of the expression N? (See also Figure 5.2.)

6.9 Given $S : *,\ P : S \to *$ and $f : S \to S$, we define in λC the expression:

$\quad M \equiv \lambda x : S.\ \Pi Q : S \to *.\ (\Pi z : S.\ (Q\,z \to Q(f\,z))) \to Q\,x.$

Give a term of type $\Pi a : S.\ (M\,a \to M(f\,a))$ and a (shortened) derivation proving this.

6.10 Given $S : *$ and $P_1, P_2 : S \to *$, we define in λC the expression:

$\quad R \equiv \lambda x : S.\ \Pi Q : S \to *.\ (\Pi y : S.\ (P_1\,y \to P_2\,y \to Q\,y)) \to Q\,x.$

We claim that R codes 'the intersection of P_1 and P_2', i.e. the predicate that holds if and only if both P_1 and P_2 hold. In order to show this, give inhabitants of the following types, plus (shortened) derivations proving this:

(a) $\Pi x : S.\ (P_1\,x \to P_2\,x \to R\,x),$

(b) $\Pi x : S.\ (R\,x \to P_1\,x),$

(c) $\Pi x : S.\ (R\,x \to P_2\,x).$

Why do (a), (b) and (c) entail that R is this intersection?

(Hint for (b): see Exercise 5.8 (a).)

6.11 Let $\Gamma \vdash M : N$ in λC and $\Gamma \equiv x_1 : A_1, \ldots, x_n : A_n$.

   (a) Prove that the $x_1, \ldots, x_n$ are distinct.

   (b) Prove the Free Variables Lemma (Lemma 6.3.3) for λC.

   (c) Prove that $FV(A_i) \subseteq \{x_1, \ldots, x_{i-1}\}$, for $1 \leq i \leq n$.

7

The encoding of logical notions in λC

7.1 Absurdity and negation in type theory

In Section 5.4, IV, we saw how *implication* can be coded in type theory (in particular, in λP). We recall: by coding the implication $A \Rightarrow B$ as the function type $A \to B$, we mimic the behaviour of 'implication', including its introduction and elimination rule, in type theory. So we also have minimal propositional logic in λC, since λP is part of λC.

In order to get more than *minimal* propositional logic, we have to be able to handle more connectives, such as negation ('$\neg$'), conjunction ('$\wedge$') and disjunction ('$\vee$'). This cannot be done in λP, but in λC there exist very elegant ways to code the respective notions, as we presently show.

We start with negation. It is natural to consider the negation $\neg A$ as the *implication* $A \Rightarrow \bot$, where $\bot$ is the 'absurdity', also called *contradiction*. So we interpret $\neg A$ as 'A implies absurdity'. But for this we first need a coding of the *absurdity* itself. (In Exercises 3.5 and 6.1 (a) we already mentioned codings of $\bot$ in $\lambda 2$ and λC, which we shall justify below.)

I. Absurdity

A characteristic property of the proposition 'absurdity', or $\bot$, is the following:

   If $\bot$ is true, then every proposition is true.

In natural deduction this property is known under the name $\bot$-elimination. It is traditionally called: '*ex falso*' or *Ex falso sequitur quodlibet*, meaning: from an absurdity follows whatever you like. It can also be expressed as follows, in a type-theoretic setting:

'If $\bot$ is inhabited, then all propositions A are inhabited.'

We can make this more constructive, by invoking a *function*:

'If we have an inhabitant M of $\bot$, then there exists a function mapping an arbitrary proposition α to an inhabitant of this same α.'

Such a function apparently has *type* $\Pi\alpha : *.\ \alpha$. And indeed, if f has type

$\Pi\alpha : * . \, \alpha$, then by the $(appl)$-rule: $fA : \alpha[\alpha := A] \equiv A$. So if f is such a function, then fA inhabits A (or: makes A true). This holds for a general proposition A, since also fB inhabits B, etcetera.

So we can rephrase again:

'Let M be an inhabitant of $\bot$. Then there is a function f which inhabits $\Pi\alpha : * . \, \alpha$.'

And the other way round: if there is such an f, then we can make *all* (!) propositions $(A, B, \ldots)$ true; this is apparently absurd, so we have an absurdity.

Summarising: $\bot$ is inhabited if and only if $\Pi\alpha : * . \, \alpha$ is inhabited.

Our problem was to find a practical coding for $\bot$. By the above, the solution is now at hand: define $\bot$ in type theory as $\Pi\alpha : * . \, \alpha$.

Remark 7.1.1 *By defining $\bot$ as $\Pi\alpha : * . \, \alpha$, we get $\bot$-elimination for free. To demonstrate this, we picture $\bot$-elimination and its type-theoretic equivalent next to each other, where A is an arbitrary inhabitant of $*$.*

$$(\bot\text{-}elim) \quad \frac{\bot}{A} \qquad\qquad \begin{array}{ll} (a) & \boxed{f \; : \; \Pi\alpha : * . \, \alpha} \\[4pt] (i) & \quad fA \; : \; A \qquad (appl) \text{ on } (a) \text{ and } A : * \end{array}$$

We discuss the counterpart of $\bot$-elimination, viz. $\bot$-introduction, after having introduced 'negation': see Remark 7.1.2 below.

To end our discussion of absurdity ($\bot$), we investigate in which system $\bot$ lives. Since $\bot \equiv \Pi\alpha : * . \, \alpha$, we see that $s_1 = \Box$ and $s_2 = *$ (cf. the diagram in Section 6.1). So we are in $\lambda 2$. Moreover, we can show using the derivation rules of $\lambda 2$, that $\bot : *$ (cf. Exercise 3.5).

II. Negation

Now that we have 'absurdity', we also have 'negation'. We define:

$\neg A \; \equiv \; A \to \bot$.

Note that $A \to \bot$ is an abbreviation for $\Pi x : A . \, \bot$. Since $A : *$ and $\bot : *$, we have here that $(s_1, s_2) = (*, *)$. However, by the involvement of $\bot$ we need at least $\lambda 2$ to code negation.

Remark 7.1.2 *The $\bot$-introduction rule employs negation:*

$$(\bot\text{-}intro) \quad \frac{A \quad \neg A}{\bot}$$

However, this rule has become superfluous by the identification of $\neg A$ and $A \to \bot$ (or $A \Rightarrow \bot$), since the $\bot$-introduction rule is now just:

$$(\bot\text{-}intro) \quad \frac{A \quad A \Rightarrow \bot}{\bot}$$

and this is a particular instance *of the* (⇒-*elim*)-*rule* (*cf. Example 2.4.9*).

Similarly, we don't need the natural deduction rule (¬-*intro*), *nor* (¬-*elim*), *since they can be replaced by* (⇒-*intro*) *and* (⇒-*elim*), *respectively* (*see Example 2.4.9, again*). *Comparing the following rules, keeping in mind that* ¬*A stands for* *A* ⇒ ⊥, *we easily see that the left-hand versions are special cases of the right-hand ones:*

$$
(\neg\text{-}intro) \quad \cfrac{\boxed{Assume : A} \\ \vdots \\ \bot}{\neg A}
\qquad\qquad
(\Rightarrow\text{-}intro) \quad \cfrac{\boxed{Assume : A} \\ \vdots \\ B}{A \Rightarrow B}
$$

$$
(\neg\text{-}elim) \quad \cfrac{\neg A \quad A}{\bot}
\qquad\qquad
(\Rightarrow\text{-}elim) \quad \cfrac{A \Rightarrow B \quad A}{B}
$$

Note: (⊥-*intro*) *and* (¬-*elim*) *are identical special cases of the* ⇒-*elim-rule. However, they serve different purposes:*

(1) (⊥-*intro*) *is meant as a rule explaining how to obtain* ⊥: *in order to get* ⊥, *find a proposition* *A* *such that* *A* *itself holds, and also its negation* ¬*A. So, as all intro-rules, it is used as a* backward *rule.*

(2) (¬-*elim*) *tells us how we can* use *a negation* ¬*A: find out whether the un-negated* *A* *holds as well, because then we have an absurdity* (⊥). *This is a* forward *rule (as all elim-rules are).*

7.2 Conjunction and disjunction in type theory

I. Conjunction

The conjunction $A \wedge B$ is true if and only if *both* A and B are true. There exists a nice encoding of the conjunction in $\lambda 2$:

$$A \wedge B \equiv \Pi C : * . \ (A \rightarrow B \rightarrow C) \rightarrow C .$$

This is a so-called 'second order' encoding of the conjunction, which is more general than a first order encoding such as $A \wedge B \equiv \neg(A \rightarrow \neg B)$. It is more general because the latter encoding only works in classical logic (see Section 7.4).

Why does the expression on the right-hand side, behind the '≡', encapsulate the same meaning (and has the same force) as '$A \wedge B$'?

Let's read the Π as 'for all' and the $\rightarrow$ as 'implies' (cf. Section 5.4). Then the expression $\Pi C : * . \ (A \rightarrow B \rightarrow C) \rightarrow C$ can be read as:

(*i*) *For all* C, (*A implies* (*B implies* C)) *implies* C.

Since we are dealing with logic, it is natural to conceive of A, B and C as propositions. Then a free interpretation of (i) is that for all propositions C:

'if A and B *together* imply C, then C holds on its own'.

This expresses that the 'condition' in the expression before the comma, namely that both A and B hold, is redundant. Such a thing can only be the case if that condition is fulfilled, so A must hold and B must hold. And the other way round: it is not hard to see that the truth of both A and B brings along that also (i) holds, since '`true` implies C' is logically equivalent to C.

Hence, it seems to be permitted to use $\Pi C : *. (A \to B \to C) \to C$ as an encoding for $A \wedge B$. One calls this the *second order encoding* of $A \wedge B$, because it generalises over propositions ('*For all propositions C...*'). And propositions (encoded as types) are second order objects.

The informal reasoning given above motivates the proposed encoding of the conjunction in $\lambda 2$. There is also a *formal* justification that this second order encoding is a proper way of treating conjunction in type theory: we shall show that the encoding satisfies the same introduction and elimination rules as $\wedge$ does in natural deduction. We recall these rules for $\wedge$, juxtaposing the type-theoretic second order encodings:

$$(\wedge\text{-}intro) \quad \frac{A \quad B}{A \wedge B} \qquad (\wedge\text{-}intro\text{-}sec) \quad \frac{A \qquad B}{\Pi C : *. (A \to B \to C) \to C}$$

$$(\wedge\text{-}elim\text{-}left) \quad \frac{A \wedge B}{A} \qquad (\wedge\text{-}elim\text{-}left\text{-}sec) \quad \frac{\Pi C : *. (A \to B \to C) \to C}{A}$$

$$(\wedge\text{-}elim\text{-}right) \quad \frac{A \wedge B}{B} \qquad (\wedge\text{-}elim\text{-}right\text{-}sec) \quad \frac{\Pi C : *. (A \to B \to C) \to C}{B}$$

In order to see that the second order rules are *derivable rules* in type theory, it suffices to give corresponding derivations in λC. Under the PAT-interpretation, this boils down to finding solutions to questions $?_1$, $?_2$ and $?_3$ in the following schemes, assuming that $\Gamma \equiv A : *, B : *$:

$$(\wedge\text{-}intro\text{-}sec\text{-}tt) \quad \frac{\Gamma \vdash a : A \qquad \Gamma \vdash b : B}{\Gamma \vdash ?_1 \; : \; \Pi C : *. (A \to B \to C) \to C}$$

$$(\wedge\text{-}elim\text{-}left\text{-}sec\text{-}tt) \quad \frac{\Gamma \vdash c \; : \; \Pi C : *. (A \to B \to C) \to C}{\Gamma \vdash ?_2 \; : \; A}$$

$$(\wedge\text{-}elim\text{-}right\text{-}sec\text{-}tt) \quad \frac{\Gamma \vdash d \; : \; \Pi C : *. (A \to B \to C) \to C}{\Gamma \vdash ?_3 \; : \; B}$$

As an example, we give a derivation corresponding to the $(\wedge\text{-}intro\text{-}sec)$-rule. So we assume that a is a term of type A and b is a term of type B, both in context Γ. Then we have to find, in the same context, a term $?_1$ having as type the second order conjunction of A and B, viz. $\Pi C : *.\,(A \to B \to C) \to C$.

In order to comply with the λC-format, we take *variables* x and y instead of the 'expressions' a and b, and add $x : A$ and $y : B$ to the context. So our start situation is:

(a) $\boxed{A : *}$

(b) $\boxed{B : *}$

(c) $\boxed{x : A}$

(d) $\boxed{y : B}$

            $\vdots$

(n) $?_1 \;:\; \Pi C : *.\,(A \to B \to C) \to C$

Filling the gap in this derivation is standard. We take the rules of the most powerful system, λC (although $\lambda 2$ would suffice). As in Chapters 4 and 5, we give a shortened derivation; in particular: we ignore the second **premiss** of the (*abst*)-rule.

(a) $\boxed{A : *}$

(b) $\boxed{B : *}$

(c) $\boxed{x : A}$

(d) $\boxed{y : B}$

(e) $\boxed{C : *}$

(f) $\boxed{z : A \to B \to C}$

(1) $z\,x : B \to C$ (*appl*) on (f) and (c)

(2) $z\,x\,y : C$ (*appl*) on (1) and (d)

(3) $\lambda z : A \to B \to C.\,z\,x\,y \;:$

                $(A \to B \to C) \to C$ (*abst*) on (2)

(4) $\lambda C : *.\,\lambda z : A \to B \to C.\,z\,x\,y \;:$

             $\Pi C : *.\,(A \to B \to C) \to C$ (*abst*) on (3)

Find yourself derivations that correspond to the two second order $\wedge$-*elim* rules (Exercise 7.4). Our final conclusion is that all these rules are already derivable in λC, and don't need to be added.

II. *Disjunction*

There is a similar second order encoding of the disjunction $A \vee B$:

$A \vee B \;\equiv\; \Pi C : *.\, (A \rightarrow C) \rightarrow (B \rightarrow C) \rightarrow C\,.$

(The usual first order encoding of disjunction is $A \vee B \equiv \neg A \rightarrow B$. But, as with the conjunction, this only works in classical logic.)

Similarly arguing as with conjunction, above, we may rephrase the right-hand expression $\Pi C : *.\, (A \rightarrow C) \rightarrow (B \rightarrow C) \rightarrow C$ as:

(ii) For all C, $(A \rightarrow C$ implies that $(B \rightarrow C$ implies $C))$.

We have to convince ourselves that *(ii)* encapsulates the same meaning as $A \vee B$. We first do this by giving an intuitive argument, as with conjunction. Think of A, B and C as propositions, again. An interpretation of *(ii)* is that for all propositions C:

'if A implies C and also B implies C, then C holds on its own'.

Logically, this means the same as

'if $(A$ *or* $B)$ implies C, then C holds'.

Clearly, the 'condition' in the expression before the comma is redundant, again. So A *or* B must hold.

The reasoning the other way round is more complicated. Assume that A *or* B holds. We may see this as the fact that there are two *cases*, one expressed as A, and the other as B. If we know now that for an arbitrary C, in *case* A we have C (i.e. $A \Rightarrow C$) and also in *case* B we have C (i.e. $B \Rightarrow C$), then we may conclude that C holds altogether. This is essentially what *(ii)* says.

Another justification is the formal proof that the encoding corresponds to the natural deduction rules for disjunction, which are:

$(\vee\text{-}intro\text{-}left) \quad \dfrac{A}{A \vee B}$

$(\vee\text{-}intro\text{-}right) \quad \dfrac{B}{A \vee B}$

$(\vee\text{-}elim) \quad \dfrac{A \vee B \quad A \Rightarrow C \quad B \Rightarrow C}{C}$

We shortly comment on these natural deduction rules.

The *intro*-rules speak for themselves: if A alone holds already, then also $A \vee B$ holds; and similarly for B.

For the *elim*-rule for $\vee$, we refer to our discussion above, in particular the part about 'case distinction'.

The type-theoretic second order versions of the $\vee$-rules look as follows.

$$(\vee\text{-}intro\text{-}left\text{-}sec) \quad \frac{A}{\Pi C : *. \ (A \to C) \to (B \to C) \to C}$$

$$(\vee\text{-}intro\text{-}right\text{-}sec) \quad \frac{B}{\Pi C : *. \ (A \to C) \to (B \to C) \to C}$$

$$(\vee\text{-}elim\text{-}sec) \quad \frac{\Pi D : *. \ (A \to D) \to (B \to D) \to D \quad A \to C \quad B \to C}{C}$$

(We use the bound variable D in the last-mentioned Π-expression in order to avoid confusion with the free C's occurring in the rest of the rule.)

Formal derivations in λC showing that the two second order $\vee$-*intro*-rules are covered by the encoding are left to the reader (Exercise 7.7).

Here follows a formal derivation in λC corresponding to the second order $\vee$-*elim*-rule:

(a)	$\boxed{A : *}$	
(b)	$\boxed{B : *}$	
(c)	$\boxed{C : *}$	
(d)	$\boxed{x : (\Pi D : *. \ (A \to D) \to (B \to D) \to D)}$	
(e)	$\boxed{y : A \to C}$	
(f)	$\boxed{z : B \to C}$	
(1)	$x \, C : (A \to C) \to (B \to C) \to C$	(*appl*) on (d), (c)
(2)	$x \, C \, y : (B \to C) \to C$	(*appl*) on (1), (e)
(3)	$x \, C \, y \, z : C$	(*appl*) on (2), (f)

Remark 7.2.1 *In the previous section and the present one, we have defined type-theoretic variants of negation, conjunction and disjunction by*

$\neg A \ \equiv \ A \to \bot \, ,$

$A \wedge B \ \equiv \ \Pi C : *. \ (A \to B \to C) \to C \, ,$

$A \vee B \ \equiv \ \Pi C : *. \ (A \to C) \to (B \to C) \to C \, .$

However, there are free variables (A and B) in these expressions. In order to be sure that these variables have the proper type ($*$), we could also have chosen to introduce the sole connectives as abbreviations for more 'abstract' expressions:

$\neg \ \equiv \ \lambda \alpha : *. \ (\alpha \to \bot) \, ,$

$\wedge \ \equiv \ \lambda \alpha : *. \ \lambda \beta : *. \ \Pi \gamma : *. \ (\alpha \to \beta \to \gamma) \to \gamma \, ,$

$\vee \ \equiv \ \lambda \alpha : *. \ \lambda \beta : *. \ \Pi \gamma : *. \ (\alpha \to \gamma) \to (\beta \to \gamma) \to \gamma \, .$

Starting from these alternative encodings, we can easily get the contents of the original ones by the (appl)-rule, for example:

$$\neg A \equiv (\lambda\alpha : *. (\alpha \to \bot))A \to_\beta A \to \bot .$$

(Note that $\neg A$ means here $\neg$ applied to A.)

So, these alternatives have the same expressivity, although we need more than $\lambda 2$. In fact, we need $\lambda\omega$ (cf. Figure 6.2). Check this yourself.

7.3 An example of propositional logic in λC

We are now able to 'do' propositional logic in type theory, since we have encodings for absurdity ($\bot$) and for the connectives $\Rightarrow$, $\neg$, $\wedge$ and $\vee$.

Remark 7.3.1 *Only the $\Leftrightarrow$ is missing, but this can be easily remedied by expressing it by means of the other connectives, in the usual way:*

$$A \Leftrightarrow B \equiv (A \Rightarrow B) \wedge (B \Rightarrow A).$$

In order to show how propositional logic 'works' in type theory, we give a type-theoretic proof of the following tautology:

$$(A \vee B) \Rightarrow (\neg A \Rightarrow B) .$$

In Figure 7.1 we give the full proof as a derivation in λC. Since we use the type-theoretic encodings of $\vee$, $\Rightarrow$ and $\neg$, the goal (see line (10) in the derivation) becomes to find an inhabitant of:

$$(*) \quad \underbrace{(\Pi C : *. ((A \to C) \to (B \to C) \to C))}_{A \vee B} \to \underbrace{(A \to \bot)}_{\neg A} \to B .$$

About this derivation, we note the following:

– In the above expression, we treat A and B as free variables, representing 'arbitrary' propositions. Hence, we must start our derivation in Figure 7.1 with the assumptions given in lines (a) and (b).
– So the set-up of the derivation is: in context (a) and (b), find an inhabitant of the expression above. Line (10) shows that we succeed in finding such an inhabitant.
– How has this been accomplished? Well, we assume to have an inhabitant of the left-hand side of the expression (see line (c)) and derive an inhabitant of the right-hand side (namely $(A \to \bot) \to B$), in the extended context (a), (b) and (c). Line (9) displays the desired (new) inhabitant.
– That inhabitant, in its turn, has been found by adding the left-hand side of the type $(A \to \bot) \to B$ as an assumption to the context (see line (d)) and deriving an inhabitant of the right-hand side, which is B. The last-mentioned inhabitant is given in line (8).

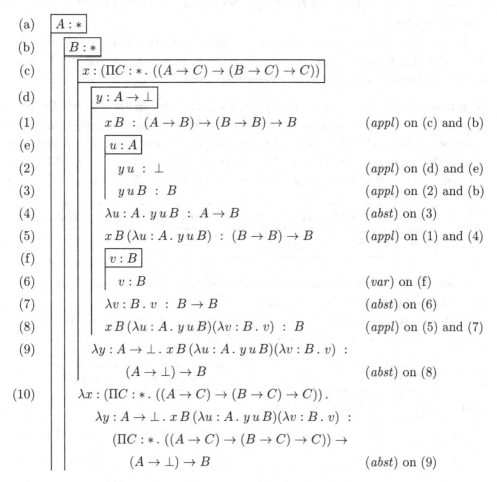

(a)	$A : *$	
(b)	$B : *$	
(c)	$x : (\Pi C : *.\,((A \to C) \to (B \to C) \to C))$	
(d)	$y : A \to \bot$	
(1)	$x\,B \; : \; (A \to B) \to (B \to B) \to B$	(*appl*) on (c) and (b)
(e)	$u : A$	
(2)	$y\,u \; : \; \bot$	(*appl*) on (d) and (e)
(3)	$y\,u\,B \; : \; B$	(*appl*) on (2) and (b)
(4)	$\lambda u : A.\,y\,u\,B \; : \; A \to B$	(*abst*) on (3)
(5)	$x\,B\,(\lambda u : A.\,y\,u\,B) \; : \; (B \to B) \to B$	(*appl*) on (1) and (4)
(f)	$v : B$	
(6)	$v : B$	(*var*) on (f)
(7)	$\lambda v : B.\,v \; : \; B \to B$	(*abst*) on (6)
(8)	$x\,B\,(\lambda u : A.\,y\,u\,B)(\lambda v : B.\,v) \; : \; B$	(*appl*) on (5) and (7)
(9)	$\lambda y : A \to \bot.\,x\,B\,(\lambda u : A.\,y\,u\,B)(\lambda v : B.\,v) \; :$	
	$\qquad (A \to \bot) \to B$	(*abst*) on (8)
(10)	$\lambda x : (\Pi C : *.\,((A \to C) \to (B \to C) \to C)).$	
	$\qquad \lambda y : A \to \bot.\,x\,B\,(\lambda u : A.\,y\,u\,B)(\lambda v : B.\,v) \; :$	
	$\qquad (\Pi C : *.\,((A \to C) \to (B \to C) \to C)) \to$	
	$\qquad (A \to \bot) \to B$	(*abst*) on (9)

Figure 7.1 A derivation of the logical tautology $(A \lor B) \Rightarrow (\neg A \Rightarrow B)$

− So the situation is now to explain why $x\,B\,(\lambda u : A.\,y\,u\,B)(\lambda v : B.\,v)$ is an inhabitant of B, in the context (a)–(d); and in particular how we found it. The flash of inspiration is to apply x to the proposition B, as has been done in line (1), which gives an inhabitant of $(A \to B) \to (B \to B) \to B$. (This ends in B, which is promising, since we look for an inhabitant of B.)

− So as soon as we have something of type $A \to B$ and something of type $B \to B$, we can use $\Rightarrow$-elimination twice, in order to obtain the desired inhabitant of B. This is exactly what we do: see lines (4) and (7) for these inhabitants.

− The rest will be obvious. Note that in line (3) we use the type-theoretic version of $(\bot\text{-}elim)$ on line (2): recall that $\bot$ is an abbreviation of $\Pi \alpha : *.\,\alpha$.

Hence, if $y\,u : \bot$, then $y\,u\,B : B$ (cf. Section 7.1). This is exactly what we put into practice.

We invite and encourage the reader to study the further details of Figure 7.1. Note that this is, again, a shortened derivation, in which the second premiss of the (*abst*)-rule has consistently been neglected.

Remark 7.3.2   *The derivation in Figure 7.1 uses the earlier described codings for expressions with $\vee$ and $\neg$. When starting from the higher order encodings described in Remark 7.2.1, we have to do a little bit more work. The translation of $A \vee B$ then is $(\lambda\alpha : *.\ \lambda\beta : *.\ \Pi\gamma : *.\ (\alpha \to \gamma) \to (\beta \to \gamma) \to \gamma)\,A\,B$, with the consequence that lines (c) and (d) in the derivation look like:*

(c′) $\boxed{x : (\lambda\alpha : *.\ \lambda\beta : *.\ \Pi\gamma : *.\ ((\alpha \to \gamma) \to (\beta \to \gamma) \to \gamma))\,A\,B}$

(d′) $\quad\boxed{y : (\lambda\alpha : *.\ (\alpha \to \bot))\,A}$

In order to continue this derivation, it is wise to execute β-reduction in each of the two types in lines (c′) and (d′).

By the conversion rule *– note that this is a good occasion to use it – we obtain the intermediate lines (i) and (ii) below:*

(c′) $\boxed{x : (\lambda\alpha : *.\ \lambda\beta : *.\ \Pi\gamma : *.\ ((\alpha \to \gamma) \to (\beta \to \gamma) \to \gamma))\,A\,B}$

(d′) $\quad\boxed{y : (\lambda\alpha : *.\ (\alpha \to \bot))\,A}$

(i) $\quad\boxed{x : (\Pi\gamma : *.\ ((A \to \gamma) \to (B \to \gamma) \to \gamma))}$ $\qquad\qquad$ (*conv*) on (c′)

(ii) $\quad\boxed{y : A \to \bot}$ $\qquad\qquad\qquad\qquad\qquad\qquad\quad$ (*conv*) on (d′)

Hence we may continue the derivation just as in lines (1) to (10) of Figure 7.1, with the only change that references to (c) and (d) should be replaced by references to (i) and (ii), respectively.

7.4 Classical logic in λC

It is worth noting that the logic we have seen until now is *constructive* logic (sometimes also referred to as *intuitionistic* logic; see van Dalen, 1994, Chapter 5). It is slightly less powerful than the usual *classical logic*. In classical logic one has the 'law of the *excluded third*' (*ET*), stating that $A \vee \neg A$ holds for any A. Also, one has the '*double negation* law' (*DN*), stating that $\neg\neg A \Rightarrow A$ holds for any A. Both ET and DN are not derivable from the rules that we have seen until now (constructive logic). For a proof of this fact, see Troelstra & van Dalen (1988), Vol. 1, p. 79.

Classical logic is what one generally wants, since this is the most commonly used kind of logic in mathematics. In order to obtain this, one has to *extend* constructive logic.

It turns out to be sufficient to add *either* ET, *or* DN. The reason is that in constructive logic plus ET we can *derive* DN. And vice versa: in constructive logic plus DN we can derive ET.

How can we *add* either ET or DN to λC? It should become a proposition which always 'holds', so it must be formalised as something which can be called upon in every derivation. The easiest way to manage this is to add it *as an assumption* in front of the context. Such an assumption can be represented in λC by means of a declaration. Let's do this, for example, for ET:

$$\boxed{i_{ET} \ : \ \Pi\alpha : * . \ \alpha \vee \neg\alpha}$$

We call this *the addition of an axiom*: we suppose that we have an *inhabitant*, i_{ET}, of the excluded-third-axiom in the right-hand side of the expression (reading: for all propositions α we have that $\alpha \vee \neg\alpha$.)

As an example, we now give the derivation corresponding to one of the two things which we claimed above: that (the type-theoretic version of) constructive logic + ET enables one to derive DN.

So we start our context with the *axiom* ET and obtain the following goal:

(a) $\boxed{i_{ET} \ : \ \Pi\alpha : * . \ \alpha \vee \neg\alpha}$

$\vdots$

(n) $\quad ? \ : \ \Pi\beta : * . \ \neg\neg\beta \rightarrow \beta$

The goal naturally brings along the following two steps:

(a) $\boxed{i_{ET} \ : \ \Pi\alpha : * . \ \alpha \vee \neg\alpha}$

(b) $\boxed{\beta : *}$

(c) $\boxed{x : \neg\neg\beta}$

$\vdots$

(l) $\quad ? \ : \ \beta$

(m) $\quad \ldots \ : \ \neg\neg\beta \rightarrow \beta$

(n) $\quad \ldots \ : \ \Pi\beta : * . \ \neg\neg\beta \rightarrow \beta$

Now we try to use (a), (b) and (c) in order to find an inhabitant of β. Line (a) appears to be a good candidate: its type is a Π-type which generalises over α of type $*$. It appears to be a good choice to *apply* i_{ET} to β, obtaining an inhabitant of $\beta \vee \neg\beta$. The latter expression is, in the type-theoretic encoding, an *abbreviation* for $\Pi\gamma : *. ((\beta \to \gamma) \to (\neg\beta \to \gamma) \to \gamma)$. So, for convenience omitting lines (m) and (n), we obtain:

(a) $\boxed{i_{ET} \; : \; \Pi\alpha : *. \alpha \vee \neg\alpha}$

(b) $\boxed{\beta : *}$

(c) $\boxed{x : \neg\neg\beta}$

(1) $i_{ET} \, \beta \; : \; \beta \vee \neg\beta$

(2) $i_{ET} \, \beta \; : \; \Pi\gamma : *. (\beta \to \gamma) \to (\neg\beta \to \gamma) \to \gamma$

$\phantom{i_{ET}}\vdots$

(l) $? \; : \; \beta$

$\phantom{i_{ET}}\vdots$

Since the type in line (2) is a Π-type, again, it appears to be a good option to apply it (again) to β. This leads to the addition of line (3):

(a) $\boxed{i_{ET} \; : \; \Pi\alpha : *. \alpha \vee \neg\alpha}$

(b) $\boxed{\beta : *}$

(c) $\boxed{x : \neg\neg\beta}$

(1) $i_{ET} \, \beta \; : \; \beta \vee \neg\beta$

(2) $i_{ET} \, \beta \; : \; \Pi\gamma : *. (\beta \to \gamma) \to (\neg\beta \to \gamma) \to \gamma$

(3) $i_{ET} \, \beta \, \beta \; : \; (\beta \to \beta) \to (\neg\beta \to \beta) \to \beta$

$\phantom{i_{ET}}\vdots$

(l) $? \; : \; \beta$

$\phantom{i_{ET}}\vdots$

What's next? Our *goal* is to obtain an inhabitant of β. Now β is also the rightmost subexpression in the type of line (3). So if we succeed in finding inhabitants of successively $\beta \to \beta$ and $\neg\beta \to \beta$, then a double use of the application rule leads from line (3) to goal (l).

The first task is easy: $\beta \to \beta$ is obviously a tautology, with an easy proof, given in line (4). (See also Figure 7.1, flag (f), and lines (6) and (7).) We fill this in, together with the (*appl*)-consequence of lines (3) and (4), stated in line (5):

(a)	$i_{ET} \; : \; \Pi\alpha : *. \; \alpha \vee \neg\alpha$
(b)	$\beta : *$
(c)	$x : \neg\neg\beta$
(1)	$i_{ET}\,\beta \; : \; \beta \vee \neg\beta$
(2)	$i_{ET}\,\beta \; : \; \Pi\gamma : *. \; (\beta \to \gamma) \to (\neg\beta \to \gamma) \to \gamma$
(3)	$i_{ET}\,\beta\,\beta \; : \; (\beta \to \beta) \to (\neg\beta \to \beta) \to \beta$
(4)	$\lambda y : \beta.\, y \; : \; \beta \to \beta$
(5)	$i_{ET}\,\beta\,\beta\,(\lambda y : \beta.\, y) \; : \; (\neg\beta \to \beta) \to \beta$
	$\vdots$
(l)	$? \; : \; \beta$
	$\vdots$

What's left is the task to find an inhabitant of $\neg\beta \to \beta$. For convenience, we isolate this part of the proof and add line (k) for the purpose mentioned. This naturally leads to assumption (d) and the new goal (j):

	$\vdots$
(c)	$x : \neg\neg\beta$
	$\vdots$
(5)	$i_{ET}\,\beta\,\beta\,(\lambda y : \beta.\, y) \; : \; (\neg\beta \to \beta) \to \beta$
(d)	$z : \neg\beta$
	$\vdots$
(j)	$? \; : \; \beta$
(k)	$\ldots \; : \; \neg\beta \to \beta$
(l)	$\ldots \; : \; \beta$
	$\vdots$

Combining assumptions (c) and (d) we obtain $\bot$, since $\neg\neg\beta$ is identical to $\neg\beta \to \bot$. And having an inhabitant of $\bot$, we have inhabitants for 'everything'. (Recall the type-theoretic version of the ($\bot$-*elim*)-rule, see Section 7.1, I.) So we have also solved the goal in line (j) and we are done (but for the filling in of a number of terms and argumentations).

This part of the proof then looks as given below. Lines (7), (8) and (9) replace goals (j), (k) and (l).

Finish the derivation yourself, including the arguments.

$\vdots$

(c) $\quad\boxed{x : \neg\neg\beta}$

$\vdots$

(5) $\quad i_{ET}\,\beta\,\beta\,(\lambda y : \beta . \, y) \; : \; (\neg\beta \to \beta) \to \beta$

(d) $\quad\boxed{z : \neg\beta}$

(6) $\qquad x\,z : \bot$

(7) $\qquad x\,z\,\beta \; : \; \beta$

(8) $\quad \lambda z : \neg\beta . \, x\,z\,\beta \; : \; \neg\beta \to \beta$

(9) $\quad i_{ET}\,\beta\,\beta\,(\lambda y : \beta . \, y)\,(\lambda z : \neg\beta . \, x\,z\,\beta) \; : \; \beta$

$\vdots$

7.5 Predicate logic in λC

Now that we have coded propositional logic (both the constructive and the classical versions), it is time to look at *predicate logic*. For this, we have to find encodings for the quantifiers $\forall$ and $\exists$. As far as $\forall$ is concerned, this has already been done in Section 5.4, part V. There we have shown that the encoding of $\forall_{x\in S}(P(x))$ as $\Pi x : S . \, Px$ is satisfactory, since it satisfies the elimination and introduction rules for $\forall$.

All that's left is the existential quantifier $\exists$. The *first order* definition of $\exists$, namely $\exists_{x\in S}(P(x)) \equiv \neg\forall_{x\in S}(\neg P(x))$, only works in classical logic. There exists a more general *second order encoding* of $\exists$ which conforms nicely with the (constructive) elimination and introduction rules for $\exists$, namely, encode

$$\exists_{x\in S}(P(x)) \quad \text{as} \quad \Pi\alpha : * . \, ((\Pi x : S . \, (P\,x \to \alpha)) \to \alpha).$$

Let's try to translate the latter expression in words, reading Π as $\forall$, and $\to$ as $\Rightarrow$:

'For all α:
    if we know that for all x in S it holds that $P\,x$ implies α,
        then α holds.'

It is not immediately clear why this statement covers the same content as the statement 'There exists an x in S with $P(x)$'. However, it is straightforward to compare the above encoding with the usual ($\exists$-*elim*)- and ($\exists$-*intro*)-rules from constructive logic, as we do next (see also van Dalen, 1994, Section 2.9).

Let's start with the elimination rule for $\exists$ as it is commonly expressed in natural deduction for first order logic. Let P be a predicate over set S, and $x \notin FV(A)$:

$$(\exists\text{-}elim) \ \frac{\exists_{x \in S} P(x) \quad \forall_{x \in S}(P(x) \Rightarrow A)}{A}$$

So this rule says:

'(**first premiss**) If there exists an x in the set S for which the predicate P holds,

(**second premiss**) and if for all x in S: *if P holds for this x, then the proposition A holds*,

(**conclusion**) then A holds altogether.'

We first give an intuitive explanation of this rule. The situation to start with is:

(1) There *is* an x with $P(x)$, and
(2) for all x we know: as soon as $P(x)$ then also A.

Then a natural reasoning is:
— we may apply (2) to 'the' x which is claimed to exist in (1);
— for this x we indeed have $P(x)$ by (1);
— hence (2) leads us to the conclusion that A holds. And this is exactly the **conclusion** in the ($\exists$-*elim*)-rule.

So this rule is intuitively acceptable.

Remark 7.5.1 *It is a general habit to apply $\exists$-elimination in a loose manner: if one knows that $\exists_{x \in S} P(x)$, one simply takes 'such an' x for which P holds, and works with 'that' x as if it has been given.*

Therefore, a mathematician tends to use the following scheme:

(1) $\exists_{x \in S} P(x)$
(2)   Let $x \in S$ be such that Px holds

(3) $\vdots$

(4) A

In mathematical texts, it is customary to simplify this scheme even more, by omitting sentence (2).

However, either of these presentations is questionable. The silent assumption about the scope of the x introduced in line (2) is that it may be used in (3), but not in (4). And when (2) is omitted, each free x in (3) can only refer to the binding variable x in (1); which clearly violates the scope of the $\exists$-symbol.

That is the reason why we consider the above (∃-elim)-rule to be the only acceptable one for a formal proof, in spite of the extra work that it requires.

Now we have to show that the type-theoretic (second order) counterpart of the (∃-*elim*)-rule is correct. So we must convince ourselves that the following rule is acceptable, for all $S : *$, $P : S \to *$ and $A : *$ with $x \notin FV(A)$:

$$(\exists\text{-}elim\text{-}sec) \quad \frac{\Pi\alpha : *.\,((\Pi x : S.\,(P\,x \to \alpha)) \to \alpha) \qquad \Pi x : S.\,(P\,x \to A)}{A}$$

A derivation to show that this rule is derivable in λC is easy and can be given right away. For the record, we spell it out:

(a) $\boxed{S : *}$

(b) $\quad\boxed{P : S \to *}$

(c) $\quad\quad\boxed{A : *}$

(d) $\quad\quad\quad\boxed{y \;:\; \Pi\alpha : *.\,((\Pi x : S.\,(P\,x \to \alpha)) \to \alpha)}$

(e) $\quad\quad\quad\quad\boxed{z \;:\; \Pi x : S.\,(P\,x \to A)}$

(1) $\quad\quad\quad\quad y\,A \;:\; (\Pi x : S.\,(P\,x \to A)) \to A$ $\qquad$ (*appl*) on (d), (c)

(2) $\quad\quad\quad\quad y\,A\,z : A$ $\qquad$ (*appl*) on (1), (e)

Note how simple this is. This does not come as a surprise, if we look again at the (∃-*elim-sec*)-rule. Let's abbreviate $\Pi x : S.\,(P\,x \to \alpha)$ as $\varphi(\alpha)$. Then the rule expresses the following, in logical terms:

'If *(i)* for all α we have that $\varphi(\alpha) \Rightarrow \alpha$ and *(ii)* $\varphi(A)$, then *(iii)* A.'

We obtain this simply by first applying *(i)* to A by means of (∀-*elim*), which gives $\varphi(A) \Rightarrow A$ (see also line (1)), and next combining this with *(ii)*, applying (⇒-*elim*). The result is *(iii)* (see line (2)).

Remark 7.5.2 *In the derivation it is essential that $x \notin FV(A)$, because otherwise the application in line (2) would be illegal (see Exercise 7.11).*

On closer inspection, we see that the second order encoding of ∃ is exactly what the (∃-*elim*)-rule expresses, namely that the *existence* of an $x \in S$ with $P(x)$ brings along that 'if $\forall_{x \in S}(P(x) \Rightarrow A)$, then A', or in type-theoretic terms: $(\Pi x : S.\,(P\,x \to A)) \to A$. This should hold for *all* A, hence we obtain $\Pi\alpha : *.\,((\Pi x : S.\,(P\,x \to \alpha)) \to \alpha)$ as the desired encoding.

Clearly, in all cases where we appeal to (∃-*elim*) in logic, we are permitted to use the second order encoding of ∃ in type theory. This brings our discussion of (∃-*elim*) to a conclusion.

How about the *introduction* rule for $\exists$? Its usual version in first order natural deduction is the following, where, as before, P is a predicate over set S; moreover, a is some fixed element (see again van Dalen, 1994, Section 2.9):

$$(\exists\text{-}intro) \quad \frac{a \in S \quad P(a)}{\exists_{x \in S}(P(x))}$$

In words:

'(first premiss) If a certain object a is element of the set S,

(second premiss) and the predicate P holds for this a,

(conclusion) then $\exists_{x \in S}(P(x))$ holds.'

This reasoning scheme is obvious and thus also intuitively acceptable: if we already *know* (first and second premisses) that a certain a in S has 'property' P, then (conclusion) there *exists* some x in S with property P (namely $x = a$).

In order to show that the type-theoretic counterpart of this ($\exists$-*intro*)-rule is correct as well, we have to convince ourselves that the following second order rule is derivable, for all $S : *$ and $P : S \to *$:

$$(\exists\text{-}intro\text{-}sec) \quad \frac{a : S \qquad P\,a}{\Pi\alpha : * . \,((\Pi x : S . \,(P\,x \to \alpha)) \to \alpha)}$$

A derivation of this can start as follows, where we code the arbitrary a as a *variable* in flag (c):

(a) $\boxed{S : *}$

(b) $\boxed{P : S \to *}$

(c) $\boxed{a : S}$

(d) $\boxed{u : P\,a}$

            $\vdots$

(n)   ? : $\Pi\alpha : * . \,((\Pi x : S . \,(P\,x \to \alpha)) \to \alpha)$

Completion of this derivation is straightforward and easy. We leave it as an exercise to the reader to derive that the following proof object is correct:

$$? \; \equiv \; \lambda\alpha : * . \, \lambda v : (\Pi x : S . \,(P\,x \to \alpha)) . \, v\,a\,u.$$

Remark 7.5.3 *We have defined a type-theoretic equivalent of the logical* $\exists$-*expression by taking:*

$$\exists_{x \in S}(P(x)) \; \equiv \; \Pi\alpha : * . \,((\Pi x : S . \,(P\,x \to \alpha)) \to \alpha).$$

As in Remark 7.2.1, we note that there are free variables in this expression, viz. S and P. Again, we could also abstract from these variables, in order to incorporate their types. Then we get the alternative representation

$$\exists \equiv \lambda S : *.\ \lambda P : S \to *.\ \Pi \alpha : *.\ ((\Pi x : S.\ (P\,x \to \alpha)) \to \alpha).$$

When using this alternative, we obtain, for given S and P of the proper types:

$$\exists\,S\,P \to_\beta \Pi \alpha : *.\ ((\Pi x : S.\ (P\,x \to \alpha)) \to \alpha),$$

so $\exists\,S\,P$ 'is' the type-theoretic encoding of $\exists_{x \in S}(P(x))$.

Check yourself that for $\Pi \alpha : *.\ ((\Pi x : S.\ (P\,x \to \alpha)) \to \alpha)$, having type $*$, we need (at least) $\lambda P2$ (see Figure 6.3). For the alternative $\exists$ described here, however, we need λC, since its type is $\Pi S : *.\ (S \to *) \to *$.

7.6 An example of predicate logic in λC

In order to demonstrate how the codings of $\forall$ and $\exists$ in λC work, we give a type-theoretic derivation of the following proposition:

$$\neg\exists_{x \in S}(P(x)) \ \Rightarrow\ \forall_{y \in S}(\neg P(y)).$$

In second order λC-encoding this becomes:

$$((\Pi \alpha : *.\ (\Pi x : S.\ (P\,x \to \alpha)) \to \alpha) \to \perp) \ \to\ \Pi y : S.\ (P\,y \to \perp).$$

In order to keep close to the formulation in logic, we write $\neg A$ for $A \to \perp$ and $A \Rightarrow B$ for $A \to B$ (see Section 7.1).

In accordance with the previous section, we also employ the $\forall$- and $\exists$-symbols, which are more familiar: we write, if appropriate,

$\forall x : S.\ P\,x$ for $\Pi x : S.\ P\,x$, and

$\exists x : S.\ P\,x$ for $\Pi \alpha : *.\ ((\Pi x : S.\ (P\,x \to \alpha)) \to \alpha)$.

With all this notational 'sugaring', our encoding in λC becomes very similar to the usual representation in logic, namely: $\neg(\exists x : S.\ P\,x) \ \Rightarrow\ \forall y : S.\ \neg(P\,y)$.

In order to give a proof of this λC-proposition, we try to find an inhabitant. Raising flags for the free variables S and P, we obtain the following start situation:

(a) $\boxed{S : *}$

(b) $\boxed{P : S \to *}$

            $\vdots$

(n) $?\ :\ \neg(\exists x : S.\ P\,x) \ \Rightarrow\ \forall y : S.\ \neg(P\,y)$

The goal type is in fact an $\twoheadrightarrow$-expression, i.e. an abbreviated Π-type. Its right-hand side $\forall y : S . \neg (P\,y)$ is a Π-expression in disguise, with an 'embedded' $\twoheadrightarrow$-expression, namely $P\,y \to \bot$. Hence, we can try to obtain line (n) by three applications of the $(abst)$-rule. See flags (c), (d) and (e) below, and the new goals (m), (l) and (k).

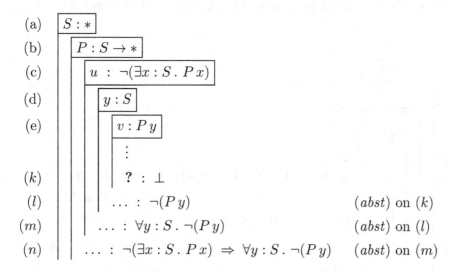

(a)	$S : *$	
(b)	$P : S \to *$	
(c)	$u : \neg(\exists x : S . P\,x)$	
(d)	$y : S$	
(e)	$v : P\,y$	
	$\vdots$	
(k)	$? : \bot$	
(l)	$\ldots : \neg(P\,y)$	$(abst)$ on (k)
(m)	$\ldots : \forall y : S . \neg(P\,y)$	$(abst)$ on (l)
(n)	$\ldots : \neg(\exists x : S . P\,x) \Rightarrow \forall y : S . \neg(P\,y)$	$(abst)$ on (m)

How can we obtain an inhabitant of $\bot$ in line (k)? A promising idea is to get it via flag (c), by finding an inhabitant of $\exists x : S . P\,x$. If we succeed, then we can apply u to this in order to get an expression of type $\bot$.

See step (j) in the incomplete derivation below.

(a)	$S : *$	
(b)	$P : S \to *$	
(c)	$u : \neg(\exists x : S . P\,x)$	
(d)	$y : S$	
(e)	$v : P\,y$	
	$\vdots$	
(j)	$? : \exists x : S . P\,x$	
(k)	$\ldots : \bot$	$(appl)$ on (c) and (j)
(l)	$\ldots : \neg(P\,y)$	$(abst)$ on (k)
(m)	$\ldots : \forall y : S . \neg(P\,y)$	$(abst)$ on (l)
(n)	$\ldots : \neg(\exists x : S . P\,x) \Rightarrow \forall y : S . \neg(P\,y)$	$(abst)$ on (m)

It is not hard to find a solution to **?** in line (j), since the second order $\exists$-introduction rule tells us that it suffices to find an a in S such that $P\,a$ holds. And such an a is obviously at hand, namely y: see flags (d) and (e).

So the derivation going with $(\exists\text{-}intro\text{-}sec)$ – see Section 7.5 – gives the answer what to take for **?** in line (j).

The rest of the derivation is no more than accurate administration:

(a) $\quad \boxed{S : *}$

(b) $\qquad \boxed{P : S \to *}$

(c) $\qquad\quad \boxed{u \;:\; \neg(\exists x : S \,.\, P\,x)}$

(d) $\qquad\qquad \boxed{y : S}$

(e) $\qquad\qquad\quad \boxed{v : P\,y}$

(1) $\qquad\qquad\qquad \lambda\alpha : * .\, \lambda w : (\Pi x : S \,.\, (P\,x \to \alpha)) \,.\, w\,y\,v \;:\; \exists x : S \,.\, P\,x$

$\qquad\qquad\qquad\qquad\qquad\qquad\qquad\qquad\qquad\qquad$ (see Section 7.5)

(2) $\qquad\qquad\qquad u\,(\lambda\alpha : * .\, \lambda w : (\Pi x : S \,.\, (P\,x \to \alpha)) \,.\, w\,y\,v) \;:\; \bot$

$\qquad\qquad\qquad\qquad\qquad\qquad\qquad\qquad\qquad$ ($appl$) on (c) and (1)

(3) $\qquad\qquad\qquad \ldots \;:\; \neg(P\,y)$ $\qquad\qquad\qquad$ ($abst$) on (2)

(4) $\qquad\qquad\quad\; \ldots \;:\; \forall y : S \,.\, \neg(P\,y)$ $\qquad\qquad$ ($abst$) on (3)

(5) $\qquad\qquad\; \ldots \;:\; \neg(\exists x : S \,.\, P\,x) \Rightarrow \forall y : S \,.\, \neg(P\,y)$ $\quad$ ($abst$) on (4)

We omitted the proof terms in lines (3) to (5), since they become longer and longer. For the record, we spell out the proof term for line (5):

$$\lambda u \;:\; \neg(\exists x : S \,.\, P\,x) \,.\, \lambda y : S \,.\, \lambda v : P\,y \,.$$
$$u\,(\lambda\alpha : * .\, \lambda w : (\Pi x : S \,.\, (P\,x \to \alpha)) \,.\, w\,y\,v) \,.$$

Without the λC-definitions of $\exists$ and $\neg$, this expression would be even longer. Since an expression of this length already occurs in the five-line example above, we can easily imagine that we soon get unintelligible long expressions in a derivation of some weight (see for example Exercise 7.14). Moreover, many (sub-)expressions become repeated in the proof terms, as one can see already in the proof objects of lines (1) and (2). These repetitions, together with the length of the expressions, hinder the understanding of what's happening. Clearly, we have to do something about this, in order to keep our derivations readable.

Another observation is that the natural deduction rules of logic are not visible in derivations represented as above, as we see for example in line (1), which is based on a 'hidden' $\exists$-introduction.

Hence, in spite of the transparency we achieved by using the flag format, we need more means to maintain the overview in complex derivations, both in logic and mathematics. In the following chapters it will turn out that a structured *definition system* will help us considerably in getting a grip on derivations.

Note that our investigations in the present chapter already hinted at such an expedient: on several occasions we used *abbreviations* for type-theoretic terms, such as $\bot$ for $\Pi\alpha : *.\ \alpha$ and $A \wedge B$ for $\Pi C : *.\ (A \to B \to C) \to C$. The usage of the $\forall$- and $\exists$-quantifiers in the example above also helped a lot.

7.7 Conclusions

In this chapter we have investigated the possibilities for encoding basic logical notions in type theory. When dealing with mathematical matters, for example when inventing, writing or reading proofs, one often uses a standard logical framework, which in more abstract form has become known as *natural deduction*. Most mathematicians apply this logical framework intuitively, since they have been acquainted with it since their first steps in mathematics.

We have succeeded in finding type-theoretic equivalents for the notions *absurdity* and *negation* and their relation with natural deduction. Next, we have introduced (second order) encodings of *conjunction* and *disjunction*. Since *implication* has already been covered in type theory, we have obtained a type-theoretic version of propositional logic (*biimplication* can be treated easily by the usual definition).

This immediately delivers an encoding of *constructive* propositional logic. In order to get *classical* logic, one has to add either ET (excluded third) or DN (double negation). This can be done with an extra assumption at the front end of the context, acting as an *axiom*.

We have also introduced the (second order) 'constructive' encoding of $\exists$ (the encoding of $\forall$ was given in an earlier chapter). So also predicate logic (either constructive or classical) is covered by type theory.

Moreover, all encodings appear to be intuitively acceptable on the one hand, and precisely correspond to the usual logical introduction and elimination rules, on the other hand. With a number of examples it has become clear how logical derivations in type theory 'work'.

We also experienced that proof terms in more complex derivations may grow to an undesirable length, making it hard to keep the derivations within reasonable bounds. This interferes with understanding and ease of survey. In following chapters, however, we shall solve these problems by an adequate usage of *definitions*.

We have showed several times how we can mimic the logical proof that a certain expression is a tautology, by giving a term of the corresponding type and a derivation that this term is of the right type. Of course, proofs in logic resemble their type-theoretic counterparts (the proof terms) to a great extent. In both cases there is an underlying derivation system which gives justifications for all the steps in the proof. This means that both a logical proof system and the here-developed type-theoretic proof system can be fully automatised, which means that the verifying check for such a proof can be left to a machine (e.g. a computer).

Advantages of the type-theoretic encodings over the usual manner, based on natural deduction, to formalise logical reasoning, are:

— Since type theory uses *inhabitants* of propositions as 'witnesses' of their validity, we are forced to give a *complete* justification of the logical facts which we are proving. In ordinary logic, the precise justifications are often not expressed at all, or only *on the meta-level*, e.g. by adding a phrase such as: 'by $\Rightarrow$-elimination'. In type theory – due to the derivation rules which use *statements* of the form $M : A$ instead of solely the *proposition* A – such justifications (the M's) are *on the object level*: one is obliged to provide such M's as inhabitants, which are type-theoretic terms (having the proper type A).

— This makes it also easy to build a *computer program* for checking logical proofs: all ingredients of reasonings are well-described and precisely formulated in type theory. Leaving gaps and 'hand waving' are not permitted when conforming to the type-theoretic rules of λC.

— One sometimes expresses this powerful property of type theory as: *proof checking = type checking*.

— By the use of type theory, it becomes feasible to extend logic *in a uniform manner* to 'full' mathematics: the same principles holding for expressing logic can be used to express mathematics in a formal way. Type theory is much more general than logic alone: one can not only represent logical notions, but also all kinds of *mathematical* notions. We give an idea of how this works in the following chapters, in particular Chapters 12 to 15.

Hence, also for wider applications in the field of mathematics, the use of type theory can be advantageous, when we think of the following features:

— Checking of mathematical theorems and proofs, or even complete theories, e.g. by the aid of a computer program.

— Helping mathematicians in filling in details in their mathematical inventions, or in developing new mathematics. This is called *proof assistance*. Computer programs designed for these purposes are called *proof assistants*. They are particularly useful in very complicated proving situations, or in the case where a proof consists of a great amount of different simple cases (when a human easily loses concentration, contrary to a computer).

Of course, there are also *disadvantages* of using type theory for logic: things become more complicated; every detail has to be spelled out in order to comply with the type-theoretic rules. This makes derivations harder to read. Reasonings in logic are usually easier to understand than their type-theoretic counterparts. So for *humans* desiring only to understand what's happening – in particular *students* – it may be disputable whether logic in type theory is preferable over 'old-time' logical systems. But type theory may certainly help to deepen understanding.

7.8 Further reading

The definition of the connectives $\vee$, $\wedge$ and $\exists$ in terms of $\Rightarrow$ and $\forall$ in second order logic is well-known from the literature and can be found e.g. in Troelstra & van Dalen, 1988, or in van Dalen, 1994 (Theorem 4.5). In Sections 1.4, 1.6, 2.8 and 2.9 of the latter book one can also find the first order natural deduction rules for the logical connectives, as we use them in this chapter. The book is a rich and useful text on mathematical logic in general.

The interesting aspect of the second order definitions is that they work in a constructive logic, so where we don't have the double negation law (or excluded middle). In the presence of the double negation axiom, one can also define $\vee$, $\wedge$ and $\exists$ in terms of $\Rightarrow$, $\neg$ and $\forall$ in the usual classical way: $A \vee B := \neg A \Rightarrow B$, $A \wedge B := \neg(\neg A \vee \neg B)$ and $\exists x . P(x) := \neg \forall x . \neg P(x)$.

Several systems for formal logic were devised in the beginning of the twentieth century. The various systems can be categorised as:

(1) *natural deduction systems*,
(2) *sequent calculi*,
(3) *axiomatic systems* (also called *Hilbert style systems*).

– The *natural deduction* systems were developed by G. Gentzen, and independently by S. Jaśkowski, to capture the natural way that mathematicians and logicians reason and to give this a formal foundation (Gentzen, 1934/5; Jaśkowski, 1934). (More about the various systems of natural deduction, their history and their use in textbooks, can be found in Pelletier, 1999.)

– In order to study his system of natural deduction, Gentzen introduced *sequent calculus*, which is much more explicit and in which one has more control over the forms of the derivations.

– *Hilbert style* systems usually have a different aim, namely to enable theoretical investigations without being bothered by an abundance of rules.

In natural deduction, a judgement is of the shape:

$$A_1, \ldots, A_n \vdash B,$$

where the A_i are seen as *hypotheses* and B as the *conclusion*. One may read this as: from A_1 to A_n we can derive B. The derivation rules say for each connective how to *introduce* it and how to *eliminate* it. This can clearly be observed from the rules for the various connectives that we have introduced in the present chapter.

In sequent calculus, a judgement is of the shape:

$$A_1, \ldots, A_n \vdash B_1, \ldots, B_k,$$

which can intuitively be read as $A_1 \wedge \ldots \wedge A_n \vdash B_1 \vee \ldots \vee B_k$, or otherwise said: (at least) one of the B_j follows from the conjunction of the A_i. The derivation rules say for each connective how to introduce it *on the left* and how to introduce it *on the right*. This gives the rules of sequent calculus a nice symmetry.

For example, here are the classical rules for conjunction and disjunction, where we abbreviate $A_1, \ldots, A_n$ to $\overline{A}$ and $B_1, \ldots, B_k$ to $\overline{B}$. Note the crosswise duality between the $\wedge$- and $\vee$-rules.

$$\frac{\overline{A} \vdash C, \overline{B} \quad \overline{A} \vdash D, \overline{B}}{\overline{A} \vdash C \wedge D, \overline{B}} \qquad \frac{\overline{A}, C, D \vdash \overline{B}}{\overline{A}, C \wedge D \vdash \overline{B}}$$

$$\frac{\overline{A} \vdash C, D, \overline{B}}{\overline{A} \vdash C \vee D, \overline{B}} \qquad \frac{\overline{A}, C \vdash \overline{B} \quad \overline{A}, D \vdash \overline{B}}{\overline{A}, C \vee D \vdash \overline{B}}$$

The rules for implication are as follows:

$$\frac{\overline{A}, C \vdash D, \overline{B}}{\overline{A} \vdash C \Rightarrow D, \overline{B}} \qquad \frac{\overline{A}, D \vdash \overline{B} \quad \overline{A} \vdash C, \overline{B}}{\overline{A}, C \Rightarrow D \vdash \overline{B}}$$

The derivation rules of sequent calculus are not devised for being 'natural', but for being able to prove properties about the system. Gentzen did this successfully, for example by proving various *consistency* results for logic using sequent calculus. It can be shown that the derivable judgements of sequent calculus and natural deduction are the same.

Another way to formalise the notion of logical derivation is via Hilbert systems, where one trades derivation rules for axioms. The idea is to introduce a number of *axiom schemes* and have only few derivation rules. The simplest instance is minimal proposition logic, which has no more than two axiom schemes:

$$A \Rightarrow (B \Rightarrow A) \quad \text{and} \quad (A \Rightarrow (B \Rightarrow C)) \Rightarrow ((A \Rightarrow B) \Rightarrow (A \Rightarrow C)),$$

where A, B and C can be instantiated with any formula; and one derivation rule, *modus ponens*:

$$\frac{A \Rightarrow B \quad A}{B}$$

However, the axiomatic method is quite unnatural to make formal derivations in. Natural deduction is the system that corresponds closest to the 'usual way of reasoning' in mathematics, so therefore we have adopted this to formalise reasoning. In fact, type theory can be seen as a more formal treatment of natural deduction, because now the derivations themselves (the proofs) are given a term representation.

The flag-style format for natural deduction was introduced by Jaśkowski (1934). Later it was further studied and popularised by F. Fitch (see Fitch, 1952) and it is therefore also often referred to as 'Fitch style natural deduction'. A practical introduction, especially for beginning students of mathematics or computer science that want to learn to use the rules, is by Nederpelt & Kamareddine (2011).

In flag-style natural deduction, a derivation is not a tree but a linear construction, where the scope of variables and hypotheses is explicitly delimited by flags. Flag-style natural deduction is not fundamentally different from tree style – also called Gentzen style. Geuvers & Nederpelt (2004) show how to translate them to each other and how to translate a proof term to a tree-style derivation or a flag-style derivation.

Natural deduction has been studied extensively by D. Prawitz (Prawitz, 1965), especially in terms of the structure of the proofs. This is the field of proof theory, which was originally devoted to studying the structure and properties of 'derivation trees', but due to the formulas-as-types/proof-as-terms analogy, this is now also very much a study of the structure and properties of (proof) terms in type theory. The β-reduction rule on terms has an interesting analogy in derivations as 'cut elimination', which makes the study of normalisation and confluence of reduction also relevant for proof theory. Similar reductions (either on the derivation level or on the term level) can be introduced for the other connectives $\wedge$, $\vee$ and the quantifier $\exists$. We refer to Girard *et al.* (1989) or Prawitz (1965) for details.

The already mentioned system Coq (Bertot & Castéran, 2004; Coq Development Team, 2012) is a proof assistant based on type theory. Originally it was based on the system λC and then the way to do logic in Coq was exactly what we describe in the present chapter. Nowadays, however, Coq also has inductive types, and the connectives are defined inductively. In a computer system like Coq, a user does not write the complete proof terms, but constructs them interactively with the system via so-called 'tactics'. This relieves the user from some of the problems that we have encountered in this chapter, where proof terms easily become very large: the Coq system doesn't show the proof terms to the user (but of course they are there!). We note, however, that the introduction of formal *definitions*, as we employ later in the present book, overcomes most of the mentioned inconveniences.

Exercises

7.1   Verify that each of the following expressions is a tautology in constructive logic, (1) by giving a proof in natural deduction, and (2) by giving a corresponding derivation in λC.

     (For the natural deduction rules concerning $\Rightarrow$, $\bot$ and $\neg$, see Section 7.1.)

     You may employ the flag style for the derivations, as in the examples given in the present chapter.

     (a) $B \Rightarrow (A \Rightarrow B)$,

     (b) $\neg A \Rightarrow (A \Rightarrow B)$,

     (c) $(A \Rightarrow \neg B) \Rightarrow ((A \Rightarrow B) \Rightarrow \neg A)$,

     (d) $\neg(A \Rightarrow B) \Rightarrow \neg B$ (hint: use part (a)).

7.2   (a) Formulate the double negation law (DN) as an axiom in λC.

     (b) Verify that the following expression is a tautology in classical logic, by giving a corresponding flag-style derivation in λC (use DN): $(\neg A \Rightarrow A) \Rightarrow A$.

7.3   Give λC-derivations proving that the following expressions are tautologies in classical logic (so you may use DN or ET):

     (a) $(A \Rightarrow B) \Rightarrow (\neg B \Rightarrow \neg A)$,

     (b) $(\neg B \Rightarrow \neg A) \Rightarrow (A \Rightarrow B)$.

7.4   Give λC-derivations to show that the following natural deduction rules are derivable in λC (cf. Section 7.2, I):

     (a) $(\wedge\text{-}elim\text{-}left\text{-}sec)$,

     (b) $(\wedge\text{-}elim\text{-}right\text{-}sec)$.

7.5   As Exercise 7.2 (b):

     (a) $\neg(A \Rightarrow B) \Rightarrow A$ (hint: use Exercise 7.1 (b)),

     (b) $\neg(A \Rightarrow B) \Rightarrow (A \wedge \neg B)$ (hint: use Exercise 7.1 (d)).

7.6   Verify that each of the following expressions is a tautology in constructive logic, by giving a ('second order') flag-style derivation in λC. Use Exercise 7.4 and Section 7.2, I.

     (a) $\neg A \Rightarrow \neg(A \wedge B)$,

     (b) $\neg(A \wedge \neg A)$,

(c) $\neg(A \wedge B) \Rightarrow (A \Rightarrow \neg B)$.

7.7 Give λC-derivations to show that the following natural deduction rules are derivable in λC:

(a) ($\vee$-*intro-left-sec*),
(b) ($\vee$-*intro-right-sec*).

7.8 Give λC-derivations verifying the following tautologies of constructive logic (hint: use Exercise 7.7 and Section 7.2):

(a) $(A \vee B) \Rightarrow (B \vee A)$,
(b) $\neg(A \vee B) \Rightarrow (\neg A \wedge \neg B)$,
(c) $(\neg A \wedge \neg B) \Rightarrow \neg(A \vee B)$.

7.9 Verify that each of the following expressions is a tautology in constructive logic, (1) by giving a proof in first order natural deduction, and (2) by giving a flag-style derivation in λC:

(a) $\forall_{x \in S}(\neg P(x) \Rightarrow (P(x) \Rightarrow (Q(x) \wedge R(x))))$,
(b) $\forall_{x \in S}(P(x)) \Rightarrow \forall_{y \in S}(P(y) \vee Q(y))$.

7.10 As Exercise 7.9:

$$\forall_{x \in S}(P(x) \Rightarrow Q(x)) \Rightarrow$$
$$\forall_{y \in S}(P(y) \Rightarrow R(y)) \Rightarrow \forall_{z \in S}(P(z) \Rightarrow (Q(z) \wedge R(z))).$$

7.11 Let $S : *$ and $P, Q : S \to *$. Let $y : \Pi \alpha : *.\ ((\Pi x : S.\ (P\,x \to \alpha)) \to \alpha)$, $z : \Pi x : S.\ (P\,x \to Q\,x)$ and $x : S$.

(a) Find a correct type for $y(Q\,x)$.
(b) Why is the application $y(Q\,x)z$ incorrect?
(c) Check that this results corresponds with Remark 7.5.2.

7.12 (a) Complete the derivation given in Section 7.5 that shows that the natural deduction rule ($\exists$-*intro-sec*) is derivable in λC.

(b) Give a flag-style λC-derivation verifying the following tautology of classical logic:

$$\neg \exists_{x \in S}(\neg P(x)) \Rightarrow \forall_{y \in S}(P(y)).$$

(Hint: use part (a) and DN.)

7.13 Verify that the following expression is a tautology in constructive logic, by giving a flag-style derivation in λC:

$$\exists_{x \in S}(P(x)) \Rightarrow (\forall_{y \in S}(P(y) \Rightarrow Q(y)) \Rightarrow \exists_{z \in S}(Q(z))).$$

7.14 Let $\Gamma \equiv S : *,\ P : S \to *,\ Q : S \to *$.

Consider the following λC-expression:
$$M \equiv \lambda u : (\exists x : S.\ (P\,x \wedge Q\,x)).\ \lambda \alpha : *.\ \lambda v : (\Pi x : S.\ (P\,x \to \alpha)).$$
$$u\,\alpha\,(\lambda y : S.\ \lambda w : (P\,y \wedge Q\,y).\ v\,y\,(w(P\,y)\,(\lambda s : P\,y.\ \lambda t : Q\,y.\ s))).$$

(a) Find a type N such that $\Gamma \vdash M : N$.

(b) Which logical tautology is expressed by N and proved by M?

(c) Give a derivation of $\Gamma \vdash M : N$.

8

Definitions

8.1 The nature of definitions

In the 'real world' of logical and mathematical texts, *definitions* are indispensable. This is particularly the case when the amount of 'knowledge' begins to grow.

Therefore we aim at an extension of λC with definitions. In the present chapter we start with an overview of what definitions are and how they are used. Gradually, we shall transform the definitions to a more formal format, in order to be able to incorporate them in λC. The derivation system that we eventually obtain when extending λC with definitions, we call λD, to be described in Chapter 10. A simpler precursor shall be named λD_0; see Chapter 9. In the following sections we describe and discuss the essential features of definitions, and how they can be formalised.

We first ask ourselves: what is the *use* of a definition? The main reason for introducing a definition is to *denote and highlight a useful concept.* Both logic and mathematics are based on certain *notions*, most of which are composed from other ones. It is very convenient to single out the noteworthy notions by giving them *names*.

We start with a number of examples of definitions as they occur in mathematics books.

Examples 8.1.1 (1) 'A *rectangle* is a quadrilateral with four right angles.'

Here the notion that we want to single out is 'a quadrilateral with four right angles'. We give it the name 'rectangle'. Note that the definition makes use of other, 'older' names of notions, such as 'quadrilateral' and 'right angle'. Each of these names has been established in earlier definitions.

(2) 'A function f from $\mathbb{R}$ to $\mathbb{R}$ is called *increasing* if, for all $x, y \in \mathbb{R}$, $x < y$ implies $f(x) < f(y)$.'

This definition says that the name 'increasing' may be used for a function $f : \mathbb{R} \to \mathbb{R}$, when it has the property described.

(3) 'We say that a relation R on a set S is *total*, if for every two elements x and y of S, either x is related to y, or y to x, or both.'

This is a definition of the notion 'totality'. Obviously, we need to have some set S and some relation R on S, before we can decide whether R is total on S. Note that S comes first: we need it for R (a relation on S).

The (new) names introduced in these definitions are words from natural language: *rectangle*, *increasing*, *total*. However, it is also possible to use newly invented 'words', or symbols, such as c or D_n; see the following examples.

Examples 8.1.2   (4) 'Define c as $\frac{1+\sqrt{5}}{2}$'.

In this definition, we use the short name c as a handy *abbreviation* of a more complex expression – thus saving space, and making it easier to speak about the object: *after* this definition, one may use the name c instead of the longer expression $\frac{1+\sqrt{5}}{2}$.

Hence it is now appropriate to say: 'It is easy to verify that $c^2 - c = 1$.'

(5) 'Let n be a natural number > 0. Then D_n is defined as the set of all positive integer divisors of n.'

Note that D *depends on* n: we need an $n > 0$ in order to determine what D_n is. So we have that $D_1 = \{1\}$, $D_2 = \{1, 2\}$, $D_3 = \{1, 3\}$, $D_4 = \{1, 2, 4\}$, ...

We may use this definition afterwards, e.g. by saying that: '$D_4 \cup D_6 = \{1, 2, 3, 4, 6\}$', or: 'if k is a divisor of l, then $D_k \subseteq D_l$'.

Names such as c and D_n are probably for temporary use, but not essentially different from more permanent names such as 'total', described earlier. An important feature of all kinds of newly defined names is that they enable the user to repeatedly refer to the related object or notion in a concise manner. In principle, all kinds of names are useable, from 'prime' or 'continuous' to 'F_3'' or '$K_i^{(0)}$'.

Apart from the reasons mentioned above, there is also a *practical reason* for introducing definitions: without definitions, logical or mathematical texts grow rapidly beyond reasonable bounds. This is an experimental fact, which can be verified by making a calculation for the 'worst case scenario'; it has been shown that definition-less mathematics may obtain a complexity that is considerably worse than exponential growth.

Hence, in order to do logic and mathematics in a feasible way, we *need* definitions.

We conclude that it is very convenient, and almost inevitable, to introduce and use definitions.

There is another case in which new names are presented, namely when introducing a *variable*, as in the sentences 'Let x be a real number' or 'Let f be a function from $\mathbb{R}$ to $\mathbb{R}$'. There is, however, an essential difference between such variables and defined names: variables (such as x, f) serve as names for '*arbitrary*' entities of a certain collection (real numbers, functions from $\mathbb{R}$ to $\mathbb{R}$), whereas defined names stand for *one specific* thing or notion, being described in the corresponding definition.

Remark 8.1.3 *One preferably chooses names which are easy to remember in connection with the notion concerned: a name often acts as a* mnemonic *('something to remember the notion by, short and clear'). For example, the word 'rectangle' combines the Latin word 'rectus', which means 'right' (cf. 'rectify': make right), with the word 'angle'. This may help to recall the notion.*

Another example is the word 'increasing', which clearly has mnemonic power: the graph *of an increasing function, viewed from left to right, reminds of a path with* increasing *height. The defined name 'total' originates from the observation that such a relation holds for the 'totality' of all pairs in $S \times S$: each pair is related in at least one of the two directions.*

This preference for names which are easy to remember also applies to the names used as a temporary aid. It is not a coincidence that the often used letter 'c' is also the first letter of the word 'constant', and a similar thing holds for the name 'D' as used above for a set of $\underline{d}$ivisors.

When more constants need to be defined (or more functions), then one usually varies a little bit on this habit: one uses primes or subscripts (not only c, but also c', c_1, ...) or letters in the same 'range' of the alphabet (a, b, d, ...).

8.2 Inductive and recursive definitions

In our type theory, we don't have *inductive definitions* or *inductive types* (see also Sections 5.7 and 6.5) as primitive constructions. In some very powerful type theories such as the Calculus of Inductive Constructions (*CIC*; see e.g. Bertot & Castéran, 2004) one can, for example, define the type of natural numbers as the type inductively built up from the constant 0 and the successor function (see Section 1.10). This automatically generates the induction proof principle and the possibility of defining functions by well-founded recursion.

We don't have inductive definitions, because they can be defined as predicates in higher order logic. Alternatively, they can be assumed axiomatically, as we will do for the integers in Section 14.2.

As for *recursive definitions*, the intention is to describe a certain object by means of an *algorithm*. For example, the factorial $n!$ of a natural number n can be described by means of the recursion scheme:

$fac(0) = 1,$

$fac(n + 1) = fac(n) \cdot (n + 1).$

Then we can, for example, *calculate* what the value of $fac(3)$ is:

$fac(3) = fac(2) \cdot 3 = (fac(1) \cdot 2) \cdot 3 = ((fac(0) \cdot 1) \cdot 2) \cdot 3 = 1 \cdot 1 \cdot 2 \cdot 3 = 6.$

Later in this book we will show that we can do without recursive definitions by making use of the descriptor ι, which gives a name to a uniquely existing entity (see Section 12.7). By not incorporating recursive definitions, we attain two goals:

− we keep our system relatively simple;
− we avoid the complications accompanying such recursive definitions, such as the necessity to show that each recursive definition represents a terminating algorithm with a unique answer for each input.

An obvious drawback is that, in our case, a function like *fac* is not a *program*, so it cannot be executed. As a consequence, $fac(3) = 6$ requires a *proof*.

For more examples of recursive definitions and of the way in which we embed these in our type-theoretic system, see Section 14.4 (about integer addition) and Section 14.11 (about integer multiplication).

8.3 The format of definitions

We borrow the following *standard format for definitions* from mathematics:

$a := \mathcal{E}.$

This expresses that a is defined as $\mathcal{E}$. So a is the name given to $\mathcal{E}$, which in its turn is an expression describing some notion which is worth being named or remembered.

Definition 8.3.1   (Definiendum, defined name, defined constant, definiens)
− In $a := \mathcal{E}$, the name a is called the *definiendum* (i.e. 'the thing to be defined'), also called the *defined name* or the *defined constant*.
− The expression $\mathcal{E}$ is the *definiens*: 'the thing that defines', or 'the expression that establishes what the meaning is'.

In this format we may rewrite two of the definitions given in Examples 8.1.1 and 8.1.2 as:

$rectangle :=$ quadrilateral with four right angles,

$c := \frac{1+\sqrt{5}}{2}.$

The situation is more complicated for the other examples, where we need some kind of 'setting' for the definitions:

— For a proper definition of 'increasing', we must have the disposal of *some function f from* $\mathbb{R}$ *to* $\mathbb{R}$.

— For the definition of 'total', we need a *set* and a *relation on this set*.

— For the definition of D_n, we need a positive natural number n.

It will be clear that such a 'setting', as in the previous chapters, can be formalised as a *context* for the definition in question. This can be expressed as in Figure 8.1. (We there code a relation on S as a predicate on $S \times S$.)

$\boxed{f : \mathbb{R} \to \mathbb{R}}$

$\qquad increasing(f) := \forall_{x,y \in \mathbb{R}} \, (x < y \Rightarrow f(x) < f(y))$

$\boxed{S : *}$

$\qquad \boxed{R : (S \times S) \to *}$

$\qquad\qquad total(S, R) := \forall_{x,y \in S} (R(x, y) \vee R(y, x))$

$\boxed{n : \mathbb{N}^+}$

$\qquad D(n) :=$ the set of all positive integer divisors of n

Figure 8.1 Examples: definitions in a context

As these examples show, each defined constant has been provided with a so-called *parameter list*: (f), (S, R) and (n), respectively. In these lists we collect the context variables (the subjects of the declarations) as appearing in the flags, in the original order. We say that the constant *'increasing'* depends on the *parameter* f, that *'total'* depends on the parameters S and R, and D on n.

Remark 8.3.2 *Parameter lists in definitions could as well be omitted: a parameter list can always be reconstructed by inspecting the context.*

We nevertheless choose to consistently append such a list to a defined constant, since addition of a parameter list to a definition makes it look more 'natural'.

Compare for example the following two versions of the same definition, expressing the function 'sum of two squares' in the context $x : \mathbb{R}$, $y : \mathbb{R}$:

(1) (without parameter list) $f := x^2 + y^2$;

(2) (with parameter list) $f(x, y) := x^2 + y^2$.

We suppose that many readers prefer the latter definition over the former.

In order to employ a consistent format in these matters, we also should add an empty parameter list to defined constants such as 'c' above, and 'rectangle', which do not need a context for their definition; or rather, which are defined in the *empty* context. Formally, we should write the following:

> *a rectangle*( ) := ...,
>
> $c( ) := \frac{1+\sqrt{5}}{2}$.

We will, however, often evade this obligation; see the following convention.

Notation 8.3.3 *A constant that has been defined in an empty context has an empty parameter list. It may be written without such an empty list, not only upon introduction (in its definition), but also when used later on.*

8.4 Instantiations of definitions

Obviously, definitions are not made for their own sake, but in order to be *used*. For example, we have already mentioned that the definition $c := \frac{1+\sqrt{5}}{2}$ may be used to state that $c^2 - c = 1$, which is easier to read than

$$(\tfrac{1+\sqrt{5}}{2})^2 - \tfrac{1+\sqrt{5}}{2} = 1 \,.$$

Moreover, the same c may be used over and over again, for example in the following calculation:

'Since $c^2 = c + 1$, we have that $c^3 = c^2 + c = c + 1 + c = 2c + 1$',

or in establishing that

'The n-th Fibonacci number f_n satisfies the equation $f_n = \frac{c^n - (1-c)^n}{\sqrt{5}}$.'

(Note that we repeatedly apply Notation 8.3.3 here, writing c for $c( )$.)

Matters become a bit more complex for definitions in a non-empty *context*. For example, consider the definition of 'increasing' as expressed in Examples 8.1.1 and formalised with context $f : \mathbb{R} \to \mathbb{R}$ in Figure 8.1. When one desires to *employ* that definition of 'increasing', one obviously must have a function from $\mathbb{R}$ to $\mathbb{R}$ at hand. For example, consider the following sentence:

'The function sending a real number to its third power, is increasing.'

In our format, this becomes: *increasing*$(\lambda x : \mathbb{R} . \, x^3)$.

What we see is that parameter f, occurring in *increasing*(f), has been *substituted* by the function $\lambda x : \mathbb{R} . \, x^3$. Such a substitution is called an *instantiation* (of the parameter). One says: 'f has been instantiated with $\lambda x : \mathbb{R} . \, x^3$'.

Remark 8.4.1 *Note that a parameter necessarily is a variable (namely a subject variable of the context), whereas an instantiation may be a variable or any other well-formed expression.*

Of course, an instantiation should respect typing requirements as given in the context: since f has been introduced in its context flag as having type $\mathbb{R} \to \mathbb{R}$, it must hold that also $\lambda x : \mathbb{R} . x^3 : \mathbb{R} \to \mathbb{R}$. This is clearly the case.

Another thing to note is that the context flag $f : \mathbb{R} \to \mathbb{R}$ is only needed in the definition itself; the flag contains the parameter on which the defined notion ('increasing') depends, plus information about the *type* of that notion. But as soon as we *use* the definition, by instantiating the parameter f, the flag itself has become superfluous (though its typing information is necessary for establishing the 'correctness' of the instantiation).

So we may use the expression '$increasing(\lambda x : \mathbb{R} . x^3)$' wherever we like, *without* the f-flag. But, of course, only *after* the definition has been given.

In the majority of the cases, we meet a more complex situation in which we have definitions with two or more parameters. Let's look at example (3) of Examples 8.1.1, in which the definition of $total(S, R)$ has been given, with the parameter list (S, R). In any 'instance' of the definition – that is, in any situation in which we 'use' this definition – we need:

(i) a *set* as instantiation of S, and

(ii) a *relation* as an instantiation of R; this relation obviously should concern the *instantiated* set, since S itself is no longer available.

For example, let's take for S the set $\mathbb{R}$ of the reals, and for R the relation '$\leq$' on that set $\mathbb{R}$. Then we obtain the correct instantiation

$total(\mathbb{R}, \leq)$.

This is a proposition, which does indeed hold in mathematics.

Instantiating S with $\mathbb{N}^+$, the positive naturals, and R with '$|$', the divisibility relation on $\mathbb{N}^+$, we obtain

$total(\mathbb{N}^+, |)$.

As an instantiation, this is correct, again. (Which has got nothing to do with the fact that, as a *proposition*, it is false: for example, neither $3|5$, nor $5|3$.)

Note that in all cases, the type conditions as given in the context of the definition should be respected in the instantiations of the parameter list, as pictured in the diagram below.

first flag		second flag		
S	: *	R	:	$(S \times S) \to *$
instantiation		instantiation		
$\mathbb{R}$	: *	$\leq$	:	$(\mathbb{R} \times \mathbb{R}) \to *$
$\mathbb{N}^+$	: *	$|$	:	$(\mathbb{N}^+ \times \mathbb{N}^+) \to *$

In definitions with more than two flags, these type conditions clearly have a cumulative effect. The precise effects will be described in Chapter 9.

Summarising: the *use* of a definition brings along that parameters become *instantiated*. A convenient manner is to record the instantiations as a list as well, in the same order as in the original parameter list.

The two different aspects of constants (their *introduction* and their *use*) imply that a constant has two different life stages:

(1) its 'birth', when introduced in a definition, e.g. total(S, R);
(2) its 'path of life', when used in different circumstances, with varying instantiations for the parameters, e.g. total$(\mathbb{R}, \leq)$ or total$(\mathbb{N}^+, \mid)$.

8.5 A formal format for definitions

Now that we know what definitions are and how they work, it is time to include them in our formal system. Look again at the three definitions in Figure 8.1. Each of these has the following general format:

$$\Gamma \,\triangleright\, a(x_1, \ldots, x_n) := \mathcal{E},$$

with Γ a context and a a constant with suffixed parameter list (together the definiendum), having been defined as $\mathcal{E}$ (the definiens). We introduce the symbol '$\triangleright$' here as a separator between the context and the rest.

The meaning of this expression clearly is:

In context Γ, we define $a(x_1, \ldots, x_n)$ as $\mathcal{E}$.

Since we work in a *typed* environment, it appears to be appropriate to add a *type* to the definiens, which is also a type for the definiendum. Therefore, our general format for a definition becomes:

$$\Gamma \,\triangleright\, a(x_1, \ldots, x_n) := M : N,$$

with M the definiens and N its type, acting as type of $a(x_1, \ldots, x_n)$, as well.

The parameter list $(x_1, \ldots, x_n)$ consists of the subject variables of the context (in the same order), so a definition looks like:

$$x_1 : A_1, \ldots, x_n : A_n \,\triangleright\, a(x_1, \ldots, x_n) := M : N.$$

Here n is a natural number, so it may be 0 (if Γ is the empty context). The parameter list $(x_1, \ldots, x_n)$ can directly be reconstructed from Γ. Nevertheless, as we discussed before (see Remark 8.3.2), our general attitude is to add a parameter list to every defined constant.

Below, we will often use an abbreviating notation for the general format, namely:

$$\overline{x} : \overline{A} \,\triangleright\, a(\overline{x}) := M : N.$$

We employ the following abbreviations in the meta-language:

Notation 8.5.1 *(1) We write $\overline{x}$ for the list $x_1, \ldots, x_n$ of variables.*
(2) We write $\overline{A}$ for the list $A_1, \ldots, A_n$ of expressions.
(3) We write $\overline{x} : \overline{A}$ for the context $x_1 : A_1, \ldots, x_n : A_n$.

As we are used to doing, we employ the flag format for the representation of this kind of formal definition. This not only gives a better overview, but also avoids annoying repetitions of context declarations.

As an example, we have listed a series of definitions regarding a set S and a relation R on S in Figure 8.2. The notions 'reflexive', 'antisymmetric' and 'transitive' have been formally expressed here by means of defined constants, and so is their conjunction: 'partially-ordered'. All four definitions depend on the same context, and therefore we suffice with one initial pair of context flags. Since each of the four defined notions is a proposition, they all have type $*$.

(a) $\boxed{S : *}$

(b) $\boxed{R : (S \times S) \to *}$

(1) $reflexive(S, R) := \forall_{x \in S}(R(x, x)) \ : \ *$

(2) $antisymmetric(S, R) := \forall_{x,y \in S}((R(x, y) \wedge R(y, x)) \Rightarrow x = y) \ : \ *$

(3) $transitive(S, R) := \forall_{x,y,z \in S}((R(x, y) \wedge R(y, z)) \Rightarrow R(x, z)) \ : \ *$

(4) $partially\text{-}ordered(S, R) :=$

         $reflexive(S, R) \wedge (antisymmetric(S, R) \wedge transitive(S, R)) \ : \ *$

Figure 8.2 A series of definitions

$\boxed{\textit{At the end of this book, we append an Index of definitions.}}$

There are many instances of the list (S, R) in this figure. Four of these lists, namely the ones left of the ':=' signs in lines (1) to (4), are *parameter lists*, as we discussed in Section 8.3. In these lists we collect the subjects S from flag (a) and R from flag (b).

The lists (S, R) behind *reflexive*, *antisymmetric* and *transitive* in line (4), however, are *instantiations*. To be precise: they are *identity* instantiations; that is: in all cases, S has been instantiated with S and R with R. Obviously, the present example contains *only* identity instantiations; although identity instantiations are very common, as we shall experience later, the really interesting instantiations occur when we instantiate with expressions that *differ* from the variables in the parameter list.

All variables S and R in (1) to (4), in particular the ones in the parameter lists and in the instantiations in line (4), are *bound* variables, being bound to the *binding* variables S and R in the flags (a) and (b). These binding variables are still within reach, as witnessed by the flag poles.

An important observation is that the flag notation involves an inherent 'overloading' of the binding variables S and R. In order to make this clear, we give the definitions of Figure 8.2 in the formal style as introduced just now, splitting up the context over the definition lines. But we do more: in order to be as exact as possible, we apply a strict renaming, avoiding the usage of different binding variables with the same name. Thereby, we avoid overloading.

We use different subscripts for all binding occurrences of the 'flag variables' S and R. To be ultimately clear, we also distinguish the different occurrences of the binding variables x, y and z accompanying the $\forall$-quantifiers.

This leads to the following four definitions-in-a-context in which all 'overloading' has been eliminated:

(i) $S_1 : *, \ R_1 : (S_1 \times S_1) \to * \ \triangleright$
$\quad$ *reflexive*$(S_1, R_1) :=$
$\quad\quad \forall_{x_1 \in S_1}(R_1(x_1, x_1)) \ : \ *$

(ii) $S_2 : *, \ R_2 : (S_2 \times S_2) \to * \ \triangleright$
$\quad$ *antisymmetric*$(S_2, R_2) :=$
$\quad\quad \forall_{x_2, y_2 \in S_2}((R_2(x_2, y_2) \wedge R_2(y_2, x_2)) \Rightarrow x_2 = y_2) \ : \ *$

(iii) $S_3 : *, \ R_3 : (S_3 \times S_3) \to * \ \triangleright$
$\quad$ *transitive*$(S_3, R_3) :=$
$\quad\quad \forall_{x_3, y_3, z_3 \in S_3}((R_3(x_3, y_3) \wedge R_3(y_3, z_3)) \Rightarrow R_3(x_3, z_3)) \ : \ *$

(iv) $S_4 : *, \ R_4 : (S_4 \times S_4) \to * \ \triangleright$
$\quad$ *partially-ordered*$(S_4, R_4) :=$
$\quad\quad$ *reflexive*$(S_4, R_4) \wedge ($*antisymmetric*$(S_4, R_4) \wedge$ *transitive*$(S_4, R_4)) \ : \ *$

An important thing that we can learn from this example is that definitions often *depend* on other definitions. Clearly, *(iv)* depends on *(i)* to *(iii)*, since the constants *reflexive*, *antisymmetric* and *transitive* are used in the definiens of *(iv)*. So there is an *order* between definitions, which must be respected. For example, we may list *(i)*, *(ii)* and *(iii)* in an arbitrary order, but *(iv)* must always follow all of these.

8.6 Definitions depending on assumptions

In the previous sections, we have encountered definitions depending on a context. The variables we met in those contexts represented sets (such as S), objects (f, n) or relations (R).

Another frequently occurring case is that such a context contains one or more *assumptions*. Such assumptions are often expressed as *conditions* imposed on context elements. For example, when defining what a *minimal element* is in a set with respect to a relation, one often already assumes that the set has been *partially ordered* by this relation:

'Let S be a set, partially ordered by a relation R. An element m of S is called *a minimal element* with respect to R, if $R(x, m)$ implies that $x = m$.'

(So the only element related to a minimal element m, is m itself.)

This definition of 'minimal element' presupposes that we have a relation R that is partially ordered. We have formalised this notion in the previous section (see Figure 8.2). We can extend this figure with a new definition: see Figure 8.3, line (5). We need two more flags, one of them (flag (c)) expressing the assumption mentioned above.

$$
\begin{array}{ll}
 & \vdots \\
(c) & \boxed{u \ : \ \textit{partially-ordered}(S, R)} \\
(d) & \boxed{m : S} \\
(5) & \textit{minimal-element}(S, R, u, m) \ := \ \forall_{x \in S}(R(x, m) \Rightarrow x = m) \ : \ *
\end{array}
$$

Figure 8.3 Definition of 'minimal element', depending on an assumption

This new definition is a flag version of the definition:

(v) $S : *, \ R : (S \times S) \to *, \ u : \textit{partially-ordered}(S, R), \ m : S \ \triangleright$
  $\textit{minimal-element}(S, R, u, m) \ := \ \forall_{x \in S}(R(x, m) \Rightarrow x = m) \ : \ *.$

8.7 Giving names to proofs

With the formal machinery described up to here, we can already express a wide range of definitions in formal form. For example, we have met definitions of constants for:

- *sets*, having $*$ as type;
- *objects*, having a set as type; and
- *propositions*, having $*$ as type.

Notation 8.7.1 *The kind $*$ is used as representing both the type of sets and of propositions. For a better understanding, it is sometimes convenient to add a subscript to $*$ in order to distinguish between these two interpretations: we then write $*_s$ for the type of all sets, and $*_p$ for the type of all propositions.*

However, this is only a kind of 'sugaring' to facilitate the interpretation: in the formal type theory discussed in this book, there are no such things as $*_s$ or $*_p$, but only $*$.

With this notation, we see that some of the example constants of Sections 8.1 and 8.3 satisfy the following typing conditions:

- (sets) *rectangle* : $*_s$ and $D(n)$: $*_s$,
- (objects) $c : \mathbb{R}$ (with $\mathbb{R} : *_s$),
- (propositions) *increasing*(f) : $*_p$ and *total*(S, R) : $*_p$.

In a schematic form, we may summarise all this in a table (see Figure 8.4), showing these three elementary kinds of definitions in an abstract setting.

(sets)	$\Gamma_1 \quad \triangleright$		$A(\ldots) := \mathcal{E}_1 \quad : \quad *_s$	
(objects)	$\Gamma_2 \quad \triangleright$	$a(\ldots) := \mathcal{E}_2 \quad :$	S	with $S : *_s$
(propositions)	$\Gamma_3 \quad \triangleright$		$B(\ldots) := \mathcal{E}_3 \quad : \quad *_p$	

Figure 8.4 Three different kinds of definitions

It is obvious that there is one line missing in Figure 8.4: a line representing a definition of a *proof* of a proposition (see Figure 8.5).

(proofs)	$\Gamma_4 \quad \triangleright \quad b(\ldots) := \mathcal{E}_4 \quad : \qquad P$	with $P : *_p$

Figure 8.5 A missing kind of definition

This is the kind of definition which gives a name, viz. $b(\ldots)$, to a proof $\mathcal{E}_4$ of a proposition P.

By means of the following example we shall make clear that this kind of definition should indeed be added, since it is very important in the formalisation of mathematics, in particular when one wants to *apply* a valid (i.e. proven) theorem.

Consider the following example from mathematics:

> '**Theorem.** *Let m and n be positive natural numbers and assume that they are coprime. Then there are integers x and y such that $mx + ny = 1$.*'

(Two positive natural numbers are *coprime* if their greatest common divisor is 1.)

Remark 8.7.2 *This theorem (or a slightly different version of it) is known under the name Bézout's Lemma. More information about it can be found in Remark 15.1.1. We shall devote Chapter 15 to Bézout's Lemma, in which we formalise a proof of it in the formal system λC extended with definitions. This serves as the major example of the system-with-definitions being developed in this book.*

The theorem states that:

$$\exists_{x,y \in \mathbb{Z}}(mx + ny = 1)$$

which depends on a context that we can summarise as:

$$m : \mathbb{N}^+, \ n : \mathbb{N}^+, \ u : coprime(m, n),$$

where $\mathbb{N}^+$ is the type of the positive naturals.

The third declaration expresses an assumption: variable u represents an assumed 'proof' (cf. Section 8.6) of the proposition $coprime(m, n)$.

Suppose that we have a correct proof of the theorem, in a formalised version; say `formalproof`. Then `formalproof` has type $\exists x, y : \mathbb{Z} . (mx + ny = 1)$, following PAT, and we obtain the following version of Bézout's Lemma, writing the context in flags:

$$\boxed{m : \mathbb{N}^+}$$
$$\boxed{n : \mathbb{N}^+}$$
$$\boxed{u : coprime(m, n)}$$
$$\textbf{formalproof} \ : \ \exists x, y : \mathbb{Z} . (mx + ny = 1)$$

An important aspect of such a theorem is that it can be *applied*. For example, we might want to use Bézout's Lemma with $m = 55$ and $n = 28$, which is allowed since their greatest common divisor is 1. Say we have a proof U of the coprimality of 55 and 28. Then we can apply the theorem by means of an *instantiation*, employing the substitution:

$$[m := 55], \ [n := 28], \ [u := U].$$

Note that we instantiate the assumption u of type $coprime(m, n)$ with the proof U of type $coprime(55, 28)$; hence, the m and n in the type of u have been instantiated, as well.

Remark 8.7.3 *We use the symbol ':=' for substitution as we did in Section 1.6. Note that the symbol ':=' is* overloaded, *since we have also decided to employ it for a definition.*

The result of applying Bézout's Lemma in this special case is that (without a context):

$$\exists x, y : \mathbb{Z} . (55x + 28y = 1).$$

How can we obtain a proof for $\exists x, y : \mathbb{Z} . (55x + 28y = 1)$? It is not hard to imagine that such a proof may be constructed by taking the expression `formalproof` *and substituting* $[m := 55], \ [n := 28], \ [u := U]$ *everywhere in this expression.* This procedure specialises the general proof `formalproof` into a proof of $\exists x, y : \mathbb{Z} . (55x + 28y = 1)$.

All this can be realised very quickly and in a formal manner, as well, when we give a *name* to that proof (as suggested in Figure 8.5), say p. In flag format:

$m : \mathbb{N}^+$
  $n : \mathbb{N}^+$
    $u : coprime(m, n)$
      $p(m, n, u) := \texttt{formalproof} \ : \ \exists x, y : \mathbb{Z} . (mx + ny = 1)$

Or, in the formal format for definitions:

$m : \mathbb{N}^+, \ n : \mathbb{N}^+, \ u : coprime(m, n) \ \triangleright$
  $p(m, n, u) := \texttt{formalproof} \ : \ \exists x, y : \mathbb{Z} . (mx + ny = 1)$.

Now we may formally conclude that, for the instantiation with $[m := 55]$, $[n := 28]$, $[u := U]$:

$p(55, 28, U) \ : \ \exists x, y : \mathbb{Z} . (55x + 28y = 1)$.

And this is a perfect *use* of a definition, exactly following the patterns as we have described earlier. Hence, it is worth while to also allow defined names for *proofs*. So all four kinds of definitions discussed in the beginning of this section have become part of our 'definition tool box'.

8.8 A general proof and a specialised version

We have expressed a version of Bézout's Lemma in the previous section, but we did not prove it there, although we gave the name $p(m, n, u)$ to a formal proof that we supposed to exist. Part of this omission will be remedied in the present section, since we shall write down a proof in the usual mathematical format: see Figure 8.6.

In the proof-in-words given here, we consider the set S of all 'linear combinations' of m and n, i.e. the numbers $mx + ny$ for integer x and y. The positive part of S has a minimum, say d. A clever calculation shows that d divides m, and also n. The desired result then follows easily.

We invite the reader to study the details of the proof and to check its correctness. The *formal* proof of this lemma, expressed in λD, will be the subject of Chapter 15.

In the previous section we also claimed that $p(55, 28, U)$ represents a proof of Bézout's Lemma in the special case when $m = 55$ and $n = 28$, where U

General theorem: (*Bézout's Lemma*)

Let m and $n \in \mathbb{N}^+$ be coprime. Then $\exists_{x,y \in \mathbb{Z}}(mx + ny = 1)$.

Proof   Let S be the set of *all* integer numbers $mx + ny$, where $x \in \mathbb{Z}$ and $y \in \mathbb{Z}$, and let S^+ be the subset of the *positive* elements of S. Let d be the minimum of S^+. Since $d \in S^+$, we have $d > 0$. Also $d \in S$, hence:

(1) $d = mx_0 + ny_0$

for certain $x_0, y_0 \in \mathbb{Z}$.

Divide m by d: we get

(2) $m = qd + r$,

for certain q and r with $0 \le r < d$ (r is the *remainder* of the division).

From (1) and (2) we obtain $m = q(mx_0 + ny_0) + r$, hence $r = m(1 - qx_0) - n(qy_0)$, implying that $r \in S$.

If r were greater than 0, then $r \in S^+$, so $r \ge d$ since $d = \min(S^+)$. But $r < d$; contradiction. Hence, $r = 0$.

So, $m = qd$ by (2), hence $d|m$.

In a similar manner we can prove $d|n$.

Since m and n are coprime, d must be 1, so $1 \in S$.

Hence there exist $x, y \in \mathbb{Z}$ such that $mx + ny = 1$. $\square$

Figure 8.6 A proof of Bézout's Lemma

represents a proof of the fact that 55 and 28 are coprime. The result is now that $\exists x, y : \mathbb{Z} . (55x + 28y = 1)$.

In order to support this claim, we also write out the *specialised* proof; see Figure 8.7.

Special theorem: (*Bézout's Lemma for $m = 55$ and $n = 28$*)

$\exists_{x,y \in \mathbb{Z}}(55x + 28y = 1)$.

Proof   Let S be the set of all integer numbers $55x + 28y$, where $x \in \mathbb{Z}$ and $y \in \mathbb{Z}$, and let S^+ be the subset of the positive elements of S. Let d be the minimum of S^+. Since $d \in S^+$, we have $d > 0$. Also $d \in S$, hence:

(1) $d = 55x_0 + 28y_0$

for certain $x_0, y_0 \in \mathbb{Z}$.

Divide 55 by d: we get

(2) $55 = qd + r$,

for certain q and r with $0 \le r < d$.

From (1) and (2) we obtain $55 = q(55x_0 + 28y_0) + r$, hence $r = 55(1 - qx_0) - 28(qy_0)$, implying that $r \in S$.

If r were greater than 0, then $r \in S^+$, so $r \ge d$ since $d = \min(S^+)$. But $r < d$; contradiction. Hence, $r = 0$.

So, $55 = qd$ by (2), hence $d|55$.

In a similar manner we can prove $d|28$.

Since 55 and 28 are coprime, d must be 1, so $1 \in S$.

Hence there exist $x, y \in \mathbb{Z}$ such that $55x + 28y = 1$. $\square$

Figure 8.7 A proof of Bézout's Lemma with $m = 55$ and $n = 28$

A proof as in Figure 8.7 is not something one easily encounters, neither in mathematics, nor in a formalisation. We give it here just to illustrate our claim: the proofs in Figures 8.6 and 8.7 are very similar, with the only difference the use of the general numbers m and n in the first case, and the special numbers 55 and 28 in the second case.

It is important to realise that both proofs may be read independently as convincing mathematical argumentations for the validity of the respective theorems: one may read, for example, the specialised proof and believe it without even being aware of the general version.

This proof specialisation works properly, but is very cumbersome. A mathematician will apply the general lemma to this special case without devoting many words to this. And in a formal setting such as λD, one can suffice with instantiating the proof name $p(m, n, u)$ to $p(55, 28, U)$, since the latter expression fully encapsulates the proof of the special theorem.

Remark 8.8.1   *For the special theorem there also exists a short, direct proof that does not use the general theorem, viz.:*

  'Since $55 . (-1) + 28 . 2 = 1$, *by elementary logic:* $\exists_{x,y \in \mathbb{Z}} (55x + 28y = 1)$.*'*

But this is irrelevant. The point that we want to make is that the specialised proof of the theorem, as presented in Figure 8.7, is indeed a correct proof; the length of the proof does not matter for this observation.

8.9 Mathematical statements as formal definitions

In Section 8.7 we have seen that giving names to *proof objects* can be useful. But this also has consequences for our formalisation of mathematical statements if we realise that every statement in the judgement-format of λC,

  $\Gamma \vdash M : N$,

can also be represented in definition format:

  $\Gamma \,\triangleright\, a(\ldots) := M : N$.

This small transformation enables us to treat *statements* and *definitions* in a similar manner, by taking the definition format as the reigning format. The only complication is then that in every statement the term M must be preceded by a constant and parameter list, $a(\ldots)$. But this small inconvenience causes great profit in the case M is a proof term proving N, because it enables us to apply theorem N in a smooth but formal manner. We have demonstrated this in Sections 8.7 and 8.8, when applying Bézout's Lemma to a special case.

In order to show how this transformation works, we give an example in which we consistently employ the definition format for the formalisation of mathematics. Consider the following text, which repeats the definition of 'total' (cf. Figure 8.1) and continues with some other notions and related statements.

> *'A relation R on a set S is called* total *if for all $x, y \in S$ we have $R(x, y)$ or $R(y, x)$.*
> *The* inverse *of a relation R is the relation R' such that $R'(x, y)$ iff $R(y, x)$.*
> *If R is total, then also the inverse of R is total.*
> *The relation R on S such that $R(x, y)$ iff $x = y$, is called the* identity relation *on S.*
> *If S has more than one element, then the identity relation on S is not total.*
> *An example of a total relation on $\mathbb{R}$ is $\leq$.'*

This text contains three definitions-in-a-context, namely of the notions 'total', 'inverse' and 'identity relation'. These definitions have been mixed with three unproven statements:

- If R is total, then also the inverse of R is total.
- If S has more than one element, then the identity relation on S is not total.
- The relation $\leq$ on $\mathbb{R}$ is a total relation.

Below we represent *all* these as formal definitions, in flag format. The three missing proof objects are provisionally called **open-term**$_1$ to **open-term**$_3$. For clearness' sake, we specialise $*$ to either $*_s$ or $*_p$ (cf. Notation 8.7.1).

(a) $\boxed{S : *_s}$

(b) $\quad \boxed{R : (S \times S) \to *_p}$

(1) $\quad total(S, R) := \forall x, y : S . (R(x, y) \vee R(y, x)) : *_p$

(2) $\quad inverse(S, R) := \lambda(x, y) : (S \times S) . (R(y, x)) : (S \times S) \to *_p$

(3) $\quad p_1(S, R) := \textbf{open-term}_1 : total(S, R) \Rightarrow total(S, inverse(S, R))$

(4) $\quad Id(S) := \lambda(x, y) : (S \times S) . (x = y) : (S \times S) \to *_p$

(5) $\quad p_2(S) := \textbf{open-term}_2 : (|S| \geq 2) \Rightarrow \neg(total(S, Id(S)))$

(6) $p_3 := \textbf{open-term}_3 : total(\mathbb{R}, \leq)$

Figure 8.8 A formalised mathematical text in definition format

This example shows that the formal definition format as we have introduced it in Section 8.5 is very powerful: formal definitions can be used as the *basic units* for expressing oneself in a type-theoretic ambiance, and a formalised mathematical text is no more than a *list of well-formed definitions*. This is a point of great importance, which we shall fruitfully exploit in the chapters to come.

But we still have to find out what the notion 'well-formedness' means for definitions. This we discuss in the following two chapters.

8.10 Conclusions

In the previous chapters there has hardly been any need for definitions or abbreviations: the logical systems that we considered were relatively simple. Remember, however, that we used a definition for $\Leftrightarrow$ (see Remark 7.3.1). Moreover, there were several 'hidden' definitions in Chapter 7: for example, $\bot$ was defined as ('identified with') $\Pi\alpha : *.\ \alpha$, and $\neg A$ was introduced as abbreviating $A \to \bot$.

When formalising more substantial parts of logic and mathematics, we cannot do without definitions. An introduction to this concept of 'definition' was given earlier in this chapter.

We have become acquainted with definitions, their nature and their usage. The main purpose of a definition is to single out a useful notion and enable one to refer to it later; this is an essential desire in both logic and mathematics. Moreover, definitions have proven to be extremely useful in the development of any mathematical theory; it is even inevitable to use definitions, since without them one very soon loses grip on the complexity of what one wishes to express.

We do not consider *inductive* and *recursive* definitions, although this kind of definitions is often used in proof assistants. But since we can do without them, we do not incorporate them in our type system. This has certain advantages: it keeps our system simpler and it relieves us of the obligation to inspect each inductive definition on its 'soundness'.

We have introduced a general format for definitions:

$$a := \mathcal{E},$$

expressing that a is defined as $\mathcal{E}$.

Since definitions are often expressed *in a context* and since we like to work with *typed* expressions, we have extended this format to:

$$\Gamma \rhd a(\ldots) := M : N,$$

with Γ a list of declarations, a the defined constant and $(\ldots)$ the *parameter list*, consisting of the subject variables of Γ, listed in the same order. In such a definition-in-a-context, $a(\ldots)$ has been defined relative to Γ as M, having type N. The parameter list is essentially superfluous, but we employ it in spite of this, for several reasons.

Using a definition amounts to calling upon the defined constant a, provided with an *instantiation* of the parameter list, each parameter substituted with an appropriate expression. Such a 'compound' substitution is rather precise work, since it has to satisfy the typing conditions as stated in the declarations, and should also be applied to all types in the variable declarations that are involved. Hence, substitution has a direct (and cumulative) effect on the typing conditions.

We have observed that it is natural to also use a definition for identifying a *proof* of a proposition. We argued that this kind of definition is desirable for being able to make use of ('apply') a valid proposition (a theorem, a lemma) in different 'situations'. Such a desire can easily be satisfied by *naming the proof* of a theorem, and instantiating this proof later, in the new circumstances, by means of a substitution.

It is interesting to see that also *statements*, e.g. expressed as λC-judgements, fit in the general format for definitions that we have developed, with only a slight adaptation. This enables us to employ a unified standard format for formally expressing mathematical texts: a satisfactory formalisation consists of an ordered list of formal definitions, and no more than that. This is a promising road, which we will follow in the chapters to come.

Now that we have investigated the pragmatic aspects of definitions, it becomes time to formalise the concept of 'definition' in one of our formal type-theoretic systems, for which we shall take λC. The desired extension of λC asks for new derivation rules, which makes the system more complex. But it also makes things easier for the formalisation of logical and mathematical content, since definitions are so handy, useful and even indispensable in 'real-life' situations. Formal derivation rules for definitions enable one to mimic the common way of thinking, in particular as regards definitions, in the formal setting of λC. This is the subject of the following two chapters.

8.11 Further reading

As we have seen in this chapter, definitions are everywhere in mathematics and they have an interesting structure with dependencies on parameters that can be sets, objects or proofs. In formal logics, definitions are left unanalysed and are used as 'meta-level' abbreviations: in a book on formal logic one finds statements like 'we define $\varphi(x, y)$ to be the formula $x + y = y + x$' or 'we abbreviate the formula $x + y = y + x$ to $\varphi(x, y)$'. But no formal rules are introduced for what is a *well-formed definition*, or rules for *instantiating* a definition or for *unfolding* it (i.e. 'undoing' a definition, by replacing a constant by its definiens, properly instantiated). For example, $\varphi(2, 3)$ can be 'unfolded' to $2+3 = 3+2$. But in a book text, $\varphi(2, 3)$ and $2+3 = 3+2$ would just be used as synonyms. (We come back to unfolding in Section 9.5.) So, definitions are treated as 'abbreviations in the meta-language'. In various mathematics texts one would even be more sloppy, writing 'we abbreviate the formula $x+y = y+x$ to φ', and then later write $\varphi(2,3)$ for $2+3 = 3+2$.

Definitions have been the subject of study by many philosophers. In ordinary language, definitions are not only used as a (parameterised) abbreviation, but have other purposes. As mathematics also uses natural language, these issues also come up when formalising mathematics. So, the question of what definitions in ordinary language mean in terms of formal mathematics is important, but this is not what is dealt with in this chapter (or book): we only deal with the correct treatment of formal *mathematical definitions*, not with the process of understanding what a *linguistic definition* means formally.

For further reading on the topic of definitions from a linguistic or philosophic perspective, the *Stanford Encyclopedia of Philosophy* is a good starting point (see Gupta, 2014). Also the paper *On Denoting* by B. Russell (Russell, 1905) is interesting, because it was the starting point for lots of discussions and research into the topic.

When implementing a system as a proof assistant, definitions are indispensable, so all proof assistants have an implementation of definitions. Unfolding of definitions is an operation that a proof assistant would do sparingly, because unlimited definition unfolding increases the size of formulas. Even though proof assistants have a formal definition mechanism implemented, the formal rules for definitions are often not described as a calculus and are thus left unexplained.

The first study of definitions in the context of λC and related type theories was by P.G. Severi and E. Poll (Severi & Poll, 1994). The rules presented there are, on the one hand, more restricted than ours, because they do not allow parameterised definitions. All definitions are of the form $c := t : A$ and if one wants to give a parameter to a definition, it has to be 'abstracted over' by a λ-abstraction. So, for example, $total(S, R) := \forall_{x,y \in S}(R(x,y) \vee R(y,x))$, cf. Figure 8.1, would have to be defined with a double λ-abstraction, e.g. as follows:

$$Total := \lambda S : *_s . \lambda R : S \to S \to *_p . \forall x, y : S . (R(x,y) \vee R(y,x)).$$

It should be noted that this method of replacing a number of parameters by λ-abstractions only works if the λ-abstractions are allowed by the type theory: there is no restriction on which variables can be used as parameters, but in general there *is* a restriction on the λ-abstractions that one can do. (However, in λC there happens to be none.) See Kamareddine *et al.* (2004) for a close investigation of the various possibilities of restrictions on abstractions and parameter use.

On the other hand, the definitions by Severi & Poll (1994) are more general, because 'local definitions' are allowed: a definition can be introduced at any time inside the context and it can be abstracted over, so definitions can occur deeper inside a term or a proof. This allows, for example, a local definition within a proof, where the scope of the definition is limited to the proof in which it is used. We see such a definition in the proof about the greatest common divisor in Figure 8.6, where the definitions of S and S^+ are local to that proof.

In systems with global and local variables, the distinction between them is part of the syntax. It will be obvious that there is a need for different rules concerning the two kinds of definitions.

For local definitions, as they are introduced by Severi & Poll (1994), without parameters, one allows contexts which contain declarations $x : A$ and definitions $c := t : A$ in arbitrary order. There are rules for ensuring the correctness of these contexts and there are the usual rules for λ, Π, etcetera. The crucial rule for allowing 'local definitions' is the following derivation rule:

$$\frac{\Gamma,\ c := t : A \vdash M : B}{\Gamma \vdash (c := t : A \text{ in } M) : (c := t : A \text{ in } B)}$$

This allows a definition to go 'deeper in a term', making it possible to have e.g. local definitions in a proof. In the setting developed in the present book, however, local definitions are not essential, since they may easily be represented by 'global' ones, as we will demonstrate later.

In the Automath project, a definition is sometimes formalised via a β-redex, following the idea that $c := t : A \text{ in } M$ is convertible with $(\lambda c : A.\ M)\, t$. (They have the same normal form.) In that case one has to consider a 'mini reduction' to allow the replacement of just one occurrence of c in M. That is, if $M[c]$ depicts M in which a specific occurrence of c is 'highlighted', we have $(\lambda c : A.\ M[c])\, t \to (\lambda c : A.\ M[t])\, t$, with $M[t]$ being M in which t replaces the specific occurrence of c.

Exercises

8.1 In Section 8.7, we gave the name $p(m, n, u)$ to a proof of the proposition

$$\exists x, y : \mathbb{Z}.\ (mx + ny = 1)$$

in the context $\Gamma \equiv m : \mathbb{N}^+,\ n : \mathbb{N}^+,\ u : coprime(m, n)$.

Assume that we have constructed, in context $m : \mathbb{N}^+,\ n : \mathbb{N}^+$, a proof (i.e. an inhabitant) $q(m, n)$ of the proposition

$$coprime(m, n) \Rightarrow coprime(n, m).$$

Find an inhabitant of $\exists x, y : \mathbb{Z}.\ (nx + my = 1)$ in context Γ.

8.2 The formal text represented below in flag format, is about a number of well-known notions in analysis, containing some statements with omitted proofs.

$\boxed{V : *_s}$

$\quad\boxed{u \ : \ V \subseteq \mathbb{R}}$

(1) $\quad\quad$ *bounded-from-above*$(V, u) :=$

$\quad\quad\quad \exists y : \mathbb{R} . \forall x : \mathbb{R} . (x \in V \Rightarrow x \leq y) \ : \ *_p$

$\quad\quad\boxed{s : \mathbb{R}}$

(2) $\quad\quad\quad$ *upper-bound*$(V, u, s) := \forall x : \mathbb{R} . (x \in V \Rightarrow x \leq s) \ : \ *_p$

(3) $\quad\quad\quad$ *least-upper-bound*$(V, u, s) := $ *upper-bound*$(V, u, s) \ \wedge$

$\quad\quad\quad\quad \forall x : \mathbb{R} . (x < s \Rightarrow \neg$*upper-bound*$(V, u, x)) \ : \ *_p$

$\quad\quad\boxed{v \ : \ V \neq \emptyset}$

$\quad\quad\quad\boxed{w : bounded\text{-}from\text{-}above(V, u)}$

(4) $\quad\quad\quad\quad p_4(V, u, v, w) := \ \ldots \ : \ \exists^1 s : \mathbb{R} . (least\text{-}upper\text{-}bound(V, u, s)$

(5) $\quad S := \{x : \mathbb{R} \mid \exists n : \mathbb{R} . (n \in \mathbb{N} \wedge x = \frac{n}{n+1})\} \ : \ *_s$

(6) $\quad p_6 := \ \ldots \ : \ S \subseteq \mathbb{R}$

(7) $\quad p_7 := \ \ldots \ : \ bounded\text{-}from\text{-}above(S, p_6)$

(8) $\quad p_8 := \ \ldots \ : \ least\text{-}upper\text{-}bound(S, p_6, 1)$

(a) Translate the text into a more usual format, as you might find in a textbook. (Note: $\exists^1$ expresses *unique existence*; 'there exists exactly one ...'.)

(b) Which of the eight lines are formalised definitions? Which are formalised mathematical statements?

(c) Which constants have been introduced in the text and which constants will have been introduced before?

(d) Underline all instantiations of parameter lists in the formal text and explain accurately what has been instantiated for what, and why that is correct.

8.3 Consider the formal text in Exercise 8.2. Describe the partial order representing the dependencies between the definitions given in this text. (Cf. the end of Section 8.5.)

8.4 The following formal text in flag format is about some well-known notions in algebra, where '*op*' means a binary operation on S, in Curried form (cf. Remark 1.2.6).

$$\boxed{S : *_s}$$

$$\boxed{op \; : \; S \to S \to S}$$

(1) $\qquad semigroup(S, op) :=$

$$\forall x, y, z : S . \; (op \; x \; (op \; y \; z) = op \; (op \; x \; y) \; z) \; : \; *_p$$

$$\boxed{u : semigroup(S, op)}$$

$$\boxed{e : S}$$

(2) $\qquad unit(S, op, u, e) := \forall x : S . \; (op \; x \; e = x \land op \; e \; x = x) \; : \; *_p$$

(3) $\qquad monoid(S, op, u) := \exists e : S . \; (unit(S, op, u, e)) \; : \; *_p$$

$$\boxed{e_1, e_2 \; : \; S}$$

(4) $\qquad p_4(S, op, u, e_1, e_2) :=$

$$\ldots \; : \; (unit(S, op, u, e_1) \land unit(S, op, u, e_2)) \Rightarrow e_1 = e_2$$

(a) Translate the text into a more usual format, as you might find in a textbook. Use infix notation when appropriate.

(b) Underline all variables that are bound to a binding variable introduced in the text.

(c) Rewrite lines (1) and (2) in the format $\Gamma \rhd a(\ldots) := M : N$ as described in Section 8.5.

8.5 Identify the definitions in the following text and rewrite the text in a formal form, using exclusively the definition format, as demonstrated in Figure 8.8. Assume that $\mathbb{R}$ is a type. Employ the flag format and the set notation $\{x : \mathbb{R} \mid P \, x\}$.

'The real number r is *rational* if there exist integer numbers p and q with $q \neq 0$ such that $r = p/q$. A real number that is not rational is called *irrational*. The set of all rational numbers is called $\mathbb{Q}$. Every natural number is rational. The number 0.75 is rational, but $\sqrt{2}$ is irrational.'

8.6 Consider the following mathematical text:

'If k, l and m are integers, m being positive, then one says that k is *congruent to l modulo m* if m divides $k - l$. We write $k \equiv l \, (mod \; m)$ to indicate that k is congruent to l modulo m.

Hence $-3 \equiv 17 \, (mod \; 5)$, but not $-3 \equiv -17 \, (mod \; 5)$.

If $k \equiv l \, (mod \; m)$, then also $l \equiv k \, (mod \; m)$.

$k \equiv l \, (mod \; m)$ if and only if there is an integer u such that $k = l + u \, m$.'

(a) Rewrite the texts in a formal form, as a list of definitions. Assume that $\mathbb{Z}$ is a type. Employ the flag format. Formalise $k \equiv l \, (mod \; m)$ as $eqv(k, l, m, u)$, with u a proof that m is positive.

(b) Indicate the scopes of all variables and constants introduced in the formal text.

(c) Identify all instantiations of the parameter lists introduced in the formal text and check that the type conditions are respected.

Extension of λC with definitions

9.1 Extension of λC to the system λD₀

In the present chapter we investigate the formal aspects of adding definitions to a type system. In this we follow the pioneering work of N.G. de Bruijn (cf. de Bruijn, 1970). As the basic system we take λC, the most powerful system in the λ-cube. System λC is suitable for the PAT-interpretation, because it encapsulates λP. But it also covers the nice second order aspects of λ2. Therefore, λC appears to be enough for the purpose of 'coding' mathematics and mathematical reasonings and is an excellent candidate for the natural extension we want, being almost inevitable for practical applications: the addition of definitions.

We start with an extension leading from λC to a system called λD₀. This system contains a formal version of definitions in the usual sense, the so-called *descriptive definitions*, so it can be used for a great amount of applications in the realm of logic and mathematics. But λD₀ does not yet allow a satisfactory representation of axioms and axiomatic notions; these will be considered in the following chapter, in which a small, further extension of λD₀ leads to our final system λD. (We have noticed before that we do not consider *inductive* and *recursive* definitions, since we can do without them; see Section 8.2.)

In order to give a proper description of λD₀, we first extend our set of *expressions*, as given in Definition 6.3.1 for λC. Since the expressions of λD₀ are the same as those for λD, we call the set $\mathcal{E}_{\lambda D}$.

We describe $\mathcal{E}_{\lambda D}$ in Definition 9.1.1. We assume that, apart from the infinite set of variables, V, we also have an infinite set of *constants*: C. We take symbols $a, a_1, a_i, a', b, \ldots$ as names of constants, just as we took $x, x_1, x_i, x', y, \ldots$ as names for variables. Moreover, we assume that variables and constants come from *disjoint* sets, and that $\Box$ and $*$ are special symbols that are distinct and not in V or C:

$$V \cap C = \emptyset, \quad * \neq \Box, \quad *, \Box \notin V \cup C.$$

Definition 9.1.1   (Expressions of λD_0 and λD, $\mathcal{E}_{\lambda D}$)
The set $\mathcal{E}_{\lambda D}$ of *expressions* of λD_0 (and λD) is defined by:
$$\mathcal{E}_{\lambda D} = V \,|\, \square \,|\, * \,|\, (\mathcal{E}_{\lambda D}\, \mathcal{E}_{\lambda D}) \,|\, (\lambda V : \mathcal{E}_{\lambda D} . \, \mathcal{E}_{\lambda D}) \,|\, (\Pi V : \mathcal{E}_{\lambda D} . \, \mathcal{E}_{\lambda D}) \,|\, C(\overline{\mathcal{E}_{\lambda D}})\,.$$

The 'overlining' in $\overline{\mathcal{E}_{\lambda D}}$ means a *list* of $\mathcal{E}_{\lambda D}$-expressions.

First we repeat from Section 8.5 what a (descriptive) *definition* is; for the meaning of the overlinings in $\overline{x} : \overline{A}$ and $a(\overline{x})$, see Notation 8.5.1. We also introduce the name 'environment' for a list of definitions.

Definition 9.1.2   (Descriptive definitions in λD_0; environment)
(1) A *(descriptive) definition* in λD_0 has the form
$$\overline{x} : \overline{A} \,\triangleright\, a(\overline{x}) := M : N,$$
with all $x_i \in V$, $a \in C$, and all $A_i, M, N \in \mathcal{E}_{\lambda D}$.
(2) An *environment* Δ is a finite (empty or non-empty) list of definitions.

We use symbols such as $\mathcal{D}, \mathcal{D}_i, \ldots$ as meta-names for definitions. An environment of length k will be denoted by e.g. $\Delta \equiv \mathcal{D}_1, \ldots, \mathcal{D}_k$.

With regards to a definition, we distinguish the following elements:

Definition 9.1.3   (Elements of a definition)
Let $\mathcal{D} \equiv \overline{x} : \overline{A} \,\triangleright\, a(\overline{x}) := M : N$ be a definition. Then:
- $\overline{x} : \overline{A}$ is the *context* of $\mathcal{D}$.
- a is the *defined constant* of $\mathcal{D}$, with $\overline{x}$ as parameter list.
- $a(\overline{x})$ is the *definiendum* of $\mathcal{D}$.
- $M : N$ is the *statement* of $\mathcal{D}$, M is the *definiens* or the *body* of $\mathcal{D}$, and N is the *type* of $\mathcal{D}$.

9.2 Judgements extended with definitions

How can we incorporate formal definitions into our most general type system, the Calculus of Constructions, i.e. λC?

Recall that the prominent expressive entity in λC is the *judgement* (also called *typing judgement*), having the form
$$\Gamma \vdash M : N.$$

In the presence of definitions, such a judgement may well depend on one or more defined constants. In particular, M and N, but also the types in the context Γ, may contain one or more constants: $a_1, a_2, \ldots$. So each judgement must have the possibility to be *preceded by* an environment, which is a list $\Delta \equiv \mathcal{D}_1, \ldots, \mathcal{D}_k$ of definitions.

Let's use meta-symbol ';' for the separation between an environment and a judgement. Then we obtain a new general format for *a judgement with definitions*:

Definition 9.2.1 (Judgement with definitions; extended judgement)
A *judgement with definitions* or *extended judgement* has the form

$\Delta \; ; \; \Gamma \vdash M : N,$

with Δ an environment, Γ a context and $M, N \in \mathcal{E}_{\lambda D}$.

We pronounce this as: 'M has type N in environment Δ and context Γ.'

By abuse of language, we will still use the simple word 'judgement' for such a 'judgement with definitions'; sometimes we'll speak of *extended judgements* to distinguish them from the judgements without definitions, as presented in the previous chapters.

By writing out the environment Δ and the context Γ we obtain:

$\mathcal{D}_1, \mathcal{D}_2, \ldots, \mathcal{D}_k \; ; \; x_1 : A_1, \ldots, x_n : A_n \vdash M : N.$

So in this format, the basic statement $M : N$ has been 'decorated' at the front with a list Δ and a list Γ:

(1) the environment Δ binding the *constants* occurring in $M : N$,
(2) the context Γ binding the *free variables* occurring in $M : N$.

Remark 9.2.2 *Note that the binding effects in the whole judgement are more complicated than this: we have 'accumulated dependencies' in a judgement with definitions. In order to make this clear, we consider the following judgement-with-definitions:*

$\mathcal{D}_1, \mathcal{D}_2, \ldots, \mathcal{D}_k \; ; \; x_1 : A_1, \ldots, x_n : A_n \vdash M : N.$

Then we have:

(1) The defined constant a_i of definition $\mathcal{D}_i$, may occur in each of the definitions $\mathcal{D}_{i+1}, \ldots, \mathcal{D}_k$, and also in each of the types $A_1, \ldots, A_n$, in M and in N.
However, this a_i may not *occur in any of the preceding $\mathcal{D}_1, \ldots, \mathcal{D}_{i-1}$.*
(2) A context variable x_j may occur in each of the types $A_{j+1}, \ldots, A_n$ of following declarations, and in M or in N.
However, x_j may not *occur in any of the $\mathcal{D}_i$'s, nor in any of the preceding types $A_1, \ldots, A_{j-1}$, nor in the type A_j itself.*

Note: in practice, it regularly happens that these matters seem to be disregarded. For example, one may find an x_j in one of the $\mathcal{D}_i$'s, but then it is clearly meant to be a 'different' one.

Similar to our notations regarding contexts, we use the following notation convention for *environments*:

Notation 9.2.3 *Let Δ be an environment (in the list representation) and $\mathcal{D}$ a definition. Then $\Delta, \mathcal{D}$ stands for the list consisting of Δ, extended on the right with $\mathcal{D}$.*

As a consequence of the extension of judgements with definitions, we have to revise the derivation rules for λC (see Figure 6.4, which contains the derivation rules for the systems of the λ-cube, so in particular for λC). First of all, the judgements in these rules must be replaced by *extended* judgements. So all judgements of the form $\Gamma \vdash K : L$ must be replaced by judgements of the form $\Delta \,;\, \Gamma \vdash K : L$. But that is obviously not all: for the extension of λC with definitions, we have to add some *new* rules. It will also turn out that we need a revision of the conversion rule.

In Section 9.8 we give a full description of λD_0, which is λC extended with (descriptive) definitions. But before we describe the new derivation system λD_0, we investigate two new rules:

- a rule for *introducing* a definition with a context, by attaching a fresh defined constant with corresponding parameter list to a definiens, and adding the newly obtained definition (including its context) to an existing environment,
- and a rule for *using* a definition by instantiating the parameter list with appropriate expressions.

These two aspects of a definition are formalised in the rules *(def)* and *(inst)*, to be developed in the following two sections, respectively.

Remark 9.2.4   *We do not consider recursive definitions. Therefore, the defined constant a in a definition $\overline{x} : \overline{A} \,\triangleright\, a(\overline{x}) := M : N$ is the only occurrence of a in that definition; so a does not occur in M (and also not in one of the types A_i in $\overline{A}$, or in N).*

We come back later to the issue of how to deal with recursive definitions; see e.g. Section 14.4, Remark 14.4.2 and Section 14.15.

9.3 The rule for adding a definition

Firstly, we describe how to extend the environment Δ of a judgement which has already been accepted as correct, say

(i) $\Delta \,;\, \Gamma \vdash K : L$.

So what we want is to append a new, well-formed definition to Δ. A provision is, of course, that the definition newly added to Δ is itself 'well-formed'.

So let's consider a 'new' definition

$$\mathcal{D} \equiv \overline{x} : \overline{A} \,\triangleright\, a(\overline{x}) := M : N$$

which we desire to add to Δ at the end.

We should allow that this $\mathcal{D}$ itself depends on the environment Δ, since the defined constants of Δ may be used in $\overline{A}$, M or N. So in order that the new definition $\mathcal{D}$ becomes 'acceptable', obviously $M : N$ itself must be derivable with respect to not only the context $\overline{x} : \overline{A}$, but also the environment Δ.

Hence, we have as a requirement that

(ii) $\Delta \; ; \; \overline{x} : \overline{A} \vdash M : N.$

This leads to the following rule:

Definition 9.3.1 (Derivation rule for adding a definition to an environment)
Let a be a fresh name with respect to Δ, and $\mathcal{D} \equiv \overline{x} : \overline{A} \triangleright a(\overline{x}) := M : N.$

$$(def) \quad \frac{\Delta \; ; \; \Gamma \vdash K : L \qquad \Delta \; ; \; \overline{x} : \overline{A} \vdash M : N}{\Delta, \mathcal{D} \; ; \; \Gamma \vdash K : L}$$

The requirement that a be *fresh* implies that a has not yet been defined in Δ. So when referring to a, there can be no confusion about which a in $\Delta, \mathcal{D}$ we mean.

9.4 The rule for instantiating a definition

Now that we know how to *insert* a definition in an environment, we investigate how to *use* a definition occurring in an environment. As mentioned in Section 8.4, this amounts to invoking the defined constant with a proper *instantiation* of the parameter list.

The instantiation process is not trivial, since instantiating a variable can change the *types* in the declaration list. See the boxed example at the end of Section 8.4, where the instantiation of S with $\mathbb{R}$ has as a consequence that the type of R changes from $(S \times S) \to *$ to $(\mathbb{R} \times \mathbb{R}) \to *$, since variable S in that type must be instantiated as well.

Let's consider a definition, of the form

$$\mathcal{D} \equiv x_1 : A_1, \ldots, x_n : A_n \triangleright a(x_1, \ldots, x_n) := M : N.$$

Assume now that we wish to instantiate the parameter list $(x_1, \ldots, x_n)$, replacing the x_i by expressions U_i, respectively. What are the requirements in order that these instantiations work out well, so that $a(U_1, \ldots, U_n)$ is a well-formed expression?

We consider the U_i one by one.
For U_1, instantiating x_1, the requirement is easy:

U_1 *must have type* A_1.

What about U_2? Note that we cannot say simply 'U_2 must have type A_2', since variable x_1 may occur in A_2, and consequently this x_1 should first be instantiated by U_1.
So the requirement becomes:

U_2 *must have type* $A_2[x_1 := U_1]$.

Things become more involved for U_3, and so on, but it is not so hard to see what the general pattern is:

U_3 *must have type* $A_3[x_1 := U_1, \ x_2 := U_2]$ (since A_3 may contain *both* x_1 and x_2), and so on.

Remark 9.4.1 *The substitutions for A_3 and higher are presented as* simultaneous *substitutions; to be executed all together, 'in one sweep'. This is, however, not essential, since variables x_1 up to x_n occurring in the A_i are bound to the context in $\mathcal{D}$, namely $x_1 : A_1, \ldots, x_n : A_n$; hence, these variables are unknown outside $\mathcal{D}$. This brings along that no x_i can occur in any U_j.*

As a consequence, it does not matter whether we use simultaneous *or* sequential *substitutions in the expressions above; so we may also say, for example:*

U_3 *must have type* $A_3[x_1 := U_1][x_2 := U_2]$.

So the general requirement is that

$U_i \ : \ A_i[x_1 := U_1, \ldots, x_{i-1} := U_{i-1}]$.

Although this requirement is clear and well argued, it does not look very nice. So we try to give it a better appearance. Note that, for each type A_i, the variables from x_i upwards to x_n do not occur in A_i. So there is no objection against *extending* the substitution list above, leading to:

$U_i \ : \ A_i[x_1 := U_1, \ldots, x_n := U_n]$,

since the added substitutions $x_i := U_i$ up to $x_n := U_n$ are 'void'; they do nothing.

Again, we propose an abbreviation (see also Notation 8.5.1):

Notation 9.4.2 *We write* $[\overline{x} := \overline{U}]$ *as an abbreviation for the simultaneous substitution* $[x_1 := U_1, \ldots, x_n := U_n]$.

This enables us to write the requirement discussed above as follows:

$U_i \ : \ A_i[\overline{x} := \overline{U}]$, for $1 \leq i \leq n$.

If these requirements have been satisfied, we may instantiate parameter list $\overline{x}$ of $a(\overline{x})$ with $\overline{U}$, obtaining $a(\overline{U})$.

So the desired derivation rule for instantiation has the following form:

$$\Delta \ ; \ \Gamma \vdash U_1 : A_1[\overline{x} := \overline{U}]$$

$$\vdots$$

$$\underline{\Delta \ ; \ \Gamma \vdash U_n : A_n[\overline{x} := \overline{U}]}$$

$$\Delta \ ; \ \Gamma \vdash a(\overline{U}) : \ldots ?$$

in which the type of the $a(\overline{U})$ in the `conclusion` still has to be filled in.

But first, we propose a condensed notation for the list of judgements being the **premisses**, by using 'overlining' again:

Notation 9.4.3 *We write* $\Delta \; ; \; \Gamma \vdash \overline{U} : \overline{V}$ *for the list of extended judgements*
$$\Delta \; ; \; \Gamma \vdash U_1 : V_1,$$
$$\vdots$$
$$\Delta \; ; \; \Gamma \vdash U_n : V_n.$$

So the **premisses** of the rule may be written in the following compact format:
$$\Delta \; ; \; \Gamma \vdash \overline{U} : \overline{A[\overline{x} := \overline{U}]}.$$

All that's left to do now, is to find a *type* for $a(\overline{U})$ in the **conclusion**:
$$\Delta \; ; \; \Gamma \vdash a(\overline{U}) : \ldots ?.$$

Since $a(\overline{x})$ has type N and the variables x_i may occur in this N, the x_i in N should be instantiated (i.e. substituted for) as well. So the type becomes $N[\overline{x} := \overline{U}]$, and the result is:
$$\Delta \; ; \; \Gamma \vdash a(\overline{U}) \; : \; N[\overline{x} := \overline{U}].$$

So now we are ready to write down the derivation rule for introducing an instantiation of the parameter list of a constant (below we discuss why we state this rule for constants with *non-empty* parameter lists only).

Definition 9.4.4 (Derivation rule for instantiation, 1)
Let a be a constant with non-empty parameter list, and let $\mathcal{D} \in \Delta$, where $\mathcal{D} \equiv \overline{x} : \overline{A} \rhd a(\overline{x}) := M : N$. Then:

$$(\textit{inst-pos}) \quad \frac{\Delta \; ; \; \Gamma \vdash \overline{U} : \overline{A[\overline{x} := \overline{U}]}}{\Delta \; ; \; \Gamma \vdash a(\overline{U}) : N[\overline{x} := \overline{U}]}$$

The appearance of this rule is quite convincing, and not *too* complicated – in particular by the adequate use of 'overlining'. However, do not forget that the upper judgement is in fact an abbreviation for a *list* of n judgements for some $n > 0$.

Remark 9.4.5 *We consider here the instantiation* $a(U_1, \ldots, U_n)$ *with respect to the environment* Δ *and the context* Γ. *It is worth noting that the constant a, being the* head *of the instantiation* $a(U_1, \ldots, U_n)$, *may also occur inside one or more of the* U_j.

For example, when we would have defined $a(n)$, *in context* $n : \mathbb{N}$, *as being some expression which represents* n^2, *then one instantiation could be* $a(a(5))$, *and another one could be* $a(\text{plus}(a(k), a(l)))$, *for some known k and l; the meaning of these expressions is obviously* $(5^2)^2$ *or* $(k^2 + l^2)^2$, *respectively.*

However, we are not yet done: there is a good reason why we forbade the parameter list of a being *empty* in the above rule. Because if it were, then there would be no x_i to instantiate, so there would be no U_i as well, and the list of n judgements on the upper side of the derivation rule would become the empty list.

The text of Definition 9.4.4 then would become:

Let a be a constant with empty *parameter list, and let $\mathcal{D} \in \Delta$, where* $\mathcal{D} \equiv \emptyset \rhd a(\,) := M : N$. *Then:*

$$(\textit{inst-zero}) \quad \frac{\langle \texttt{no requirements} \rangle}{\Delta\,;\,\Gamma \vdash a(\,) : N} \quad ??$$

This rule is not what we want, because it permits us to derive the judgement $\Delta\,;\,\Gamma \vdash a(\,) : N$ for *any* Δ and Γ: we have no check on the correctness of Δ and Γ in the **conclusion**. It is important to recognise that in Definition 9.4.4, the correctness of Δ and Γ is a consequence of the correctness of the **premisses**: each of these already implies the correctness of both Δ and Γ.

So we have to find something to mend these possible sources of incorrectness. It is obviously sufficient to ensure that environment Δ and context Γ together are correct.

A clever way out is the following: if we are able to determine the derivability of *any* statement with respect to environment Δ and context Γ, then automatically $\Delta;\Gamma$ itself must be well-formed. So why not take the simplest statement that we know, namely $* : \square$? Our requirement then becomes:

$\Delta\,;\,\Gamma \vdash * : \square$.

Note that, since the definition under consideration ($\mathcal{D} \equiv \emptyset \rhd a(\,) := M : N$) is an element of this Δ, well-formedness of Δ immediately implies that $\mathcal{D}$ is well-formed.

So now we have a **premiss** to ensure well-formedness in the case of an empty parameter list. Hence, for definitions $\mathcal{D}$ in which the defined constant has an *empty* parameter list, the derivation rule becomes amazingly simple:

Definition 9.4.6   (Derivation rule for instantiation, 2)
Let a be a constant with empty parameter list, and let $\mathcal{D} \in \Delta$, where $\mathcal{D} \equiv \emptyset \rhd a(\,) := M : N$. Then:

$$(\textit{inst-zero}) \quad \frac{\Delta\,;\,\Gamma \vdash * : \square}{\Delta\,;\,\Gamma \vdash a(\,) : N}$$

We can combine this rule (*inst-zero*) with the rule (*inst-pos*) into one, to obtain the following instantiation rule (*inst*) for λD_0, covering both cases:

Definition 9.4.7 (Derivation rule for instantiation)

Let a be a constant and let $\mathcal{D} \in \Delta$, where $\mathcal{D} \equiv \overline{x} : \overline{A} \triangleright a(\overline{x}) := M : N$. Then:

$$(inst) \ \frac{\Delta \, ; \, \Gamma \vdash * : \Box \quad \Delta \, ; \, \Gamma \vdash \overline{U} : \overline{A[\overline{x} := \overline{U}]}}{\Delta \, ; \, \Gamma \vdash a(\overline{U}) : N[\overline{x} := \overline{U}]}$$

In this combined instantiation rule, we find literally the (*inst-zero*)-rule in case the parameter list of a is empty (because then all but the first **premiss** vanishes). If this parameter list is non-empty, we recognise the (*inst-pos*)-rule, but with an *extra* requirement: the newly added first **premiss**. It is not hard to show, however, that in this case the first **premiss** is a *consequence* of each of the remaining ones; so it does not enlarge the amount of effort required: we may just ignore that first **premiss** if the parameter list is not empty.

So the reason to insert the **premiss** $\Delta \, ; \, \Gamma \vdash * : \Box$ in the general (*inst*)-rule is that we desire the rule to have a simple appearance, and yet cover both cases. In this we succeeded; the additional burden in the latter case is only apparently a nuisance.

9.5 Definition unfolding and δ-conversion

There is an important aspect of definitions that we have not yet formalised: our intention that a defined constant 'takes the place of' ('stands for', 'abbreviates') the definiens. The intended meaning of the definiendum and the definiens is that they are the same.

For example, in Figure 8.1 we have defined $D(n)$ as follows, considering it to be an abbreviation for a set depending on natural number n:

$\boxed{n : \mathbb{N}^+}$

$D(n) :=$ the set of all positive integer divisors of n

We clearly intend that, by this definition, $D(n)$ *denotes* that set, so – as a set – they are *the same*; for arbitrary k in $\mathbb{N}$ we obtain (after instantiation) that:

$$D(k) \ = \ \{d \in \mathbb{N}^+ \mid d \mid k\},$$

and this remains so for other instantiations, for example:

$$D(15) \ = \ \{d \in \mathbb{N}^+ \mid d \mid 15\} \ (\text{so } D(15) = \{1, 3, 5, 15\}).$$

In the same manner, we wish to identify the definiendum 'total (S, R)' (see Definition 8.1) with '$\forall_{x,y \in S}(xRy \vee yRx)$', and consequently

$$\text{total}\,(\mathbb{N}, \leq) \ \Leftrightarrow \ \forall_{x,y \in \mathbb{N}}(x \leq y \vee y \leq x).$$

These kinds of equalities/equivalencies have not yet found their way into our system. This is, however, necessary. For example, if we want to *prove* that total $(\mathbb{N}, \leq)$, then all we can do is to prove that $\forall_{x,y \in \mathbb{N}}(x \leq y \vee y \leq x)$. Suppose that we succeed in the latter task:

$\Delta \; ; \; \emptyset \vdash \texttt{formalproof} \; : \; \forall_{x,y \in \mathbb{N}}(x \leq y \vee y \leq x)$.

Then we are apparently 'almost ready', but the final step to

$\Delta \; ; \; \emptyset \vdash \texttt{formalproof} \; : \; \text{total}\,(\mathbb{N}, \leq)$

cannot yet be made.

So our first thought is to introduce a rule that says: if $a(\overline{x})$ has been defined as K, then $a(\overline{x})$ may be replaced by K (and vice versa). But this is not enough: the above example shows that something like this should also hold for an instantiation $a(\overline{U})$:

If we have a definition

$\mathcal{D} \equiv \Gamma \rhd a(\overline{x}) := M : N$,

where $\mathcal{D} \in \Delta$ for some well-formed Δ, then it must be permitted to replace $a(\overline{U})$ by $M[\overline{x} := \overline{U}]$.

And there is more: such a replacement of an expression by some definitional equivalent one should clearly be permitted on a wider scale, since their intended meaning is the same. For example, since the expressions total $(\mathbb{N}, \leq)$ and $\forall_{x,y \in \mathbb{N}}(x \leq y \vee y \leq x)$ have the same meaning, a replacement of either of them by the other should be admitted, also when occurring as a subexpression.

This reminds us of the *Conversion rule* for systems in the λ-cube (cf., for example, Section 4.7), which permitted replacement of any expression by a (well-formed) β-convertible one. And indeed, in Section 9.7 we shall adapt the conversion rule in such a manner that also *definitional equivalence* will be covered.

But we have to start with giving a neat description of the mentioned notion of definitional equivalence, which we shall call δ-conversion. We make this notion precise in a number of steps, comparable to the transition from β-reduction to β-conversion, as discussed in Section 1.8.

First, we introduce a relation called *one-step definition unfolding* or δ-reduction; note that this unfolding is always relative to the environment Δ in which the definition occurs.

Definition 9.5.1   (One-step definition unfolding; one-step δ-reduction, $\overset{\Delta}{\to}$)
If $\Gamma \rhd a(\overline{x}) := M : N$ is an element of environment Δ, then:

(1) (Basis) $a(\overline{U}) \overset{\Delta}{\to} M[\overline{x} := \overline{U}]$,

(2) (Compatibility) If $M \overset{\Delta}{\to} M'$, then $ML \overset{\Delta}{\to} M'L$, $LM \overset{\Delta}{\to} LM'$, $\lambda x \, . \, M \overset{\Delta}{\to} \lambda x \, . \, M'$ and $b(\ldots, M, \ldots) \overset{\Delta}{\to} b(\ldots, M', \ldots)$.

As usual (cf. Definitions 1.5.2 and 1.8.1), compatibility (2) is the formal counterpart of the informal desire that (1) extends to subexpressions:

If $a(\overline{U})$ is a subexpression of K (say $K \equiv \ldots a(\overline{U}) \ldots$), then $a(\overline{x}) := M$ implies:

$$K \equiv \ldots a(\overline{U}) \ldots \overset{\Delta}{\rightarrow} \ldots M[\overline{x} := \overline{U}] \ldots .$$

Remark 9.5.2 *We use the notation $\overset{\Delta}{\rightarrow}$ for one-step δ-reduction with respect to environment Δ, without mentioning the δ. This is not consistent with our notation $\rightarrow_\beta$ for one-step β-reduction. A better notation would probably be $\overset{\Delta}{\rightarrow}_\delta$; but in the presence of the Δ, we take the liberty to leave out subscript δ, thus simplifying the image for the human eye.*

A similar remark holds for the notations to be introduced below: $\overset{\Delta}{\twoheadrightarrow}$ and $\overset{\Delta}{=}$.

In case $M \overset{\Delta}{\rightarrow} M'$, we say that M' is obtained from M by *one-step unfolding* in M a certain definition registered in Δ. If this regards an occurrence of the constant a (so $a(\overline{U})$ is replaced by $M[\overline{x} := \overline{U}]$, as above), then one also says that this occurrence of constant a *gets unfolded*.

Remark 9.5.3 *Unfolding concerns one occurrence at a time: other occurrences of the same constant are left untouched in the described unfolding step. And this is what we want, since one is usually only 'locally' interested in what a constant represents. This differs from β-reduction in an essential manner, since β-reduction requires that all bound occurrences of the variable are replaced by the argument. Hence, although the mechanisms of reduction and unfolding are tightly connected to the same basic notion, namely substitution, they behave differently and therefore we treat them in a different manner. That this can be realised in our formalisation is an advantage of the style with parameters that we employ, over the style with λ-abstractions as described in Section 8.11.*

The process the other way round, corresponding to the inverse relation of $\overset{\Delta}{\rightarrow}$, is called (one-step) *folding*: if $M \overset{\Delta}{\rightarrow} M'$, then M is the result of folding a certain instantiated constant in M'.

Similarly to what we did in Sections 1.8 and 1.9 regarding $\rightarrow_\beta$, which we extended to $\twoheadrightarrow_\beta$ and $=_\beta$, we define the notions 'zero-or-more-step δ-reduction relative to Δ', or $\overset{\Delta}{\twoheadrightarrow}$, and 'δ-conversion relative to Δ', or $\overset{\Delta}{=}$:

Definition 9.5.4 (δ-reduction (zero-or-more-step), $\overset{\Delta}{\twoheadrightarrow}$)
$M \overset{\Delta}{\twoheadrightarrow} N$ if there is an n and there are expressions M_0 to M_n such that $M_0 \equiv M$, $M_n \equiv N$ and for all i such that $0 \leq i < n$:

$$M_i \overset{\Delta}{\rightarrow} M_{i+1} .$$

Definition 9.5.5 (δ-conversion, $\overset{\triangle}{=}$)

$M \overset{\triangle}{=} N$ (to be read as: 'M and N are convertible with respect to Δ') if there is an n and there are expressions M_0 to M_n such that $M_0 \equiv M$, $M_n \equiv N$ and for all i such that $0 \leq i < n$:

$$\text{either } M_i \overset{\triangle}{\rightarrow} M_{i+1} \text{ or } M_{i+1} \overset{\triangle}{\rightarrow} M_i .$$

So M and N are δ-convertible (or $M \overset{\triangle}{=} N$) if the one can be obtained from the other by successively folding or unfolding a number of definitions occurring in it.

Remark 9.5.6 *The relation $\overset{\triangle}{=}$ is an* equivalence relation *on expressions, just as $=_\beta$ is (cf. Lemma 1.8.6). It is:*

- reflexive: *for all L: $L \overset{\triangle}{=} L$,*
- symmetric: *for all L, M: if $L \overset{\triangle}{=} M$, then $M \overset{\triangle}{=} L$, and*
- transitive: *for all L, M and N: if $L \overset{\triangle}{=} M$ and $M \overset{\triangle}{=} N$, then $L \overset{\triangle}{=} N$.*

Comparable to what we have said in the case of β-reduction (see Section 1.9), we define the δ-*normal form* of an expression, with respect to an environment Δ:

Definition 9.5.7 (Unfoldable, δ-normal form, δ-nf)

Let Δ be an environment.

(1) A constant a is *unfoldable* with respect to Δ, if a is bound to a descriptive definition in Δ, say: $\overline{x} : \overline{A} \rhd a(\overline{x}) := M : N$.
(2) K *is in δ-normal form* (or: is in δ-nf) with respect to Δ, if there occurs no constant in K that is unfoldable with respect to Δ.
(3) K *has a δ-normal form* (has a δ-nf) with respect to Δ, if there is an L in δ-nf with respect to Δ such that $K \overset{\triangle}{=} L$. One also says in this case: K is δ-*normalising*, and L is a δ-normal form of K (with respect to Δ).

9.6 Examples of δ-conversion

We continue with giving examples of the notions (un-)folding, δ-reduction and δ-conversion.

Let's assume that we have started to compose a mathematics book in λD_0, in which defined constants are included for *addition, multiplication* and *squaring* of integer numbers, and a defined constant for *equality* on the integers. For convenience, we denote them with the usual symbols ('$+$', '$\cdot$', '$.^2$' and '$=$'), written in *infix* notation (as to the symbols '$+$', '$\cdot$' and '$=$') and with *superscript* (for '$.^2$'), respectively.

Then we can add the following λD_0-text to our formal mathematics book:

$(\mathcal{D}_1)$ $x : \mathbb{Z}, y : \mathbb{Z} \ \triangleright \ a(x, y)$ $:= x^2 + y^2$ $: \mathbb{Z}$
$(\mathcal{D}_2)$ $x : \mathbb{Z}, y : \mathbb{Z} \ \triangleright \ b(x, y)$ $:= 2 \cdot (x \cdot y)$ $: \mathbb{Z}$
$(\mathcal{D}_3)$ $x : \mathbb{Z}, y : \mathbb{Z} \ \triangleright \ c(x, y)$ $:= a(x, y) + b(x, y)$ $: \mathbb{Z}$
$(\mathcal{D}_4)$ $x : \mathbb{Z}, y : \mathbb{Z} \ \triangleright \ lemma(x, y) := c(x, y) = (x + y)^2$ $: \ *_p$

Now take $\Delta \equiv \mathcal{D}_1, \ldots, \mathcal{D}_4$ and consider the expression

$\mathcal{E} \equiv a(a(x, x), a(y, y))$,

with respect to Δ, in the context $\Gamma \equiv x : \mathbb{Z}, y : \mathbb{Z}$. This expression $\mathcal{E}$ is well-formed with respect to Γ and Δ, since each of the three occurrences of a is followed by an instantiated parameter list of the proper length (viz. 2), and in each case, the two parameters have the proper type (viz. $\mathbb{Z}$).

For example: subexpression $a(x, x)$ of $\mathcal{E}$ is a correct instantiation of $a(x, y)$ as defined in $\mathcal{D}_1$; the instantiation substitutions are $[x := x]$ and $[y := x]$. The following subtlety is worth noting: in $[x := x]$, the *first* occurrence of x is the one bound in $\mathcal{D}_1$, but the *second* occurrence of x is another copy of x: it is the one bound in the context Γ of $\mathcal{E}$.

The mentioned instantiation $a(x, x)$ has the type $\mathbb{Z}$, again, as is desired by the rules for well-formedness (w.r.t. Δ and Γ) as given in Section 9.4.

In expression $\mathcal{E}$, there are three ways to start 'unfolding', i.e. to apply a single δ-reduction. We picture these three possibilities in Figure 9.1.

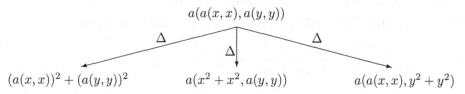

$$a(a(x, x), a(y, y))$$

$(a(x, x))^2 + (a(y, y))^2$ $a(x^2 + x^2, a(y, y))$ $a(a(x, x), y^2 + y^2)$

Figure 9.1 Possible first steps of unfolding $\mathcal{E} \equiv a(a(x, x), a(y, y))$

From this figure we can see that, for example:

$a(x^2 + x^2, a(y, y)) \stackrel{\Delta}{=} a(a(x, x), y^2 + y^2)$.

Continue the diagram yourself, until you have a picture of the complete δ-reduction behaviour of $\mathcal{E}$ with respect to Δ. The bottom expression in that diagram will be:

$(x^2 + x^2)^2 + (y^2 + y^2)^2$,

being a δ-normal form of $\mathcal{E}$ with respect to Δ. (Such a δ-normal form is unique, as we shall see in Corollary 10.5.4.)

In Figure 9.2, we picture one of the two possible complete δ-reduction 'paths' (cf. Definition 1.9.5) of the expression $lemma(u, v)$, for given $u, v : \mathbb{Z}$. Here the path ends in the expression $(u^2 + v^2) + 2 \cdot (u \cdot v) = (u + v)^2$, which is a δ-normal form with respect to Δ, again.

$$lemma(u, v)$$
$$\downarrow_\Delta$$
$$c(u, v) = (u + v)^2$$
$$\downarrow_\Delta$$
$$a(u, v) + b(u, v) = (u + v)^2$$
$$\downarrow_\Delta$$
$$(u^2 + v^2) + b(u, v) = (u + v)^2$$
$$\downarrow_\Delta$$
$$(u^2 + v^2) + 2 \cdot (u \cdot v) = (u + v)^2$$

Figure 9.2 A reduction path for $lemma(u, v)$

9.7 The conversion rule extended with $\overset{\Delta}{\to}$

Now that we have introduced δ-conversion, we can include it in the Conversion rule. From the discussion in Section 9.5 it can easily be concluded that this is what we want:

If $\Delta; \Gamma \vdash A : B$ and $B \overset{\Delta}{=} B'$, then also $\Delta; \Gamma \vdash A : B'$.

Now B is well-formed, since it is part of the judgement $\Delta; \Gamma \vdash A : B$. But just as in the original Conversion rule dealing with β-conversion only (see e.g. Section 4.7), it is not guaranteed that B' is well-formed as well. So again, we have to add an extra requirement about B': we require that $\Delta; \Gamma \vdash B' : s$, for s a sort, in order to ensure well-formedness of B'.

Hence, we obtain the following conversion rule for δ-conversion:

$$(\delta\text{-}conv) \quad \frac{\Delta; \Gamma \vdash A : B \quad \Delta; \Gamma \vdash B' : s}{\Delta; \Gamma \vdash A : B'} \quad \text{if } B \overset{\Delta}{=} B'.$$

We are not yet done, because it is quite natural to combine this rule for δ-conversion with the β-conversion rule in λC (see Figure 6.4). So we permit that B and B' are related by β-conversion, by δ-conversion, or by a *combination* thereof.

Before we discuss this further, we extend the formal definition of one-step β-reduction (cf. Definitions 1.8.1, 2.11.2, 3.6.2 and the comment to Theorem 6.3.11) to λD_0. In particular, we add a compatibility rule for constants with instantiated parameter lists:

Definition 9.7.1 (One-step β-reduction for expressions in λD_0, $\to_\beta$)
(1) (Basis) $(\lambda x : K . M)N \to_\beta M[x := N]$.
(2) (Compatibility) Assume $M \to_\beta N$, then also $ML \to_\beta NL$, $LM \to_\beta LN$, $\lambda x : M . K \to_\beta \lambda x : N . K$, $\lambda x : K . M \to_\beta \lambda x : K . N$, $\Pi x : M . K \to_\beta \Pi x : N . K$, $\Pi x : K . M \to_\beta \Pi x : K . N$ and $a(\overline{U}, M, \overline{V}) \to_\beta a(\overline{U}, N, \overline{V})$.

The definitions of zero-or-more-step β-reduction ($\twoheadrightarrow_\beta$) and β-conversion ($=_\beta$)

can remain as they are (see Definitions 1.8.3 and 1.8.5), albeit that they concern the *new* one-step β-reduction as given in the above definition.

Now we can give the appropriate definition for the new relation $\overset{\Delta}{=}_\beta$, which combines β- and δ-conversion:

Definition 9.7.2   ($\beta\delta$-conversion, $\overset{\Delta}{=}_\beta$)

We say that M $\beta\delta$-converts to N with respect to Δ, or $M \overset{\Delta}{=}_\beta N$, if there is an n and there are expressions M_0 to M_n such that $M_0 \equiv M$, $M_n \equiv N$ and for all i such that $0 \le i < n$:

$$M_i \to_\beta M_{i+1} \ or \ M_i \overset{\Delta}{\to} M_{i+1} \ or \ M_{i+1} \to_\beta M_i \ or \ M_{i+1} \overset{\Delta}{\to} M_i \,.$$

This leads us to the following general conversion rule for λD_0:

Definition 9.7.3   (Derivation rule for β-δ-conversion):

$$(\beta\delta\text{-}conv) \ \frac{\Delta;\Gamma \vdash A : B \quad \Delta;\Gamma \vdash B' : s}{\Delta;\Gamma \vdash A : B'} \quad \text{if } B \overset{\Delta}{=}_\beta B'.$$

9.8 The derivation rules for λD_0

Now we can summarise what we have developed in this chapter, by giving the full system of derivation rules for λD_0 (see Figure 9.3), as an extension of λC. All judgements are in the λD_0-format, hence in the form $\Delta;\Gamma \vdash K : L$. Obviously, the new element in comparison with λC (see Figure 6.4) is the environment Δ. Let's inspect the new rules.

(var), *(weak)*, *(form)*, *(appl)*, *(abst)*   As compared with Figure 6.4, the environment Δ is the *only* extension for these five rules, which therefore need no further explanation. Just as in Section 6.2, sort s ranges over $*$ and $\square$, and the pair (s_1, s_2) may be each of the pairs composed from these two sorts: $(*, *)$, $(\square, *)$, $(\square, \square)$ or $(*, \square)$.

(def) and *(inst)*   These two rules were treated in Sections 9.3 and 9.4.

(sort)   With regard to the *(sort)*-rule, it will be no surprise that we take the environment $\Delta \equiv \emptyset$, reflecting the empty *context* appearing in the corresponding λC-rule. So both Δ and Γ are empty, which brings along that there is nothing to be checked when invoking this rule. This is in agreement with the fact that *(sort)* acts as the start of every derivation: it is the only rule without premisses.

(conv)   For the conversion rule, we need, apart from the new Δ, another extension with respect to λC, as we explained in the previous section (see Definition 9.7.2): the relation $=_\beta$ must be upgraded to $\overset{\Delta}{=}_\beta$. For the sake of simplicity, we rename $(\beta\delta\text{-}conv)$ to *(conv)*.

This comment makes the rules in Figure 9.3 understandable and acceptable as a 'natural' extension of the λC-rules, suitable for satisfying our desire to include definitions.

$(sort)$ $\emptyset$; $\emptyset \vdash * : \square$

(var) $\dfrac{\Delta\,;\,\Gamma \vdash A : s}{\Delta\,;\,\Gamma,\,x : A \vdash x : A}$ if $x \notin \Gamma$

$(weak)$ $\dfrac{\Delta\,;\,\Gamma \vdash A : B \quad \Delta\,;\,\Gamma \vdash C : s}{\Delta\,;\,\Gamma,\,x : C \vdash A : B}$ if $x \notin \Gamma$

$(form)$ $\dfrac{\Delta\,;\,\Gamma \vdash A : s_1 \quad \Delta\,;\,\Gamma,\,x : A \vdash B : s_2}{\Delta\,;\,\Gamma \vdash \Pi x : A.\,B \;:\; s_2}$

$(appl)$ $\dfrac{\Delta\,;\,\Gamma \vdash M \;:\; \Pi x : A.\,B \quad \Delta\,;\,\Gamma \vdash N : A}{\Delta\,;\,\Gamma \vdash MN \;:\; B[x := N]}$

$(abst)$ $\dfrac{\Delta\,;\,\Gamma,\,x : A \vdash M : B \quad \Delta\,;\,\Gamma \vdash \Pi x : A.\,B \;:\; s}{\Delta\,;\,\Gamma \vdash \lambda x : A.\,M \;:\; \Pi x : A.\,B}$

$(conv)$ $\dfrac{\Delta\,;\,\Gamma \vdash A : B \quad \Delta\,;\,\Gamma \vdash B' : s}{\Delta\,;\,\Gamma \vdash A : B'}$ if $B \stackrel{\Delta}{=}_\beta B'$

(def) $\dfrac{\Delta\,;\,\Gamma \vdash K : L \quad \Delta\,;\,\overline{x} : \overline{A} \vdash M : N}{\Delta\,,\,\overline{x} : \overline{A} \vartriangleright a(\overline{x}) := M : N\,;\,\Gamma \vdash K : L}$ if $a \notin \Delta$

$(inst)$ $\dfrac{\Delta;\Gamma \vdash * : \square \quad \Delta;\Gamma \vdash \overline{U} : \overline{A[\overline{x} := \overline{U}]}}{\Delta\,;\,\Gamma \vdash a(\overline{U}) : N[\overline{x} := \overline{U}]}$ if $\overline{x} : \overline{A} \vartriangleright a(\overline{x}) := M : N \in \Delta$

Figure 9.3 Derivation rules for λD$_0$

9.9 A closer look at the derivation rules of λD$_0$

On closer examination, there is more to be said about some of the λD$_0$-rules. Firstly, we observe that the $(weak)$-rule and the (def)-rule have notable similarities:

- The $(weak)$-rule makes it possible to weaken the *context* Γ of a judgement $\Delta;\Gamma \vdash A : B$, by adding a new entry at the end of Γ (viz. the declaration $x : C$).
- The (def)-rule makes it possible to weaken the *environment* Δ of a judgement $\Delta;\Gamma \vdash K : L$, by adding a new entry at the end of Δ (viz. the definition $\overline{x} : \overline{A} \vartriangleright a(\overline{x}) := M : N$).

This implies that *(weak)* and *(def)* may both be considered as *weakening rules* (cf. Section 4.3): one for contexts, the other for environments.

Another correspondence exists between the rules *(var)* and *(inst)*, albeit more hidden than between *(weak)* and *(def)*:

− The *(var)*-rule tells us what the type of a *variable* x is (namely A), provided that this variable is the subject of the last declaration $x : A$ in the context and that A is 'correct' with respect to Δ and Γ.
− The *(inst)*-rule tells us what the type of an *instantiated constant* $a(\ldots)$ is, provided that $a(\overline{x})$ is the definiens of a definition somewhere in Δ and that the list $(\ldots)$ contains an instantiation $\overline{U}$ of the parameter list $\overline{x}$. The condition is that $\overline{U}$ must be 'correct' with respect to Δ and Γ.

Hence, *(var)* and *(inst)* establish types for the 'basic' expressions in λD_0, namely: (*i*) a *variable*, and (*ii*) an expression starting with *a constant*. From these basic expressions, one builds more complex ones by means of *(appl)*, *(abst)*, *(form)* and *(inst)* (again).

The rules left are the 'initial' rule *(sort)* and the rule for manipulating the type: *(conv)*.

There is a second view on the *(var)*-rule: one may also consider this rule as stating that *the final declaration, $x : A$, in a context Γ is itself derivable* with respect to a 'legal' Δ–Γ-pair.

A counterpart of this option for environment Δ appears to be missing. It would be something like '*The final definition $\mathcal{D} \in \Delta$ is itself derivable* with respect to "legal" Δ and Γ'. This is, of course, not realisable, since a definition $\mathcal{D} \equiv \overline{x} : \overline{A} \vartriangleright a(\overline{x}) := M : N$ is not a *statement*, and therefore it does not fit in the format for what we allow behind the '$\vdash$'.

One can, however, extract two acceptable statements out of this definition, namely $a(\overline{x}) : N$ and $M : N$. Both are intuitively 'valid' statements, in a proper environment and with context $\overline{x} : \overline{A}$, because: (1) $M : N$ is the observation upon which the definition has been based in the mentioned context, and (2) $a(\overline{x}) : N$ follows from our intention that $a(\overline{x})$ is a new *name* for M, and hence inherits all its properties.

It turns out that we do not need new derivation rules for this pair of statements: both statements are derivable from the rules we already have. We state this as a lemma.

Lemma 9.9.1 *Assume* $\Delta \,;\, \overline{x} : \overline{A} \,\vdash\, M : N$. *Let* $\mathcal{D} \equiv \overline{x} : \overline{A} \vartriangleright a(\overline{x}) := M : N$. *Then:*

(1) $\Delta, \mathcal{D} \,;\, \overline{x} : \overline{A} \,\vdash\, M : N$, *and*
(2) $\Delta, \mathcal{D} \,;\, \overline{x} : \overline{A} \,\vdash\, a(\overline{x}) : N$.

Proof Consider the (*def*)-rule. In the first **premiss**, take $\Gamma \equiv \overline{x} : \overline{A}$ and take $M : N$ for $K : L$; then the first and the second **premisses** are two identical copies of the assumption. Hence we obtain (1) as an immediate result.

The Start Lemma, to be formulated in the following chapter (Lemma 10.4.7, part (1b)), gives us (2) (see Exercise 10.6).   □

As will turn out in the following chapters, the second part of Lemma 9.9.1 is worth singling out as an extra rule. We give it the name (*par*) because it is about the typing of a defined constant in its 'pure' form – i.e. followed by a parameter list instantiated in the simplest manner, namely with *variables* $x_1, \ldots, x_n$; these 'mimic' exactly the original *parameters* $x_1, \ldots, x_n$.

Hence, we add the rule given in Figure 9.4:

$$(par) \quad \frac{\Delta \; ; \; \overline{x} : \overline{A} \; \vdash \; M : N}{\Delta, \mathcal{D} \; ; \; \overline{x} : \overline{A} \; \vdash \; a(\overline{x}) : N} \quad \text{if } \mathcal{D} \equiv \overline{x} : \overline{A} \rhd a(\overline{x}) := M : N \text{ and } a \notin \Delta$$

Figure 9.4 The derived rule (*par*) for λD_0

Remember that (*par*) does not belong to the basic rules; so it may be *used* whenever we like, but we need not consider it in our theoretical investigations.

9.10 Conclusions

In this chapter we have investigated the formal format for so-called *descriptive* definitions, which connect the defined constant a to an explicit definiens M. Our main concern has been the addition of such definitions to the type system λC. This eventually results in a formal type system called λD_0.

Because of the presence of defined constants in judgements, we have extended the typing judgements in front with a list of useable definitions (an *environment* Δ). This has led to a general format for judgements-with-definitions, also called *extended judgements*:

$\Delta \; ; \; \Gamma \vdash M : N$.

We have discussed several derivation rules for such extended judgements. We started with the rule (*def*) for adding a definition to an environment of a judgement. Next, we investigated the conditions necessary for a 'neat' instantiation of the parameters of a defined constant. This turned out to be an intricate process. The rule for describing what appropriate instantiations are has first been given in two separate versions: one for a non-empty parameter list and one for an empty list. But it turned out that these two parts can also be presented together, in one (*inst*)-rule.

Next, we have described the necessity of definition unfolding. We considered the consequences of the definition mechanism for convertibility: a descriptive definition naturally may be *unfolded* in an expression (by replacing a defined name by its definiens), without altering its meaning. In formalising this process of unfolding, we have to take the instantiations of the parameters into account. These instantiations reflect the necessary updating caused by the actual situation.

For the formalisation of unfolding, we have introduced the notion of (one-step) δ-reduction, and its generalisation: δ-conversion. The latter was obtained similarly to the way in which β-conversion has been based on β-reduction. We have also considered the notion of δ-normal form, being an expression in which there are no unfoldable constants. After giving examples of δ-reduction, we have formalised an extended Conversion rule, (*conv*), which takes both β-conversion and δ-conversion into account.

Finally, we have given the list of derivation rules of λD_0. We observed several correspondences between these rules. One of these correspondences was the reason for the formulation of a useful *derived rule*, called (*par*).

9.11 Further reading

N.G. de Bruijn was the first to draw explicit attention to definitions and to make definitions part of the formal language itself, not just a 'meta-notion'. Formal rules for definitions in type theory were first spelled out explicitly in his Automath project (de Bruijn, 1970), which has an elaborate, formal mechanism of definitions (see also van Daalen, 1973). The rules we give here are reminiscent of the ones of Automath.

A comparison between the Automath systems and Pure Type Systems (including type theories like λC) is given by Kamareddine *et al.* (2003), where the notion of parameterised definitions, as we have introduced in the present chapter, is added to the Pure Type Systems framework.

The type theory λC by Th. Coquand and G. Huet (Coquand & Huet, 1988) does not include a mechanism for definitions, but the first implementation of the system as a proof assistant obviously had one. The definitions were seen as an 'abbreviation mechanism' that didn't need a formal description or analysis; this opinion differs from our vision on definitions, as we have amply set out in the previous chapters.

The idea of progressively extending a 'book', as a document containing mathematical knowledge, by adding 'lines', is of course the basis of almost every mathematical text. In Automath (and in λD) the book consists of definition-like expressions; the added lines contain new constructions that are given a name, via a definition again.

We see the same pattern of development in the flag-style – also called Fitch style – way of doing natural deduction (see Section 7.8 and Fitch, 1952).

In the present chapter – and the whole book – we employ the transformation from tree style to flag style in an implicit manner: we give the formal derivation rules of the type theory in a tree style, writing all the contexts in full. But when we do examples of type derivations, we mostly prefer to use a flag style. This saves us from copying the contexts, because they are in the flags. See, for example, Chapter 7; we shall also employ the flag style in Chapter 11 and further.

Exercises

9.1   Consider the environment $\Delta \equiv \mathcal{D}_1, \mathcal{D}_2, \mathcal{D}_3, \mathcal{D}_4$ of Section 9.6. Describe the dependencies between the four definitions and give all possible linearisations of the corresponding partial order.

9.2   Consider the following two definitions, $\mathcal{D}_i$ and $\mathcal{D}_j$:

$$\overline{x} : \overline{A} \;\triangleright\; a(\overline{x}) := K : L,$$
$$\overline{y} : \overline{B} \;\triangleright\; b(\overline{y}) := M : N.$$

Let $\Delta \,;\, \Gamma \vdash U \,:\, V$ and assume that $\mathcal{D}_i$ and $\mathcal{D}_j$ are elements of the list Δ, where $\mathcal{D}_i$ precedes $\mathcal{D}_j$.

(a) Describe exactly where the constant a may occur in $\mathcal{D}_i$ and $\mathcal{D}_j$.
(b) Describe where the constant b may occur in Δ.

9.3   The text in Exercise 8.2 contains eight new definitions. Let Δ be the corresponding environment. Rewrite the type in line (8) in such a manner that all definitions of Δ have been unfolded.

9.4   See Section 9.6. Let $\Delta \equiv \mathcal{D}_1, \ldots, \mathcal{D}_4$.

Give the full δ-reduction diagram of $c(a(u, v), b(w, w))$.

9.5   Check that all instantiations of the parameters of constants defined and used in Exercise 8.2 satisfy the requirements imposed by the (*inst*)-rule.

9.6   Consider the following environment Δ consisting of six definitions, in which we use, for the sake of convenience, some well-known formats such as the Σ and infix-notations:

$$\mathcal{D}_1 \equiv f : \mathbb{N} \to \mathbb{R},\, n : \mathbb{N} \;\triangleright\; a_1(f, n) := \Sigma_{i=0}^{n}(f\, i) : \mathbb{R},$$
$$\mathcal{D}_2 \equiv f : \mathbb{N} \to \mathbb{R},\, d : \mathbb{R} \;\triangleright\; a_2(f, d) := \forall_{n:\mathbb{N}}(f\,(n+1) - f\, n = d) : *_p,$$
$$\mathcal{D}_3 \equiv f : \mathbb{N} \to \mathbb{R},\, d : \mathbb{R},\, u : a_2(f, d),\, n : \mathbb{N} \;\triangleright$$
$$a_3(f, d, u, n) := \texttt{formalprf}_3 : f\, n = f\, 0 + n \cdot d,$$

$\mathcal{D}_4 \equiv f : \mathbb{N} \to \mathbb{R},\ d : \mathbb{R},\ u : a_2(f,d),\ n : \mathbb{N} \rhd$
$\qquad a_4(f,d,u,n) := \texttt{formalprf}_4 : a_1(f,n) = \frac{1}{2}\cdot(n+1)\cdot(f\,0 + f\,n),$
$\mathcal{D}_5 \equiv f : \mathbb{N} \to \mathbb{R},\ d : \mathbb{R},\ u : a_2(f,d),\ n : \mathbb{N} \rhd$
$\qquad a_5(f,d,u,n) := \texttt{formalprf}_5 :$
$$a_1(f,n) = (n+1)\cdot f\,0 + \tfrac{1}{2}\cdot n\cdot(n+1)\cdot d,$$
$\mathcal{D}_6 \equiv \emptyset \rhd a_6 := \texttt{formalprf}_6 : \Sigma_{i=0}^{100}(i) = 5050.$

Assume that $\texttt{formalprf}_3$ to $\texttt{formalprf}_6$ are meta-terms, standing for real proof terms.

(a) Rewrite this environment in flag format.
(b) What is a name used for a_2 in the standard literature?
(c) Find the δ-normal form with respect to Δ of $a_5(\lambda x : \mathbb{N}.\ 2x, 2, u, 100)$, where u is an inhabitant of $a_2(\lambda x : \mathbb{N}.\ 2x, 2)$.

9.7 We call a definition $\mathcal{D}$ *correct* in environment Δ if $\Delta, \mathcal{D}\,;\,\emptyset \vdash * : \square$.
Consider $\mathcal{D}_1$ to $\mathcal{D}_6$ as in Exercise 9.6.

(a) On what condition can you derive that $\mathcal{D}_1$ is correct in environment $\emptyset$?
(b) How do you prove that $\mathcal{D}_2$ is correct in environment $\mathcal{D}_1$?
(c) The same question for $\mathcal{D}_3$ in environment $\mathcal{D}_1, \mathcal{D}_2$.

9.8 See Exercises 9.6 and 9.7.

(a) Let $\Delta' \equiv \mathcal{D}_1, \dots, \mathcal{D}_5$. Assume that $\mathcal{D}_6$ is correct in environment Δ' and $\Delta'\,;\,\emptyset \vdash (a_1(\lambda x : \mathbb{N}.\ x,\ 100) = (\lambda x : \mathbb{N}.\ x)5050) : *_p$. Derive:
$\Delta\,;\,\emptyset \vdash \texttt{formalprf}_6 : a_1(\lambda x : \mathbb{N}.\ x,\ 100) = (\lambda x : \mathbb{N}.\ x)5050$.
(b) Assume that the conditions mentioned in Exercise 9.7(a) have been satisfied. What is the fastest manner to prove
$\mathcal{D}_1\,;\,f : \mathbb{N} \to \mathbb{R},\ n : \mathbb{N} \vdash a_1(f,n) : \mathbb{R}$?

9.9 Let $\Gamma \equiv A : *,\ B : *,\ C : *$. Prove, by giving full derivations in $\lambda\mathrm{D}_0$:

(a) $\emptyset\,;\,\Gamma \vdash * : \square$,
(b) $\emptyset\,;\,\Gamma \vdash A : *$,
(c) $\emptyset\,;\,\Gamma \vdash B : *$,
(d) $\emptyset\,;\,\Gamma \vdash C : *$.

9.10 Let $\mathcal{J}_1, \dots, \mathcal{J}_n$ be judgements such that, listed in this order, they form a derivation. Let
$$\mathcal{J}_n \equiv \Delta_n\,;\,\Gamma_n \vdash M_n : N_n \mid J_n$$
be the final judgement in this derivation, with J_n its justification in $\lambda\mathrm{D}_0$.
Assume that for all $i < j$: if $\mathcal{J}_i \equiv \Delta_i\,;\,\Gamma_i \vdash M_i : N_i$, then we have that $\Delta_i\,;\,\Gamma_i \vdash * : \square$.

(a) Let J_n be a case of the (*weak*)-rule. Prove that
$\Delta_n\,;\,\Gamma_n \vdash * : \square$.
(b) The same if J_n is a case of the (*var*)-rule.

(c) The same if J_n is a case of the (def)-rule.

(d) The same if J_n is a case of one of the other λD_0-rules as given in Figure 9.3.

10

Rules and properties of λD

10.1 Descriptive versus primitive definitions

As we have explained before, our intention is to switch over from λC to an extended formal system with definitions that can be fruitfully used for the formalisation of mathematical texts (including logic).

In the previous chapter we have defined the system λD_0, an extension of λC with definitions as 'first class citizens'. We have based λD_0 on so-called *descriptive definitions*. The word 'descriptive' means that each defined constant is connected to an *explicit definiens*, giving a formal description of what the constant represents. The new name (the constant), so to say, 'stands for' the 'describing' expression to which it has been coupled in its definition.

When it comes to mathematics (and logic) in general, there is still one thing that we miss: the possibility to express so-called *primitive* notions, necessary for the incorporation of axioms and axiomatic notions. These appear as soon as we go beyond the so-called *constructive logic* (cf. Sections 7.4 and 11.8), or when we incorporate mathematics in a style based on axioms, as often happens.

The constants introduced in primitive definitions – as opposed to those in descriptive definitions – are *not* accompanied by a descriptive expression. These so-called *primitive constants* are only provided with a *type* to which the constant belongs, but there is no further restriction or characterisation. Consequently, primitive constants *cannot* be unfolded, simply because there is nothing to unfold them to.

A primitive definition can be seen as the axiomatic introduction of a logical or mathematical object one assumes to exist, but cannot construct. It can also be used for an axiom one assumes to hold but cannot prove in the (limited) framework of λC. An example is the axiom DN from classical logic, the 'double negation law' (see Section 7.4).

So we are dealing with the following two kinds of definitions:

– *descriptive definitions*, being the 'genuine', well-known ones, which are coupled to a description (the definiens) and a type;
– *primitive definitions*, not being definitions in the original sense, since they miss a description and are only confined to a type.

In their formal appearance, the essential *difference* between the two kinds of definition is the presence or non-presence of a definiens. The points of *agreement* are:

– both kinds of constants have similar behaviour as to the instantiation of their *parameter lists*; and
– both kinds of constants are connected to a *type*.

Because of these similarities, we have chosen to put the introduction process of the two kinds of constants on a par. This implies that we *extend* the common meaning of the word 'definition' to the primitive or axiomatic names. *Hence, our word 'definition' from now on also encompasses the cases where there exists no description, but only a type.*

As you may imagine, descriptive definitions form the great majority in an average formalised piece of mathematics; primitive definitions tend to be rather exceptional, particularly in the long run.

In the remainder of the present chapter we extend λD_0 with primitive definitions. The resulting system is called λD.

System λD is our ultimate formal machinery, which we firstly show to be a nice vehicle for the formalisation of logical notions, together with a corresponding deduction system (see Chapter 11). The system is also very suited for the formalisation of a larger body of mathematics (as the following chapters will demonstrate). Hence, λD fulfils our desire to have a powerful machinery for the formalisation of mathematical theories – the great profit being that the formalisation process enforces the formal content to become thoroughly verified.

10.2 Axioms and axiomatic notions

Let's have a closer look at *axioms*, or – in general – *primitive entities*. These are concepts or principles that are *postulated* to exist or to hold. They form the *fundamentals* of a certain theory, which are necessary as a kind of basis. They are so elementary that they are not constructible or derivable from other entities.

Examples of such primitive entities are:

– the set $\mathbb{N}$ of natural numbers, as a basis of Peano arithmetic;
– the number 0 in $\mathbb{N}$ and the successor function $s : \mathbb{N} \to \mathbb{N}$, as basic with respect to $\mathbb{N}$;

– the axiom of induction in Peano arithmetic;
– the axioms of Zermelo–Fraenkel set theory; for example: the Extensionality Axiom (sets with the same elements are equal), or the Empty Set Axiom (there exists a set with no elements).

These entities are all primitive in the respective theories. Note that the entities in the examples are varying in nature: they may be a set ($\mathbb{N}$), an element of a set (0, s) or the assertion of a proposition which one accepts as elementary and hence should be accepted without a proof (Induction, Extensionality, Empty Set).

We have already met such primitive entities in Section 7.4, where we discussed the laws of the excluded third (ET) and double negation (DN). Both propositions cannot be proved in constructive logic. So, when we want to do classical logic, we need to add them (or at least one of them; see the relevant passages in the beginning of the mentioned section).

In Section 7.4 we proposed to add ET as an assumption in front of the context – a kind of *pre-context*. This worked out fine there. However, this solution of the problem has definitely disadvantages:

– It complicates derivations in more complex situations, in particular when *several* primitive entities must be accounted for: then we always need to drag along a sizeable pre-context.
– It is not immediately clear how to deal with primitive entities that are themselves presented in a context. For example, we can express Induction with a context (instead of with universal quantification over P), as follows:

 'Let P be any predicate on $\mathbb{N}$. We *axiomatically* assume that induction holds for P.'

More formally, we can express this as follows:

 Induction property: In context $P : \mathbb{N} \to *_p$, we assume
 $$P\,0 \Rightarrow (\forall_{n \in \mathbb{N}}(P\,n \Rightarrow P(s\,n)) \Rightarrow \forall_{n \in \mathbb{N}}(P\,n)).$$

For these reasons, we have chosen another approach to primitive entities: we do *not* regard them as overall *assumptions*, but as a kind of *definitions*. To be precise, we regard them as definitions *without definientes* (see Section 10.1). We speak in these cases of a *definition of a primitive entity* or a *primitive definition*.

Formally, we use the symbol $\perp\!\!\!\perp$ for the non-existing definiens in such a primitive definition. This enables us to use the same format as for the usual descriptive definitions (cf. Definition 9.1.2).

Definition 10.2.1 (Primitive definition, definition, environment)
(1) A *primitive definition* has the form $\overline{x} : \overline{A} \,\triangleright\, a(\overline{x}) := \perp\!\!\!\perp : N$.
(2) A *definition* is either a descriptive or a primitive one.

(3) As a consequence, an *environment*, being a list of definitions, can now also include primitive definitions.

Example 10.2.2   Some of the above examples can be expressed as follows in this format (we suppress empty parameter lists):

$$
\begin{array}{llllll}
\emptyset & \triangleright & \mathbb{N} & := & \perp & : & *_s \\
\emptyset & \triangleright & 0 & := & \perp & : & \mathbb{N} \\
\emptyset & \triangleright & s & := & \perp & : & \mathbb{N} \to \mathbb{N} \\
P : \mathbb{N} \to *_p & \triangleright & ind(P) & := & \perp & : & \\
& & & & & & P0 \Rightarrow (\forall n : \mathbb{N}.\ (Pn \Rightarrow P(sn)) \Rightarrow \forall n : \mathbb{N}.\ Pn \\
\emptyset & \triangleright & i_{ET} & := & \perp & : & \Pi\alpha : *.\ (\alpha \vee \neg(\alpha))
\end{array}
$$

We can now *use* $ind(P)$ for any predicate P on $\mathbb{N}$, by employing the derivation rule $(inst)$.

For example: say that we have defined the functions 'cube' and $+$ on $\mathbb{N}$, and that we have derived the relevant properties of arithmetic. Now we want to prove by induction that

$\forall_{n\in\mathbb{N}}(9 \mid n^3 + (n+1)^3 + (n+2)^3)$, where $a \mid b$ means: a divides b.

We can *define* property Q as $\lambda n : \mathbb{N}.\ (9 \mid n^3+(n+1)^3+(n+2)^3)$, a predicate of type $\mathbb{N} \to *_p$, and take as our new goal:

$\forall n : \mathbb{N}.\ Qn$.

Now using the primitive definition $ind(P)$, we get with $(inst)$ that:

$ind(Q)\ :\ Q0 \Rightarrow (\forall n : \mathbb{N}.\ (Qn \Rightarrow Q(sn))) \Rightarrow \forall n : \mathbb{N}.\ Qn$.

Hence, it suffices to find an inhabitant (say r) of $Q0$ and an inhabitant (say t) of $\forall n : \mathbb{N}.\ (Qn \Rightarrow Q(sn))$, in order to derive, using $(appl)$ twice, that $ind(Q)\,r\,t : \forall n : \mathbb{N}.\ Qn$, so $ind(Q)\,r\,t : \forall n : \mathbb{N}.\ (9 \mid n^3 + (n+1)^3 + (n+2)^3)$ by $(conv)$. (See Exercise 10.1.)

10.3 Rules for primitive definitions

All we need to make this operational in λD_0 is to provide the derivation rules for primitive definitions. First we give the rule for including a primitive definition in the environment Δ. This rule is an adapted version of (def), given in Definition 9.3.1.

It is obvious that we do not copy the second **premiss** $\Delta\ ;\ \overline{x} : \overline{A} \vdash M : N$ of the rule (def): in the case of *primitive* entities there is no M available. Hence, we switch to a second **premiss** as given below, which guarantees the well-formedness of N, with respect to the environment Δ and the context $\overline{x} : \overline{A}$.

$$
(def\text{-}prim)\ \frac{\Delta\ ;\ \Gamma \vdash K : L \qquad \Delta\ ;\ \overline{x} : \overline{A} \vdash N : s}{\Delta\ ,\ \overline{x} : \overline{A} \triangleright a(\overline{x}) := \perp : N\ ;\ \Gamma \vdash K : L}\ \text{if } a \notin \Delta
$$

With respect to the *instantiation* rule (*inst*), the only modification is the
$\perp\!\!\!\perp$ in the definition. So we obtain the following (*inst-prim*)-rule, in which the
first **premiss** is necessary for the case $\Gamma \equiv \emptyset$, just as in the λD_0-rule (see Section 9.4):

$$(inst\text{-}prim) \quad \frac{\Delta; \Gamma \vdash *: \square \quad \Delta; \Gamma \vdash \overline{U} : \overline{A[\overline{x} := \overline{U}]}}{\Delta \; ; \; \Gamma \; \vdash \; a(\overline{U}) : N[\overline{x} := \overline{U}]}$$
$$\text{if } \overline{x} : \overline{A} \vartriangleright a(\overline{x}) := \perp\!\!\!\perp : N \in \Delta$$

Since these new rules (*def-prim*) and (*inst-prim*) for primitive definitions
are so similar to the 'general' rules (*def*) and (*inst*) for descriptive definitions,
it is worthwhile to put them side by side. See Figure 10.1, in which we have
boxed the relevant statements, containing the differences between the 'proper'
and the 'primitive' cases.

$$(def) \quad \frac{\Delta; \Gamma \vdash K : L \quad \Delta; \overline{x} : \overline{A} \vdash \boxed{M : N}}{\Delta, \overline{x} : \overline{A} \vartriangleright a(\overline{x}) := \boxed{M : N}; \Gamma \vdash K : L} \quad \text{if } a \notin \Delta$$

$$(def\text{-}prim) \quad \frac{\Delta; \Gamma \vdash K : L \quad \Delta; \overline{x} : \overline{A} \vdash \boxed{N : s}}{\Delta, \overline{x} : \overline{A} \vartriangleright a(\overline{x}) := \boxed{\perp\!\!\!\perp : N}; \Gamma \vdash K : L} \quad \text{if } a \notin \Delta$$

$$(inst) \quad \frac{\Delta; \Gamma \vdash *: \square \quad \Delta; \Gamma \vdash \overline{U} : \overline{A[\overline{x} := \overline{U}]}}{\Delta \; ; \; \Gamma \; \vdash \; a(\overline{U}) : N[\overline{x} := \overline{U}]}$$
$$\text{if } \overline{x} : \overline{A} \vartriangleright a(\overline{x}) := \boxed{M : N} \in \Delta$$

$$(inst\text{-}prim) \quad \frac{\Delta; \Gamma \vdash *: \square \quad \Delta; \Gamma \vdash \overline{U} : \overline{A[\overline{x} := \overline{U}]}}{\Delta \; ; \; \Gamma \; \vdash \; a(\overline{U}) : N[\overline{x} := \overline{U}]}$$
$$\text{if } \overline{x} : \overline{A} \vartriangleright a(\overline{x}) := \boxed{\perp\!\!\!\perp : N} \in \Delta$$

Figure 10.1 Comparing the derivation rules for (*def*) and (*inst*) in λD

The system λD_0 extended with primitive definitions and the (*def-prim*)-
and (*inst-prim*)-rules is called λD.

$$\boxed{\textit{The full set of derivation rules for } \lambda D \textit{ is listed in Appendix D.}}$$

10.4 Properties of λD

When it comes to the properties of λD, it turns out that many of them are
a straightforward extension of the corresponding properties of λC (see Sec-

tion 6.3). Of course, since *definitions* enter the stage, there is more to be
said. In particular, this concerns statements about definition unfolding and
δ-conversion. Below we give the relevant lemmas for λD.

The statements are very much like the ones in Section 6.3. The proofs are
also very similar, and for the extension with definitions the proofs are like the
ones in Severi & Poll (1994). As λD is not exactly the same as the system
in that paper, we give full proofs of the properties below in the note Geuvers
(2014a). Concerning δ-conversion, we only give the relevant normalisation and
confluence properties.

The set of expressions of λD is the same as the set of expressions of $λD_0$:
$\mathcal{E}_{λD}$ (see Definition 9.1.1). So it is important to note that we do not consider
'⊥' as an expression: it is a meta-symbol in judgements, on a par with e.g. ':='
and '▷'.

Next, we establish that $λD_0$ is indeed an extension of λC and that λD, in
its turn, extends $λD_0$. Each of these three systems has its own notion of derivability, implied by the specific rules of each system. By abuse of notation, we
use the symbol '⊢' for each of these three notions. If this may cause confusion,
we add a phrase to mend this, such as: '$Γ; Δ ⊢ K : L$ in λD'.

Lemma 10.4.1   (*Inclusion of λC in $λD_0$, and of $λD_0$ in λD.*)
   (1) If $Γ ⊢ K : L$ in λC, then $∅; Γ ⊢ K : L$ in $λD_0$; and
   (2) If $Δ; Γ ⊢ K : L$ in $λD_0$, then $Δ; Γ ⊢ K : L$ in λD.

Next, we focus on λD; we use the notation $a(\overline{x}) := K/⊥ : L$ to indicate that
it does not matter whether a is attached to a *description*, viz. K, or has
primitively been defined as a constant.

The following definition is an extension of Definition 9.1.3.

Definition 10.4.2   (Elements of a definition in λD)
Let $\mathcal{D} ≡ Γ ▷ a(\overline{x}) := K/⊥ : L$ be a definition.

− $Γ$ is the *context* of $\mathcal{D}$.
− a is the *defined constant* of $\mathcal{D}$, with $\overline{x}$ as parameter list.
− $a(\overline{x})$ is the *definiendum* of $\mathcal{D}$.
− $K/⊥ : L$ is the *statement* of $\mathcal{D}$.
− K resp. ⊥ is the *definiens* (also called: *body*) of $\mathcal{D}$.
− L is the *type* of $\mathcal{D}$.

If $\mathcal{D} ≡ Γ ▷ a(\overline{x}) := K : L$, then the definition is called a *descriptive* or *proper*
definition, and a is a *proper* constant.
If $\mathcal{D} ≡ Γ ▷ a(\overline{x}) := ⊥ : L$, then the definition is called a *primitive* definition,
and a is a *primitive* constant.

The following lemma concerns (free) variable and constant occurrences:

Lemma 10.4.3 *(Free Variables and Constants Lemma)*
Let $\Delta\,;\Gamma \vdash M : N$, where $\Delta \equiv \Delta_1, \mathcal{D}, \Delta_2$ with $\mathcal{D} = \overline{x} : \overline{A} \rhd a(\overline{x}) := K/\bot : L$, and $\Gamma \equiv \overline{y} : \overline{B}$. Then:
(1) For all i, $FV(A_i) \subseteq \{x_1,\ldots,x_{i-1}\}$; $FV(K), FV(L) \subseteq \{\overline{x}\}$.
(2) For all j, $FV(B_j) \subseteq \{y_1,\ldots,y_{j-1}\}$; $FV(M), FV(N) \subseteq \{\overline{y}\}$.
(3) Constant a does not occur in Δ_1.
(4) If constant b occurs in $\overline{A}$, K or L, then $b \neq a$ and b is the defined constant of some $\mathcal{D} \in \Delta_1$.
(5) If constant b occurs in $\overline{B}$, M or N, then b is the defined constant of some $\mathcal{D} \in \Delta$.

Next, we define *legality* for expressions, environments or contexts, which in each case means that they are 'accepted' in some derivation (cf. Definition 6.3.7 and Lemma 6.3.8):

Definition 10.4.4 (Legal expression, legal environment, legal combination, legal context)
(1) An expression M is called legal, if there exist an environment Δ, a context Γ, and N such that $\Delta;\Gamma \vdash M : N$ or $\Delta;\Gamma \vdash N : M$. (For such Δ and Γ, we call M legal *with respect to* Δ *and* Γ.)
(2) An environment Δ is called legal, if there exist a context Γ, and M and N such that $\Delta\,;\Gamma \vdash M : N$.
(3) An environment Δ and a context Γ form a *legal combination*, if there exist M and N such that $\Delta\,;\Gamma \vdash M : N$.
(4) A context Γ is called legal, if there exist an environment Δ, and M and N such that $\Delta\,;\Gamma \vdash M : N$.

We have the following extension of the Subexpression Lemma (6.3.8):

Lemma 10.4.5 *(Legality Lemma)*
(1) If $\Delta \equiv \Delta_1, \Delta_2$ and Δ is legal, then Δ_1 is legal.
(2) If $\Gamma \equiv \Gamma_1, \Gamma_2$ and Γ is legal, then Γ_1 is legal.
(3) If M is legal, then every subexpression of M is legal.

There is more to be said about legal environments:

Lemma 10.4.6 *(Legal Environment Lemma)*
If $\mathcal{D} \equiv \overline{x} : \overline{A} \rhd a(x) := M/\bot : N$ occurs in a legal Δ, say $\Delta \equiv \Delta_1, \mathcal{D}, \Delta_2$, then:
(1) each A_i is legal with respect to Δ_1 and $x_1 : A_1,\ldots,x_{i-1} : A_{i-1}$;
(2) both M and N are legal with respect to Δ_1 and $\overline{x} : \overline{A}$.

Legality is also used in the following lemmas:

Lemma 10.4.7 *(Start Lemma for declarations and definitions)*

(1) (Start for contexts) If $\Delta ; \Gamma$ *is a legal combination and* $(x : A) \in \Gamma$, *then we have* $\Delta ; \Gamma \vdash x : A$.

(2) (Start for environments) Let $\mathcal{D} \equiv \overline{x} : \overline{A} \rhd a(\overline{x}) := M : N$. *If* Δ *is legal and* $\mathcal{D} \in \Delta$, *then both (1a)* $\Delta ; \overline{x} : \overline{A} \vdash M : N$ *and (1b)* $\Delta ; \overline{x} : \overline{A} \vdash a(\overline{x}) : N$.

Lemma 10.4.8 *(Thinning Lemma, Condensing Lemma)*

(1) (Thinning) Let $\Delta_1 \subseteq \Delta_2$, $\Gamma_1 \subseteq \Gamma_2$, *and let* $\Delta_2 ; \Gamma_2$ *be a legal combination. Now if* $\Delta_1 ; \Gamma_1 \vdash M : N$, *then* $\Delta_2 ; \Gamma_2 \vdash M : N$.

(2) (Condensing of environments) If $\Delta_1, \mathcal{D}, \Delta_2 ; \Gamma \vdash M : N$, *where definition* $\mathcal{D}$ *is* $\Gamma' \rhd a(\overline{x}) := K/\perp : L$, *and* a *does not occur in either* Δ_2, Γ, M *or* N, *then* $\Delta_1, \Delta_2 ; \Gamma \vdash M : N$.

(3) (Condensing of contexts) If $\Delta ; \Gamma_1, x : A, \Gamma_2 \vdash M : N$ *and* x *does not occur in* Γ_2, M *or* N, *then* $\Delta ; \Gamma_1, \Gamma_2 \vdash M : N$.

For 'backtracking' a derivation from a certain judgement, we have the following lemma; parts (1) to (4) are 'λD-copies' of the corresponding parts of Lemma 6.3.6; part (5), concerning an instantiated constant, is new:

Lemma 10.4.9 *(Generation Lemma)*

(1) If $\Delta ; \Gamma \vdash x : C$, *then there exist a sort* s *and an expression* B *such that* $B \stackrel{\Delta}{=}_\beta C$, $\Delta ; \Gamma \vdash B : s$ *and* $x : B \in \Gamma$.

(2) If $\Delta ; \Gamma \vdash MN : C$, *then there are* A, B *such that* $\Delta ; \Gamma \vdash M : \Pi x : A \,.\, B$ *and* $\Delta ; \Gamma \vdash N : A$ *and* $C \stackrel{\Delta}{=}_\beta B[x := N]$.

(3) If $\Delta ; \Gamma \vdash \lambda x : A \,.\, b : C$, *then there are a sort* s *and an expression* B *such that* $C \stackrel{\Delta}{=}_\beta \Pi x : A \,.\, B$ *and* $\Delta ; \Gamma \vdash \Pi x : A \,.\, B : s$ *and* $\Delta ; \Gamma, x : A \vdash b : B$.

(4) If $\Delta ; \Gamma \vdash \Pi x : A \,.\, B : C$, *then there are* s_1 *and* s_2 *such that* $C \stackrel{\Delta}{=}_\beta s_2$ *and* $\Delta ; \Gamma \vdash A : s_1$ *and* $\Delta ; \Gamma, x : A \vdash B : s_2$.

(5) If $\Delta ; \Gamma \vdash a(\overline{U}) : C$, *then constant* a *must be the defined constant in a definition* $\mathcal{D} \equiv \overline{x} : \overline{A} \rhd a(\overline{x}) := M/\perp : N$ *in* Δ, *and* $C \stackrel{\Delta}{=}_\beta N[\overline{x} := \overline{U}]$; *moreover:*

– *if* $|\Gamma| = n > 0$, *then there is* $\overline{B}$ *such that* $\Delta ; \Gamma \vdash \overline{U} : \overline{B}$ *and, for all* $1 \le i \le n$, $B_i \stackrel{\Delta}{=}_\beta A_i[\overline{x} := \overline{U}]$;

– *if* $|\Gamma| = 0$ *and* $\mathcal{D}$ *is a descriptive definition, then there is* N' *such that* $N \stackrel{\Delta}{=}_\beta N'$ *and* $\Delta ; \Gamma \vdash M : N'$;

– *if* $|\Gamma| = 0$ *and* $\mathcal{D}$ *is a primitive definition, then* $\Delta ; \Gamma \vdash N : s$ *for some sort* s.

The relation β-reduction in λD is the same as in λD_0 (see Definition 9.7.1). In a similar manner we have $\twoheadrightarrow_\beta$, $=_\beta$ and $\stackrel{\Delta}{=}_\beta$ for the expressions of λD. We have the following extension of Lemma 6.3.9:

Lemma 10.4.10 *(Uniqueness of Types up to* $\beta\delta$-*conversion)*

If $\Delta ; \Gamma \vdash K : L_1$ *and* $\Delta ; \Gamma \vdash K : L_2$, *then* $L_1 \stackrel{\Delta}{=}_\beta L_2$.

And also (cf. Lemma 6.3.10):

Lemma 10.4.11   *(Substitution Lemma)*
   Let $\Delta \, ; \Gamma_1, x : A, \Gamma_2 \vdash M : N$ *and* $\Delta \, ; \Gamma_1 \vdash L : A$.
   Then $\Delta \, ; \Gamma_1, \Gamma_2[x := L] \vdash M[x := L] : N[x := L]$.

The importance of the following lemma has already been explained after Lemma 2.11.5; see also Lemma 6.3.13:

Lemma 10.4.12   *(Subject Reduction)*
   If $\Delta \, ; \Gamma \vdash M : N$ *and* $M \overset{\Delta}{\twoheadrightarrow} M'$ *or* $M \twoheadrightarrow_\beta M'$, *then* $\Delta \, ; \Gamma \vdash M' : N$.

Consequently, the lemma also holds if $M \overset{\Delta}{\twoheadrightarrow}_\beta M'$, where $\overset{\Delta}{\twoheadrightarrow}_\beta$ is the symbol for a sequence of β- and δ-reductions (with respect to Δ), in an arbitrary mixture.

10.5 Normalisation and confluence in λD

We continue with the investigation of the normalisation and confluence properties of λD. We don't give proofs in this section, but refer for those to Geuvers (2014a). As we saw earlier (e.g. in Sections 1.9 and 6.3), 'normalisation' is another word for 'termination'. So we are interested in the *termination behaviour* of the reduction relations $\rightarrow_\beta$ and $\overset{\Delta}{\twoheadrightarrow}$, both separately and combined. Termination is desirable as a property, since it prevents infinite reduction paths. We recall that 'weak normalisation' of a term M only ensures the *existence* of a reduction path to a term in β-normal form (see Definition 1.9.6); 'strong normalisation' holds if *all* reduction paths terminate after a finite number of steps – which number may vary according to the path chosen.

Firstly, we consider the new relation $\overset{\Delta}{\twoheadrightarrow}$, which formalises the 'unfolding' of a definition. Given a legal expression L in λD, does there always exist a δ-reduction path starting with L which terminates? This is indeed the case. (A proof can be given by considering a clever order for unfolding the proper constants in an expression, and eliminating them one by one.)

Theorem 10.5.1   *(Weak Normalisation of* $\overset{\Delta}{\twoheadrightarrow}$*)*
   For each legal Δ, *the relation* $\overset{\Delta}{\twoheadrightarrow}$ *is weakly normalising.*

It requires more effort to prove that strong normalisation holds for $\overset{\Delta}{\twoheadrightarrow}$:

Theorem 10.5.2   *(Strong Normalisation of* $\overset{\Delta}{\twoheadrightarrow}$*)*
   For each legal Δ, *the relation* $\overset{\Delta}{\twoheadrightarrow}$ *is strongly normalising.*

We also have confluence for λD with respect to definition unfolding; so if

$M \overset{\Delta}{\twoheadrightarrow} N_1$ and $M \overset{\Delta}{\twoheadrightarrow} N_2$, then there is N_3 such that $N_1 \overset{\Delta}{\twoheadrightarrow} N_3$ and $N_2 \overset{\Delta}{\twoheadrightarrow} N_3$ (cf. Theorem 1.9.8):

Theorem 10.5.3   *(δ-confluence in $(\lambda D, \overset{\Delta}{\twoheadrightarrow})$)*
  For each legal Δ, the relation $\overset{\Delta}{\twoheadrightarrow}$ is confluent.

And this, in its turn, brings along that δ-normal forms are unique (cf. Lemma 1.9.10):

Corollary 10.5.4   *(Uniqueness of δ-normal forms in $(\lambda D, \overset{\Delta}{\twoheadrightarrow})$)*
  For every $L \in \lambda D$ that is legal with respect to Δ and Γ, there is a unique expression M such that $L \overset{\Delta}{\twoheadrightarrow} M$ and M is in δ-normal form with respect to Δ.

Note that M is in δ-normal form if (and only if) M contains no proper constants; there may, however, occur *primitive* constants in such an M.

We have now investigated the behaviour of λD with respect to definition unfolding (δ-reduction). But we are not yet done, because there still is a more fundamental reduction relation in λD, namely β-reduction. And although we observed that both β- and δ-reduction, separately, satisfy nice properties (viz. WN and SN, i.e. weak and strong normalisation), this is no guarantee that these properties also hold for a *combination* of the two reductions, $\overset{\Delta}{\twoheadrightarrow}_\beta$. For a reduction $L_0 \overset{\Delta}{\twoheadrightarrow}_\beta \ldots$, which may for example start as follows:

$$L_0 \overset{\Delta}{\twoheadrightarrow} L_1 \rightarrow_\beta L_2 \rightarrow_\beta L_3 \overset{\Delta}{\twoheadrightarrow} L_4 \rightarrow_\beta \ldots,$$

it is not clear whether it will end after a finite number of steps. We now turn to WN and SN for $\overset{\Delta}{\twoheadrightarrow}_\beta$.

Our first concern is whether the property CR (or Confluence; cf. Theorem 1.9.8) holds for $\overset{\Delta}{\twoheadrightarrow}_\beta$.

Theorem 10.5.5   *(Church–Rosser for $\overset{\Delta}{\twoheadrightarrow}_\beta$ in λD; CR; $\beta\delta$-confluence)*
  Suppose that for an expression $L \in \mathcal{E}_{\lambda D}$ holds that $L \overset{\Delta}{\twoheadrightarrow}_\beta L_1$ and $L \overset{\Delta}{\twoheadrightarrow}_\beta L_2$. Then there is an expression $L_3 \in \mathcal{E}_{\lambda D}$ such that $L_1 \overset{\Delta}{\twoheadrightarrow}_\beta L_3$ and $L_2 \overset{\Delta}{\twoheadrightarrow}_\beta L_3$.

A consequence of $\beta\delta$-confluence is, as before (cf. Lemma 1.9.10 (2)):

Corollary 10.5.6   *(Uniqueness of $\beta\delta$-normal form)*
  If $L \in \mathcal{E}_{\lambda D}$ has a $\beta\delta$-normal form, then this normal form is unique.

What remains are the questions of weak and strong normalisation. Both properties hold in λD. The first one follows from Weak Normalisation for λC.

The second one is also a consequence of the corresponding theorem for λC, but the proof is more complicated.

Theorem 10.5.7 *(Weak Normalisation for $\overset{\Delta}{\twoheadrightarrow}_\beta$ in λD)*

If $L \in \mathcal{E}_{\lambda D}$ and L is legal, then there is a $\beta\delta$-reduction sequence starting with L which ends in a $\beta\delta$-normal form after a finite number of steps.

Theorem 10.5.8 *(Strong Normalisation for $\overset{\Delta}{\twoheadrightarrow}_\beta$ in λD)*

If $L \in \mathcal{E}_{\lambda D}$ and L is legal, then there is no infinite $\beta\delta$-reduction sequence starting with L.

10.6 Conclusions

In this chapter we have argued that it is desirable to have a possibility for the handling of axioms and axiomatic (also called 'primitive') notions. This has led us to a distinction between the *descriptive* definitions, as dealt with in the previous chapter, and the *primitive* ones.

A descriptive definition $\Delta\,;\Gamma \vdash a(\overline{x}) := M : N$ has a *body* M, which opens the possibility to *unfold* an instantiation $a(\overline{U})$ into $M[\overline{x} := \overline{U}]$. In a primitive definition $\Delta\,;\Gamma \vdash a(\overline{x}) := \perp\!\!\!\perp : N$, however, such unfolding is impossible (and not intended).

We have given several examples of axioms and primitive notions, to emphasise that such entities really form part of a natural build-up of logic and mathematics.

For the formalisation of such notions, we added two more rules to system λD_0: a *(def-prim)*-rule for adding a primitive definition to the tail of an environment, and an *(inst-prim)*-rule for instantiating the parameter list of a primitive constant. These rules are similar to the corresponding *(def)*- and *(inst)*-rules already present in λD_0, but since they miss the definiens parts in the definitions, some changes in the shape of the rules are required.

Altogether, we have thus obtained our final system: λD. We have concluded with an overview of the relevant properties of λD, including the desired normalisation and confluence properties, which are very important for λD to behave well.

10.7 Further reading

The use of a definition-like mechanism for adding parameterised axioms to a type theory originates from the Automath project (de Bruijn, 1970). There, a definition without body is called a 'primitive notion', PN. So a definiens can either be an expression or 'PN', in which case it is an axiom or an axiomatic notion. The Automath approach views a formalisation as a *book* with *lines*. Each line builds on the previous ones and contains a definition or a primitive notion. That is, it contains either a definition with or a definition without a body. So, from Automath we inherit the idea to treat definitions and axioms very much on a par, and we formalise them in λD with a similar syntactic construction.

Normalisation and *confluence* are important properties to establish the logical consistency of a type theory. They also are crucial to make an implementation of the type theory as a proof assistant or proof checker possible. Let us expand on these two issues.

In a type theory like λD, proofs are represented as λ-terms. So in an implementation of λD as a proof checker, the basic functionality would be to *verify the well-formedness of a term*, which is done by *type-checking the term* (i.e. computing the type of the term). A general description of type checking algorithms (and their correctness) for Pure Type Systems can be found in van Benthem Jutting (1993) and van Benthem Jutting *et al.* (1994). The algorithms and proofs described therein apply directly to λD.

Here we outline the connection with confluence and normalisation of the reduction relation. The crucial point is that, when type-checking a term, one has to check $\beta\delta$-convertibility. For example, to compute the type of the term $F\,M$, one has to

(1) compute the type of M, say A,

(2) compute the type of F, say B,

(3) check if the type B can be $\beta\delta$-reduced to a type of the shape $\Pi x : C\,.\,D$,

(4) if yes, then check whether $C \stackrel{\triangle}{=}_\beta A$,

(5) if yes, then the type of $F\,M$ is $D[x := M]$.

In the third step, normalisation guarantees that this check terminates: we can continue reducing the so-called 'outermost' redex (see Terese, 2003) of B until we either arrive at an expression of the shape $\Pi x : C\,.\,D$ or we arrive at a normal form which is not of this shape. (The uniqueness of the normal form is a consequence of confluence.) In the fourth step, normalisation and confluence guarantee that this check is decidable: just compute the normal form on both sides and check if they are the same. For this to work, we only need weak normalisation in steps (3) and (4), because this implies that we have a strategy (see above) for computing the normal form.

It should be noted that *in practice* a proof checker would not reduce two terms to normal form to check their $\beta\delta$-convertibility, because this would be too expensive (in time and space). An '*equality checker*' tries to decide convertibility as fast as possible without doing too many reductions.

Strong normalisation is important because it guarantees the termination of the reduction process, whatever reduction strategy one prefers, so it allows one to *choose* the reduction path in order to establish the convertibility of two terms. This can be profitable, since a clever choice of the reduction path may speed up the reduction process considerably.

To prove the logical consistency of a type theory, one way to reason is as follows: suppose the system is inconsistent. Then $\vdash M : \bot$ for some M. It follows that there also is an M' in normal form with $\vdash M' : \bot$, because of normalisation and subject reduction. And then we derive a contradiction from the fact that a term of type $\bot$ in the empty context cannot be in normal form (see Proposition 5.2.31 of Barendregt, 1992). For λD, this argument works: we can show that there is no term of type $\bot$ in the empty context. To show that a specific environment (containing primitive notions) is consistent, a similar argument can be applied. For example, we can show that the environment that introduces classical logic as a primitive notion is consistent: there is no term M in normal form of type $\bot$ in this environment.

Exercises

10.1 See Section 10.2. Show that
$$\forall_{n\in\mathbb{N}} \, (9 \mid n^3 + (n+1)^3 + (n+2)^3)$$
by giving an informal proof based on induction.

10.2 A 'contradiction' is formalised in λD as being an inhabitant of $\bot$.

    (a) Show that the following primitive definition causes inconsistency, because it enables the derivation of a contradiction in λD:
$$A, B : *_p \, \triangleright \, k(A, B) := \bot \!\!\!\bot : (A \Rightarrow B) \Rightarrow A.$$

    (b) Show that the following pair of primitive definitions causes inconsistency:
$$\emptyset \, \triangleright \, \iota_{DN} := \bot \!\!\!\bot : \forall A : *_p . \, (\neg\neg A \Rightarrow A),$$
$$\emptyset \, \triangleright \, neg\text{-}imp := \bot \!\!\!\bot : \forall A : *_p . \, (A \Rightarrow \neg A).$$

    (c) Show that the following definition, resembling the induction axiom, causes inconsistency:
$$P : \mathbb{N} \to *_p \, \triangleright \, ind\text{-}s(P) := \forall n : \mathbb{N} . \, (P\,n \Rightarrow P(s\,n)) \Rightarrow \forall n : \mathbb{N} . \, P\,n.$$

10.3 (a) Give a modified version of Lemma 9.9.1 (1) for primitive definitions and prove it.

    (b) Formulate a *(par-prim)*-rule for primitive definitions, as a natural companion to the *(par)*-rule for descriptive definitions (cf. Figure 9.4).

10.4 Let $\Delta \, ; \, \Gamma$ be a legal combination. Give a proof of
$$\Delta \, ; \, \Gamma \vdash * : \square.$$
(Use induction on the structure of the derivation of $\Delta \, ; \, \Gamma \vdash M : N$.)

10.5 Prove Lemma 10.4.7 (1).

10.6 Prove that Lemma 9.9.1 (2) is a consequence of Lemma 9.9.1 (1) and Lemma 10.4.7 (2).

10.7 Let $\Delta \,;\, \Gamma$ be a legal combination. Prove the following (hint: see Exercise 10.4 and Lemma 10.4.7 (1)):

(a) If $(x : A) \in \Gamma$, then $\Delta \,;\, \Gamma \vdash A : s$ for some sort s.

(b) If x is fresh, then also $\Delta \,;\, \Gamma, x : *$ is a legal combination.

(c) If $(x : *) \in \Gamma$ and y is fresh, then also $\Delta \,;\, \Gamma, y : x$ is a legal combination.

10.8 Prove Lemma 10.4.5 (1).

11

Flag-style natural deduction in λD

11.1 Formal derivations in λD

Now that we have developed system λD, being the Calculus of Constructions enriched with definitions and primitive notions, we can do better when expressing logic. In particular, we can now do constructive logic in an efficient and elegant manner. This can be done already in λD$_0$, since there are no axioms in constructive logic.

In Sections 7.1 and 7.2, we encountered a number of 'hidden' definitions dealing with logic in λC. As examples, we repeat three of them below, now using the standard format of λD as described in the previous sections.

Absurdity

In Section 7.1, we identified the absurdity $\bot$ with $\Pi\alpha : *.\,\alpha$. The symbol $\bot$ was not part of the λC syntax; it acted as a 'new name' (or shorthand) for the expression $\Pi\alpha : *.\,\alpha$. This is exactly what a descriptive definition does, so we write this now as:

$\emptyset \,\rhd\, \bot() := \Pi\alpha : *.\,\alpha \,:\, *.$

(Since this is our first exercise with the system λD, we do not omit the empty parameter list, as would have been allowed by Notation 8.3.3.)

Negation

In the same Section 7.1, we took $\neg A$ as an abbreviation for $A \to \bot$. This clearly is a descriptive definition again, but this time one with a non-empty context, since we silently presupposed that $A : *$ (the definition holds *for all* propositions A):

$A : * \,\rhd\, \neg(A) := A \to \bot() \,:\, *.$

The flag-manner to write this definition is:

$\boxed{A : *}$

$\quad \neg(A) := A \to \bot() \,:\, *$

Conjunction

In Section 7.2 we considered the second order encodings for ∧ and ∨. Let's consider conjunction here. Its definition depends on *two* parameters, viz. the free variables A and B. (Note that C is a *bound* variable, and not a parameter of the definition.)

$$\boxed{A : *}$$
$$\quad \boxed{B : *}$$
$$\qquad \wedge(A, B) \ := \ \Pi C : * . \ (A \to B \to C) \to C \ : \ *$$

How can logical definitions like the ones above be formally *derived* in λD? Let's consider how they fit into the λD scheme (Figure 9.3).

First look at the absurdity definition $\emptyset \ \triangleright \ \bot() \ := \ \Pi \alpha : * . \ \alpha \ : \ *$. If we want to incorporate this definition into an environment, e.g. by means of the *(par)*-rule, it suffices to construct a derivation of

$$\emptyset \ ; \ \emptyset \ \vdash \ \Pi \alpha : * . \ \alpha \ : \ *.$$

It will be clear that we can simply start with the corresponding derivation in λC and 'copy' it in λD-style:

	λC		λD$_0$	
(1)	$\emptyset \vdash * : \square$	*(sort)*	$\emptyset \ ; \ \emptyset \vdash * : \square$	*(sort)*
(2)	$\alpha : * \vdash \alpha : *$	*(var)*	$\emptyset \ ; \ \alpha : * \vdash \alpha : *$	*(var)*
(3)	$\emptyset \vdash \Pi \alpha : * . \ \alpha \ : \ *$	*(form)*	$\emptyset \ ; \ \emptyset \vdash \Pi \alpha : * . \ \alpha \ : \ *$	*(form)*

Figure 11.1 'Copying' a λC-derivation into λD$_0$

After this, we may append the definition of $\bot$ to the (still empty) environment in line (3), right-hand side. In order to keep things clear for the reader, we abbreviate the definition by

$$\mathcal{D}_1 \ \equiv \ \emptyset \ \triangleright \ \bot() \ := \ \Pi \alpha : * . \ \alpha \ : \ *,$$

and we derive in λD with the rule *(par)* (see Figure 9.4):

(4) $\mathcal{D}_1 \ ; \ \emptyset \vdash \bot() \ : \ *$ *(par)*.

The next task is to incorporate the above definition of $\neg$ into λD. We abbreviate it by $\mathcal{D}_2$:

$$\mathcal{D}_2 \ \equiv \ A : * \ \triangleright \ \neg(A) \ := \ A \to \bot() \ : \ *.$$

As we want to introduce this definition $\mathcal{D}_2$ in the environment as well, just as we did in (4) with $\mathcal{D}_1$, we try to derive the following judgement:

$$\mathcal{D}_1, \mathcal{D}_2 \ ; \ A : * \vdash \neg(A) \ : \ *.$$

Note that we need $\mathcal{D}_1$ in the environment, because we use $\bot$ in $\mathcal{D}_2$.

The above judgement is indeed derivable, as we demonstrate in Figure 11.2.

$$
\begin{array}{lll}
\mathcal{D}_1 & \equiv & \emptyset \quad \triangleright \ \bot() \quad := \ \Pi\alpha : * . \, \alpha \ : \ * \\
\mathcal{D}_2 & \equiv & A : * \ \triangleright \ \neg(A) \ := \ A \to \bot() \ : \ *
\end{array}
$$

(1)	$\emptyset$	;	$\emptyset$	$\vdash$	$*$	:	$\Box$	(*sort*)
(2)	$\emptyset$	;	$\alpha : *$	$\vdash$	α	:	$*$	(*var*) on (1)
(3)	$\emptyset$	;	$\emptyset$	$\vdash$	$\Pi\alpha : * . \, \alpha$	:	$*$	(*form*) on (1), (2)
(4)	$\mathcal{D}_1$	;	$\emptyset$	$\vdash$	$\bot()$	:	$*$	(*par*) on (3)
(5)	$\mathcal{D}_1$	;	$\emptyset$	$\vdash$	$*$	:	$\Box$	(*def*) on (1), (3)
(6)	$\mathcal{D}_1$	;	$A : *$	$\vdash$	A	:	$*$	(*var*) on (5)
(7)	$\mathcal{D}_1$	;	$A : *$	$\vdash$	$\bot()$	:	$*$	(*weak*) on (4), (5)
(8)	$\mathcal{D}_1$	;	$A : *, \, y : A$	$\vdash$	$\bot()$	:	$*$	(*weak*) on (7), (6)
(9)	$\mathcal{D}_1$	;	$A : *$	$\vdash$	$A \to \bot()$	:	$*$	(*form*) on (6), (8)
(10)	$\mathcal{D}_1, \mathcal{D}_2$	;	$A : *$	$\vdash$	$\neg(A)$	:	$*$	(*par*) on (9)

Figure 11.2 A λD_0-derivation for the definition of $\neg$

We take some time to look deeper into this derivation. First note that, for convenience's sake, we list the two definitions in a kind of *preamble* at the beginning of the derivation, together with their 'meta-names' $\mathcal{D}_1$ and $\mathcal{D}_2$. This permits us to write the derivation in the condensed form as given in Figure 11.2; officially, the 'meta-names' $\mathcal{D}_1$ and $\mathcal{D}_2$ in lines (4) to (10) should be replaced by the unabbreviated definitions they represent.

As is usual with the development of derivations (cf. Chapters 2 to 7, and in particular Section 2.6), we start at the bottom end. So we ask ourselves the question: how can we *arrive at* the final judgement, being:

(10) $\mathcal{D}_1, \, A : * \ \triangleright \ \neg(A) \ := \ A \to \bot() \ : \ * \ ; \ A : * \ \vdash \ \neg(A) \ : \ *$.

This judgement is a consequence of the (*par*)-rule, if we can derive:

(9) $\mathcal{D}_1 \ ; \ A : * \ \vdash \ A \to \bot() \ : \ *$,

which in its turn, since $A \to \bot()$ is an abbreviation of $\Pi y : A . \, \bot()$, can be obtained from the (*form*)-rule applied on the judgements

(6) $\mathcal{D}_1 \ ; \ A : * \ \vdash \ A : *$, and

(8) $\mathcal{D}_1 \ ; \ A : *, \, y : A \ \vdash \ \bot() : *$.

We leave it to the reader to continue this bottom-up analysis of the derivation above.

In a similar manner, one can derive the formal λD-version of the definition of conjunction. See Figure 11.3 for an outline; the details are left to the reader (Exercise 11.2). Note that this derivation does not appeal to definitions $\mathcal{D}_1$ or $\mathcal{D}_2$, because neither $\bot$ nor $\neg$ play a role in the definition of $\wedge$. There would be, however, no objection against maintaining $\mathcal{D}_1$ and $\mathcal{D}_2$ in the environment of the judgement.

$$\mathcal{D}_3 \; \equiv \; A : *, \; B : * \; \rhd \; \wedge(A, B) \; := \; \Pi C : * . \; (A \to B \to C) \to C \; : \; *$$

$$\vdots \quad \vdots \qquad\qquad\qquad\qquad\qquad\qquad\quad\Big|$$

$$(..) \quad \mathcal{D}_3 \; ; \quad A : *, B : * \;\; \vdash \;\; \wedge(A, B) \; : \; * \;\Big|\; (par)$$

Figure 11.3 The shape of a λC-derivation for the definition of $\wedge$

11.2 Comparing formal and flag-style λD

In Chapter 4 – to be precise, in Section 4.6 – we decided to suppress less interesting steps in derivations, when this does not harm the cogency. In particular, we tended to omit applications of the rules $(sort)$, (var), $(weak)$ and $(form)$. This enabled us to develop derivations in flag style that have a nice and convincing appearance, without having to bother about the more administrative steps that the type systems require. We have maintained this procedure in later chapters, which includes the examples in λC given in Chapter 7.

We do the same in λD: we suppress, if we desire so, the occurrences of not-so-interesting steps (in particular, the ones mentioned above, plus (def)), so we can concentrate on the steps that really matter. Applying this to our derivation in Figure 11.2, we can skip lines (1), (2), (5) and (7).

An interesting question is how a derivation in the linear format as employed in Figure 11.2 relates to a *flag-style* derivation. In order to demonstrate this, we make a faithful copy in flag format of the derivation in Figure 11.2. We take the shortened version as described just now, but for ease of reference we maintain the original line numbers:

(3)	$\Pi\alpha : * . \; \alpha \; : \; *$	$(form)$
$(\mathcal{D}_1)$	$\bot() \; := \; \Pi\alpha : * . \; \alpha \; : \; *$	definition
(4)	$\bot() : *$	(par) on (3) and $(\mathcal{D}_1)$
(a)	$\boxed{A : *}$	
(6)	$A : *$	(var)
(b)	$\boxed{y : A}$	
(8)	$\bot() \; : \; *$	$(weak)$, twice, on (4) and (6)
(9)	$A \to \bot() \; : \; *$	$(form)$ on (6) and (8)
$(\mathcal{D}_2)$	$\neg(A) \; := \; A \to \bot() \; : \; *$	definition
(10)	$\neg(A) \; : \; *$	(par) on (9) and $(\mathcal{D}_2)$

There clearly is a close resemblance between this flag version and the 'official' λD_0 version of Figure 11.2 (in the shortened form).

When looking closer at the *flag* version above, it strikes the eye that in line $(\mathcal{D}_1)$ there appears an almost-duplication of the information contained in the embracing lines (3) and (4), and similarly with $(\mathcal{D}_2)$ and lines (9) and (10). It appears reasonable to maintain only definitions $(\mathcal{D}_1)$ and $(\mathcal{D}_2)$, and erase lines (3), (4), (9) and (10).

For example, when condensing the triple (3), $(\mathcal{D}_1)$ and (4) into $(\mathcal{D}_1)$ alone:

$$\perp() := \Pi\alpha : *.\ \alpha\ :\ *,$$

we should agree on the convention that this single line *incorporates* derivability of the omitted statements (3) and (4).

A second observation is that lines (6) and (8) are more or less superfluous: line (9) can also be seen as an obvious consequence of assumption (a) and line (4). So we may skip lines (6) and (8), and therefore also assumption (b).

Implementing the mentioned adaptations, we obtain the following flag-style derivation:

$(\mathcal{D}_1)$	$\perp() := \Pi\alpha : *.\ \alpha\ :\ *$	*(form)* and *(par)*
(a)	$\boxed{A : *}$	
$(\mathcal{D}_2)$	$\neg(A) := A \to \perp()\ :\ *$	*(form)* and *(par)*

Hence, by rewriting the λD proof into flag format, and omitting some very obvious lines, we obtain a flag derivation that is identical to the presentation of the corresponding definitions in the beginning of Section 11.1. It is tempting to conjecture, albeit based on very little evidence, that the formal derivation system λD as we developed it, can be fruitfully employed for a faithful reflection of the more intuitive approach towards definitions as we have employed, for example, in Chapter 7.

11.3 Conventions about flag-style proofs in λD

The examples in the previous section, in particular in the 'condensed form' of the final paragraphs, show how specific lines in the flag-style presentation have a specific 'meaning'.

For example, a line of the form

$$c(\overline{x}) := M : N$$

in an environment Δ and a context Γ, where parameter list $\overline{x}$ is the list of the subject variables in Γ, has a *triple* meaning:

(1) the statement $M : N$ is derivable with respect to Δ and Γ,

(2) the definition $\mathcal{D} \equiv \Gamma \rhd c(\overline{x}) := M : N$ is added at the end of Δ,

(3) the statement $c(\overline{x}) : N$ is derivable in the extended environment $\Delta, \mathcal{D}$ and context Γ.

This kind of 'multiple meaning' of assumptions, definitions and other lines in λD_0 can be made more formal by explicitly giving a sort of 'operational semantics' to flag-style derivations. We confine ourselves to an illustrative situation to show how this semantics works. In this example we record the *state* of a derivation as a pair $\{\mathcal{D} \mid \Gamma\}$ of an environment and a context. This state changes when the context changes, and when a new definition is added.

$\{\emptyset \mid \emptyset\}$

(a) $\boxed{x_1 : A_1}$

$\{\emptyset \mid x_1 : A_1\}$

(b) $\boxed{x_2 : A_2}$

$\{\emptyset \mid x_1 : A_1, x_2 : A_2\}$

(1) $a(x_1, x_2) := M_1 : N_1$

$\{x_1 : A_1, x_2 : A_2 \rhd a(x_1, x_2) := M_1 : N_1 \mid x_1 : A_1, x_2 : A_2\}$

$\{x_1 : A_1, x_2 : A_2 \rhd a(x_1, x_2) := M_1 : N_1 \mid x_1 : A_1\}$

(2) $b(x_1) := M_2 : N_2$

$\{x_1 : A_1, x_2 : A_2 \rhd a(x_1, x_2) := M_1 : N_1, \; x_1 : A_1 \rhd b(x_1) := M_2 : N_2 \mid$

$x_1 : A_1\}$

In this example we see that:

— each time *a flag is raised*, the context is extended; when the flag is *hauled down* (at the end of a flagpole), context Γ accordingly shrinks;

— a *definition* $a(\overline{x}) := M : N$ under a context of flags expresses that the corresponding definition $\mathcal{D} \equiv \Gamma \rhd a(\overline{x}) := M : N$ is added to the environment Δ, where Γ corresponds to the flag context.

Moreover, the statements $M : N$ and $a(\overline{x}) : N$, implicitly present within $\mathcal{D}$, correspond to the following two derivable judgements: $\Delta \; ; \; \Gamma \vdash M : N$ and $\Delta, \mathcal{D} \; ; \; \Gamma \vdash a(\overline{x}) : N$.

When constructing a single derivation, either in the official λD format or in the flag format, we gradually build up an environment Δ. One may choose at any time to start a new derivation *from scratch*, thus 'throwing away' previous information; an example of this is given in Section 11.1, where definition $\mathcal{D}_3$ did not depend on the derivations leading to definitions $\mathcal{D}_1$ and $\mathcal{D}_2$ (see Figures 11.2 and 11.3).

An alternative working method, which we prefer to follow in the chapters to come, is to condense all obtained derivations into *one* big overall derivation. This can easily be done by *attaching* new derivations to old ones. Such a continuous-derivation approach is advantageous, since then *all* judgements, including the definitions, stay 'alive' (i.e. valid and attainable), and therefore remain serviceable in a later stage. A *disadvantage* may of course be that there is a good chance that we 'drag along' judgements (in particular definitions) that are superfluous.

Remark 11.3.1 *In the latter approach, when building one big coherent derivation, context* Γ *may grow and shrink from line to line, just like a stack in a computer, but the environment* Δ *only becomes bigger and bigger: once added, a definition is never erased.*

This non-erasing situation for definitions is standard in our system λD, *since, as one may easily check, there is no derivation rule for deleting a definition.*

A reader not content with this fact may easily design an extra derivation rule – being a provable consequence *of the official rules – which makes it possible to eliminate superfluous definitions from an environment. This is allowed by the Condensing Lemma, 10.4.8 (2).*

That we do not erase definitions in λD may be justified as follows. An environment may be seen as a listing of all facts that matter or *may* matter: a judgement recorded as a definition can always be called upon at a later stage, by using its *name* and instantiating its parameters. Therefore, the environment acts as a kind of *log-book* of our achievements. And indeed, there is a natural correspondence between the 'knowledge' built up in a (logic or mathematics) *book* and the mentioned log-book of a derivation. We'll see this better in the examples of the following chapters.

In order to streamline the presentation of flag derivations, we shall from now on only use the *definition format*. That is, we present derivations consistently as a *list of definitions*, in agreement with our informal discussion in Section 8.9.

> *In a flag derivation, we turn every statement relative to a certain context, into a definition, by choosing a new defined name and appending that name in front of the statement.*

So instead of $\Gamma \vdash M : N$ we write $\Gamma \triangleright c(\overline{x}) := M : N$ in flag derivations.

Remark 11.3.2 *This approach is followed in the pioneering system* Automath, *devised and exploited in the late 1960s and the 1970s by N.G. de Bruijn and his group in Eindhoven, the Netherlands. (Cf. de Bruijn, 1970; Nederpelt et al., 1994.)*

We are aware that application of the above convention may introduce non-essential defined names; i.e. names that are never used after they have been defined. On the other hand, this approach enables a simplified version of system λD, in particular when presented in flag format, since there are no longer statements-as-such: statements are all embedded into definitions.

11.4 Introduction and elimination rules

In this chapter we consider λD-formalised *logic* as a start for the exploration of the *usefulness* of λD as a system for the formalisation of *mathematics*. We go even further: in the present chapter and the ones to come we investigate whether it is true that such a formalisation can be made in a '*natural*' manner; that is, close to the way a mathematician is used to develop theories.

In order to pave our survey of how to encode *logic* in λD, we recall our endeavours in Chapter 7, where we have shown that logic, in particular *natural deduction*, can be fruitfully embedded into the Calculus of Constructions, λC. Presently, with λD, we have more expressive power, which enables us to precisely register *inside the formal derivation* which natural deduction rules are used during the development of a derivation. This makes it easier for the writer to communicate the logical background of a step in a derivation; and thereby enables the reader to follow the proof with better understanding.

We demonstrate this point with an example from predicate logic. We give a λD-derivation in flag format embodying a proof of the following tautology:

if $\forall_{x \in S}(A \Rightarrow P(x))$, then $A \Rightarrow \forall_{x \in S}(P(y))$,

for a given predicate P over a set S, and a proposition A.

A formal derivation of this tautology in λD is easy, as the reader can see in Figure 11.4. As before (see Section 7.6) we write $\forall$ for Π, and $\Rightarrow$ for $\rightarrow$.

Remark 11.4.1 *We have added defined constants to every statement, in conformity with Remark 11.3.2. The names a_1 to a_3 do not play a further role in the present derivation. This is, however, exceptional: defined constants turn out to be very useful and will regularly be called upon; see, for example, line (5).*

There are two lines in this derivation that are a result of the (*appl*)-rule:

- Line (1) is a consequence of $\forall$-elimination, since we apply the proposition $\forall_{x \in S}(A \Rightarrow P(x))$ to y in S, which results in $A \Rightarrow P(y)$. Formally: the u inhabiting the coded $\forall$-expression is applied to the y inhabiting S, resulting in $u\,y$ inhabiting the coded version of $A \Rightarrow P(y)$.

- It is followed by line (2), in which the obtained $u\,y$ has been applied to v, being an inhabitant of A. From a logical point of view, we have a case of $\Rightarrow$-elimination here: $A \Rightarrow P(y)$ and A lead to $P(y)$.

(a) $\boxed{S : *}$

(b) $\quad\boxed{P \,:\, S \to *}$

(c) $\qquad\boxed{A : *}$

(d) $\qquad\boxed{u \ :\ \forall x : S . \, (A \Rightarrow P\,x)}$

(e) $\qquad\qquad\boxed{v : A}$

(f) $\qquad\qquad\boxed{y : S}$

(1) $\qquad\qquad\quad a_1(S, P, A, u, v, y) \ := \ u\,y \ : \ A \Rightarrow P\,y \qquad (appl)$ on (d) and (f)

(2) $\qquad\qquad\quad a_2(S, P, A, u, v, y) \ := \ u\,y\,v \ : \ P\,y \qquad (appl)$ on (1) and (e)

(3) $\qquad\qquad a_3(S, P, A, u, v) \ := \ \lambda y : S . \, u\,y\,v \ : \ \forall y : S . \, P\,y \qquad (abst)$ on (2)

(4) $\qquad\quad a_4(S, P, A, u) \ := \ \lambda v : A . \, \lambda y : S . \, u\,y\,v \ :$

$$A \Rightarrow \forall y : S . \, P\,y \qquad (abst) \text{ on } (3)$$

(5) $\qquad a_5(S, P, A) \ := \ \lambda u : (\forall x : S . \, (A \Rightarrow P\,x)) . \, a_4(S, P, A, u) \ :$

$$(\forall x : S . \, (A \Rightarrow P\,x)) \Rightarrow A \Rightarrow \forall y : S . \, P\,y \qquad (abst) \text{ on } (4)$$

Figure 11.4 A λD-derivation of a logical tautology

Hence, the annotation (*appl*) used in both lines is in a sense too general: it hides the information that in line (1) the logical $\forall$-elimination rule has been used, and in line (2) the logical $\Rightarrow$-elimination rule. This makes the given derivation less transparent than one might desire.

A similar remark can be made about lines (3) to (5): all these are annotated with (*abst*), concealing that we have, from a logical point of view, a case of $\forall$-introduction in line (3) and of $\Rightarrow$-introduction in lines (4) and (5).

In the present chapter we demonstrate how the definition mechanism may help us to disclose such information if we wish so, as part of the derivation and on the spot where it 'happens'. Therefore it is worthwhile to redo our systematic discussion of the so-called 'logical constants' that we have discussed earlier, notably in Chapter 7 and (as examples of definitions) in Section 11.1. We shall introduce a number of *definitions* that embody the logical introduction- and elimination-rules. We have to choose which rules to include: it is not immediately clear which ones to insert and which to omit. We try to be concise but also practical.

Another thing is that we do *not* make the fundamental choice to only consider constructive logic. Hence, we admit the axiom of the *excluded third* or that of the *double negation* – see Section 7.4. The reason is that mathematicians often employ *classical logic*, and we respect this preference.

Below, we start with the rules of *constructive* propositional logic, but cross over to *classical* propositional logic as soon as this is appropriate. Definitions and rules for predicate logic will be given thereafter, again in the two versions.

In between, we give examples in order to demonstrate how these introduction and elimination rules 'work'. A summary of the presented rules for constructive and classical natural deduction in λD will be given in Appendix A.

11.5 Rules for constructive propositional logic

We start with the connectives closest connected to type theory, namely *implication*, *absurdity* and *negation*. The logical introduction and elimination rules for $\Rightarrow$, $\bot$ and $\neg$ are described in Remarks 7.1.1 and 7.1.2. We recall from Section 5.4, IV, that $A \Rightarrow B$ may simply be encoded as $A \to B$, being an abbreviation for $\Pi x : A . B$ if $x \notin FV(B)$ (which is here the case).

In λD we can *give a name* to each of the corresponding natural deduction rules. For example, we shall introduce the λD-constant $\bot\text{-}in$ for the $\bot$-introduction rule. See Figures 11.5, 11.6 and 11.7 below.

Notation 11.5.1 *For reasons of space, we sometimes combine flags. In Figure 11.5 we employ such a condensed representation on two occasions:*
- *we combine the two flags $A : *_p$ and $B : *_p$, concerning declarations that have the same type $*_p$;*
- *we use a double flag between lines (2) and (3) for the subsequent declarations $u : A \Rightarrow B$ and $v : A$, presented horizontally instead of vertically.*

In order to emphasise that we are dealing with *propositions*, we write $*_p$ instead of $*$ (see Notation 8.7.1).

$$
\begin{array}{ll}
& \boxed{A, B : *_p} \\
(1) & \quad \Rightarrow(A, B) \ := \ A \to B \ : \ *_p \\
& \quad \text{Notation: } A \Rightarrow B \text{ for } \Rightarrow(A, B) \\
& \quad \boxed{u : A \to B} \\
(2) & \quad\quad \Rightarrow\text{-}in(A, B, u) \ := \ u \ : \ A \Rightarrow B \\
& \quad \boxed{u : A \Rightarrow B \mid v : A} \\
(3) & \quad\quad \Rightarrow\text{-}el(A, B, u, v) \ := \ u\,v \ : \ B
\end{array}
$$

Figure 11.5 Definition and rules for $\Rightarrow$

Notation 11.5.2 *We make our formalised versions of mathematics more readable by inserting notation conventions as extra lines in a derivation. See the 'Notation' following line (1): thereby we agree to write expressions like $\Rightarrow(A, B)$ as $A \Rightarrow B$, in infix notation, which is more reader-friendly. Such a convention is just made for our comfort; it is not meant to be an actual extension of the language. Otherwise said: we suppose that such notational abbreviations have been undone in the 'real' λD-text.*

(1) $\quad \perp := \Pi A : *_p . \ A : *_p$

$\boxed{A : *_p}$

$\qquad \boxed{u : A \mid v : A \Rightarrow \perp}$

(2) $\qquad \perp\text{-}in(A, u, v) := v\, u \ : \ \perp$

$\qquad \boxed{u : \perp}$

(3) $\qquad \perp\text{-}el(A, u) := u\, A \ : \ A$

Figure 11.6 Definition and rules for $\perp$

Note that we could as well have defined $\perp\text{-}in(A, u, v)$ as $\Rightarrow\text{-}in(A, u, v)$ in line (2) of Figure 11.6, since $\perp\text{-}in$ is a special case of $\Rightarrow\text{-}in$. The rule $\neg\text{-}in$ in Figure 11.7 is also a special case of $\Rightarrow\text{-}in$, with $\perp$ for B. Similarly, $\neg\text{-}el$ is a special case of $\Rightarrow\text{-}el$. (Cf. Remark 7.1.2.)

$\boxed{A : *_p}$

(1) $\qquad \neg(A) := A \Rightarrow \perp \ : \ *_p$

$\qquad$ Notation: $\neg A$ for $\neg(A)$

$\qquad \boxed{u : A \rightarrow \perp}$

(2) $\qquad \neg\text{-}in(A, u) := u \ : \ \neg A$

$\qquad \boxed{u : \neg A \mid v : A}$

(3) $\qquad \neg\text{-}el(A, u, v) := u\, v \ : \ \perp$

Figure 11.7 Definition and rules for $\neg$

Names for the proof objects corresponding to introduction and elimination rules, as introduced above, can be particularly informative when we are interested in the natural deduction background of a derivation. See the following example, demonstrating that A implies $\neg\neg A$.

$\boxed{A : *_p}$

$\qquad \boxed{u : A}$

$\qquad \qquad \boxed{v : \neg A}$

(1) $\qquad\qquad a_1(A, u, v) := \neg\text{-}el(A, v, u) \ : \ \perp$

(2) $\qquad\quad a_2(A, u) := \neg\text{-}in(\neg A, \lambda v : \neg A . \ a_1(A, u, v)) \ : \ \neg\neg A$

(3) $\qquad a_3(A) := \Rightarrow\text{-}in(A, \neg\neg A, \lambda u : A . \ a_2(A, u)) \ : \ A \Rightarrow \neg\neg A$

Figure 11.8 Derivation of $A \Rightarrow \neg\neg A$ in natural deduction style

In Figure 11.8 we clearly see that the rules $\neg$-elimination, $\neg$-introduction and $\Rightarrow$-introduction have consecutively been used to obtain the result.

Such a presentation may be useful for the goal described. However, in case we are dealing with $\Rightarrow$, $\bot$ or $\neg$, the usual *type-theoretic style* is often more attractive. This is particularly the case when one is interested in the derivation as such, and not so much in the logical structure. The reason is that the original (unfolded) proof objects are considerably shorter. See Figure 11.9, in which we condensed the derivation of Figure 11.8 still further by omitting line (1).

$\boxed{A : *_p}$

$\qquad \boxed{u : A}$

(2) $\qquad a_2(A, u) := \lambda v : \neg A \,.\, v\, u \;:\; \neg\neg A$

(3) $\qquad a_3(A) := \lambda u : A \,.\, a_2(A, u) \;:\; A \Rightarrow \neg\neg A$

Figure 11.9 Derivation of $A \Rightarrow \neg\neg A$ in type-theoretic style

That the unfolded proof objects are *shorter* than the folded ones, as we see in Figures 11.9 vs. 11.8, is not the usual situation. In the natural deduction rules concerning conjunction, disjunction and biimplication, a definiendum such as $\wedge(A, B)$ is considerably *shorter* than $\Pi C : *_p \,.\, (A \Rightarrow B \Rightarrow C) \Rightarrow C$, the definiens. In these cases we can make good use of the *natural deduction style*.

We first give the relevant rules for $\wedge$ and $\vee$, corresponding to the introduction and elimination rules as discussed and explained in Section 7.2, I and II. The proof objects in line (2) of Figure 11.10 and line (4) of Figure 11.11 have been copied from that section. See also Section 11.1. Check the remaining lines in these figures yourself.

$\boxed{A, B : *_p}$

(1) $\qquad \wedge(A, B) := \Pi C : *_p \,.\, (A \Rightarrow B \Rightarrow C) \Rightarrow C \;:\; *_p$

$\qquad$ Notation: $A \wedge B$ for $\wedge(A, B)$

$\qquad \boxed{u : A \mid v : B}$

(2) $\qquad\quad \wedge\text{-}in(A, B, u, v) := \lambda C : *_p \,.\, \lambda w : A \Rightarrow B \Rightarrow C \,.\, w\, u\, v \;:\; A \wedge B$

$\qquad \boxed{u : A \wedge B}$

(3) $\qquad\quad \wedge\text{-}el_1(A, B, u) := u\, A\, (\lambda v : A \,.\, \lambda w : B \,.\, v) \;:\; A$

(4) $\qquad\quad \wedge\text{-}el_2(A, B, u) := u\, B\, (\lambda v : A \,.\, \lambda w : B \,.\, w) \;:\; B$

Figure 11.10 Definition and rules for $\wedge$

$\boxed{A, B : *_p}$

(1) $\lor(A, B) := \Pi C : *_p . (A \Rightarrow C) \Rightarrow (B \Rightarrow C) \Rightarrow C : *_p$
        Notation: $A \lor B$ for $\lor(A, B)$

$\boxed{u : A}$

(2) $\lor\text{-}in_1(A, B, u) := \lambda C : *_p . \lambda v : A \Rightarrow C . \lambda w : B \Rightarrow C . v\,u : A \lor B$

$\boxed{u : B}$

(3) $\lor\text{-}in_2(A, B, u) := \lambda C : *_p . \lambda v : A \Rightarrow C . \lambda w : B \Rightarrow C . w\,u : A \lor B$

$\boxed{C : *_p}$

$\boxed{u : A \lor B \mid v : A \Rightarrow C \mid w : B \Rightarrow C}$

(4) $\lor\text{-}el(A, B, C, u, v, w) := u\,C\,v\,w : C$

Figure 11.11 Definition and rules for $\lor$

Note that the $\lor\text{-}el$-rule in Figure 11.11 has, exceptionally, a body $(u\,C\,v\,w)$ that is shorter than the definiendum.

The definition of *biimplication* as the conjunction of the implications in both directions immediately leads to the introduction and elimination rules concerned. See Figure 11.12.

$\boxed{A, B : *_p}$

(1) $\Leftrightarrow(A, B) := (A \Rightarrow B) \land (B \Rightarrow A) : *_p$
        Notation: $A \Leftrightarrow B$ for $\Leftrightarrow(A, B)$

$\boxed{u : A \Rightarrow B \mid v : B \Rightarrow A}$

(2) $\Leftrightarrow\text{-}in(A, B, u, v) := \land\text{-}in(A \Rightarrow B, B \Rightarrow A, u, v) : A \Leftrightarrow B$

$\boxed{u : A \Leftrightarrow B}$

(3) $\Leftrightarrow\text{-}el_1(A, B, u) := \land\text{-}el_1(A \Rightarrow B, B \Rightarrow A, u) : A \Rightarrow B$
(4) $\Leftrightarrow\text{-}el_2(A, B, u) := \land\text{-}el_2(A \Rightarrow B, B \Rightarrow A, u) : B \Rightarrow A$

Figure 11.12 Definition and rules for $\Leftrightarrow$

11.6 Examples of logical derivations in λD

We give two examples in order to demonstrate how (constructive) natural deduction works in λD. For that purpose we firstly revisit the example from Section 7.3 (see Figure 7.1): a derivation of the logical tautology

$$(A \lor B) \Rightarrow (\neg A \Rightarrow B).$$

Having the introduction and elimination rules available in λD (see the previous section), we first give the derivation in the explicit natural deduction style. See Figure 11.13. In this presentation, it is clearly visible how the derivation is driven by natural deduction as the system for logic: in every line we find one instance of a logical introduction or elimination rule, which is more informative than the λC-rules (*appl*) and (*abst*) used in Figure 7.1.

(a) $\boxed{A, B : *_p}$

(b) $\boxed{x : A \lor B}$

(c) $\boxed{y : \neg A}$

(d) $\boxed{u : A}$

(1) $a_1(A, B, x, y, u) := \neg\text{-}el(A, y, u) : \bot$

(2) $a_2(A, B, x, y, u) := \bot\text{-}el(B, a_1(A, B, x, y, u)) : B$

(3) $a_3(A, B, x, y) := \Rightarrow\text{-}in(A, B, \lambda u : A \, . \, a_2(A, B, x, y, u)) : A \Rightarrow B$

(4) $a_4(A, B, x, y) := \Rightarrow\text{-}in(B, B, \lambda v : B \, . \, v) : B \Rightarrow B$

(5) $a_5(A, B, x, y) := \lor\text{-}el(A, B, B, x, a_3(A, B, x, y), a_4(A, B, x, y)) : B$

(6) $a_6(A, B, x) := \Rightarrow\text{-}in(\neg A, B, \lambda y : \neg A \, . \, a_5(A, B, x, y)) : \neg A \Rightarrow B$

(7) $a_7(A, B) := \Rightarrow\text{-}in(A \lor B, \neg A \Rightarrow B, \lambda x : A \lor B \, . \, a_6(A, B, x)) :$
$\qquad (A \lor B) \Rightarrow (\neg A \Rightarrow B)$

Figure 11.13 A derivation in natural deduction style of $(A \lor B) \Rightarrow (\neg A \Rightarrow B)$

Remark 11.6.1   *The names* a_1 *to* a_3 *already appeared in Figures 11.8 and 11.9, although they are obviously intended to refer to other constants than the ones in Figure 11.13. This is a case of* reuse of constant names *which is not in agreement with the rules of* λD. *We do it nevertheless, in order to keep the number of constant names within reasonable bounds. We are aware, however, that such overloading of names is not without danger.*

It is worthwhile to compare this derivation with the one expressed in Section 7.3. There are many correspondences: the derivation given in Figure 7.1 follows lines similar to those in Figure 11.13, although the reasonings deviate in some details. In the following section (Figure 11.15) we shall reproduce the same λD-derivation, but with the shorter proof objects corresponding to the type-theoretic style, according to the following convention.

> *In a flag derivation, we shall often use the type-theoretic style for proof objects corresponding to the natural deduction rules for* $\Rightarrow$, $\bot$ *and* $\neg$.

We continue with a second example: the commutativity of $\vee$. That is, we prove the simple fact that $A \vee B$ implies $B \vee A$.

The derivation in Figure 11.14 is based on the two introduction rules for $\vee$ (lines (1) and (2)) and the elimination rule for $\vee$ (line (3)). In the proof, we use the type-theoretic style. We leave it to the reader to formulate the four proof objects in natural deduction style (Exercise 11.7).

$$
\boxed{A, B : *_p}
$$

$$
\boxed{u : A \vee B}
$$

(1)	$a_1(A, B, u) := \lambda v : A.\ \vee\text{-}in_2(B, A, v) : A \Rightarrow (B \vee A)$
(2)	$a_2(A, B, u) := \lambda w : B.\ \vee\text{-}in_1(B, A, w) : B \Rightarrow (B \vee A)$
(3)	$a_3(A, B, u) := u\,(B \vee A)\ a_1(A, B, u)\ a_2(A, B, u) : B \vee A$
(4)	$sym\text{-}\vee(A, B) := \lambda u : A \vee B.\ a_3(A, B, u) : (A \vee B) \Rightarrow (B \vee A)$

Figure 11.14 Commutativity of $\vee$

Note that $sym\text{-}\vee(A, B)$ *inhabits* the property $(A \vee B) \Rightarrow (B \vee A)$; it is not the property itself.

11.7 Suppressing unaltered parameter lists

When looking back at the example derivation in Figure 11.13, we notice that the presence of parameter lists following the constants a_1 to a_7 obscures the general picture. The more so, because in the proof objects occurring in these examples, the corresponding parameter lists bear no interesting information: in all cases we see 'identical' instantiations for the parameters: A for A, B for B, and so on.

Hence, no information is lost when we *omit* such non-interesting parameter lists, both in the definienda (so before the ':='-sign) as in the proof objects. And without these lists, we can better concentrate on the things that matter, such as the course of the derivation. We realise that this contradicts our arguments to consistently mention the parameter lists in the definienda; see Remark 8.3.2. The advantages of suppressing unessential parameter lists are, however, too important to neglect.

To show the effects of this convention, we rewrite the derivation of Figure 11.13 in this novel format. We also take the opportunity to apply the type-theoretic style for the $\Rightarrow$-, $\bot$- and $\neg$-rules, and for the $\vee$-*el*-rule. See Figure 11.15.

Hence, we adopt the following notational option, which we call the *parameter list convention*:

(a)	$A, B : *_p$
(b)	$x : A \vee B$
(c)	$y : \neg A$
(d)	$u : A$
(1)	$a_1^\dagger := y\,u \ : \ \bot$
(2)	$a_2 := a_1\,B \ : \ B$
(3)	$a_3 := \lambda u : A .\, a_2 \ : \ A \Rightarrow B$
(4)	$a_4 := \lambda v : B .\, v \ : \ B \Rightarrow B$
(5)	$a_5 := x\,B\,a_3\,a_4 \ : \ B$
(6)	$a_6 := \lambda y : \neg A .\, a_5 \ : \ \neg A \Rightarrow B$
(7)	$a_7 := \lambda x : A \vee B .\, a_6 \ : \ (A \vee B) \Rightarrow (\neg A \Rightarrow B)$

†*parameters suppressed*

Figure 11.15 Suppressed parameter lists and short proof objects

Notation 11.7.1 *(Parameter list convention)*
  Parameter lists that literally reflect the context in which they have been introduced may be suppressed completely.

This applies not only when *introducing* a defined constant, as in the left-hand sides of lines (1) to (7) of Figure 11.13, but also when *using* a constant with *unaltered* parameter list in the proof objects.

The result is convincing. In the text to come, we shall employ the parameter list convention whenever we consider it useful. This will mostly be in *examples*, not in the derivations that are essential for the development of this course. If we employ the convention, we shall mention this in a footnote accompanying the first constant with suppressed parameter list (cf. Figure 11.15).

Note, however, that this convention makes it harder to distinguish between variables and constants: some constants now deceptively resemble variables, since they do not show their parameter lists.

11.8 Rules for classical propositional logic

When one wishes to do *classical* logic, we need to add an axiom. In λD we do this by the addition of a primitive definition. We may choose, as we already mentioned in Section 7.4, either the law of the excluded third $A \vee \neg A$ (ET) or the double negation law $\neg\neg A \Rightarrow A$ (DN).

Since we add an axiom, we go beyond λD_0 and employ the extra rules of λD. In Figure 11.16, we formulate axiom ET in λD and subsequently derive

DN. In line (1) we primitively introduce ET, by giving a name, *exc-thrd*, to an *inhabitant*. So *exc-third* is an axiomatically assumed constant of *type* ET. We express it as an axiom *in a context*, namely $A : *_p$. This differs from the approach in Section 7.4, where we introduced proof object i_{ET} of the type $\Pi A : *. \, A \vee \neg A$.

$\boxed{A : *_p}$

(1) $\quad$ *exc-thrd*$(A) \; := \; \perp\!\!\!\perp \; : \; A \vee \neg A$

(2) $\quad a_2(A) \; := \; \lambda v : A . \, v \; : \; A \Rightarrow A$

$\quad \boxed{u : \neg\neg A}$

$\quad\quad \boxed{v : \neg A}$

(3) $\quad\quad a_3(A, u, v) \; := \; u\, v \; : \; \perp$

(4) $\quad\quad a_4(A, u, v) \; := \; a_3(A, u, v) \, A \; : \; A$

(5) $\quad\quad a_5(A, u) \; := \; \lambda v : \neg A . \, a_4(A, u, v) \; : \; \neg A \Rightarrow A$

(6) $\quad\quad a_6(A, u) \; := \; \textit{exc-thrd}(A) \, A \, a_2(A) \, a_5(A, u) \; : \; A$

(7) $\quad \textit{doub-neg}(A) \; := \; \lambda u : \neg\neg A . \, a_6(A, u) \; : \; \neg\neg A \Rightarrow A$

Figure 11.16 The law of the excluded third, entailing the double negation law

The derivation resembles the λC version given in Section 7.4. We use the type-theoretic style discussed in Section 11.5. This enables us to produce a short derivation, albeit that it is not immediately clear which natural deduction rules have been applied. Find out yourself which introduction or elimination rules apply to lines (2) to (7).

Note that *doub-neg* may be conceived as implying a kind of *elimination rule* concerning the double negation symbol ($\neg\neg$): if we have a proof of $\neg\neg A$, then we can obtain a proof of A with the help of *doub-neg* (by the aid of $\Rightarrow$-*el*). In the same vein, we may consider an *introduction rule* for $\neg\neg$, since we have derived in Figure 11.9 (without the *exc-thrd*-axiom, hence constructively) that from A we may conclude $\neg\neg A$.

Since both transitions (from A to $\neg\neg A$ and vice versa) occur so often, we devote two extra rules to them: $\neg\neg$-*in* and $\neg\neg$-*el*. See Figure 11.17.

We continue with a derivation of the tautology $(\neg A \Rightarrow B) \Rightarrow (A \vee B)$, the 'reversal' of the tautology derived in Figure 11.13 (see Figure 11.18). This is a *non-constructive* tautology: it can only be proved with the help of DN (or ET); and indeed, in line (10) of Figure 11.18 we use the non-constructive rule $\neg\neg$-*el*. We suppress parameters as explained in the previous section, and use

	$A : *_p$
	$\quad u : A$
	$\qquad v : \neg A$
(1)	$\qquad \neg\neg\text{-}in(A, u) := \lambda v : \neg A . \, v \, u \; : \; \neg\neg A$
	$\qquad u : \neg\neg A$
(2)	$\qquad \neg\neg\text{-}el(A, u) := doub\text{-}neg(A) \, u \; : \; A$

Figure 11.17 Natural deduction rules for $\neg\neg$

a mixture of the type-theoretic style and the natural deduction style, choosing what is convenient.

(a)	$A, B : *_p$
(b)	$\quad u : \neg A \Rightarrow B$
(c)	$\qquad v : \neg(A \vee B)$
(d)	$\qquad\quad w : A$
(1)	$\qquad\qquad a_1^\dagger := \vee\text{-}in_1(A, B, w) \; : \; A \vee B$
(2)	$\qquad\qquad a_2 := v \, a_1 \; : \; \bot$
(3)	$\qquad\quad a_3 := \lambda w : A . \, a_2 \; : \; \neg A$
(e)	$\qquad\quad w : B$
(4)	$\qquad\qquad a_4 := \vee\text{-}in_2(A, B, w) \; : \; A \vee B$
(5)	$\qquad\qquad a_5 := v \, a_4 \; : \; \bot$
(6)	$\qquad\quad a_6 := \lambda w : B . \, a_5 \; : \; \neg B$
(7)	$\qquad\quad a_7 := u \, a_3 \; : \; B$
(8)	$\qquad\quad a_8 := a_6 \, a_7 \; : \; \bot$
(9)	$\qquad a_9 := \lambda v : \neg(A \vee B) . \, a_8 \; : \; \neg\neg(A \vee B)$
(10)	$\qquad a_{10} := \neg\neg\text{-}el(A \vee B, a_9) \; : \; A \vee B$
(11)	$\quad a_{11} := \lambda u : (\neg A \Rightarrow B) . \, a_{10} \; : \; (\neg A \Rightarrow B) \Rightarrow (A \vee B)$

†*parameters suppressed*

Figure 11.18 A derivation in natural deduction of $(\neg A \Rightarrow B) \Rightarrow (A \vee B)$

    We leave most of the reasoning employed in the derivation of Figure 11.18 to the reader. There is only one aspect to which we pay special attention. The original goal $(\neg A \Rightarrow B) \Rightarrow (A \vee B)$, line (11), induces assumption (b) and the new goal $A \vee B$, line (10). For attaining the latter goal, we try *proof by contradiction*: we assume the opposite, $\neg(A \vee B)$ (see assumption (c)) and try to derive $\bot$ (see line (8)), in which we succeed.

Remark 11.8.1 *Proof by contradiction (or 'indirect proof') is a standard strategy in classical logic. It has the following pattern.*

To prove A, we can try the following scheme:

It suffices to fill the dots with a proper proof. The motivation in natural deduction style is that after filling the dots, ¬-in followed by ¬¬-el indeed gives A as a result (check this; see also lines (9) and (10) in Figure 11.18).

A proof by contradiction may be called upon in every step of a proof. It is, however, wise to use it with considerable care – namely only when no direct proof appears to be at hand. The reason for this prudence is that a rash use of 'proof by contradiction' may easily lead to an unnecessary detour.

11.9 Alternative natural deduction rules for ∨

The two example derivations we gave in Figures 11.13 and 11.18 may be combined into one derivable biimplication:

$(A \lor B) \Leftrightarrow (\neg A \Rightarrow B)$.

Hence, $A \lor B$ and $\neg A \Rightarrow B$ are interchangeable in classical logic. This has the following strategic consequences for the disjunction:

– If $A \lor B$ occurs in a reasoning-under-construction as the *goal* to be proved, it is possible to prove the implication $\neg A \Rightarrow B$ instead. This 'classical' method can be applied in many more cases than the original ∨-*in*-rule, which asks for a proof of either A or B; such a proof is seldom at hand.

– And vice versa: if we are allowed to *use* $A \lor B$ (it is part of our 'knowledge' at a certain point in a reasoning), we may as well appeal to the implication $\neg A \Rightarrow B$.

Both strategies for dealing with disjunction are current in mathematics. Therefore, we shall extend our set of introduction and elimination rules in λD one more time.

Since ∨ is commutative (see Figure 11.14), we may interchange A and B in $A \lor B$; this brings along that $A \lor B$ is also equivalent to $\neg B \Rightarrow A$. Hence, the new introduction and elimination rules for ∨ come in pairs, as one can see in Figure 11.19.

Remark 11.9.1 *In several lines of the derivation in Figure 11.19, we refer to constants with non-specific names that were defined earlier. In order to* *prevent confusion, we add an extra subscript to such constants. For example,* $a_{10[Fig.\ 11.18]}$ *in line (1) is the constant* a_{10} *in Figure 11.18.*

$$\boxed{A, B : *_p}$$

$$\boxed{u : \neg A \Rightarrow B}$$

(1) $\quad \vee\text{-}in\text{-}alt_1(A, B, u) := a_{10[Fig.\ 11.18]}(A, B, u) \;:\; A \vee B$

$$\boxed{v : \neg B \Rightarrow A}$$

(2) $\quad a_2(A, B, v) := \vee\text{-}in\text{-}alt_1(B, A, v) \;:\; B \vee A$

(3) $\quad \vee\text{-}in\text{-}alt_2(A, B, v) := a_{3[Fig.\ 11.14]}(B, A, a_2(A, B, v)) \;:\; A \vee B$

$$\boxed{u : A \vee B}$$

$$\boxed{v : \neg A}$$

(4) $\quad \vee\text{-}el\text{-}alt_1(A, B, u, v) := a_{5[Fig.\ 11.13]}(A, B, u, v) \;:\; B$

$$\boxed{w : \neg B}$$

(5) $\quad \vee\text{-}el\text{-}alt_2(A, B, u, w) := \vee\text{-}el\text{-}alt_1(B, A, a_{3[Fig.\ 11.14]}(A, B, u), w) \;:\; A$

Figure 11.19 Alternative rules for $\vee$

Remark 11.9.2 *The alternative introduction rules* $\vee\text{-}in\text{-}alt_1$ *and* $\vee\text{-}in\text{-}alt_2$ *start from the assumption that a certain implication holds: in the first case* $\neg A \Rightarrow B$, *in the second case* $\neg B \Rightarrow A$.

In actual usage of these rules, such implications will often result from a derivation themselves. So, for example, a typical use of the first alternative introduction rule for $\vee$ *may have the format as depicted below. (We give an example of this procedure in Figure 11.20.)*

$$\vdots$$

$$\boxed{x : \neg A}$$

$$\vdots$$

$$a(\ldots, x) := \ldots \;:\; B$$

$$\vee\text{-}in\text{-}alt_1(A, B, \lambda x : \neg A . \, a(\ldots, x)) \;:\; A \vee B$$

We continue with two examples of the use of the alternative $\vee$-rules, which together justify the well-known biimplication

$$\neg(A \wedge B) \Leftrightarrow (\neg A \vee \neg B).$$

We advise the reader to study the content of the derivations in Figures 11.20 and 11.21 'from bottom to top', since that is the way they were devised.

$$A, B : *_p$$

$$u : \neg(A \wedge B)$$

$$v : \neg\neg A$$

(1) $\quad a_1^\dagger := \neg\neg\text{-}el(A, v) \; : \; A$

$$w : B$$

(2) $\quad a_2 := \wedge\text{-}in(A, B, a_1, w) \; : \; A \wedge B$

(3) $\quad a_3 := u\, a_2 \; : \; \bot$

(4) $\quad a_4 := \lambda w : B.\, a_3 \; : \; \neg B$

(5) $\quad a_5(A, B, u) := \vee\text{-}in\text{-}alt_1(\neg A, \neg B, \lambda v : \neg\neg A.\, a_4) \; : \; \neg A \vee \neg B$

†*parameters suppressed*

Figure 11.20 Proof of the lemma: $\neg(A \wedge B)$ entails $\neg A \vee \neg B$

$$A, B : *_p$$

$$u : \neg A \vee \neg B$$

$$v : A \wedge B$$

(1) $\quad a_1^\dagger := \wedge\text{-}el_1(A, B, v) \; : \; A$

(2) $\quad a_2 := \wedge\text{-}el_2(A, B, v) \; : \; B$

(3) $\quad a_3 := \neg\neg\text{-}in(A, a_1) \; : \; \neg\neg A$

(4) $\quad a_4 := \vee\text{-}el\text{-}alt_1(\neg A, \neg B, u, a_3) \; : \; \neg B$

(5) $\quad a_5 := a_4\, a_2 \; : \; \bot$

(6) $\quad a_6(A, B, u) := \lambda v : A \wedge B.\, a_5 \; : \; \neg(A \wedge B)$

†*parameters suppressed*

Figure 11.21 Proof of the lemma: $\neg A \vee \neg B$ entails $\neg(A \wedge B)$

Remark 11.9.3 *A proof as in Figure 11.20 can also be read from top to bottom: start with propositions A and B, make the assumptions $\neg(A \wedge B)$ and $\neg\neg A$, then conclude to A in line (1); next, assume B, conclude to $A \wedge B$ in line (2); and so forth. In this manner one may definitely* check *that the derivation is correct, from start to end.*

This manner of reading a proof does, however, not give much insight *into how such a proof has been constructed and what its intuitive ideas are. Almost every proof, and certainly the more sophisticated ones, has been devised in a non-linear manner: one usually starts at the end (the goal), develops intermediate results, sets new goals, and so on. Regularly, there have been attempts that have failed (and therefore have not been recorded).*

This art of 'proof finding' is illustrated in various parts of this book. Altogether, finding a proof is an ingenuous mixture of routine and bright ideas. And when studying a proof, it is the task of the reader to value it at its true worth.

11.10 Rules for constructive predicate logic

Predicate logic is the logic obtained by extending propositional logic with the quantifiers $\forall$ and $\exists$. We start with the constructive rules for the universal quantifier $\forall$.

As we have already discussed in Section 5.4, V, an expression $\forall_{x \in S}(P(x))$ is naturally coded as $\Pi x : S . P x$ in type theory. This makes it easy to find out what the introduction and elimination rules for $\forall$ become in λD (see Figure 11.22). For a clear exposition, we write $*$ as either $*_s$ (when dealing with sets) or $*_p$ (for propositions); see Notation 8.7.1.

$$
\begin{array}{ll}
& \boxed{S : *_s \mid P : S \to *_p} \\[4pt]
(1) & \quad \forall(S, P) := \Pi x : S . P x \; : \; *_p \\[4pt]
& \quad \text{Notation: } \forall x : S . P x \text{ for } \forall(S, P) \\[4pt]
& \quad \boxed{u : \Pi x : S . P x} \\[4pt]
(2) & \quad \forall\text{-}in(S, P, u) := u \; : \; \forall x : S . P x \\[4pt]
& \quad \boxed{u : \forall x : S . P x \mid v : S} \\[4pt]
(3) & \quad \forall\text{-}el(S, P, u, v) := u v \; : \; P v
\end{array}
$$

Figure 11.22 Definition and rules for $\forall$

Remark 11.10.1 *We only formulate the $\forall$-rules in the first order case, with x ranging over a set S, because this is the standard situation. Similar rules can be developed for the second order case, when the variable ranges over e.g. propositions. Such a situation occurs, for example, in previously mentioned second order definitions such as $\perp := \Pi A : *_p . A \; : \; *_p$ (see Section 11.5).*

We noticed in Section 11.5 that we use the λD-versions of the natural deduction rules for $\Rightarrow$, $\perp$ and $\neg$ only sparingly, since the type-theoretic style gives shorter proof objects. The same holds for the $\forall$-rules: we only employ the rules as defined above if we want to emphasise that a $\forall$-introduction or a $\forall$-elimination takes place. So, the constructed proof objects in these cases will usually be given in the type-theoretic style, i.e. u instead of $\forall\text{-}in(S, P, u)$ and $u\,v$ instead of $\forall\text{-}el(S, P, u, v)$.

We continue with the constructive rules for the existential quantifier $\exists$. The corresponding natural deduction rules are discussed in Section 7.5, together with their λC-translations.

Below we recapitulate these results, but now in λD. We employ the *second order definition* of $\exists$, which we repeat (with slight adaptations) in line (1). The proof object in line (2) is easy to find; see Exercise 7.12 (a). The proof object in line (3) was derived in Section 7.5.

(1) $\quad$ $\boxed{S : *_s \mid P : S \to *_p}$

$\quad\quad$ $\exists(S, P) \ := \ \Pi A : *_p \,.\, ((\forall x : S \,.\, (P\,x \Rightarrow A)) \Rightarrow A) \ : \ *_p \,.$

$\quad\quad$ Notation: $\exists x : S \,.\, P\,x$ for $\exists(S, P)$

(2) $\quad$ $\boxed{u : S \mid v : P\,u}$

$\quad\quad\quad$ $\exists\text{-}in(S, P, u, v) \ := \ \lambda A : *_p \,.\, \lambda w : (\forall x : S \,.\, (P\,x \Rightarrow A)) \,.\, w\,u\,v \ :$

$\quad\quad\quad\quad\quad\quad$ $\exists x : S \,.\, P\,x$

(3) $\quad$ $\boxed{u \,:\, \exists x : S \,.\, P\,x \mid A : *_p \mid v \,:\, \forall x : S \,.\, (P\,x \Rightarrow A)}$

$\quad\quad\quad$ $\exists\text{-}el(S, P, u, A, v) \ := \ u\,A\,v \ : \ A$

Figure 11.23 Definition and rules for $\exists$

The usage of the $\exists$-*introduction* rule will be obvious: in order to establish that $\exists x : S \,.\, P\,x$, it suffices to *find* a u in S satisfying P. This is precisely what the expression suggests. The $\exists$-*elimination* rule is more complicated. For its justification, see Section 7.5. Note that the five assumptions in line (3) are a well-formed context. This implies that x does not occur as a free variable in A, as is required in Section 7.5.

The $\exists$-elimination rule of Figure 11.23 is commonly used as follows.

Suppose that we are engaged in constructing a derivation and that the reigning goal is proposition A, while we have detected that $\exists x : S \,.\, P\,x$ is a usable fact. In order to fill the gap between $\exists x : S \,.\, P\,x$ and A, the rule $\exists\text{-}el$ suggests to us to find an inhabitant of $\forall x : S \,.\, (P\,x \Rightarrow A)$ (becoming the new goal). A natural strategy to attain this is to assume $x : S$ and $P\,x$, and to find an inhabitant of A. Note that this is the same goal A as before, *but now in a context enlarged with the mentioned two extra assumptions*. If we succeed in fulfilling this assignment, then $\exists\text{-}el$ enables us to conclude the original goal A.

A schematic picture of this strategy in type theory is:

$$\vdots$$

$a(\ldots) := \ldots : \exists x : S . P x$

> $\boxed{x : S}$
>
> > $\boxed{u : P x}$
> >
> > $\vdots$
> >
> > $b(\ldots, x, u) := \ldots : A$
> >
> > $c(\ldots, x) := \lambda u : P x . b(\ldots, x, u) : P x \Rightarrow A$

$d(\ldots) := \lambda x : S . c(\ldots, x) : \forall x : S . (P x \Rightarrow A)$

$e(\ldots) := \exists\text{-}el(S, P, a(\ldots), A, d(\ldots)) : A$

We continue with an example in which both $\exists$-*in* and $\exists$-*el* play a role, and for which a λC-derivation was asked in Exercise 7.13. See Figure 11.24. The lemma we prove is:

$$\exists x : S . P x \Rightarrow \forall y : S . (P y \Rightarrow Q y) \Rightarrow \exists z : S . Q z.$$

In the derivation, the flags $x : S$ and $w : P x$ are raised since we have an inhabitant (viz. u) of $\exists x : S . P x$. This conforms with the schematic picture of the $\exists$-elimination strategy sketched just now. Check the details.

> $\boxed{S : *_s \mid P : S \to *_p \mid Q : S \to *_p}$
>
> > $\boxed{u : \exists x : S . P x \mid v : \forall y : S . (P y \Rightarrow Q y)}$
> >
> > > $\boxed{x : S \mid w : P x}$

(1)	$a_1^\dagger := v\, x : P x \Rightarrow Q x$
(2)	$a_2 := a_1\, w : Q x$
(3)	$a_3 := \exists\text{-}in(S, Q, x, a_2) : \exists z : S . Q z$
(4)	$a_4 := \lambda x : S . \lambda w : P x . a_3 : \forall x : S . (P x \Rightarrow \exists z : S . Q z)$
(5)	$a_5 := \exists\text{-}el(S, P, u, \exists z : S . Q z, a_4) : \exists z : S . Q z$
(6)	$a_6(S, P, Q) := \lambda u : (\exists x : S . P x) . \lambda v : (\forall y : S . (P y \Rightarrow Q y)) . a_5 :$
	$\qquad \exists x : S . P x \Rightarrow \forall y : S . (P y \Rightarrow Q y) \Rightarrow \exists z : S . Q z$

†*parameters suppressed*

Figure 11.24 An example concerning the rules for $\exists$

Remark 11.10.2 *The two assumptions in the second flag, viz.* $\exists x : S . P x$ *and* $\forall y : S . (P y \Rightarrow Q y)$*, do not match the* $\exists$*-el-rule: although it appears tempting to conclude* $Q y$ *as a result of this rule, this is incorrect since* y *occurs free in* $Q y$*. See Remark 7.5.2.*

As another example, we consider the following well-known proposition:

$$\exists_{x \in S}(P(x)) \;\Rightarrow\; \neg\forall_{x \in S}(\neg P(x)).$$

In a λD-derivation of this proposition, the $\exists$-*el* rule can be used directly: see Figure 11.25.

	$S : *_s \mid P : S \to *_p$
	$\quad u \;:\; \exists x : S \,.\, P\,x$
	$\qquad v \;:\; \forall y : S \,.\, \neg(P\,y)$
(1)	$\qquad\quad a_1^\dagger \;:=\; \exists\text{-}el(S, P, u, \bot, v) \;:\; \bot$
(2)	$\qquad a_2 \;:=\; \lambda v : (\forall y : S \,.\, \neg(P\,y)) \,.\, a_1 \;:\; \neg\forall y : S \,.\, \neg(P\,y)$
(3)	$\qquad a_3(S, P) \;:=\; \lambda u : (\exists x : S \,.\, P\,x) \,.\, a_2 \;:\; (\exists x : S \,.\, P\,x) \Rightarrow \neg(\forall y : S \,.\, \neg(P\,y))$

†*parameters suppressed*

Figure 11.25 Example: $\exists$ implies $\neg\forall\neg$

In setting up this derivation, we have the disposal of $\exists x : S \,.\, P\,x$ in one of the flags. So, when we wish to apply $\exists$-elimination, aiming at goal $\bot$ in line (1), we have to derive an inhabitant of $\forall x : S \,.\, (P\,x \Rightarrow \bot)$. But such an inhabitant is already *at hand*, namely v in the last flag, because $\neg P\,y$ is equivalent to $P\,y \Rightarrow \bot$.

The rest of the derivation will speak for itself.

11.11 Rules for classical predicate logic

When combining the introduction and elimination rules for the quantifiers with constructive propositional logic, we obtain *constructive predicate logic*. In that system, similarly to the situation with constructive propositional logic, we miss some tautologies with quantifiers that mathematicians intuitively accept to hold. An example is the reversal of the last example in the previous section, namely:

$$\neg\forall_{x \in S}(\neg P(x)) \;\Rightarrow\; \exists_{x \in S}(P(x)).$$

This expression is naturally considered to be true, since it says: 'If not all elements of S do *not* satisfy P, then there must be an element of S that *does* so.' But it is not derivable in (first or second order) constructive predicate calculus.

Adding the propositional axiom DN (or ET), we obtain *classical predicate logic*, in which the above expression *can* be derived, as we show below. As a consequence, we may combine the two propositions into the classical predicate-logical fact (in shorthand): $\exists \Leftrightarrow \neg\forall\neg$.

Remark 11.11.1   *There exists a counterpart of the equivalence $\exists \Leftrightarrow \neg\forall\neg$ mentioned above, to the effect that also $\forall \Leftrightarrow \neg\exists\neg$ is valid in classical predicate logic. This is left to the reader (Exercise 11.16; see also Exercise 7.12 (b)).*

In the proof we make good use of another simple equivalence regarding quantifiers, which admits a constructive proof:

$\neg\exists_{x \in S}(P(x)) \Rightarrow \forall_{x \in S}(\neg P(x))$.

We first give a derivation of the latter proposition (Figure 11.26), and next for the former one (Figure 11.27).

For the last-mentioned proposition, we have already given a proof in λC (see Section 7.6). But there we did not yet have a formal definition apparatus. The derivation in Figure 11.26 enables the reader to compare the λC- and the λD-approach to formal proof development. It is a simple exercise with natural deduction. We only mention that the goal $\bot$ in line (2) can easily be derived from assumption $\neg\exists x : S . P x$, and the fact that $y : S$ and $v : P y$ imply $\exists z : S . P z$ (line (1)). The rest is routine.

$\boxed{S : *_s \mid P : S \to *_p}$

    $\boxed{u : \neg \exists x : S . P x}$

        $\boxed{y : S}$

            $\boxed{v : P y}$

(1) $a_1^\dagger := \exists\text{-}in(S, P, y, v) \; : \; \exists z : S . P z$

(2) $a_2 := u \, a_1 \; : \; \bot$

(3) $a_3 := \lambda v : P y . a_2 \; : \; \neg(P y)$

(4) $a_4 := \lambda y : S . a_3 \; : \; \forall y : S . \neg(P y)$

(5) $a_5(S, P) := \lambda u : (\neg\exists x : S . P x) . a_4 \; : \; (\neg\exists x : S . P x) \Rightarrow \forall y : S . \neg(P y)$

     $^\dagger parameters\ suppressed$

Figure 11.26 Example: $\neg\exists$ implies $\forall\neg$

The derivation in Figure 11.27 is a consequence: it uses line (4) of Figure 11.26. We apply the method *proof by contradiction* (see Remark 11.8.1) by adding flag $v : \neg\exists y : S . P y$ in order to obtain $\exists y : S . P y$ in line (4), via line (3) and $\neg\neg\text{-}el$. We recall that $\neg\neg\text{-}el$ is based on the axiom DN, hence the derivation is non-constructive.

In classical predicate logic it appears advantageous to add alternative rules for $\exists$, inspired by the equivalence of $\exists$ and $\neg\forall\neg$ that we have established above.

The motivation for adding these alternative rules is similar to the situation with disjunction (cf. Section 11.9). In practical proof finding, the constructive

$$S : *_s \mid P : S \to *_p$$

$$u : \neg\forall x : S . \neg(P\,x)$$

$$v : \neg\exists y : S . P\,y$$

(1) $\quad a_1^\dagger := a_{4[Fig.\ 11.26]}(S, P, v) \; : \; \forall z : S . \neg(P\,z)$

(2) $\quad a_2 := u\,a_1 \; : \; \bot$

(3) $\quad a_3 := \lambda v : (\neg\exists y : S . P\,y) . a_2 \; : \; \neg\neg\exists y : S . P\,y$

(4) $\quad a_4 := \neg\neg\text{-}el(\exists y : S . P\,y, a_3) \; : \; \exists y : S . P\,y$

(5) $\quad a_5(S, P) := \lambda u : (\neg\forall x : S . \neg(P\,x)) . a_4 \; : \; \neg\forall x : S . \neg(P\,x) \Rightarrow \exists y : S . P\,y$

†*parameters suppressed*

Figure 11.27 Example: $\neg\forall\neg$ implies $\exists$

rule $\exists$-*in* turns out to be rather restrictive, just as $\lor$-*in* is: in order to obtain a proof of $\exists x : S . P\,x$, the procedure suggested by $\exists$-*in* is to *find* a so-called 'witness', i.e. a certain entity a of type S that satisfies P. But *existence* of an x satisfying $P\,x$ does not always imply that we can *point out* a witness.

In *classical* logic we can derive $\exists x : S . P\,x$ without a witness if we can prove $\neg\forall x : S . \neg(P\,x)$, as Figure 11.27 demonstrates.

For reasons of symmetry, we also add an alternative $\exists$-*el*-rule, leading (the other way round) from $\exists$ to $\neg\forall\neg$. This rule is based on the constructive example derivation of Figure 11.25, which uses the original $\exists$-*el*.

Both alternative rules for $\exists$ are given in Figure 11.28.

$$S : *_s \mid P : S \to *_p$$

$$u : \neg\forall x : S . \neg(P\,x)$$

(1) $\quad \exists\text{-}in\text{-}alt(S, P, u) := a_{4[Fig.\ 11.27]}(S, P, u) \; : \; \exists x : S . P\,x$

$$u : \exists x : S . P\,x$$

(2) $\quad \exists\text{-}el\text{-}alt(S, P, u) := a_{2[Fig.\ 11.25]}(S, P, u) \; : \; \neg\forall x : S . \neg(P\,x)$

Figure 11.28 Alternative rules for $\exists$

We conclude this section with an example concerning the alternative $\exists$-*in*-rule. We prove the following lemma in λD:

$$\neg\forall_{x \in S}(P(x)) \Rightarrow \exists_{x \in S}(\neg P(x)).$$

The 'natural' bottom-up construction of the derivation depicted in Figure 11.29 soon leads to the goal $\exists y : S . \neg(P\,y)$ (see line (6)). We replace it by the goal $\neg\forall y : S . \neg\neg(P\,y)$ (line (5)), in order to be able to apply $\exists$-*in*-*alt*.

The rest of the derivation will speak for itself.

$$\boxed{S : *_s \mid P : S \to *_p}$$

$\boxed{u : \neg \forall x : S . P x}$

$\boxed{v : \forall y : S . \neg\neg(P y)}$

$\boxed{x : S}$

(1) $a_1^\dagger := v x : \neg\neg(P x)$

(2) $a_2 := \neg\neg\text{-}el(P x, a_1) : P x$

(3) $a_3 := \lambda x : S . a_2 : \forall x : S . P x$

(4) $a_4 := u\, a_3 : \bot$

(5) $a_5 := \lambda v : (\forall y : S . \neg\neg(P y)) . a_4 : \neg \forall y : S . \neg\neg(P y)$

(6) $a_6 := \exists\text{-}in\text{-}alt(S, \lambda y : S . \neg(P y), a_5) : \exists y : S . \neg(P y)$

(7) $a_7(S, P) := \lambda u : (\neg \forall x : S . P x) . a_6 : (\neg \forall x : S . P x) \Rightarrow \exists y : S . \neg(P y)$

†*parameters suppressed*

Figure 11.29 Example: $\neg\forall$ implies $\exists\neg$

Remark 11.11.2 *In Figures 11.26 and 11.29 we derived* $\neg\exists \Rightarrow \forall\neg$ *and* $\neg\forall \Rightarrow \exists\neg$. *These implications are actually biimplications (Exercise 11.15).*

11.12 Conclusions

In the present chapter we embarked upon a first investigation into the potential of λD. We started with logic and discovered that λD is a framework as convincing for the expression of logical connectives and quantifiers, as λC. It turned out that, when using the tree format of the λD-rules, one is obliged to proceed in a meticulous manner. The positive news is that this leads to the desired results, but this is obviously not so pleasant for a human user.

Therefore, we have reintroduced the flag style that we have already employed in our λC-presentation. By permitting to omit a number of obvious derivation steps, and by condensing the steps concerned with definitions, we have succeeded in developing a useful and feasible flag format for λD.

As we mentioned already in Chapter 7, it is worthwhile to investigate the precise nature of natural deduction as a logical apparatus. This may facilitate understanding and clarify what's really happening in the *logical* steps of a proof; insight in these matters makes proofs more convincing, since the logical background highly contributes to the reliability of a piece of mathematics.

Another tool of logic often used in mathematics is that of *rewriting* an expression into a logically equivalent one. For example, an expression such as $\neg(x > 0 \land x < 10)$ may be replaced by $\neg(x > 0) \lor \neg(x < 10)$, and vice versa.

The rationale behind this is again *logical*, since the mentioned proof steps can be traced back to the logical equivalence $\neg(A \wedge B) \Leftrightarrow (\neg A \vee \neg B)$. The *validity* of such a logical tautology can well be shown by means of a proof in natural deduction (cf. Figures 11.20 and 11.21). This is a general observation. Hence, one may consider natural deduction to be the *essential* logical framework underlying mathematical reasoning; and rewriting to be a *secondary* method – albeit a very useful one.

Natural deduction as a formal logical method has already been a major topic in Chapter 7, with a view to λC. In the present section we have investigated whether a definition mechanism in type theory can help to make natural deduction still more accessible and usable. It has turned out that, indeed, natural deduction may be successfully incorporated in λD. We have encapsulated the λD-versions of the introduction and elimination rules for the basic symbols of logic ($\Rightarrow$, $\bot$, $\neg$, $\wedge$, $\vee$, $\Leftrightarrow$, $\forall$ and $\exists$), and have illustrated their use in (logical) derivations. The mentioning of the natural deduction rules makes a reasoning more transparent and understandable for a human being. It turned out, however, that for the natural deduction rules concerning $\Rightarrow$, $\bot$, $\neg$ and $\forall$, and for the $\vee$- and $\exists$-elimination rules, the type-theoretic style of λC is often more appropriate, since this gives shorter proof objects.

In order to be able to also work with *classical* logic in λD, we have added the axiom ET ('excluded third') as a primitively inhabited proposition. We have also given a practical set of alternative rules for the disjunction which are derivable in classical logic. Examples showed how these alternative rules may enter into the matter. Other alternative rules were introduced for the use of quantifiers in classical logic and we added several examples of logical derivations in which the quantifier rules play a role.

In the process of developing a natural deduction framework in the setting of type theory, we have furthermore studied several strategies to successfully exploit the rules presented.

The given examples foreshadow how the natural deduction rules may be used in *mathematics*; and indeed, these logical rules are frequently employed in a mathematical ambiance, as we shall see in the chapters to come.

We recall that the λD-version of all natural deduction rules that have been discussed in the present section (both constructive and classical) are summarised in Appendix A, as a service to the reader.

11.13 Further reading

The rules we use for natural deduction are the standard ones that can be found e.g. in van Dalen (1994). The difference is that now they are presented in a flag style, which was popularised by F. Fitch (Fitch, 1952), and can also be found in the textbook of Nederpelt & Kamareddine (2011). The presence of definitions in λD gives yet more possibilities to apply natural deduction in a flexible manner.

Natural deduction systems, and other systems for formal logic, have already been discussed in Section 7.8.

There are various source books in mathematical logic, of which *Logic and Structure* (van Dalen, 1994) is still a good introduction. A more philosophical introduction to logic is Kneale & Kneale (1962), a substantial book which also nicely describes the history of logic.

Exercises

11.1 Let Δ be an environment containing the definitions of $\bot$, $\neg$, $\Rightarrow$, $\wedge$, $\vee$ and $\exists$ as presented in this chapter.

    (a) Prove: $(\wedge(\bot, \bot)) \bot \stackrel{\Delta}{=}_\beta \neg(\bot \Rightarrow \neg(\bot))$.

    (b) Give the δ-normal form of $\exists(S, \lambda x : S . (P\,x \vee Q\,x))$.

11.2 Take $\Gamma \equiv A : *, \ B : *, \ C : *$. For $\mathcal{D}_3$ see Figure 11.3. Extend the derivations given in Exercise 9.9 in order to prove:

    (a) $\emptyset ; \Gamma \vdash (A \to B \to C) \to C : *$,

    (b) $\mathcal{D}_3 ; A : *, B : * \vdash \wedge(A, B) : *$.

11.3 Let $\Gamma \equiv S : *, P : S \to *$ and $\mathcal{D}_4 \equiv \Gamma \triangleright \forall(S, P) := \Pi x : S . P\,x : *$.

    Give a full derivation in λD_0 of $\mathcal{D}_4 ; \Gamma \vdash \forall(S, P) : *$.

11.4 Describe the 'states' (see Section 11.3) corresponding to the derivation given in Figure 11.4.

11.5 Let $\mathcal{D}_1 \equiv \emptyset \triangleright \mathbb{N} := \bot\!\bot : *$ and $\mathcal{D}_2 \equiv \emptyset \triangleright s := \bot\!\bot : \mathbb{N} \to \mathbb{N}$ (cf. Example 10.2.2).

    (a) Prove that $\mathcal{D}_1$ is a legal environment in λD.

    (b) Derive $\mathcal{D}_1, \mathcal{D}_2 ; \emptyset \vdash s : \mathbb{N} \to \mathbb{N}$ in λD.

11.6 Let $\mathcal{D}'$ and $\mathcal{D}''$ be the definitions in λD-format of $\neg$ and $\vee$ as given in this chapter. Assume that we already have a derivation showing that $\mathcal{D}', \mathcal{D}'' ; \emptyset \vdash * : \square$.

    (a) Give a full derivation in λD of the judgement
        $\mathcal{D}', \mathcal{D}'' ; \emptyset \vdash \Pi\alpha : * . \vee (\alpha, \neg(\alpha)) : *$.

    (b) Prove that the definition of i_{ET} (see Example 10.2.2) may be appended to $\mathcal{D}', \mathcal{D}''$; i.e. the resulting environment is legal, again.

11.7 Write the proof objects in the λD-derivation of Figure 11.14 in natural deduction style (cf. Section 11.5).

11.8 Write the derivation of $(\neg A \Rightarrow B) \Rightarrow (A \vee B)$, as given in Figure 11.18, in natural deduction style.

11.9 Redo the following exercises of Chapter 7 in the λD-style of Section 11.6, hence with flags. You may use a mixture of the natural deduction style and the type-theoretic style, and you may apply the parameter list convention (Notation 11.7.1).

(a) Exercise 7.6 (b),
(b) Exercise 7.8 (b),
(c) Exercise 7.12 (b).

11.10 Give a λD-derivation in classical logic, in the style as employed from Section 11.6 onwards, of the following tautology:

$$((A \Rightarrow B) \Rightarrow A) \Rightarrow A.$$

(Hint: see Remark 11.8.1 and Exercise 7.1 (b).)

11.11 As the previous exercise (note: Exercises 7.1 (a) and 7.1 (b) and the alternative rules for $\vee$ may be helpful):

(a) $(A \Rightarrow B) \vee A$,
(b) $(A \Rightarrow B) \vee \neg B$.

11.12 Give λD-derivations of the following tautologies:

(a) In constructive logic: $(A \Leftrightarrow B) \Rightarrow (\neg A \Leftrightarrow \neg B)$,
(b) In classical logic: $(A \Leftrightarrow B) \Rightarrow ((A \wedge B) \vee (\neg A \wedge \neg B))$,
(c) $\neg(A \vee B) \Leftrightarrow (\neg A \wedge \neg B)$. (Can this be done constructively?)

11.13 Give λD$_0$-derivations (so using constructive logic only) of the following lemmas:

(a) ET implies DN (see also Section 7.4),
(b) DN implies ET.

11.14 Let S and T be sets and R a predicate on $S \times T$, coded $R : S \to T \to *_p$. Give a λD-derivation of the following tautology of constructive logic:

$$\neg \exists_{x \in S} \exists_{y \in T} (R(x, y)) \Rightarrow \forall_{x \in S} \forall_{y \in T} (\neg R(x, y)).$$

11.15 Let S be a set and P a predicate on S. Give λD-derivations for the following tautologies of classical logic; you may use the alternative rules given in Figure 11.28:

(a) $\exists_{x \in S}(\neg P(x)) \Rightarrow \neg \forall_{x \in S}(P(x))$,
(b) $\forall_{x \in S}(\neg P(x)) \Rightarrow \neg \exists_{x \in S}(P(x))$.

11.16 As the previous exercise:

$$\forall_{x \in S}(P(x)) \Leftrightarrow \neg \exists_{x \in S}(\neg P(x)).$$

11.17 As Exercise 11.15:

$$\forall_{x \in S}[\neg \exists_{y \in S}(P(y)) \Rightarrow \exists_{z \in S}(\neg P(z))].$$

11.18 Let S and T be sets, P and Q predicates on S, and R a predicate on $S \times T$. Give λD-derivations of the following tautologies:

(a) $\exists_{x \in S}(P(x) \vee Q(x)) \Rightarrow (\exists_{x \in S}(P(x)) \vee \exists_{x \in S}(Q(x)))$,

(b) $\exists_{x \in S}\forall_{y \in T}(R(x, y)) \Rightarrow \forall_{y \in T}\exists_{x \in S}(R(x, y))$.

12

Mathematics in λD: a first attempt

12.1 An example to start with

Logic, a fundamental part of many sciences, can be fruitfully expressed and used in an appropriate type-theory-with-definitions such as λD. We have demonstrated this extensively in Chapter 11. Our conclusion is that a flag-style approach, which is still fully formal, is very similar to the common *informal* style of deduction which is standard for reasoning in both logic and mathematics. The type theory λD can be fruitfully exploited for expressing the logical system of *natural deduction* in a feasible and practical manner.

In the present chapter, we turn to mathematics. The deductive framework of logic is essential for doing mathematics, since it embodies the principles of reasoning, but mathematics itself is much more than logic (or reasoning) alone.

In order to explore these matters, we start with some illustrative examples, showing the possibilities *and* the problems connected with doing mathematics in type theory. Our purpose is to investigate whether (or rather: to show how) λD 'works' in mathematical practice.

It will turn out that a formal translation of a mathematical text into the λD-format may demand more effort than expected. This is due, of course, to the very precise nature of the 'formal language' λD, requiring *all* aspects to be spelled out, sometimes even to an annoying degree of detail; although the flag style alleviates the burden to some extent.

For the time being, we accept these inconveniences as inevitable – in the hope that the gains of ultimate precision will prove to be greater than the losses. We come back to this subject in the course of the following chapters.

We begin with a simple example about partially ordered sets, namely the proof that there can be at most one minimum in such a set. This proof, based on the corresponding definition, is straightforward; see below.

We recall that a relation R on a set S is a *partial order* if it is *reflexive*, *antisymmetric* and *transitive*; see Section 8.5 for the mathematical definitions of these notions.

> **Definition 12.1.1**   Let S be a set and $\leq$ a binary relation on S. Then $m \in S$ is a *least element* of S with respect to $\leq$ if $\forall_{n \in S}(m \leq n)$.

> **Lemma 12.1.2**   *Let S be a set, partially ordered by $\leq$. Assume that S has a least element with respect to $\leq$. Then this least element is unique.*

> *Proof*   Assume that m_1 and m_2 are elements of S and that both are *least* elements. Then $\forall_{n \in S}(m_1 \leq n)$ and $\forall_{n \in S}(m_2 \leq n)$. In particular, $m_1 \leq m_2$ and $m_2 \leq m_1$. Hence, $m_1 = m_2$, by antisymmetry of $\leq$. It follows that, if S has a least element, then this element is unique.   □

Let's formalise this proof in λD. We use the flag format (see Section 11.2).

The first attempt is represented in Figure 12.1, in which we combine the flags of m_1 and m_2 (see Notation 11.5.1). In the flags of u and v we express the assumption that both m_1 and m_2 are least elements. (See also Remark 12.6.1.)

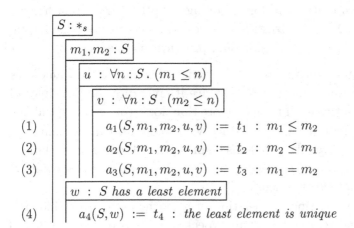

Figure 12.1 A first attempt of proving Lemma 12.1.2 in λD

Browsing through this derivation-like figure, we note several problems. Some of them can be solved in a straightforward manner:

- The symbol '$\leq$' stands for an arbitrary relation on S, being a partial order. These implicit assumptions will be made explicit in Section 12.4.
- The $\forall$-quantifier is not 'basic' in λD, but in Section 5.4 we proposed to code $\forall$ as Π.
- This also solves the question of what to take for the unknown terms t_1 and t_2 in lines (1) and (2): these must be instances of the $\forall$-elimination rule (see Figure 11.22).

So we may take

$$t_1 \equiv \forall\text{-}el(S, \lambda x : S . m_1 \leq x, u, m_2) \text{ and}$$
$$t_2 \equiv \forall\text{-}el(S, \lambda y : S . m_2 < y, v, m_1),$$

or simply $t_1 \equiv u\,m_2$ and $t_2 \equiv v\,m_1$.

The remaining problems appear to be more serious. The questions are:

Q1 The symbol '=' in line (3) denotes the basic *equality relation*, which is fundamental in all areas of mathematics, but is *not* yet a part of our system. How can this be remedied?

Q2 What has to be taken for t_3?

Q3 How to express that S has a least element, as required in the last flag?

Q4 What about its *uniqueness*?

Q5 And how to prove it, i.e. what is the proof object t_4?

12.2 Equality

We start with equality (*Q1*). (Question *Q2* will be answered in Section 12.4, questions *Q3* to *Q5* in Section 12.6.) An easy way out is to suppose that the notion 'equality' belongs to what we call *foreknowledge*. But this attitude does not solve our question, because we have to know the formal rules for dealing with equality.

Equality obviously is a relation between two arguments: for each pair of elements x and y, we have a proposition (namely that $x = y$). But since we work with a system in *type theory*, each element should have a type; so suppose that S is the type of both x and y. Then we can see equality as a binary predicate on S. We write $x =_S y$ for the equality of x and y in S.

So, equality is a parameterised binary relation: for every type S we have an equality relation $=_S : S \to S \to *$, which is a binary relation on terms of type S. We may have equality in $\mathbb{N}$, equality in $\mathbb{Z}$, and so on.

Now the core question is: what does it *mean* that elements x and y of S are 'equal'? A fertile philosophical answer, due to the German mathematician G.W. Leibniz (1646–1716), is that two objects are equal if they are *indiscernible* in all conceivable circumstances. This indiscernibility of x and y can be expressed more concisely as follows: 'For any predicate P on S, the validity of $P\,x$ is equivalent to the validity of $P\,y$'; that is, for given P either both $P\,x$ and $P\,y$ hold, or neither of them holds. If this is the case, then there is no possibility to discriminate between x and y. Hence, they are equal.

Now one could decide to take this equality as a *primitive* relation. In that case we consider it as a *'law'* or axiom, which is then usually called *Leibniz's law*. But the nice thing is that Leibniz's view on equality can be formalised as a *descriptive definition* in λD, so that we do not need an axiom. We take the Π for expressing the generalisation over all predicates, and formally define $eq(S, x, y)$, expressing the equality of x and y (for $x, y : S$), as

$$\Pi P : S \to *_p . (P\, x \Leftrightarrow P\, y).$$

See Figure 12.2, line (1).

Remark 12.2.1   *Even a simpler definition would do, namely:*

$$\Pi P : S \to *_p . (P\, x \Rightarrow P\, y),$$

with $\Rightarrow$ *instead of* $\Leftrightarrow$. *See Exercise 12.2.*

We also use Figure 12.2 to show that this defined equality is a *reflexive* relation, as expected (see line (3)). We use the name $eq\text{-}refl(S, x)$ for the *proof* of reflexivity (hence not for the property itself).

	$S : *_s$
	$\quad x : S$
	$\qquad y : S$
(1)	$\qquad eq(S, x, y) := \Pi P : S \to *_p . (P\, x \Leftrightarrow P\, y) \; : \; *_p$
	$\qquad P : S \to *_p$
(2)	$\qquad a_2(S, x, P) := \ldots ? \ldots \; : \; P\, x \Leftrightarrow P\, x$
(3)	$\quad eq\text{-}refl(S, x) := \lambda P : S \to *_p . a_2(S, x, P) \; : \; eq(S, x, x)$

Figure 12.2 Definition of equality, and the reflexivity property for equality

Remark 12.2.2   *We obtain a* second order *definition of equality, since the* Π *ranges over predicates P, and $P : S \to * : \square$. Hence, the* Π *in the formula is a second order* ∀*-quantifier. This cannot be covered by the* first order ∀*-symbol dealt with in Sections 5.4, part V, and 7.5. See also Remark 11.10.1.*

There is one *hole* in the derivation: the proof object of line (2) is still open. We need a proof of $P\, x \Leftrightarrow P\, x$. There are two obvious strategies to fill the hole:

(1) *The ad-hoc approach:* immediately find an inhabitant of $P\, x \Leftrightarrow P\, x$. This is not hard: we may take the expression

$$\Leftrightarrow\text{-}in(P\, x, P\, x, \lambda u : P\, x . u, \lambda u : P\, x . u),$$

which is appropriate since $\lambda u : P\, x . u$ is an inhabitant of both $P\, x \Rightarrow P\, x$ and $P\, x \Leftarrow P\, x$.

(2) *The general approach:* first prove a lemma to the effect that $A \Leftrightarrow A$ holds for arbitrary A of type $*_p$, give its proof a name (say $\Leftrightarrow\text{-}refl(A)$), and then fill the hole with the instantiated expression $\Leftrightarrow\text{-}refl(P\, x)$.

The formalisation of such a lemma and its proof is easy; we leave it to the reader. Both strategies solve the problem. We suppose that one of these has been chosen in line (2) of Figure 12.2.

Since formal equality plays such an important role in mathematics, we introduce a *notation convention* in our λD-text, for a smoother representation (see Figure 12.3, which replaces Figure 12.2). Denoting $eq(S, x, y)$ as $x =_S y$, being more reader-friendly, we employ the usual symbol ' $=$ ', subscripted with the set in which the equality is taken; moreover, we use infix notation (see also Notation 11.5.2).

$\boxed{S : *_s}$

$\boxed{x : S}$

$\boxed{y : S}$

(1) $\quad eq(S, x, y) := \Pi P : S \to *_p . (Px \Leftrightarrow Py) : *_p$

$\quad\quad$ Notation : $x =_S y$ for $eq(S, x, y)$

$\quad\quad \vdots$

(3) $\quad eq\text{-}refl(S, x) := \lambda P : S \to *_p . a_2(S, x, P) : x =_S x$

Figure 12.3 A notation convention for equality, and its use

It is not hard to also prove symmetry and transitivity for this equality, by proving $x =_S y \Rightarrow y =_S x$, and $(x =_S y \wedge y =_S z) \Rightarrow x =_S z$, in appropriate contexts.

These proofs may be based on the corresponding properties for biimplication:

- (symmetry) if $A \Leftrightarrow B$, then $B \Leftrightarrow A$, and
- (transitivity) if $A \Leftrightarrow B$ and $B \Leftrightarrow C$, then $A \Leftrightarrow C$.

We leave the corresponding proofs to the reader.

A simple consequence of the definition of equality is that it satisfies *substitutivity*. This notion can be expressed as follows:

'One always may substitute equals for equals',

or, more formally:

'For all predicates P on S, if $x =_S y$ and P holds for x, then P also holds for y'.

This implies the following: if an expression t_1 occurs in any proposition, and we know that $t_1 =_S t_2$, then one may replace t_1 by t_2 without influencing the truth value. (This explains the name 'substitutivity'.)

We formalise substitutivity in Figure 12.4.

$$\boxed{S : *_s}$$

$$\boxed{P : S \to *_p}$$

$$\boxed{x, y : S}$$

$$\boxed{u : x =_S y}$$

(1)　　　　　　　$a_1(S, P, x, y, u) := u\,P : P\,x \Leftrightarrow P\,y$

(2)　　　　　　　$a_2(S, P, x, y, u) := \Leftrightarrow\text{-}el_1(P\,x, P\,y, a_1(S, P, x, y, u)) : P\,x \Rightarrow P\,y$

$$\boxed{v : P\,x}$$

(3)　　　　　　　$eq\text{-}subs(S, P, x, y, u, v) := a_2(S, P, x, y, u)\,v : P\,y$

Figure 12.4 Substitutivity as property of equality

12.3 The congruence property of equality

There are several properties of equality that can be derived from the definitions in the previous section. One of them is called the *congruence property*. It has some similarities with substitutivity, but congruence concerns ordinary functions (with a *set* as co-domain), and not predicates (which are functions with a *proposition* as co-domain). But again, the idea is to allow the substitution of a t_1 by a t_2 that is equal to t_1.

This congruence property can be phrased as follows:

'For all functions $f : S \to T$ and $x, y : S$, if $x =_S y$, then $f x =_T f y$.'

One says in this case: 'equality is a congruence for function application'.

Again, this is a property we obviously should have. A promising attempt is to try substitutivity (see Figure 12.4): use $x =_S y$ to derive the result $f x =_T f y$. Therefore we must find an appropriate predicate.

One possibility is to unfold the goal $f x =_T f y$. This gives:

$$\Pi Q : T \to *_p \,.\, (Q(f\,x) \Leftrightarrow Q(f\,y)).$$

Hence, we raise a flag $Q : T \to *_p$ and try to prove $Q(f\,x) \Leftrightarrow Q(f\,y)$. This is easy now: substitutivity (using $x =_S y$) on the predicate $\lambda z : S \,.\, Q(f\,z)$ transforms a proof of $Q(f\,x)$ into one of $Q(f\,y)$ (see line (1) in Figure 12.5).

The final part of this derivation serves to dismiss the last two flags, one with $\Rightarrow$-*in* and one with the (*abst*)-rule. Note that we cannot take $\forall$-*in* instead of the λ-expression in line (3), since the Π in the unfolding of $f\,x =_T f\,y$ is second order (cf. Remark 12.2.2). Line (4) is a consequence of the (*conv*)-rule.

We can also derive the congruence property directly from substitutivity by making a smart choice for the predicate involved in substitutivity. This leads to a second proof of congruence.

$$\boxed{S, T : *_s}$$

$$\boxed{f : S \to T}$$

$$\boxed{x, y : S}$$

$$\boxed{u \ : \ x =_S y}$$

$$\boxed{Q \ : \ T \to *_p}$$

$$\boxed{v : Q(f\,x)}$$

(1) $\quad a_1^\dagger \ := \ eq\text{-}subs(S, \lambda z : S\,.\, Q(f\,z), x, y, u, v) \ : \ Q(f\,y)$

(2) $\quad a_2 \ := \ \lambda v : Q(f\,x)\,.\, a_1 \ : \ Q(f\,x) \Rightarrow Q(f\,y)$

(3) $\quad a_3 \ := \ \lambda Q : T \to *_p\,.\, a_2 \ : \ \Pi Q : T \to *_p\,.\, (Q(f\,x) \Rightarrow Q(f\,y))$

(4) $\quad eq\text{-}cong_1(S, T, f, x, y, u) \ := \ a_3 \ : \ f\,x =_T f\,y$

† *parameters suppressed*

Figure 12.5 First proof of the congruence property for equality

This time we take predicate Q_1, with the following description:

$$Q_1 \equiv \lambda z : S\,.\, (f\,x =_T f\,z),$$

where Q_1 obviously depends on S, T, f and x. Note that x is a 'free' variable in this expression, whereas variable z is *bound* by the λ; so Q_1 is a predicate 'about' a z of type S.

Now $Q_1\,x$ is convertible to $f\,x =_T f\,x$, which is valid by reflexivity; and $Q_1\,y$ is convertible to $f\,x =_T f\,y$, the desired equality in the congruence property. Substitutivity gives that $x =_S y$ and $Q_1\,x$ imply $Q_1\,y$. Hence, substitutivity gives (again) the result desired (see Figure 12.6).

$$\boxed{S, T : *_s}$$

$$\boxed{f : S \to T}$$

$$\boxed{x : S}$$

(1) $\quad Q_1(S, T, f, x) \ := \ \lambda z : S\,.\, (f\,x =_T f\,z) \ : \ S \to *_p$

$$\boxed{y : S}$$

$$\boxed{u \ : \ x =_S y}$$

(2) $\quad eq\text{-}cong_2(S, T, f, x, y, u) \ :=$

$\qquad eq\text{-}subs(S, Q_1(S, T, f, x), x, y, u, eq\text{-}refl(T, f\,x)) \ : \ f\,x =_T f\,y$

Figure 12.6 Second proof of the congruence property for equality

So we have a formally defined equality, together with three important properties: reflexivity, substitutivity and the congruence property.

In the previous section we have already mentioned 'symmetry' and 'transitivity', two other properties that are very fundamental for equality. In Section 12.5 we deal with these. But first we note that (variants of) symmetry and transitivity are important in a more general setting, namely with respect to *orders*. This is the subject of the following section.

12.4 Orders

Now that we know how to code 'equality', we need to say more about the other relation playing a role in the proof of Lemma 12.1.2, namely the ordering relation denoted '$\leq$'. First, $\leq$ must have a type. For this we take $S \to S \to *_p$, so the relation between x and y is represented by the twofold application $\leq x\, y$.

We start with a formalisation of this notion 'partial order' (see Figure 12.7). In line (5) is expressed what a partial order *means*, i.e. what it is as a type (namely, an antisymmetric preorder).

Remark 12.4.1 *We are fairly liberal in employing notation conventions (see also Chapter 11 and Figure 12.3). For example, we shall take identical binding symbols (such as quantifiers) 'together', as is usual in the mathematical notation: we write $\forall x, y : S\,.\,P\,x$ instead of $\forall x : S\,.\,\forall y : S\,.\,P\,x$. Similarly, we write $\lambda x, y : S\,.\,\ldots$ for $\lambda x : S\,.\,\lambda y : S\,.\,\ldots$. See e.g. Figure 12.9, line (9).*

Earlier (Figure 12.3), we introduced $x =_S y$ for $eq(S, x, y)$. We now allow a similar infix notation $x \leq_S y$ (see Figure 12.7) for a very different syntactical structure: the twofold application $\leq x\, y$ (which is $(\leq x)\, y$) on elements x and y of a set S. The symbol S is not part of the original expression $\leq x\, y$.

$S : *_s$

$\leq\, : S \to S \to *_p$

    Notation : $x \leq_S y$ for $\leq x\, y$ (on S)

(1) $refl(S, \leq) := \forall x : S\,.\,(x \leq_S x)\ :\ *_p$

(2) $trans(S, \leq) :=$

        $\forall x : S\,.\,\forall y : S\,.\,\forall z : S\,.\,(x \leq_S y \Rightarrow y \leq_S z \Rightarrow x \leq_S z)\ :\ *_p$

(3) $pre\text{-}ord(S, \leq) := refl(S, \leq) \wedge trans(S, \leq)\ :\ *_p$

(4) $antisymm(S, \leq) := \forall x : S\,.\,\forall y : S\,.\,(x \leq_S y \Rightarrow y \leq_S x \Rightarrow x =_S y)\ :\ *_p$

(5) $part\text{-}ord(S, \leq) := pre\text{-}ord(S, \leq) \wedge antisymm(S, \leq)\ :\ *_p$

Figure 12.7 Definitions regarding partial orders

We now try to formalise the proof attempt of Figure 12.1. The final part of the proof, expressed in line (4) of that figure, will be dealt with in Section 12.6, in which we explain how to formalise 'uniqueness'.

First we give a *skeleton proof*, which only contains the necessary *flags* and the *types* (see Figure 12.8). The proof skeleton expresses the basic ideas and the course of the derivation being expressed in the informal proof of Lemma 12.1.2 (but for the last sentence).

(a) $\boxed{S \,:\, *_s}$

(b) $\boxed{\leq \,:\, S \to S \to *_p}$

(c) $\boxed{r \,:\, \textit{part-ord}(S, \leq)}$

(d) $\boxed{m_1, m_2 \,:\, S}$

(e) $\boxed{u \,:\, \forall n : S.\,(m_1 \leq_S n) \mid v \,:\, \forall n : S.\,(m_2 \leq_S n)}$

(1) $\ldots \,:\, m_1 \leq_S m_2$

(2) $\ldots \,:\, m_2 \leq_S m_1$

(3) $\ldots \,:\, \textit{pre-ord}(S, \leq) \wedge \textit{antisymm}(S, \leq)$

(4) $\ldots \,:\, \textit{antisymm}(S, \leq)$

(5) $\ldots \,:\, \forall x : S.\,\forall y : S.\,(x \leq_S y \Rightarrow y \leq_S x \Rightarrow x =_S y)$

(6) $\ldots \,:\, m_1 \leq_S m_2 \Rightarrow m_2 \leq_S m_1 \Rightarrow m_1 =_S m_2$

(7) $\ldots \,:\, m_2 \leq_S m_1 \Rightarrow m_1 =_S m_2$

(8) $\ldots \,:\, m_1 =_S m_2$

(9) $\ldots \,:\, \forall m_1, m_2 : S.\,((\forall n : S.\,(m_1 \leq_S n)) \Rightarrow (\forall n : S.\,(m_2 \leq_S n)) \Rightarrow (m_1 =_S m_2))$

Figure 12.8 A skeleton proof for the first part of Lemma 12.1.2

The proof is a consequence of antisymmetry (line (4), elaborated in line (5)), combined with lines (1) and (2). This is the leading idea in the incomplete derivation of Figure 12.8.

We invite the reader to compare the given skeleton proof with the informal proof in Section 12.1, and with lines (1) to (3) of the proof attempt given in Figure 12.1. (In flags (d) and (e) we combine flags, as proposed in Notation 11.5.1.)

In Figure 12.9 we have filled in all proof objects in the skeleton proof, and given them names. For the sake of clarity, we *underline* the types, so that this derivation can be easily compared with the proof skeleton in Figure 12.8.

The problem in this part of the derivation is question *Q2* of Section 12.1:

to find t_3, which is a proof (in the form of an inhabitant) of $m_1 =_S m_2$. The solution is the proof object in line (8).

(a)	$S : *_s$
(b)	$\leq\, :\, S \to S \to *_p$
(c)	$r\, :\, part\text{-}ord(S, \leq)$
(d)	$m_1, m_2 : S$
(e)	$u\, :\, \forall n : S.\,(m_1 \leq_S n)\ \|\ v\, :\, \forall n : S.\,(m_2 \leq_S n)$
(1)	$a_1^\dagger := u\, m_2\, :\, \underline{m_1 \leq_S m_2}$
(2)	$a_2 := v\, m_1\, :\, \underline{m_2 \leq_S m_1}$
(3)	$a_3 := r\, :\, \underline{pre\text{-}ord(S, \leq) \wedge antisymm(S, \leq)}$
(4)	$a_4 := \wedge\text{-}el_2(pre\text{-}ord(S, \leq)\,,\, antisymm(S, \leq)\,,\, a_3)\ :$
	$\qquad antisymm(S, \leq)$
(5)	$a_5 := a_4\ :\ \forall x : S.\,\forall y : S.\,(x \leq_S y \Rightarrow y \leq_S x \Rightarrow x =_S y)$
(6)	$a_6 := a_5\, m_1\, m_2\ :\ \underline{m_1 \leq_S m_2 \Rightarrow m_2 \leq_S m_1 \Rightarrow m_1 =_S m_2}$
(7)	$a_7 := a_6\, a_1\ :\ \underline{m_2 \leq_S m_1 \Rightarrow m_1 =_S m_2}$
(8)	$a_8 := a_7\, a_2\ :\ \underline{m_1 =_S m_2}$
(9)	$a_9(S, \leq, r) := \lambda m_1, m_2 : S.\,\lambda u : \ldots .\,\lambda v : \ldots .\,a_8\ :$
	$\qquad \forall m_1, m_2 : S.\,((\forall n : S.\,(m_1 \leq_S n)) \Rightarrow (\forall n : S.\,(m_2 \leq_S n)) \Rightarrow$
	$\qquad\qquad\qquad\qquad\qquad\qquad\qquad\qquad \underline{m_1 =_S m_2})$

† *parameters suppressed*

Figure 12.9 A formal proof of the first part of Lemma 12.1.2 in λD

We give little comment on Figure 12.9, since most of it will speak for itself:
- We suppress parameters, following Notation 11.7.1.
- We use the type-theoretic style whenever we find this convenient.
- Lines (3) and (5) are only meant to help the reader: we repeat earlier statements (given in flag (c) and line (4), respectively), but with an unfolded type. This is permitted by the (*conv*)-rule.

12.5 A proof about orders

In Figures 12.2 and 12.4, we have formally introduced the properties *reflexivity* and *substitutivity* for equality. Proofs of the properties *symmetry* and *transitivity* are suggested in Section 12.2, but not spelled out. In the present section we show an alternative manner to obtain these results, since both properties can be *derived* from the first two. We do not claim that the methods presented here are either shorter or easier than the proofs suggested in Section 12.2 – on the contrary. Our endeavours appear, however, to be a useful exercise with substitutivity.

We first show that *symmetry* follows from reflexivity and substitutivity: see Figure 12.10 (at the end of this section we do the same for transitivity).

The idea behind the proof is the following. Assume $x =_S y$. Then we have to prove that also $y =_S x$. Now first recall that *reflexivity* gives: $x =_S x$. Secondly, focus on the first x of this equality, which we underline for the sake of clarity: $\underline{x} =_S x$. Then apply *substitutivity*: since $x =_S y$, we may replace $\underline{x}$ by y, thus obtaining $y =_S x$. So we are done.

Formally: consider the predicate $Q_2(S, x) := \lambda z : S . (z =_S x)$, for which we have that $(Q_2(S, x)) x \to_\beta (x =_S x)$ and $(Q_2(S, x)) y \to_\beta (y =_S x)$; the definition of *eq-subs* in Figure 12.4, with $Q_2(S, x)$ substituted for P, then does the job.

$$\boxed{S : *_s}$$

$\quad\boxed{x : S}$

(1) $\quad Q_2(S, x) := \lambda z : S . (z =_S x) : S \to *_p$

(2) $\quad a_2(S, x) := eq\text{-}refl(S, x) : x =_S x$

$\quad\quad\boxed{y : S}$

$\quad\quad\quad\boxed{u : x =_S y}$

(3) $\quad\quad\quad eq\text{-}sym(S, x, y, u) :=$
$\quad\quad\quad\quad eq\text{-}subs(S, Q_2(S, x), x, y, u, a_2(S, x)) :$
$\quad\quad\quad\quad y =_S x$

(4) $\quad a_4(S) := \lambda x, y : S . \lambda u : (x =_S y) . eq\text{-}sym(S, x, y, u) :$
$\quad\quad\quad \forall x, y : S . (x =_S y \Rightarrow y =_S x)$

Figure 12.10 Symmetry of equality follows from reflexivity and substitutivity

In line (4) of Figure 12.10, we give a λ-term as inhabitant, which is shorter than what we would obtain with the (more natural) logical introduction rules for $\Rightarrow$ and $\forall$.

The definitions in lines (1) and (2) are inserted to make the proof more comprehensible for a human reader: the formal proof now narrowly follows the informal explanation given above. There is no objection against condensing the essence of the proof into one proof term, by the *unfolding* of the constants Q_2 and a_2 in line (3). This permits us to omit lines (1) and (2). The result is depicted in Figure 12.11.

$$S : *_s \mid x, y : S \mid u : x =_S y$$

$$eq\text{-}sym'(S, x, y, u) :=$$

$$eq\text{-}subs(S, \lambda z : S . (z =_S x), x, y, u, eq\text{-}refl(S, x)) : y =_S x$$

Figure 12.11 A shorter version of the core of the derivation of Figure 12.10

We conclude this section with the promised derivation of *transitivity* of equality, using similar methods as in the above derivation of symmetry.

We give an alternative to the proof suggested in Section 12.2 (see Figure 12.12). The important thing is, again, to devise an appropriate predicate Q. It turns out that $Q_3(S, x) := \lambda w : S . (x =_S w)$ does the job together with Substitutivity, since $(Q_3(S, x))y$ converts to $x =_S y$ and $(Q_3(S, x))z$ to $x =_S z$. Hence, the essence of the proof is the following: given that $x =_S y$ (i.e. $(Q_3(S, x))y$), then if also $y =_S z$ we may substitute z for y in $x =_S y$, to obtain $x =_S z$ (i.e. $(Q_3(S, x))z$).

We leave it to the reader to check the details (Exercise 12.3 (a)).

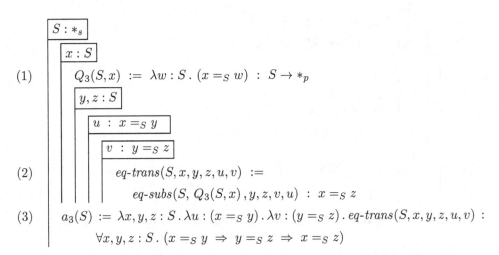

Figure 12.12 Transitivity of equality follows from substitutivity

12.6 Unique existence

We have succeeded (see Figure 12.9) in translating the main part of the *proof* of Lemma 12.1.2, but the final statement of the proof, the lemma itself, and the related Definition 12.1.1, have not yet been transferred to λD. In this section we investigate how this can be done.

The first thing that we consider is a formal description of the property 'being-a-least-element', which is the subject of Definition 12.1.1. See Figure 12.13.

(For a 'least element' it is not necessary that the relation is a partial order.)

(a) $\quad\boxed{S : *_s \mid \; \leq \; : S \to S \to *_p \mid m : S}$

(1) $\quad\boxed{\quad Least(S, \leq, m) := \forall n : S . (m \leq n) : *_p}$

Figure 12.13 A formal version of Definition 12.1.1

We use the name *Least*, with a capital '*L*', because m is intended to be a least element of the type S. Later, we use '*least*' to denote a least element of a *subset* of S (see Figure 15.1).

So now we can express '*m is a least element of S with respect to relation $\leq$*'.

Remark 12.6.1 *This definition also enables us to rephrase the flags in* (e) *of Figure 12.9 as $u : Least(S, \leq, m_1)$ and $v : Least(S, \leq, m_2)$, thus bringing our formal proof and the informal one of Section 12.1 closer together.*

We have not yet formally expressed that such an m is *unique* when $\leq$ is a partial order, which is the conclusion of Lemma 12.1.2. How about this *uniqueness of existence*? Let's investigate the various modes of existence:

- To begin with, we already have the property *existence* as such, expressible by means of the quantifier $\exists$. (See Section 7.5 for its λC-version and Figure 11.23, line (1), for its definition in λD.)
- Obviously, $\exists_{x \in S}(P(x))$ means 'there exists *at least one* x in S satisfying P'. Hence, we sometimes write $\exists^{\geq 1}$ instead of just $\exists$.
- A counterpart of $\exists^{\geq 1}$ is 'there exists *at most one*', which we express as $\exists^{\leq 1}$. So $\exists^{\leq 1}_{x \in S}(P(x))$ means that there either are no x's in S satisfying P, or just one. A common way of establishing 'at most one' is by proving that 'two is impossible' (and hence also three, four, ... are impossible). In formal form:

  $$\forall y, z : S . (P(y) \Rightarrow P(z) \Rightarrow y =_S z);$$

  or, in words: if we observe 'two' elements of S satisfying P, then they are necessarily equal.

- It is now easy to express '*exactly one*', as the conjunction of 'at most one' and 'at least one'.

It is clear how to formalise all this in λD; see Figure 12.14.

Notation 12.6.2 *In Figure 11.23 we agreed to allow the common notation $\exists x : S . P x$ as an alternative notation for $\exists(S, P)$.*

Similarly, we allow $\exists^{\leq 1} x : S . P x$ as alternative notation for $\exists^{\leq 1}(S, P)$, and also $\exists^1 x : S . P x$ for $\exists^1(S, P)$.

$$\boxed{S : *_s}$$

$$\boxed{P : S \to *_p}$$

(1) $\exists(S,P) := \Pi A : *_p . \, ((\forall x : S . \, (P\,x \Rightarrow A)) \Rightarrow A) \; : \; *_p$

(2) $\exists^{\geq 1}(S,P) := \exists(S,P) \; : \; *_p$

(3) $\exists^{\leq 1}(S,P) := \forall y, z : S . \, (P\,y \Rightarrow P\,z \Rightarrow (y =_S z)) \; : \; *_p$

(4) $\exists^1(S,P) := \exists^{\geq 1}(S,P) \wedge \exists^{\leq 1}(S,P) \; : \; *_p$

Figure 12.14 Various existential quantifiers

With respect to the proof in Figure 12.9, we observe that the type in line (9) of that figure, viz.

$$\forall m_1, m_2 : S . \, ((\forall n : S . \, (m_1 \leq_S n)) \Rightarrow (\forall n : S . \, (m_2 \leq_S n)) \Rightarrow m_1 =_S m_2),$$

corresponds to $\forall y, z : S . \, (P\,y \Rightarrow P\,z \Rightarrow (y =_S z))$, if P is the 'least-element-predicate':

$\lambda m : S . \, Least(S, \leq, m).$

Hence, $a_9(S, \leq, r)$ of Figure 12.9 is by line (3) of Figure 12.14 and the $(conv)$-rule also an inhabitant of $\exists^{\leq 1} x : S . \, Least(S, \leq, x)$.

So all we need now is the assumption that *there is* a least element of S (i.e. $\exists^{\geq 1} x : S . \, Least(S, \leq, x)$), to be able to conclude that *there is exactly one* least element ($\exists^1 x : S . \, Least(S, \leq, x)$). This observation corresponds precisely to the last sentence of the informal proof in Section 12.1.

Hence, we now can express the full Lemma 12.1.2 and its proof in a formal λD-version (see Figure 12.15, which is an extension of Figure 12.9).

(10) $a_{10} := a_{9[Fig.\ 12.9]} \; : \; \exists^{\leq 1} x : S . \, Least(S, \leq, x)$

(d) $\boxed{w \; : \; \exists^{\geq 1} x : S . \, Least(S, \leq, x)}$

(11) $a_{11}(S, \leq, r, w) := \wedge\text{-}in(\exists^{\geq 1} \ldots, \exists^{\leq 1} \ldots, w, a_{10}) \; :$

$\exists^1 x : S . \, Least(S, \leq, x)$

Figure 12.15 A completed formal version of Lemma 12.1.2 and its proof

So $a_{11}(S, \leq, r, w)$ in Figure 12.15 (or the connected definiens, which has the same meaning), together with context (a)–(d) of Figure 12.9, is a representation of the *full* proof of that lemma. The lemma itself is represented by the *type* of line (11) in Figure 12.15, since this line may be read as:

'In context (a)–(d), $a_{11}(S, \leq, r, w)$ inhabits $\exists^1 x : S . \, Least(S, \leq, x)$.'

We have here a good example of the following general observation about formal theorems and formal proofs in λD, which corresponds to the PAT-interpretation (see Section 5.4):

Theorems and proofs

Let the following judgements be both derivable in λD:

$\Gamma \vdash a(\overline{x}) := N : *_p$ and

$\Gamma \vdash b(\overline{x}) := M : N.$

Then, in context Γ:

$a(\overline{x})$ (or N) represents a *theorem* and
$b(\overline{x})$ (or M) represents a *proof* of that theorem.

(Remember that a *lemma* is formally the same as a *theorem*; the difference is that a lemma is considered to be less important, or only a stepping stone to a theorem.)

Remark 12.6.3 *In the present chapter we have done a lot of work to achieve a relatively small result: one definition, one lemma and one proof have been formalised. This may be disappointing to a newcomer in the area of formal proving.*

Note, however, that our take-off in Section 12.1 was a bit naive. We started boldly with an example that was simple, but not standing on its own. Hence, we had to account for several basic notions that had no formal representation yet: equality was one of these notions, the partial order relation $\leq$ another one. Many basic properties of equalities had to be expressed in formal form, which took some time.

The necessity to deliver every 'dirty detail' is sometimes not very pleasant, but inevitable for a justified formalisation. Some of these annoyances can be avoided, e.g. by choosing a more deliberate build-up of the mathematical edifice. For the time being, we are happy with the progress we make.

12.7 The descriptor ι

In the previous section we saw how to express that m is a *least element* with respect to relation $\leq$ on set S: that is the case if we have an inhabitant of *Least* $(S, \leq, m)$. We proved, informally and formally, that such an m (if it exists) is *unique* when $\leq$ is a partial order on S. In the traditional mathematical setting, this implies that we can *identify* such a least element with a name: it is usual to talk about *the minimum* of S with respect to $\leq$, or to reserve a special notation for it, e.g. $Min(S)$ (or rather: $Min(S, \leq)$).

Note that, as long as the uniqueness hasn't been proved, we only may speak of *a* minimum (which is the same as a least element); whereas uniqueness only allows us to call it *the* minimum.

In some fields of mathematics, the *descriptor* ι (pronounced 'ióta' and first proposed by F.L.G. Frege, who lived 1848–1925) is used for naming ('describing') such a uniquely existing element: $\iota_{x \in S}(P(x))$ then represents *the (unique) element x of S that has property* $P(x)$.

So in this notation, we have that the minimum of set S with respect to relation $\leq$ is $\iota_{m \in S}(Least(S, \leq, m))$.

In λD, we can easily add the ι-operator as a primitive constant. This constant depends on a set S, a predicate P, and a proof u that there exists *exactly one* element in S that satisfies predicate P. In Figure 12.16, we call it $\iota(S, P, u)$ (that is: *the* element of S for which P holds, being unique because of u).

A characteristic property of $\iota(S, P, u)$ is that it satisfies predicate P. To express this, we must also add a primitive inhabitant of $P(\iota(S, P, u))$, being a (primitive) *proof* of this property.

In Figure 12.16 we propose an alternative notation $\iota_{x:S}^{u}(P\,x)$ that is quite similar to the usual one: $\iota_{x \in S}(P(x))$, the main difference being that the obligatory proof u for the unique existence of such an x is added as a superscript. In line (2), we give the name $\iota\text{-}prop(S, P, u)$ to the primitively assumed *inhabitant* of the proposition that P holds for the element described by means of the iota.

$$
\begin{array}{|l}
\hline
S : *_s \\
\quad \begin{array}{|l}
\hline
P : S \to *_p \\
\quad \begin{array}{|l}
\hline
u : (\exists^1 x : S \,.\, P\,x) \\
\hline
\end{array} \\
\hline
\end{array}
\end{array}
$$

(1) $\qquad\qquad \iota(S, P, u) \;:=\; \bot \;:\; S$

$\qquad\qquad\quad$ Notation : $\iota_{x:S}^{u}(P\,x)$ for $\iota(S, P, u)$

(2) $\qquad\qquad \iota\text{-}prop(S, P, u) \;:=\; \bot \;:\; P\,(\iota_{x:S}^{u}(P\,x))$

Figure 12.16 The descriptor ι

As a general example of the use of this formal ι-operator, we prove the following obvious (and useful) property: if there is exactly one element in S satisfying P, then an element x of S for which P holds must necessarily be equal to $\iota_{x:S}^{u}(P\,x)$. This is expressed in the following lemma.

Lemma 12.7.1 *Let S be a set, P a predicate on S and assume $\exists^1_{x \in S}(P(x))$. Then $\forall_{z \in S}(P(z) \Rightarrow (z =_S \iota_{x \in S}(P(x))))$.*

The proof of Lemma 12.7.1 is given in Figure 12.17. The judgements in lines (1) and (3) are 'Notes for the reader', as we have used earlier.

(a)	$\boxed{S : *_s \mid P : S \rightarrow *_p \mid u : (\exists^1 x : S . P x)}$
(1)	$a_1^\dagger := u : (\exists^{\geq 1} x : S . P x \wedge \exists^{\leq 1} x : S . P x)$
(2)	$a_2 := \wedge\text{-}el_2(\exists^{\geq 1} x : S . P x, \exists^{\leq 1} x : S . P x, u) : \exists^{\leq 1} x : S . P x$
(3)	$a_3 := a_2 : \forall x, y : S . (P x \Rightarrow P y \Rightarrow (x =_S y))$
(b)	$\boxed{z : S \mid v : P z}$
(4)	$\quad a_4 := a_3 \ z \ (\iota^u_{x:S}(P x)) \ v \ \iota\text{-}prop(S, P, u) : z =_S \iota^u_{x:S}(P x)$
(5)	$a_5(S, P, u) := \lambda z : S . \lambda v : P z . a_4 : \forall z : S . (P z \Rightarrow (z =_S \iota^u_{x:S}(P x)))$

†*parameters suppressed*

Figure 12.17 Lemma 12.7.1 and its proof

The proof in Figure 12.17 is not hard to understand. The final result stated in line (5) is the combined derivation of the lemma (the type) *and* its proof (the definiens), both in context (a). This exemplifies the observation about 'Theorems and proofs' in the previous section.

Remark 12.7.2 *Seemingly, $\iota(S, P, u)$ depends on the proof u of $\exists^1 x : S . P x$. Now assume that we have two different proofs u_1 and u_2 of this uniqueness. Then it is imaginable that $\iota(S, P, u_1)$ and $\iota(S, P, u_2)$ are also* different; *which is clearly undesirable. We can easily prove, however, that this does not occur: both $\iota(S, P, u_1)$ and $\iota(S, P, u_2)$ satisfy predicate P, as a consequence of $\iota\text{-}prop(S, P, u_1)$ and $\iota\text{-}prop(S, P, u_2)$, respectively. But since there is* exactly one *element satisfying P (of which fact we even have two proofs!), we can derive in λD that $\iota(S, P, u_1)$ must be equal to $\iota(S, P, u_2)$, using either of these proofs.*

One calls such a situation irrelevance of proof: *$\iota^u_{x:S}(P x)$ only depends on the* existence *of proof u, not on its exact content. See also Section 14.13 for this matter.*

We are now able to define *the* (unique) minimum of a set S with respect to the partial order $\leq$ on S, provided that *there is* a least element of S. See line (1) in Figure 12.18. Since we use the ι, we need that $\exists^1 m : S . Least(S, \leq, m)$, which is a consequence of assumption (b). We proved this in Figure 12.15.

We also take the opportunity to give a compact rephrasing of the original example, Lemma 12.1.2 (and its proof), with the new minimum-operator. See line (2) of Figure 12.18. This lemma can be expressed in words as follows: 'Let $\leq$ be a partial order on S; if S has a least element x, then x is the minimum of S.'

(a) $\boxed{S \,:\, *_s \mid\, \leq\, :\, S \to S \to *_p \mid r \,:\, \textit{part-ord}(S, \leq)}$

(b) $\quad \boxed{w \,:\, \exists^{\geq 1} x : S \,.\, \textit{Least}(S, \leq, x)}$

(1) $\qquad \textit{Min}(S, \leq, r, w) \,:=$

$\qquad\qquad \iota(S, \lambda m : S \,.\, \textit{Least}(S, \leq, m), a_{11\,[\textit{Fig. 12.15}]}(S, \leq, r, w)) \,:\, S$

(2) $\qquad a_2(S, \leq, r, w) \,:=$

$\qquad\qquad a_{5\,[\textit{Fig. 12.17}]}(S, \lambda m : S \,.\, \textit{Least}(S, \leq, m), a_{11\,[\textit{Fig. 12.15}]}(S, \leq, r, w)) \,:$

$\qquad\qquad\qquad \forall x : S \,.\, (\textit{Least}(S, \leq, x) \,\Rightarrow\, (x =_S \textit{Min}(S, \leq, r, w)))$

Figure 12.18 The minimum-operator, and a lemma with proof

12.8 Conclusions

In the present chapter we have given a first introduction to the formalisation of mathematics in λD. We selected an example from mathematics, dealing with a definition, a lemma and a proof (all about the notion 'least element').

As could be expected, we immediately became confronted with a lack of formalised *foreknowledge* about common notions in mathematics that play a role in this example, such as equality and inequalities. Hence, we had to introduce these notions.

With regard to *equality*, it appeared indispensable to also discuss notions such as reflexivity, substitutivity and the congruence property. For the formalisation of more general relations, we have considered orders in general, together with their characteristic properties: reflexivity, transitivity and antisymmetry.

As another example, we have given a λD-proof of the lemma that symmetry of equality follows from reflexivity and substitutivity. We also gave a formal proof that transitivity of equality follows from substitutivity.

As a demonstration of how these formal notions work in practice, we have elaborated a complete formal proof of the original example, which turned out well. In the course of the formalisation, we introduced a formal quantifier for unique existence, which enabled us to accurately express the contents of the example lemma.

Next, reconsidering the original example, we have noticed that the *unique existence* of an entity enables one to identify it. For example, the uniqueness of a least element permits us to speak about *the* minimum. Since it is natural to give a *name* to a uniquely existing entity, we have added the descriptor ι as a primitive extension to our formal machinery. *The* unique element of set S satisfying property P is denoted $\iota(S, P, u)$ (or $\iota^u_{T \cdot S}(P\,x)$), where u codes a proof of the uniqueness. We concluded the chapter with a few short demonstrations of use and utility of the descriptor ι.

Altogether, our first confrontation of λD with a part of mathematics has led to convincing results. Hence, our investigations described in the present chapter inspire confidence that we are on the right path with our endeavours to use λD as a well-designed backbone for the formalisation of mathematics.

In the following chapters we will be fortified in this opinion. But before we start exploring this in a more systematic manner, in a build-up from the ground, we consider the relation between sets and subsets. This is basic in mathematics, but its formalisation seems to conflict with a fundamental property of type theory, namely: decidability of typing. The following chapter is devoted to an adequate formalisation of the set-notion.

12.9 Further reading

In the present chapter we see that some actual mathematics can be done in λD, but that, in order to do that in a smooth way, we need to introduce a notion of equality and a description operator, ι. The formal treatment of these notions, roughly in the way we do in λD, goes back to A. Church (Church, 1940), where he introduces the simple theory of types and uses it to define a system for higher order logic. The idea of descriptions – also called *definite descriptions* – dates further back to 1905 (Russell, 1905). In Church's system, equality is also *defined* as Leibniz-equality. A definite description operator is introduced axiomatically by Church (1940), similar to our introduction of ι as a primitive notion.

From a logical point of view, the definite description operator ι can be seen as a convenient abbreviation mechanism: in case we can prove that there is a *unique* x satisfying a certain property P, we give it a name and refer to it via that name. This does not extend the power of the logic in terms of the formulas that are provable: it is a *conservative extension*. This can be seen from the fact that alternatively one can 'reason under an $\exists$-elimination': suppose one wants to prove C, given a proof of $\exists x : A \,.\, (P(x))$. Now, one raises flags $x : A$ and $q : P(x)$ and tries to construct a proof of C. Upon success, one eliminates the flags and concludes C out of the scope of these flags. With *unique* existence, and by the use of the description operator, this becomes simpler, because one can just refer to 'the element $a : A$ that satisfies $P(a)$', without having to raise these flags. The uniqueness guarantees that every time we eliminate a proof of $\exists x : A \,.\, (P(x))$, we get *the same* element of type A that satisfies property P.

The ι-operator is related to D. Hilbert's ε-operator (Hilbert & Bernays, 1939), also called the *choice operator*, which gives *an* element $\varepsilon_x(P(x))$ that satisfies P in case one can prove $\exists_x(P(x))$. This is stronger than the description operator, because it does not require uniqueness. However, the ε-operator is usually only considered in relatively weak logical systems and then the aim is to show that it can be eliminated. This is also one of the aims of Hilbert's Program, where the ε-terms are the 'ideal elements'; the aim of Hilbert is to show that these can be eliminated, thus showing that the extension with ε-terms is a conservative extension. Hilbert & Bernays (1939) show this, for example, for quantifier-free predicate logic.

It should be noted that both the choice and the description operator are much weaker than the Axiom of Choice (see van Dalen *et al.*, 1978). This is a crucial axiom in set theory that states that, if we have a collection of non-empty sets A_i, indexed by $i \in I$, then *there exists a choice function f* that assigns to every $i \in I$ an element of A_i. The Axiom of Choice cannot be eliminated in the way mentioned above and it is debated in the foundation of mathematics.

Exercises

12.1 Give a proof of the symmetry of equality in λD as suggested in Section 12.2, by first proving the symmetry property for biimplication.

12.2 Let $S : *_s,\ x, y : S \ \triangleright\ eq\text{-}alt(S, x, y)\ :=\ \Pi P : S \to *_p\ .\ (P\,x \Rightarrow P\,y)\ :\ *_p$ be a definition.

    (a) Prove that *eq-alt* is a reflexive relation.

    (b) Prove that *eq-alt* is a symmetric relation. (Hint: consider, given $x : S$ and $y : S$, the predicate $\lambda z : S\ .\ eq\text{-}alt(S, z, x)$.)

    (c) Prove that *eq-alt* is a transitive relation.

    (d) Check the substitutivity property for *eq-alt*. What can you conclude about the predicate *eq-alt*?

12.3 (a) Check that line (3) of Figure 12.10 and line (2) of Figure 12.12 satisfy the derivation rules of λD.

    (b) The same question for lines (1) and (2) of Figure 12.18.

12.4 Let S be a set, partially ordered by $\leq$. For $m, n \in S$, define $m < n$ as $m \leq n \wedge (m \neq n)$.

    (a) Formalise the definition of $<$ in λD and introduce the notation $x <_S y$.

    Prove the following by giving derivations in λD (in parts (c) and (d) you may suffice with *skeleton proofs*, cf. Figure 12.8):

    (b) $<$ is irreflexive, i.e. $\forall_{m \in S}(\neg(m < m))$,

    (c) $<$ is strictly antisymmetric, i.e. $\forall_{m,n \in S}(\neg((m < n) \wedge (n < m)))$,

    (d) $<$ is transitive.

12.5 Let S be a set, P a predicate on S and let n be an element of S such that $P(n)$ and $\forall_{x \in S}(P(x) \Rightarrow (x = n))$. Prove the following by giving λD-derivations, first as skeleton proofs, and then as complete proofs:

(a) $\exists^1_{x \in S}(P(x))$,

(b) $n =_S \iota_{x \in S}(P(x))$. (Hint: use Lemma 12.7.1.)

12.6 Let S be a set, partially ordered by $\leq$. An element m in S is called a *minimal* element of S (with respect to $\leq$), if $\forall_{x \in S}(x \leq m \Rightarrow x =_S m)$ (cf. Section 8.6).

(a) If m is a minimal element of S, is this necessarily the only one?

(b) Prove the following (you may suffice with a skeleton proof in λD): if m is a least element of S (with respect to $\leq$), then m also is a minimal element of S.

(c) As in part (b): if m is a least element of S, then m is the *only* minimal element of S.

(You may use classical logic and Exercise 12.5.)

12.7 A *monoid* is a set S with a binary operation $\circ : (S \times S) \to S$ that is *associative*, i.e. $\forall_{x,y,z \in S}((x \circ y) \circ z = x \circ (y \circ z))$.

Let $(S, \circ)$ be a monoid. Assume that $(S, \circ)$ has a *unit*, i.e. an element e such that $e \circ x = x$ and $x \circ e = x$, for all x in S.

(a) Formalise these notions by giving the corresponding λD-definitions. (Take $S \to S \to S$ as the type of $\circ$.)

(b) Prove in λD that the unit is unique.

(c) Assume that every element x of S has an *inverse*, i.e. an element y such that $x \circ y = e$ and $y \circ x = e$. Give a skeleton proof in λD to show that every x has a *unique* inverse.

(d) Raise a flag with $x : S$ and express the inverse of x in λD.

12.8 'Invert' the implication arrow in the type of line (2) of Figure 12.18 and prove that also this type is inhabited in context (a), (b). (Use substitutivity; see Section 12.2.)

12.9 Assume that the set $\mathbb{R}$ of real numbers has been formalised as a type in λD. Moreover, assume that the number 0 has been formalised as a term of type $\mathbb{R}$, the binary subtraction operation '$-$' as a term of type $\mathbb{R} \to \mathbb{R} \to \mathbb{R}$, the relations $>_\mathbb{R}$, $\geq_\mathbb{R}$ and $<_\mathbb{R}$ as terms of type $\mathbb{R} \to \mathbb{R} \to *_p$, and the unary absolute value operator $|\ldots|$ as a term of type $\mathbb{R} \to \mathbb{R}$.

Moreover, let the set $\mathbb{N}$ be formalised as a type in λD, and the relation $>_\mathbb{N}$ as a term of type $\mathbb{N} \to \mathbb{N} \to *_p$.

An (infinite) sequence of reals is then represented by a map f from $\mathbb{N}$ to $\mathbb{R}$.

(a) Express in λD the convergence property for a sequence:
$f : \mathbb{N} \to \mathbb{R}$ has *limit* l if $\forall_{\varepsilon>0}\exists_{N\in\mathbb{N}}\forall_{n>N}(|f(n) - l| < \varepsilon)$.
(Hint: formalise $\forall_{\varepsilon>0}(P(\varepsilon))$ as $\forall\varepsilon : \mathbb{R}. (\varepsilon >_{\mathbb{R}} 0 \Rightarrow P\varepsilon)$.)

(b) Give a mathematical proof, using classical logic, of the following proposition:
If sequence $f : \mathbb{N} \to \mathbb{R}$ has limit l, then this limit is unique.
(Hint: Assume that f has two *different* limits l_1 and l_2. Define ε as $\frac{1}{2}|l_1 - l_2|$ and derive a contradiction, using the *triangle inequality*, viz.
$\forall_{x,y,z\in\mathbb{R}}(|x - y| + |x - z| \geq |y - z|)$.)

(c) Transform the proof in (b) into a skeleton proof in λD. (You may use infix notation.) Indicate where it is not yet possible to provide an appropriate proof object, because formalised mathematical foreknowledge is missing.

13

Sets and subsets

13.1 Dealing with subsets in λD

In type theory, *sets* are not directly represented, although we have often treated sets as types (i.e. objects of type $*$) in the previous chapters. We wrote $*_s$ instead of $*$ to underline this. However, types and sets have very different backgrounds. In Chapters 2 to 6, we introduced *types* as formal expressions, in order to eliminate undesired properties from the ('free') untyped lambda calculus. *Sets*, on the other hand, are *mathematical constructs*, meant to enable us to talk about collections of mathematical objects.

Until now, considering sets as types has worked out fine. But we may expect serious problems when it comes to *subsets*. The reason is that the Uniqueness of Types property (see e.g. Lemma 10.4.10) conflicts with the 'natural' view on subsets. For example, let S be a set and T a proper subset of S. Now let c be an element of S. In type theory this could be expressed as $c : S$. But what if we wish to express that c is also an element of the subset T? Then $c : T$ doesn't work, because types S and T are different, hence Uniqueness of Types would be violated.

As another example, let P be a property of elements in S. Then one can form the set $\{x \in S \,|\, P\,x\}$ of all elements of S satisfying P. Now, for $c : S$, to decide $c : \{x \in S \,|\, P\,x\}$, we would have to decide if $P\,c$ holds, which is undecidable in general. Hence, treating subsets as types violates decidability of typing. To make this example more concrete, let S be $\mathbb{R}$, let P be $\lambda x : \mathbb{R} \,.\, x \geq 0$ and suppose $F : \{x \in \mathbb{R} \,|\, x \geq 0\} \to \mathbb{R}$ is the square root function. Now, if we need to type-check the term $F\,M$ with $M : \mathbb{R}$, we have to verify that $M : \{x \in \mathbb{R} \,|\, x \geq 0\}$; that is, we have to find a proof of $M \geq 0$. This is undecidable: following the famous results by Church (1936b) and Turing (1936) there is no general algorithm to decide if something is provable.

This is a serious issue in type theory. On the one hand, we are content with *decidability* of typing, as we argued in earlier chapters. This makes type theory strong as a system for proof checking, which can be executed with a definite answer (either 'ok', or 'not ok', but never 'we don't know'). Decidability of typing is also helpful in proof finding.

On the other hand, decidability of typing prevents the usual handling of subsets. This is strange for the average mathematician, who is used to considering an object of a set as naturally belonging to every 'superset'. So we conclude that sets cannot be identified with types in a straightforward manner. Researchers have developed several views on how to deal with (sub-)sets in type theory, leading to different starting points, each with their own advantages and disadvantages. (We mention the most prominent views in Section 13.8.)

So in order to be able to fruitfully incorporate set theory in our type-theoretic framework of λD, we have to make a choice about the treatment of subsets. In doing so, we have to take a decision about one fundamental issue, which has been mentioned several times before: whether or not to stick to *decidability* of typing, and to Uniqueness of Types.

It is tempting to abandon Uniqueness of Types in order to treat types in the way mathematics treat sets. Then an element can belong to several types; for example, the number 3 may have type $\mathbb{N}$, and also $\mathbb{Z}$, and $\mathbb{R}$; moreover, the same 3 may also have type 'the odd natural numbers', and 'the interval of all reals between -2 and 10'.

This would give us great freedom in typing a term, and would solve many of our problems with subsets. However, this has serious drawbacks for the *effectivity* of a type system as a basis for proof checking.

Remember that we want proof checking to be decidable. In our type-theoretic framework, this means that given a pre-term p it should be decidable if it is a well-formed *proof term*, and if so, what proposition A it is a proof of (so $p : A$). In particular, *proof checking* is decidable, through the fact that *type checking* is decidable.

Therefore, we hereby declare to *maintain decidability of typing*, and consequently to accept all the consequences arising from this choice, in particular with respect to subsets.

Before describing our choice for the representation of subsets, we mention a number of notions related to sets in mathematics. *Sets* are mathematical entities that embody the idea of 'collecting objects together'. So a set S may be thought of as being the collection of its *elements*. The notion *elementhood* is expressed by the symbol $\in$; so $x \in S$ if and only if x is one of S's elements. One says that S is a *subset* of T (notation: $S \subseteq T$) if all elements of S are also elements of T.

Further notions related to sets are equality of sets, subsets, union, intersection, difference, complement, powerset and Cartesian product.

The notion 'complement' of a set is a *relative* notion: one considers 'the complement of S *with respect to* T'.

The *powerset* $\mathcal{P}(S)$ of some set S is defined as the set of all its subsets. Note that the notions 'set' and 'element' are not absolute: an *element* of $\mathcal{P}(S)$ is itself a *set*, which may have elements again. For example, $\{x \in \mathbb{N} \mid x \text{ is even}\}$ is both a set *and* an element (e.g. of $\mathcal{P}(\mathbb{N})$).

Another essential aspect of set theory is the existence of a *set building construct* (enabling the so-called *Set Comprehension*). This is usually denoted by curly brackets: $\{x \in S \mid P(x)\}$ denotes all elements of set S that satisfy predicate P. For example, $\{x \in \mathbb{R} \mid -2 < x < 10\}$ is the 'interval' of all real numbers between -2 and 10.

Now we discuss how to incorporate subsets in our type theory λD. A smooth and fruitful manner to do this is to use *predicates* for representing subsets. Let's assume that we have a type S which we consider as our basic set of entities, and that we want to isolate a *subset* V of S. Let P be the predicate describing whether x is element of subset V or not, so we can define P as $P = \lambda x : S . \, (x \in V)$, having type $S \to *_p$. There clearly is a straightforward correspondence between this *subset* V and the mentioned *predicate* P, since for arbitrary $x : S$ we have: $x \in V \Leftrightarrow P(x)$.

Hence, it is not a great step to consider the predicate P as *representing* the subset V. This is a fruitful identification, since predicates are already part of our formal system λD, so there is no need for new symbols or operations to deal with the notion of subset.

In this *subset-as-predicate view* we start with a type, say S, acting as a set. Next, subsets of S are represented as predicates over S. Consequently, the powerset $ps(S)$ coincides with the collection $S \to *_p$ of all predicates over S (see Figure 13.1, line (1)).

How about *elementhood*? This is easy, again: x is an element of subset V of S if x satisfies predicate V over S, i.e. if $V\,x$ holds. We express this in Figure 13.1, line (2). In order to emphasise the correspondence between 'x is an element of subset V' and 'x satisfies predicate V', we introduce the new symbol ε, resembling the usual elementhood-symbol $\in$, but not being identical: we wish to keep the difference in mind. We write $x \, \varepsilon_S V$ in this situation, or $x \, \varepsilon \, V$ if it is clear what the type S is (see the Notation following line (2)).

Figure 13.1 also contains the definition of inclusion of a subset in another, and the definition of the union of subsets. These have a natural appearance, and the more so if we add some sugaring notation, for example: $V \subseteq_S W$ and $V \cup_S W$, for $\subseteq (S, V, W)$ and $\cup (S, V, W)$, respectively.

This looks promising. Hence, we follow the subset-is-predicate approach of Figure 13.1, where subsets of a type S are coded as predicates over this S.

$$\boxed{S \; : \; *_s}$$

(1) $\quad ps(S) \; := \; S \to *_p \; : \; \square$

$$\boxed{x : S}$$

$$\boxed{V : ps(S)}$$

(2) $\quad\quad element(S, x, V) \; := \; V\,x \; : \; *_p$

$\quad\quad$ Notation : $x \,\varepsilon_S V$ or $x \,\varepsilon\, V$ for $element(S, x, V)$

$$\boxed{V, W : ps(S)}$$

(3) $\quad\quad \subseteq(S, V, W) \; := \; \forall x : S\,.\,(x \,\varepsilon\, V \Rightarrow x \,\varepsilon\, W) \; : \; *_p$

(4) $\quad\quad \cup(S, V, W) \; := \; \lambda x : S\,.\,(x \,\varepsilon\, V \vee x \,\varepsilon\, W) \; : \; ps(S)$

Figure 13.1 Subsets as predicates over a type

13.2 Basic set-theoretic notions

In this section we consider a number of basic notions about (sub-)sets and see how these can be formalised in λD by means of the subset-as-predicate approach chosen in the previous section (see Figure 13.1). The crucial point is that in this approach there are *only subsets*, which are formalised as predicates. The notion $x \in V$ should not be identified with $x : V$ but with $x \,\varepsilon\, V$, which is a type. To establish $x \in V$ we have to give a proof; that is, we have to construct a proof term $p \; : \; x \,\varepsilon\, V$.

We now consider quantifications. Let S be a type representing a set. If V is a subset of S, then we formalise V *not* as a type, but as a predicate on S. Hence, we have $S : *_s$, but $V : S \to *_p$. Now suppose that we want to quantify over the 'subset' V, for example by expressing that $\forall_{x \in V}(P(x))$ for some predicate P. Then we cannot formalise this immediately in λD as $\forall x : V\,.\,P\,x$, since V is not a type (cf. the rule (*form*); recall that $\forall$ is a sugared version of Π).

An elegant way out is to quantify over the type S, and restrict the domain of the x's by means of the extra condition that x must satisfy V. So we have the following translation convention:

$\forall_{x \in V}(P(x)) \; \rightsquigarrow \; \forall x : S\,.\,(x \,\varepsilon\, V \Rightarrow P\,x)$.

There is a similar solution for the existential quantifier. This time we need an $\wedge$ instead of an $\Rightarrow$ (examine why):

$\exists_{x \in V}(P(x)) \; \rightsquigarrow \; \exists x : S\,.\,(x \,\varepsilon\, V \wedge P\,x)$.

So in our formalisation *every quantifier ranges over a type*.

Example 13.2.1   The expression $\forall x \,\varepsilon\, V\,.\,(x \,\varepsilon\, W)$ has an illegal format, hence we cannot use it for the definition of the inclusion $V \subseteq W$. But we can write $\forall x : S\,.\,(x \,\varepsilon\, V \Rightarrow x \,\varepsilon\, W)$ (see line (3) of Figure 13.1).

In Figure 13.2 we build further on lines (1) and (2) of Figure 13.1. In order to get the complete picture, we repeat the definitions of inclusion and union, and add other ones. We also incorporate the customary notation for subset comprehension $\{x : S \mid V\,x\}$ (cf. the previous section) for the subset-as-predicate $\lambda x : S . V\,x$. Writing $x\,\varepsilon\,V$ instead of $V\,x$, we obtain $\{x : S \mid x\,\varepsilon\,V\}$ as a recognisable notation for the subset-as-predicate.

Inclusion between subsets of S and *equality* of subsets are propositions (see lines (1) and (2) of Figure 13.2).

Note that we apply the following translations:

V is a subset of the type S $\rightsquigarrow$	$V : ps(S)$ (or $V : S \to *_p$)
V is a subset of W for V and W subsets of the type S $\rightsquigarrow$	$V \subseteq W$ (or $\forall x : S . (x\,\varepsilon\,V \Rightarrow x\,\varepsilon\,W)$)

Next, we define in Figure 13.2 the *union*, *intersection* and *difference* of two subsets of S; which are subsets, again. And we consider the *complement* of a subset, with respect to S.

$\boxed{S : *_s}$

$\quad\boxed{V : ps(S)}$

$\qquad$ `Notation :` $\{x : S \mid x\,\varepsilon\,V\}$ `for` $\lambda x : S . V\,x$

$\qquad\boxed{W : ps(S)}$

(1) $\qquad \subseteq(S,V,W) := \forall x : S . (x\,\varepsilon\,V \Rightarrow x\,\varepsilon\,W) : *_p$

$\qquad$ `Notation :` $V \subseteq W$ `for` $\subseteq(S,V,W)$

(2) $\qquad IS(S,V,W) := V \subseteq W \wedge W \subseteq V : *_p$

(3) $\qquad \cup(S,V,W) := \{x : S \mid x\,\varepsilon\,V \vee x\,\varepsilon\,W\} : ps(S)$

(4) $\qquad \cap(S,V,W) := \{x : S \mid x\,\varepsilon\,V \wedge x\,\varepsilon\,W\} : ps(S)$

(5) $\qquad \backslash(S,V,W) := \{x : S \mid x\,\varepsilon\,V \wedge \neg(x\,\varepsilon\,W)\} : ps(S)$

$\qquad$ `Notation :` $V = W,\ V \cup W,\ V \cap W,\ V \backslash W,$ `respectively`

(6) $\qquad {}^c(S,V) := \{x : S \mid \neg(x\,\varepsilon\,V)\} : ps(S)$

$\qquad$ `Notation :` V^c `for` ${}^c(S,V)$

Figure 13.2 Propositions and operations concerning sets

The new notation enables us, for example, to define the union of V and W in a familiar manner:

$$\cup(S,V,W) := \{x : S \mid x\,\varepsilon\,V \vee x\,\varepsilon\,W\} : ps(S).$$

For convenience's sake, we allow the usual infix notations in Figure 13.2.

The base set S is not mentioned in these sugared notations. Furthermore, we *overload* the symbol '=', since this equality symbol, earlier having been defined for *elements*, is now also employed for *subsets*.

Consider the expression $y \, \varepsilon \, \{x : S \,|\, P\,x\}$. Undoing the sugaring concerning both ε and $\{\ldots|\ldots\}$, we obtain $(\lambda x : S \,.\, P\,x)\,y$, which is β-equal to $P\,y$. This β-equality is used in Figure 13.3. Line (1) can be considered as an introduction rule for ε, and line (2) as its elimination rule.

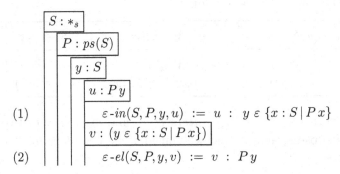

Figure 13.3 Introduction and elimination rules for the new element symbol

In order to demonstrate how one works with these set notions, we give the proof of a simple set-theoretic theorem in λD (see Figure 13.4). We prove the following:

For all subsets V and W of S: if $V \subseteq W^c$, then $V \backslash W = V$.

Since the proof is an easy exercise with logic and with the definition mechanism of λD, we only make some remarks about the way in which the proof terms are constructed.

We start in Figure 13.4 (lines (1) to (4)) with the first part of the proof, showing that we always have the *inclusion* $V \backslash W \subseteq V$ (independent of whether or not $V \subseteq W^c$). In line (1) we use that $(x \, \varepsilon \, V \backslash W) \overset{\triangle}{=}_\beta (x \, \varepsilon \, V \wedge \neg(x \, \varepsilon \, W))$. An alternative to proof term v in line (1) is a proof term based on ε-*el* (construct it yourself).

The second part of the proof (lines (5) to (10)), proving $V \subseteq V \backslash W$, is slightly more complicated. Now we need that $V \subseteq W^c$. Lines (11) and (12) conclude the proof.

We omit several proof terms based on logical rules: from Figure 13.4 onwards we will often only *mention* the logical rule employed, by giving a *hint*, without bothering about the details. We take it that the reader is by now sufficiently accustomed to the use of the logical (natural deduction) rules in λD. Hence, we will often omit the detailed arguments for these rules, since they can be easily constructed following familiar patterns. Of course, a hint can lead to several solutions; for example, the logical hint $\ldots$ **use** $\Rightarrow$-*in* on $a_2 \ldots$ in line (3) can be filled in with

$-$ $\Rightarrow$-$in(x \; \varepsilon \; V \backslash W, x \; \varepsilon \; V, \lambda v : (x \; \varepsilon \; V \backslash W) \, . \, a_2)$ (in the natural deduction style), or directly with

$-$ $\lambda v : (x \; \varepsilon \; V \backslash W) \, . \, a_2$ (in the type-theoretic style).

$$\boxed{S : *_s \mid V, W : ps(S)}$$

> $\boxed{x \; : \; S}$
>
> > $\boxed{v \; : \; (x \; \varepsilon \; V \backslash W)}$
> >
> > (1) $\quad a_1^\dagger := v$ (or: **use** ε-*el*) $: x \; \varepsilon \; V \wedge \neg(x \; \varepsilon \; W)$
> > (2) $\quad a_2 := \ldots$ **use** $\wedge$-el_1 on $a_1 \ldots : x \; \varepsilon \; V$
> >
> > (3) $\quad a_3 := \ldots$ **use** $\Rightarrow$-*in* on $a_2 \ldots : x \; \varepsilon \; V \backslash W \Rightarrow x \; \varepsilon \; V$
>
> (4) $a_4(S, V, W) := \ldots$ **use** $\forall$-*in* on $a_3 \ldots : V \backslash W \subseteq V$
>
> > $\boxed{u \; : \; V \subseteq W^c}$
> >
> > > $\boxed{x \; : \; S}$
> > >
> > > > $\boxed{v \; : \; x \; \varepsilon \; V}$
> > > >
> > > > (5) $\quad a_5 := u \, x \, v : x \; \varepsilon \; W^c$
> > > > (6) $\quad a_6 := a_5 : \neg(x \; \varepsilon \; W)$
> > > > (7) $\quad a_7 := \ldots$ **use** $\wedge$-*in* on v and $a_6 \ldots : x \; \varepsilon \; V \wedge \neg(x \; \varepsilon \; W)$
> > > > (8) $\quad a_8 := a_7 : x \; \varepsilon \; V \backslash W$
> > >
> > > (9) $\quad a_9 := \ldots$ **use** $\Rightarrow$-*in* on $a_8 \ldots : (x \; \varepsilon \; V) \Rightarrow (x \; \varepsilon \; V \backslash W)$
> >
> > (10) $a_{10}(S, V, W, u) := \ldots$ **use** $\forall$-*in* on $a_9 \ldots : V \subseteq V \backslash W$
> > (11) $a_{11}(S, V, W, u) := \ldots$ **use** $\wedge$-*in* on $a_4(S, V, W)$ **and** $a_{10}(S, V, W, u) \ldots :$
> > $\quad V \backslash W = V$
>
> (12) $a_{12}(S, V, W) := \ldots$ **use** $\Rightarrow$-*in* on $a_{11} \ldots :$
> $\quad (V \subseteq W^c) \Rightarrow (V \backslash W = V)$

†*parameters suppressed*

Figure 13.4 An example proof about sets

We invite the reader to study the details. We confine ourselves to two commentary remarks:

$-$ It would be more in line with logic (but also more involved) to replace the proof term $u \, x \, v$ in line (5) by a $\forall$-*el*-step, followed by an $\Rightarrow$-*el*-step.
$-$ In lines (6) and (8), we could also have used ε-*el* and ε-*in*, respectively.

A proof as given in Figure 13.4 requires some effort to construct, but on completion its course is clearly visible, in particular when we omit everything but the skeleton proof – otherwise said: when we concentrate on the *types*. Some conventions for syntactic sugaring make the proof more transparent, as this derivation demonstrates; using dots or only hints for obvious arguments simplifies matters considerably.

Remark 13.2.2 *A representation of a proof in λD-style can shed light on interesting aspects. As a small example: in Figure 13.4 we see in line (11) a reference to two proof objects: a_4 and a_{10}. Note that the parameter list of a_4 is one entry shorter than that of a_{10}; this corresponds to what we have noticed earlier: that the proof of $V \backslash W \subseteq V$ does not depend on the assumption of $V \subseteq W^c$, but the proof of $V \subseteq V \backslash W$ does.*

Reflecting on the notions introduced in this section, there remains one question: we have defined subset-equality $IS(S, V, W)$ (in sugared version: $V = W$) in Figure 13.2 as the conjunction of $V \subseteq W$ and $W \subseteq V$. How does this equality relate to the Leibniz-equality as discussed in Section 12.2?

Since we have $S : *_p$, but $ps(S) : \Box$, we cannot write $V =_{ps(S)} W$ for Leibniz-equality of V and W by using the definition of $x =_S y$ as given in line (1) of Figure 12.3. We can, however, define a similar Leibniz-equality on the powerset of S as $\Pi K : ps(S) \to *_p \cdot (K V \Leftrightarrow K W)$ – in words: for all predicates K on the powerset of S, if V satisfies K, then also W; and vice versa. Let's denote this Leibniz-equality of V and W by $V \mathrel{\widehat{=}}_{ps(S)} W$.

Now it would obviously be desirable that the subset-equality $V = W$ implies the Leibniz-equality $V \mathrel{\widehat{=}}_{ps(S)} W$, and vice versa.

It is easy to show (Exercise 13.1) that Leibniz-equality implies subset-equality. For the implication the other way round, however, no proof can be constructed with what we have. So it is necessary to add another axiom. This we do in Figure 13.5.

(1) $\boxed{S : *_s}$

    $\boxed{V, W \ : \ ps(S)}$

(1) $eq\text{-}subset(S, V, W) \ := \ \Pi K : ps(S) \to *_p \cdot (K V \Leftrightarrow K W) \ : \ *_p$

    Notation : $V \mathrel{\widehat{=}}_{ps(S)} W$ for $eq\text{-}subset(S, V, W)$

    $\boxed{u \ : \ V = W}$

(2) $IS\text{-}prop(S, V, W, u) \ := \ \bot \ : \ V \mathrel{\widehat{=}}_{ps(S)} W$

Figure 13.5 $V = W$ implies $V \mathrel{\widehat{=}}_{ps(S)} W$

13.3 Special subsets

Another basic notion connected with sets is that of the 'empty set', the set having no elements. In our powerset approach we cannot suffice with *one empty set* relative to a universe; we have to define, for every type $S : *_s$, an empty set $\emptyset(S)$ *with respect to* that S. Such an $\emptyset(S)$ (denoted $\emptyset_S$) is a subset of S, coded as the predicate $\lambda x : S . \perp$ on S (Figure 13.6).

We also define the 'full subset' of S, which contains all elements of S. It is coded as the predicate $\lambda x : S . \neg\perp$. (Note that *full-set*$(S)$ is the complement of $\emptyset_S$ relative to S; see Exercise 13.6 (a).)

$$\boxed{S : *_s}$$

(1) $\quad \emptyset(S) := \{x : S \mid \perp\} : ps(S)$
$\qquad$ Notation : $\emptyset_S$ for $\emptyset(S)$

(2) $\quad$ *full-set*$(S) := \{x : S \mid \neg\perp\} : ps(S)$

Figure 13.6 The empty set and full set as subsets of a type S

As a simple exercise, we prove that the empty set is included in every subset of S, and that every subset is included in the full set (see Figure 13.7). In line (3) we use that $x \ \varepsilon \ \emptyset_S$ is β-equal to $\perp$, and in line (7) that $x \ \varepsilon \ $ *full-set*(S) is β-equal to $\neg\perp$.

$$\vdots$$

$\boxed{V : ps(S)}$

$\quad \boxed{x : S \mid u : x \ \varepsilon \ \emptyset_S}$

(3) $\qquad a_3^\dagger := u \ : \ \perp$

(4) $\qquad a_4 := \ ... \ \text{use } \perp\text{-el on } a_3 \ ... \ : x \ \varepsilon \ V$

(5) $\qquad a_5 := \ ... \ \text{use } \Rightarrow\text{-in and } \forall\text{-in} \ ... \ : \ \emptyset_S \subseteq V$

$\quad \boxed{x : S \mid v : x \ \varepsilon \ V}$

(6) $\qquad a_6 := \lambda y : \perp . y \ : \ \neg\perp$

(7) $\qquad a_7 := a_6 \ : \ x \ \varepsilon \ $ *full-set*(S)

(8) $\quad a_8 := \ ... \ \text{use } \Rightarrow\text{-in and } \forall\text{-in} \ ... \ : \ V \subseteq $ *full-set*(S)

†*parameters suppressed*

Figure 13.7 Lemma: $\emptyset_S \subseteq V \subseteq $ *full-set*(S), for all subsets V

In Figure 13.8 we practise with the empty-set notion. We prove that if a subset of S is not the empty set, then it has at least one element; and vice versa. In the derivation we have omitted several proof objects, and replaced them by hints.

In line (6) we apply $\exists$-*in-alt* (see Figure 11.28), making the derivation non-constructive. So we use classical logic. This is in accordance with our earlier decision (see Section 11.4) to take classical logic as our basic system for logic.

$S : *_s$

$V : ps(S)$

$u : V \neq \emptyset_S$

$v : V \subseteq \emptyset_S$

(1) $\quad a_1^\dagger := \ldots$ use $\wedge$-*in* on v and a_5 [*Fig. 13.7*] $\ldots : V = \emptyset_S$

(2) $\quad a_2 := u\, a_1 : \perp$

(3) $\quad a_3 := \ldots$ use $\neg$-*in* $\ldots : \neg(V \subseteq \emptyset_S)$

(4) $\quad a_4 := a_3 : \neg \forall x : S . (x \,\varepsilon\, V \Rightarrow x \,\varepsilon\, \emptyset_S)$

(5) $\quad a_5 := a_4 : \neg \forall x : S . (\neg(x \,\varepsilon\, V))$

(6) $\quad a_6 := \exists\text{-}in\text{-}alt(S, \lambda x : S . (x \,\varepsilon\, V), a_5) : \exists x : S . (x \,\varepsilon\, V)$

(7) $\quad a_7 := \ldots$ use $\Rightarrow$-*in* $\ldots : (V \neq \emptyset_S) \Rightarrow \exists x : S . (x \,\varepsilon\, V)$

$u : \exists x : S . (x \,\varepsilon\, V)$

$v : V = \emptyset_S$

$x : S \mid w : x \,\varepsilon\, V$

(8) $\quad a_8 := \ldots$ use $\wedge$-*el*$_1$ on $v \ldots : V \subseteq \emptyset_S$

(9) $\quad a_9 := a_8 \, x \, w : x \,\varepsilon\, \emptyset_S$

(10) $\quad a_{10} := a_9 : \perp$

(11) $\quad a_{11} := \ldots$ use $\exists$-*el* on u and $a_{10} \ldots : \perp$

(12) $\quad a_{12} := \ldots$ use $\neg$-*in* on $a_{11} \ldots : V \neq \emptyset_S$

(13) $\quad a_{13} := \ldots$ use $\Rightarrow$-*in* on $a_{12} \ldots : (\exists x : S . (x \,\varepsilon\, V)) \Rightarrow (V \neq \emptyset_S)$

(14) $\quad a_{14}(S, V) := \ldots$ use $\Leftrightarrow$-*in* on a_7 and $a_{13} \ldots :$

$\qquad (V \neq \emptyset_S) \Leftrightarrow \exists x : S . (x \,\varepsilon\, V)$

†*parameters suppressed*

Figure 13.8 Properties of the empty set

13.4 Relations

Now that we have seen how to represent sets in λD, the time has come to look at notions which are connected with sets. The first matter that we study is the notion *relation*.

As we have observed before, a relation on S is a binary predicate over S.

In line with type theory, we employ Currying for binary functions (see Remark 1.2.6) and write binary predicates over S as composite unary predicates, of type $S \to S \to *_p$.

We mentioned earlier that relations may have specific properties such as reflexivity, symmetry or transitivity. These properties are easily expressible in λD (see Figure 13.9). A relation having all three properties is called an equivalence relation.

Remark 13.4.1 *We have added a bit of sugar in line (4) of Figure 13.9: $\rho \wedge \sigma \wedge \tau$ is not official syntax; it should be read as $(\rho \wedge \sigma) \wedge \tau$.*

$$\boxed{S : *_s}$$

$$\boxed{R : S \to S \to *_p}$$

(1) $\quad reflexive(S, R) \; := \; \forall x : S \,.\, (R\,x\,x) \; : \; *_p$

(2) $\quad symmetric(S, R) \; := \; \forall x, y : S \,.\, (R\,x\,y \Rightarrow R\,y\,x) \; : \; *_p$

(3) $\quad transitive(S, R) \; := \; \forall x, y, z : S \,.\, (R\,x\,y \Rightarrow R\,y\,z \Rightarrow R\,x\,z) \; : \; *_p$

(4) $\quad equivalence\text{-}relation(S, R) \; :=$
$$\qquad reflexive(S, R) \wedge symmetric(S, R) \wedge transitive(S, R) \; : \; *_p$$

Figure 13.9 Basic notions connected to relations

Remark 13.4.2 *We have defined the relations in Figure 13.9 on the 'full' S, being a type. If we want to consider such relations for a subset of S (i.e. a predicate over S), say V, we can employ a coding similar to the one used in the beginning of Section 13.2. For example, reflexivity on subset V of S can be defined as:*

$$refl\text{-}subset(S, V, R) \; := \; \forall x : S \,.\, (x \,\varepsilon\, V \Rightarrow R\,x\,x).$$

An equivalence relation enables one to divide a set into non-empty *equivalence classes*. These can be defined as in Figure 13.10: the equivalence class of x consists of all y's related to x. We abbreviate $class(S, R, u, x)$ by $[x]_R$, thus hiding two parameters.

Equivalence classes have three important characteristics:

(1) $\forall x : S \,.\, ([x]_R \neq \emptyset_S)$,
(2) $\forall x, y : S \,.\, ([x]_R = [y]_R \vee ([x]_R \cap [y]_R = \emptyset_S))$,
(3) $\forall y : S \,.\, \exists x : S \,.\, (y \,\varepsilon\, [x]_R)$.

We can express this in words as follows:
(1) No class is empty.
(2) If the intersection of two classes is non-empty, then the classes coincide.
(3) Every element of S belongs to some class; otherwise said: the union of all classes is the full S. (See also Exercises 13.10 and 13.11.)

$\boxed{S : *_s}$
$\boxed{R : S \to S \to *_p}$
$\boxed{u : \textit{equivalence-relation}(S, R)}$
$\boxed{x : S}$

$$class(S, R, u, x) := \{y : S \mid R\,x\,y\} : ps(S)$$
Notation : $[x]_R$ for $class(S, R, u, x)$

Figure 13.10 Equivalence classes

Together, (2) and (3) imply: each x belongs to *exactly one* class.

As a demonstration of what we have achieved now, and also as an exercise, we prove (2) in the following form, which is equivalent (Exercise 13.9):

$$\forall x, y, z : S . (z \; \varepsilon \; [x]_R \Rightarrow z \; \varepsilon \; [y]_R \Rightarrow ([x]_R = [y]_R)).$$

In words: if there is a z that belongs to both class $[x]_R$ and class $[y]_R$, then these classes must be the same – hence, we never have 'partial overlap' between two classes, but either *no* overlap or *full* overlap. (Note that this does not imply that $x = y$; it only entails that x and y belong to the same class.)

The proof is given as a derivation in Figure 13.11.

Remark 13.4.3 *Since we assume that R is an equivalence relation on S, we have symmetry and transitivity of R. We do not spell this out, but only mention it (see lines (4)–(6)). Note that we do not need reflexivity.*

We only give a short comment and leave it to the reader to study the details of how this proof has been developed.

– Start from the bottom upwards: the type of line (12) contains our goal.

– Decomposition of the goal leads to a number of flags and to the goals registered in the types of lines (9) and (10).

– The first of these new goals is rephrased in line (8) and leads to the flags in (d) and the goal $m \; \varepsilon \; [y]_R$ in line (7). This goal type can be rewritten to $m \; \varepsilon \; \{n : S \mid R\,y\,n\}$, so a proof of $R\,y\,m$ will do.

– We get $R\,y\,m$ by using assumptions w, u and v, which give us $R\,x\,m$, $R\,x\,z$ and $R\,y\,z$ (lines (1) to (3)). These three together lead to $R\,y\,m$ via symmetry and transitivity of R (lines (4) to (6)).

– Finally, note how nicely we can use line (9), in order to obtain the 'mirror result' in line (10): a swap of two pairs of parameters suffices.

The rest is routine.

(a)	$S : *_s \mid R : S \to S \to *_p \mid u : equivalence\text{-}relation(S, R)$
(b)	$x, y, z : S$
(c)	$u : (z \; \varepsilon \; [x]_R) \mid v : (z \; \varepsilon \; [y]_R)$
(d)	$m : S \mid w : (m \; \varepsilon \; [x]_R)$
(1)	$a_1^\dagger := \ldots$ use ε-el on w $\ldots$: $R \, x \, m$
(2)	$a_2 := \ldots$ use ε-el on u $\ldots$: $R \, x \, z$
(3)	$a_3 := \ldots$ use ε-el on v $\ldots$: $R \, y \, z$
(4)	$a_4 := \ldots$ use symmetry on a_2 $\ldots$: $R \, z \, x$
(5)	$a_5 := \ldots$ use transitivity on a_3 and a_4 $\ldots$: $R \, y \, x$
(6)	$a_6 := \ldots$ use transitivity on a_5 and a_1 $\ldots$: $R \, y \, m$
(7)	$a_7 := a_6 \; : \; m \; \varepsilon \; [y]_R$
(8)	$a_8 := \ldots$ use $\Rightarrow$-in and $\forall$-in on a_7 $\ldots$:
	$\forall m : S . \, (m \; \varepsilon \; [x]_R \Rightarrow m \; \varepsilon \; [y]_R)$
(9)	$a_9 := a_8 \; : \; [x]_R \subseteq [y]_R$
(10)	$a_{10}(S, R, u, x, y, z, u, v) := a_9(S, R, u, y, x, z, v, u) \; : \; [y]_R \subseteq [x]_R$
(11)	$a_{11} := \ldots$ use $\wedge$-in on a_9 and a_{10} $\ldots$: $[x]_R = [y]_R$
(12)	$a_{12}(S, R, e) := \ldots$ use $\Rightarrow$-in and $\forall$-in on a_{11} $\ldots$:
	$\forall x, y, z : S . \, (z \; \varepsilon \; [x]_R \; \Rightarrow \; z \; \varepsilon \; [y]_R \; \Rightarrow \; [x]_R = [y]_R)$

† *parameters suppressed*

Figure 13.11 Proof of a lemma about equivalence classes

Until now, we have discussed relations R on a single type S, represented as binary predicates over this S, so $R : S \to S \to *_p$ (using Currying). A natural extension is to consider relations on a *pair* of types, say S and T. (In such a case one also speaks of a relation *between* S and T.) The obvious representation of such a relation has type $S \to T \to *_p$.

Examples 13.4.4 Assume that we have $\mathbb{N}$ and $\mathbb{Z}$ as types. Consider the relation R between $\mathbb{N}$ and $\mathbb{Z}$ that holds between $n : \mathbb{N}$ and $x : \mathbb{Z}$ if $n = x^2 + 1$. So we have $R \, 5 \, 2$, $R \, 5 \, (-2)$, and $\neg(R \, 5 \, x)$ for any other $x : \mathbb{Z}$. This relation can be coded as $R := \lambda n : \mathbb{N} . \, \lambda x : \mathbb{Z} . \, (n = x^2 + 1) \; : \; \mathbb{N} \to \mathbb{Z} \to *_p$.

13.5 Maps

A map can be seen as a special kind of relation. To be precise: a map from set S to set T is a relation $F : S \to T \to *_p$, such that:

$$\forall_{x \in S} \exists^1_{y \in T} (F \, x \, y).$$

So the essential property that turns a relation into a map is that each $x \in S$ has a relation with *exactly one* $y \in T$. We call such a relation a *functional* relation. Because of the uniqueness of the y related to such an x, one usually prefers to consider F as a unary symbol and one writes $F(x) = y$ instead of $F\,x\,y$.

Remark 13.5.1 *One can consider a wider notion of 'map' and speak of a map if there is, for each x, at most one related y (so there may be none). Such a relation is also called a* partial map. *In the present text, however, maps are always 'total', in the sense explained above.*

We have already seen that the notion of a map is a core concept in type theory: we write $F : A \to B$ in order to express that F is a map from A to B; where $A \to B$ is also an abbreviation of $\Pi x : A\,.\,B$ (cf. Notation 5.2.1).

Fortunately, the connection between a map as an inhabitant of a (functional) Π-type and a map as a functional relation (a predicate) is easy to establish. Given the map $F : S \to T$, we have the relation $R = \lambda x : S\,.\,\lambda y : T\,.\,(y = F\,x)$; and vice versa, given $R : S \to T \to *_p$ with $u : \forall x : S\,.\,\exists^1 y : T\,.\,R\,x\,y$, we have the function $F = \lambda x : S\,.\,\iota_{y:T}^{ux}(R\,x\,y)$. (For the ι, see Figure 12.16.) This is expressed in lines (1) and (3) of Figure 13.12. In line (2) we add some more information (we leave it to the reader to derive the proof object).

$$
\begin{array}{l}
\boxed{S, T : *_s} \\
\quad \boxed{F : S \to T} \\
(1) \quad\quad R(S, T, F) := \lambda x : S\,.\,\lambda y : T\,.\,(y =_T F\,x)\ :\ S \to T \to *_p \\
(2) \quad\quad a_2(S, T, F) := \ \ldots\ \texttt{Exerc. 13.12 (a)}\ \ldots\ : \\
\quad\quad\quad\quad\quad\quad \forall x : S\,.\,\exists^1 y : T\,.\,(R(S, T, F)\,x\,y) \\
\quad \boxed{R : S \to T \to *_p} \\
\quad\quad \boxed{u : \forall x : S\,.\,\exists^1 y : T\,.\,R\,x\,y} \\
(3) \quad\quad\quad F(S, T, R, u) := \ \lambda x : S\,.\,\iota_{y:T}^{ux}(R\,x\,y)\ :\ S \to T
\end{array}
$$

Figure 13.12 The connection between a functional relation and a type-theoretic function

Remark 13.5.2 *In mathematics, the words 'function' and 'map' often mean the same thing, albeit that 'map' sometimes suggests a more abstract viewpoint.*

We shall continue to represent maps in the type-theoretic format, which is – in our framework – more basic than the functional relation format.

It is easy to express some properties that maps $F : S \to T$ may have, such as injectivity, surjectivity and bijectivity (see Figure 13.13). Another directly expressible notion is that of the *inverse* of a bijective map (again, see Figure 13.13).

$$\boxed{S, T : *_s}$$

$$\boxed{F : S \to T}$$

(1) $injective(S, T, F) := \forall x_1, x_2 : S . (F x_1 =_T F x_2 \Rightarrow x_1 =_S x_2) : *_p$

(2) $surjective(S, T, F) := \forall y : T . \exists x : S . (F x =_T y) : *_p$

(3) $bijective(S, T, F) := injective(S, T, F) \wedge surjective(S, T, F) : *_p$

$$\boxed{u : bijective(S, T, F)}$$

(4) $a_4(S, T, F, u) := \dots$ **Exerc. 13.12 (b)** $\dots :$
         $\forall y : T . \exists^1 x : S . (F x =_T y)$

(5) $inv(S, T, F, u) := \lambda y : T . \iota_{x:S}^{a_4(S,T,F,u)\, y}(F x =_T y) : T \to S$

Figure 13.13 Some well-known notions connected with maps

Things become a bit more complicated when the domain of function F is not the type S, but a subset V of S. Following the line that we have taken earlier, the type of such an F then becomes $\Pi x : S . ((x \,\varepsilon\, V) \to T)$, with an extra argument, $x \,\varepsilon\, V$.

As an example of the extra administration necessary for such a function F on a subset, we give the corresponding definition of injectivity in Figure 13.14.

$$\boxed{S, T : *_s}$$

$$\boxed{V : ps(S)}$$

$$\boxed{F : \Pi x : S . ((x \,\varepsilon\, V) \to T)}$$

(1) $inj\text{-}subset(S, T, V, F) := \forall x_1, x_2 : S . \Pi p : (x_1 \,\varepsilon\, V) . \Pi q : (x_2 \,\varepsilon\, V) .$
         $((F x_1\, p =_T F x_2\, q) \Rightarrow x_1 =_S x_2) : *_p$

Figure 13.14 Injectivity of a map on a subset

Other notions that can relatively easily be formalised, are, given sets S and T, and a function $F : S \to T$:

- The F-*image* of a subset V of source set S; the image of V is the subset of T consisting of all the F-values of elements in V.

- The F-*origin* of a subset W of range set T; the origin of W is the subset of S consisting of all elements which have F-values in W.

$$\boxed{S, T : *_s}$$

$$\boxed{F : S \to T}$$

$$\boxed{V : ps(S)}$$

(1) $image(S, T, F, V) := \{y : T \mid \exists x : S . (x \; \varepsilon \; V \wedge F x =_T y)\} \; : \; ps(T)$

$$\boxed{W : ps(T)}$$

(2) $origin(S, T, F, W) := \{x : S \mid F x \; \varepsilon \; W\} \; : \; ps(S)$

Figure 13.15 Image and origin of a subset

See Figure 13.15 for a formal description of *image* and *origin*.

We conclude this section with an example concerning these notions. We prove the following lemma in λD:

For $F : S \to T$ and $V \subseteq S$, we have that $V \subseteq origin(image(V))$.

The idea behind the proof is simple: let $s \; \varepsilon \; V$, then $F s \; \varepsilon \; image(V)$ (by the definition of *image*), hence (by the definition of *source*) $s \; \varepsilon \; origin(image(V))$.

The λD-proof – see Figure 13.16 – is hardly more complicated than that. The justification for the formal proof is directly based on the definitions of *image* and *origin* as given in Figure 13.15. It is a good exercise for the reader to check precisely that the given proof is a correct λD-derivation (Exercise 13.16 (a)).

$$\boxed{S, T : *_s}$$

$$\boxed{F : S \to T}$$

$$\boxed{V : ps(S)}$$

$$\boxed{s : S \mid u : (s \; \varepsilon \; V)}$$

(1) $a_1^\dagger := eq\text{-}refl_{[Fig.\ 12.2]}(T, F s) \; : \; F s =_T F s$

(2) $a_2 := \ldots \text{ use } \wedge\text{-}in \ldots : \; s \; \varepsilon \; V \wedge F s =_T F s$

(3) $a_3 := \ldots \text{ use } \exists\text{-}in \; \ldots : \; \exists x : S . (x \; \varepsilon \; V \wedge F x =_T F s)$

(4) $a_4 := a_3 \; : \; F s \; \varepsilon \; image(S, T, F, V)$

(5) $a_5 := a_4 \; : \; s \; \varepsilon \; origin(S, T, F, image(S, T, F, V))$

(6) $a_6(S, T, F, V) := \ldots \text{ use } \Rightarrow\text{-}in \text{ and } \forall\text{-}in \ldots :$

         $V \subseteq origin(S, T, F, image(S, T, F, V))$

$^\dagger parameters\ suppressed$

Figure 13.16 A lemma about image and origin of a subset

13.6 Representation of mathematical notions

In the present chapter we have investigated how to represent a subset of a type S in type theory, and we have decided to identify a subset of S with a predicate on S, representing both as $\lambda x : S \, . \, P\,x$. Such a many-to-one map of mathematical notions into λD-constructs occurs more often. In the diagram below (Figure 13.17) we give a list of some basic notions which have a different meaning in mathematics, but are represented by the same λD-constructs. (Compare this with the way in which logical notions are represented in type theory; see Figure 5.2.)

mathematics	the type theory of λD	
function space $A \to B$	$\Pi x : A \, . \, B$	$A : *_s, \ B : *_s$
implication $A \Rightarrow B$	$\Pi x : A \, . \, B$	$A : *_p, \ B : *_p$
universal statement $\forall_{x \in A}(B(x))$	$\Pi x : A \, . \, B$	$A : *_s, \ B : *_p$
function from A to B	$\lambda x : A \, . \, t$	$A : *_s, \ t : B : *_s$
predicate on A	$\lambda x : A \, . \, t$	$A : *_s, \ t : *_p$
subset of A	$\lambda x : A \, . \, t$	$A : *_s, \ t : *_p$
two-valued function from $A \times B$ to C	$\lambda x : A . \, \lambda y : B . \, t$	$A, B : *_s, \ t : C : *_s$
binary relation R over $A \times B$	$\lambda x : A . \, \lambda y : B . \, t$	$A, B : *_s, \ t : *_p$

Figure 13.17 Coding mathematics in λD

There are clearly *advantages* of this 'compression' of different notions into the same form. For example, this enables us to keep the system λD relatively simple and 'lean'. Moreover, similar calculational patterns in mathematics and logic coincide in λD, as we have already noticed before; see e.g. Examples 2.4.8 and 2.4.9.

On the other hand, a clear *disadvantage* is that the interpretation of λD-expressions becomes ambiguous. When confronted, for example, with $\lambda x : A \, . \, t$, it is not clear whether this represents a function, a predicate or a subset. This can be cumbersome when we want to decipher the mathematical meaning of a certain text given purely in λD-coded form, without further comment.

This disadvantage disappears almost completely, however, when one takes the precaution to divide the $*$'s into $*_s$ and $*_p$, as advocated in Section 8.7 (cf. Notation 8.7.1). This simple sugaring, albeit not official syntax of λD, enables one to give an unambiguous interpretation of almost all of the mentioned notions (see Figure 13.17, final column). The only exception is that predicates over a type and subsets of that type cannot be distinguished, as a consequence of our choice in Section 13.1 to identify these notions in the λD-coding.

13.7 Conclusions

We have seen that it is not straightforward how to deal with subsets in type theory, since there is a potential conflict of interests between two visions:

— the liberal view of the mathematical community towards set-membership, which is undecidable in general and allows an element to be a member of several sets;
— the strict typing discipline in type theory (and in particular, in λD), which is decidable and where terms have a unique type.

The differences are explainable because of the divergent perspectives:

— In mathematics, one is usually not focused on a mechanised verification. It suffices that a fellow mathematician (or a student) can follow the reasoning and thereby obtains confidence in the correctness of the mathematical content that is presented. Hence, the *conviction* that a viable proof path exists is enough; mathematical training enables one to choose the effective steps necessary to complete a mathematical argument, and thus one obtains a great, tradition-honoured trust in the results. The experienced *mind* makes the proper choices – in general – for a fruitful processing of the mathematical material.
— The perspective of type theory, on the other hand, is different. Its centre of interest is *all* imaginable proofs, including the extremely complex ones, or the tedious ones, or the long ones (e.g. concerning the correctness of computer programs), where humans tend to lose their concentration. Here the crucial thing is that an *automatic* verification can be executed by a computer program. This introduces the point of *decidability*, which is crucial for a fluid advancement of the verification process. Human interventions should be minimised; preferably, to the level of non-interference. Decidability makes this possible, at least in principle: it may still happen that a decidable procedure takes an unknown amount of time or space, which may cause problems as long as the procedure is not finished. So *feasibility* is another point. However, experiences with the use of type theory have demonstrated that the verification of mathematical content in formal form does not tend to last forbiddingly long or to cost too much memory space.

Decidability and feasibility are particularly important for proof checking, so also for type checking. Subsets are amply present in mathematics, in particular in proofs. Hence, a careful treatment of the formalisation of the notions 'set' and 'subset' is very relevant. We have chosen the subset-as-predicate approach, since there is a direct correspondence between subsets and predicates, and since predicates are already part of our λD machinery.

We have put the chosen approach to the test by formalising several notions connected with subsets, such as the basic notions of inclusion, union and intersection. Moreover, we have practised with the formal apparatus by considering examples. We have also formalised a number of relations on (sub-)sets, in particular equivalence relations and equivalence classes, maps between sets and a number of notions connected with maps. It worked out well, which gives us confidence in the rightness of our choice.

In Section 13.6 we explained that there is a many-to-one map of mathematics into λD, meaning that different mathematical notions are represented by the same λD-constructs. The interpretation of a piece of λD-code as originally intended remains, however, possible, if one has added a bit of sugar during the coding process, in the sense that one writes $*_s$ instead of $*$ for the type of sets, and $*_p$ for the type of propositions.

In the forthcoming chapters we continue the endeavour to deal with subsets via the subsets-as-predicates approach, as we did in the present chapter. It will turn out that our choice is fruitful. Sometimes we shall find that it is not easy to force mathematics into this jacket, but it is doable and does not create insurmountable problems. The more we practise, the better it goes. And sometimes, the meticulous formalisation that we pursue has, also when considering subsets, unexpected consequences: it may evoke new insights and a deeper view of mathematics and its meaning. These are the real moments of satisfaction – or beauty, for some of us.

So indeed, there is a price to be paid for maintaining decidability of typing and Uniqueness of Types, but it appears not to be too high. And we still *do* succeed – so we've got nothing serious to complain about, the more so as we realise that the profits of decidability are impressive.

13.8 Further reading

The standard for set theory is Zermelo–Fraenkel axiomatic set theory (ZF), sometimes extended with the Axiom of Choice (AC). This is a first order theory about the $\in$-relation, that axiomatises which sets exist and how sets can be formed from other sets. Axiomatic set theory is one of the answers to the foundational and consistency questions that arose around 1900. The foundational question is whether all of mathematics can be based on one simple basic set of assumptions and constructions. G. Cantor (Cantor, 1874) was the first to develop set theory for this, as early as 1874, where he also showed that there exist various levels of infinity. Cantor's first set theory is inconsistent, as was noticed by C. Burali-Forti and later by B. Russell, using his famous paradox, which he discovered in 1901 (see van Heijenoort, 1967, pp. 124–125; Russell, 1903). Since then the question of creating a consistent foundation for mathematics has become a major topic of research.

Russell developed his *Ramified Type Theory*, first in *The Principles of Mathematics* (Russell, 1903), and later it was shown by A.N. Whitehead and Russell in the famous three volumes of *Principia Mathematica* (Whitehead & Russell, 1910) that one can actually formalise many essential parts of mathematics in this type theory. (For a modern view on these matters, see Kamareddine *et al.*, 2002, 2004.) For Russell, this shows the viability of the so-called logicist approach, which asserts that all of mathematics can be based on (reduced to) logic.

The *Principia Mathematica* has been very influential, even though the subtle ramification of its type theory is sometimes felt as awkward and Whitehead and Russell had to resort to an additional 'axiom of reducibility' to make their approach viable. It was later shown, first by F.P. Ramsey (Ramsey, 1926), that the addition of the axiom of reducibility makes the ramification superfluous. In 1940, A. Church defined the *simple theory of types* (Church, 1940), which can be seen as a 'deramification' of Russell's type theory. Church used it to define the language of higher order logic. On top of it he defined the natural deduction derivation rules of higher order logic, so proofs in his system are 'external': they are derivation trees. Compared to the simple theory of types, our system λD *internalises* derivations as typed λ-terms. On top of that, we add type dependency (allowing the definition of objects that depend on proofs) and we add a definition mechanism.

To overcome paradoxes and regain consistency, E.F.F. Zermelo chose another way: he axiomatised set theory in 1908. His axioms were later (around 1921) adapted by A.H. Fraenkel, which led to a system now known as ZF (see e.g. Jech, 2003, or van Heijenoort, 1967, where the original papers of Zermelo and Fraenkel can be found). This axiom system is widely used, albeit mostly in theoretical investigations: mathematicians hardly ever base their work explicitly on ZF. The system describes which sets exist, where sets are just 'collections of things' that don't have any structure. So, one can recover the natural numbers in set theory by describing it as the set $\{\emptyset, \{\emptyset\}, \{\{\emptyset\}\}, \ldots\}$, but also in different ways. There is no 'typing' involved in the sense that one can recognise a natural number from the shape of the expression. This makes formalising mathematics in pure set theory relatively unnatural. See van Dalen *et al.* (1978) for a clear exposition of ZF.

The advantage of set theory over type theory is that various 'natural constructions' are directly available, like the union of two sets. In the present chapter we have looked at ways to also include these in our type theory, starting from a practical point of view: which set-operations are needed when formalising mathematics and how we include them in our type theory by providing the proper primitive notions.

There are various ways of formalising sets in type theory, each of which has its own advantages and disadvantages. In the present chapter we have chosen 'sets as predicates', which works well, as we have indicated by showing how to deal with the basic set-theoretic constructions. We now overview some other possible approaches and we briefly indicate why we have not chosen them.

(1) *Follow the approach of Russell and Whitehead to use their Ramified Type Theory to formalise sets.* They also follow the 'sets-as-predicates' approach, but their predicates live in a different type theory. As we have already indicated above, Ramsey and Church have shown that the ramification is unnecessarily complicated, so we don't follow that approach.

(2) *Formalize Zermelo–Fraenkel axiomatic set theory directly, by declaring a fixed basic type $V : *$ of all sets and letting the sets be terms of this type V.* Then both elements and sets are represented as terms of type V and elementhood is a relation on V, so $\in : V \to V \to *$. By assuming the axioms of Zermelo and Fraenkel we obtain ZF. The ZF-approach is widely employed to settle foundational issues, but it is not used for the real formalisation of mathematics, because the intrinsic untyped behaviour of ZF does not reflect everyday mathematics, where a type-like classification forms a natural and widely used concept. The $\in$-relation in ZF set theory relates entities of the same level, where everyday mathematical practice views it as relating an object to a collection. This idea is much better reflected in the type-theoretic framework. Also, using set theory for formalising mathematics involves a lot of coding: numbers are encoded as sets and so are functions, relations, etcetera. In type theory we make an attempt to avoid too much coding and we feel that using Zermelo–Fraenkel axiomatic set theory for formal mathematics is not a natural thing.

(3) *Treat powersets as types, by letting $ps(S)$, defined as $S \to *$, be of type $*$.* This is an attractive idea, because now the powerset of a type is again a type, which feels closer to axiomatic set theory. We then immediately have $ps(ps(S)) : *$, etcetera, so all powersets of types are again types. In van Benthem Jutting (1977) it is shown that this formalization of set theory, together with a number of primitive definitions about equality and pairing, is enough to deal with sets as they occur in the foundations of mathematics precisely described by E. Landau in his early and influential book *Foundations of Analysis* (Landau, 1930). It is a bit unusual that in this approach an element a of type S is on the same level as an element V of type $ps(S)$, while V plays the role of a set (namely a subset of S). This

mixture of elements and sets on the same level does not cause problems in Jutting's formalisation, using the system Automath, since Automath has a logical strength that is comparable to λP. However, when copying Jutting's primitive definitions to λD (or λC), the resulting system turns out to be inconsistent, as J.H. Geuvers has proved (see Geuvers, 2013). The problem arises here since we basically have $S \to * \; : \; *$. This is comparable to $* : *$, which is known to cause inconsistency.

(4) *Formalize subsets as Σ-types.* A much-used solution in type theory to deal with subsets is to add so-called Σ-types (we have already mentioned them in Sections 5.7 and 6.5). A Σ-type consists of *dependent pairs*. To be precise, for $S : *$, and $P : S \to *$, the Σ-type $\Sigma x : S . P x$ is the type of all pairs $\langle a, q \rangle$ where $a : S$ and $q : P a$. One can view $\Sigma x : S . P x$ as the subset of S consisting of all elements a for which $P a$ holds, where the *proof* of $P a$, i.e. the term q of type $P a$, is attached to a. So, if $a : S$ and $q : P a$, we don't just have $a : \Sigma x : S . P x$, but $\langle a, q \rangle : \Sigma x : S . P x$.

To have Σ-types in λD, we need four new derivation rules:

$$(\Sigma\text{-}form) \quad \frac{\Delta; \Gamma \vdash S : *_s \qquad \Delta; \Gamma, x : S \vdash B : *_p}{\Delta; \Gamma \vdash \Sigma x : S . B \; : \; *_s}$$

$$(\Sigma\text{-}pair) \quad \frac{\Delta; \Gamma \vdash M : S \quad \Delta; \Gamma \vdash N : B[x := M] \quad \Delta; \Gamma \vdash \Sigma x : S . B \; : \; *_s}{\Delta; \Gamma \vdash \langle M, N \rangle \; : \; \Sigma x : S . B}$$

$$(\Sigma\text{-}proj_1) \quad \frac{\Delta; \Gamma \vdash K \; : \; \Sigma x : S . B}{\Delta; \Gamma \vdash \pi_1 K : S}$$

$$(\Sigma\text{-}proj_2) \quad \frac{\Delta; \Gamma \vdash K \; : \; \Sigma x : S . B}{\Delta; \Gamma \vdash \pi_2 K \; : \; B[x := \pi_1 K]}$$

The rule (Σ-*form*) serves for the *formation* of Σ-types. The rule (Σ-*pair*) states that if M is of type S and it satisfies the predicate $\lambda x : S . B$, which is proved by N (since $N : B[x := M]$), then the pair $\langle M, N \rangle$ is of type $\Sigma x : S . B$. The rules (Σ-*proj*$_1$) and (Σ-*proj*$_2$) tell how to project information out of a pair: one can either project to the first component (via π_1) or the second component (via π_2) of a pair.

The type system of the well-known proof assistant Coq (see Coq Development Team, 2012) contains Σ-types, which are defined as inductive types. The usual notation $\{x : S \mid B\}$ is used there for $\Sigma x : S . B$.

In a competing system, called *PVS* (see PVS, 1992), a term M of type S may be of type $\{x : S \mid B\}$ as well. The derivation rule in PVS is:

$$\frac{M \,:\, S \qquad N \,:\, B[x :- N]}{M \,:\, \{x : S \mid B\}}$$

Although this looks a lot more familiar, this approach has serious drawbacks: one does not have decidability of typing and there is no Uniqueness of Types.

In both approaches, one needs to add symbols and rules to λD if one wants to have Σ-types. Since we intend to keep the system as simple as possible, we choose not to use Σ-types.

(5) *Subsets via embeddings.* Yet another approach is to simulate a subset of S by considering a different type, V, that is related to S by an injective embedding $in : V \to S$. The image $in(V)$ of V is the subset of S that we wish to capture. This image may be considered to be a 'copy' of V, since V and $in(V)$ are bijectively ('one-to-one') related. One may also define the map $out : in(V) \to V$ as the inverse of in, and we have, among other things, that $out(in(y)) =_V y$. Given such an embedding in of V into S, we may consider V itself to represent the subset (instead of $in(V)$), thus avoiding a 'typing clash' caused by the situation that a term both has type $in(V)$ and S (which is impossible, since $in(V)$ is not a type). If one wants to see a y of type V as also having type S, then this can be done via the injection in: consider the 'copy' $in(y)$ of y. Hence, by shifting back and forth between V and $in(V)$, we can deal with elements of type V as if they were of type S as well. Of course, this involves a lot of extra administration; but it works, and we don't have to abandon decidability of typing and Uniqueness of Types.

This approach can be applied nicely to the general situation where we wish to represent a set $\{x : S \mid P\,x\}$. Suppose $S : *$ and $P : S \to *$. We can now primitively assume a type $subtype(S, P) : *$, which takes the role of V above. We declare, primitively again, the embedding function in from $subtype(S, P)$ to S, having the property of being an injection. If desired, we may combine this with the inverse function out, defined on those x's in S for which P holds. A concrete implementation of this approach in type theory was given by L.S. van Benthem Jutting (see Nederpelt *et al.*, 1994, pp. 763/4). There are close correspondences between Σ-types and the subtypes obtained via embeddings. For example, the Σ-type $\Sigma x : S \,.\, P\,x$ finds its counterpart in the type $subtype(S, P)$.

Because a lot more primitive notions have to be added to λD, we have not followed this approach.

Exercises

13.1 Let V and W be subsets of S that are Leibniz-equal ($V \cong_{ps(S)} W$) as described in the final part of Section 13.2. Give a λD-derivation to prove that V and W are also subset-equal ($V = W$; see Figure 13.2).

If a λD-derivation is required in this exercise or one of the following ones, you may suffice with only mentioning the logical arguments in 'hints', as we have done regularly in the present chapter (cf. Section 13.2).

13.2 Let $S : *_s$ and $V, W : ps(S)$.

 (a) Show that the following is an immediate consequence of *eq-refl* (see Figure 12.2):
 $$\forall x : S . ((x \ \varepsilon \ V^c) \Leftrightarrow \neg(x \ \varepsilon \ V)).$$
 (b) Prove in λD: $(V \subseteq W) \Rightarrow (W^c \subseteq V^c)$.

13.3 Let $S : *_s$.

 (a) We have that *full-set*$(S) : ps(S)$. Why is S itself not a subset of S, i.e. not $S : ps(S)$?
 (b) Show that S not a member of its own powerset (i.e. show that $S \ \varepsilon \ ps(S)$ is not derivable).
 (c) Explain why we cannot code the powerset of the powerset of S as $ps(ps(S))$.
 (d) For $T : \square$, define $PS(T)$ as $T \to *_p$. Give a legal λD-expression representing the powerset of the powerset of the powerset of S.

13.4 Prove in λD, for $S : *_s$ and $V : ps(S)$:

 (a) $V \cup \emptyset_S = V$,
 (b) $V \cap \emptyset_S = \emptyset_S$,
 (c) $V \cup \textit{full-set}(S) = \textit{full-set}(S)$,
 (d) $V \cap \textit{full-set}(S) = V$.

13.5 Prove in λD, for $S : *_s$ and $V : ps(S)$:

 (a) $V \cup V^c = \textit{full-set}(S)$,
 (b) $V \cap V^c = \emptyset_S$.

13.6 Let S be a type.

 (a) Prove in λD: $\textit{full-set}(S) = (\emptyset_S)^c$.
 (b) Let V be a subset of S. Prove: $V \neq \textit{full-set}(S) \Leftrightarrow \exists x : S . \neg(x \ \varepsilon \ V)$.

13.7 Prove the following lemmas in λD, for $S : *_s$ and $V, W : ps(S)$:

 (a) $(V \cap W = V) \Rightarrow V \subseteq W$,
 (b) $V \backslash W = V \cap W^c$,
 (c) $V \subseteq W \Leftrightarrow V \backslash W = \emptyset_S$ (see Figure 13.7).

13.8 Let R be a binary relation on the set S that is symmetric and transitive. Assume that $\forall x : S . \exists y : S . (R\,x\,y)$. Prove in λD that R is also reflexive.

13.9 See Section 13.4. Prove in λD that the following two versions of the second characteristic of an equivalence class are indeed equivalent:

(2a) $\forall x, y : S . ([x]_R = [y]_R \vee ([x]_R \cap [y]_R = \emptyset_S))$,

(2b) $\forall x, y, z : S . (z \, \varepsilon \, [x]_R \Rightarrow z \, \varepsilon \, [y]_R \Rightarrow ([x]_R = [y]_R))$.

13.10 Let the binary relation R be an equivalence relation on S. Prove the following lemmas in λD:

(a) No class is empty (hint: see Figure 13.8),

(b) $\forall x, y, z : S . ((y \, \varepsilon \, [x]_R \wedge z \, \varepsilon \, [x]_R) \Rightarrow R\,y\,z)$,

(c) $\forall y : S . \exists x : S . (y \, \varepsilon \, [x]_R)$.

13.11 (a) Let $S, T : *_s$ and $F : T \to ps(S)$. Give a λD-definition of the 'big union' $\bigcup(S, T, F)$, notation $\bigcup_{z:T}(F\,z)$, being the subset of S consisting of all 'elements' of the subsets $F(z)$, for all $z : T$.

(b) Rewrite characteristic (3) for a partition in equivalence classes, as described in Section 13.4, using the $\bigcup$-symbol.

(c) Prove in λD that this new version of characteristic (3) is equivalent to the original one.

13.12 Fill the following gaps:

(a) In line (2) of Figure 13.12.

(b) In line (4) of Figure 13.13.

13.13 Let $S_1, S_2, S_3 : *_s$. Let $F : S_1 \to S_2$ and $G : S_2 \to S_3$. Then the *composition* of F and G is the function $G \circ F := \lambda x : S_1 . (G(F\,x))$. Prove the following lemmas in λD:

(a) If F and G are injective, then $G \circ F$ is injective.

(b) If F and G are surjective, then $G \circ F$ is surjective.

13.14 Let $S, T : *_s$, $F : S \to T$ and assume that u proves that F is a bijection. Prove in λD:
$$\forall y : T . (F(inv(S, T, F, u)\,y) =_T y).$$

13.15 (a) Extend Figure 13.14 with definitions for surjectivity and bijectivity of a function F on subset V, i.e. $F : \Pi x : S . ((x \, \varepsilon \, V) \to T)$.

(b) Also give a definition of the inverse in case F is bijective (cf. Figure 13.13); first prove that such an inverse is indeed a function, i.e. each y of type T has a unique function value under 'inverse'.

13.16 (a) Check lines (4) and (5) of Figure 13.16.

(b) Let $S, T : *_s$, let $F : S \to T$ be an injection and $V : ps(S)$. Prove the following in λD:
$$\forall x : S . (F\,x \, \varepsilon \, image(S, T, F, V) \Rightarrow x \, \varepsilon \, V).$$

14
Numbers and arithmetic in λD

14.1 The Peano axioms for natural numbers

In the previous chapters we have become acquainted with the use of λD for doing mathematics, by selecting a few examples and investigating the issues that we came across.

Let's now make a fresh start by thoroughly exploring the most fundamental entities in mathematics: natural and integer numbers. This will not be easy, since in the process of development we have to pretend that we 'know nothing' about subjects we are so familiar with. As a consequence, we have to build up our knowledge from scratch, which may seem cumbersome, but it is also quite interesting, since we are obliged to scrutinise the foundations of mathematics.

In the present section, we start with the basis: natural numbers. Integers will be the main topic of following sections.

In Chapter 1 we saw how natural numbers, and operations on naturals such as addition and multiplication, can be coded in untyped lambda calculus, as so-called *Church numerals* (see Exercise 1.10). There also exist encodings of these notions in *typed* lambda calculi: in the chapter about λ2 we have discussed the so-called *polymorphic Church numerals*; see, for example, Section 3.8 and Exercise 3.13. (For Church numerals in λ→: see Section 2.14.)

Therefore, it would be a type-theoretically justified choice to introduce the natural numbers in this manner. This can be done by writing down the appropriate definitions, since λ2 is a subsystem of λD. An immediate advantage of this choice is that calculations using basic operations such as addition and multiplication may be handed over to the inherent β-reduction mechanism of λD.

There are, however, several objections against this choice.

— Firstly, it has been shown that induction, one of the most fundamental proof principles of natural numbers, cannot be derived by means of the polymorphic Church numerals, not in $\lambda 2$ or $\lambda P2$ (Geuvers, 2001), and also not in λD. Hence, we need an extra *axiom* to represent it.

– Secondly, the representation of some basic functions on the naturals is difficult. For example, the encoding of the predecessor in Church-numeral style is inefficient and far from natural (see e.g. Geuvers & Nederpelt, 1994, Exercise 32.11). The reason is that Church numerals facilitate iteration, but not primitive recursion as a construction scheme.

– Thirdly, the Church numerals are not appropriate to also deal with *integers*, so we have to introduce integers in a different manner, which appears neither elegant nor convenient.

– Finally, the approach to introduce naturals in the Church format is not very 'natural' for mathematicians, who are used to older and more intuitively acceptable formats. The most accepted one is via the axioms of G. Peano (Peano, 1889), which include induction. This is the approach that we will follow henceforth.

We now elucidate this fundamental view of the mathematician G. Peano (1858–1932). He introduces the natural numbers as a set equipped with a zero element and a successor function, similar to Church's set-up, but with a different elaboration. Formally, Peano *postulates* the existence of a set $\mathbb{N}$, a singled-out element 0 in it and a function s from $\mathbb{N}$ to $\mathbb{N}$. So in $\mathbb{N}$ we have elements 0, $s(0)$, $s(s(0))$, etcetera, representing the numbers we are acquainted with: 0, 1, 2, etcetera. Of course, it is quite sensible to identify these two lists.

Next, Peano enforces by means of *axioms* that these formal numbers behave as expected. An important property is that the successor function must deliver new numbers, over and over again. Therefore, Peano adds two axioms. The aim of these axioms is to prevent the 'chain of numbers' retracing its own footsteps:

$ax\text{-}nat_1 : \forall_{x \in \mathbb{N}}(s(x) \neq 0),$

$ax\text{-}nat_2 : \forall_{x,y \in \mathbb{N}}(s(x) = s(y) \Rightarrow x = y).$

By $ax\text{-}nat_1$, none of the elements $s(s(\ldots(0)\ldots))$ (i.e. with at least one s), can be equal to 0. By $ax\text{-}nat_2$, two elements of the form $s(s(\ldots(0)\ldots))$ with a different number of s's are unequal. (Check this informally; you will need $ax\text{-}nat_1$.) Axiom $ax\text{-}nat_2$ expresses that s is an *injective* function (cf. Figure 13.13), but $ax\text{-}nat_1$ implies that s is not *surjective*.

Remark 14.1.1 *Although natural numbers are fundamental, there are things that are still 'more fundamental', namely logic and equality: see the negation sign occurring in $ax\text{-}nat_1$, the implication symbol in $ax\text{-}nat_2$ and the $\forall$-quantifiers and the equality symbols appearing in both axioms. Of course, also the rules of logic and the characteristic properties of equality belong to this primeval material. (See Chapters 7, 11 and 12 for the formal representation of these matters.)*

Peano recognised another thing as essential for the set of natural numbers, namely the possibility to establish a property for all natural numbers by *(mathematical) induction*. Induction is the well-known principle which enables the transfer of the validity of both $P(0)$ and $P(n) \to P(n+1)$, for all $n \in \mathbb{N}$, to the validity of P on the full $\mathbb{N}$ (see also Section 10.2). Formally:

axiom of induction for $\mathbb{N}$: for all predicates P on $\mathbb{N}$,
$$(P(0) \wedge \forall_{x \in \mathbb{N}}(P(x) \Rightarrow P(s(x)))) \Rightarrow \forall_{x \in \mathbb{N}}(P(x)).$$

In Figure 14.1 you find the fundamental notions and the three axioms of Peano for the naturals, in the setting of λD.

(1) $\mathbb{N} := \perp\!\!\!\perp : *_s$

(2) $0 := \perp\!\!\!\perp : \mathbb{N}$

(3) $s := \perp\!\!\!\perp : \mathbb{N} \to \mathbb{N}$

(4) $ax\text{-}nat_1 := \perp\!\!\!\perp : \forall x : \mathbb{N}. \neg(s\,x =_\mathbb{N} 0)$

(5) $ax\text{-}nat_2 := \perp\!\!\!\perp : \forall x : \mathbb{N}. \forall y : \mathbb{N}. (s\,x =_\mathbb{N} s\,y \Rightarrow x =_\mathbb{N} y)$

$\boxed{P : \mathbb{N} \to *_p}$

(6) $\quad ax\text{-}nat_3(P) := \perp\!\!\!\perp : (P\,0 \wedge \forall x : \mathbb{N}. (P\,x \Rightarrow P(s\,x))) \Rightarrow \forall x : \mathbb{N}. P\,x$

Figure 14.1 The Peano-axioms for natural numbers

Remark 14.1.2 *The names ax-nat$_1$ and ax-nat$_2$ are given to inhabitants of the axioms (which themselves are expressed as types); similarly, ax-nat$_3(P)$ names an inhabitant of the induction property for P, not the property itself.*

Apparently, we have succeeded in formalising the Peano-naturals in λD. Note that we need six *primitive* definitions in Figure 14.1, which are only 'justified' by a nowadays generally accepted view on the basics of natural numbers. This gives us a sufficient guarantee with regards to their acceptability.

Remark 14.1.3 *We remind the reader that all primitive definitions have to be scrupulously accounted for, since they contain notions or statements of an axiomatic nature; hence, their content is not formally justified (and more than that: formal justification is mostly impossible).*

So we have to be very careful with primitive definitions. For example, there is no formal objection against a primitive definition declaring that true $(\neg\perp)$ is equivalent to false $(\perp)$; nor is there any formal objection against an axiom stating that $0 =_\mathbb{N} s(0)$. But in both cases we have a big problem: either logic collapses (since $\perp \equiv \neg\perp$ implies that 'everything is provable'), or mathematics breaks down (because $0 =_\mathbb{N} s(0)$ implies that all natural numbers are equal).

Hence, there are several lessons to learn from this discussion:

(1) There should be a separate justification for all primitive definitions in a λD-text.

(2) It appears wise to use primitive definitions only sparingly.

(3) Even a full check of a λD-text on its compliance to the syntactical requirements imposed by the derivation rules, does not guarantee that it contains sensible mathematical content, since the primitive notions could be contradictory or meaningless.

These observations do by no means hold exclusively for λD: every mathematical exposition has the same provisos, and to the same extent, since there are always fundamental concepts *that must be introduced without formal justification.*

It is obvious that each $s(s(\ldots(0)\ldots))$, including 0 itself, has type $\mathbb{N}$. One might wonder whether the Peano-axioms are not too *weak*, in the sense that there may be more elements in $\mathbb{N}$ than the ones of the form $s(s(\ldots(0)\ldots))$. This fear is taken away by the following lemma:

Lemma 14.1.4   *For all* $n \in \mathbb{N}$: $n = 0 \lor \exists_{m \in \mathbb{N}}(n = s(m))$.

A proof of this lemma is amazingly simple, even when formalised in λD: all we have to do is apply induction on the predicate

$P \equiv \lambda n : \mathbb{N}.\, (n =_{\mathbb{N}} 0 \lor \exists m : \mathbb{N}.\, (n =_{\mathbb{N}} s\, m))$.

We sketch the proof of Lemma 14.1.4 in the usual mathematical style, albeit with flags (see Figure 14.2). Note that induction works perfectly, although we do not appeal to the induction hypothesis $P(k)$ in the body of the proof. This is exceptional, but yet in accordance with the induction principle.

The formal λD-version follows exactly the same pattern, although it needs more explicit proof terms. We leave it to the reader.

14.2 Introducing integers the axiomatic way

In the previous section we investigated how natural numbers can be dealt with in type theory, on the basis of the Peano-axioms. The basic number system in many mathematical applications, however, is the larger set $\mathbb{Z}$ of *integer numbers*. In particular, most of *number theory* is about integer numbers. In mathematical analysis, one prefers even larger systems, such as real numbers or complex numbers.

Since this book aims at giving an impression of how type theory can be used for mathematics and proofs, we decide to focus on integer numbers. Our justification is that we analyse one major example in the following chapter, namely Bézout's Lemma (cf. Remark 8.7.2), for which we need more than natural numbers alone, but no more than *integer* arithmetic.

Define, for $n \in \mathbb{N}$, $P(n) := (n = 0 \vee \exists_{m \in \mathbb{N}}(n = s(m)))$

step (i) $P(0)$, since $0 = 0$; use $\vee$-*in*.

step (ii)

> $k \in \mathbb{N}$
>
> > $P(k)$
> >
> > > $s(k) = s(k)$ (by reflexivity of $=$)
> > >
> > > $\exists_{m \in \mathbb{N}}(s(k) = s(m))$ (by $\exists$-*in*)
> > >
> > > $s(k) = 0 \vee \exists_{m \in \mathbb{N}}(s(k) = s(m))$ (by $\vee$-*in*)
> > >
> > > $P(s(k))$ (by definition of P)
> >
> $\forall_{k \in \mathbb{N}}(P(k) \Rightarrow P(s(k)))$ (by $\Rightarrow$-*in* and $\forall$-*in*)

step (iii) $\forall_{n \in \mathbb{N}}(P(n))$ (by induction on (i) and (ii))

Figure 14.2 An informal proof of Lemma 14.1.4

Hence, we take the integers as our basic number system, of which the naturals are a subset. In the remainder of the present chapter we find out how that vision can be expressed in type theory, borrowing the formal notion 'subset' from the previous chapter.

So we put aside the Peano-axioms for the naturals as dealt with in Section 14.1 (in particular: Figure 14.1) and start from scratch. As with the naturals, we prefer to introduce the integer numbers primitively, by giving a number of determining axioms. It will not come as a surprise that these axioms are a kind of extension of the Peano-axioms.

The five primitive definitions for the introduction of integers that we present below are an adaptation of the ones given by A. Margaris (Margaris, 1961), elaborated with the help of A. Visser and R. Iemhoff (2009, pers. comm.).

The axiomatisation of the integers postulates a set ($\mathbb{Z}$) with a specific element (0) and again a successor function (s), this time from $\mathbb{Z}$ to $\mathbb{Z}$ (see Figure 14.3, lines (1) to (3)).

The axiom *ax-int$_1$* in line (4) declares that s is a *bijection*: not only an injection (cf. *ax-nat$_2$*), but also a surjection (cf. Figure 13.13).

A consequence of *surjectivity* is that for all y in $\mathbb{Z}$ there is an x in $\mathbb{Z}$ such that $s(x) = y$; see line (7). So $\mathbb{Z}$ not only stretches out to the right, but also to the left. This is of course what we expect.

By the *injectivity*, such an x with $s(x) = y$ is *unique*. This is proven in lines (8) to (12). So we conclude (line (13)):

$\forall_{y \in \mathbb{Z}} \exists^1_{x \in \mathbb{Z}} (s(x) = y)$.

Consequently (cf. Section 12.7), we may give a *name* to such an x, uniquely existing as a companion for each y in $\mathbb{Z}$. Clearly, this x is the *predecessor* of y, which we call $p(y)$ (see line (14)).

Then ι-*prop* (see Figure 12.16, line (2)) immediately gives: $s(p(y)) = y$ (line (15)), and an easy consequence is that also $p(s(y)) = y$ (line (17)). Hence, successor and predecessor *cancel* each other, which is obvious since p is the inverse of s. We call this *s-p-annihilation* and *p-s-annihilation*, respectively.

(1) $\mathbb{Z} := \perp : *_s$

(2) $0 := \perp : \mathbb{Z}$

(3) $s := \perp : \mathbb{Z} \to \mathbb{Z}$

(4) $ax\text{-}int_1 := \perp : bijective(\mathbb{Z}, \mathbb{Z}, s)$

(5) $inj\text{-}suc := \ldots \text{ use } \wedge\text{-}el_1 \ldots : injective(\mathbb{Z}, \mathbb{Z}, s)$

(6) $surj\text{-}suc := \ldots \text{ use } \wedge\text{-}el_2 \ldots : surjective(\mathbb{Z}, \mathbb{Z}, s)$

> $y : \mathbb{Z}$
>
> (7) $a_7(y) := surj\text{-}suc \, y : \exists^{\geq 1} x : \mathbb{Z} . \, (s \, x =_{\mathbb{Z}} y)$
>
> > $x_1, x_2 : \mathbb{Z} \mid u : s \, x_1 =_{\mathbb{Z}} y \mid v : s \, x_2 =_{\mathbb{Z}} y$
> >
> > (8) $a_8(\ldots) := eq\text{-}sym(\mathbb{Z}, s \, x_2, y, v) : y =_{\mathbb{Z}} s \, x_2$
> >
> > (9) $a_9(\ldots) := eq\text{-}trans(\mathbb{Z}, s \, x_1, y, s \, x_2, u, a_8(\ldots)) : s \, x_1 =_{\mathbb{Z}} s \, x_2$
> >
> > (10) $a_{10}(\ldots) := inj\text{-}suc \, x_1 \, x_2 \, a_9(\ldots) : x_1 =_{\mathbb{Z}} x_2$
>
> (11) $a_{11}(y) := \ldots \text{ use } \Rightarrow\text{-}in \text{ and } \forall\text{-}in \ldots : \exists^{\leq 1} x : \mathbb{Z} . \, (s \, x =_{\mathbb{Z}} y)$
>
> (12) $a_{12}(y) := \ldots \text{ use } \wedge\text{-}in \text{ on } a_7(y) \text{ and } a_{11}(y) \ldots :$
>
> $\qquad \exists^1 x : \mathbb{Z} . \, (s \, x =_{\mathbb{Z}} y)$

(13) $a_{13} := \ldots \text{ use } \forall\text{-}in \ldots : \forall y : \mathbb{Z} . \, \exists^1 x : \mathbb{Z} . \, (s \, x =_{\mathbb{Z}} y)$

(14) $p := \lambda y : \mathbb{Z} . \, \iota(\mathbb{Z}, \lambda x : \mathbb{Z} . \, (s \, x =_{\mathbb{Z}} y), a_{12}(y)) : \mathbb{Z} \to \mathbb{Z}$

> $y : \mathbb{Z}$
>
> (15) $s\text{-}p\text{-}ann(y) := \iota\text{-}prop(\mathbb{Z}, \lambda x : \mathbb{Z} . \, (sx =_{\mathbb{Z}} y), a_{12}(y)) : s(p \, y) =_{\mathbb{Z}} y$
>
> (16) $a_{16}(y) := s\text{-}p\text{-}ann(s \, y) : s(p(s \, y)) =_{\mathbb{Z}} s \, y$
>
> (17) $p\text{-}s\text{-}ann(y) := inj\text{-}suc \, (p(s \, y)) \, y \, a_{16}(y) : p(s \, y) =_{\mathbb{Z}} y$

Figure 14.3 A formal set-up for integer numbers in λD and some consequences

> *In Appendix B we give a list of the interesting statements and lemmas dealt with in the present chapter, starting with the ones in Figure 14.3.*

We obviously also want an axiom about *induction* for the integers, $ax\text{-}int_2$, which replaces $ax\text{-}nat_3$ in Figure 14.1. For $\mathbb{Z}$ we need the so-called '*symmetric induction*' axiom, extending the usual induction axiom in 'both directions': apart from the prerequisites $P(0)$ and $\forall_{x \in \mathbb{Z}}(P(x) \Rightarrow P(s(x)))$, we also require the implication in the 'opposite' direction: $\forall_{x \in \mathbb{Z}}(P(x) \Rightarrow P(p(x)))$. Only then, one is allowed to conclude the universal validity of P on $\mathbb{Z}$. This leads to the following induction axiom for $\mathbb{Z}$ (compare it with the induction axiom for $\mathbb{N}$ as given in the previous section):

axiom of induction for $\mathbb{Z}$: for all predicates P on $\mathbb{Z}$,
$$[P(0) \wedge \forall_{x \in \mathbb{Z}}(P(x) \Rightarrow (P(s(x)) \wedge P(p(x))))] \Rightarrow \forall_{x \in \mathbb{Z}}(P(x)).$$

We introduce this as a primitive proposition in Figure 14.4, with proof object $ax\text{-}int_2$.

$$
\begin{array}{|l}
\hline
P : \mathbb{Z} \to *_p \\
\hline
\quad ax\text{-}int_2(P) := \perp\!\!\!\perp : \\
\qquad [P\,0 \wedge \forall x : \mathbb{Z}.\,(P\,x \Rightarrow (P(s\,x) \wedge P(p\,x)))] \Rightarrow \forall x : \mathbb{Z}.\,P\,x
\end{array}
$$

Figure 14.4 The induction axiom for integer numbers

Remark 14.2.1 *In this axiom, the 'starting point' of the induction is* 0, *since we must have* $P\,0$. *But any other integer number than* 0 *would do as well. Prove this variant of induction for* $\mathbb{Z}$ *yourself (Exercise 14.18).*

Next, we single out the integers from 0 'upwards', the *natural numbers*, as a subset $\mathbb{N}$ of $\mathbb{Z}$. This asks for one definition and an axiom, as expressed in Figures 14.5 and 14.6.

In line (2) of Figure 14.5, we present $\mathbb{N}$ as a predicate over $\mathbb{Z}$ (i.e. a subset), by means of a definition:
$$\mathbb{N} := \lambda x : \mathbb{Z}.\,\Pi P : \mathbb{Z} \to *_p.\,(nat\text{-}cond(P) \Rightarrow P\,x).$$

We explain what this definition expresses. First, we look at the *condition*
$$nat\text{-}cond := P\,0 \wedge \forall y : \mathbb{Z}.\,(P\,y \Rightarrow P(s\,y))$$
occurring in $\mathbb{N}$. If *nat-cond* holds for P, then, in particular, 0 and all its successors satisfy P. This implies intuitively that P contains all natural numbers.

Now the above definition says that $\mathbb{N}$ satisfies x if *all* predicates P over $\mathbb{Z}$ satisfying *nat-cond* also satisfy x. Hence, under the subset-interpretation, $\mathbb{N}$ is *included* in all P's that satisfy *nat-cond*.

Remark 14.2.2 *If we imagine* $\mathbb{Z}$ *in the usual manner as a straight line, infinite in both directions, then each predicate* P *that satisfies nat-cond represents an interval* $[x, \infty)$, *i.e. a set of integers greater than or equal to a certain* x. *Since* 0 *is an element of all these* P's, *we always have* $x \leq 0$. *The predicate* $\mathbb{N}$ *is the intersection of all these* P.

It is not hard to prove that $\mathbb{N}$ itself satisfies *nat-cond*, since $\mathbb{N}\,0$ holds and $\forall x : \mathbb{Z}.\,(\mathbb{N}\,x \Rightarrow \mathbb{N}(s\,x))$ (Exercise 14.2). See lines (3) and (4) of Figure 14.5.

(Recall that $x \, \varepsilon \, \mathbb{N}$ is an alternative notation for $\mathbb{N} \, x$; see Figure 13.1.) It follows in line (6) that $\mathbb{N}$ is the *smallest subset* of $\mathbb{Z}$ satisfying *nat-cond* (Exercise 14.3).

$\boxed{P : \mathbb{Z} \to *_p}$

(1) $\quad nat\text{-}cond(P) := P\,0 \wedge \forall x : \mathbb{Z} . \, (P\,x \Rightarrow P(s\,x)) \; : \; *_p$

(2) $\quad \mathbb{N} := \lambda x : \mathbb{Z} . \, \Pi P : \mathbb{Z} \to *_p . \, (nat\text{-}cond(P) \Rightarrow P\,x) \; : \; \mathbb{Z} \to *_p$

(3) $\quad zero\text{-}prop := \, \ldots \, [Exerc. \; 14.2(a)] \, \ldots \; : \; 0 \, \varepsilon \, \mathbb{N}$

(4) $\quad clos\text{-}prop := \, \ldots \, [Exerc. \; 14.2(b)] \, \ldots \; : \; \forall x : \mathbb{Z} . \, (x \, \varepsilon \, \mathbb{N} \Rightarrow s\,x \, \varepsilon \, \mathbb{N})$

(5) $\quad a_5 := \, \ldots \, \text{use} \; \wedge\text{-}in \, \ldots \; : \; nat\text{-}cond(\mathbb{N})$

(6) $\quad nat\text{-}smallest := \, \ldots \, [Exerc. \; 14.3] \, \ldots \; :$

$$\Pi Q : \mathbb{Z} \to *_p . \, (nat\text{-}cond(Q) \Rightarrow (\mathbb{N} \subseteq Q))$$

Figure 14.5 The natural numbers as a subset of $\mathbb{Z}$

There is still one fundamental problem with the formal presentation of $\mathbb{Z}$ as given up to now: it does not enforce that this $\mathbb{Z}$ conforms to the intuitive 'picture' of $\mathbb{Z}$, in which it stretches out infinitely to the right and to the left – without loops or repetitions. There are *models* (i.e. mathematical structures) satisfying the formal axioms of $\mathbb{Z}$ as we have presented so far that do not comply with this picture. For example, every *finite* set satisfies the above formalisation, if we choose one element as representing 0 and let the successor function s 'rotate' through this set. Take e.g. $S \equiv \{a, b, c, d\}$, take $a = 0$ and s such that $s(a) = b$, $s(b) = c$, $s(c) = d$ and $s(d) = a$, again. Then 0 is in S, the function s is bijective and symmetric induction holds. So S is a *model* of the axioms of $\mathbb{Z}$ we have given so far. In this model, the $\mathbb{N}$ as defined above *coincides* with $\mathbb{Z}$.

This means that our formalisation so far does not capture the integers as we imagine them. So we have to do something about it. The solution is simple, as follows from Margaris (1961) and Visser and Iemhoff (2009): add one extra axiom to the effect that $p\,0$, the predecessor of 0, is not in $\mathbb{N}$. This prevents loops as above, and finite models in general (Exercise 14.4).

And this is what we do in Figure 14.6.

$$ax\text{-}int_3 := \perp\!\!\!\perp \; : \; \neg(p\,0 \, \varepsilon \, \mathbb{N})$$

Figure 14.6 The third axiom for natural numbers

So now we have the integers (expressions of type $\mathbb{Z}$), the natural numbers (being those n of type $\mathbb{Z}$ for which $n \, \varepsilon \, \mathbb{N}$)) and the negative integers (the n of type $\mathbb{Z}$ for which $\neg(n \, \varepsilon \, \mathbb{N})$).

14.3 Basic properties of the 'new' $\mathbb{N}$

The next thing that we have to do is to convince ourselves that the Peano-axioms (see Figure 14.1) 'hold' for the new $\mathbb{N}$.

Let's consider them one by one:

ax-nat$_1$: $\quad \forall x : \mathbb{N} . \ \neg(s\,x =_{\mathbb{N}} 0)$.

In the new setting, this expression becomes: $\forall x : \mathbb{Z} . \ (x \ \varepsilon \ \mathbb{N} \Rightarrow \neg(s\,x =_{\mathbb{Z}} 0))$.

This is easy to prove: let $x : \mathbb{Z}$, assume $x \ \varepsilon \ \mathbb{N}$. If $s\,x =_{\mathbb{Z}} 0$, then $p(s\,x) =_{\mathbb{Z}} p\,0$, hence $x =_{\mathbb{Z}} p\,0$ (since p and s annihilate each other; Figure 14.3, line (17)). It follows that $p\,0 \ \varepsilon \ \mathbb{N}$, contradicting *ax-int$_3$*. So $\neg(s\,x =_{\mathbb{Z}} 0)$. (Fill in the details by giving the corresponding λD-derivation.)

The next Peano-axiom is:

ax-nat$_2$: $\quad \forall x : \mathbb{N} . \ \forall y : \mathbb{N} . \ (s\,x =_{\mathbb{N}} s\,y \Rightarrow x =_{\mathbb{N}} y)$.

This becomes: $\forall x, y : \mathbb{Z} . \ (x \ \varepsilon \ \mathbb{N} \Rightarrow (y \ \varepsilon \ \mathbb{N} \Rightarrow (s\,x =_{\mathbb{Z}} s\,y \Rightarrow x =_{\mathbb{Z}} y)))$, which follows directly from *ax-int$_1$* (cf. line (5) in Figure 14.3).

We record the $\mathbb{Z}$-equivalents of *ax-nat$_1$* and *ax-nat$_2$*, being *theorems* now, as *nat-prop$_1$* and *nat-prop$_2$* in Figure 14.7. (We omit the corresponding proof objects.)

(1) $\quad$ *nat-prop$_1$* $:= \ \ldots \ : \ \forall x : \mathbb{Z} . \ (x \ \varepsilon \ \mathbb{N} \Rightarrow \neg(s x =_{\mathbb{Z}} 0))$

(2) $\quad$ *nat-prop$_2$* $:= \ \ldots \ : \ \forall x, y : \mathbb{Z} . \ (x \ \varepsilon \ \mathbb{N} \Rightarrow (y \ \varepsilon \ \mathbb{N} \Rightarrow (s x =_{\mathbb{Z}} s y \Rightarrow x =_{\mathbb{Z}} y)))$

Figure 14.7 The first two Peano-axioms for $\mathbb{N}$ in the new setting

Finally, we have the third Peano-axiom:

ax-nat$_3$(induction): for all predicates P of type $\mathbb{N} \to *_p$:
$\quad (P\,0 \wedge \forall x : \mathbb{N} . \ (P\,x \Rightarrow P(s\,x))) \Rightarrow \forall x : \mathbb{N} . \ P\,x$.

First, we note that the type $\mathbb{N} \to *_p$, which is $\Pi x : \mathbb{N} . \ *_p$, is not available now ($\mathbb{N}$ is no longer a type, so Π-abstraction over $\mathbb{N}$ is not permitted).

In the present setting, all predicates must be over the type of the *integers*. For predicates over $\mathbb{N}$, we apply the solution developed in the beginning of Section 13.2: we include the condition $x \ \varepsilon \ \mathbb{N}$ in the body of the two $\forall$-expressions.

This leads to the following rephrasing of the induction axiom:

induction for $\mathbb{N}$ *as subset of* $\mathbb{Z}$: $\quad$ for all predicates P of type $\mathbb{Z} \to *_p$:
$\quad (P\,0 \wedge \forall x : \mathbb{Z} . \ (x \ \varepsilon \ \mathbb{N} \Rightarrow (P\,x \Rightarrow P(s\,x)))) \Rightarrow \forall x : \mathbb{Z} . \ (x \ \varepsilon \ \mathbb{N} \Rightarrow P\,x)$.

Again, it is not necessary to formulate this as an extra axiom, because it is a *theorem*: it can be derived from our axioms for integers and the definition of $\mathbb{N}$. The proof is given in Figure 14.8.

The start is familiar by now: we raise a flag with an arbitrary P and a second one assuming the left-hand side of the main implication. We have to prove the right-hand side of this implication, namely $\forall x : \mathbb{Z} . (x \, \varepsilon \, \mathbb{N} \Rightarrow P \, x)$. However, assuming an x of type $\mathbb{Z}$ such that $x \, \varepsilon \, \mathbb{N}$ does not immediately lead to the desired result $P \, x$: an obvious option is to use the definition of $\mathbb{N}$ for this x and P, but this does not work. The reason is that the definition of $\mathbb{N}$ has $\forall x : \mathbb{Z} . (P \, x \Rightarrow P(s \, x))$ in its 'condition', whereas we have in the second flag the weaker statement $\forall x : \mathbb{Z} . (x \, \varepsilon \, \mathbb{N} \Rightarrow (P \, x \Rightarrow P(s \, x)))$.

The solution that works is to 'upgrade' the predicate P by adding $z \, \varepsilon \, \mathbb{N}$, and consider the predicate $Q := \lambda z : \mathbb{Z} . (z \, \varepsilon \, \mathbb{N} \wedge P \, z)$ (see line (1) of the derivation), for which we *can* prove $\forall x : \mathbb{Z} . (Q \, x \Rightarrow Q(s \, x))$ (line (11)). This enables us to apply the definition of $\mathbb{N}$ (see line (13), where w inhabits $\mathbb{N} \, x$). The remainder of the proof is mainly technique.

$$\boxed{P : \mathbb{Z} \rightarrow *_p}$$

(1) $\quad Q^\dagger := \lambda z : \mathbb{Z} . (z \, \varepsilon \, \mathbb{N} \wedge P \, z) \; : \; \mathbb{Z} \rightarrow *_p$

$\qquad \boxed{u : \; P 0 \wedge \forall x : \mathbb{Z} . (x \, \varepsilon \, \mathbb{N} \Rightarrow (P \, x \Rightarrow P(s \, x)))}$

(2) $\qquad a_2 := \ldots$ **use** $\wedge\text{-}el_1$ **on** $u \ldots : \; P 0$

(3) $\qquad a_3 := \ldots$ **use** $\wedge\text{-}el_2$ **on** $u \ldots : \; \forall x : \mathbb{Z} . (x \, \varepsilon \, \mathbb{N} \Rightarrow (P \, x \Rightarrow P(s \, x)))$

(4) $\qquad a_4 := \ldots$ **use** $\wedge\text{-}in$ **on** *zero-prop* **and** $a_2 \ldots : \; Q 0$

$\qquad \quad \boxed{y : \mathbb{Z} \mid v : Q \, y}$

(5) $\qquad \quad a_5 := \ldots$ **use** $\wedge\text{-}el_1$ **on** $v \ldots : \; y \, \varepsilon \, \mathbb{N}$

(6) $\qquad \quad a_6 := \ldots$ **use** $\wedge\text{-}el_2$ **on** $v \ldots : \; P \, y$

(7) $\qquad \quad a_7 := clos\text{-}prop \; y \; a_5 \; : \; s \, y \, \varepsilon \, \mathbb{N}$

(8) $\qquad \quad a_8 := a_3 \, y \, a_5 \; : \; P \, y \Rightarrow P(s \, y)$

(9) $\qquad \quad a_9 := a_8 \, a_6 \; : \; P(s \, y)$

(10) $\qquad \quad a_{10} := \ldots$ **use** $\wedge\text{-}in$ **on** a_7 **and** $a_9 \ldots : \; Q(s \, y)$

(11) $\qquad a_{11} := \ldots$ **use** $\Rightarrow\text{-}in$ **and** $\forall\text{-}in \ldots : \; \forall y : \mathbb{Z} . (Q \, y \Rightarrow Q(s \, y))$

(12) $\qquad a_{12} := \ldots$ **use** $\wedge\text{-}in$ **on** a_4 **and** $a_{11} \ldots : \; nat\text{-}cond(Q)$

$\qquad \quad \boxed{x : \mathbb{Z} \mid w : x \, \varepsilon \, \mathbb{N}}$

(13) $\qquad \quad a_{13} := w \, Q \, a_{12} \; : \; Q \, x$

(14) $\qquad \quad a_{14} := \ldots$ **use** $\wedge\text{-}el_2$ **on** $a_{13} \ldots : \; P \, x$

(15) $\qquad a_{15} := \ldots$ **use** $\Rightarrow\text{-}in$ **and** $\forall\text{-}in \ldots : \; \forall x : \mathbb{Z} . (x \, \varepsilon \, \mathbb{N} \Rightarrow P \, x)$

(16) $\quad nat\text{-}ind(P) := \ldots$ **use** $\Rightarrow\text{-}in$ **on** $a_{15} \ldots :$

$\qquad \quad (P 0 \wedge \forall x : \mathbb{Z} . (x \, \varepsilon \, \mathbb{N} \Rightarrow (P \, x \Rightarrow P(s \, x)))) \Rightarrow \forall x : \mathbb{Z} . (x \, \varepsilon \, \mathbb{N} \Rightarrow P \, x)$

† *parameters suppressed*

Figure 14.8 Induction over the natural numbers

So we have adapted versions of all three Peano-axioms for natural numbers available as *theorems* in $\mathbb{Z}$, with proofs *nat-prop*$_1$, *nat-prop*$_2$ (see Figure 14.7) and *nat-ind* (Figure 14.8, line (16)).

We recall an important property of natural numbers, given in Lemma 14.1.4: for all $n \in \mathbb{N}$ we have $n = 0$ or $\exists_{m \in \mathbb{N}}(n = s(m))$. Obviously, we now may replace the part $\exists_{m \in \mathbb{N}}(n = s(m))$ by $p(n) \in \mathbb{N}$.

In order to make this formal, we again quantify over $\mathbb{Z}$ (not over $\mathbb{N}$) and add $n \; \varepsilon \; \mathbb{N}$ as a condition. This leads to the following λD-reformulation of Lemma 14.1.4:

Lemma 14.3.1 $\forall x : \mathbb{Z}. \, (x \; \varepsilon \; \mathbb{N} \Rightarrow (x =_{\mathbb{Z}} 0 \vee p\,x \; \varepsilon \; \mathbb{N})).$

A proof of this lemma uses *nat-ind* (see Figure 14.8). For the predicate P we take:

$$P \; := \; \lambda x : \mathbb{Z}. \, (x =_{\mathbb{Z}} 0 \vee p\,x \; \varepsilon \; \mathbb{N}),$$

since induction for $\mathbb{N}$ as a subset of $\mathbb{Z}$, which we described above, eventually leads to $\forall x : \mathbb{Z}. \, (x \; \varepsilon \; \mathbb{N} \Rightarrow P\,x)$, and this is the content of Lemma 14.3.1 after substitution of P.

A formal proof in λD, following these lines, is not too hard. We leave it to the reader (Exercise 14.5). In order to be able to give a formal reference to Lemma 14.3.1, we register the λD-version (without proof object) under the name *nat-split* in line (1) of Figure 14.9.

Using elementary logic, we can rewrite this as in line (2). Since we may view $p\,x \; \varepsilon \; \mathbb{N}$ as 'x is positive', and $\neg(x \; \varepsilon \; \mathbb{N})$ as 'x is negative', line (2) expresses that an integer is negative, zero or positive. This is known as the *tripartition* property of the integers. See line (5) of Figure 14.9.

(1)   *nat-split* $:= \; \ldots \; : \; \forall x : \mathbb{Z}. \, (x \; \varepsilon \; \mathbb{N} \Rightarrow (x =_{\mathbb{Z}} 0 \vee p\,x \; \varepsilon \; \mathbb{N}))$

(2)   *nat-split-alt* $:= \; \ldots \; : \; \forall x : \mathbb{Z}. \, (\neg(x \; \varepsilon \; \mathbb{N}) \vee x =_{\mathbb{Z}} 0 \vee p\,x \; \varepsilon \; \mathbb{N})$

$\boxed{x : \mathbb{Z}}$

(3) $\quad pos(x) := p\,x \; \varepsilon \; \mathbb{N}$

(4) $\quad neg(x) := \neg(x \; \varepsilon \; \mathbb{N})$

(5)   *trip* $:=$ *nat-split-alt* $: \; \forall x : \mathbb{Z}. \, (neg(x) \vee x =_{\mathbb{Z}} 0 \vee pos(x))$

Figure 14.9 Positive and negative numbers, and the tripartition property

Below, we list a number of useful lemmas about positive and negative numbers. The proofs are left to the reader (Exercise 14.7). By combining parts (a) and (b) of Lemma 14.3.2, we see that the '$\Rightarrow$' in *nat-split* can be replaced by a '$\Leftrightarrow$'.

Lemma 14.3.2   *(a)* $\forall x : \mathbb{Z}.\ (pos(s\,x) \Leftrightarrow x\ \varepsilon\ \mathbb{N})$,
  (b) $\forall x : \mathbb{Z}.\ (pos(s\,x) \Leftrightarrow (x =_{\mathbb{Z}} 0 \vee pos(x)))$,
  (c) $\forall x : \mathbb{Z}.\ (neg(p\,x) \Leftrightarrow (x =_{\mathbb{Z}} 0 \vee neg(x)))$.

Lemma 14.3.3 implies that the disjunctions in *trip* are 'exclusive': an integer is either negative, or 0, or positive.

Lemma 14.3.3   *(a)* $\forall x : \mathbb{Z}.\ (pos(x) \Leftrightarrow x \neq_{\mathbb{Z}} 0 \wedge \neg neg(x))$,
  (b) $\forall x : \mathbb{Z}.\ (neg(x) \Leftrightarrow x \neq_{\mathbb{Z}} 0 \wedge \neg pos(x))$,
  (c) $\forall x : \mathbb{Z}.\ (x =_{\mathbb{Z}} 0 \Leftrightarrow \neg pos(x) \wedge \neg neg(x))$.

14.4 Integer addition

Now that we have formalised the integers in λD, with the naturals as a subset, the next thing is to investigate how *arithmetical operations* can be formalised for these numbers, since we want to *compute* with them. Our first aim is *addition*: the computation of a sum of two numbers. Usually, computational operations are introduced by means of a *recursive definition*. That's also the case with addition.

Let's consider the recursive definition for adding two *natural* numbers. The standard approach is the following. In order to compute $x + y$, one uses recursion over the *second* argument, i.e. y. (This is an arbitrary choice: it could just as well be the first argument.) One then distinguishes two cases for this argument, in accordance with Lemma 14.1.4: it may be either 0 or the successor of another natural number (see also *nat-split* in Figure 14.9).

The standard recursive definition then has the following shape:

  (i) $m + 0 = m$,
  (ii) $m + s(n) = s(m + n)$.

We do an example to see how this works.

Example 14.4.1   For the computation of the sum $2 + 3$, or, more precisely, $s(s(0)) + s(s(s(0)))$, we obtain from *(ii)* that

  $2 + 3 = s(s(0)) + s(s(s(0))) = s[s(s(0)) + s(s(0))]$.

(In the third expression we use one pair of square brackets, for clarity.)

Repetition of the procedure on $s(s(0)) + s(s(0))$ results in $s[s(s(0)) + s(0)]$, hence $2 + 3 = s(s[s(s(0)) + s(0)])$.

One step further, we get $2 + 3 = s(s(s[s(s(0)) + 0]))$.

Then, finally, we use *(i)* for the computation of the subexpression $s(s(0)) + 0$. Hence, $2 + 3 = s(s(s(s(s(0)))))$, which is 5 by definition; so altogether we get $2 + 3 = 5$, just as expected.

Note that we have used substitutivity and transitivity of $=$ in this calculation.

Since the number m in (i) and (ii) does not change in the recursion, we can view this recursive definition as a *family* of many *unary* $+$-operations, one for each $m \in \mathbb{N}$. To make this explicit, we write down the recursive equations for each of these $+_m$-operations separately, as follows:

(i) $+_m(0) = m$,

(ii) $+_m(s(n)) = s(+_m(n))$.

Hence, the recursive equations tell us, for fixed m, what function $+_m$ does with n:

- in (i), the case $n = 0$ is given;
- in (ii), the situation for n is 'scaled up' to the situation for $s(n)$: if we know what $+_m$ does with n, then the equation tells us the effect on $s(n)$.

The word 'recursion' literally refers to the reverse process: not scaling 'up', but scaling 'down'. (*Recursion* literally means 'walking back'.) This is how an actual computation works. In the example above, for the computation of $+_2(3)$, we need (by (ii)) to compute $+_2(2)$. But in order to compute this $+_2(2)$, we need $+_2(1)$. Finally we have to compute $+_2(0)$; for this, (i) gives an answer. So the recursion *stops* and delivers a result.

Remark 14.4.2 *Characteristic for recursive definitions is that the definiens occurs left and right of the definitional $=$-sign. See equation (ii), where the $+_m$ occurs on both sides. So the function $+_m$ is not expressed as a 'new' symbol: it is defined in terms of itself.*

It is essential for recursion that the process comes to a halt. When the recursion stops, there should be a unique 'outcome', in which the definiens is no longer present. In general, this requires a so-called well-founded *recursion. Such a well-founded recursion delivers a 'proper' function as a result – in this case: an operator $+_m$ that gives a unique answer when applied to an argument n.*

Until now, we have silently assumed that m and n are natural numbers. It will be clear that the same recursive equations also apply to integers, but they apparently do not suffice. The scheme above appears to be tailored for 'upwards' counting from 0 via (ii): $+_m(1) = s(+_m(0))$, $+_m(2) = s(+_m(1))$, etcetera. When extending m and n to the *integers*, it is not immediately clear what $+_m$ does when applied to a *negative* number.

Since we want to be able to add integer numbers, our first impulse is to add a third entry to the recursion scheme, allowing 'downwards' counting:

(iii) $m + p(n) = p(m + n)$.

However, this turns out to be superfluous, since (iii) is a consequence of (ii), as we show now. Assume (ii) $m + s(n) = s(m + n)$. Since this equation holds for all n, also $m + s(p(n)) = s(m + p(n))$. By *s-p-ann*, $m + n = s(m + p(n))$, so $p(m + n) = p(s(m + p(n)))$, which is $m + p(n)$ by *p-s-ann*.

So also for $\mathbb{Z}$, equations (i) and (ii) are enough.

To incorporate definitions such as $+_m$ by *well-founded* recursion (see Remark 14.4.2; see also Exercise 14.9) into the format of λD, we need a kind of Recursion Theorem for $\mathbb{Z}$. Such a theorem indeed exists, as an immediate generalisation of the Recursion Theorem for natural numbers (see van Dalen *et al.*, 1978). Both theorems, the original one and the generalised one, are provable in λD with the formalised knowledge that we have developed in the previous sections and chapters. We do not demonstrate this here because of the complexity of the proofs. See Geuvers (2014b) for details.

The theorem for $\mathbb{Z}$ reads as follows:

Theorem 14.4.3   *(Recursion Theorem for $\mathbb{Z}$)*
  Let A be a type, $a : A$ and let $f_1, f_2 : A \to A$.
  Then there exists exactly one function $g : \mathbb{Z} \to A$ such that

$-$ $g\,0 =_A a,$
$-$ $g(s\,x) =_A f_1(g\,x)$ *if $x : \mathbb{Z}$ and $pos(s\,x)$,*
$-$ $g(p\,x) =_A f_2(g\,x)$ *if $x : \mathbb{Z}$ and $neg(p\,x)$.*

Let's investigate the content of the theorem. For the unique g that must exist according to this theorem, we have:

  $g\,0 =_A a,$
  $g\,1 =_A g(s\,0) =_A f_1(g\,0) =_A f_1\,a$ since $s\,0$ is positive,
  $g\,2 =_A g(s\,1) =_A f_1(g\,1) =_A f_1(f_1\,a)$, etcetera.

How about $g(k)$ for *negative* k?

  $g(-1) =_A g(p\,0) =_A f_2(g\,0) =_A f_2(a)$ since $p\,0$ is negative,
  $g(-2) =_A \cdots =_A f_2(f_2\,a)$, etcetera.

So a is the value of g in 0, function f_1 provides the g-values for positive numbers and f_2 for negative numbers. The theorem says that the recursive process produces a unique g-value for each integer, so g is indeed a function on $\mathbb{Z}$.

Remark 14.4.4   *Theorem 14.4.3 enables one to recursively define a function with different descriptions for positive and negative numbers. For example, the absolute-value-function abs, with*

$$abs(x) \ := \ \begin{cases} x & \text{if } x \geq 0, \\ -x & \text{if } x < 0, \end{cases}$$

can easily be defined by means of the Recursion Theorem for $\mathbb{Z}$ (Exercise 14.6).

Although we give no proof of Theorem 14.4.3, we state it in λD, under the name *spec-rec-th*, but without a proof object (see Figure 14.10).

$$\boxed{A : *_s \mid a : A \mid f_1, f_2 : A \to A}$$

$$spec\text{-}rec\text{-}th(A, a, f_1, f_2) := \ldots :$$
$$\exists^1 g : \mathbb{Z} \to A . [g\, 0 =_A a \land$$
$$\forall x : \mathbb{Z} . [(pos(s\, x) \Rightarrow (g(s\, x) =_A f_1(g\, x))) \land$$
$$(neg(p\, x) \Rightarrow (g(p\, x) =_A f_2(g\, x)))]]$$

Figure 14.10 The Recursion Theorem for $\mathbb{Z}$ in λD

When recursively defining addition $+_m$ as we have done above, we apparently have to take $\mathbb{Z}$ for A, integer m for a, the successor function s for f_1 and the predecessor function p for f_2. The Recursion Theorem for $\mathbb{Z}$ then states that there exists *exactly one* $g : \mathbb{Z} \to \mathbb{Z}$ such that

- $g\, 0 =_{\mathbb{Z}} m$,
- $\forall x : \mathbb{Z} . (pos(s\, x) \Rightarrow g(s\, x) =_{\mathbb{Z}} s(g\, x))$ and
- $\forall x : \mathbb{Z} . (neg(p\, x) \Rightarrow g(p\, x) =_{\mathbb{Z}} p(g\, x))$.

By giving the name $+_m$ to this g, we get what we want, albeit that we like to omit the conditions '$pos(s\, x)$' and '$neg(p\, x)$', respectively. This is indeed permitted, because s is a *bijection* according to $ax\text{-}int_1$, and function p is the inverse of function s. What we thus obtain is a restricted version of the Recursion Theorem for $\mathbb{Z}$:

Theorem 14.4.5 *(Recursion Theorem for $\mathbb{Z}$, with bijection)*
Let A be a type, $a : A$ and $f : A \to A$, a bijection.
Then there exists exactly one function $g : \mathbb{Z} \to A$ such that
- $g\, 0 =_A a$,
- $g(s\, x) =_A f(g\, x)$ *for all $x : \mathbb{Z}$.*

This theorem is an immediate consequence of Theorem 14.4.3: given a bijective f, take $f_1 := f$ and $f_2 := f^{-1}$ in that theorem (see Exercise 14.10).

The restricted theorem is suitable for the addition operator $+_m$, since s is a bijection. It permits applying the simple recursion scheme that we had before, when taking m for a, function s for f and writing $+_m$ for g:

- $+_m 0 =_{\mathbb{Z}} m$,
- $\forall x : \mathbb{Z} . (+_m(s\, x) =_{\mathbb{Z}} s(+_m x))$.

Formally, we can express this as in Figure 14.11. For convenience's sake, in line (2) we have given a name to the predicate involved: $rec\text{-}add\text{-}prop(m)$. In line (4), the function $plus(m)$ is defined as *the* function that satisfies the predicate, i.e. the unique function satisfying the properties $plus(m)\, 0 = m$ and, for all integers n, $plus(m)\, (s(n)) = s(plus(m)\, n)$. By means of a Notation Convention, we introduce $+_m$ as notation for $plus(m)$.

(1) $a_1 := ax\text{-}int_1 : bijective(\mathbb{Z}, \mathbb{Z}, s)$

> $\boxed{m : \mathbb{Z}}$
>
> (2) $rec\text{-}add\text{-}prop(m) := \lambda g : \mathbb{Z} \to \mathbb{Z}.\ (g\,0 =_{\mathbb{Z}} m \land \forall x : \mathbb{Z}.\ (g(s\,x) =_{\mathbb{Z}} s(g\,x))) :$
> $(\mathbb{Z} \to \mathbb{Z}) \to *_p$
>
> (3) $rec\text{-}add\text{-}lem(m) := \ldots$ use Theorem 14.4.5... :
> $\exists^1 g : \mathbb{Z} \to \mathbb{Z}.\ (rec\text{-}add\text{-}prop(m)\ g)$
>
> (4) $plus(m) := \iota(\mathbb{Z} \to \mathbb{Z}, rec\text{-}add\text{-}prop(m), rec\text{-}add\text{-}lem(m)) : \mathbb{Z} \to \mathbb{Z}$
> Notation : $+_m$ for $plus(m)$

Figure 14.11 Addition $+_m : \mathbb{Z} \to \mathbb{Z}$ in λD

Now we are in the position to define the *binary* plus-operation; see line (1) of Figure 14.12. In lines (2) and (3), the recursive equations for $+$ are expressed, which can be *derived* since $+_m$ has been defined as *the* function satisfying *rec-add-prop*. Line (4) contains the consequence that we have discussed above. We leave the proof terms in lines (2) to (4) to the reader (Exercise 14.11).

(1) $+ := \lambda x : \mathbb{Z}.\ \lambda y : \mathbb{Z}.\ (+_x\, y) : \mathbb{Z} \to \mathbb{Z} \to \mathbb{Z}$
  Notation : $x + y$ for $+\, x\, y$

> $\boxed{x : \mathbb{Z}}$
>
> (2) $plus\text{-}i(x) := \ldots : x + 0 =_{\mathbb{Z}} x$
>
> > $\boxed{y : \mathbb{Z}}$
> >
> > (3) $plus\text{-}ii(x, y) := \ldots : x + s\,y =_{\mathbb{Z}} s(x + y)$
> >
> > (4) $plus\text{-}iii(x, y) := \ldots : x + p\,y =_{\mathbb{Z}} p(x + y)$

Figure 14.12 Properties of addition in $\mathbb{Z}$, formalised in λD

14.5 An example of a basic computation in λD

In order to show how computations are executed on this fundamental level, we give a formal λD-proof for the statement that $1 + 2$ equals 3. This is not simple (see Figure 14.13). For *eq-refl*, *eq-trans* and *eq-cong*$_1$, see Figures 12.2, 12.12 and 12.5, respectively.

In the proof, there are only three really interesting lines, namely lines (2), (4) and (5), in which we appeal to the two definition lines for addition, with constants *plus-i* and *plus-ii* (see Figure 14.12). The other eight lines in the proof are meant to establish the necessary 'administration' related to the naming of numbers 1, 2 and 3, and to the use of reflexivity, transitivity and congruence as properties of equality.

Notation 14.5.1 *Since equality of numbers concerns integers only in the remainder of this book, we simply write '=' instead of '$=_{\mathbb{Z}}$' in the λD-texts to come.*

(i) $1 := s\,0 : \mathbb{Z}$

(ii) $2 := s\,1 : \mathbb{Z}$

(iii) $3 := s\,2 : \mathbb{Z}$

(1) $a_1 := eq\text{-}refl(\mathbb{Z}, 1+2) : 1+2 = 1+s1$

(2) $a_2 := plus\text{-}ii(1,1) : 1+s1 = s(1+1)$

(3) $a_3 := eq\text{-}refl(\mathbb{Z}, s(1+1)) : s(1+1) = s(1+s0)$

(4) $a_4 := eq\text{-}cong_1(\mathbb{Z}, \mathbb{Z}, s, 1+s0, s(1+0), plus\text{-}ii(1,0)) :$
       $s(1+s0) = s(s(1+0))$

(5) $a_5 := eq\text{-}cong_1(\mathbb{Z}, \mathbb{Z}, \lambda n : \mathbb{Z}.\, s(s(n)), 1+0, 1, plus\text{-}i(1)) :$
       $s(s(1+0)) = s(s\,1)$

(6) $a_6 := eq\text{-}refl(\mathbb{Z}, s(s\,1)) : s(s(1)) = 3$

(7) $a_7 := eq\text{-}trans(\mathbb{Z}, 1+2, 1+s1, s(1+1), a_1, a_2) : 1+2 = s(1+1)$

(8) $a_8 := eq\text{-}trans(\mathbb{Z}, 1+2, s(1+1), s(1+s0), a_7, a_3) : 1+2 = s(1+s0)$

(9) $a_9 := eq\text{-}trans(\mathbb{Z}, 1+2, s(1+s0), s(s(1+0)), a_8, a_4) : 1+2 = s(s(1+0))$

(10) $a_{10} := eq\text{-}trans(\mathbb{Z}, 1+2, s(s(1+0)), s(s\,1), a_9, a_5) : 1+2 = s(s1)$

(11) $a_{11} := eq\text{-}trans(\mathbb{Z}, 1+2, s(s\,1), 3, a_{10}, a_6) : 1+2 = 3$

Figure 14.13 A proof in λD that $1+2 = 3$

A condensed version of the proof reads as follows:

$$1+2 \overset{(1)}{=} 1+s1 \overset{(2)}{=} s(1+1) \overset{(3)}{=} s(1+s0) \overset{(4)}{=} s(s(1+0)) \overset{(5)}{=} s(s(1)) \overset{(6)}{=} 3.$$

The lines (1), (3) and (6) use reflexivity of equality, together with the *definitions* in lines (i) to (iii), which imply that

- $s\,1 \overset{\Delta}{=} 2$, hence $1+2 = 1+s1$,
- $1 \overset{\Delta}{=} s\,0$, hence $s(1+1) = s(1+s0)$, and
- $s(s(1)) \overset{\Delta}{=} 3$, respectively.

The underlying derivation rule is *(conv)* in all three cases.

The conclusions based on the transitivity of equality (lines (7) to (11)) are straightforward – albeit annoying.

Remark 14.5.2 *A human text writer would immediately (even without mentioning this) infer $A = G$ from the chain of equalities $A = B = C = D = E = F = G$ (see above).*

But formally, we have to do this step by step:

– from $A = B$ and $B = C$, follows $A = C$ (line (7));

– *from $A = C$ and $C = D$, follows $A = D$ (line (8)); and so on, until*
– *from $A = F$ and $F = G$, follows $A = G$ (line (11)).*

This makes the derivation in Figure 14.13 rather lengthy.

It might help to generalise transitivity (eq-trans) to several lemmas for many-fold transitivity, expressing e.g. that:

– *Lemma eq-trans-4. From $A = B = C = D$ follows $A = D$;*
– *Lemma eq-trans-5. From $A = B = C = D = E$ follows $A = E$; and so on, to a reasonable limit.*

(Find out yourself how, for example, eq-trans-4 can be defined by a double use of eq-trans.)

With eq-trans-7, we can condense lines (7) to (11) into one line, of the form: eq-trans-7(...) : $1 + 2 = 3$.

14.6 Arithmetical laws for addition

We continue with an exposition in λD-style of several arithmetical laws concerning addition. First, as a preparation for the proof that $+$ is a commutative operation, we establish the 'reversals' of *plus-i*, *plus-ii* and *plus-iii* as defined in Figure 14.12. The proofs of parts (a) and (b) are by (symmetric) induction, hence based on the axiom *ax-int$_2$* (Figure 14.4) for integers. In order to give a good impression of how this symmetric induction works, we spell out these induction proofs in words. We leave it to the reader to provide the corresponding λD-proofs.

Lemma 14.6.1 *(a)* $\forall x : \mathbb{Z} . (0 + x = x)$,
  (b) $\forall x, y : \mathbb{Z} . (s\,x + y = s(x + y))$,
  (c) $\forall x, y : \mathbb{Z} . (p\,x + y = p(x + y))$.

Proof (a) We use symmetric induction for integers.
Take $P \equiv \lambda x : \mathbb{Z} . (0 + x = x)$, then:

(1) $P\,0$ because $0 + 0 = 0$ by *plus-i*.
(2) Induction hypothesis: $P\,x$, i.e. $0 + x = x$.
   Then $P(s\,x)$, since $0 + s\,x = s(0 + x) = s\,x$, by *plus-ii* and the induction hypothesis, respectively.
   Also $P(p\,x)$, since $0 + p\,x = p(0 + x) = p\,x$, by *plus-iii* and the induction hypothesis.
   Hence: $\forall x : \mathbb{Z} . (P\,x \Rightarrow (P(s\,x) \land P(p\,x)))$.

Final conclusion by *ax-int$_2$*: $\forall x : \mathbb{Z} . (P\,x)$, i.e. $\forall x : \mathbb{Z} . (0 + x = x)$.

(b) Let x be fixed in $\mathbb{Z}$. We proceed by symmetric induction on y in $\mathbb{Z}$. Let $Q := \lambda y : \mathbb{Z} . (s\,x + y = s(x + y))$. Then:

(1) $Q\,0$, since $s\,x + 0 = s\,x = s(x + 0)$ by *plus-i* (twice).
(2) Induction hypothesis: $Q\,y$, i.e. $s\,x + y = s(x + y)$.

Then $Q(s\,y)$, since $s\,x + s\,y = s(s\,x + y) = s(s(x + y)) = s(x + s\,y)$, by *plus-ii*, induction hypothesis and *plus-ii*, respectively.

Also $Q(p\,y)$, since on the one hand: $s\,x + p\,y = p(s\,x + y) = p(s(x + y)) = x + y$ by *plus-iii*, induction hypothesis and *p-s*-annihilation. On the other hand: $s(x + p\,y) = s(p(x + y)) = x + y$, by *plus-iii* and *s-p*-annihilation. It follows that $s\,x + p\,y = s(x + p\,y)$, i.e. $Q(p\,y)$.

Hence $\forall y : \mathbb{Z} . \ (Q\,y \Rightarrow (Q(s\,y) \wedge Q(p\,y)))$.

Conclusion by induction $(ax\text{-}int_2)$: $\forall y : \mathbb{Z} . \ (s\,x + y = s(x + y))$.
Final conclusion by $\forall$-*in*: $\forall x, y : \mathbb{Z} . \ (s\,x + y = s(x + y))$.

(c) We have shown in Section 14.4 that $+_m(p\,n) = p(+_m(n))$ is a consequence of $+_m(s\,n) = s(+_m(n))$. Similarly, $\forall x, y : \mathbb{Z} . \ (p\,x + y = p(x + y))$ is a consequence of (b) (show it yourself). $\qquad\square$

We leave it to the reader (Exercise 14.12 (a)) to give a proof of the *commutativity* of addition; that is:

Lemma 14.6.2 $\quad \forall x, y : \mathbb{Z} . \ (x + y = y + x)$.

We give two more properties of addition:

Lemma 14.6.3 $\quad$ *(a)* $\forall x, y : \mathbb{Z} . \ (p\,x + s\,y = x + y)$,
$\quad$ *(b)* $\forall x, y : \mathbb{Z} . \ (s\,x + p\,y = x + y)$.

Proof (a) We have: $p\,x + s\,y = p(x + s\,y) = p(s(x + y)) = x + y$, by Lemma 14.6.1 (c), *plus-ii* and annihilation.

(b) Prove it yourself. $\qquad\square$

Addition is also *associative*:

Lemma 14.6.4 $\quad \forall x, y, z : \mathbb{Z} . \ (x + (y + z) = (x + y) + z)$.

The proof of associativity is straightforward and therefore omitted. Do it yourself (Exercise 14.12 (b)).

We continue with the so-called Cancellation Laws, which allow us to 'strike out' an identical added value at both sides of an equality:

Lemma 14.6.5 $\quad$ *(Cancellation Laws for addition)*
$\quad$ *(a) (Right Cancellation)* $\forall x, y, z : \mathbb{Z} . \ (x + z = y + z \Rightarrow x = y)$,
$\quad$ *(b) (Left Cancellation)* $\forall x, y, z : \mathbb{Z} . \ (x + y = x + z \Rightarrow y = z)$.

A proof of the Right Cancellation Law is left to the reader (Exercise 14.12 (c)). The Left Cancellation Law then follows directly from the commutativity of addition (Lemma 14.6.2).

Note that the converses of both Cancellation Laws also hold:

$$\forall x, y, z : \mathbb{Z} . \ (x = y \Rightarrow x + z = y + z)$$

and

$$\forall x, y, z : \mathbb{Z} . \ (y = z \Rightarrow x + y = x + z),$$

since both are a consequence of the congruence property of functions (see Figure 12.6).

We list most of the extra results obtained in this section, in λD-format but without proof objects, in Figure 14.14.

	$\boxed{x : \mathbb{Z}}$
(1)	$plus\text{-}i\text{-}alt(x) \ := \ \ldots \ : \ 0 + x = x$
	$\boxed{y : \mathbb{Z}}$
(2)	$plus\text{-}ii\text{-}alt(x, y) \ := \ \ldots \ : \ s \, x + y = s(x + y)$ ·
(3)	$plus\text{-}iii\text{-}alt(x, y) \ := \ \ldots \ : \ p \, x + y = p(x + y)$
(4)	$comm\text{-}add(x, y) \ := \ \ldots \ : \ x + y = y + x$
	$\boxed{z : \mathbb{Z}}$
(5)	$assoc\text{-}add(x, y, z) \ := \ \ldots \ : \ x + (y + z) = (x + y) + z$
(6)	$right\text{-}canc\text{-}add(x, y, z) \ := \ \ldots \ : \ x + z = y + z \Rightarrow x = y$
(7)	$left\text{-}canc\text{-}add(x, y, z) \ := \ \ldots \ : \ x + y = x + z \Rightarrow y = z$

Figure 14.14 More properties of addition in $\mathbb{Z}$

14.7 Closure under addition for natural and negative numbers

We now focus on an important property of addition for elements of the subset $\mathbb{N}$, namely the nice property that $\mathbb{N}$ is *closed* under addition; that is:

Lemma 14.7.1 *(Closure of* $\mathbb{N}$ *under addition)*
$\forall x, y : \mathbb{Z} . \ ((x \ \varepsilon \ \mathbb{N} \wedge y \ \varepsilon \ \mathbb{N}) \Rightarrow x + y \ \varepsilon \ \mathbb{N}).$

Proof The proof is by induction for the *natural* numbers (*nat-ind*; see Figure 14.8). We take x fixed and apply induction on y. Therefore we first reformulate Lemma 14.7.1 in order to facilitate induction (check that the two expressions are equivalent):

To prove: $\forall x : \mathbb{Z} . \ (x \ \varepsilon \ \mathbb{N} \Rightarrow \forall y : \mathbb{Z} . \ (y \ \varepsilon \ \mathbb{N} \Rightarrow x + y \ \varepsilon \ \mathbb{N})).$

So take x of type $\mathbb{Z}$ fixed, and assume $x \ \varepsilon \ \mathbb{N}$. To prove:

$\forall y : \mathbb{Z} . \ (y \ \varepsilon \ \mathbb{N} \Rightarrow x + y \ \varepsilon \ \mathbb{N}).$

For the proof by induction on y, we consider an appropriate induction predicate, viz. $P := \lambda y : \mathbb{Z} . \ (x + y \ \varepsilon \ \mathbb{N}).$

We now obtain:

(1) $P\,0$, since $x + 0 = x$ and $x\ \varepsilon\ \mathbb{N}$, by assumption.

(2) Let $y\ :\ \mathbb{Z}$ such that $y\ \varepsilon\ \mathbb{N}$ and $P\,y$. To prove: $P(s\,y)$. Now $P\,y$ means $x + y\ \varepsilon\ \mathbb{N}$; then also $s(x + y)\ \varepsilon\ \mathbb{N}$ by *clos-prop* (Figure 14.5), so $x + s\,y\ \varepsilon\ \mathbb{N}$, which is $P(s\,y)$.

Hence, $\forall y\ :\ \mathbb{Z}.\ (y\ \varepsilon\ \mathbb{N} \Rightarrow (P\,y \Rightarrow P(s\,y)))$.

By *nat-ind* we may conclude that $\forall y\ :\ \mathbb{Z}.\ (y\ \varepsilon\ \mathbb{N} \Rightarrow P\,y)$, as desired. $\qquad\square$

We formalise this proof and its conclusion in Figure 14.15, in the style to which we are now used: many proof objects are not actually given, but only hinted at. Note that P depends on the 'fixed' x: the parameter list, (x), has been suppressed in accordance with Notation 11.7.1.

$\boxed{x : \mathbb{Z}}$

(1) $\quad P^{\dagger} := \lambda y : \mathbb{Z}.\ (x + y\ \varepsilon\ \mathbb{N})\ :\ \mathbb{Z} \to *_p$

$\quad\boxed{u\ :\ x\ \varepsilon\ \mathbb{N}}$

(2) $\quad\quad a_2 := \ldots$ **use** *plus-i* **and** *eq-sym* $\ldots\ :\ x = x + 0$

(3) $\quad\quad a_3 := \ldots$ **use** *eq-subs* **on** a_2 **and** u $\ldots\ :\ P\,0$

$\quad\quad\boxed{y : \mathbb{Z}\ |\ v\ :\ y\ \varepsilon\ \mathbb{N}}$

$\quad\quad\quad\boxed{w : P\,y}$

(4) $\quad\quad\quad\quad a_4 := \textit{clos-prop}\ (x + y)\ w\ :\ s(x + y)\ \varepsilon\ \mathbb{N}$

(5) $\quad\quad\quad\quad a_5 := \ldots$ **use** *plus-ii* **and** *eq-sym* $\ldots\ :\ s(x + y) = x + s\,y$

(6) $\quad\quad\quad\quad a_6 := \ldots$ **use** *eq-subs* **on** a_5 **and** a_4 $\ldots\ :\ P\,(s\,y)$

(7) $\quad\quad\quad a_7 := \ldots$ **use** $\Rightarrow$*-in* **twice, and** $\forall$*-in,* **on** a_6 $\ldots\ :$

$\quad\quad\quad\quad \forall y : \mathbb{Z}.\ (y\ \varepsilon\ \mathbb{N} \Rightarrow (P\,y \Rightarrow P\,(s\,y)))$

(8) $\quad\quad\quad a_8 := \ldots$ **use** $\wedge$*-in* **on** a_3 **and** a_7, **and** $\Rightarrow$*-el* **on** *nat-ind*(P) $\ldots\ :$

$\quad\quad\quad\quad \forall y : \mathbb{Z}.\ (y\ \varepsilon\ \mathbb{N} \Rightarrow x + y\ \varepsilon\ \mathbb{N})$

(9) $\quad a_9 := \ldots$ **use** $\Rightarrow$*-in* **and** $\forall$*-in* **on** a_8 $\ldots\ :$

$\quad\quad \forall x : \mathbb{Z}.\ (x\ \varepsilon\ \mathbb{N} \Rightarrow \forall y : \mathbb{Z}.\ (y\ \varepsilon\ \mathbb{N} \Rightarrow x + y\ \varepsilon\ \mathbb{N}))$

$\boxed{x, y : \mathbb{Z}\ |\ u\ :\ x\ \varepsilon\ \mathbb{N}\ |\ v\ :\ y\ \varepsilon\ \mathbb{N}}$

(10) $\quad \textit{plus-clos-nat} := a_9\ x\ u\ y\ v\ :\ x + y\ \varepsilon\ \mathbb{N}$

†*parameters suppressed*

Figure 14.15 Closure property of addition in $\mathbb{N}$

We also give the fully formalised version, so without hints and with complete parameter lists. This we do in Appendix C, Section C.1. Thus we enable the reader to compare the complete and the shortened versions.

There is a companion to the closure of the natural numbers under addition, namely the closure of the *negative* numbers under addition. In order to prove this, we first give the following characterisation of negative numbers:

Lemma 14.7.2   *(Characterisation of negative numbers)*
  $\forall x : \mathbb{Z}. (neg(x) \Leftrightarrow \exists y : \mathbb{Z}. (pos(y) \wedge x + y = 0))$.

We give the proof below as an extra exercise with symmetric induction for integer numbers (see Figure 14.4). Since it is a bit involved, we suffice with a proof *in words*.

Proof   *(Part I: left to right)* $\forall x : \mathbb{Z}. (neg(x) \Rightarrow \exists y : \mathbb{Z}. (pos(y) \wedge x + y = 0))$?
  The induction predicate P is $\lambda x : \mathbb{Z}. (neg(x) \Rightarrow \exists y : \mathbb{Z}. (pos(y) \wedge x + y = 0))$.

(1) $P\,0$? Yes, since $0 \,\varepsilon\, \mathbb{N}$, hence $\neg(neg(0))$.

(2) $\forall x : \mathbb{Z}. (P\,x \Rightarrow (P(s\,x) \wedge P(p\,x)))$? Assume $x : \mathbb{Z}$ and $P\,x$.

  (a) To prove: $P(s\,x)$.
  So assume $neg(s\,x)$. Is there a $z : \mathbb{Z}$ such that $pos(z)$ and $s\,x + z = 0$?
  Since $neg(s\,x)$, also $neg(p(s\,x))$ (Lemma 14.3.2 (c)), so $neg(x)$. From the induction hypothesis $P\,x$ then follows: there is $y : \mathbb{Z}$ such that $pos(y)$ and $x + y = 0$, hence $s\,x + p\,y = 0$ by Lemma 14.6.3 (b).
  It follows that $p\,y \neq 0$, since otherwise $s\,x = 0$, contradicting $neg(s\,x)$. Lemma 14.3.2 (b) implies (take $p\,y$ for x) that from $pos(y)$ and $p\,y \neq 0$ we can infer that $pos(p\,y)$.
  Hence, $p\,y$ is a witness showing that $\exists z : \mathbb{Z}. (pos(z) \wedge s\,x + z = 0)$.

  (b) To prove: $P(p\,x)$.
  So assume $neg(p\,x)$. Is there a $z : \mathbb{Z}$ such that $pos(z)$ and $p\,x + z = 0$?
  We can use Lemma 14.3.2 (c) to derive $x = 0 \vee neg(x)$. We continue with using $\vee$-*el*:
  Case $x = 0$: then $p\,x + s\,0 = x + 0 = 0$ by Lemma 14.6.3 (a), and $pos(s\,0)$, so $s\,0$ is a witness for $\exists z : \mathbb{Z}. (pos(z) \wedge p\,x + z = 0)$.
  Case $neg(x)$: then by induction hypothesis $P\,x$ there is $y : \mathbb{Z}$ such that $pos(y)$ and $x + y = 0$. Hence, $pos(s\,y)$ (Lemma 14.3.2 (b)) and $p\,x + s\,y = 0$ (Lemma 14.6.3 (a)), so $s\,y$ is a witness for $\exists z : \mathbb{Z}. (pos(z) \wedge p\,x + z = 0)$.

  So altogether, with $\vee$-*el* we obtain $\exists z : \mathbb{Z}. (pos(z) \wedge p\,x + z = 0)$.

  (Part II: right to left) $\forall x : \mathbb{Z}. ((\exists y : \mathbb{Z}. (pos(y) \wedge x + y = 0)) \Rightarrow neg(x))$?
  Left to the reader (Exercise 14.13).   □

As a consequence, we have the closure property for negative integers:

Lemma 14.7.3   *(Closure for negative integers)*
  $\forall x, y : \mathbb{Z}. (neg(x) \wedge neg(y) \Rightarrow neg(x + y))$.

Proof Let x and y be negative integers. Then by Lemma 14.7.2:

- there is $z_1 : \mathbb{Z}$ such that $pos(z_1)$ and $x + z_1 = 0$, and
- there is $z_2 : \mathbb{Z}$ such that $pos(z_2)$ and $y + z_2 = 0$.

Use commutativity and associativity of addition to get $(x+y)+(z_1+z_2) = 0$.

From $pos(z_1)$ and $pos(z_2)$ follows $p\, z_1\ \varepsilon\ \mathbb{N}$ (so $s(p\, z_1) = z_1\ \varepsilon\ \mathbb{N}$ by *clos-prop*) and $p\, z_2\ \varepsilon\ \mathbb{N}$. Hence, by Lemma 14.7.1, $z_1 + p\, z_2\ \varepsilon\ \mathbb{N}$, so $p(z_1 + z_2)\ \varepsilon\ \mathbb{N}$, i.e. $pos(z_1 + z_2)$. It follows that there is $z : \mathbb{Z}$ (namely $z_1 + z_2$) such that $pos(z)$ and $(x + y) + z = 0$. So $neg(x + y)$ by Lemma 14.7.2. $\qquad\square$

14.8 Integer subtraction

After we have studied addition for integers, it is natural to consider its inverse: subtraction. Note that subtraction is easier for integers than for natural numbers: each pair of integers has a difference in $\mathbb{Z}$, but not every pair of natural numbers has a difference in $\mathbb{N}$.

The *difference* of x and y in $\mathbb{Z}$ is a unique number, namely the number z such that when y is added to it, gives x:

$$x - y := \iota_{z:\mathbb{Z}}(z + y = x).$$

Since the ι is part of our λD-syntax (see Section 12.6), we define subtraction in this manner, but first we have to prove the uniqueness of such a z:

Lemma 14.8.1 *(Uniqueness of difference)*
$\forall x, y : \mathbb{Z}.\ \exists^1 z : \mathbb{Z}.\ (z + y = x).$

We prove this lemma below in the informal style to which we are now used. (It can be transformed relatively easily into a formal λD-derivation.) As expected, we split the proof of this lemma into two parts: first we show existence, then uniqueness of existence.

Proof (Part I: Existence) $\forall x, y : \mathbb{Z}.\ \exists z : \mathbb{Z}.\ (z + y = x)$?

Take x in $\mathbb{Z}$ fixed; we proceed by symmetric induction on y. As a shorthand, we write P for $\lambda y : \mathbb{Z}.\ \exists z : \mathbb{Z}.\ (z + y = x)$. To prove: $\forall y : \mathbb{Z}.\ (P y)$.

(1) $P\, 0$? Since $x + 0 = x$, we have by $\exists$-*in* that $\exists z : \mathbb{Z}.\ (z + 0 = x)$. Hence $P\, 0$.

(2) $\forall y : \mathbb{Z}.\ (P y \Rightarrow (P(s\, y) \wedge P(p\, y)))$? Assume $y : \mathbb{Z}$ and $P y$. To prove: $P(s\, y)$ (i.e. $\exists z' : \mathbb{Z}.\ (z' + s\, y = x)$) and $P(p\, y)$ (i.e. $\exists z'' : \mathbb{Z}.\ (z'' + p\, y = x)$).

We assumed $P y$, which means $\exists z : \mathbb{Z}.\ (z + y = x)$. Use $\exists$-*el*, or in words: take a z in $\mathbb{Z}$ with $z + y = x$.

Now $p\, z + s\, y = z + y$ and $s\, z + p\, y = z + y$ (see Lemma 14.6.3 (b) and (c)). Hence we found the z' such that $z' + s\, y = x$ (viz. $z' = p\, z$) and the z'' such that $z'' + p\, y = x$ (viz. $z'' = s\, z$). Consequently $P(s\, y)$ and $P(p\, y)$ hold, as desired.

Hence, by symmetric induction, $\forall y : \mathbb{Z} . (P y)$.
Final conclusion: $\forall x, y : \mathbb{Z} . \exists z : \mathbb{Z} . (z + y = x)$.

(*Part II: Uniqueness of existence*) $\forall x, y : \mathbb{Z} . \exists^1 z : \mathbb{Z} . (z + y = x)$?
Let x and y be in $\mathbb{Z}$. Assume z_1 and z_2 in $\mathbb{Z}$ such that $z_1 + y = x$ and $z_2 + y = x$.
Obviously, $z_1 + y = z_2 + y$, so (by Right Cancellation, Lemma 14.6.5 (a)) $z_1 = z_2$.
This implies the uniqueness of the z such that $z + y = x$ (cf. Section 12.6). □

The corresponding λD-proof is straightforward, but slightly involved because
of the instances of $\exists$-*in* and $\exists$-*el*. We shall not give it here.

Since $x - y$ is *the* z in $\mathbb{Z}$ such that $z + y = x$, it follows from *ι-prop* (cf.
Figure 12.16) that $x - y$ satisfies the last-mentioned equation; hence we have:

Lemma 14.8.2 $\forall x, y : \mathbb{Z} . ((x - y) + y = x)$.

The following counterpart is an easy consequence:

Lemma 14.8.3 $\forall x, y : \mathbb{Z} . ((x + y) - y = x)$.

Proof   Since $((x + y) - y) + y = x + y$ by Lemma 14.8.2, the result follows by
Right Cancellation.   □

In Figure 14.16 we record all this in λD-format.

$\boxed{x : \mathbb{Z}}$

$\quad\boxed{y : \mathbb{Z}}$

(1) $uni\text{-}dif(x, y) := \ \ldots\ \textbf{see Lemma 14.8.1}\ \ldots\ : \ \exists^1 z : \mathbb{Z} . (z + y = x)$

(2) $minus(x, y) := \iota_{z : \mathbb{Z}}^{uni\text{-}dif(x,y)} (z + y = x) : \mathbb{Z}$

$\quad\ \ \textbf{Notation} : \ x - y \ \textbf{for}\ minus(x, y)$

(3) $subtr\text{-}prop_1(x, y) := \iota\text{-}prop(\mathbb{Z}, \lambda z : \mathbb{Z} . (z + y = x), uni\text{-}dif(x, y)) \ :$
$\qquad\qquad (x - y) + y = x$

(4) $subtr\text{-}prop_2(x, y) := \ \ldots\ \textbf{see Lemma 14.8.3}\ \ldots\ : \ (x + y) - y = x$

Figure 14.16 Subtraction of integers

It follows from Lemma 14.8.2 that, for every x in $\mathbb{Z}$: $(x - x) + x = x$. And
since we also know that $0 + x = x$ (Lemma 14.6.1 (a)), we may conclude that
$\forall x : \mathbb{Z} . ((x - x) + x = 0 + x)$, by symmetry and transitivity of $=$. Hence, by
Right Cancellation:

Lemma 14.8.4 $\forall x : \mathbb{Z} . (x - x = 0)$.

Another consequence of Lemma 14.8.2 is:

Lemma 14.8.5 $\forall x : \mathbb{Z} . (x - 0 = x)$.

The proof is easy: $x - 0 = (x - 0) + 0 = x$, by *plus-i* and Lemma 14.8.2.

The same Lemma 14.8.2 can also be used for proofs of the following counterparts of *plus-ii* and *plus-iii*:

Lemma 14.8.6 *(a)* $\forall x, y : \mathbb{Z} . \ (x - sy = p(x - y))$,
(b) $\forall x, y : \mathbb{Z} . \ (x - py = s(x - y))$.

Proof of part (a):

– First consider the left-hand side: $x - sy$. It is a subtraction, so its characteristic property (cf. Lemma 14.8.2) is that adding sy to it delivers x:
$$(x - sy) + sy = x.$$

– Adding sy to the right-hand side of the equation gives $p(x - y) + sy$, which may be rewritten by Lemmas 14.6.3 (a) and 14.8.2 to:
$$p(x - y) + sy = (x - y) + y = x.$$

Combining this, we get that $(x - sy) + sy = p(x - y) + sy$, so by Right Cancellation: $x - sy = p(x - y)$.

The proof of part (b) is similar. □

Counterparts of *plus-ii-alt* and *plus-iii-alt* are:

Lemma 14.8.7 *(a)* $\forall x, y : \mathbb{Z} . \ (sx - y = s(x - y))$,
(b) $\forall x, y : \mathbb{Z} . \ (px - y = p(x - y))$.

Prove this lemma yourself.

As a consequence (Exercise 14.15 (a)), we have the following facts, which will not come as a surprise (recall from Figure 14.13 that 1 has been defined as $s\,0$):

Lemma 14.8.8 *(a)* $\forall x : \mathbb{Z} . \ (x + 1 = sx)$,
(b) $\forall x : \mathbb{Z} . \ (x - 1 = px)$.

There are many arithmetical lemmas concerning addition and subtraction, which can be proved using our definitions. Each new lemma, once proved, has the potential to simplify proofs of further lemmas and theorems. If one desires to formally develop a substantial body of arithmetic in λD-style, it is worthwhile to formulate and prove a considerable number of these arithmetical laws. (See also some of the exercises at the end of the present chapter.) An example are the Cancellation Laws for subtraction, which are similar to the ones for addition (Lemma 14.6.5):

Lemma 14.8.9 *(Cancellation Laws for subtraction)*
(a) (Right Cancellation) $\forall x, y, z : \mathbb{Z} . \ (x - z = y - z \Rightarrow x = y)$,
(b) (Left Cancellation) $\forall x, y, z : \mathbb{Z} . \ (x - y = x - z \Rightarrow y = z)$.

Proof The proof of part (a) is easy: if $x - z = y - z$, then by the congruence property for plus: $(x - z) + z = (y - z) + z$, hence by Lemma 14.8.2 (twice): $x = y$.

The proof of part (b) is more complicated; it is left to the reader (Exercise 14.15 (b)). □

The following lemma contains variants of associativity (Lemma 14.6.4), but now with subtraction involved. Prove it yourself (Exercise 14.16), following the strategy employed in the proof of Lemma 14.8.6.

Lemma 14.8.10 (a) $\forall x, y, z : \mathbb{Z}.\ (x + (y - z)\ =\ (x + y) - z)$,
(b) $\forall x, y, z : \mathbb{Z}.\ (x - (y + z)\ =\ (x - y) - z)$,
(c) $\forall x, y, z : \mathbb{Z}.\ (x - (y - z)\ =\ (x - y) + z)$.

Finally, we mention and prove the following lemma, which we can use well in the following section:

Lemma 14.8.11 $\forall x, y : \mathbb{Z}.\ (pos(x - y) \Leftrightarrow neg(y - x))$.

Proof Let $x, y : \mathbb{Z}$.
(*Part I: left to right*) Assume $pos(x - y)$, so $p(x - y)\ \varepsilon\ \mathbb{N}$.
Assume $y - x\ \varepsilon\ \mathbb{N}$. Then by closure, $p(x - y) + (y - x)\ \varepsilon\ \mathbb{N}$. After some calculational steps, using the lemmas given earlier, we obtain from this: $p\,0\ \varepsilon\ \mathbb{N}$, contradicting *ax-int₃*. Hence $neg(y - x)$.
(*Part II: right to left*) Assume $neg(y - x)$.
Then by Lemma 14.7.2, there is $z : \mathbb{Z}$ such that $pos(z)$ and $(y - x) + z = 0$. Calculation (do it yourself) leads to $z = x - y$. Hence, $pos(x - y)$. □

14.9 The opposite of an integer

The minus-sign, employed for subtraction of two integers, is also used as a sign for constructing the *opposite* of an integer: to make $-m$ out of m. This is clearly 'overloading' of the symbol '$-$'. In practice, however, this is no problem, since the parsing of an arithmetical expression should make it clear whether an occurrence of a minus-sign is meant as a *binary* symbol (denoting subtraction) or a *unary* one (for 'taking-the-opposite').

A standard definition for the opposite is: $-x$ is the number that, when added to x, delivers 0. (It is not hard to show that there always is such a number, and that it is unique; Exercise 14.17.) Another approach is to define the opposite as a special case of subtraction, namely: $-x$ is $0 - x$. We follow the latter option, which is easier to implement in λD (see Figure 14.17).

Again, there are many basic arithmetical laws that can be proved now, about (a combination of) addition, subtraction and opposites of integers. We only discuss a few of them in Lemma 14.9.1, but a useful 'library' of arithmetical facts should contain many more. (See again the exercises for some other laws of arithmetic.) Proofs are only sketched; the details and λD-versions of the proofs are left to the reader.

Lemma 14.9.1 *(a)* $\forall x : \mathbb{Z} . ((-x) + x = 0)$,
(b) $\forall x, y : \mathbb{Z} . (x + (-y) = x - y)$,
(c) $\forall x, y : \mathbb{Z} . (-(x + y) = (-x) - y)$.

Proof sketch
(a) $(-x) + x = (0 - x) + x = 0$ by *subtr-prop₁* (see Figure 14.16).

(b) $(x + (-y)) + y = x + ((-y) + y) = x + 0 = x$ by associativity and part (a), and $(x - y) + y = x$ by *subtr-prop₁*; use Right Cancellation.

(c) $(-(x + y)) + (x + y) = 0$, and $((-x) - y) + (x + y) = ((-x) - y) + (y + x) = (((-x) - y) + y) + x = (-x) + x = 0$ by *subtr-prop₁* and part (a); use Right Cancellation. $\qquad\square$

The equalities mentioned in Lemma 14.9.1 are entered in Figure 14.17.

$$
\begin{array}{l|l}
\hline
\multicolumn{2}{l}{\boxed{x : \mathbb{Z}}} \\
(1) & opp(x) := 0 - x \ : \ \mathbb{Z} \\
& \text{Notation}: \ -x \text{ for } opp(x) \\
(2) & a_2(x) := \ \ldots \ : \ (-x) + x = 0 \\
& \quad \boxed{y : \mathbb{Z}} \\
(3) & \quad a_3(x, y) := \ \ldots \ : \ x + (-y) = x - y \\
(4) & \quad a_4(x, y) := \ \ldots \ : \ -(x + y) = (-x) - y \\
\hline
\end{array}
$$

Figure 14.17 The opposite of an integer number and some lemmas

It will turn out in the following chapter that when dealing with an example of a mathematical theorem of importance ('Bézout's Lemma'), we need more properties concerning the opposite of an integer. Therefore, we list some fundamental properties of opposites in the following lemmas.

Informal proofs of these lemmas, and formal proofs in λD, are left to the reader (cf. Exercise 14.19).

Lemma 14.9.2 *(a)* $-0 = 0$,
(b) $\forall x : \mathbb{Z} . (-(-x) = x)$,
(c) $\forall x : \mathbb{Z} . (x = 0 \Leftrightarrow -x = 0)$.

Lemma 14.9.3 *(a)* $\forall x : \mathbb{Z} . (-(s\,x) = p(-x))$,
(b) $\forall x : \mathbb{Z} . (-(p\,x) = s(-x))$.

We conclude this section with a number of useful lemmas. In the first lemma, we make good use of Lemma 14.8.11.

Lemma 14.9.4   *(a)* $\forall x : \mathbb{Z} . \, (pos(x) \Leftrightarrow neg(-x))$,
   (b) $\forall x : \mathbb{Z} . \, (neg(x) \Leftrightarrow pos(-x))$.

Proof of part (b): $neg(x)$ if and only if $neg(x-0)$ by Lemma 14.8.5, if and only if $pos(0-x)$ by Lemma 14.8.11, if and only if $pos(-x)$ by definition of $-x$.

Part (a) is an easy consequence (use Lemma 14.9.2 (b)).   □

From *trip* (Figure 14.9) we may now infer:

Lemma 14.9.5   *(a)* $\forall x : \mathbb{Z} . \, (pos(x) \vee pos(-x) \vee x = 0)$,
   (b) $\forall x : \mathbb{Z} . \, (neg(x) \vee neg(-x) \vee x = 0)$.

The following lemma describes a characterising condition, in terms of earlier sections, for the opposite of x to be a natural number.

Lemma 14.9.6 $\forall x : \mathbb{Z} . \, (-x \, \varepsilon \, \mathbb{N} \Leftrightarrow (neg(x) \vee x = 0))$.

Proof   Let $x : \mathbb{Z}$.
   (Part I: left to right) Assume $-x \, \varepsilon \, \mathbb{N}$.
   Assume $x \neq 0$. Then $-x \neq 0$ (see Lemma 14.9.2 (a)), hence $p(-x) \, \varepsilon \, \mathbb{N}$ by Lemma 14.3.1. So $pos(-x)$, hence $neg(x)$ by Lemma 14.9.4.
   So $neg(x) \vee x = 0$ by $\vee$-*in-alt*$_2$.
   (Part II: right to left) Assume $neg(x) \vee x = 0$.
   (1) Case $neg(x)$: then by Lemma 14.9.4 (b): $pos(-x)$, i.e. $p(-x) \, \varepsilon \, \mathbb{N}$. Hence, also $s(p(-x)) = -x \, \varepsilon \, \mathbb{N}$.
   (2) Case $x = 0$: then $-x = 0$ by Lemma 14.9.2 (a), so $-x \, \varepsilon \, \mathbb{N}$.
   So altogether we obtain $-x \, \varepsilon \, \mathbb{N}$ by $\vee$-*el*.   □

Consequences are (Exercise 14.19 (c)):

Lemma 14.9.7   *(a)* $\forall x : \mathbb{Z} . \, (x \, \varepsilon \, \mathbb{N} \vee -x \, \varepsilon \, \mathbb{N})$,
   (b) $\forall x : \mathbb{Z} . \, ((x \, \varepsilon \, \mathbb{N} \wedge -x \, \varepsilon \, \mathbb{N}) \Rightarrow x = 0)$.

Notice that this brings along that $\mathbb{Z}$ consists of all natural numbers together with their opposites, where -0 is the only opposite of a natural number that remains a natural number; just as we had in mind when setting out the formalisation of integers in λD.

14.10 Inequality relations on $\mathbb{Z}$

We now consider the inequality relations $\leq$ and $<$ and how to include them in the λD-version of $\mathbb{Z}$. A standard approach is to define $\leq$ in the following manner:

$$x \leq_{\mathbb{Z}} y := \exists z : \mathbb{Z}. \, (z \; \varepsilon \; \mathbb{N} \wedge x + z = y).$$

An easier way of defining inequalities, without the $\exists$-quantifier, is by making a direct use of subtraction and the natural numbers (see Figure 14.18).

(1) $\leq_{\mathbb{Z}} := \lambda x : \mathbb{Z}. \, \lambda y : \mathbb{Z}. \, (y - x \; \varepsilon \; \mathbb{N}) \; : \; \mathbb{Z} \rightarrow \mathbb{Z} \rightarrow *_p$

     `Notation`: $\; x \leq_{\mathbb{Z}} y$ or $x \leq y$ `for` $\; \leq_{\mathbb{Z}} x \, y$

(2) $<_{\mathbb{Z}} := \lambda x : \mathbb{Z}. \, \lambda y : \mathbb{Z}. \, (x \leq_{\mathbb{Z}} y \wedge x \neq y) \; : \; \mathbb{Z} \rightarrow \mathbb{Z} \rightarrow *_p$

     `Notation`: $\; x <_{\mathbb{Z}} y$ or $x < y$ `for` $\; <_{\mathbb{Z}} x \, y$

Figure 14.18 Inequalities between integer numbers in λD

Again, there are many lemmas about inequalities, containing addition, subtraction and opposites. We restrict ourselves to some examples.

Lemma 14.10.1   *(a)* $\forall x : \mathbb{Z}. \, (x \leq x)$,
   (b) $\forall x, y, z : \mathbb{Z}. \, ((x \leq y \wedge y \leq z) \Rightarrow (x \leq z))$,
   (c) $\forall x, y, z : \mathbb{Z}. \, ((x + z \leq y + z) \Leftrightarrow (x \leq y))$,
   (d) $\forall x, y, z : \mathbb{Z}. \, ((x < y \wedge y \leq z) \Rightarrow (x < z))$,
   (e) $\forall x, y, z : \mathbb{Z}. \, ((x + z < y + z) \Leftrightarrow (x < y))$.

In order to demonstrate how inequalities work in the present setting, we give informal proofs of the first three parts; these proofs can be transposed without too much effort into formal λD-proofs.

Proof   (a) Let $x : \mathbb{Z}$. Then $x \leq x$ if and only if $x - x \; \varepsilon \; \mathbb{N}$, and Lemma 14.8.4 implies that $x - x = 0 \; \varepsilon \; \mathbb{N}$.

(b) Let $x, y, z : \mathbb{Z}$, with $x \leq y$ and $y \leq z$. This means that $y - x \; \varepsilon \; \mathbb{N}$ and $z - y \; \varepsilon \; \mathbb{N}$, so by the closure of $\mathbb{N}$ under addition (Figure 14.15) also $(y - x) + (z - y) \; \varepsilon \; \mathbb{N}$. It is not hard to show that $(y - x) + (z - y) = z - x$ (use e.g. Lemmas 14.6.2, 14.8.10 and 14.8.2). Hence, $x \leq z$.

(c) Let $x, y, z : \mathbb{Z}$, with $x + z \leq y + z$. Then $(y + z) - (x + z) \; \varepsilon \; \mathbb{N}$. We can prove that $(y + z) - (x + z) = y - x$, for example in the following manner: add $x + z$ to both sides, then:

– $((y + z) - (x + z)) + (x + z)$ is equal to $y + z$;
– and $(y - x) + (x + z) = ((y - x) + x) + z$ by Lemma 14.6.4, which is equal to $y + z$ by Lemma 14.8.2.

Hence, Right Cancellation gives the desired equality, hence also $y - x \; \varepsilon \; \mathbb{N}$. This proves $(x + z \leq y + z) \Rightarrow (x \leq y)$.

A proof of the reverse, $(x \leq y) \Rightarrow (x + z \leq y + z)$, follows immediately.

(d), (e) Proofs are left to the reader (Exercise 14.26).   □

It is now straightforward to show that $\leq$ is a partial order (see Figure 8.2) and that $<$ is a strict partial order (see Section 2.5), both on $\mathbb{Z}$. We leave this to the reader.

We can define the related notions $\geq$ and $>$ directly as the reverses of $\leq$ and $<$ (see Figure 14.19).

(1) $\geq_\mathbb{Z} := \lambda x : \mathbb{Z}.\, \lambda y : \mathbb{Z}.\, (y \leq_\mathbb{Z} x) \; : \; \mathbb{Z} \to \mathbb{Z} \to *_p$

      `Notation:` $x \geq_\mathbb{Z} y$ `or` $x \geq y$ `for` $\geq_\mathbb{Z} x\, y$

(2) $>_\mathbb{Z} := \lambda x : \mathbb{Z}.\, \lambda y : \mathbb{Z}.\, (y <_\mathbb{Z} x) \; : \; \mathbb{Z} \to \mathbb{Z} \to *_p$

      `Notation:` $x >_\mathbb{Z} y$ `or` $x > y$ `for` $>_\mathbb{Z} x\, y$

Figure 14.19 More inequalities between integers

The following lemma is a consequence (Exercise 14.27):

Lemma 14.10.2   *(a)* $\forall x : \mathbb{Z}.\, (pos(x) \Leftrightarrow x > 0)$,
  (b) $\forall x : \mathbb{Z}.\, (neg(x) \Leftrightarrow x < 0)$,
  (c) $\forall x : \mathbb{Z}.\, (x < 0 \vee x = 0 \vee x > 0)$.

Finally, we give two examples of the interplay between the inequality relation and the opposites of integers:

Lemma 14.10.3   *(a)* $\forall x, y : \mathbb{Z}.\, (x < y \Leftrightarrow -y < -x)$,
  (b) $\forall x : \mathbb{Z}.\, (x < 0 \Leftrightarrow -x > 0)$.

Again, we give informal proofs in order to demonstrate what the relevant proof steps are (see also Exercise 14.28).

Proof   (a) On the one hand, $x < y$ is equivalent to $(y - x \; \varepsilon \; \mathbb{N}) \wedge (x \neq y)$, and on the other hand, $-y < -x$ is equivalent to $(-x - (-y) \; \varepsilon \; \mathbb{N}) \wedge (-y \neq -x)$. Now it is not hard to show that $y - x = -x - (-y)$ (use a_3 of Figure 14.17, and Lemma 14.9.2 (b)).
Moreover, $x \neq y \Leftrightarrow -y \neq -x$.

(b) This is an easy consequence of part (a). $\square$

As an application, we give the definition of *lower bound* for a subset of a set S relative to a relation R on S. Often we take $\mathbb{Z}$ for S and $\leq$ for R. We introduce a separate name for the lower bound in this special case, in order to shorten the parameter list. We also prove that 0 is a lower bound for every subset of $\mathbb{Z}$ that consists of natural numbers only (see Figure 14.20).

$$\boxed{S : *_s \mid R : S \to S \to *_p \mid T : ps(S) \mid l : S}$$

(1) $\quad \boxed{lw\text{-}bnd(S, R, T, l) \; :- \; \forall t : S \,.\, (t \,\varepsilon\, T \Rightarrow R\,l\,t) \; : \; *_p}$

$$\boxed{T : ps(\mathbb{Z}) \mid l : \mathbb{Z}}$$

(2) $\quad \boxed{lw\text{-}bnd_{\mathbb{Z}}(T, l) \; := \; lw\text{-}bnd(\mathbb{Z}, \leq_{\mathbb{Z}}, T, l) \; : \; *_p}$

$$\boxed{T : ps(\mathbb{Z}) \mid u : T \subseteq \mathbb{N}}$$

$$\boxed{t : \mathbb{Z} \mid w : t \,\varepsilon\, T}$$

(3) $\qquad a_3(T, u, t, w) \; := \; u\,t\,w \; : \; t \,\varepsilon\, \mathbb{N}$

(4) $\qquad a_4(T, u, t, w) \; := \; \dots \textbf{ use Lemma } 14.8.5 \; \dots \; : \; 0 \leq t$

(5) $\quad\; a_5(T, u) \; := \; \dots \textbf{ use } \Rightarrow\textit{-in} \textbf{ and } \forall\textit{-in} \; \dots \; : \; lw\text{-}bnd_{\mathbb{Z}}(T, 0)$

Figure 14.20 The number 0 is lower bound of every subset of $\mathbb{N}$

14.11 Multiplication of integers

We also consider multiplication of integers, in a similar manner as we have done in Section 14.4 for addition. This is the basic recursion scheme for multiplication:

(i) $\;m \cdot 0 = 0$,

(ii) $\;m \cdot s(n) = (m \cdot n) + m$.

Obviously, the recursion takes place in the second operand of $m \cdot n$, again, so taking m constant we obtain for integers m and n:

(i) $\;\times_m(0) = 0$,

(ii) $\;\times_m(s(n)) = \times_m(n) + m$.

The same question arises as with addition: is this 'upward' definition of multiplication sufficient to also cover the negative numbers? Otherwise said: do we need a third recursive equation, to the effect that:

(iii) $\;m \cdot p(n) = (m \cdot n) - m$?

The answer is no, again, just as in the addition case (cf. Section 14.4). We leave a proof of this to the reader (Exercise 14.30).

We can define multiplication for integers similarly to what we have done for addition in Section 14.4. In Figure 14.21 we give the relevant lines, in which we refer to the Recursion Theorem 14.4.5 (for $\mathbb{Z}$). In line (1), we define f as $\lambda v : \mathbb{Z} \,.\, (v + m)$, which is a bijective function (prove it yourself; the inverse of f is $\lambda v : \mathbb{Z} \,.\, (v - m)$).

In Figure 14.22 we define the binary multiplication operation and we list the most important properties of multiplication.

$$\boxed{m : \mathbb{Z}}$$

(1) $\quad f := \lambda v : \mathbb{Z}. (v + m) \; : \; \mathbb{Z} \to \mathbb{Z}$

(2) $\quad a_2 := \ldots : \; bijective(\mathbb{Z}, \mathbb{Z}, f)$

(3) $\quad rec\text{-}mult\text{-}prop(m) := \lambda g : \mathbb{Z} \to \mathbb{Z}. (g\,0 = 0 \wedge \forall x : \mathbb{Z}. (g(s\,x) = f(g\,x))) \; :$
$\qquad (\mathbb{Z} \to \mathbb{Z}) \to *_p$

(4) $\quad rec\text{-}mult\text{-}lem(m) := \ldots \textbf{ use Theorem } 14.4.5 \ldots :$
$\qquad \exists^1 g : \mathbb{Z} \to \mathbb{Z}. (rec\text{-}mult\text{-}prop(m)\,g)$

(5) $\quad times(m) := \iota(\mathbb{Z} \to \mathbb{Z}, rec\text{-}mult\text{-}prop(m), rec\text{-}mult\text{-}lem(m)) \; : \; \mathbb{Z} \to \mathbb{Z}$
$\qquad \textbf{Notation}: \; \times_m \; \textbf{ for } \; times(m)$

Figure 14.21 Multiplication $\times_m : \mathbb{Z} \to \mathbb{Z}$ in λD

(1) $\quad \times := \lambda x : \mathbb{Z}. \lambda y : \mathbb{Z}. (\times_x y) \; : \; \mathbb{Z} \to \mathbb{Z} \to \mathbb{Z}$
$\qquad \textbf{Notation}: \; x \cdot y \; \textbf{ for } \; \times \, x \, y$

$$\boxed{x : \mathbb{Z}}$$

(2) $\quad times\text{-}i(x) := \ldots : \; x \cdot 0 = 0$

$$\boxed{y : \mathbb{Z}}$$

(3) $\quad times\text{-}ii(x, y) := \ldots : \; x \cdot s\,y = (x \cdot y) + x$

(4) $\quad times\text{-}iii(x, y) := \ldots : \; x \cdot p\,y = (x \cdot y) - x$

Figure 14.22 Properties of multiplication in $\mathbb{Z}$

Again, we may consider the 'reversals' of (2), (3) and (4) in Figure 14.22 (cf. Lemma 14.6.1):

Lemma 14.11.1 *(a)* $\forall x : \mathbb{Z}. (0 \cdot x = 0)$,
(b) $\forall x, y : \mathbb{Z}. (s\,x \cdot y = (x \cdot y) + y)$,
(c) $\forall x, y : \mathbb{Z}. (p\,x \cdot y = (x \cdot y) - y)$.

The proofs are left to the reader (Exercise 14.31).

There is an important lemma that considers the combining of addition and multiplication in $\mathbb{Z}$. This lemma is called *Distributivity*. It tells us how multiplication distributes over addition; this means that the x together with the multiplication symbol '$\cdot$' in the left-hand side of the following equation may be distributed over *both* operands of the '+'-symbol: $x \cdot (y + z) = (x \cdot y) + (x \cdot z)$.

Multiplication also distributes over subtraction. Both facts are expressed in the following lemma.

Lemma 14.11.2 *(Right Distributivity Laws for multiplication)*
(a) $\forall x, y, z : \mathbb{Z}. (x \cdot (y + z) = (x \cdot y) + (x \cdot z))$,
(b) $\forall x, y, z : \mathbb{Z}. (x \cdot (y - z) = (x \cdot y) - (x \cdot z))$.

There are, of course, also *Left Distributivity Laws*. All proofs are left to the reader again (cf. Exercise 14.32).

Consequences of Lemmas 14.11.1 and 14.11.2 are the *commutativity* and *associativity* of multiplication:

Lemma 14.11.3 *(a)* $\forall x, y : \mathbb{Z} . (x \cdot y = y \cdot x),$
(b) $\forall x, y, z : \mathbb{Z} . ((x \cdot y) \cdot z = x \cdot (y \cdot z)).$

Again, the proofs are omitted (Exercise 14.33).

Various other lemmas about multiplication in combination with addition, subtraction, opposites and inequality relations can be formulated. Some of them you may find in the exercises at the end of this chapter.

We conclude with a selection of interesting examples of such lemmas, with instructive (informal) proofs. We start with a lemma about the interplay between multiplication and the opposite of an integer:

Lemma 14.11.4 $\forall x, y : \mathbb{Z} . (x \cdot (-y) = -(x \cdot y)).$

Proof On the one hand, $x \cdot (-y) + x \cdot y = x \cdot ((-y) + y) = x \cdot 0 = 0$ (by Lemma 14.11.2 (a), a_2 of Figure 14.17 and *times-i*). On the other hand, also $-(x \cdot y) + x \cdot y = 0$ (by a_2 of Figure 14.17, again). So $x \cdot (-y) = -(x \cdot y)$ by Right Cancellation. □

We prove that $\mathbb{N}$ is closed under multiplication (cf. Lemma 14.7.1), and some related matters:

Lemma 14.11.5 *(a)* $\forall x, y : \mathbb{Z} . ((x \,\varepsilon\, \mathbb{N} \wedge y \,\varepsilon\, \mathbb{N}) \Rightarrow x \cdot y \,\varepsilon\, \mathbb{N}),$
(b) $\forall x, y : \mathbb{Z} . ((x > 0 \wedge y > 0) \Rightarrow x \cdot y > 0),$
(c) $\forall x, y : \mathbb{Z} . ((x > 0 \wedge y < 0) \Rightarrow x \cdot y < 0),$
(d) $\forall x, y : \mathbb{Z} . ((x < 0 \wedge y < 0) \Rightarrow x \cdot y > 0).$

Proof (a) The proof can be given by induction, similarly to the proof of closure under addition (cf. Figure 14.15). Do it yourself (Exercise 14.36; you can use the addition-closure property in the multiplication-closure proof).

(b) Let $x, y : \mathbb{Z}$. Assume $x > 0$ and $y > 0$. The latter implies that $py \,\varepsilon\, \mathbb{N}$ by Lemma 14.10.2 (a). Hence (use Lemma 14.10.1 (e)): $x \cdot y = x \cdot s(py) = x \cdot (py) + x > x \cdot (py) + 0 = x \cdot (py)$. Since both x and py are in $\mathbb{N}$, we have by part (a) that $x \cdot py \,\varepsilon\, \mathbb{N}$, so $x \cdot py \geq 0$. Using Lemma 14.10.1 (d), we obtain that $x \cdot y > 0$.

(c) Let $x, y : \mathbb{Z}$. Assume $x > 0$ and $y < 0$. Then Lemma 14.10.3 (b) implies that $-y > 0$, hence $x \cdot (-y) > 0$ by part (b). But $x \cdot (-y) = -(x \cdot y)$ by Lemma 14.11.4, hence $-(x \cdot y) > 0$, so $x \cdot y < 0$ (use Lemma 14.10.3 (b), again).

(d) Prove it yourself. (Hint: use Lemma 14.10.3 (b) and part (b).) □

The following lemma says that a product is zero if and only if one of the factors is zero:

Lemma 14.11.6 $\forall x, y : \mathbb{Z} . \ (x \cdot y = 0 \Rightarrow (x = 0 \vee y = 0))$.

Prove it yourself (Exercise 14.37).

There are also Cancellation Laws for multiplication. They have an extra condition compared to the Cancellation Laws for addition (Lemma 14.6.5), namely that the 'cancelled' argument should not be zero:

Lemma 14.11.7   *(Right Cancellation Law for multiplication)*
$\forall x, y, z : \mathbb{Z} . \ ((x \cdot z = y \cdot z \wedge z \neq 0) \Rightarrow x = y)$.

A counterpart is, of course, the *Left Cancellation Law* for multiplication. These laws can be proved using Lemma 14.11.6 (cf. Exercise 14.38).

14.12 Divisibility

Another relation between integers is *divisibility*: m divides n (or m is a *divisor* of n) if there exists q in $\mathbb{Z}$ such that $m \cdot q = n$. The relation, called $div(m, n)$, can easily be defined in λD, as demonstrated in Figure 14.23, line (1). We employ the usual notation $m \mid n$ for this.

Note that this definition concerns all integer numbers, including 0. Check the following properties for divisibility in relation with the number zero:

Lemma 14.12.1   *(a)* $\forall m : \mathbb{Z} . \ (m \mid 0)$,
(b) In particular: $0 \mid 0$,
(c) $\forall n : \mathbb{Z} . \ (0 \mid n \Rightarrow n = 0)$.

So *all* integers divide 0, whereas 0 divides *no* integer number except itself.

It is also worthwhile to derive some more basic lemmas about divisibility, such as the following ones:

Lemma 14.12.2   *(a)* $\forall l, m : \mathbb{Z} . \ (l \mid m \Leftrightarrow -l \mid m)$,
(b) $\forall m : \mathbb{Z} . \ (1 \mid m)$.

The following lemma implies that $\mid$ is a partial order (see Figure 12.7) on the naturals.

Lemma 14.12.3   *(a)* $\forall m : \mathbb{Z} . \ (m \mid m)$,
(b) $\forall l, m, n : \mathbb{Z} . \ ((l \mid m \wedge m \mid n) \Rightarrow l \mid n)$,
(c) $\forall m, n : \mathbb{Z} . \ ((m \ \varepsilon \ \mathbb{N} \wedge n \ \varepsilon \ \mathbb{N}) \Rightarrow ((m \mid n \wedge n \mid m) \Rightarrow m = n))$.

Remark 14.12.4   *Parts (a) and (b) of Lemma 14.12.3 hold for arbitrary integers, but the integer variant for part (c) is:*

$\forall m, n : \mathbb{Z} . \, ((m \mid n \wedge n \mid m) \Rightarrow (m = n \vee m = -n)).$

Hence, the relation $\mid$ is not a partial order on the integers.

A proof of Lemma 14.12.3 is left to the reader (cf. Exercise 14.42).

We can define several notions related to divisibility, and prove lemmas about them. In Figure 14.23 we define the common divisor property (line (2)), co-primality (see Section 8.7; line (4)) and the greatest common divisor ('*gcd*') of two numbers (line (7)). We restrict the definition of *gcd* to *positive natural* numbers m and n, as is usual in mathematics. (It is possible to extend the gcd-notion to *integers*, but we shall not do that here.)

$\boxed{m, n : \mathbb{Z}}$

(1) $\quad div(m, n) := \exists q : \mathbb{Z} . \, (m \cdot q = n) \, : \, *_p$

$\quad$ Notation : $m \mid n$ for $div(m, n)$

$\boxed{k, m, n : \mathbb{Z}}$

(2) $\quad com\text{-}div(k, m, n) := k \mid m \wedge k \mid n \, : \, *_p$

(3) $\quad gcd\text{-}prop(k, m, n) := com\text{-}div(k, m, n) \, \wedge$

$\qquad \forall l : \mathbb{Z} . \, (com\text{-}div(l, m, n) \Rightarrow l \leq k) \, : \, *_p$

$\boxed{m, n : \mathbb{Z}}$

(4) $\quad coprime(m, n) := \forall k : \mathbb{Z} . \, ((com\text{-}div(k, m, n) \wedge k > 0) \Rightarrow k = 1) \, : \, *_p$

$\boxed{s \, : \, m > 0 \mid t \, : \, n > 0}$

(5) $\quad gcd\text{-}unq(m, n, s, t) := \ldots \, : \, \exists^1 k : \mathbb{Z} . \, gcd\text{-}prop(k, m, n)$

(6) $\quad gcd(m, n, s, t) := \iota(\mathbb{Z}, \lambda k : \mathbb{Z} . \, gcd\text{-}prop(k, m, n), gcd\text{-}unq(m, n, s, t)) \, : \, \mathbb{Z}$

(7) $\quad gcd\text{-}pos(m, n, s, t) := \ldots \, : \, gcd(m, n, s, t) > 0$

Figure 14.23 Notions related to divisibility

The definition we use is the most commonly used: a *gcd* of two positive naturals m and n is a common divisor that is larger than all other common divisors. Such a number is *unique* (see line (6)), according to a fact about integers that we mention without proof: each non-empty subset of $\mathbb{Z}$ that has an upper bound also has a (unique) *maximum*. (This theorem and its mirror image, the Minimum Theorem, are discussed and proved in λD-style in the following chapter.) The set that we consider here is the set of all common divisors of m and n, which is non-empty because it always contains 1, and bounded above by m (or n) (Exercise 14.44). Its maximum is the unique *gcd* that we are looking for.

We note, again without proof (Exercise 14.45), that the *gcd* of (positive) m and n is positive.

14.13 Irrelevance of proof

We have argued that *proofs-as-terms* (one of the two meanings of 'PAT') is an important feature for the formalisation of mathematics. With proofs-as-terms, proofs become 'first-class citizens' of the system, which can be studied, manipulated and checked. This also means that when we define an object that depends on a property (e.g. the definition of $1/x$, which depends on the fact that $x \neq 0$), then we make this dependency explicit by carrying a proof of $x \neq 0$ into the definition of $1/x$. But of course, the number $1/x$ should not really depend on that proof.

We have also encountered such a situation in the previous section (Figure 14.23, line (6)), when defining the greatest common divisor: we have introduced $gcd(m, n, s, t)$ as an integer number that depends on integers m and n which are *positive*, s and t being proofs of the positivity of m and n, respectively. Now it is undesirable that the value of the gcd can be influenced by the nature of the *proofs* s and t: even if s_1 and t_1 are 'essentially different' (i.e. not $\beta\Delta$-convertible) proofs of the positivity of m and n, then we do not want that $gcd(m, n, s_1, t_1)$ differs from $gcd(m, n, s, t)$. The only thing that matters for such proofs s and t should be that they *exist*. It should be *irrelevant* what these proofs exactly look like: one must be free to trade one proof for another, without external effects. For the gcd, this is the case: $gcd(m, n, s_1, t_1) = gcd(m, n, s_2, t_2)$ for any $s_1, s_2 : m > 0$ and $t_1, t_2 : n > 0$.

That gcd is proof-irrelevant is a consequence of a similar observation we have made in Section 12.7: in Remark 12.7.2 we have shown that $\iota(S, P, u)$ (the unique object of type S satisfying P, where u is a proof of the uniqueness) does not depend on the nature of the proof u: for proofs u_1 and u_2 we can formally prove that $\iota(S, P, u_1) =_S \iota(S, P, u_2)$. This is a general phenomenon in this case: if we always use the ι-operator to define an object that depends on a proof, there is never a real dependency on a proof. This conforms with mathematical practice: we only allow ourselves to talk about 'the object x that satisfies P' if we have first shown that there is a unique object satisfying P.

The fact that objects can depend on proofs is a consequence of the use of type theory for formalising mathematics and is often considered unnatural and even undesirable from a mathematical perspective. Therefore, one sometimes introduces a principle of *proof-irrelevance* in type theory to avoid an effective dependency of objects on proofs. In all our examples, we use the ι-operator (of unique existence) in cases where we define an object (or function) that depends on a proof (see Section 12.7). Therefore, these objects are proof-irrelevant and we don't need to add a separate principle.

In more complicated circumstances it may well happen that 'irrelevance of proof' is not a natural consequence of the theory being developed in λD. In such cases, it should be handled with care and – if necessary – proof irrelevance may be explicitly stipulated, for example by means of an axiom. It may also happen that one encounters a situation where the dependency of an object on a proof is desired, and one doesn't want irrelevance of proofs. Therefore we don't wish to add proof irrelevance as a general principle to λD.

Remark 14.13.1   *The terminology* irrelevance of proof *was introduced by N.G. de Bruijn in the 1970s. More about 'irrelevance of proof' can be found in Nederpelt et al. (1994); see for example the following reprints in that book: Zucker, 1977, Section 3; de Bruijn, 1980, Section 24; van Benthem Jutting, 1977, Sections 4.0.1 and 4.0.2.*

14.14 Conclusions

In the present section we have formally constructed a set-up for arithmetic, right from the ground. One of the most fundamental concepts in mathematics is that of *number*, so we have first investigated how to represent natural numbers in λD. The standard approach of Peano apparently provides a good foundation, including the important method of *induction*.

We soon abandoned this view, however, and changed the focus to *integer numbers*, being the basis of many mathematical disciplines. For integers there also exists a Peano-like set-up, which we have discussed in detail before formalising it in λD. This axiomatisation of the integers was inspired by Margaris (1961) and elaborated by the authors, with valuable help from A. Visser and R. Iemhoff (Visser and Iemhoff, 2009). The idea is to introduce the operation *predecessor* on a par with the *successor* of a number. In this formalisation, every integer has exactly one successor and exactly one predecessor. A core notion in this approach, mathematical induction for the integers, turns out to have the form of a 'symmetric' axiom, expanding to both sides on the number line. The natural numbers ($\mathbb{N}$) can now be *defined* as a subset of the integers ($\mathbb{Z}$). It turns out that $\mathbb{Z}$ and $\mathbb{N}$ only have the desired behaviour if we add one more axiom, stating that the predecessor of 0 is not a natural number.

The given axiomatisation possesses the relevant basic properties. It enables, for example, suitable translations of the original Peano-axioms for natural numbers (including induction for $\mathbb{N}$) into provable *theorems*. We have also mentioned the *tripartition* property of the integers.

Altogether, this test case for our earlier chosen manner to formalise sets and subsets works out well, with satisfactory results.

But there is more to say about numbers as operational objects in mathematics. The first thing is the wish to compute with integer (and natural) numbers. Therefore one needs the usual operations addition and multiplication. The usual recursive definitions of these operations cannot immediately be translated to λD, since λD does not have recursion in its definition apparatus. However, by appealing to (a special form of) the Recursion Theorem, derivable in λD (albeit with a proof too complex for the present book), we have succeeded in incorporating both arithmetical operations in a smooth and convincing manner.

An example computation shows that proofs of even the simplest facts of arithmetic ('$1 + 2 = 3$') require quite some effort in this approach. This is unpleasant, but does not come as a surprise: we know that every single step must be accounted for in λD. It is good to realise that this is intentionally so, being a consequence of our starting point. We recall that our original plan was to build a formal system with a limited number of built-in principles, that gives a maximal guarantee of correctness for everything expressible in it. So it is almost unavoidable to encounter a number of obstacles.

We have also explored the formalisation of some other basic notions concerning integers, such as subtraction, taking the opposite, inequalities and divisibility. We have accompanied the definitions with helpful lemmas, often with informal proofs and sometimes with (a sketch of) a λD-derivation. Induction, of course, plays a central role in the definitions and proofs concerning these operations.

We finally discussed the notion 'irrelevance of proof', which has consequences for type theory in general, but not for the investigations of λD that we encounter in this book. This is due to our introduction of the descriptor ι, which prevents many of the difficulties connected with the possible dependency of objects on proofs.

The general lemmas and theorems that have been discussed in this chapter are useful in a wider mathematical environment, as we shall show in Chapter 15.

On several occasions we have decided in this chapter not to give all the precise, formal details. The reason is definitely not that this is insurmountable or not feasible. On the contrary, it is precisely the *definition mechanism* that enables the user of λD to provide a complete formalisation and yet stay in control of the mathematical material being formalised, concentrating on the overall picture.

It is, however, no more than honest to realise that the gains of formalisation also have a counterpart. Therefore we have decided to sometimes adapt the formal presentation of a derivation by omitting proof objects or by restricting ourselves to only give *hints* concerning the holes in the derivations.

In the present chapter we went even further by often not giving the λD-proofs, but only *informal* proofs, assuming that the reader is by now capable of transforming these into real λD-proofs. The reason is that we want to protect readers from an overdose of formal information, keeping their attention focused on the things that really matter. In the following chapter, however, we will turn back to formal λD-proofs (albeit with hints and holes).

This is not the place for a deeper examination of the advantages or disadvantages for humans confronted with proofs that have been presented in λD. Nor do we try to find solutions at this moment, in order to alleviate the negative effects of a λD-translation on 'understanding'. We come back to these matters in the conclusive chapter of this book (Chapter 16), without pretending to have the final say in the matter.

14.15 Further reading

The formal treatment of natural numbers goes back to G. Peano in 1889 (a translation of the original paper of Peano can be found in van Heijenoort, 1967). This description is axiomatic, so it does not describe functions as programs or algorithms, but as symbols that satisfy certain equations. In the beginning of the twentieth century, the issues of *computability* and *decidability* came up, when D. Hilbert asked the question whether there exists a procedure to mechanically decide whether a formula is true or not. Later this was further refined by differentiating between the question whether a formula A is *true* (in all models or in some specific model) and the question whether a formula A is *derivable* in a certain formal system. It was shown by A.M. Turing (Turing, 1936) and A. Church (Church, 1936b) that these questions are *undecidable*: there is no machine (computer program) that will decide on input A whether it is true, respectively derivable (unless one restricts to a logic of limited expressivity, like proposition calculus). With respect to 'truth' the situation is even more subtle: the famous *incompleteness theorem* of K.F. Gödel (Gödel, 1932) shows that there is no derivation system that can capture all formulas that are true in $\mathbb{N}$.

This also gave rise to a characterisation of the *computable functions*, first by Turing (Turing, 1936), as the class of functions that can be computed via (what later became known as) a *Turing machine*. After Turing, various 'models' of computation have been defined with the remarkable property that they all capture the same class of computable functions. This led Turing and Church to formulate the thesis that any function that can be computed by a mechanical device can be computed by a Turing machine. See e.g. Lewis & Papadimitriou (1981) or Sudkamp (2006) for an introduction.

The class of computable functions can be defined in various ways. A popular way that abstracts from a 'machine model' is to define it as the class of μ-recursive functions. This is the class of functions that contains the zero function and the successor and is closed under the operations of *function composition*, *primitive recursion* and *minimisation*. Again, see Sudkamp (2006). The scheme of primitive recursion basically states that a function f that has a value for input 0, and for input $n + 1$ only uses its output on input n (i.e. $f(n)$), is computable.

Our text is not about *computability* of functions but merely about *well-definedness*. We use recursive definitions as a mechanism to define a function, e.g. addition. To make sure that such a recursive definition actually defines something meaningful, we have to ensure that recursive calls in the definitions have 'smaller' arguments. Therefore we use a simple instance of the scheme for primitive recursion to have a proper mechanism for *defining* functions by recursion. Our *Recursion Theorem for* $\mathbb{Z}$ (Theorem 14.4.3) states that an instance of the scheme for primitive recursion yields a well-defined function. In the text of Section 14.4, we have argued this in detail for the example of addition.

In real mathematics, and notably in number theory, one works more often with the integers than with the natural numbers. However, the natural numbers are a nice inductively defined set, which gives rise to proofs by induction and definitions by well-founded recursion. In the present chapter we use the work of A. Margaris (Margaris, 1961) to axiomatically introduce the integers, an induction principle over the integers and also a scheme for defining functions by recursion over the integers. As a matter of fact, the approach of Margaris is very close in style to Peano's original one for the natural numbers.

A possible alternative is to define the set of integers $\mathbb{Z}$ as a *quotient* of the set of pairs of natural numbers $\mathbb{N} \times \mathbb{N}$. This approach can be found in e.g. van Dalen *et al.*, 1978, Chapter 11. We repeat the essential points: one defines the equivalence relation $\sim$ over $\mathbb{N} \times \mathbb{N}$ by $(k, l) \sim (m, n)$ if $k + n = l + m$. (Intuitively: the difference between k and l is the same as between m and n.) Now one defines $\mathbb{Z}$ as the set of equivalence classes of $\mathbb{N} \times \mathbb{N}$ modulo $\sim$. In abstract mathematics, this works fine, but if one really needs to use this in type theory, it is cumbersome. First of all, this needs the notion 'equivalence class'. This can be introduced (see Section 13.4), but we prefer not to do it if it isn't needed. A second disadvantage is that one has to define all functions 'modulo the equivalence relation' $\sim$: a function from $\mathbb{N} \times \mathbb{N}$ to $\mathbb{N} \times \mathbb{N}$ only gives rise to a function from $\mathbb{Z}$ to $\mathbb{Z}$ if it respects $\sim$ and this is a property to check every time.

Exercises

14.1 (a) See Section 14.2. Prove in λD: $\forall x : \mathbb{Z} . (\neg(x \; \varepsilon \; \mathbb{N}) \Rightarrow \neg(p\,x \; \varepsilon \; \mathbb{N}))$.

    (b) Give an informal proof of the following: if $x = p(\ldots(p\,0)\ldots)$, with at least one occurrence of p in the right-hand side, then $\neg(x \; \varepsilon \; \mathbb{N})$.

*Just as in the exercises for the previous chapter, you may confine your-
self in these exercises to only mentioning the logical rules you use in λD-
derivations (cf. Section 13.2). This also applies to instances of equality-
rules, such as eq-subs, eq-cong₁ and eq-subs. In proving a numbered
lemma from the book text, you may appeal to earlier lemmas, but not
to later ones.*

14.2 See Figure 14.5. Derive proof terms corresponding to:

(a) *zero-prop*,
(b) *clos-prop*.

(You may add intermediate judgements.)

14.3 See Figure 14.5. Prove in λD that $\mathbb{N}$ is the smallest subset satisfying
nat-cond, by finding an inhabitant of

$$\Pi Q : \mathbb{Z} \to *_p . \, (nat\text{-}cond(Q) \Rightarrow \mathbb{N} \subseteq Q).$$

14.4 If $\mathbb{Z}$ has been formalised as in Section 14.2, including *ax-int₃*, then all
models for $\mathbb{Z}$ are infinite. Give an informal proof for this.

14.5 Give a λD-proof of Lemma 14.3.1.

14.6 Give a λD-proof of: $\forall x : \mathbb{Z} . \, (neg(p\,x) \vee pos(s\,x))$.

14.7 Give λD-proofs of all parts of Lemma 14.3.2.

14.8 Give a λD-proof of Lemma 14.3.3 (a).

14.9 See Remark 14.4.2. A relation $R : S \to S \to *_p$ is called *well-founded* if
there exists no infinite 'descending' sequence $x_0, x_1, x_2, \ldots$ of elements of
S such that $x_{i+1} R x_i$ for all i.

(a) Give an informal description of a well-founded relation on $\mathbb{Z}$ that
corresponds to the recursion scheme in Theorem 14.4.3.
(b) Explain why the relation defined in part (a) is no longer well-founded
when we delete the conditions '$pos(s\,x)$' and '$neg(p\,x)$' from the recursion scheme in Theorem 14.4.3.

14.10 (a) Let A be a type, $f : A \to A$ a bijection and $g : \mathbb{Z} \to A$. Consider the
following statements:
(1) $\forall x : \mathbb{Z} . \, [(pos(s\,x)) \Rightarrow g(s\,x) =_A f(g\,x)) \wedge$
$\qquad (neg(p\,x)) \Rightarrow g(p\,x) =_A f^{-1}(g\,x))],$
(2) $\forall x : \mathbb{Z} . \, (g(s\,x) =_A f(g\,x)).$

Prove (1) $\Leftrightarrow$ (2) (hint for (1) $\Rightarrow$ (2): see Exercise 14.6, Lemma 14.3.2 (c)
and Exercise 13.14).
(b) Prove informally that Theorem 14.4.5 is a consequence of the Recursion Theorem for $\mathbb{Z}$, i.e. Theorem 14.4.3.

14.11 Fill the holes in lines (2) to (4) of Figure 14.12.

14.12 Give informal proofs of the following properties of addition:

(a) Commutativity (Lemma 14.6.2) (hint: take x fixed, and apply symmetric induction on y; use Lemma 14.6.1),

(b) Associativity (Lemma 14.6.4) (hint: take x and y fixed, and apply symmetric induction on z),

(c) the Right Cancellation Law (Lemma 14.6.5 (a)).

14.13 Give a proof in λD-format of part II of Lemma 14.7.2.

14.14 Represent the proof of Lemma 14.8.6 (b) in λD-format.

14.15 Give informal proofs of:

(a) Lemma 14.8.8 (a) and (b),

(b) the Left Cancellation Law for subtraction (Lemma 14.8.9 (b)) (hint: start with using Lemma 14.8.2 twice).

14.16 Give informal proofs of Lemma 14.8.10 (a) and (c).

14.17 Prove in λD that for each x in $\mathbb{Z}$, there exists exactly one y in $\mathbb{Z}$ such that $x + y = 0$.

14.18 See Remark 14.2.1. Prove in λD that *ax-int$_2$* implies the following *variant of induction for* $\mathbb{Z}$, with an arbitrary $P\,l$ instead of $P\,0$:

$$((\exists l : \mathbb{Z}.\ P\,l) \wedge \forall x : \mathbb{Z}.\ (P\,x \Rightarrow (P(s\,x) \wedge P(p\,x)))) \ \Rightarrow\ \forall x : \mathbb{Z}.\ P\,x.$$

14.19 Give informal proofs and sketches of the λD-versions for:

(a) the three parts of Lemma 14.9.2,

(b) the two parts of Lemma 14.9.3,

(c) the two parts of Lemma 14.9.7.

14.20 Give proof sketches in λD-style of the following lemmas:

(a) $\forall x, y : \mathbb{Z}.\ (x - (-y) = x + y)$,

(b) $\forall x, y : \mathbb{Z}.\ (-(x - y) = (-x) + y)$,

(c) $\forall x, y : \mathbb{Z}.\ (x - y = -(y - x))$.

14.21 See Remark 14.4.4.

(a) Define the absolute-value-function $abs : \mathbb{Z} \to \mathbb{Z}$ by the aid of the Recursion Theorem for $\mathbb{Z}$.

(b) Prove in λD that $\forall x : \mathbb{Z}.\ (x\ \varepsilon\ \mathbb{N} \Rightarrow abs\,x = x)$.

(c) Prove in λD that $\forall x : \mathbb{Z}.\ (x\ \varepsilon\ \mathbb{N} \Rightarrow abs(-x) = x)$.

14.22 Give a proof sketch of the following lemma:

$$\forall x, y : \mathbb{Z}.\ (abs(x - y) = abs(y - x)).$$

(Hint: see Exercise 14.20 (c) and Lemma 14.8.11).

14.23 Prove in λD:

(a) $\forall x : \mathbb{Z}.\ (x < s\,x)$,

(b) $\forall x : \mathbb{Z}.\ (x > p\,x)$.

14.24 Prove in λD:

    (a) $\forall x, y : \mathbb{Z}. \, (x < y \Leftrightarrow s\,x < s\,y)$,

    (b) $\forall x, y : \mathbb{Z}. \, (x < y \Leftrightarrow p\,x < p\,y)$.

14.25 Give proof sketches in λD-style of the following lemmas:

    (a) $\forall x, y : \mathbb{Z}. \, ((x \, \varepsilon \, \mathbb{N} \wedge x \leq y) \Rightarrow y \, \varepsilon \, \mathbb{N})$,

    (b) $\forall x, y : \mathbb{Z}. \, ((neg(y) \wedge x \leq y) \Rightarrow neg(x))$.

14.26 Give proof sketches of Lemma 14.10.1 (d) and (e).

14.27 Give proof sketches of Lemma 14.10.2 (a) and (b).

14.28 Convert the informal proofs of Lemma 14.10.3 (a) and (b) into λD-proofs.

14.29 Give proof sketches in λD-style of the following lemmas:

    (a) $\forall x, y : \mathbb{Z}. \, ((x \leq y \wedge y \leq x) \Rightarrow x = y)$,

    (b) $\forall x, y : \mathbb{Z}. \, (x < y \Rightarrow s\,x \leq y)$.

14.30 In the beginning of Section 14.11 we claimed that the recursive equation

    $(ii) \quad m \cdot s(n) = (m \cdot n) + m$

implies the equation

    $(iii) \quad m \cdot p(n) = (m \cdot n) - m$.

Show this.

14.31 Give informal proofs and give sketches of the λD-versions for the three parts of Lemma 14.11.1.

14.32 Give informal proofs of the two parts of Lemma 14.11.2.

14.33 Give informal proofs of the two parts of Lemma 14.11.3.

14.34 Give sketches of λD-proofs for:

    (a) $1 \cdot 1 = 1$,

    (b) $2 \cdot 2 = 4$,

    (c) $(-1) \cdot (-1) = 1$.

14.35 Give derivations in λD of the following lemmas:

    (a) $\forall x : \mathbb{Z}. \, (x \cdot 1 = x)$,

    (b) $\forall x : \mathbb{Z}. \, (x \cdot (-1) = -x)$.

14.36 Give an informal proof and a proof sketch in λD for the statement that $\mathbb{N}$ is closed under multiplication (Lemma 14.11.5 (a)).

14.37 Give an informal proof of Lemma 14.11.6 (hint: use Lemmas 14.10.2 (c) and 14.11.5).

14.38 Give an informal proof of Lemma 14.11.7.

14.39 Give informal proofs of the following lemmas:

    (a) $\forall x, y, z : \mathbb{Z}. \, ((x \leq y \wedge z \, \varepsilon \, \mathbb{N}) \Rightarrow x \cdot z \leq y \cdot z)$,

    (b) $\forall x, y, z : \mathbb{Z}. \, ((x \cdot z \leq y \cdot z \wedge pos(z)) \Rightarrow x \leq y)$,

    (c) $\forall x, y, z : \mathbb{Z}. \, ((x \cdot z \leq y \cdot z \wedge neg(z)) \Rightarrow x \geq y)$.

14.40 Give informal proofs of:

  (a) Lemma 14.12.1 (a) and (c),
  (b) Lemma 14.12.2 (a).

14.41 Give informal proofs of the following lemmas:

  (a) $\forall x : \mathbb{Z} . \ (x \ \varepsilon \ \mathbb{N} \Rightarrow (x = 0 \vee x \geq 1))$,
  (b) $\forall x, y : \mathbb{Z} . \ (x \ \varepsilon \ \mathbb{N} \Rightarrow (x \cdot y = 1 \Rightarrow x = 1))$ (hint: use part (a)).

14.42 Give an informal proof of Lemma 14.12.3 (c).
     (Hint: use Exercise 14.41 (b).)

14.43 Prove the following in λD:
     $\forall m, n : \mathbb{Z} . \ (coprime(m, n) \Rightarrow coprime(n, m))$.

14.44 Let $k, m : \mathbb{Z}$ be such that $k > 0$, $m > 0$ and $k | m$. Prove that $k \leq m$.
     (Hint: use Exercises 14.41 (a) and 14.39 (a).)

14.45 Give an informal proof of the lemma expressed in Figure 14.23, line (7).

15

An elaborated example

15.1 Formalising a proof of Bézout's Lemma

In Section 8.7, we considered a well-known theorem from number theory, and we have given a mathematical proof of it in Section 8.8. We now revisit this theorem and its proof, which are reproduced below, and translate it into the formal λD-format.

A thorough inspection of what we need for the formalisation of the proof in its entirety will take up the space of a full chapter: the present one. It acts as a final exercise, showing several important aspects of λD.

In the process, we will encounter various questions and problems. We'll try to foresee some of these questions and solve them before we start the actual proof. Other problems we solve 'on the fly'. On some occasions, we come across situations of missing foreknowledge that is either too laborious or too uninspiring to be dealt with in this book; in those cases we resort to only summarising what is lacking. Hence, we decide neither to fill every gap, nor to always supply the relevant details.

The mentioned theorem reads as follows:

'**Theorem ("Bézout's Lemma"**, *restricted version*)
Let $m, n \in \mathbb{N}^+$ be coprime. Then $\exists_{x,y \in \mathbb{Z}}(mx + ny = 1)$.'

Remark 15.1.1 *The lemma has been attributed to the French mathematician É. Bézout (1730–1783), although it already appeared in earlier work of others. Actually, in order to make our example less complicated, we have chosen a special case of Bézout's Lemma, by adding the restriction that m and n be coprime, i.e. their greatest common divisor is 1. The original version applies to all pairs of positive natural numbers m and n, and expresses that there exist integer numbers x and y such that $mx + ny = gcd(m, n)$.*

The general version with the gcd is only seemingly more general: in fact, it easily follows from the restricted version that we consider in this chapter (see Exercise 15.1).

There is a well-known constructive *manner (i.e. a procedure) to find such x and y for given positive numbers m and n. This procedure works for both the restricted and the general version of the lemma. It is called the* Euclidean algorithm, *based on a method attributed to Euclid, a mathematician who lived around 300 BC in Alexandria (Egypt).*

Euclid became famous for his standard work 'The Elements', which is a bundle of 13 books on geometry and number theory. The theorem-and-proof approach he employed is now a standard in the mathematical world, as is also demonstrated in the present book. Another notion that Euclid introduced, is that of axiom, which corresponds to our notion of 'primitive definition' (see Section 10.2).

We restate the proof of Bézout's Lemma (restricted version) as given in Figure 8.6:

> *Proof* Let m and n be positive natural numbers that have no other positive common divisor than 1.
>
> Consider the set of *all* integers $mx + ny$, where $x \in \mathbb{Z}$ and $y \in \mathbb{Z}$. Call this set S.
>
> Define S^+ as $S \cap \mathbb{N}^+$. This S^+ has a minimum, call it d.
>
> Since $d \in S^+$, also $d \in S$, hence (i) $d = mx_0 + ny_0$ for certain $x_0, y_0 \in \mathbb{Z}$. Moreover, $d > 0$ since $d \in \mathbb{N}^+$.
>
> Divide m by d. This gives q and r such that (ii) $m = qd + r$, with $0 \leq r < d$.
>
> By inserting d of (i) into (ii) we get $m = q(mx_0 + ny_0) + r$, from which follows that $r = m(1 - qx_0) - n(qy_0)$. Hence $r \in S$.
>
> Suppose $r > 0$. Then $r \in S^+$, so $r \geq d$ since $d = \min(S^+)$. But $r < d$: contradiction. Hence, $r = 0$.
>
> From (ii) now follows that $m = qd$, hence $d|m$.
> In a similar manner we can prove that $d|n$.
>
> Since m and n are coprime, d must be 1, implying that $1 \in S$.
>
> Hence there exist $x, y \in \mathbb{Z}$ such that $mx + ny = 1$.   □

Browsing through this proof with a view to a λD-formalisation, there are certain things that catch the eye. First of all, we observe that there are *two* number systems involved in this proof: we encounter integers (elements of $\mathbb{Z}$) and positive natural numbers (elements of $\mathbb{N}^+$).

Since $\mathbb{N}^+$ is a subset of $\mathbb{Z}$, and also the other sets defined in the proof (S, S^+), our choice in Chapter 14 to take $\mathbb{Z}$ as our basic set appears to be appropriate. We shall consider these subsets as predicates on $\mathbb{Z}$ (cf. Section 13.1).

We recall that Chapter 14 contains a number of notions connected with integer numbers, many of which are used in this proof, such as the basic operations addition, subtraction and multiplication, and the inequality relations.

By observing the above proof somewhat closer, we notice the following details. Some of these appear to be problematic and should preferably be solved before we give a formalisation in λD:

- For the notions *common divisor*, *coprime* and the divisibility operator '$\,|\,$', see Section 14.12.
- The notion *intersection* ($\cap$) of subsets was dealt with in Figure 13.2.
- The proof mentions a *minimum d* of subset S^+. We have dealt with minimum values before (Section 12.7), but only for a type $*_s$, not for a *subset* of type $\mathbb{Z} \to *_p$. So we have to adapt this notion to the new situation.
- In order to be able to speak about *the* minimum d, we have to prove its *existence* and *uniqueness*. This requires a piece of 'foreknowledge', in the form of the so-called *Minimum Theorem*, stating that each non-empty subset of $\mathbb{Z}$ that is bounded from below, has a (unique) minimum. These two requirements (non-emptiness, being bounded from below) are neither mentioned nor explicitly verified in the informal proof text. In the λD-formalisation, however, this is indispensable.
- For the Minimum Theorem we need the notion of 'non-emptiness'. But *empty sets* were discussed in Section 13.3, so non-emptiness appears to be no problem.
- Another property of numbers was used when *dividing* m by d (both in $\mathbb{N}^+$): there exist (unique) q and r such that $m = q \cdot d + r$, where $0 \le r < d$. This amounts, again, to an important theorem (the *Division Theorem*) that belongs to the necessary foreknowledge.
- Finally, several *computations* are executed, based on properties of arithmetic. It appears instructive to unravel what these properties are, and how they can be proved; the lemmas developed in Chapter 14 may be convenient.

We treat the mentioned points of interest that we miss as foreknowledge, in the preparatory Section 15.2:

- We first redefine the minimum operator, this time for *subsets*.
- Next, we *formulate* the Minimum Theorem and the Division Theorem in λD, in order to be able to use them in the proof of Bézout's Lemma; we do not (yet) give formal *proofs* of these theorems: this we postpone to Sections 15.7 and 15.8, respectively. (A full proof of the Minimum Theorem will be given in Appendix C, Section C.2.)

The remainder of the chapter will be devoted to a λD-formalisation of the proof of Bézout's Lemma and related subjects:

(1) We provide a thorough description of the full λD-proof of Bézout's

Lemma in Sections 15.3 to 15.5. For many subjects in these sections, we refer to earlier chapters, in particular to Chapter 14 for a number of arithmetical laws.

(2) We reserve Section 15.6 for discussing a variety of 'loose ends' concerning computational laws and other special subjects that we encounter in the proof of Bézout's Lemma, and which have not yet been covered by earlier chapters.

15.2 Preparatory work

I. The minimum operator for subsets

The minimum operator *Min* developed in Section 12.7 (see Figure 12.18) does not suffice for our present purposes: it denotes a *global* minimum operator for the $\leq$-ordered type S; it is not immediately transferable to *subsets* of S.

Hence, we start by reformulating the notion 'minimum' for subsets of S. We assume a type $S : *_s$ that is partially ordered by a relation $R : S \to S \to *_p$. (The letter R we use instead of the symbol $\leq$ in order to emphasise the general character of this relation; for the notion 'partial order', see Figure 12.7.)

Now we express for subset $T : ps(S)$ what it means to have a minimum; this is done by defining when m is a *least element* of T with respect to R, or formally: $least(S, R, T, m)$. This is the case if m belongs to subset T and is a lower bound of T (see Figure 14.20 for the notion 'lower bound'). We express this in Figure 15.1, line (1); compare this with the proposition $Least(S, \leq, m)$ in Figure 12.13. In line (2) we introduce constant $least_\mathbb{Z}$ with a shorter parameter list, for the special case that S is $\mathbb{Z}$ and R is $\leq$ on $\mathbb{Z}$ (compare this with $lw\text{-}bnd_\mathbb{Z}$ in Figure 14.20).

Next, we can prove that there is at most one least element of T. Consequently, if we also assume that there is *at least* one such element of T, then there is *exactly one* such element, and we can baptise this unique element 'the minimum of the subset', $min(S, R, T, r, w)$, by the aid of the descriptor ι introduced in Section 12.7. This is done quite similarly to what we have done in Figures 12.15 and 12.18.

Summarising this, we obtain Figure 15.1; as in Figure 12.15, we leave the proof objects in lines (3) and (4) to the reader (Exercise 15.2).

II. Formulation of the Minimum Theorem

The Minimum Theorem says that every non-empty set of integers that is bounded from below has a (unique) minimum. The theorem can be expressed in λD as in Figure 15.2. We use the $\leq$-relation as defined in Figure 14.18. For $lw\text{-}bnd_\mathbb{Z}$, see Figure 14.20; for $least_\mathbb{Z}$ and min, see Figure 15.1.

The *existence* of a minimum is the Minimum Theorem; it is expressed in

$$\boxed{S \; : \; *_s \; | \; R : S \to S \to *_p \; | \; T : ps(S) \; | \; m : S}$$

(1) $least(S, R, T, m) \; := \; m \; \varepsilon \; T \wedge lw\text{-}bnd(S, R, T, m) \; : \; *_p$

$$\boxed{T : ps(\mathbb{Z}) \; | \; m : \mathbb{Z}}$$

(2) $least_{\mathbb{Z}}(T, m) \; := \; least(\mathbb{Z}, \leq, T, m) \; : \; *_p$

$$\boxed{S \; : \; *_s \; | \; R : S \to S \to *_p \; | \; T : ps(S) \; | \; r \; : \; part\text{-}ord(S, R)}$$

(3) $a_3(S, R, T, r) \; := \; \dots \; : \; \exists^{\leq 1} m : S \, . \, least(S, R, T, m)$

$$\boxed{w \; : \; \exists m : S \, . \, least(S, R, T, m)}$$

(4) $a_4(S, R, T, r, w) \; := \; \dots \; : \; \exists^1 m : S \, . \, least(S, R, T, m)$

(5) $min(S, R, T, r, w) \; := \; \iota(S, \lambda m : S \, . \, least(S, R, T, m), a_4(S, R, T, r, w)) \; : \; S$

Figure 15.1 The minimum of a subset of a partially ordered set

line (1) of Figure 15.2 and will be proved in Section 15.7. The *uniqueness* of such a minimum (line (2)) is stated in Figure 15.1, hence we can name that minimum (line (3)). A proof that $\leq$ is a partial order on $\mathbb{Z}$ is left open in the proof objects of lines (2) and (3); we call it *hole #1* and come back to it in Section 15.6. In line (4) we derive a decisive property of the minimum. Check yourself that this derivation is correct, assuming that the omitted parts have been properly filled.

Note again that constant names such as *min-the* and *min-uni-the* are somewhat deceiving, since they are *inhabitants* (proofs) of the two theorems, not the theorems themselves.

$$\boxed{T : ps(\mathbb{Z}) \; | \; u : T \neq \emptyset_{\mathbb{Z}} \; | \; v \; : \; \exists x : \mathbb{Z} \, . \, lw\text{-}bnd_{\mathbb{Z}}(T, x)}$$

(1) $min\text{-}the(T, u, v) \; := \; \dots \; \textbf{see } Figure \; 15.18, \; line \; (29) \; \dots \; :$
       $\exists m : \mathbb{Z} \, . \, least_{\mathbb{Z}}(T, m)$

(2) $min\text{-}uni\text{-}the(T, u, v) \; := \; a_{4[Fig.15.1]}(\mathbb{Z}, \leq, T, hole \; \#1, min\text{-}the(T, u, v)) \; :$
       $\exists^1 m : \mathbb{Z} \, . \, least_{\mathbb{Z}}(T, m)$

(3) $minimum(T, u, v) \; := \; min(\mathbb{Z}, \leq, T, hole \; \#1, min\text{-}the(T, u, v)) \; : \; \mathbb{Z}$

(4) $min\text{-}prop(T, u, v) \; :=$
       $\iota\text{-}prop(\mathbb{Z}, \lambda m : \mathbb{Z} \, . \, least_{\mathbb{Z}}(T, m), min\text{-}uni\text{-}the(T, u, v)) \; :$
       $minimum(T, u, v) \; \varepsilon \; T \wedge lw\text{-}bnd_{\mathbb{Z}}(T, minimum(T, u, v))$

Figure 15.2 Formulation of the Minimum Theorem, and some consequences

III. Formulation of the Division Theorem

It is obvious how to formulate the Division Theorem in λD; see Figure 15.3. For 'addition' and 'multiplication' we refer to Sections 14.4 and 14.11.

The expression $0 \leq r < d$ is obviously an abbreviation of $(0 \leq r) \wedge (r < d)$.

The Division Theorem expresses the possibility to *divide* a positive m by a positive d in such a manner that the 'remainder' after division is a natural number smaller than this d. Otherwise said, when inspecting the infinite series $0 \cdot d$, $1 \cdot d$, $2 \cdot d \ldots$, from left to right, and comparing each entry with m, there comes a point where $q \cdot d$ is smaller than or equal to m, whereas $(q + 1) \cdot d$ is greater than m. That q is called the *quotient*. It has the property that the difference $m - q \cdot d$ (which is the *remainder* r) is a natural number that is less than d itself.

Note that the Division Theorem holds for all integer numbers m and positive naturals d. We restrict it here to $m > 0$, since that is what we need in Bézout's Lemma.

The proof of this theorem is postponed to Section 15.8.

$$m, d : \mathbb{Z} \mid u : m > 0 \mid v : d > 0$$
$$\text{div-the}(m, d, u, v) := \ldots \textbf{ see } \textit{Section 15.8} \ldots :$$
$$\exists q, r : \mathbb{Z} . \ (m = q \cdot d + r \ \wedge \ 0 \leq r < d)$$

Figure 15.3 Formulation of the Division Theorem

Remark 15.2.1 *The Division Theorem only expresses the existence of q and r with the mentioned properties; it does not state that both are unique (for given $m, d \in \mathbb{N}^+$). This uniqueness can be shown to hold. (Try yourself to give a proof sketch.) So we may speak about the quotient q and the remainder r. But the proof of the uniqueness is not particularly useful for our present purposes: in the proof of Bézout's Lemma, the pure existence of q and r is enough.*

15.3 Part I of the proof of Bézout's Lemma

The proof of Bézout's Lemma (see Section 15.1) starts quite naturally, with the introduction of two variables and an assumption:

'Let m and n be positive natural numbers that have no other positive common divisors than 1.'

Hence, the overall *context* consists of two numbers m and n, both positive and being *coprime* (see Figure 14.23, line (4)). Since $\mathbb{Z}$ is our basic set, we take $m, n : \mathbb{Z}$. We express the positiveness of a number x as '$x > 0$', which is permitted by Lemma 14.10.2 (a).

Hence, we commence our formal version as follows:

$$m, n : \mathbb{Z} \mid ass_1 \, : \, m > 0 \mid ass_2 \, : \, n > 0 \mid ass_3 \, : \, coprime(m, n)$$
$$\vdots$$

Figure 15.4 Start of the proof of Bézout's Lemma

Remark 15.3.1 *The assumption* $coprime(m, n)$ *is not used in the proof of Figure 8.6 until the second but last sentence. Hence, in order to save on parameters, we could decide to postpone the corresponding flag until the final part of the formalisation (Section 15.5). Since we want to keep close to the proof text, we do not choose this option.*

It is clear that an important part of the proof-to-come will depend on the parameter list $(m, n, ass_1, ass_2, ass_3)$ containing the five parameters of the overall context of Bézout's Lemma, although they will never be instantiated in the proof. Since we have adopted the *parameter list convention* (see Section 11.7), this is no problem: we simply write S, for example, instead of $S(m, n, ass_1, ass_2, ass_3)$ (see Figure 15.5).

The proof continues with the definition of the subset S of $\mathbb{Z}$ consisting of all so-called *linear combinations* of m and n:

> 'Consider the set of *all* integers $mx + ny$, where $x \in \mathbb{Z}$ and $y \in \mathbb{Z}$. Call this set S.'

The corresponding *subset* S coincides with the predicate 'being a linear combination of m and n'. For the *subset*-notation, $\{\ldots \mid \ldots\}$, see Figure 13.2.

$$\vdots$$

(1) $\quad S^\dagger := \{k : \mathbb{Z} \mid \exists x, y : \mathbb{Z} . \, (k = m \cdot x + n \cdot y)\} \; : \; ps(\mathbb{Z})$

†*parameters suppressed*

Figure 15.5 Step 1 of the proof

Remark 15.3.2 *Since S depends on m and n only, we could have restricted ourselves to a shorter context. However, we have decided to follow the proof text as closely as possible. The longer parameter list does not bother us because of the parameter list convention.*

The following paragraph of the proof of Bézout's Lemma starts by defining the subset S^+, containing the positive elements of S. It is constructed as the intersection of S and $\mathbb{N}^+$:

'Define S^+ as $S \cap \mathbb{N}^+$.'

So another well-known subset of $\mathbb{Z}$ is required, next to $\mathbb{N}$, namely the set of *positive* naturals, $\mathbb{N}^+$. This set has obviously been 'imported' in the proof, so we may assume that it was defined earlier, outside the context. In order to record this, we temporarily suppress the flagpole started in Figure 15.4; see Figure 15.6, line (2). After that, we reopen the flagpole and define S^+, with the help of the formal intersection operator $\cap$ introduced in Figure 13.2. (These manipulations of the flag poles are permitted; cf. Sections 2.5 and 11.1.)

$$\vdots$$

(2) $\mathbb{N}^+ := \{k : \mathbb{Z} \mid k > 0\}$

(3) $\big|$ $S^+ := S \cap \mathbb{N}^+ \ : \ ps(\mathbb{Z})$

Figure 15.6 Step 2 of the proof

Recall that $S \cap \mathbb{N}^+$ is an abbreviation of $\cap(\mathbb{Z}, S, \mathbb{N}^+)$, being of type $ps(\mathbb{Z})$ by the (*inst*)-rule.

The next sentence in the proof is only a short observation followed by a definition:

'This S^+ has a minimum, call it d.'

This proof step requires the Minimum Theorem, as we have explained in the previous sections (S^+ has a minimum because it is a non-empty subset of $\mathbb{Z}$ being bounded from below). So we try to use Figure 15.2, line (3), and define d as $minimum(S^+, ?_1, ?_2)$, where $?_1$ must be of type $S^+ \neq \emptyset_{\mathbb{Z}}$ and $?_2$ of type $\exists x : \mathbb{Z} . \ lw\text{-}bnd_{\mathbb{Z}}(S^+, x)$.

For the first proof object, $?_1$, it suffices to provide a positive element of S. This set is, as we recall, the collection of all linear combinations of m and n. Now m itself is such a linear combination, since $m = m \cdot 1 + n \cdot 0$, and m is positive by the assumption named ass_1, so m is a witness for the non-emptiness of S^+. We do not spell out here the arithmetical proof of $m = m \cdot 1 + n \cdot 0$, since this is an easy consequence of what we discussed in the previous chapter. We leave it open in line (4) of Figure 15.7, marking it as *hole #2*.

The second required proof object, $?_2$, is not hard to find, since 1 acts as a lower bound of S^+. We decide to also leave this proof open, since the derivation is straightforward. We therefore register it as *hole #3*. We come back to all open 'holes' in Section 15.6.

As a result of all this, we can formalise the above proof sentence and many of the needed details as in Figure 15.7.

$$\vdots$$

(4) $\quad a_4 := hole\ \#2 \ : \ m = m \cdot 1 + n \cdot 0$

(5) $\quad a_5 := \dots$ use $\exists$-*in* (twice) on a_4 and use that $1 : \mathbb{Z}$ and $0 : \mathbb{Z} \dots$:

$\qquad \exists x, y : \mathbb{Z} . \ (m = m \cdot x + n \cdot y)$

(6) $\quad a_6 := a_5 \ : \ m \ \varepsilon \ S$

(7) $\quad a_7 := ass_1 \ : \ m \ \varepsilon \ \mathbb{N}^+$

(8) $\quad a_8 := \dots$ use $\wedge$-*in* on a_6 and $a_7 \dots$: $\ m \ \varepsilon \ S^+$

(9) $\quad a_9 := \dots$ use $\exists$-*in* on m and $a_8 \dots$: $\ \exists k : \mathbb{Z} . \ (k \ \varepsilon \ S^+)$

(10) $\quad a_{10} := a_{13\,[Fig.13.8]}(\mathbb{Z}, S^+)\, a_9 \ : \ S^+ \neq \emptyset_{\mathbb{Z}}$

(11) $\quad a_{11} := hole\ \#3 \ : \ \exists x : \mathbb{Z} . \ lw\text{-}bnd_{\mathbb{Z}}(S^+, x)$

(12) $\quad d := minimum(S^+, a_{10}, a_{11}) \ : \ \mathbb{Z}$

Figure 15.7 Step 3 of the proof

15.4 Part II of the proof

The proof of Bézout's Lemma continues with a number of observations concerning the minimum d defined just now:

> 'Since $d \in S^+$, also $d \in S$, hence (i) $d = m x_0 + n y_0$ for certain $x_0, y_0 \in \mathbb{Z}$. Moreover, $d > 0$ since $d \in \mathbb{N}^+$.'

Proofs of these things are formalised in Figure 15.8, in a straightforward manner. For *min-prop*, see Figure 15.2. In line (18) we add a simple consequence of line (13) that we need later (line (29)).

$$\vdots$$

(13) $\quad a_{13} := min\text{-}prop(S^+, a_{10}, a_{11}) \ : \ d \ \varepsilon \ S^+ \wedge lw\text{-}bnd_{\mathbb{Z}}(S^+, d)$

(14) $\quad a_{14} := \dots$ use $\wedge$-*el*$_1$ on $a_{13} \dots$: $\ d \ \varepsilon \ S \wedge d \ \varepsilon \ \mathbb{N}^+$

(15) $\quad a_{15} := \dots$ use $\wedge$-*el*$_1$ on $a_{14} \dots$: $\ d \ \varepsilon \ S$

(16) $\quad a_{16} := a_{15} \ : \ \exists x_0, y_0 : \mathbb{Z} . \ (d = m \cdot x_0 + n \cdot y_0)$

(17) $\quad a_{17} := \dots$ use $\wedge$-*el*$_2$ on $a_{14} \dots$: $\ d > 0$

(18) $\quad a_{18} := \dots$ use $\wedge$-*el*$_2$ on $a_{13} \dots$: $\ \forall x : \mathbb{Z} . \ (x \ \varepsilon \ S^+ \Rightarrow d \leq x)$

Figure 15.8 Step 4 of the proof

Next, the informal proof appeals to the Division Theorem:

> 'Divide m by d. This gives q and r such that (ii) $m = qd + r$, with $0 \leq r < d$.'

This is an easy application of Figure 15.3; see Figure 15.9. Recall that ass_1 is the assumption that $m > 0$.

$$\vdots$$

(19) $\quad a_{19} := \textit{div-the}(m, d, ass_1, a_{17}) :$
$$\exists q, r : \mathbb{Z} . \, (m = q \cdot d + r \, \wedge \, (0 \le r \wedge r < d))$$

Figure 15.9 Step 5 of the proof

The informal proof goes on with a computation, leading to the result that the remainder r must be in S:

'By inserting d of (i) into (ii) we get $m = q(mx_0 + ny_0) + r$, from which follows that $r = m(1-qx_0)-n(qy_0)$. Hence $r \in S$.'

This part of the proof is formally expressed in Figure 15.10.

Remember that the mentioned equation (i) was formalised in the type of line (16), stating that $\exists x_0, y_0 : \mathbb{Z} . \, (d = m \cdot x_0 + n \cdot y_0)$. So we have a double existential quantifier. Moreover, equation (ii), expressing that $m = q \cdot d + r$, is part of the type of line (19), *within* the scope of another double existence quantifier: $\exists q, r : \mathbb{Z}$. Hence, we have four $\exists$-quantifiers and hence we have to employ the structure of $\exists$-*el four times* in order to be able to 'work' with the mentioned x_0, y_0, q and r. Therefore we start with extra flags introducing these variables and their properties (see Figure 15.10).

Remark 15.4.1 *The statement $\exists x_0, y_0 : \mathbb{Z} . \, (d = m \cdot x_0 + n \cdot y_0)$ in line (16) should actually read $\exists x_0 : \mathbb{Z} . \, (\exists y_0 : \mathbb{Z} . \, \ldots)$. Hence, a proper usage of the $\exists$-el procedure obliges us to introduce* four *flags, two for the first $\exists$-quantifier:*

$- x_0 : \mathbb{Z}$,
$- v_0 \, : \, \exists y_0 : \mathbb{Z} . \, (d = m \cdot x_0 + n \cdot y_0)$,

and subsequently, two for the second $\exists$-quantifier:

$- y_0 : \mathbb{Z}$,
$- v \, : \, d = m \cdot x_0 + n \cdot y_0$.

This is one more flag (with variable v_0) than we give in Figure 15.10. We expect, however, that the reader can deal with this omission (Exercise 15.4 (b)). A similar observation holds for the double $\exists$-proposition in line (19).

The equality $m = q(mx_0 + ny_0) + r$ obtained in the informal proof can be formally derived by the aid of *substitutivity*, as described in Section 12.2 (see Figure 12.4). This is done in line (23).

For the other equality, $r = m(1 - qx_0) - n(qy_0)$, we need arithmetical (or computational) laws. For the time being, we denote the relevant proof term as a hole; see line (24). In line (25) we slightly modify the result of line (24) in order to make it ready for line (26). Again, we mark the proof term in line (25) as a hole.

$$\vdots$$

$$\boxed{x_0, y_0 : \mathbb{Z} \mid v : (d = m \cdot x_0 + n \cdot y_0)}$$

$$\boxed{q, r : \mathbb{Z} \mid w : (m = q \cdot d + r \ \wedge \ (0 \le r \wedge r < d))}$$

(20) $\quad a_{20} := \ldots$ **use** $\wedge\text{-}el_1$ **on** $w \ldots : \ m = q \cdot d + r$

(21) $\quad a_{21} := \ldots$ **use** $\wedge\text{-}el_2$ **and** $\wedge\text{-}el_1$ **on** $w \ldots : \ 0 \le r$

(22) $\quad a_{22} := \ldots$ **use** $\wedge\text{-}el_2$, **twice, on** $w \ldots : \ r < d$

(23) $\quad a_{23} := eq\text{-}subs(\mathbb{Z}, \lambda z : \mathbb{Z}. \ m = q \cdot z + r, \ d, \ m \cdot x_0 + n \cdot y_0, \ v, \ a_{20}) \ :$
$$m = q \cdot (m \cdot x_0 + n \cdot y_0) + r$$

(24) $\quad a_{24} := hole\#4 \ : \ r = m \cdot (1 - q \cdot x_0) - n \cdot (q \cdot y_0)$

(25) $\quad a_{25} := hole\#5 \ : \ r = m \cdot (1 - q \cdot x_0) + n \cdot (-(q \cdot y_0))$

(26) $\quad a_{26} := \ldots$ **use** $\exists\text{-}in$ **(twice) on** $a_{25} \ldots : $
$$\exists x, y : \mathbb{Z}. \ (r = m \cdot x + n \cdot y)$$

(27) $\quad a_{27} := a_{26} \ : \ r \ \varepsilon \ S$

Figure 15.10 Step 6 of the proof

The proof continues with the following text:

'Suppose $r > 0$. Then $r \in S^+$, so $r \ge d$ since $d = \min(S^+)$.
But $r < d$: contradiction. Hence, $r = 0$.'

It is not hard to formalise this piece of text; see Figure 15.11. The holes in Step 7 of the proof are:
- $hole\#6$: a proof that $r < d$ and $d \le r$ entail $\bot$;
- $hole\#7$: a proof that $0 \le r$ and $\neg(r > 0)$ result in $r = 0$.

$$\vdots$$

$$\boxed{z : r > 0}$$

(28) $\quad a_{28} := \ldots$ **use** $\wedge\text{-}in$ **on** a_{27} **and** $z \ldots : \ r \ \varepsilon \ S^+$

(29) $\quad a_{29} := \ldots$ **use** $\forall\text{-}el$ **and** $\Rightarrow\text{-}el$ **on** a_{18}, r **and** $a_{28} \ldots : \ d \le r$

(30) $\quad a_{30} := hole\#6$ (math on a_{22} and a_{29}) $: \ \bot$

(31) $\quad a_{31} := \ldots$ **use** $\neg\text{-}in$ **on** $a_{30} \ldots : \ \neg(r > 0)$

(32) $\quad a_{32} := hole\#7$ (math on a_{21} and a_{31}) $: \ r = 0$

Figure 15.11 Step 7 of the proof

15.5 Part III of the proof

The informal proof goes on with the sentence:

'From (ii) now follows that $m = q \cdot d$, hence $d|m$.'

This can be formalised in the λD-format as illustrated in Figure 15.12 (see Figure 14.23 for the divisibility operator '$|$').

$$\vdots$$

(33) $a_{33} := hole\#8 \ (\text{math on } a_{20} \text{ and } a_{32}) \ : \ d \cdot q = m$

(34) $a_{34} := \ldots \ \text{use } \exists\text{-}in \text{ on } a_{33} \ \ldots \ : \ \exists x : \mathbb{Z} . \, (d \cdot x = m)$

(35) $a_{35} := a_{34} \ : \ d \,|\, m$

(36) $a_{36} := \ldots \ \text{use } \exists\text{-}el \text{ on } a_{19} \ \ldots \ : \ d \,|\, m$

(37) $a_{37} := \ldots \ \text{use } \exists\text{-}el \text{ on } a_{16} \ \ldots \ : \ d \,|\, m$

Figure 15.12 Step 8 of the proof

The informal proof continues with:

'In a similar manner we can prove that $d \,|\, n$.'

This statement is not accompanied by an explanation. Clearly, the proof author supposes that the reader can easily see that a proof of $d \,|\, n$ is very similar to the one of $d \,|\, m$, given in line (37).

And this is indeed the case, if we realise that interchanging m and n delivers the result desired. For example, $n = n \cdot 1 + m \cdot 0$ is the 'mirror image' of the equation $m = m \cdot 1 + n \cdot 0$ stated in line (4), and proceeding with copying the derivation above with a swap of m and n eventually gives what we want.

This is, however, a long way to go, and it neglects one of the powerful aspects of λD: the definitional structure, and the use of parameter lists. Recall that a_{37} is actually accompanied by a parameter list, marked by the flag pole preceding it: it should read $a_{37}(m, n, ass_1, ass_2, ass_3)$. Now all we have to do is to swap m and n in this parameter list and perform appropriate substitutions for ass_1, ass_2 and ass_3); so we have to solve the question marks in $a_{37}(n, m, ?_1, ?_2, ?_3)$.

Check that the derivation rule (*inst*) (see Section 9.8) requires that $?_1$ must be of type $n > 0$ and $?_2$ of type $m > 0$. Hence, we may simply take $?_1 \equiv ass_2$ and $?_2 \equiv ass_1$ (hence, ass_1 and ass_2 are swapped, as well). Finally, $?_3$ must be of type $coprime(n, m)$. But we already have the assumption ass_3 of type $coprime(m, n)$. From this easily follows $coprime(n, m)$, which we denote as a hole in line (38) of Figure 15.13.

This solves all our problems and we are ready in no time (see Figure 15.13).

$$\vdots$$

(38) $a_{38} := hole\#9 : coprime(n, m)$

(39) $a_{39} := a_{37}(n, m, ass_2, ass_1, a_{38}) : d \,|\, n$

Figure 15.13 Step 9 of the proof

The remainder of the informal proof is:

'Since m and n are coprime, d must be 1, implying that $1 \in S$.
Hence there exist $x, y \in \mathbb{Z}$ such that $mx + ny = 1$. '

The formalisation of this final part of the proof is given in Figure 15.14. It is an easy consequence of the assumption ass_3 that m and n are coprime, and the fact that $d \; \varepsilon \; S$ (line (15)). (For *com-div* and *coprime*, see Figure 14.23.)

$$\vdots$$

(40) $a_{40} := \ldots$ **use** $\wedge\text{-}in$ **on** a_{37} **and** a_{39}**, and again on** $a_{17} \ldots$:

        $com\text{-}div(d, m, n) \wedge d > 0$

(41) $a_{41} := ass_3 \, d \, a_{40} : d = 1$

(42) $a_{42} := \ldots$ **use** $eq\text{-}subs$ **on** a_{15} **and** $a_{41} \ldots : 1 \; \varepsilon \; S$

(43) $a_{43} := a_{42} : \exists x, y : \mathbb{Z}. \, (1 = m \cdot x + n \cdot y)$

(44) $a_{44} := \ldots$ **use symmetry of** $=$ **on** $a_{43} \ldots$:

        $\exists x, y : \mathbb{Z}. \, (m \cdot x + n \cdot y = 1)$

Figure 15.14 Step 10 of the proof of Bézout's Lemma

So we have brought the formalisation of Bézout's Lemma to a conclusion: the informal proof reproduced in Section 15.1 has (almost) completely been formalised in λD. By following the text as a guideline, we succeeded in expressing the details of the proof in a formalised setting.

The formal proof is not yet ready for computer verification, for two reasons:

– The many shortcuts we made by inserting '*hints*', introduced by the phrase '**use** ...', must be adjusted by providing the intended formal expressions. This can be done straightforwardly; it just requires a certain amount of precise administrative work.

– There are a number of specific *holes* in the described formalisation. Most of these are due to the absence of a sufficient amount of arithmetical fore-knowledge. In Section 15.6 we discuss these holes one by one and suggest how they may be filled.

We conclude this section with a number of general remarks.

It is good to realise that the simple expression $a_{44}(m, n, ass_1, ass_2, ass_3)$ in the final line is a condensed version of the *full* (and completely formalised) proof of Bézout's Lemma. Hence, an extremely short answer to the assignment 'prove Bézout's Lemma' could consist of one judgement only, composed of an appropriate environment Δ, the five relevant declarations (corresponding to the five parameters), plus the statement

$$a_{44}(m, n, ass_1, ass_2, ass_3) \ : \ \exists x, y : \mathbb{Z} . \, (m \cdot x + n \cdot y = 1).$$

By repeatedly unfolding the visible constants, starting with a_{44} itself, we obtain more and more details of the proof as it has been presented in this chapter. In principle, we may proceed this unfolding until all of a_4 to a_{44}, plus S, $\mathbb{N}^+$, S^+ and d, have disappeared. As a final result of such a complete unfolding, we obtain one (very long) expression containing all the details that were reviewed in this chapter. This, of course, is the other extreme.

Both extremes themselves are not very revealing: they are either too compact or too detailed to convey what the essential elements of the proof are. Somewhere in between these extremes is the full flag-style proof represented in Figures 15.4 up to 15.14. We hope that the reader agrees with the authors that the presented derivation, albeit rather elaborate, contains a clear and instructive formal exposition of the proof.

Another interesting observation is that the final result in line (44), named $a_{44}(m, n, ass_1, ass_2, ass_3)$, may be *instantiated* in accordance with the derivation rules of λD. For example, we may take 55 for m and 28 for n. Next, we need proofs for the positivity of 55 and 28, plus a proof for $coprime(55, 28)$.

When we have these proofs, we can extend the 44 lines of the proof above with the four lines given in Figure 15.15, which can be derived in the empty context.

(45)	$a_{45} := \ \ldots \ :$	$55 > 0$
(46)	$a_{46} := \ \ldots \ :$	$28 > 0$
(47)	$a_{47} := \ \ldots \ :$	$coprime(55, 28)$
(48)	$a_{48} := a_{44}(55, 28, a_{45}, a_{46}, a_{47}) \ :$	$\exists x, y : \mathbb{Z} . \, (55 \cdot x + 28 \cdot y = 1)$

Figure 15.15 Specialising the proof of Bézout's Lemma

So as a consequence of Bézout's Lemma, we have obtained the proof object $a_{48}(55, 28, a_{45}, a_{46}, a_{47})$, coding a proof of

$$\exists_{x, y \in \mathbb{Z}} (55 \cdot x + 28 \cdot y = 1).$$

Note that a_{48} (with empty parameter list) stands for the specialised proof described in Figure 8.7, just as $a_{44}(m, n, ass_1, ass_2, ass_3)$, together with the accompanying context, abbreviates the general proof of Bézout's Lemma as expressed in Figure 8.6. A suitable unfolding of $a_{44}(m, n, ass_1, ass_2, ass_3)$ gives us all details described in Figure 8.6; the corresponding unfolding of a_{48} gives us the content of Figure 8.7.

So now our attempts to fully formalise the proof of Bézout's Lemma have come to an end. As already said, there remain a number of promises that we must hold: in particular, to deal with several loose ends that have to be tied together, and to give proofs of the Minimum Theorem and the Division Theorem. These will be the subjects of the remaining sections of the present chapter.

15.6 The holes in the proof of Bézout's Lemma

In the previous four sections we have given a formal λD-proof of Bézout's Lemma, in which we have skipped a number of details, called *holes*. We now come back to these holes in order to fill them.

Altogether, we have recorded nine holes. They all have the status of *proof objects* that still have to be found. The propositions they prove are of different character, but none of them is really difficult to prove, as we show below.

We list the propositions-to-prove one by one and discuss what the λD-proofs of these (mostly small) problems look like by describing them informally. These proofs should be inserted in the respective holes.

All variables mentioned below $(m, n, x, y, q, r \ldots)$ have type $\mathbb{Z}$.

I. Hole #1 (line (2), Figure 15.2): $\mathbb{Z}$ is partially ordered by $\leq$
For the notion of partial order: see Figure 12.7, line (5). Informal proofs of reflexivity and transitivity of $\leq$ are given in Section 14.10 (Lemma 14.10.1 (a) and (b)). Antisymmetry of $(\mathbb{Z}, \leq)$ was dealt with in Exercise 14.29 (a).

II. Hole #2 (line (4), Figure 15.7): $m = m \cdot 1 + n \cdot 0$
This follows directly from (1) $m \cdot 1 = m$, (2) $n \cdot 0 = 0$ and (3) $m + 0 = m$.

For the proof of equation (1): note that $m \cdot s0 = (m \cdot 0) + m = 0 + m = m$ (use *times-ii*, *times-i* (Figure 14.22) and *plus-i-alt* (Figure 14.14)).

For (2): use *times-i*, again; and for (3): *plus-i* (Figure 14.12).

III. Hole #3 (line (11), Figure 15.7): $\exists x : \mathbb{Z}. \ lw\text{-}bnd_{\mathbb{Z}}(S^+, x)$
See Exercise 15.3.

IV. Hole #4 (line (24), Figure 15.10): $m = q \cdot (m \cdot x_0 + n \cdot y_0) + r$ implies $r = m \cdot (1 - q \cdot x_0) - n \cdot (q \cdot y_0)$
This is the result of simple computation steps. It is good to realise that the

number of basic steps involved is larger than one might expect. To illustrate this, we give some of the intermediate results below:

(1) $m = q \cdot (m \cdot x_0 + n \cdot y_0) + r$,
(2) $m = (q \cdot (m \cdot x_0) + q \cdot (n \cdot y_0)) + r$,
(3) $(m - m \cdot (q \cdot x_0)) - n \cdot (q \cdot y_0) = r$,
(4) $r = m \cdot (1 - q \cdot x_0) - n \cdot (q \cdot y_0)$.

We have left out several easy steps, in particular all necessary calls to associativity and commutativity of both multiplication and addition. When writing out the full proof, these calls would add about ten more steps to the chain of computations.

V. Hole #5 (line (25), Figure 15.10): $r = m \cdot (1 - q \cdot x_0) - n \cdot (q \cdot y_0)$ implies $r = m \cdot (1 - q \cdot x_0) + n \cdot (-(q \cdot y_0))$

This is a consequence of $x - y \cdot z = x + (y \cdot (-z))$. Informal proof, based on Figure 14.17, line (3) and Lemma 14.11.4:

$$x - y \cdot z = x + (-(y \cdot z)) = x + (y \cdot (-z)).$$

VI. Hole #6 (line (30), Figure 15.11): $r < d$ and $d \leq r$ imply $\bot$
See Exercise 15.4 (a).

VII. Hole #7 (line (32), Figure 15.11): $0 \leq r$ and $\neg(r > 0)$ imply $r = 0$
See Exercise 15.4 (a).

VIII. Hole #8 (line (33), Figure 15.12): $m = q \cdot d + r$ and $r = 0$ imply $d \cdot q = m$
See Exercise 15.4 (b).

IX. Hole #9 (line (38), Figure 15.13): $coprime(m, n) \Rightarrow coprime(n, m)$
See Exercise 14.43.

15.7 The Minimum Theorem for $\mathbb{Z}$

In Section 15.1 we noticed that the proof of Bézout's Lemma uses a form of the Minimum Theorem, a basic theorem in integer arithmetic. We gave a formal version of this theorem, but without a proof, in Figure 15.2. Note that this Minimum Theorem has a complementary Maximum Theorem for non-empty subsets of $\mathbb{Z}$ being bounded from above (Exercise 15.7).

We consider it instructive to investigate the Minimum Theorem more thoroughly and give a formal proof, independently from the rest of this chapter. So we have to convince ourselves by means of a λD-proof that each non-empty subset of $\mathbb{Z}$, if bounded from below, has a minimum with respect to the relation $\leq$ (defined in Figure 14.18). We recall that $\leq$ is a partial order on $\mathbb{Z}$, as we already mentioned in Section 14.10. See also Hole #1 discussed in Section 15.6.

So let T be a non-empty subset of $\mathbb{Z}$, bounded from below. Then it's intuitively clear that it must have a minimum value. But why? We have to ground our argument on the *formal* version of $\mathbb{Z}$ as given in Chapter 14 (in particular, Section 14.2), together with the fact that the relation $\le$ on $\mathbb{Z}$ is a partial order.

Let's start with a sketch of the situation in λD-format (see Figure 15.16). We have subset T of $\mathbb{Z}$, a proof that T is non-empty and the assumption that T is bounded from below. By the aid of Figure 13.8, we may rewrite the non-emptiness of T as in line (1).

Assumption v and conclusion a_1 both have $\exists$-expressions as types. Hence, the $\exists$-*el*-rule suggests to add two pairs of new flags, as depicted below.

(1)

$$\boxed{T : ps(\mathbb{Z}) \mid u : T \ne \emptyset_{\mathbb{Z}} \mid v : \exists x : \mathbb{Z}.\ lw\text{-}bnd_{\mathbb{Z}}(T, x)}$$

$a_1^{\dagger} := \ldots$ use $a_{6\,[Fig.13.8]}$ on $u\ldots : \exists n : \mathbb{Z}.\ n \,\varepsilon\, T$

$\boxed{l : \mathbb{Z} \mid ass_1 : lw\text{-}bnd_{\mathbb{Z}}(T, l)}$

$\boxed{n : \mathbb{Z} \mid ass_2 : n \,\varepsilon\, T}$

$\vdots$

†*parameters suppressed*

Figure 15.16 Start of the proof of the Minimum Theorem

Our goal is to find a least element of T in this setting.

There are several ways to achieve this. One possibility is to prove this by contradiction: assume that T does *not* have a least element and derive $\bot$. This approach works well and was elaborated in Exercise 15.5.

In order to demonstrate the flexibility of the λD-format, we follow another strategy for the continuation of our proof attempt, which goes as follows. In order to find the minimum of T, we start with the lower bound l of T, which is 'below' (to be precise: $\le$) all elements of T. Now we climb upwards through the integer numbers, one by one, until we strike upon a member of T. This element must be the minimum of T.

Another way of expressing this method is that we browse upward, from l, through other lower bounds of T, until we meet an element of T. This is a lower bound which belongs to T, and consequently is the desired minimum of T (cf. Figures 15.1 and 15.2). Note that all integers greater than this minimum are no longer lower bounds of T. So, we can also phrase our strategy in terms of lower bounds only: we look for *a lower bound of T such that its successor is not a lower bound of T*.

Hence our upward search may be expressed as follows: we try to prove that

(i) $\exists y : \mathbb{Z}.\ (lw\text{-}bnd_{\mathbb{Z}}(T, y) \wedge \neg lw\text{-}bnd_{\mathbb{Z}}(T, s\,y))$.

We prove this by contradiction: we assume that such a y does *not* exist, and derive $\bot$. The *negation* of (i) can be rewritten by means of logical equivalences to:

(ii) $\forall y : \mathbb{Z}.\ (lw\text{-}bnd_{\mathbb{Z}}(T, y) \Rightarrow lw\text{-}bnd_{\mathbb{Z}}(T, s\, y))$.

So (ii) is our assumption and our goal is to prove $\bot$. We derive a contradiction by showing that from (ii) we can derive that *every* $x : \mathbb{Z}$ is a lower bound of T, i.e. $\forall x : \mathbb{Z}.\ lw\text{-}bnd_{\mathbb{Z}}(T, x)$; and this can be easily refuted.

So we take the predicate

$P := \lambda x : \mathbb{Z}.\ lw\text{-}bnd_{\mathbb{Z}}(T, x)$,

and first prove from assumption (ii) by (symmetric) induction over $\mathbb{Z}$, that $\forall x : \mathbb{Z}.\ P\, x$.

Clearly, P holds for the lower bound l introduced above, so $\exists x : \mathbb{Z}.\ P\, x$ by $\exists$-*in*. To make a good use of that fact, we take the *variant of induction for* $\mathbb{Z}$ as mentioned in Remark 14.2.1, with l as the 'start value' for P. Then left to prove is

(iii) $\forall x : \mathbb{Z}.\ (P\, x \Rightarrow (P(s\, x) \wedge P(p\, x)))$.

Now (ii), our extra assumption, is $\forall x : \mathbb{Z}.\ (P\, x \Rightarrow P(s\, x))$. So in order to obtain (iii) we only have to prove $\forall x : \mathbb{Z}.\ (P\, x \Rightarrow P(p\, x))$. The proof of the latter expression is not difficult: if x is a lower bound of T, then a *predecessor* of x must clearly also be a lower bound of T.

The conclusion by induction is $\forall x : \mathbb{Z}.\ P\, x$. This conflicts with the non-emptiness of T: we have $n\ \varepsilon\ T$ (see ass_2 of Figure 15.16) and albeit that n itself may happen to be a lower bound of T, this is certainly not the case for $s\, n$, which is greater than $n\ \varepsilon\ T$ and hence not a lower bound of T.

This argumentation was formalised in Figure 15.17, which is a continuation of Figure 15.16.

So now our proof has reached an important point: we have shown that there exists an integer z such that z itself is a lower bound of T, but its successor $s\, z$ is not. Hence, this z is a good candidate for being the minimum of T. We prove this conjecture in Figure 15.18, which we shall discuss in more detail below.

Recall (see Figure 15.2, line (1)) that we have to find a proof for the expression

$\exists m : \mathbb{Z}.\ least_{\mathbb{Z}}(T, m)$,

where $least_{\mathbb{Z}}$ has been defined in Figure 15.1, line (2).

Triggered by the $\exists$-quantifier in the type of line (14) of Figure 15.17, we first raise flags for assumptions with variables z and ass_6, in order to be able to appeal to $\exists$-*el* with respect to line (14) (what we shall do in line (27)).

It suffices to show that z satisfies the predicate of being a minimum of T, so

$$\vdots$$

(2) $\qquad P := \lambda x : \mathbb{Z}.\ lw\text{-}bnd_{\mathbb{Z}}(T, x)\ :\ \mathbb{Z} \to *_p$

(3) $\qquad a_3 := \ldots$ use $\exists\text{-}in$ on l and $ass_1 \ldots :\ \exists x : \mathbb{Z}.\ P\,x$

> $ass_3\ :\ \forall x : \mathbb{Z}.\ (P\,x \Rightarrow P(s\,x))$
>
> > $x : \mathbb{Z} \mid ass_4 : P\,x$
> >
> > (4) $\qquad a_4 := \ldots$ use Exercise $14.23\,(b) \ldots :\ p\,x \le x$
> >
> > > $t : \mathbb{Z} \mid ass_5 : t \,\varepsilon\, T$
> > >
> > > (5) $\qquad a_5 := \ldots$ use $\forall\text{-}el$ and $\Rightarrow\text{-}el$ on ass_4, t and $ass_5 \ldots :\ x \le t$
> > >
> > > (6) $\qquad a_6 := \ldots$ use Lemma $14.10.1\,(b)$ on a_4 and $a_5 \ldots :\ p\,x \le t$
> > >
> > (7) $\qquad a_7 := \ldots$ use $\Rightarrow\text{-}in$ and $\forall\text{-}in$ on $a_6 \ldots :\ P(p\,x)$
> >
> (8) $\qquad a_8 := \ldots$ use $\Rightarrow\text{-}in$ and $\forall\text{-}in$ on $a_7 \ldots :\ \forall x : \mathbb{Z}.\ (P\,x \Rightarrow P(p\,x))$
>
> (9) $\qquad a_9 := \ldots$ use logical laws on ass_3 and $a_8 \ldots :$
> $$\forall x : \mathbb{Z}.\ (P\,x \Rightarrow (P(s\,x) \wedge P(p\,x)))$$

(10) $\qquad a_{10} := \ldots$ use variant of induction for $\mathbb{Z}$ on a_3 and $a_9 \ldots :$
$$\forall x : \mathbb{Z}.\ P\,x$$

(11) $\qquad a_{11} := \ldots$ use $\forall\text{-}el$ on a_{10} and $s\,n \ldots :\ P(s\,n)$

(12) $\qquad a_{12} := \ldots$ use $\forall\text{-}el$ and $\Rightarrow\text{-}el$ on a_{11}, n and $ass_2 \ldots :\ s\,n \le n$

(13) $\qquad a_{13} := \ldots$ use arithmetic on $a_{12} \ldots :\ \bot$

(14) $\qquad a_{14} := \ldots$ use $\neg\text{-}in$ and logic on $a_{13} \ldots :$
$$\exists z : \mathbb{Z}.\ (lw\text{-}bnd_{\mathbb{Z}}(T, z) \wedge \neg lw\text{-}bnd_{\mathbb{Z}}(T, s\,z))$$

Figure 15.17 The existence of a maximal lower bound of T

$least_{\mathbb{Z}}(T, z)$ (see line (25)), because from this follows line (26) via $\exists\text{-}in$. A triple use of $\exists\text{-}el$ then permits us to let the type of line (26) 'descend' to the original context consisting of T, u and v, and we have proved the Minimum Theorem: see the concluding line (29).

But how can we obtain $least_{\mathbb{Z}}(T, z)$, being the proof obligation in line (25)? Let's unfold it:

$$z \,\varepsilon\, T \wedge \forall t : \mathbb{Z}.\ (t \,\varepsilon\, T \Rightarrow z \le t).$$

The part behind the $\wedge$ in the last-mentioned expression is δ-equivalent to $lw\text{-}bnd_{\mathbb{Z}}(T, z)$, which is the left-hand side of the assumption called ass_6. So all that's left to prove is $z \,\varepsilon\, T$ (see line (24)). This we prove by contradiction: if $\neg(z \,\varepsilon\, T)$, then we can show that not only z, but also $s\,z$ is a lower bound of T (line (22)); and this contradicts the right-hand side of the assumption called ass_6.

(A more complete proof of the Minimum Theorem, with the 'hints' worked out, can be found in Appendix C, Section C.2.)

$$\vdots$$

$$z : \mathbb{Z} \mid ass_6 \ : \ (lw\text{-}bnd_{\mathbb{Z}}(T, z) \wedge \neg lw\text{-}bnd_{\mathbb{Z}}(T, s\,z))$$

(15) $a_{15} := \ \ldots \ \textbf{use } \wedge\text{-}el_1 \textbf{ on } ass_6 \ \ldots \ : \ lw\text{-}bnd_{\mathbb{Z}}(T, z)$

(16) $a_{16} := \ \ldots \ \textbf{use } \wedge\text{-}el_2 \textbf{ on } ass_6 \ \ldots \ : \ \neg lw\text{-}bnd_{\mathbb{Z}}(T, s\,z)$

$$ass_7 \ : \ \neg(z \ \varepsilon \ T)$$

$$y : \mathbb{Z} \mid ass_8 \ : \ y \ \varepsilon \ T$$

(17) $a_{17} := \ \ldots \ \textbf{use } \forall\text{-}el \textbf{ and } \Rightarrow\text{-}el \textbf{ on } a_{15}, \ y \textbf{ and } ass_8 \ \ldots \ :$
$$z \le y$$

$$ass_9 \ : \ z = y$$

(18) $a_{18} := \ \ldots \ \textbf{use } ass_9, \ ass_7 \textbf{ and } ass_8 \ \ldots \ : \ \bot$

(19) $a_{19} := \ \ldots \ \textbf{use } \neg\text{-}in \textbf{ on } a_{18} \ \ldots \ : \ \neg(z = y)$

(20) $a_{20} := \ \ldots \ \textbf{use } \wedge\text{-}in \textbf{ on } a_{17} \textbf{ and } a_{19} \ \ldots \ : \ z < y$

(21) $a_{21} := \ \ldots \ \textbf{use Exercise } 14.29 \, (b) \textbf{ on } a_{20} \ \ldots : \ s\,z \le y$

(22) $a_{22} := \ \ldots \ \textbf{use } \Rightarrow\text{-}in \textbf{ and } \forall\text{-}in \textbf{ on } a_{21} \ \ldots \ : \ lw\text{-}bnd_{\mathbb{Z}}(T, s\,z)$

(23) $a_{23} := \ \textbf{use } \neg\text{-}el \textbf{ on } a_{16} \textbf{ and } a_{22} \ \ldots \ : \ \bot$

(24) $a_{24} := \ \ldots \ \textbf{use } \neg\text{-}in \textbf{ and } \neg\neg\text{-}el \textbf{ on } a_{23} \ \ldots \ : \ z \ \varepsilon \ T$

(25) $a_{25} := \ \ldots \ \textbf{use } \wedge\text{-}in \textbf{ on } a_{24} \textbf{ and } a_{15} \ \ldots \ : \ least_{\mathbb{Z}}(T, z)$

(26) $a_{26} := \ \ldots \ \textbf{use } \exists\text{-}in \textbf{ on } z \textbf{ and } a_{25} \ \ldots \ : \ \exists m : \mathbb{Z}. \ least_{\mathbb{Z}}(T, m)$

(27) $a_{27} := \ \ldots \ \textbf{use } \exists\text{-}el \textbf{ on } a_{14} \ \ldots \ : \ \ldots$

(28) $a_{28} := \ \ldots \ \textbf{use } \exists\text{-}el \textbf{ on } a_1 \ \ldots \ : \ \ldots$

(29) $min\text{-}the(T, u, v) := \ \ldots \ \textbf{use } \exists\text{-}el \textbf{ on } v \ \ldots \ : \ \exists m : \mathbb{Z}. \ least_{\mathbb{Z}}(T, m)$

Figure 15.18 The remaining part of the proof of the Minimum Theorem

The proof as described in Figures 15.16 to 15.18 is not difficult to follow. The reader is invited to study it in detail and compare it with the full proof in Appendix C.

We recall from Figure 15.2 that the existence of the minimum of T implies its uniqueness (line (2)), so that we can give it a name, viz. $minimum(T, u, v)$ (see line (3)). Moreover, this *minimum* has some obvious characteristic properties, which are also accounted for in the same figure (line (4)).

15.8 The Division Theorem

In Section 15.1 we also mentioned a second fundamental theorem from arithmetic needed in the proof of Bézout's Lemma, namely the Division Theorem. For a formal version, see Figure 15.3. It expresses that, for integers m and d both greater than 0, there exist integers q and r such that $m = q \cdot d + r$ and $0 \leq r < d$. It can also be shown that such a q must be non-negative and that the numbers q and r are *unique*.

Otherwise said: when dividing the so-called *dividend* m by *divisor* d, we obtain *the quotient* $q \geq 0$ and *the remainder* r. The quotient q is such that $q \cdot d$ is the greatest multiple of d that is $\leq m$. This implies that r, the difference between m and $q \cdot d$, is ≥ 0 but $< d$.

How can we formally *prove* this theorem? We have to show the *existence* of q and r with the desired properties.

A promising approach is to consider multiples of d: start with $0 \cdot d$, which is 0 so less than m, and continue with $1 \cdot d$, $2 \cdot d$, and so on. Since $d > 0$, we must have $0 \cdot d < 1 \cdot d < 2 \cdot d < \ldots$, so somewhere these multiples must cross the 'border' m: then $(k + 1) \cdot d$ exceeds m, whereas $k \cdot d$ did not yet do so. This k is then the quotient desired, and $m - k \cdot d$ is the remainder of the division.

This process recalls what we did in the previous section, when searching for the minimum of a non-empty subset T of $\mathbb{N}$. There we also looked for a maximal element with a certain property (namely: to be a lower bound of T).

Obviously, we might give a proof of the Division Theorem by copying the ideas described in the previous section. But we prefer not to *redo* the work we already have done before. It appears more profitable, and more in the line of type theory, to *apply the results* of the previous section.

One way of doing this is to appeal to the mirror-image of the Minimum Theorem, called the *Maximum Theorem* (which we have mentioned already in the beginning of the previous section):

Each non-empty subset of $\mathbb{Z}$ that is bounded from above, has a maximum.

The theorem can be proven by the aid of the Minimum Theorem; see Exercise 15.7.

In order to be able to refer formally to the Maximum Theorem and its consequences, we list the relevant notions, without proofs, in Figure 15.19. Note that an *upper* bound for $T \subseteq \mathbb{Z}$ with respect to relation '$\leq$' can be defined as a *lower* bound for T with respect to the reverse relation '$\geq$'. Similarly, a *greatest* element of T with respect to $\leq$ is a *least* element for $\geq$.

The Maximum Theorem implies that the set of *all* multiples $l \cdot d$ that are smaller than or equal to m, has a maximum. And this, with a view to our discussion above, suffices for the proof of the Division Theorem.

$$\boxed{T : ps(\mathbb{Z})}$$

$$\boxed{l : \mathbb{Z}}$$

(1) $up\text{-}bnd_{\mathbb{Z}}(T, l) := lw\text{-}bnd(\mathbb{Z}, \geq, T, l) : *_p$

(2) $grtst_{\mathbb{Z}}(T, l) := least(\mathbb{Z}, \geq, T, l) : *_p$

$$\boxed{u : T \neq \emptyset_{\mathbb{Z}} \mid v : \exists x : \mathbb{Z} . \, up\text{-}bnd_{\mathbb{Z}}(T, x)}$$

(3) $max\text{-}the(T, u, v) := \ldots : \exists m : \mathbb{Z} . \, grtst_{\mathbb{Z}}(T, m)$

(4) $max\text{-}uni\text{-}the(T, u, v) := \ldots : \exists^1 m : \mathbb{Z} . \, grtst_{\mathbb{Z}}(T, m)$

(5) $maximum(T, u, v) := \ldots : \mathbb{Z}$

(6) $max\text{-}prop(T, u, v) := \ldots :$

         $maximum(T, u, v) \; \varepsilon \; T \; \wedge \; up\text{-}bnd_{\mathbb{Z}}(T, maximum(T, u, v))$

Figure 15.19 The Maximum Theorem, related notions and consequences

We limit ourselves, again, to an elaborate *sketch* of the formalised proof in λD, leaving a full formalisation to the reader. We start the proof of the Division Theorem with a context consisting of two positive integers, m and d, and divide the proof into three parts:

I. We define the set D of all multiples of d that are $\leq m$

This subset D of $\mathbb{Z}$ is: $D := \{x : \mathbb{Z} \mid (\exists k : \mathbb{Z} . \, (x = k \cdot d)) \wedge x \leq m\}$.

See Figure 15.20 for a formalisation. We also prove that D is non-empty and bounded from above: we show that $0 \; \varepsilon \; D$ (line (5)), so $D \neq \emptyset$ (line (7)), and that there is an upper bound of D, namely m (lines (9) and (10)).

$$\boxed{m, d : \mathbb{Z} \mid u : m > 0 \mid v : d > 0}$$

(1) $D^{\dagger} := \{x : \mathbb{Z} \mid (\exists k : \mathbb{Z} . \, (x = k \cdot d)) \wedge x \leq m\} : ps(\mathbb{Z})$

(2) $a_2 := \ldots$ **use Lemma** $14.11.1\,(a) \; \ldots : 0 = 0 \cdot d$

(3) $a_3 := \ldots$ **use** $\exists\text{-}in \; \ldots : \exists k : \mathbb{Z} . \, (0 = k \cdot d)$

(4) $a_4 := \ldots$ **use** $\wedge\text{-}el_1$ **on** $u \; \ldots : 0 \leq m$

(5) $a_5 := \ldots$ **use** $\wedge\text{-}in$ **on** a_3 **and** $\tilde{a}_4 \; \ldots : 0 \; \varepsilon \; D$

(6) $a_6 := \ldots$ **use** $\exists\text{-}in$ **on** $a_5 \; \ldots : \exists z : \mathbb{Z} . \, (z \; \varepsilon \; D)$

(7) $a_7 := a_{12[Fig.\ 13.8]}(\mathbb{Z}, D, a_6) : D \neq \emptyset_{\mathbb{Z}}$

$$\boxed{x : \mathbb{Z} \mid w : x \; \varepsilon \; D}$$

(8) $a_8 := \ldots$ **use** $\wedge\text{-}el_2$ **on** $w \; \ldots : x \leq m$

(9) $a_9 := \ldots$ **use** $\Rightarrow\text{-}in$ **and** $\forall\text{-}in$ **on** $a_8 \; \ldots : up\text{-}bnd_{\mathbb{Z}}(D, m)$

(10) $a_{10} := \ldots$ **use** $\exists\text{-}in$ **on** $a_9 \; \ldots : \exists x : \mathbb{Z} . \, up\text{-}bnd_{\mathbb{Z}}(D, x)$

†*parameters suppressed*

Figure 15.20 The set D and some of its properties

II. We define the maximum l of D and define the quotient q

The Maximum Theorem implies that D has a unique maximum, say l. We list some relevant properties of l; among other things, l belongs to D, hence there is a k such that $l = k \cdot d$. We prove that this k is unique and call it q (see Figure 15.21).

$$\vdots$$

(11) | $l := maximum(D, a_7, a_{10}) : \mathbb{Z}$

(12) | $a_{12} := max\text{-}prop(D, a_7, a_{10}) : l \; \varepsilon \; D \wedge up\text{-}bnd_{\mathbb{Z}}(D, l)$

(13) | $a_{13} := \dots$ use $\wedge\text{-}el_1$ on $a_{12} \dots : (\exists k : \mathbb{Z}. (l = k \cdot d)) \wedge l \leq m$

(14) | $a_{14} := \dots$ use $\wedge\text{-}el_2$ on $a_{12} \dots : \forall t : \mathbb{Z}. (t \; \varepsilon \; D \Rightarrow t \leq l)$

(15) | $a_{15} := \dots$ use $\wedge\text{-}el_1$ on $a_{13} \dots : \exists k : \mathbb{Z}. (l = k \cdot d)$

(16) | $a_{16} := \dots$ use $\wedge\text{-}el_2$ on $a_{13} \dots : l \leq m$

| $k_1, k_2 : \mathbb{Z} \mid w_1 : l = k_1 \cdot d \mid w_2 : l = k_2 \cdot d$

(17) | $a_{17} := \dots$ use properties of $=$ on w_1 and $w_2 : k_1 \cdot d = k_2 \cdot d$

(18) | $a_{18} := \dots$ use $\wedge\text{-}el_2$ on $v \dots : d \neq 0$

(19) | $a_{19} := \dots$ use Lemma 14.11.7 on a_{17} and $a_{18} \dots : k_1 = k_2$

(20) | $a_{20} := \dots$ use $\Rightarrow\text{-}in$ and $\forall\text{-}in \dots : \exists^{\leq 1} k : \mathbb{Z}. (l = k \cdot d)$

(21) | $a_{21} := \dots$ use $\wedge\text{-}in$ on a_{15} and $a_{20} \dots : \exists^1 k : \mathbb{Z}. (l = k \cdot d)$

(22) | $q := \iota(\mathbb{Z}, \lambda x : \mathbb{Z}. (l = x \cdot d), a_{21}) : \mathbb{Z}$

Figure 15.21 The maximum l of D and its properties

III. We define the remainder r and prove that $0 \leq r < d$

We define r as the difference $m - q \cdot d$. Since $q \cdot d$ is equal to the maximum l of D, which is $\leq m$, we conclude that $r \geq 0$. What is left, is to prove that $r < d$. We show this by contradiction: if $r \geq d$, then $(q + 1) \cdot d$ would also be in D, implying that $q \cdot d$ is not the maximum of D (see Figure 15.22).

Hence our investigation of how to prove the Division Theorem in λD-style has come to an end. The transformation of the presented proof into a complete λD-proof is not difficult.

15.9 Conclusions

In the present chapter we have put system λD to the test, by trying to formalise a substantial piece of mathematics, namely Bézout's Lemma; to be more precise: a proof of it. The proof itself is not very sizeable; but it involves a number of implicit notions that require a more explicit treatment, prior to the formalisation of the lemma itself. Altogether, this has accumulated into a challenging

$$\vdots$$

(23) $\quad a_{23} := \iota\text{-}prop(\mathbb{Z}, \lambda x : \mathbb{Z}.\,(l = x \cdot d), a_{21}) \;:\; l = q \cdot d$

(24) $\quad a_{24} := \dots$ use *eq-subs* on a_{16} and $a_{23} \dots \;:\; q \cdot d \leq m$

(25) $\quad r := m - q \cdot d \;:\; \mathbb{Z}$

(26) $\quad a_{26} := \dots$ use arithm. on a_{24} and $r \dots \;:\; r \geq 0$

(27) $\quad a_{27} := \dots$ use arithm. on the definition of $r \dots \;:\; m = q \cdot d + r$

$\boxed{w \;:\; d \leq r}$

(28) $\qquad a_{28} := \dots$ use arithm. on w and $a_{27} \dots \;:\; q \cdot d + d \leq m$

(29) $\qquad a_{29} := \dots$ use arithm. on $a_{28} \dots \;:\; (q+1) \cdot d \leq m$

(30) $\qquad a_{30} := \dots$ use *eq-refl* $\dots \;:\; (q+1) \cdot d = (q+1) \cdot d$

(31) $\qquad a_{31} := \dots$ use $\exists\text{-}in$ on $a_{30} \dots \;:\; \exists k : \mathbb{Z}.\,((q+1) \cdot d = k \cdot d)$

(32) $\qquad a_{32} := \dots$ use $\wedge\text{-}in$ on a_{31} and $a_{29} \dots \;:\; (q+1) \cdot d \;\varepsilon\; D$

(33) $\qquad a_{33} := a_{14}\,((q+1) \cdot d)\, a_{32} \;:\; (q+1) \cdot d \leq l$

(34) $\qquad a_{34} := \dots$ use *eq-subs* on a_{33} and $a_{23} \dots \;:\; (q+1) \cdot d \leq q \cdot d$

(35) $\qquad a_{35} := \dots$ use arithm. on $a_{34} \dots \;:\; d \leq 0$

(36) $\qquad a_{36} := \dots$ use arithm. on v and $a_{35} \dots \;:\; \bot$

(37) $\quad a_{37} := \dots$ use $\neg\text{-}in$ and arithm. $\dots \;:\; r < d$

(38) $\quad a_{38} := \dots$ use $\wedge\text{-}in$ (twice) on a_{27}, a_{26} and $a_{37} \dots \;:$
$$(m = q \cdot d + r) \wedge (r \geq 0 \wedge r < d)$$

(39) $\quad div\text{-}the(m, d, n, v) := \;$ use $\exists\text{-}in$ (twice) on $a_{38} \;:$
$$\exists q, r : \mathbb{Z}.\,((m = q \cdot d + r) \wedge (r \geq 0 \wedge r < d))$$

Figure 15.22 The completion of the proof of the Division Theorem

exercise, in which various aspects of the formalisation process have come to the surface. Hence, the task we have set ourselves has appeared to be a good test case; and now, in retrospect, it is sensible to conclude that we have succeeded in this investigation concerning the useability of λD.

We may well conclude, albeit provisionally due to the restricted test setting, that λD has sufficient power to formalise large amounts of mathematical content. What convinces us still more is that previous endeavours with the λD-like system Automath have shown that a large corpus of mathematical texts could effectively and successfully be translated into formal form, without insurmountable problems (see also de Bruijn, 1968, 1970; van Benthem Jutting, 1977). Hence, such formal translations are not only theoretically possible, but also practically feasible.

We have started the 'real work' in this chapter with the formal definition of a general minimum operator for certain subsets. We continued with λD-formulations (provisionally without proofs) of the Minimum Theorem and the Division Theorem, to be used in the proof of Bézout's Lemma.

Then we embarked upon the proof of Bézout's Lemma, which we have split into three parts: Sections 15.3 to 15.5. In the process of developing the proof, we took the liberty to introduce several shortcuts, for reasons of economy and readability:

- We have applied the parameter list convention (Notation 11.7.1).
- As in previous chapters, we did not write out proof terms based on logical (natural deduction) rules, but instead we only gave hints about the relevant rules.
- We introduced 'holes', being omitted proof terms, to be constructed at a later stage; many of these holes are based on mathematical (or computational) lemmas being more or less out of scope for the progress of the proof, or too complex to be filled in on the spot.

At the end of Section 15.5 it turned out that our formalisation task had come to a successful end. We could immediately use this to derive a formal proof of the *instantiated* Bézout Lemma, in which we have chosen specific m and n. This shows all the more how powerful the parameter system of λD is when it comes to 'specialising' a theorem or a lemma.

We have also seen in which manner the holes in the proof may be filled; this was the subject of Section 15.6. Many small tasks of a varying nature have been reviewed, with satisfactory results.

In Section 15.7 we considered the Minimum Theorem and how to prove it. A formal approach by the aid of symmetric induction has delivered a viable solution, which could be formalised in λD, as required. The notion 'lower bound' played a prominent role in the process.

The Division Theorem was the focus in Section 15.8. It turned out that a formal proof of this theorem could be built on the Maximum Theorem, a 'mirror image' of the Minimum Theorem, by choosing the proper perspective on the mathematical content of the theorem. The proof, presented in three parts, turned out to be, again, a fruitful exercise in formalisation.

15.10 Further reading

This chapter shows that a real mathematical proof of a real mathematical result can be fully formalised in λD. An early successful attempt of a formalisation of a serious piece of mathematics into a λD-like setting was made by L.S. van Benthem Jutting and is described in his PhD thesis (van Benthem Jutting, 1977).

In today's proof assistants there are a number of formalisations of Bézout's

Lemma, which is often called *Bézout's Theorem* or occurs without being explicitly named. F. Wiedijk has a web-page called *Formalizing 100 Theorems*, (Wiedijk, 2013), where he keeps a list of the 'top 100' mathematical theorems and the systems in which they have been formalised. Bézout's Theorem is number 60 in the list, so we can see that it has been formalised (status of November 2013) in

- HOL Light, by J. Harrison,
- Mizar, by R. Kwiatek,
- Isabelle, by A. Chaieb,
- Coq, in the standard library,
- ProofPower, by R.D. Arthan.

The precise statement varies in the various systems, so it is interesting to see what exactly has been formalised. We first recall that in our setting (see Figure 14.23) we define, for $m, n : \mathbb{Z}$ with $m > 0$ and $n > 0$, the $gcd(m, n)$ to be the unique $k : \mathbb{Z}$ for which

$$k \mid m \wedge k \mid n \wedge \forall l : \mathbb{Z}. \, (l \mid m \wedge l \mid n \Rightarrow l \leq k)$$

and we have introduced the name *gcd-prop* in the same figure for this determining property of the *gcd*.

In various proof assistants (e.g. Mizar) the notion of *gcd* that is used is different from ours. (Ours seems to be the standard one and can be found in various textbooks.) The alternative definition, which we denote for clarity as $gcd'(m, n)$, is that, given $m, n : \mathbb{Z}$, $gcd'(m, n)$ is defined to be the unique natural number k for which

$$k \mid m \wedge k \mid n \wedge \forall l : \mathbb{Z}. \, (l \mid m \wedge l \mid n \Rightarrow l \mid k).$$

So, $gcd'(m, n)$ is again the 'greatest' common divisor of m and n, but now *greatest* in the ordering of 'divisibility'. (Note that, if we allow k to be an integer instead of a natural number, then the uniqueness is lost.) Let us use $gcd\text{-}prop'(k, m, n)$ for the alternative gcd property displayed above.

It can be proved that, for $m, n > 0$, the definitions of *gcd* and *gcd'* coincide. The nice thing about *gcd'* is that it also works for $m = n = 0$: we have $gcd'(0, 0) = 0$, because 0 is the 'greatest' factor of 0 in the 'divides' relation.

The general form of Bézout's Theorem states that for $m, n : \mathbb{Z}$ with $m > 0$ and $n > 0$,

$$\exists x, y : \mathbb{Z}. \, (mx + ny = gcd(m, n)).$$

In the present chapter we prove the 'restricted form', which states that for $m, n : \mathbb{Z}$ with $m > 0$ and $n > 0$ and $coprime(m, n)$,

$$\exists x, y : \mathbb{Z}. \, (mx + ny = 1),$$

where $coprime(m, n)$ is defined as $\forall k : \mathbb{Z}. \, ((k \mid m \wedge k \mid n \wedge k > 0) \Rightarrow k = 1)$ (see

Figure 14.23, again). (It can be proved that $coprime(m, n) \Leftrightarrow gcd(m, n) = 1$ for either one of the definitions of gcd.) So we prove Bézout's Theorem for the case where $gcd(m, n) = 1$.

Let's now look at the formalisations of the theorem in the various proof assistants.

HOL Light The theorem is called `INT_GCD_EXISTS_POS`, and it states in mathematical terms:

$$\forall a \, b \, \exists d \, (0 \leq d \wedge d \,|\, a \wedge d \,|\, b \wedge \exists x \, y \, (d = ax + by)).$$

Here, a, b, d, x, y range over the integers. The theorem does not explicitly refer to the notion of gcd, but states that there exists a positive d that is a linear combination of a and b.

It can be proven that, if $0 \leq d \wedge d \,|\, a \wedge d \,|\, b \wedge \exists \, x \, y \, (d = ax + by)$, then d satisfies $gcd\text{-}prop'(d, a, b)$ (and also the other way around), which implies the uniqueness of the d in the theorem.

Mizar The theorem is called `NEWTON:67` and occurs in Kwiatek (1990). It states in mathematical terms:

$$\forall m, n : nat \, (m > 0 \vee n > 0 \Rightarrow \exists i, i_1 : \mathbb{Z} \, (im + i_1 n = gcd'(m, n))).$$

Note that m, n range over nat and i, i_1 range over $\mathbb{Z}$ and that the theorem is proved under the hypothesis that $m > 0$ or $n > 0$, which is a bit more liberal than in our case ($m > 0$ *and* $n > 0$). The general form of Bézout's Theorem is proved, for the natural numbers.

The notion of greatest common divisor in Mizar is the one that we called gcd' above, so we have used that notation in the mathematical statement (where Mizar of course writes gcd).

Isabelle The Isabelle system has its own list of the 100 formalised theorems (Klein, 2013). Bézout's Theorem states in mathematical terms:

$$\forall a, b \, \exists d, x, y \, (d \,|\, a \wedge d \,|\, b \wedge (ax - by = d \vee bx - ay = d)),$$

where a, b, d, x, y range over nat. So, just like in HOL Light, the theorem does not use the notion of gcd explicitly. The Isabelle formalisation circumvents having to deal with integers (instead of the naturals) by making a case distinction: either $ax \geq by$ or $bx \geq ay$.

Coq The Coq system also has its own list of the 100 formalised theorems (Madiot, 2013). Bézout's Theorem is part of the standard library, and it is formalised using inductive types. We translate it in standard mathematical terms:

$$\forall a, b, d : \mathbb{Z} \, (gcd\text{-}prop'(d, a, b) \Rightarrow \exists u, v : \mathbb{Z} \, (ua + vb = d)),$$

where $gcd\text{-}prop'(d, a, b)$ denotes the alternative gcd property discussed above (uniqueness is not explicitly proven). So, Coq has the same definition of *gcd* as Mizar, using the 'divisibility' ordering.

ProofPower The ProofPower system (Arthan, 2013) by R.D. Arthan also maintains a web-page (Jones, 2013) of the theorems from the 'famous 100 theorems' list that have been formalised in it. Bézout's Theorem in mathematical form reads

$$\forall m, n \, (0 < m \wedge 0 < n \Rightarrow$$
$$\exists a, b \, (bn \leq am \wedge gcd(m, n) = am - bn) \, \vee$$
$$\exists a, b \, (am \leq bn \wedge gcd(m, n) = bn - am)).$$

The variables m, n, a, b range over *nat*, and just like in Isabelle, the integers are circumvented by making a case distinction in the conclusion.

Exercises

15.1 Let $m, n \in \mathbb{N}^+$ and define d as $gcd(m, n)$.

(a) Prove in λD that $d|m$ and $d|n$.
(b) Let $m = k \cdot d$ and $n = l \cdot d$. Give an informal proof of $gcd(k, l) = 1$.
(c) Give an informal proof to show that the restricted version of Bézout's Lemma entails the general version (cf. Remark 15.1.1).

15.2 Find the proof objects in lines (3) and (4) of Figure 15.1.

15.3 See Section 15.6. Give a λD-proof leading to the missing proof object in Hole #3.

15.4 Give a complete λD-version of the following derivations, by elaborating the hints and filling the holes:

(a) Figure 15.11,
(b) Figure 15.12. (Apply $\exists$-*el* two times to obtain line (36), and two times for line (37), in accordance with Remark 15.4.1.)

15.5 Consider the Minimum Theorem, as stated in Section 15.2, part II.

(a) Show that the following biimplication holds:
$$\neg \exists x : \mathbb{Z}. \, least_{\mathbb{Z}}(T, x) \iff \forall x : \mathbb{Z}. \, (x \, \varepsilon \, T \Rightarrow \exists t : \mathbb{Z}. \, (t \, \varepsilon \, T \wedge t < x)),$$
by 'rewriting' the left-hand side in a number of steps to the right-hand side, using definition unfolding and logical and arithmetical lemmas.
(b) Extend Figure 15.16 with the assumption $\neg \exists x : \mathbb{Z}. \, least_{\mathbb{Z}}(T, x)$. Give a λD-proof of $\forall x : \mathbb{Z}. \, \exists y : \mathbb{Z}. \, (y \, \varepsilon \, T \wedge y < k)$ in this setting. (Hint: use part (a) and the variant of induction for $\mathbb{Z}$ as described in Remark 14.2.1.)
(c) Prove the Minimum Theorem by taking Figure 15.16 as the proof setting, and showing that the assumption $\neg \exists x : \mathbb{Z}. \, least_{\mathbb{Z}}(T, x)$ then leads to a contradiction.

15.6 Give a proof sketch for the uniqueness of the quotient and the remainder in the Division Theorem.

15.7 Give a proof sketch of the Maximum Theorem, by making use of the Minimum Theorem. (Hint: for subset T of $\mathbb{Z}$, define T' as the set of all opposites of elements of T, i.e. $T' \equiv \{x : \mathbb{Z} \mid -x \; \varepsilon \; T\}$.)

15.8 Replace all hints in Figure 15.20 by proof objects in λD-style.

15.9 Give a full description of the arithmetical lemmas used in the hints of Figure 15.22 and give informal proofs for each of them.

16

Further perspectives

16.1 Useful applications of λD

The type theory λD provides a system in which mathematical definitions, statements and proofs can be completely spelled out in a very structured way that is still close to ordinary mathematical practice. This enables and facilitates the formalisation of mathematics and the checking of its correctness. Below, we summarise the main features of type theory, and in particular λD, as a system for formalising mathematics.

Formalisation of mathematics via type theory In λD-like type theory, a mathematical notion can be defined precisely in full detail and the definition can be reasoned with in a logically sound way. The type system enforces a very high level of precision, which gives additional insight into mathematical and logical constructs. Nevertheless, formalising mathematics in λD is still very close to what is standard in mathematics.

Checking of mathematics The high level of precision of type theory greatly improves the level of correctness of the formalised mathematics: incomplete proofs, or proofs using illegal logical steps, are not accepted and a definition has to be syntactically correct. The *soundness* of course still depends on the axioms that one has assumed: if the axioms do not correspond to what one wants to formalise, or if they are inconsistent, the derived results are still useless. This already applies to informal mathematics, so the formalisation in type theory is separate from the question of whether the axioms are sound. So in general, one should use axioms sparingly.

Also the *relevance* of the results is up to the user, that is: do the definitions and theorems correspond to notions that are considered interesting? Here again, the fact that the formalised mathematics in λD is close to standard mathematics makes it easier to verify the correspondence between the formalised notions and the intended ones. In summary, type theory shifts attention from *correctness* (which is dealt with by the system and therefore doesn't have to be discussed anymore) to *relevance*. Once formalised, the correctness of a piece of mathematics can be left to λD.

Proof development The precision of λD guides the proof development. The context structure (that we have depicted using flags) clearly indicates the hypotheses and the variables that are 'in scope' and clarifies and guides the thought process. This is particularly helpful for students that start to learn logic or mathematics: at any time in the proof development it is clear what has already been done (the definitions that are in scope), what is still left to do (the open goals) and what is available to proceed (the previous theorems and lemmas plus the assumptions that are in scope). The context structure of proofs with flags to indicate the scope of variables and assumptions provides a partial proof, which is ready to be completed in a step-wise process.

Libraries In mathematics, the basic activities are doing proofs and giving definitions. Both should be stored for reuse and it should be possible to refer to them. The system λD provides these facilities: both definitions and theorems are stored in a perspicuous way, for easy access and referral. In λD, definitions can depend on a context of parameters that are instantiated when the definition is used. A crucial point of type theory is that giving proofs and introducing definitions is very much the same type of activity: when proving, one creates a 'proof-term' of a certain type, and then a name is introduced for that proof-term. This name is what is being referred to later when using the proved result. The specific situation in which a result is used is reflected by the instantiations of the parameter list. (A difference between defining a proof and defining a mathematical notion is that in the latter case one wants to be able to unfold the definition, whereas in the case of a proof, one hardly ever wants to do that.) Due to the naming of definitions and proofs, it is also easy to find the dependencies: which proof depends on which notion or other result? All together, one obtains a large 'environment': a library of formalised mathematics, consisting of definitions of mathematical concepts and theorems with proofs.

16.2 Proof assistants based on type theory

We have shown that the type theory λD can be used to formalise mathematics. The system includes various basic constructs to define mathematical notions and also a mechanism to declare primitive notions that one wants to add. The power of such a system does not just lie in doing formalisations on paper. Its real strength lies in the fact that the theory can be cast into a computer program that can serve as a *proof assistant* to interactively build up theorems and proofs, eventually leading to a computer-supported library of formalised and computer-checked mathematics.

Computer-checked proofs A crucial aspect of λD (and type theory in general) is that a term can be type-checked by a computer: there is a – not too difficult – algorithm that, given a term p, an environment Δ of definitions and a context Γ of declarations, can compute the type of p in Γ, if it exists, and decide that p is not typable in case no such type exists. This means that a user doesn't have to provide the type, but can leave that to the computer. So, λD is a system that allows *proof checking*: an alleged proof (a term p) can be proposed and an algorithm can check what formula it is a proof of (the type of p), if any.

Schematically we depict the proof checking situation as follows:

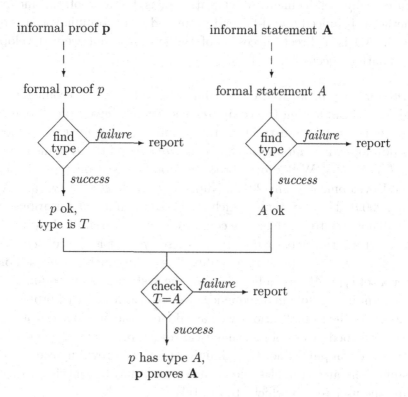

Figure 16.1 Checking correctness by means of type theory

Figure 16.1 describes the following procedure. The informal proof **p** and the statement it is supposed to prove, **A**, are translated to formal expressions p and A. This step itself is not carried out by the computer – hence the dashed arrows. (Of course, there can be computer support for this step, but at present there are no computer programs that can fully translate a proof in natural language to a formal proof term.) Then the type of p is computed, which returns T. (If p is not typable, the computer will report that.) Also, A is checked for well-formedness, which is also done by computing the type of A. These steps are carried out by the computer. After this, we know that T and A are well-formed types, and T is a type for p. The final step, which is also carried out by the computer, is to check whether T and A are equal; that is, whether these types are $\beta\Delta$-convertible. If so, then the computer has executed proof checking successfully, which entails that **p** indeed proves **A**.

This was the basic idea behind the Automath project, started around 1970 by N.G. de Bruijn (de Bruijn, 1970, 1980; Nederpelt *et al.*, 1994): develop a computer program that can check mathematics and mathematical proofs for their correctness. For an expression, this means checking whether it is syntactically well-formed and what its type is. For a proof, this means checking whether it is indeed a well-formed proof and what formula it is a proof of. The system λD is a direct successor of the systems that were developed in the Automath project of the 1970s.

Interactive proving In the meantime, computers have become more powerful, and apart from letting the computer just check a given proof, one can let the computer assist in constructing the proof. The technology of proof checking has developed into *interactive theorem proving* and the systems used are called *proof assistants*. Well-known proof assistants based on type theory are Coq (Coq Development Team, 2012), Nuprl (Constable *et al.*, 1986) and Agda (Bove *et al.*, 2009). These systems, which are based on different variations of λD (that we will not go into here) use the computer not just to check the type, but also to construct a term. A basic concept in these systems is that of *term refinement*. One starts with a type A in a context Γ and an 'open place' (a 'hole'), where a term (of type A) has to be filled in. The system provides *refinement steps* to fill a term in the hole in a sequence of steps. Basically, this provides computer support for the formalisations we have done in the previous chapters, where we have developed proofs of mathematical results in a step-wise manner. The idea is that the computer does the administration, by providing the bookkeeping of assumptions and variables that can be used, and by showing the open goals, while the user tells it which step to take next.

In the Agda system, one is editing the term directly: one starts from just a hole, which is then replaced by a part of a term, with still some holes left; then one focuses on another hole and fills that in until there are no holes left. The Agda system gives support for what can be filled in the hole (which depends on the type of the hole) and checks the types of the unfinished proof terms along the way. In the Coq system, one just looks at the holes themselves: these are filled in by refinement steps, but the user doesn't see the term that is being constructed (in the background): the user only sees a sequence of holes with their own context.

Automation and tactics In proof assistants based on type theory, the computer is used to check the types and to store the terms, plus the environment of definitions and the context of declarations. But maybe most importantly, the system is used to *construct* terms. For example, the Coq system has powerful *tactics* to refine proof terms, and users are supported to write their own tactics in a special 'tactic language' (or directly in the implementation language of Coq). In this way, a significant amount of automation can be (and has been) added to the various proof assistants. A crucial aspect of a system like Coq is that, no matter what (smart) tactic one writes to create proof terms, in the end the completed term has to be typable in the type theory, with as type the formula that one claims to prove. So, in the end everything is checked by the *kernel*, which is just the type-checking algorithm for the type theory of Coq. This feature, that a proof assistant generates *proof terms* that can be checked for correctness by a *small kernel*, was named the 'de Bruijn criterion' by H.P. Barendregt (Barendregt & Geuvers, 2001), in honour of the pioneering work of Automath, whose systems all satisfy this property.

Technical assistance The computer can provide various additional features for theorem-proving support. An obvious desire is to enable sugared notation, such as, for example, infix notation for defined binary operation and relation symbols. Current proof assistants provide that. They also provide shorthand facilities for invoking standard techniques for definitions or proofs and sometimes pull-down menus to select applicable tactics. Basically, these are all interface features that are important for enhancing the proof process, but do not affect the underlying type theory and the formalised mathematics that is stored. The primitives of the type theory already provide the mechanisms for type checking and definition look-up, so one can always ask for the type of a term and of the definiens of a defined notion. Slightly more advanced proof assistants also provide 'search' mechanisms, e.g. to search for a lemma about a certain relation, or a lemma of a certain shape.

Additional type-theoretic features The type theory of λD is simpler than that of Coq, which also has a scheme for *inductive types* (see Bertot & Castéran, 2004). These are important for defining e.g. data types from computer science, but also mathematical notions like the closure of a property, or 'the smallest set X satisfying property Φ'. For mathematical applications, this is not crucial, because in λD one can define 'closure' or 'smallest set satisfying ...' using the higher order predicate logic that is included. Data types can be encoded using higher order logic as well, but one doesn't get the full computation rules for these data types as term-conversion. To be more precise: in the presence of an inductive type for the natural numbers with an associated scheme for structural recursion, one has a (small) programming language, and the evaluation of programs is part of the term-reduction, just like β-reduction in λD. In λD we can specify recursive functions using equations, but these do not compute within λD: computation is done using equational reasoning. Given our focus on the formalisation of mathematics in this book, we don't see that as a serious limitation.

State of the art In recent times, proof assistants have become more mature and the research and development of the systems have enabled various big formalisations, both in mathematics and computer science. The topics range from formalisations of pure mathematics to correctness of software or operating systems. Usually, these are not isolated formalisation efforts anymore, but part of the building up of a large library of formalised mathematical results.

The practical work on implementing proof assistants based on type theory has gone hand in hand with foundational studies of the underlying theory. Also, results in computer science, concerning the variety of type notions present in programming languages, have stimulated research in the essence and the 'power' of these type systems, and into the connections between the various notions of type. The theoretical consequences for implementing mathematics and logic, as sketched above, provide a firm backbone to these investigations.

16.3 Future of the field

Various impressive computer formalisations of substantial bodies of mathematics have been done, which shows the maturity of this field. We mention the formalisation of the Four Color Theorem in Coq by G. Gonthier (Gonthier, 2005, 2008). Another impressive result is the formalisation of the Feit-Thompson Theorem in Coq by a team led by G. Gonthier (Gonthier *et al.*, 2013). The latter theorem, an important step in the classification of finite simple groups, is also known as the Odd-Order Theorem, and it states that every finite group of odd order is solvable. Yet another major formalisation of mathematics is the Flyspeck project led by T.C. Hales (Hales, 2006; Hales *et al.*, 2010), in order to formalise a proof of the Kepler Conjecture in the proof assistant HOL Light (HOL system, 1988; Gordon & Melham, 1993; Gordon, 2000).

All older proof assistants have a basic 'standard library' of formalised mathematics and a number of larger 'deep' results based on that. Mizar (Mizar, 1989) is the system with the largest library of formalised mathematics.

An important application of proof assistants is in verifying computer systems: software and hardware. The ultimate level of correctness of a program or a hardware design is obtained by proving it formally correct using a proof assistant. In recent years we have seen a strong increase of computer-formalised correctness proofs of artefacts from computer science.

Increasing use of proof assistants In the future, we expect an enormous increase in the use of proof assistants. Our vision is that formalising a mathematical proof may become as easy as writing mathematics in a mathematical text editor such as LaTeX (Lamport, 1985) and that a mathematical proof will only be accepted for publication when it has been formally checked. This means that a large library of formalised mathematics will be built up, which allows all results now appearing in journals and books to be accompanied by formal proof code. Such formalised proofs can be inspected, experimented with and be used in other proofs. This will vastly increase the use of formal (computer-supported) verification of computer science artefacts.

Right now, the above vision is far from a reality. There are some clear challenges ahead.

Automation All proof assistants provide a basic level of automation, but this is not enough to let a large part of mathematical reasoning be done by the machine. Proof steps that the average mathematician would skip and leave unexplained are often not understood by the proof assistant and need further elaboration. This is felt as a hindrance by users. Also, the proof assistant is mostly unable to propose useful lemmas (from the library of known results). We believe that these problems can be solved by a combination of powerful automated theorem proving (using symbolic techniques) and machine learning (using statistical inference). A considerable part of undergraduate mathematics should be 'known' to the proof assistant, in the sense that it can use it instantly without further assistance.

High-level explanation of formal proofs There is a considerable gap between what a user of a proof assistant sees on the screen and what the mathematics looks like on paper. This is to a great extent a direct consequence of the fact that a proof assistant is a computer program that deals with formal syntax (computer code), whereas mathematics on paper is informal text (in natural language), with snippets of formal text (formulas) inside it. Some users can easily relate the computer code to the informal mathematics, but in general this turns out to be difficult. So there is a need for better relating formalised mathematics and formal proofs to their informal counterparts.

Also, fully detailed formal proofs and definitions contain so much detail that the overview is lost and the 'message' of a proof (e.g. the crucial important step) gets hidden. It is important that parts of proofs can be made invisible, being available for further inspection on demand. So, one needs to be able to fold and unfold sub-parts.

Step-wise proof development A mathematical proof is usually presented (and also often found) by starting from a high-level argument and then filling in the various details, which may take several iterations. This is close to a step-wise refinement method of programming. In type theory, this amounts to constructing terms with holes which can later be selected to be filled in further. In the proof assistant community this is known as a *formal proof sketch*: an outline of a formal proof, with precise statements and definitions that are formally verified for syntactic correctness by the proof assistant, with a clear indication of which parts of the argument need to be filled in. A proof assistant that provides this method of working is also easier for novice users that currently experience a steep learning curve.

Export between proof assistants Mathematical research consists of developing new notions and results on top of existing ones, reusing and referring to earlier work in the literature. With formalised mathematics, the situation is different. Various proof assistants have impressive libraries of formal mathematics and proofs of deep mathematical theorems. However, it is not possible to reuse results between different proof assistants. It is even difficult in practice to reuse an existing library in the same proof assistant. The latter issue is related to the lack of high-level explanation of formal proofs, which we have already addressed. The impossibility to reuse results between different proof assistants is more fundamental and due to the use of different mathematical foundations (set theory, higher order logic, type theory) and different computer representations (e.g. the language the proof assistant is programmed in). This means that a proven theorem in one proof assistant cannot easily be transferred to another; it may even be inconsistent to do so. The seamless combining of results from different proof assistants is a big challenge.

Didactics As we have already pointed out, for novices the learning curve to use a proof assistant is very steep. One should know a bit of mathematics and logic and quite a bit of the peculiarities of the system before one can start using a proof assistant. In our ideal vision, that situation should be turned around: a proof assistant should be easy to start using and would help to *learn* logic and mathematics.

16.4 Conclusions

In this book, we have advocated the use of type theory as a vehicle for formalising mathematics. In particular, we have introduced the system λD for that purpose and we have shown how to do mathematics in it: logic, sets, arithmetic. We highlight the main points that support the formalisation of mathematics in λD.

– We have a *relatively simple syntax* that is built on the λ-calculus, and therefore well suited to the function-based approach underlying many mathematical topics.

– We use *types* that are appropriate for a natural translation of the set-and-element ideas present in a great number of mathematical fields.

– We use *propositions-as-types, proofs-as-terms* and hence we incorporate the usually informal notion of 'proof' into the formal system, so theorems and proofs become first-class citizens.

– We have *decidability of type checking* and, consequently, decidability of proof checking; every well-typed term has a unique type that can be computed by a relatively simple algorithm.

– *Definitions* are formally incorporated, so they are also first-class citizens.

– We use explicit *contexts* to record assumptions and free variables.

– The economic display of contexts via *flags* provides a feasible mechanism of developing and representing proofs; this is close to the mathematical practice using a natural deduction format.

In the present chapter we first highlighted the further applications of λD, starting by answering the questions: why formalise mathematics and why use type theory for it? An important bonus of a formal system is that one can develop a computer tool to actually work with the formal system. For type theory, that has been one of the goals from the start: to implement the formal system as a *proof checker*. This has developed into mature *proof assistants* based on type theory. We have reviewed the developments in this field. Then, of course, we have asked the question of where this is all heading. Proof assistants have not yet developed into a standard tool for mathematicians, but we strongly believe they will in the future.

16.5 Further reading

Type theory appears in various forms in the literature and has a variety of purposes, mostly related to programming languages, logic and proof theory, or formalising mathematics. B. Russell and A.N. Whitehead were the first to use type theory as a language for mathematics in their *Principia Mathematica* (Whitehead & Russell, 1910), but the Ramified Theory of Types of Russell (Russell, 1908) is now seen as unnecessarily complicated. The introduction of Russell and Whitehead's book still provides a nice motivation and discussion of the problems with paradoxes that were manifest at the time and that they tried to circumvent with their system. A. Church's simple theory of types is a simpler system that uses type theory to define higher order logic; the article (Church, 1940) is still very readable.

Interest in type theory has grown in the past decades, both in university curricula and in circles of researchers (computer scientists, logicians, mathematicians). In this section we make no attempt at giving a complete historic overview. Instead we mention the important ideas and point to further literature in which these ideas are developed and discussed in more detail.

The Automath system by N.G. de Bruijn and his co-workers was the first to use type theory for formalising mathematics. The book (Nederpelt *et al.*, 1994) is an overview of the scientific work, including descriptions of formalisations. See also the Automath Archive (2004). The article (Dechesne & Nederpelt, 2012) explores de Bruijn's motivation for the development of Automath. The paper (Geuvers & Nederpelt, 2013) gives a high-level introduction to the ideas of de Bruijn and the concepts of Automath.

Around the same time as de Bruijn, P. Martin Löf developed his intuitionistic theory of types, which was originally intended to give a constructive account of the foundations of mathematics, in the style of L.E.J. Brouwer and A. Heyting (see Troelstra & van Dalen, 1988), but it also turned out to serve as a logical framework that incorporates programming and proving. There have been various implementations of Martin-Löf type theory (Martin-Löf, 1980) developed in Göteborg (Magnusson & Nordström, 1994), as ALF and Agda, and in Ithaca (NY), as the Nuprl proof development system of R.L. Constable and his team (Constable *et al.*, 1986). The notes from Padova (Martin-Löf, 1980) give a good introduction into the system, while Nordström *et al.* (1990) also provide various examples from programming.

A third source of influential research in type theory is the work of J.-Y. Girard (Girard, 1972), from the beginning of the 1970s, who introduced the concept of impredicativity into type theory, which enables various data types (like the Church numerals) and logical connectives (like $\wedge$ and $\vee$) to be definable inside the type system. A good reference text is *Proofs and Types* (Girard *et al.*, 1989).

Research in type theory has gained momentum by the efforts of various research groups to build interactive *proof assistants* based on type theory. As we have already remarked, λD has, as a type theory, most resemblances with the Calculus of Constructions, first implemented as a proof assistant by Th. Coquand and G. Huet (Coquand & Huet, 1988). The mentioned paper is still a good reference and well readable. Later, the Calculus of Constructions was extended with inductive types, obtaining the Calculus of Inductive Constructions, CIC, which is also implemented in the proof assistant Coq (Coq Development Team, 2012). There is not really a standard reference for the rules of CIC, but the introductory book to Coq (Bertot & Castéran, 2004) provides a very comprehensible overview of Coq and CIC.

Another system is Lego (Pollack, 1994; Pollack *et al.*, 2001), implemented by R. Pollack (Edinburgh) and based on the so-called Extended Calculus of Constructions of Z. Luo (Luo, 1990). Coq and Lego originate from the end of the 1980s.

We also mention the Logical Framework implementation, based on the type theory λP in Edinburgh (Harper *et al.*, 1987; see also Pfenning, 2002).

In the last decades of the twentieth century, types have also obtained a prominent role in programming language research, especially due to the pioneering work of R. Milner (Milner, 1978), J.R. Hindley (Hindley, 1969) and J.C. Reynolds (Reynolds, 1974) in the 1970s, who firmly based functional programming languages on typed λ-calculus. Milner also developed the so-called LCF approach to theorem proving (Milner, 1972), which uses – basically – an abstract data type approach: there is an abstract data type 'theorem' and the only way to create an object of this type is by using the rules of logic. The proof assistants from the HOL family (HOL system, 1988; Gordon & Melham, 1993; Gordon, 2000) and the interactive theorem prover Isabelle (Paulson, 1993; Nipkow *et al.*, 2002) are based on this approach and also originate from the 1980s.

There are various other proof assistants, some of them based purely on type theory, others based on higher order logic (which uses type theory as its language) and others based on set theory. Apart from Coq, the proof assistants closest to using a type theory like λD are Agda (Bove *et al.*, 2009), Matita (Asperti *et al.*, 2011) and Nuprl (Constable *et al.*, 1986). For a more general account of proof assistants (with a focus on the ones using dependent types), presenting general ideas and comparison of approaches, see Barendregt & Geuvers (2001) and Geuvers (2009). Wiedijk (2006) also gives a nice comparison of proof assistants by showing how the irrationality of $\sqrt{2}$ can be proved in 17 different systems. Interesting overview papers can be found in the Special Issue on Formal Proof published in the *Notices of the American Mathematical Society* (AMS, 2008), with contributions of T.C. Hales, G. Gonthier, J. Harrison and F. Wiedijk.

Type theory is still developing, both within computer science (theory of programming languages) and within mathematics. Also on the level of non-dependent type theory, there is still a lot of research going on (see e.g. Barendregt *et al.*, 2013).

The focus of the present book is the formalisation of mathematics. A series of papers on this matter can be found in the *Journal of Automated Reasoning: Special Issue on Formal Mathematics for Mathematicians* (JAR, 2013). In this direction, the latest development is 'Homotopy Type Theory', a field founded by V.A. Voevodsky, who interprets objects $a, b : A$ as points in a space and a proof of the identity $a =_A b$ as a *path* from a to b. This gives a new perspective on formalising mathematics and on the foundations of mathematics, the so-called 'Univalent Foundations'. A good reference is the Univalent Foundations Program (2013). See also the introductory lecture of Voevodsky (2014).

We observe that nowadays type theory is a mature and respected topic, and that a lot of research is going on in the field, ranging from foundational studies to applications in computer science, proof assistants and mathematical logic.

Appendix A

Logic in λD

A.1 Constructive propositional logic

Implication (cf. Figure 11.5)

(1) $\quad\boxed{A, B : *_p}$

$\quad\Rightarrow (A, B) := A \to B : *_p$

$\quad$ Notation: $A \Rightarrow B$ for $\Rightarrow (A, B)$

(2) $\quad\boxed{u : A \to B}$

$\quad\quad\Rightarrow\text{-}in(A, B, u) := u : A \Rightarrow B$ (**see** $(2)^*$)

(3) $\quad\boxed{u : A \Rightarrow B \mid v : A}$

$\quad\quad\Rightarrow\text{-}el(A, B, u, v) := u\,v : B$

$(2)^*$ **Strategy for** $\Rightarrow$**-introduction:**

$\vdots$

$\boxed{x : A}$

$\quad\vdots$

$\quad a(\ldots, x) := \ldots : B$

$b(\ldots) := \lambda x : A . a(\ldots, x) : A \Rightarrow B$

Absurdity (cf. Figure 11.6)

(4) $\quad \perp := \Pi A : *_p . A : *$

> $\boxed{A : *_p}$
>
> > $\boxed{u : A \mid v : A \Rightarrow \perp}$
> >
> > (5) $\quad \perp\text{-}in(A, u, v) := v\,u : \perp$
> >
> > $\boxed{u : \perp}$
> >
> > (6) $\quad \perp\text{-}el(A, u) := u\,A : A$

Negation (cf. Figure 11.7)

> $\boxed{A : *_p}$
>
> (7) $\quad \neg(A) := A \Rightarrow \perp : *_p$
>
> $\quad$ Notation: $\neg A$ for $\neg(A)$
>
> > $\boxed{u : A \to \perp}$
> >
> > (8) $\quad \neg\text{-}in(A, u) := u : \neg A$
> >
> > $\boxed{u : \neg A \mid v : A}$
> >
> > (9) $\quad \neg\text{-}el(A, u, v) := u\,v : \perp$

Conjunction (cf. Figure 11.10)

> $\boxed{A, B : *_p}$
>
> (10) $\quad \wedge(A, B) := \Pi C : *_p . (A \Rightarrow B \Rightarrow C) \Rightarrow C : *_p$
>
> $\quad$ Notation: $A \wedge B$ for $\wedge(A, B)$
>
> > $\boxed{u : A \mid v : B}$
> >
> > (11) $\quad \wedge\text{-}in(A, B, u, v) := \lambda C : *_p . \lambda w : A \Rightarrow B \Rightarrow C . w\,u\,v : A \wedge B$
> >
> > $\boxed{u : A \wedge B}$
> >
> > (12) $\quad \wedge\text{-}el_1(A, B, u) := u\,A\,(\lambda v : A . \lambda w : B . v) : A$
> >
> > (13) $\quad \wedge\text{-}el_2(A, B, u) := u\,B\,(\lambda v : A . \lambda w : B . w) : B$

Disjunction (cf. Figure 11.11)

$\boxed{A, B : *_p}$

(14) $\vee(A, B) := \Pi C : *.\,(A \Rightarrow C) \Rightarrow (B \Rightarrow C) \Rightarrow C \;:\; *_p$

    Notation: $A \vee B$ for $\vee(A, B)$

$\boxed{u : A}$

(15) $\vee\text{-}in_1(A, B, u) := \lambda C : *_p.\,\lambda v : A \Rightarrow C.\,\lambda w : B \Rightarrow C.\,v\,u \;:\; A \vee B$

$\boxed{u : B}$

(16) $\vee\text{-}in_2(A, B, u) := \lambda C : *_p.\,\lambda v : A \Rightarrow C.\,\lambda w : B \Rightarrow C.\,w\,u \;:\; A \vee B$

$\boxed{C : *_p}$

     $\boxed{u : A \vee B \mid v : A \Rightarrow C \mid w : B \Rightarrow C}$

(17) $\vee\text{-}el(A, B, C, u, v, w) := u\,C\,v\,w \;:\; C$

Biimplication (cf. Figure 11.12)

$\boxed{A, B : *_p}$

(18) $\Leftrightarrow(A, B) := (A \Rightarrow B) \wedge (B \Rightarrow A) \;:\; *_p$

    Notation: $A \Leftrightarrow B$ for $\Leftrightarrow(A, B)$

$\boxed{u : A \Rightarrow B \mid v : B \Rightarrow A}$

(19) $\Leftrightarrow\text{-}in(A, B, u, v) := \wedge\text{-}in(A \Rightarrow B, B \Rightarrow A, u, v) \;:\; A \Leftrightarrow B$

$\boxed{u : A \Leftrightarrow B}$

(20) $\Leftrightarrow\text{-}el_1(A, B, u) := \wedge\text{-}el_1(A \Rightarrow B, B \Rightarrow A, u) \;:\; A \Rightarrow B$

(21) $\Leftrightarrow\text{-}el_2(A, B, u) := \wedge\text{-}el_2(A \Rightarrow B, B \Rightarrow A, u) \;:\; B \Rightarrow A$

A.2   Classical propositional logic

Excluded Third axiom (cf. Figure 11.16)

$\boxed{A : *_p}$

(22) $exc\text{-}thrd(A) := \perp\!\!\!\perp \;:\; A \vee \neg A$

Double Negation (cf. Figure 11.17)

$$\boxed{A : *_p}$$

$$\boxed{u : A}$$

(23) $\neg\neg\text{-}in(A, u) := \lambda v : \neg A \,.\, v\, u \;:\; \neg\neg A$

(24) $doub\text{-}neg(A) := \;\ldots\; \textsf{see Figure 11.16} \;\ldots\; : \; \neg\neg A \Rightarrow A$

$$\boxed{u : \neg\neg A}$$

(25) $\neg\neg\text{-}el(A, u) := doub\text{-}neg(A)\, u \;:\; A$

Alternatives for Disjunction (cf. Figure 11.19)

$$\boxed{A, B : *_p}$$

$$\boxed{u : \neg A \Rightarrow B}$$

(26) $\vee\text{-}in\text{-}alt_1(A, B, u) := a_{10[Fig.\ 11.18]}(A, B, u) \;:\; A \vee B \;\; (\text{see } (26)^*)$

$$\boxed{v : \neg B \Rightarrow A}$$

(27) $\vee\text{-}in\text{-}alt_2(A, B, v) := \;\ldots\; \textsf{see Figure 11.19} \;\ldots\; : \; A \vee B$

$$\boxed{u : A \vee B}$$

$$\boxed{v : \neg A}$$

(28) $\vee\text{-}el\text{-}alt_1(A, B, u, v) := a_{5[Fig.\ 11.13]}(A, B, u, v) \;:\; B$

$$\boxed{w : \neg B}$$

(29) $\vee\text{-}el\text{-}alt_2(A, B, u, w) := \;\ldots\; \textsf{see Figure 11.19} \;\ldots\; : \; A$

$(26)^*$ **Strategy for alternative $\vee$-introduction, first version:**

$$\vdots$$

$$\boxed{x : \neg A}$$

$$\vdots$$

$a(\ldots, x) := \;\ldots\; : \; B$

$b(\ldots) := \vee\text{-}in\text{-}alt_1(A, B, \lambda x : \neg A \,.\, a(\ldots, x)) \;:\; A \vee B$

A.3 Constructive predicate logic

Universal Quantification (cf. Figure 11.22)

$$\boxed{S : *_s \mid P : S \to *_p}$$

(30) $\forall(S, P) := \Pi x : S . P x \; : \; *_p$

   Notation: $\forall x : S . P x$ for $\forall(S, P)$

   $$\boxed{u : \Pi x : S . P x}$$

(31) $\forall\text{-}in(S, P, u) := u \; : \; \forall x : S . P x$ (see (31)*)

   $$\boxed{u : \forall x : S . P x \mid v : S}$$

(32) $\forall\text{-}el(S, P, u, v) := u v \; : \; P v$

(31)* **Strategy for $\forall$-introduction:**

$\vdots$

$$\boxed{x : S}$$

   $\vdots$

   $a(\ldots, x) := \ldots \; : \; P x$

   $b(\ldots) := \lambda x : S . a(\ldots, x) \; : \; \forall x : S . P x$

Existential Quantification (cf. Figure 11.23)

$$\boxed{S : *_s \mid P : S \to *_p}$$

(33) $\exists(S, P) := \Pi A : *_p . ((\forall x : S . (P x \Rightarrow A)) \Rightarrow A) \; : \; *_p$

   Notation: $\exists x : S . P x$ for $\exists(S, P)$

   $$\boxed{u : S \mid v : P u}$$

(34) $\exists\text{-}in(S, P, u, v) := \lambda A : *_p . \lambda w : (\forall x : S . (P x \Rightarrow A)) . w u v \; :$
              $\exists x : S . P x$

   $$\boxed{u : \exists x : S . P x \mid A : *_p \mid v : \forall x : S . (P x \Rightarrow A)}$$

(35) $\exists\text{-}el(S, P, u, A, v) := u A v \; : \; A$ (see (35)*)

(35)* Strategy for ∃-elimination:

$\vdots$

$a(\ldots) := \ldots : \exists x : S . P x$

$\boxed{x : S}$

> $\boxed{u : P x}$
>
> $\vdots$
>
> $b(\ldots, x, u) := \ldots : A$
>
> $c(\ldots, x) := \lambda u : P x . b(\ldots, x, u) : P x \Rightarrow A$

$d(\ldots) := \lambda x : S . c(\ldots, x) : \forall x : S . (P x \Rightarrow A)$

$e(\ldots) := \exists \text{-}el(S, P, a(\ldots), A, d(\ldots)) : A$

A.4 Classical predicate logic

Alternatives for Existential Quantification (cf. Figure 11.28)

$\boxed{S : *_s \mid P : S \to *_p}$

> $\boxed{u : \neg \forall x : S . \neg (P x)}$

(36) $\quad \exists\text{-}in\text{-}alt(S, P, u) := a_{4[Fig.\ 11.27]}(S, P, u) : \exists x : S . P x$

> $\boxed{u : \exists x : S . P x}$

(37) $\quad \exists\text{-}el\text{-}alt(S, P, u) := a_{2[Fig.\ 11.25]}(S, P, u) : \neg \forall x : S . \neg (P x)$

Appendix B

Arithmetical axioms, definitions and lemmas

Below we list axioms, definitions and lemmas concerning arithmetic in $\mathbb{Z}$ and its subset $\mathbb{N}$, as stated in Chapter 14.

Axiom (Fig. 14.3)
 s is a bijection $(ax\text{-}int_1)$.

Lemma (Fig. 14.3)
 (a) s is an injection $(inj\text{-}suc)$,
 (b) s is a surjection $(surj\text{-}suc)$.

Lemma (Fig. 14.3)
 (a) $\forall y : \mathbb{Z} . \, (s(p\,y) = y)$ $(s\text{-}p\text{-}ann)$,
 (b) $\forall y : \mathbb{Z} . \, (p(s\,y) = y)$ $(p\text{-}s\text{-}ann)$.

Axiom (Fig. 14.4)
 For all $P : \mathbb{Z} \to *_p$, $[P\,0 \wedge \forall x : \mathbb{Z} . \, (P\,x \Rightarrow (P(s\,x) \wedge P(p\,x)))] \Rightarrow \forall x : \mathbb{Z} . \, P\,x$
 $(ax\text{-}int_2$, symmetric induction over $\mathbb{Z})$.

Definition (Fig. 14.5)
 (a) For $P : \mathbb{Z} \to *_p$, $nat\text{-}cond(P) := P\,0 \wedge \forall x : \mathbb{Z} . \, (P\,x \Rightarrow P(s\,x))$,
 (b) $\mathbb{N} := \lambda x : \mathbb{Z} . \, \Pi P : \mathbb{Z} \to *_p . \, (nat\text{-}cond(P) \Rightarrow P\,x)$.

Lemma (Fig. 14.5)
 (a) $0 \, \varepsilon \, \mathbb{N}$ $(zero\text{-}prop)$,
 (b) $\forall x : \mathbb{Z} . \, (x \, \varepsilon \, \mathbb{N} \Rightarrow s\,x \, \varepsilon \, \mathbb{N})$ $(clos\text{-}prop)$,
 (c) $\Pi Q : \mathbb{Z} \to *_p . \, (nat\text{-}cond(Q) \Rightarrow (\mathbb{N} \subseteq Q))$ $(nat\text{-}smallest)$.

Axiom (Fig. 14.6)
 $\neg(p\,0 \, \varepsilon \, \mathbb{N})$ $(ax\text{-}int_3)$.

Lemma (Fig. 14.7)
 (a) $\forall x : \mathbb{Z} . \, (x \, \varepsilon \, \mathbb{N} \Rightarrow \neg(s\,x = 0))$ $(nat\text{-}prop_1)$,
 (b) $\forall x, y : \mathbb{Z} . \, (x \, \varepsilon \, \mathbb{N} \Rightarrow (y \, \varepsilon \, \mathbb{N} \Rightarrow (s\,x = s\,y \Rightarrow x = y)))$ $(nat\text{-}prop_2)$.

Lemma (Fig. 14.8)
For all $P : \mathbb{Z} \to *_p$,
$[P\,0 \wedge \forall x : \mathbb{Z}.\,(x\,\varepsilon\,\mathbb{N} \Rightarrow (P\,x \Rightarrow P\,(s\,x)))] \Rightarrow \forall x : \mathbb{Z}.\,(x\,\varepsilon\,\mathbb{N} \Rightarrow P\,x)$
(*nat-ind, induction over* $\mathbb{N}$).

Lemma 14.3.1
$\forall x : \mathbb{Z}.\,(x\,\varepsilon\,\mathbb{N} \Rightarrow (x = 0 \vee p\,x\,\varepsilon\,\mathbb{N}))$.

Definition (Fig. 14.9) For $x : \mathbb{Z}$:
(a) $pos(x) := p\,x\,\varepsilon\,\mathbb{N}$,
(b) $neg(x) := \neg(x \in \mathbb{N})$.

Lemma (Fig. 14.9)
(a) $\forall x : \mathbb{Z}.\,(x\,\varepsilon\,\mathbb{N} \Rightarrow (x = 0 \vee p\,x\,\varepsilon\,\mathbb{N}))$ (*nat-split*),
(b) $\forall x : \mathbb{Z}.\,(\neg(x\,\varepsilon\,\mathbb{N}) \vee x = 0 \vee p\,x\,\varepsilon\,\mathbb{N})$ (*nat-split-alt*),
(c) $\forall x : \mathbb{Z}.\,(neg(x) \vee x = 0 \vee pos(x))$ (*trip*).

Lemma 14.3.2
(a) $\forall x : \mathbb{Z}.\,(pos(s\,x) \Leftrightarrow x\,\varepsilon\,\mathbb{N})$,
(b) $\forall x : \mathbb{Z}.\,(pos(s\,x) \Leftrightarrow (x = 0 \vee pos(x)))$,
(c) $\forall x : \mathbb{Z}.\,(neg(p\,x) \Leftrightarrow (x = 0 \vee neg(x)))$.

Lemma 14.3.3
(a) $\forall x : \mathbb{Z}.\,(pos(x) \Leftrightarrow x \neq 0 \wedge \neg neg(x))$,
(b) $\forall x : \mathbb{Z}.\,(neg(x) \Leftrightarrow x \neq 0 \wedge \neg pos(x))$,
(c) $\forall x : \mathbb{Z}.\,(x = 0 \Leftrightarrow \neg pos(x) \wedge \neg neg(x))$.

Lemma (Fig. 14.12)
(a) $\forall x : \mathbb{Z}.\,(x + 0 = x)$ (*plus-i*),
(b) $\forall x, y : \mathbb{Z}.\,(x + s\,y = s(x + y))$ (*plus-ii*),
(c) $\forall x, y : \mathbb{Z}.\,(x + p\,y = p(x + y))$ (*plus-iii*).

Lemma 14.6.1
(a) $\forall x : \mathbb{Z}.\,(0 + x = x)$ (*plus-i-alt, Fig. 14.14*),
(b) $\forall x, y : \mathbb{Z}.\,(s\,x + y = s(x + y))$ (*plus-ii-alt, Fig. 14.14*),
(c) $\forall x, y : \mathbb{Z}.\,(p\,x + y = p(x + y))$ (*plus-iii-alt, Fig. 14.14*).

Lemma 14.6.2
$\forall x, y : \mathbb{Z}.\,(x + y = y + x)$ (*comm-add, Fig. 14.14*).

Lemma 14.6.3
(a) $\forall x, y : \mathbb{Z}.\,(p\,x + s\,y = x + y)$,
(b) $\forall x, y : \mathbb{Z}.\,(s\,x + p\,y = x + y)$.

Lemma 14.6.4
$\forall x, y, z : \mathbb{Z}.\,(x + (y + z) = (x + y) + z)$ (*assoc-add, Fig. 14.14*).

Lemma 14.6.5 (Cancellation Laws for addition)
(a) $\forall x, y, z : \mathbb{Z}.\,(x + z = y + z \Rightarrow x = y)$ (*right-canc-add, Fig. 14.14*),
(b) $\forall x, y, z : \mathbb{Z}.\,(x + y = x + z \Rightarrow y = z)$ (*left-canc-add, Fig. 14.14*).

Lemma 14.7.1 (Closure of $\mathbb{N}$ under addition)
$\forall x, y : \mathbb{Z} . \, ((x \, \varepsilon \, \mathbb{N} \wedge y \, \varepsilon \, \mathbb{N}) \Rightarrow x + y \, \varepsilon \, \mathbb{N})$ $\;$ (*plus-clos-nat*, *Fig. 14.15*).

Lemma 14.7.2 (Characterisation of negative numbers)
$\forall x : \mathbb{Z} . \, (neg(x) \Leftrightarrow \exists y : \mathbb{Z} . \, (pos(y) \wedge x + y = 0))$.

Lemma 14.7.3 (Closure for negative integers)
$\forall x, y : \mathbb{Z} . \, (neg(x) \wedge neg(y) \Rightarrow neg(x + y))$.

Lemma 14.8.1 (Uniqueness of difference)
$\forall x, y : \mathbb{Z} . \, \exists^1 z : \mathbb{Z} . \, (z + y = x)$ $\;$ (*uni-dif*, *Fig. 14.16*).

Lemma 14.8.2
$\forall x, y : \mathbb{Z} . \, ((x - y) + y = x)$ $\;$ (*subtr-prop$_1$*, *Fig. 14.16*).

Lemma 14.8.3
$\forall x, y : \mathbb{Z} . \, ((x + y) - y = x)$ $\;$ (*subtr-prop$_2$*, *Fig. 14.16*).

Lemma 14.8.4
$\forall x : \mathbb{Z} . \, (x - x = 0)$.

Lemma 14.8.5
$\forall x : \mathbb{Z} . \, (x - 0 = x)$.

Lemma 14.8.6
(a) $\forall x, y : \mathbb{Z} . \, (x - s\,y = p(x - y))$,
(b) $\forall x, y : \mathbb{Z} . \, (x - p\,y = s(x - y))$.

Lemma 14.8.7
(a) $\forall x, y : \mathbb{Z} . \, (s\,x - y = s(x - y))$,
(b) $\forall x, y : \mathbb{Z} . \, (p\,x - y = p(x - y))$.

Lemma 14.8.8
(a) $\forall x : \mathbb{Z} . \, (x + 1 = s\,x)$,
(b) $\forall x : \mathbb{Z} . \, (x - 1 = p\,x)$.

Lemma 14.8.9 (Cancellation Laws for subtraction)
(a) $\forall x, y, z : \mathbb{Z} . \, (x - z = y - z \Rightarrow x = y)$,
(b) $\forall x, y, z : \mathbb{Z} . \, (x - y = x - z \Rightarrow y = z)$.

Lemma 14.8.10
(a) $\forall x, y, z : \mathbb{Z} . \, (x + (y - z) \; = \; (x + y) - z)$,
(b) $\forall x, y, z : \mathbb{Z} . \, (x - (y + z) \; = \; (x - y) - z)$,
(c) $\forall x, y, z : \mathbb{Z} . \, (x - (y - z) \; = \; (x - y) + z)$.

Lemma 14.8.11
$\forall x, y : \mathbb{Z} . \, (pos(x - y) \Leftrightarrow neg(y - x))$.

Lemma 14.9.1
(a) $\forall x : \mathbb{Z} . \, ((-x) + x = 0)$,
(b) $\forall x, y : \mathbb{Z} . \, (x + (-y) = x - y)$,
(c) $\forall x, y : \mathbb{Z} . \, (-(x + y) = (-x) - y)$.

Lemma 14.9.2
(a) $-0 = 0$,
(b) $\forall x : \mathbb{Z} . (-(-x) = x)$,
(c) $\forall x : \mathbb{Z} . (x = 0 \Leftrightarrow -x = 0)$.

Lemma 14.9.3
(a) $\forall x : \mathbb{Z} . (-(s\,x) = p(-x))$,
(b) $\forall x : \mathbb{Z} . (-(p\,x) = s(-x))$.

Lemma 14.9.4
(a) $\forall x : \mathbb{Z} . (pos(x) \Leftrightarrow neg(-x))$,
(b) $\forall x : \mathbb{Z} . (neg(x) \Leftrightarrow pos(-x))$.

Lemma 14.9.5
(a) $\forall x : \mathbb{Z} . (pos(x) \vee pos(-x) \vee x = 0)$,
(b) $\forall x : \mathbb{Z} . (neg(x) \vee neg(-x) \vee x = 0)$.

Lemma 14.9.6
$\forall x : \mathbb{Z} . (-x \;\varepsilon\; \mathbb{N} \Leftrightarrow (neg(x) \vee x = 0))$.

Lemma 14.9.7
(a) $\forall x : \mathbb{Z} . (x \;\varepsilon\; \mathbb{N} \vee -x \;\varepsilon\; \mathbb{N})$,
(b) $\forall x : \mathbb{Z} . ((x \;\varepsilon\; \mathbb{N} \wedge -x \;\varepsilon\; \mathbb{N}) \Rightarrow x = 0)$.

Definition (Fig. 14.18)
(a) $\leq_{\mathbb{Z}} := \lambda x : \mathbb{Z} . \lambda y : \mathbb{Z} . (y - x \;\varepsilon\; \mathbb{N})$,
(b) $<_{\mathbb{Z}} := \lambda x : \mathbb{Z} . \lambda y : \mathbb{Z} . (x \leq_{\mathbb{Z}} y \wedge x \neq y)$.

Definition (Fig. 14.19)
(a) $\geq_{\mathbb{Z}} := \lambda x : \mathbb{Z} . \lambda y : \mathbb{Z} . (y \leq_{\mathbb{Z}} x)$,
(b) $>_{\mathbb{Z}} := \lambda x : \mathbb{Z} . \lambda y : \mathbb{Z} . (y <_{\mathbb{Z}} x)$.

Lemma 14.10.1
(a) $\forall x : \mathbb{Z} . (x \leq x)$,
(b) $\forall x, y, z : \mathbb{Z} . ((x \leq y \wedge y \leq z) \Rightarrow (x \leq z))$,
(c) $\forall x, y, z : \mathbb{Z} . ((x + z \leq y + z) \Leftrightarrow (x \leq y))$,
(d) $\forall x, y, z : \mathbb{Z} . ((x < y \wedge y \leq z) \Rightarrow (x < z))$,
(e) $\forall x, y, z : \mathbb{Z} . ((x + z < y + z) \Leftrightarrow (x < y))$.

Lemma 14.10.2
(a) $\forall x : \mathbb{Z} . (pos(x) \Leftrightarrow x > 0)$,
(b) $\forall x : \mathbb{Z} . (neg(x) \Leftrightarrow x < 0)$,
(c) $\forall x : \mathbb{Z} . (x < 0 \vee x = 0 \vee x > 0)$.

Lemma 14.10.3
(a) $\forall x, y : \mathbb{Z} . (x < y \Leftrightarrow -y < -x)$,
(b) $\forall x : \mathbb{Z} . (x < 0 \Leftrightarrow -x > 0)$.

Lemma (Fig. 14.22)
(a) $\forall x : \mathbb{Z} . (x \cdot 0 = 0)$ *(times-i)*,
(b) $\forall x, y : \mathbb{Z} . (x \cdot s\,y = (x \cdot y) + x)$ *(times-ii)*,
(c) $\forall x, y : \mathbb{Z} . (x \cdot p\,y = (x \cdot y) - x)$ *(times-iii)*.

Lemma 14.11.1
(a) $\forall x : \mathbb{Z} . (0 \cdot x = 0)$,
(b) $\forall x, y : \mathbb{Z} . (s\,x \cdot y = (x \cdot y) + y)$,
(c) $\forall x, y : \mathbb{Z} . (p\,x \cdot y = (x \cdot y) - y)$.

Lemma 14.11.2 (Right Distributivity Laws for multiplication)
(a) $\forall x, y, z : \mathbb{Z} . (x \cdot (y + z) = (x \cdot y) + (x \cdot z))$,
(b) $\forall x, y, z : \mathbb{Z} . (x \cdot (y - z) = (x \cdot y) - (x \cdot z))$.

Lemma 14.11.3
(a) $\forall x, y : \mathbb{Z} . (x \cdot y = y \cdot x)$,
(b) $\forall x, y, z : \mathbb{Z} . ((x \cdot y) \cdot z = x \cdot (y \cdot z))$.

Lemma 14.11.4
$\forall x, y : \mathbb{Z} . (x \cdot (-y) = -(x \cdot y))$.

Lemma 14.11.5
(a) $\forall x, y : \mathbb{Z} . ((x \;\varepsilon\; \mathbb{N} \wedge y \;\varepsilon\; \mathbb{N}) \Rightarrow x \cdot y \;\varepsilon\; \mathbb{N})$,
(b) $\forall x, y : \mathbb{Z} . ((x > 0 \wedge y > 0) \Rightarrow x \cdot y > 0)$,
(c) $\forall x, y : \mathbb{Z} . ((x > 0 \wedge y < 0) \Rightarrow x \cdot y < 0)$,
(d) $\forall x, y : \mathbb{Z} . ((x < 0 \wedge y < 0) \Rightarrow x \cdot y > 0)$.

Lemma 14.11.6
$\forall x, y : \mathbb{Z} . (x \cdot y = 0 \Rightarrow (x = 0 \vee y = 0))$.

Lemma 14.11.7 (Right Cancellation Law for multiplication)
$\forall x, y, z : \mathbb{Z} . ((x \cdot z = y \cdot z \wedge z \neq 0) \Rightarrow x = y)$.

Definition (Fig. 14.23)
For $m, n : \mathbb{Z}$,
$div(m, n) := \exists q : \mathbb{Z} . (m \cdot q = n)$ *(Notation: $m \mid n$)*.

Lemma 14.12.1
(a) $\forall m : \mathbb{Z} . (m \mid 0)$,
(b) $0 \mid 0$,
(c) $\forall n : \mathbb{Z} . (0 \mid n \Rightarrow n = 0)$.

Lemma 14.12.2
(a) $\forall l, m : \mathbb{Z} . (l \mid m \Leftrightarrow -l \mid m)$,
(b) $\forall m : \mathbb{Z} . (1 \mid m)$.

Lemma 14.12.3
(a) $\forall m : \mathbb{Z} . (m \mid m)$,
(b) $\forall l, m, n : \mathbb{Z} . ((l \mid m \wedge m \mid n) \Rightarrow l \mid n)$,
(c) $\forall m, n : \mathbb{Z} . ((m \;\varepsilon\; \mathbb{N} \wedge n \;\varepsilon\; \mathbb{N}) \Rightarrow ((m \mid n \wedge n \mid m) \Rightarrow m = n))$.

Definition (Fig. 14.23)

For $k, m, n : \mathbb{Z}$,

(a) $com\text{-}div(k, m, n) := k \mid m \wedge k \mid n$,

(b) $gcd\text{-}prop(k, m, n) :=$
$$com\text{-}div(k, m, n) \wedge \forall l : \mathbb{Z} . \, (com\text{-}div(l, m, n) \Rightarrow l \leq k),$$

(c) $coprime(m, n) := \forall k : \mathbb{Z} . \, ((com\text{-}div(k, m, n) \wedge k > 0) \Rightarrow k = 1)$.

Lemma (Fig. 14.23)

For $m, n : \mathbb{Z}$, $s : m > 0$, $t : n > 0$,

$\exists^1 k : \mathbb{Z} . \, gcd\text{-}prop(k, m, n) \quad (gcd\text{-}unq)$.

Definition (Fig. 14.23)

For $m, n : \mathbb{Z}$, $s : m > 0$, $t : n > 0$,

$gcd(m, n, s, t) := \iota(\mathbb{Z}, \lambda k : \mathbb{Z} . \, gcd\text{-}prop(k, m, n), gcd\text{-}unq(m, n, s, t))$.

Lemma (Fig. 14.23)

For $m, n : \mathbb{Z}$, $s : m > 0$, $t : n > 0$,

$gcd(m, n, s, t) > 0 \quad (gcd\text{-}pos)$.

Appendix C

Two complete example proofs in λD

In this appendix we repeat two λD-derivations, but now with the 'hints' having been worked out. The examples give an impression of what one might come across in this process.

C.1 Closure under addition in $\mathbb{N}$

We start with a *full* proof of the Closure property of addition in $\mathbb{N}$, corresponding to Figure 14.15. In the logical steps, we apply the rules for natural deduction in λD-format as summarised in Appendix A. We do not use the short versions of the proof objects as explained in Sections 11.5 and 11.10. Notational conventions such as *infix* notation are maintained in the λD-derivation, in order to keep a good view on the mathematical background.

	$x : \mathbb{Z}$
(1)	$P(x) := \lambda y : \mathbb{Z} . (x + y \; \varepsilon \; \mathbb{N}) \; : \; \mathbb{Z} \to *_p$
	$u \; : \; x \; \varepsilon \; \mathbb{N}$
(2)	$a_2(x, u) := eq\text{-}sym(\mathbb{Z}, x + 0, x, plus\text{-}i(x)) \; : \; x = x + 0$
(3)	$a_3(x, u) := eq\text{-}subs(\mathbb{Z}, \mathbb{N}, x, x + 0, a_2(x, u), u) \; : \; P(x) \, 0$
	$y : \mathbb{Z}$
	$v \; : \; y \; \varepsilon \; \mathbb{N}$
	$w \; : \; P(x) \, y$
(4)	$a_4(x, u, y, v, w) := clos\text{-}prop \, (x + y) \, w \; : \; s(x + y) \; \varepsilon \; \mathbb{N}$
(5)	$a_5(x, u, y, v, w) := eq\text{-}sym(\mathbb{Z}, x + s\,y, s(x + y), plus\text{-}ii(x, y)) \; :$
	$s(x + y) = x + s\,y$

$\vdots$

(6) $a_6(x, u, y, v, w) := eq\text{-}subs(\mathbb{Z}, \mathbb{N}, s(x + y), x + s\,y,$

         $a_5(x, u, y, v, w), a_4(x, u, y, v, w))$:

           $P(x)\,(s\,y)$

(6a) $a_{6a}(x, u, y, v) := \Rightarrow\text{-}in(P(x)\,y, P(x)\,(s\,y),$

         $\lambda w : P(x)\,y \,.\, a_6(x, u, y, v, w))$:

           $P(x)\,y \Rightarrow P(x)\,(s\,y)$

(6b) $a_{6b}(x, u, y) := \Rightarrow\text{-}in(y \;\varepsilon\; \mathbb{N}, P(x)\,y \Rightarrow P(x)\,(s\,y),$

         $\lambda v \;:\; y \;\varepsilon\; \mathbb{N} \,.\, a_{6a}(x, u, y, v))$:

           $y \;\varepsilon\; \mathbb{N} \Rightarrow (P(x)\,y \Rightarrow P(x)\,(s\,y))$

(7) $a_7(x, u) := \forall\text{-}in(\mathbb{Z}, \lambda y : \mathbb{Z} \,.\, (y \;\varepsilon\; \mathbb{N} \Rightarrow (P(x)\,y \Rightarrow P(x)\,(s\,y))),$

       $\lambda y : \mathbb{Z} \,.\, a_{6b}(x, u, y))$:

         $\forall y : \mathbb{Z} \,.\, (y \;\varepsilon\; \mathbb{N} \Rightarrow (P(x)\,y \Rightarrow P(x)\,(s\,y)))$

(7a) $a_{7a}(x, u) := \wedge\text{-}in(P(x)\,0, \forall y : \mathbb{Z} \,.\, (y \;\varepsilon\; \mathbb{N} \Rightarrow (P(x)\,y \Rightarrow P(x)\,(s\,y))),$

       $a_3(x, u), a_7(x, u))$:

         $P(x)\,0 \wedge \forall y : \mathbb{Z} \,.\, (y \;\varepsilon\; \mathbb{N} \Rightarrow (P(x)\,y \Rightarrow P(x)\,(s\,y)))$

(8) $a_8(x, u) := nat\text{-}ind(P(x))\,a_{7a}(x, u)$:

         $\forall y : \mathbb{Z} \,.\, (y \;\varepsilon\; \mathbb{N} \Rightarrow x + y \;\varepsilon\; \mathbb{N})$

(8a) $a_{8a}(x) := \Rightarrow\text{-}in(x \;\varepsilon\; \mathbb{N}, \forall y : \mathbb{Z} \,.\, (y \;\varepsilon\; \mathbb{N} \Rightarrow x + y \;\varepsilon\; \mathbb{N}),$

       $\lambda u : x \;\varepsilon\; \mathbb{N} \,.\, a_8(x, u))$:

         $x \;\varepsilon\; \mathbb{N} \Rightarrow \forall y : \mathbb{Z} \,.\, (y \;\varepsilon\; \mathbb{N} \Rightarrow x + y \;\varepsilon\; \mathbb{N})$

(9) $a_9 := \forall\text{-}in(\mathbb{Z}, \lambda x : \mathbb{Z} \,.\, (x \;\varepsilon\; \mathbb{N} \Rightarrow \forall y : \mathbb{Z} \,.\, (y \;\varepsilon\; \mathbb{N} \Rightarrow x + y \;\varepsilon\; \mathbb{N})),$

       $\lambda x : \mathbb{Z} \,.\, a_{8a}(x))$:

         $\forall x : \mathbb{Z} \,.\, (x \;\varepsilon\; \mathbb{N} \Rightarrow \forall y : \mathbb{Z} \,.\, (y \;\varepsilon\; \mathbb{N} \Rightarrow x + y \;\varepsilon\; \mathbb{N}))$

C.2 The Minimum Theorem

We now give a full proof of the Minimum Theorem (see Section 15.7). The only incompletions that we tolerate are the justifications of 'foreknowledge' that were dealt with earlier in this book: we regard these results as proven facts.

We start with a list in λD-format of the lemmas and exercises that are used in the proof, leaving out the proof objects. Then we give an elaborated proof of the Minimum Theorem, as a completion of Figures 15.16–15.18.

We use the notational conventions that we described and employed earlier, for example in making free use of infix notations (cf. Chapter 12, in particular Remark 12.4.1) and by omitting unaltered parameter lists in part II (cf. Section 11.7).

In the logical steps, we apply the rules for natural deduction in λD-format as described in Chapter 11 and summarised in Appendix A. In order to save on space, we often employ the 'shorter' version of the proof terms accompanying these rules, as mentioned in Sections 11.5 and 11.10.

I. Foreknowledge: lemmas and exercises

$$\boxed{A, B : *_p}$$

(1) $Exerc\text{-}7.5.(b)(A, B) := \ldots : \neg(A \Rightarrow B) \Rightarrow (A \wedge \neg B)$

$$\boxed{S : *_s}$$

$$\boxed{P, Q, R : S \rightarrow *_p}$$

(2) $Exerc\text{-}7.10(S, P, Q, R) := \ldots : (\forall x : S . (P x \Rightarrow Q x)) \Rightarrow$
$$(\forall y : S . (P y \Rightarrow R y)) \Rightarrow \forall z : S . (P z \Rightarrow (Q z \wedge R z))$$

$$\boxed{P, Q : S \rightarrow *_p}$$

(3) $Exerc\text{-}7.13(S, P, Q) := \ldots :$
$$(\exists x : S . P x) \Rightarrow (\forall y : S . (P y \Rightarrow Q y)) \Rightarrow \exists z : S . Q z$$

$$\boxed{P : S \rightarrow *_p}$$

(4) $Fig\text{-}11.29(S, P) := \ldots : (\neg \forall x : S . P x) \Rightarrow (\exists y : S . \neg(P y))$

(5) $Lem\text{-}14.8.4 := \ldots : \forall x : \mathbb{Z} . (x - x = 0)$

(6) $Lem\text{-}14.8.6.(a) := \ldots : \forall x, y : \mathbb{Z} . (x - s y = p(x - y))$

(7) $Lem\text{-}14.10.1.(b) := \ldots : \forall x, y, z : \mathbb{Z} . ((x \leq y \wedge y \leq z) \Rightarrow x \leq z)$

$$\boxed{P : \mathbb{Z} \rightarrow *_p}$$

(8) $Exerc\text{-}14.18(P) := \ldots :$
$$((\exists l : \mathbb{Z} . P l) \wedge \forall x : \mathbb{Z} . (P x \Rightarrow (P(s x) \wedge P(p x)))) \Rightarrow \forall x : \mathbb{Z} . P x$$

(9) $Exerc\text{-}14.23.(b) := \ldots : \forall x : \mathbb{Z} . (x > p x)$

(10) $Exerc\text{-}14.29.(b) := \ldots : \forall x, y : \mathbb{Z} . (x < y \Rightarrow s x \leq y)$

II. A full proof of the Minimum Theorem

$$T : ps(\mathbb{Z}) \mid u : T \neq \emptyset_{\mathbb{Z}} \mid v : \exists x : \mathbb{Z}.\ lw\text{-}bnd_{\mathbb{Z}}(T, x)$$

(1) $a_1 := a_{6\,[Fig.13.8]}(\mathbb{Z}, T, u)\ :\ \exists n : \mathbb{Z}.\ n\ \varepsilon\ T$

$$l : \mathbb{Z} \mid ass_1 : lw\text{-}bnd_{\mathbb{Z}}(T, l)$$

$$n : \mathbb{Z} \mid ass_2 : n\ \varepsilon\ T$$

(2) $P := \lambda x : \mathbb{Z}.\ lw\text{-}bnd_{\mathbb{Z}}(T, x)\ :\ \mathbb{Z} \to *_p$

(3) $a_3 := \exists\text{-}in(\mathbb{Z}, P, l, ass_1)\ :\ \exists x : \mathbb{Z}.\ P\,x$

$$ass_3 :\ \forall x : \mathbb{Z}.\ (P\,x \Rightarrow P(s\,x))$$

$$x : \mathbb{Z} \mid ass_4 : P\,x$$

(4) $a_4 := \wedge\text{-}el_1(p\,x \leq x, p\,x \neq x, Exerc\text{-}14.23.(b)\,x)\ :\ p\,x \leq x$

$$t : \mathbb{Z} \mid ass_5 : t\ \varepsilon\ T$$

(5) $a_5 := ass_4\,t\,ass_5\ :\ x \leq t$

(5a) $a_{5a} := \wedge\text{-}in(p\,x \leq x, x \leq t, a_4, a_5) := p\,x \leq x \wedge x \leq t$

(6) $a_6 := Lem\text{-}14.10.1.(b)\,(p\,x)\,x\,t\,a_{5a}\ :\ p\,x \leq t$

(7) $a_7 := \lambda t : \mathbb{Z}.\ \lambda\,ass_5 : (t\ \varepsilon\ T).\ a_6\ :\ P(p\,x)$

(8) $a_8 := \lambda x : \mathbb{Z}.\ \lambda\,ass_4 : P\,x.\ a_7\ :\ \forall x : \mathbb{Z}.\ (P\,x \Rightarrow P(p\,x))$

(9) $a_9 := Exerc\text{-}7.10\,(\mathbb{Z}, P, \lambda x : \mathbb{Z}.\ P(s\,x), \lambda x : \mathbb{Z}.\ P(p\,x))\,ass_3\,a_8\ :$
         $\forall x : \mathbb{Z}.\ (P\,x \Rightarrow (P(s\,x) \wedge P(p\,x)))$

(9a) $a_{9a} := \wedge\text{-}in(\exists x : \mathbb{Z}.\ P\,x,$
         $\forall x : \mathbb{Z}.\ (P\,x \Rightarrow (P(s\,x) \wedge P(p\,x))), a_3, a_9)\ :$
         $(\exists x : \mathbb{Z}.\ P\,x) \wedge \forall x : \mathbb{Z}.\ (P\,x \Rightarrow (P(s\,x) \wedge P(p\,x)))$

(10) $a_{10} := Exerc\text{-}14.18(P)\,a_{9a}\ :\ \forall x : \mathbb{Z}.\ P\,x$

(11) $a_{11} := a_{10}\,(s\,n)\ :\ P(s\,n)$

(12) $a_{12} := a_{11}\,n\,ass_2\ :\ s\,n \leq n$

(12a) $a_{12a} := eq\text{-}subs(\mathbb{Z}, \lambda x : \mathbb{Z}.\ (x\ \varepsilon\ \mathbb{N}), n - s\,n, p(n - n),$
         $Lem\text{-}14.8.6.(a)\,n\,n, a_{12})\ :\ p(n - n)\ \varepsilon\ \mathbb{N}$

(12b) $a_{12b} := eq\text{-}subs(\mathbb{Z}, \lambda x : \mathbb{Z}.\ (p\,x\ \varepsilon\ \mathbb{N}), n - n, 0,$
         $Lem\text{-}14.8.4\,n, a_{12a})\ :\ p0\ \varepsilon\ \mathbb{N}$

(13) $a_{13} := ax\text{-}int_3\,a_{12b}\ :\ \bot$

(13a) $a_{13a} := \lambda\,ass_3 : (\forall x : \mathbb{Z}.\ (P\,x \Rightarrow P(s\,x))).\ a_{13}\ :$
         $\neg\forall x : \mathbb{Z}.\ (P\,x \Rightarrow P(s\,x))$

(13b)
$$a_{13b} := Fig\text{-}11.29(\mathbb{Z}, \lambda y : \mathbb{Z} . (P\,y \Rightarrow P(s\,y)))\, a_{13a} :$$
$$\exists x : \mathbb{Z} . \neg(P\,x \Rightarrow P(s\,x))$$

(13c)
$$a_{13c} := \lambda y : \mathbb{Z} . Exerc\text{-}7.5.(b)(P\,y, P(s\,y)) :$$
$$\forall y : \mathbb{Z} . (\neg(P\,y \Rightarrow P(s\,y)) \Rightarrow (P\,y \wedge \neg P(s\,y)))$$

(14)
$$a_{14} := Exerc\text{-}7.13(\mathbb{Z}, \lambda x : \mathbb{Z} . \neg(P\,x \Rightarrow P(s\,x)),$$
$$\lambda z : \mathbb{Z} . (P\,z \wedge \neg P(s\,z)))\, a_{13b}\, a_{13c} :$$
$$\exists z : \mathbb{Z} . (lw\text{-}bnd_{\mathbb{Z}}(T, z) \wedge \neg lw\text{-}bnd_{\mathbb{Z}}(T, s\,z))$$

$$\boxed{z : \mathbb{Z} \mid ass_6 : (lw\text{-}bnd_{\mathbb{Z}}(T, z) \wedge \neg lw\text{-}bnd_{\mathbb{Z}}(T, s\,z))}$$

(15)
$$a_{15} := \wedge\text{-}el_1(lw\text{-}bnd_{\mathbb{Z}}(T, z), \neg lw\text{-}bnd_{\mathbb{Z}}(T, s\,z), ass_6) :$$
$$lw\text{-}bnd_{\mathbb{Z}}(T, z)$$

(16)
$$a_{16} := \wedge\text{-}el_2(lw\text{-}bnd_{\mathbb{Z}}(T, z), \neg lw\text{-}bnd_{\mathbb{Z}}(T, s\,z), ass_6) :$$
$$\neg lw\text{-}bnd_{\mathbb{Z}}(T, sz)$$

$$\boxed{ass_7 : \neg(z\,\varepsilon\,T)}$$

$$\boxed{y : \mathbb{Z} \mid ass_8 : y\,\varepsilon\,T}$$

(17)
$$a_{17} := a_{15}\, y\, ass_8 : z \le y$$

$$\boxed{ass_9 : z = y}$$

(18)
$$a_{18} := eq\text{-}subs(\mathbb{Z}, \lambda x : \mathbb{Z} . \neg(x\,\varepsilon\,T), z, y, ass_9, ass_7)\, ass_8 :$$
$$\bot$$

(19)
$$a_{19} := \lambda\, ass_9 : (z = y) . a_{18} : \neg(z = y)$$

(20)
$$a_{20} := \wedge\text{-}in(z \le y, \neg(z = y), a_{17}, a_{19}) : z < y$$

(21)
$$a_{21} := Exerc\text{-}14.29.(b)\, z\, y\, a_{20} : s\,z \le y$$

(22)
$$a_{22} := \lambda y : \mathbb{Z} . \lambda\, ass_8 : (y\,\varepsilon\,T) . a_{21} : lw\text{-}bnd_{\mathbb{Z}}(T, s\,z)$$

(23)
$$a_{23} := a_{16}\, a_{22} : \bot$$

(24)
$$a_{24} := \neg\neg\text{-}el(z\,\varepsilon\,T, \lambda\, ass_7 : \neg(z\,\varepsilon\,T) . a_{23}) : z\,\varepsilon\,T$$

(25)
$$a_{25} := \wedge\text{-}in(z\,\varepsilon\,T, lw\text{-}bnd_{\mathbb{Z}}(T, z), a_{24}, a_{15}) : least_{\mathbb{Z}}(T, z)$$

(26)
$$a_{26} := \exists\text{-}in(\mathbb{Z}, \lambda y : \mathbb{Z} . least_{\mathbb{Z}}(T, y), z, a_{25}) :$$
$$\exists m : \mathbb{Z} . least_{\mathbb{Z}}(T, m)$$

(27)
$$a_{27} := \exists\text{-}el(\mathbb{Z}, \lambda x : \mathbb{Z} . (lw\text{-}bnd_{\mathbb{Z}}(T, z) \wedge \neg lw\text{-}bnd_{\mathbb{Z}}(T, sz)), a_{14},$$
$$\exists m : \mathbb{Z} . least_{\mathbb{Z}}(T, m),$$
$$\lambda z : \mathbb{Z} . \lambda\, ass_6 : (lw\text{-}bnd_{\mathbb{Z}}(T, z) \wedge \neg lw\text{-}bnd_{\mathbb{Z}}(T, sz)) . a_{26}) :$$
$$\exists m : \mathbb{Z} . least_{\mathbb{Z}}(T, m)$$

(28) $\quad a_{28} \;:=\; \exists\text{-}el(\mathbb{Z}, \lambda x : \mathbb{Z}.\ (x\ \varepsilon\ T), a_1, \exists m : \mathbb{Z}.\ least_{\mathbb{Z}}(T, m),$

$\qquad \lambda n : \mathbb{Z}.\ \lambda\, ass_2 : (n\ \varepsilon\ T).\ a_{27})\ :$

$\qquad\quad \exists m : \mathbb{Z}.\ least_{\mathbb{Z}}(T, m)$

(29) $min\text{-}the(T, u, v) \;:=\; \exists\text{-}el(\mathbb{Z}, \lambda x : \mathbb{Z}.\ lw\text{-}bnd_{\mathbb{Z}}(T, x), v,$

$\qquad \exists m : \mathbb{Z}.\ least_{\mathbb{Z}}(T, m), \lambda l : \mathbb{Z}.\ \lambda\, ass_1 : lw\text{-}bnd_{\mathbb{Z}}(T, l).\ a_{28})\ :$

$\qquad\quad \exists m : \mathbb{Z}.\ least_{\mathbb{Z}}(T, m)$

Appendix D

Derivation rules for λD

$(sort)$ $\emptyset \; ; \; \emptyset \vdash * : \square$

(var) $\dfrac{\Delta \; ; \; \Gamma \vdash A : s}{\Delta \; ; \; \Gamma, \, x : A \vdash x : A}$ if $x \notin \Gamma$

$(weak)$ $\dfrac{\Delta \; ; \; \Gamma \vdash A : B \quad \Delta \; ; \; \Gamma \vdash C : s}{\Delta \; ; \; \Gamma, \, x : C \vdash A : B}$ if $x \notin \Gamma$

$(form)$ $\dfrac{\Delta \; ; \; \Gamma \vdash A : s_1 \quad \Delta \; ; \; \Gamma, \, x : A \vdash B : s_2}{\Delta \; ; \; \Gamma \vdash \Pi x : A. \, B \; : \; s_2}$

$(appl)$ $\dfrac{\Delta \; ; \; \Gamma \vdash M \; : \; \Pi x : A. \, B \quad \Delta \; ; \; \Gamma \vdash N : A}{\Delta \; ; \; \Gamma \vdash MN \; : \; B[x := N]}$

$(abst)$ $\dfrac{\Delta \; ; \; \Gamma, \, x : A \vdash M : B \quad \Delta \; ; \; \Gamma \vdash \Pi x : A. \, B \; : \; s}{\Delta \; ; \; \Gamma \vdash \lambda x : A. \, M \; : \; \Pi x : A. \, B}$

$(conv)$ $\dfrac{\Delta \; ; \; \Gamma \vdash A : B \quad \Delta \; ; \; \Gamma \vdash B' : s}{\Delta \; ; \; \Gamma \vdash A : B'}$ if $B \stackrel{\Delta}{=}_\beta B'$

(def) $\dfrac{\Delta \; ; \; \Gamma \vdash K : L \quad \Delta \; ; \; \overline{x} : \overline{A} \vdash M : N}{\Delta , \, \overline{x} : \overline{A} \vartriangleright a(\overline{x}) := M : N \; ; \; \Gamma \vdash K : L}$ if $a \notin \Delta$

$(def\text{-}prim)$ $\dfrac{\Delta \; ; \; \Gamma \vdash K : L \quad \Delta \; ; \; \overline{x} : \overline{A} \vdash N : s}{\Delta , \, \overline{x} : \overline{A} \vartriangleright a(\overline{x}) := \perp\!\!\!\perp : N \; ; \; \Gamma \vdash K : L}$ if $a \notin \Delta$

$(inst)$ $\dfrac{\Delta ; \Gamma \vdash * : \square \quad \Delta ; \Gamma \vdash \overline{U} : \overline{A[\overline{x} := \overline{U}]}}{\Delta \; ; \; \Gamma \vdash a(\overline{U}) : N[\overline{x} := \overline{U}]}$ if $\overline{x} : \overline{A} \vartriangleright a(\overline{x}) := M : N \in \Delta$

$(inst\text{-}prim)$ $\dfrac{\Delta ; \Gamma \vdash * : \square \quad \Delta ; \Gamma \vdash \overline{U} : \overline{A[\overline{x} := \overline{U}]}}{\Delta \; ; \; \Gamma \vdash a(\overline{U}) : N[\overline{x} := \overline{U}]}$ if $\overline{x} : \overline{A} \vartriangleright a(\overline{x}) := \perp\!\!\!\perp : N \in \Delta$

Derived rule:

(par) $\dfrac{\Delta \; ; \; \overline{x} : \overline{A} \vdash M : N}{\Delta, \mathcal{D} \; ; \; \overline{x} : \overline{A} \vdash a(\overline{x}) : N}$ if $\mathcal{D} \equiv \overline{x} : \overline{A} \vartriangleright a(\overline{x}) := M : N$ and $a \notin \Delta$

References

AMS, 2008: *Notices of the American Mathematical Society*, 55 (11).

Arthan, R.D., 2013: *ProofPower*,
www.lemma-one.com/ProofPower/index/index.html.

Asperti, A., Ricciotti, W., Sacerdoti Coen, C. and Tassi, E., 2011: The Matita Interactive Theorem Prover. In Bjørner, N. and Sofronie-Stokkermans, V., eds, *Automated Deduction: CADE 23*, 23rd International Conference on Automated Deduction, Wroclaw, Poland, 31 July – 5 August 2011, pp. 64–69, Springer. See also matita.cs.unibo.it/.

Automath Archive, 2004: Home Page, www.win.tue.nl/automath/.

Barendregt, H.P., 1981: *The Lambda Calculus: Its Syntax and Semantics*, North-Holland Publishing Company.

Barendregt, H.P., 1992: Lambda calculi with types. In Abramski, S., Gabbay, D. and Maibaum, T., eds, *Handbook of Logic in Computer Science*, pp. 117–309, Oxford University Press.

Barendregt, H. and Geuvers, H., 2001: Proof assistants using dependent type systems. In Robinson, A. and Voronkov, A., eds, *Handbook of Automated Reasoning*, Vol. 2, pp. 1149–1238, Elsevier.

Barendregt, H.P., Dekkers, W. and Statman, R., eds, 2013: *Lambda Calculus with Types*, Cambridge University Press.

van Benthem Jutting, L.S., 1977: *Checking Landau's 'Grundlagen' in the AUTOMATH system*, PhD thesis, Eindhoven University of Technology. See also Nederpelt *et al.*, 1994, pp. 763–780.

van Benthem Jutting, L.S., 1993: Typing in Pure Type Systems, *Information and Computation*, 105 (1), pp. 30–41.

van Benthem Jutting, L.S., McKinna, J. and Pollack, R., 1994: Checking algorithms for Pure Type Systems. In Barendregt, H.P. and Nipkow, T., eds, *Types for Proofs and Programs*, International Workshop TYPES'93, Nijmegen, The Netherlands, pp. 19–61, Springer.

Bertot, Y. and Castéran, P., 2004: *Interactive Theorem Proving and Program Development: Coq'Art: the Calculus of Inductive Constructions*, Springer.

Böhm, C. and Berarducci, A., 1985: Automatic synthesis of typed Λ-programs on term algebras, *Theoretical Computer Science*, 39, pp. 135–154.

Bove, A., Dybjer, P. and Norell, U., 2009: A brief overview of Agda: a functional language with dependent types. In Ierghofer, S., Nipkow, T., Irban, C. and Wenzel, M., eds, *Proceedings of the 22nd International Conference on Theorem*

Proving in Higher Order Logics, TPHOLs 2009, Munich, Germany, 17–20 August 2009, pp. 73–78, Springer. See also `wiki.portal.chalmers.se/agda/`.

de Bruijn, N.G., 1968: *Example of a text written in Automath*. In Nederpelt *et al.*, 1994, pp. 687–700.

de Bruijn, N.G., 1970: The mathematical language AUTOMATH, its usage and some of its extensions. In Laudet, M., Lacombe, D., Nolin, L. and Schützenberger, M., eds, *Symposium on Automatic Demonstration*, Versailles, pp. 29–61, Springer. Reprinted in Nederpelt *et al.*, 1994, pp. 73–100.

de Bruijn, N.G., 1972: Lambda calculus notation with nameless dummies, a tool for automatic formula manipulation, with application to the Church–Rosser Theorem, *Indagationes Mathematicae*, 34 (5), pp. 381–392, Elsevier.

de Bruijn, N.G., 1980: *A survey of the project AUTOMATH*. In Seldin & Hindley, 1980, pp. 579–606.

Cantor, G., 1874: Über eine Eigenschaft des Inbegriffes aller reellen algebraischen Zahlen, *Journal für die Reine und Angewandte Mathematik*, 77, pp. 258–262, Georg Reimer Verlag. English translation in Ewald, W., ed., *From Kant to Hilbert: A Source Book in the Foundations of Mathematics*, 1996, pp. 840–843, Clarendon Press.

Cardone, F. and Hindley, J.R., 2009: Lambda-calculus and combinators in the 20th century. In Gabbay, D.M. and Woods, J., eds, *Handbook of the History of Logic*, Vol. 5, pp. 723–817, Elsevier.

Church, A., 1933: A set of postulates for the foundation of logic, *Annals of Mathematics*, 33, pp. 346–366, and 34, pp. 839–864.

Church, A., 1935: An unsolvable problem of elementary number theory, preliminary report (abstract), *Bulletin of the American Mathematical Society*, 41, pp. 332–333.

Church, A., 1936a: A note on the Entscheidungsproblem, *Journal of Symbolic Logic*, 1, pp. 40–41.

Church, A., 1936b: An unsolvable problem of elementary number theory, *American Journal of Mathematics*, 58, pp. 345–363.

Church, A., 1940: A formulation of the simple theory of types, *Journal of Symbolic Logic*, 5, pp. 56–68.

Constable, R.L., Allen, S.F., Bromley, H.M., Cleaveland, W.R., Cremer, J.F., Harper, R.W., Howe, D.J., Knoblock, T.B., Mendler, N.P., Panangaden, P., Sasaki, J.T. and Smith, S.F., 1986: *Implementing Mathematics with the Nuprl Development System*, Prentice-Hall.

Coq Development Team, 2012: *The Coq Proof Assistant, Reference Manual*, Version 8.4. See `coq.inria.fr/refman/`.

Coquand, Th., 1985: *Une théorie des constructions*, PhD thesis, University of Paris VII.

Coquand, Th. and Huet, G., 1988: The Calculus of Constructions, *Information and Computation*, 76, pp. 95–120.

Curry, H.B., 1930: Grundlagen der Kombinatorischen Logik, *American Journal of Mathematics*, 52 (3), pp. 509–536, and (4), pp. 789–834.

Curry, H.B., 1969: Modified basic functionality in combinatory logic, *Dialectica*, 23, pp. 83–92.

Curry, H.B. and Feys, R., 1958: *Combinatory Logic*, Vol. 1, North-Holland Publishing Company.

van Daalen, D.T., 1973: A description of AUTOMATH and some aspects of its language theory. In Braffort, P., ed., *Proceedings of the Symposium APLASM*, Orsay, France. Reprinted in Nederpelt *et al.*, 1994, pp. 101–126.

van Dalen, D., 1994: *Logic and Structure*, 3rd augmented edition, Springer.

van Dalen, D., Doets, H.C. and de Swart, H., 1978: *Sets: Naive, Axiomatic and Applied*, Pergamon Press.

Damas, L. and Milner, R., 1982: Principal type-schemes for functional programs. In DeMillo, R.A., ed., *POPL '82: Proceedings of the 9th ACM SIGPLAN-SIGACT Symposium on Principles of Programming Languages*, pp. 207–212, ACM.

Davis, M., ed., 1965: *The Undecidable, Basic Papers on Undecidable Propositions, Unsolvable Problems and Computable Functions*, Raven Press.

Dechesne, F. and Nederpelt, R.P., 2012: N.G. de Bruijn (1918–2012) and his road to Automath, the earliest proof checker, *The Mathematical Intelligencer*, 34 (4), pp. 4–11.

Fitch, F., 1952: *Symbolic Logic, An Introduction*, The Ronald Press Company.

Frege, F.L.G., 1893: *Grundgesetze der Arithmetik*, Verlag Hermann Pohle. Facsimile reprints in 1962 and 1998, Georg Olms Verlag.

Gandy, R.O., 1980: *An early proof of normalization by A.M. Turing*. In Seldin & Hindley, 1980, pp. 453–455, Academic Press.

Gentzen, G., 1934/5: Untersuchungen über das logische Schliessen, I, *Mathematische Zeitschrift*, 39 (2).

Geuvers, J.H., 1995: A short and flexible proof of Strong Normalization for the Calculus of Constructions. In Dybjer, P., Nordström, B. and Smith, J., eds, *Types for Proofs and Programs*, International Workshop TYPES '94, Bastad, Sweden, pp. 14–38, Springer.

Geuvers, J.H., 2001: Induction is not derivable in second order dependent type theory. In Abramsky, S., ed., *Proceedings of Typed Lambda Calculus and Applications*, TLCA 2001, Krakow, Poland, May 2001, pp. 166–181, Springer.

Geuvers, J.H., 2009: Proof assistants: history, ideas and future, *Sadahana Journal, Academy Proceedings in Engineering Sciences, Indian Academy of Sciences*, 34 (1), Special Issue on Interactive Theorem Proving and Proof Checking, pp. 3–25.

Geuvers, J.H., 2013: *Inconsistency of 'Automath powersets' in impredicative type theory*, Short note, www.cs.ru.nl/~herman/PUBS/InconsAutSetTh.pdf .

Geuvers, J.H., 2014a: *Properties of a lambda calculus with definitions*, Short note, www.cs.ru.nl/~herman/PUBS/PropLamCDef.pdf .

Geuvers, J.H., 2014b: *A formalization of the integers*, Short note, www.cs.ru.nl/~herman/PUBS/FormInt.pdf .

Geuvers, J.H. and Nederpelt, R.P., 1994: Typed λ-calculus. In de Swart, H.C.M., *Logic: Mathematics, Language, Computer Science and Philosophy*, Vol. 2, Section 33, pp. 168–199, Peter Lang GmbH.

Geuvers, J.H. and Nederpelt, R.P., 2004: Rewriting for Fitch style natural deductions. In van Oostrom, V., ed., *Proceedings of RTA 2004*, 15th International Conference on Rewriting Techniques and Applications, Aachen, Germany, pp. 134–154, Springer.

Geuvers, J.H. and Nederpelt, R.P., 2013: N.G. de Bruijn's contribution to the formalization of mathematics, *Indagationes Mathematicae*, 24, pp. 1034–1049.

Girard, J.-Y., 1971: Une extension de l'interprétation de Gödel à l'analyse et son application à l'élimination des coupures dans l'analyse et la théorie des types. In Fenstad, J.E., ed., *Proceedings of the Second Scandinavian Logic Symposium*, pp. 63–92, North-Holland Publishing Company.

Girard, J.-Y., 1972: *Interprétation fonctionelle et élimination des coupures dans l'arithmétique d'ordre supérieur*, PhD thesis, Université Paris VII.

Girard, J.-Y., 1986: The system F of variable types, fifteen years later, *Theoretical Computer Science*, 45, pp. 159–192.

Girard, J.-Y., Lafont, Y. and Taylor, P., 1989: *Proofs and Types*, Cambridge University Press.

Gödel, K., 1932: Über formal unentscheidbare Sätze der Principia Mathematica und verwandter Systeme, I, *Monatshefte für Mathematik und Physik*, 38, pp. 173–198. Also in van Heijenoort, 1967.

Gonthier, G., 2005: *A Computer-checked Proof of the Four Colour Theorem*, research.microsoft.com/en-us/people/gonthier/4colproof.pdf.

Gonthier, G., 2008: Formal proof: the Four Color Theorem, *Notices of the American Mathematical Society*, 55 (11), pp. 1370–1381.

Gonthier, G., Asperti, A., Avigad, J., Bertot, Y., Cohen, C., Garillot, F., Le Roux, S., Mahboubi, A., O'Connor, R., Ould Biha, S., Pasca, I., Rideau, L., Solovyev, A., Tassi, E. and Théry, L., 2013: A machine-checked proof of the odd order theorem. In Blazy, S., Paulin-Mohring, C. and Pichardie, D., eds, *Interactive Theorem Proving: 4th International Conference*, ITP 2013, 22–26 July 2013, Rennes, France, pp. 163–179, Springer.

Gordon, M.J.C., 2000: From LCF to HOL: a short history. In Plotkin, G., Stirling, C.P. and Tofte, M., eds, *Proof, Language, and Interaction, Essays in Honour of Robin Milner (Foundations of Computing)*, pp. 169–185, MIT Press.

Gordon, M.J.C. and Melham, T.F., eds, 1993: *Introduction to HOL: A Theorem-Proving Environment for Higher-Order Logic*, Cambridge University Press.

Gupta, A., 2014: Definitions. In Zalta, E.N., ed., *The Stanford Encyclopedia of Philosophy*, plato.stanford.edu/archives/spr2014/entries/definitions/.

Hales, T.C., 2006: *Introduction to the Flyspeck Project*, Dagstuhl Seminar Proceedings 05021, Mathematics, Algorithms, Proofs, pdf.aminer.org/000/137/477/introduction_to_the_flyspeck_project.pdf.

Hales, T.C., Harrison, J., McLaughlin, S., Nipkow, T., Obua, S. and Zumkeller, R., 2010: A revision of the proof of the Kepler conjecture, *Discrete & Computational Geometry*, 44 (1), pp. 1–34.

Harper, R., Honsell, F. and Plotkin, G., 1987: A framework for defining logics. In *Proceedings of the Second Annual Symposium on Logic in Computer Science*, Ithaca, NY, pp. 194–204, IEEE.

van Heijenoort, J., 1967: *From Frege to Gödel: A Source Book in Mathematical Logic, 1879–1931*, Harvard University Press.

Hilbert, D., 1927: *The Foundations of Mathematics*. Reproduced in van Heijenoort, 1967.

Hilbert, D. and Bernays, P., 1939: *Grundlagen der Mathematik*, Vol. 2, Springer.

Hindley, J.R., 1969: The principal type-scheme of an object in combinatory logic, *Transactions of the American Mathematical Society*, 146, pp. 29–60.

Hindley, J.R., 1997: *Basic Simple Type Theory*, Cambridge University Press.

Hindley, J.R. and Seldin, J.P., 2008: *Lambda-Calculus and Combinators, an Introduction*, Cambridge University Press.

HOL system, 1988: www.cl.cam.ac.uk/research/hvg/HOL/.

Howard, W., 1980: *The formulas-as-types notion of construction*. In Seldin & Hindley, 1980, pp. 479–490.

JAR, 2013: *Journal of Automated Reasoning*, 50 (2), Special Issue: Formal Mathematics for Mathematicians.

Jaśkowski, S., 1934: On the rules of suppositions in formal logic, *Studia Logica*, 1, pp. 5–32. Reprinted in McCall, S., ed., *Polish Logic 1920–1939*, Oxford University Press, 1967, pp. 232–258.

Jech, Th., 2003: *Set Theory: The Third Millennium Edition*, revised and expanded edition, Springer.

Jones, R.B., 2013: *42 Famous Theorems in ProofPower*, www.rbjones.com/rbjpub/pp/rda001.html.

Kamareddine, F.D., Laan, T.D.L. and Nederpelt, R.P., 2002: Types in logic and mathematics before 1940, *The Bulletin of Symbolic Logic*, 8 (2), pp. 185–245. Reprinted as 'A history of types' in Gabbay, D.M., Pelletier, F.J. and Woods, J., eds, *Handbook of the History of Logic*, Vol. 11, pp. 451–511, Elsevier, 2012.

Kamareddine, F.D., Laan, T.D.L. and Nederpelt, R.P., 2003: De Bruijn's Automath and Pure Type Systems. In Kamareddine, F.D., ed., *Thirty Five Years of Automating Mathematics*, pp. 71–123, Kluwer.

Kamareddine, F.D., Laan, T.D.L. and Nederpelt, R.P., 2004: *A Modern Perspective on Type Theory, From its Origins until Today*, Kluwer.

Klein, G., 2013: *Isabelle Top 100*, www.cse.unsw.edu.au/~kleing/top100/.

Kneale, W. and Kneale, M., 1962: *The Development of Logic*, Clarendon Press.

Kwiatek, R., 1990: Factorial and Newton coefficients, *Journal of Formalized Mathematics*, 1 (5), pp. 887–890.

Lamport, L., 1985: LATEX: *A Document Preparation System*, Addison-Wesley Publishing Company.

Landau, E., 1930: *Grundlagen der Analysis*, Akademische Verlagsgesellschaft; 3rd edition, 1960, Chelsea Publishing Company.

Lewis, H. and Papadimitriou, C.H., 1981: *Elements of the Theory of Computation*, Prentice-Hall.

Luo, Z., 1990: *An Extended Calculus of Constructions*, PhD thesis, University of Edinburgh.

Luo, Z., 1994: *Computation and Reasoning: A Type Theory for Computer Science*, Oxford University Press.

Madiot, J.-M., 2013: *Formalizing 100 theorems in Coq*, perso.ens-lyon.fr/jeanmarie.madiot/coq100/.

Magnusson, L. and Nordström, B., 1994: The ALF proof editor and its proof engine. In Barendregt, H. and Nipkow, T., eds, *Types for Proofs and Programs*, International Workshop TYPES'93, Nijmegen, The Netherlands, pp. 213–237, Springer.

Margaris, A., 1961: Axioms for the integers, *American Mathematical Monthly*, 68 (5), pp. 441–444.

Martin-Löf, P., 1980: *Intuitionistic Type Theory*, Bibliopolis.

McCarthy, J., Abrahams, P.W., Edwards, D.J., Hart, T.P. and Levin, M.I., 1985: *LISP 1.5 Programmer's Manual*, MIT Press.

Mendelson, E., 2009: *Introduction to Mathematical Logic*, 5th edition, Chapman and Hall/CRC.

Milner, R., 1972: *Logic for Computable Functions: Description of a Machine Implementation*, Technical Report, Stanford University.

Milner, R., 1978: A theory of type polymorphism in programming, *Journal of Computer and System Sciences*, 17, pp. 348–375.

Mizar, 1989: Home Page, www.mizar.org.

Nederpelt, R.P., 1987: *De Taal van de Wiskunde* (The Language of Mathematics), Versluys.

Nederpelt, R.P., Geuvers, J.H. and de Vrijer, R.C., eds, 1994: *Selected Papers on Automath*, North-Holland, Elsevier.

Nederpelt, R.P. and Kamareddine, F.D., 2011: *Logical Reasoning: A First Course*, 2nd revised edition, College Publications.

Nipkow, T., Paulson, L.C. and Wenzel, M., 2002: *Isabelle/HOL – A Proof Assistant for Higher-Order Logic*, Springer.

Nordström, B., Petersson, K. and Smith, J., 1990: *Programming in Martin-Löf's Type Theory, An Introduction*, Oxford University Press.

Paulson, L.C., 1993: *The Isabelle Reference Manual*, Computer Laboratory, University of Cambridge.

Peano, G., 1889: *The Principles of Arithmetic, Presented by a New Method*. Reproduced in van Heijenoort, 1967, pp. 83–97.

Pelletier, F.J., 1999: A brief history of natural deduction, *History and Philosophy of Logic*, 20, pp. 1–31.

Peyton Jones, S. *et al.*, eds, 1998: *Revised Report on Haskell 98*, haskell.org/onlinereport/.

Pfenning, F., 2002: Logical frameworks: a brief introduction. In Schwichtenberg, H. and Steinbrüggen, R., eds, *Proof and System-Reliability*, Kluwer.

Pierce, B.C., 2002: *Types and Programming Languages*, MIT Press.

Pierce, B.C., 2004: *Advanced Topics in Types and Programming Languages*, MIT Press.

Plotkin, G., 1977: LCF considered as a programming language, *Theoretical Computer Science*, 5, pp. 223–255.

Pollack, R., 1994: *The Theory of LEGO: A Proof Checker for the Extended Calculus of Constructions*, PhD thesis, University of Edinburgh.

Pollack, R. *et al.*, 2001: The LEGO Proof Assistant, www.dcs.ed.ac.uk/home/lego/.

Prawitz, D., 1965: *Natural Deduction, A Proof-Theoretic Study*, Almqvist & Wiksell.

PVS, 1992: pvs-wiki.csl.sri.com/index.php/Main_Page.

Ramsey, F.P., 1926: The foundations of mathematics, *Proceedings of the London Mathematical Society*, 2nd series, 25, pp. 338–384.

Reynolds, J.C., 1974: Towards a theory of type structure. In Robinet, B., ed., *Programming Symposium, Proceedings Colloque sur la Programmation*, Paris, France, 9–11 April 1974, pp. 408–423, Springer.

Reynolds, J.C., 1984: Polymorphism is not set-theoretic. In Kahn, G., MacQueen, D.B. and Plotkin, G., eds, *Semantics of Data Types*, International Symposium, Sophia-Antipolis, France, 27–29 June 1984, pp. 145–156, Springer.

Robinson, J.A., 1965: A machine-oriented logic based on the resolution principle, *Journal of the ACM*, 12 (1), pp. 23–41.

Russell, B., 1903: *The Principles of Mathematics*, Cambridge University Press.

Russell, B., 1905: On Denoting, *Mind*, 14, pp. 479–493.

Russell, B., 1908: Mathematical logic as based on the theory of types, *American Journal of Mathematics*, 30, pp. 222–262.

Sanchis, L.E., 1967: Functionals defined by recursion, *Notre Dame Journal of Formal Logic*, 8, pp. 161–174.

Schönfinkel, M., 1924: *Über die Bausteine der mathematischen Logik*. Translated as 'On the building blocks of mathematical logic' in van Heijenoort, 1967.

Schwichtenberg, H., 1976: Definierbare Funktionen im λ-Kalkül mit Typen, *Archiv für Mathematische Logik und Grundlagenforschung*, 17, pp. 113–114.

Seldin, J.P., 1979: Progress report on generalized functionality, *Annals of Mathematical Logic*, 17, pp. 29–59.

Seldin, J.P. and Hindley, J.R., eds, 1980: *To H.B. Curry: Essays on Combinatory Logic, Lambda-Calculus and Formalism*, Academic Press.

Severi, P.G. and Poll, E., 1994: Pure Type Systems with definitions. In Nerode, A. and Matiyasevich, Yu. V., eds, *Proceedings of the Symposium on Logical Foundations of Computer Science, LFCS '94*, pp. 316–328, Springer.

Simmons, H., 2000: *Derivation and Computation: Taking the Curry–Howard Correspondence Seriously*, Cambridge University Press.

Sørensen, M.H. and Urzyczyn, P., 2006: *Lectures on the Curry–Howard Isomorphism*, Elsevier.

Sudkamp, Th., 2006: *Languages and Machines: An Introduction to the Theory of Computer Science*, 3rd edition, Addison-Wesley Publishing Company.

Tait, W.W., 1967: Intensional interpretation of functionals of finite type, *Journal of Symbolic Logic*, 32 (2), pp. 187–199.

Takahashi, M., 1995: Parallel reductions in lambda calculus, *Information and Computation*, 118 (1), pp. 120–127.

Terese (Bezem, M.A., Klop, J.W. and de Vrijer, R.C., eds), 2003: *Term Rewriting Systems*, Cambridge University Press.

Troelstra, A.S. and van Dalen, D., 1988: *Constructivism in Mathematics: An Introduction*, 2 vols, Elsevier.

Turing, A.M., 1936: On computable numbers, with an application to the Entscheidungsproblem, *Proceedings of the London Mathematical Society*, 42 (2), pp. 230–265; a correction, 43 (1937), pp. 544–546.

Twelf Project, 1999: `twelf.plparty.org/wiki/Main_Page`.

Univalent Foundations Program, 2013: *Homotopy Type Theory, Univalent Foundations of Mathematics*, Institute for Advanced Study, `homotopytypetheory.org/book/`.

Visser, A. and Iemhoff, R., 2009: personal communication.

Voevodsky, V.A., 2014: *Univalent Foundations: New Foundations of Mathematics*, video lecture, Institute for Advanced Study, Princeton, `video.ias.edu/node/6395`.

Wand, M., 1987: A simple algorithm and proof for type inference, *Fundamenta Informaticae*, X, pp. 115–122.

Wells, J.B., 1994: Typability and type-checking in the second-order λ-calculus are equivalent and undecidable, *Proceedings of the 9th Annual Symposium on Logic in Computer Science*, Paris, France, pp. 176–185, IEEE Computer Society Press.

Whitehead, A.N. and Russell, B., 1910: *Principia Mathematica*, 3 vols, Cambridge University Press, 1910, 1912 and 1913. 2nd edition, 1925 (Vol. 1), 1927 (Vols 2, 3).

Wiedijk, F., 1999: *Automath*, Home Page: `www.cs.ru.nl/~freek/aut/`.

Wiedijk, F., ed., 2006: *The Seventeen Provers of the World*, Springer.

Wiedijk, F., 2013: *Formalizing 100 Theorems*, `www.cs.ru.nl/~freek/100/index.html`.

Zermelo, E., 1908: Untersuchungen über die Grundlagen der Mengenlehre, I, *Mathematische Annalen*, 65, pp. 261–281.

Zucker, J., 1977: Formalization of classical mathematics in Automath. In *Colloque International de Logique*, Colloques Internationaux du Centre National de la Recherche Scientifique, 249. Reprinted in Nederpelt *et al.*, 1994, pp. 127–139.

Index of names

Index of definitions

Index of subjects

Printed in the United States
By Bookmasters